W9-APH-791

Public Speaking

Concepts and Skills for a Diverse Society

SIXTH EDITION

Public Speaking

Concepts and Skills for a Diverse Society

SIXTH
EDITION

CLELLA JAFFE

GEORGE FOX UNIVERSITY

Australia • Brazil • Canada • Mexico • Singapore • Spain
United Kingdom • United States

WADSWORTH
CENGAGE Learning

Public Speaking: Concepts and Skills for a Diverse Society, Sixth Edition
Clella Jaffe

Publisher: Lyn Uhl

Executive Editor: Monica Eckman

Senior Development Editor: Greer Lleuad

Assistant Editor: Rebekah Matthews

Editorial Assistant: Colin Solan

Associate Media Editor: Jessica Badiner

Marketing Manager: Erin Mitchell

Marketing Coordinator: Darlene Macanan

Marketing Communications Manager: Christine Dobberpuhl

Project Manager, Editorial Production: Kristy Zamagni

Art Director: Linda Helcher

Print Buyer: Susan Carroll

Image Manager: Audrey Pettengill

Text Permissions Manager: Mardell Glinski Schultz

Production Service: Pre-Press PMG

Cover Image: Tim Timmerman

Compositor: Pre-Press PMG

© 2010, 2007 Wadsworth, Cengage Learning

ALL RIGHTS RESERVED. No part of this work covered by the copyright herein may be reproduced, transmitted, stored, or used in any form or by any means graphic, electronic, or mechanical, including but not limited to photocopying, recording, scanning, digitizing, taping, Web distribution, information networks, or information storage and retrieval systems, except as permitted under Section 107 or 108 of the 1976 United States Copyright Act, without the prior written permission of the publisher.

For product information and technology assistance, contact us at **Cengage Learning Customer & Sales Support, 1-800-354-9706**

For permission to use material from this text or product, submit all requests online at **www.cengage.com/permissions** Further permissions questions can be e-mailed to **permissionrequest@cengage.com**

Library of Congress Control Number: to come

Student Edition:

ISBN-13: 978-0-495-56664-9

ISBN-10: 0-495-56664-0

Wadsworth
20 Channel Center Street
Boston, MA 02210
USA

Cengage Learning products are represented in Canada by Nelson Education, Ltd.

To learn more about Wadsworth, visit **www.cengage.com/wadsworth**

Purchase any of our products at your local college store or at our preferred online store **www.ichapters.com**

Printed in China by China Translation & Printing Services Limited
4 5 6 7 13 12 11 10

BRIEF CONTENTS

CONTENTS

C H A P T E R   1 4

Delivering Your Speech   253

C H A P T E R   1 5

Telling Narratives   270

LIST OF SPEECHES

Please Note: *A transcript or outline of the following additional speeches does not appear in the book, but the text refers to most of these speeches, and a video of each is on the book's website along with transcripts, outlines, and note cards.*

Hillary Carter-Liggett, *Shakespeare [informative]*

Brittany Farrer, *Limiting Alcohol Ads [persuasive]*

Nikki Giovanni, *Closing remarks at the convocation for the Virginia Tech shooting victims [commemorative]*

Barack Obama, *A More Perfect Union [commemorative]*

Paul Southwick, *Embryo Adoption [persuasive]*

PREFACE

The civilization of the dialogue is the only civilization worth having and the only civilization in which the whole world can unite. It is, therefore, the only civilization we can hope for, because the world must unite or be blown to bits.

Robert Hutchins, 1967

IT IS A PLEASURE to write the preface to the sixth edition of *Public Speaking: Concepts and Skills for a Diverse Society.* I am grateful to all who have used the first five editions and to the many professors and students who have given helpful suggestions to keep the text on the cutting edge of research and practice. I'm proud to say that this was the first public speaking textbook to focus on diversity, include an interpreted speech (given in Spanish and translated into English), describe invitational rhetoric, and show alternative patterns of speech organization.

This edition, like previous editions, is a culturally informed book that never loses sight of its fundamental purpose: to train students to be effective public speakers and listeners in a world filled with monumental cultural, political, and technological changes. It applies 2,500-year-old principles with up-to-date research into concepts, skills, theories, applications, and critical thinking proficiencies essential for listening and speaking in today's world. Its discussions of classic public speaking topics are all grounded in an awareness of the impact of cultural nuances—ranging from gender differences to co-cultures within the United States to the traditions of other nations. This provides students with a key element in being an effective public speaker: a heightened awareness of and sensitivity to the audience.

New to This Edition

Each edition has maintained several proven emphases:

- Cultural influences on public speaking and public speakers' influence on culture
- Gender, ethnic, and global diversity
- Civility and ethics in speaking and listening
- Communication as dialogue
- The importance of narrative speaking
- Technological advances and public speaking
- Traditions dating back to classical rhetoric
- Nontraditional organizational patterns

This edition retains these features and includes a number of important changes in response to reviewer feedback. Here are some highlights of what's new:

Practically Speaking boxes. Reviewers asked for more practical applications to situations outside the classroom. Consequently, most chapters now feature an example of "ordinary" people who share tips on how they use concepts developed in the chapter in their daily lives. In addition, there are more references to workplace situations and topics throughout the text, and more workplace-related speeches are included.

Ethics in Practice boxes. This text has always emphasized ethical speaking and listening. This edition includes an ethics box in most chapters. These boxes present short examples or cases that invite students to contemplate the ethical implications of chapter concepts, using probing questions that are appropriate for class discussions.

New sample speeches. I have replaced or updated the sample speeches for currency, variety, and even greater effectiveness. Several of the sample speeches, by both student and professional speakers, are new, and most of the speeches are available on video. For more information about the speech videos for this book, see the Student Resources section.

New chapter arrangement. In response to reviewer feedback, Chapter 5 (topic choice) now precedes Chapter 6 (audience analysis), and Chapter 12 (language) now precedes Chapter 13 (visual aids).

More how-to tips. Several chapters have new and updated practical information describing how to develop specific skills. Chapter 14 (delivery) has been substantially revised to include less theory and more practical tips on how to prepare and deliver speeches, using each delivery mode. Chapter 11 (outlining) shows the difference between the content outline, the speaking outline, and the actual speech. Chapter 3 (ethics and diversity) includes a new exercise on appropriate and inappropriate paraphrases. Chapter 7 (research) includes a new section on source citation.

Updated research. Communication scholars continue to expand our understanding of listening and reasoning. Information on receiver apprehension (Chapter 4), visual evidence (Chapter 8), and narrative and thinking (Chapter 15) are just a few examples of research updates.

Updated references to popular culture. New references to popular culture, such as YouTube and movies, show how the principles in the text apply in a variety of contexts.

Proven Chapter-by-Chapter Features

In addition to chapter-opening lists of learning objectives, key term definitions in the margins of each chapter, and chapter-ending summaries, each chapter includes several acclaimed pedagogical features that improve student learning and performance.

▶ **Stop and Check boxes.** These critical thinking and skill-building exercises help students check their progress throughout the chapter. Often, they refer to an article on the InfoTrac College Edition™ database, which helps students better understand the topic and gives them practice in researching and locating quality supporting material online. These activities are also available in an interactive format on the book's online resources.

▶ **Diversity in Practice boxes.** These boxes enhance the book's emphasis on diversity by presenting brief summaries of public speaking traditions from a range of perspectives. Examples include ancient cultures (Chapters 1 and 17), global groups (Chapters 7 and 13), ethnic groups (Chapters 10 and 15), and co-cultures (Chapters 12 and 14).

▶ **Build Your Speech boxes.** These skill-building activities help students apply text concepts to actual speechmaking. They can serve as starting points for completing speech assignments. Many of these activities offer students the option of completing the activities by accessing Speech Builder Express™ 3.0, an online speech coach. For more information about Speech Builder Express, see the Student Resources section.

▶ **Application and Critical Thinking Exercises.** Suitable for individual or group assignments, and for in-class discussion, these end-of-chapter questions help students better understand and critically evaluate the chapter content and further apply the skills they've learned.

▶ **Diverse student speeches.** Most chapters include an outline or text of a student speech, accompanied by marginal commentary. These speeches provide positive models showing how other students fulfilled a typical assignment. Chapter 18 provides a cautionary, negative model, and Chapters 3 and 12 feature speeches by professional speakers. Many of these speeches are available on video. For more information about this book's speech resources, see the Student Resources section.

Accompanying Resources: An Exclusive Teaching and Learning Package

Public Speaking: Concepts and Skills for a Diverse Society, Sixth Edition, offers a comprehensive array of supplements to assist in helping students succeed and in making the public speaking course as meaningful and enjoyable as possible for both students and instructors.

Resources for Students

Many of these student resources are available free of charge when instructors order them (or access to them) for students bundled with the text. Other users or students whose instructors do not order these resources with the text may purchase them at **cengage.com/communication**.

Resource Center. The Resource Center for *Public Speaking: Concepts and Skills for a Diverse Society* offers a variety of rich learning resources designed to enhance the student experience. These resources include Audio Study Tools chapter downloads, Interactive Video Activities, Speech Builder Express 3.0, self-assessments, InfoTrac College Edition with InfoMarks™, and web resources. All resources are mapped to both key discipline learning concepts as well as specific chapter learn lists.

Companion Website. Features chapter-by-chapter study tools, including weblinks, quizzes, glossary, flash cards, and online versions of the book's Stop and Check skill-building and critical thinking activities. Students can complete activities and quizzes online and, if requested, submit them to their instructors electronically.

Interactive Video Activities. Presented within Wadsworth Cengage Learning's unique interactive user interface, the speech videos help students gain experience evaluating and critiquing introductory, informative, persuasive, and special occasion speeches so that they can more effectively provide feedback to their peers and improve their own speeches and delivery. Features of this highly praised resource include critical thinking questions that prompt students to apply concepts discussed in the book to the speech; transcripts for all speech videos; full-sentence and key word outlines, as well as notecards, for student speech videos; and a scrolling function that students may choose to turn on or off. When the scroll feature is on, synchronized highlighting tracks each speaker's progress through his or her outline or transcript as the video of the speaker's delivery plays alongside. In addition, a "notes" function lets students insert written comments while watching the video. At a student's command, the program pauses, enters a time-stamp that indicates where the video was paused, and offers the student prewritten notes to choose from or modify as well as the option of composing completely original notes.

Audio Study Tools. These tools provide a fun and easy way for students to download audio files and review chapter content whenever and wherever. For each chapter, students will have access to a chapter review consisting of the learning objectives for the chapter, a brief summary of the main points in the text, audio of a speech, and critical-thinking questions. Students can download files to their computers, iPods, or other MP3 players.

Speech Builder Express 3.0. This online program coaches students through the entire process of preparing speeches and provides the additional support of built-in video speech models, a tutor feature for concept review, and an online dictionary and thesaurus. Equipped with their speech type or purpose, a general topic, and preliminary research, students respond to the program's customized prompts to complete interactive activities that require critical thinking about all aspects of creating an effective speech. Students are able to specify a specific speech purpose, identify an organizational pattern, write a thesis statement or central idea, establish main points, integrate support material, craft transitions, plan visual aids, compose their speech introduction and conclusion, and prepare their bibliography to complete formal speech outlines. Students are also able to stop and start work whenever they choose. They can complete, save online, export to Microsoft® Word®, or email their outlines.

InfoTrac College Edition with InfoMarks. This online library provides access to more than 18 million reliable, full-length articles from more than 5,000 academic and popular periodicals. Students also have access to InfoMarks—stable URLs that can be linked to articles, journals, and searches to save valuable time when doing research—and to the InfoWrite online resource center, where students can access grammar help, critical-thinking guidelines, guides to writing research papers, and much more. For more information about InfoTrac College Edition and the InfoMarks linking tool, visit **infotrac-college.com** and click on "InfoTrac Demo."

A Guide to the Basic Course for ESL Students is also available bundled with the book. Specifically for communicators whose first language is not English, it features FAQs, helpful URLs, and strategies for managing communication anxiety.

The Art and Strategy of Service Learning Presentations, Second Edition. Available bundled with *Public Speaking: Concepts and Skills for a Diverse Society*. Authored by Rick Isaacson and Jeff Saperstein of San Francisco State University, this handbook provides guidelines for connecting service-learning work with classroom concepts and advice for working effectively with agencies and organizations.

Resources for Instructors

Public Speaking: Concepts and Skills for a Diverse Society, Sixth Edition, also features a full suite of resources for instructors. The following class preparation, classroom presentation, assessment, and course management resources are available:

Instructor's Resource Manual. The Instructor's Resource Manual provides a comprehensive teaching guide. Written by Clella Jaffe, this manual features sample syllabi, as well as suggested speaking assignments and criteria for evaluation. Each text chapter has the following resources: transition notes to the sixth edition, chapter goals, a chapter outline, suggestions correlating supplements and online resources, supplementary research notes, suggested discussion questions and specific suggestions for integrating student workbook activities and videos. The manual also includes a printed test bank that features class-tested multiple-choice, true-false, short-answer, essay, and fill-in-the-blank test questions.

Instructor's Website. The password-protected instructor's website includes electronic access to the Instructor's Resource Manual and downloadable versions of the book's PowerPoint slides. To gain access to the website, simply request a course key by opening the site's home page.

PowerLecture CD-ROM. This includes an electronic version of the Instructor's Resource Manual, ExamView® Computerized Testing, predesigned and customizable Microsoft PowerPoint® presentations, and the book's video footage. This resource is available to qualified adopters. Please consult your local sales representative for details.

ExamView Computerized Testing. ExamView enables you to create, deliver, and customize tests and study guides (both print and online) in minutes using the test bank questions from the Instructor's Resource Manual. ExamView offers both a Quick Test Wizard and an Online Test Wizard that guide you step-by-step through the process of creating tests, while its "what you see is what you get" interface allows you to see the test you are creating on-screen exactly as it will print or display online. You can build tests of up to 250 questions using up to twelve question types. Using the complete word processing capabilities of ExamView, you can also enter an unlimited number of new questions or edit existing ones.

ExamView®

Wadsworth Cengage Learning Communication Video and DVD Library. Wadsworth Cengage Learning's video and DVD series for Speech Communication includes Student Speeches for Critique and Analysis, Communication Scenarios for Critique and Analysis, and ABC News videos and DVDs for Public Speaking, Human Communication, and Interpersonal Communication.

The Teaching Assistant's Guide to the Basic Course. Katherine G. Hendrix, who is on the faculty at the University of Memphis, prepared this resource specifically for new instructors. Based on leading communication teacher training programs, this guide discusses some of the general issues that accompany a teaching role and offers specific strategies for managing the first week of classes, leading productive discussions, managing sensitive topics in the classroom, and grading students' written and oral work.

These resources are available to qualified adopters, and ordering options for student supplements are flexible. Please consult your local Wadsworth Cengage Learning sales representative for more information, to evaluate examination copies of any of these instructor or student resources, or for product demonstrations. You may also contact the Cengage Learning Academic Resource Center at 800-423-0563 or visit us at **cengage.com/communication**.

Acknowledgments

Every book is a cocreated product in which an author relies on the encouragement of others. I owe a longstanding debt to former Oregon State University colleagues (Victoria O'Donnell, Sean Patrick O'Rourke, Anne Zach Ferguson, and dozens of graduate teaching instructors). My colleagues at George Fox University, Richard Engnell, Craig Johnson, and Ray Anderson, have consistently and patiently supported my writing, for which I am grateful. I also thank generations of students at Oregon State, St. John's (New York), and George Fox University who provided insights, examples, speeches, and support. Scott Johnson (Bethel College) and Mark Parravecchio deserve special recognition for their insights on the text. I extend special thanks too to Michael McNamara of George Fox University, who taped the new student speeches; Melissa Meyer, who created the web quizzes for students on the book's companion website; Sherry Lewis of University of Texas, El Paso, who created the critical thinking questions and outlines for the new student speeches; and Kim Cowden of North Dakota State University, who created the audio study tools.

Likewise, I want to thank the many people at or working with Wadsworth Cengage Learning who helped bring this new edition and its many supplements to fruition: Jessica Badiner, Rita Dienst, Christine Dobberpuhl, Monica Eckman, Larry Goldberg, Linda Helcher, Megan Lessard, Greer Lleuad, Rebekah Matthews, Darlene Macanan, Erin Mitchell, Audrey Pettengill, Jessica Rasile, Mardell Glinski Schultz, Colin Solan, Lyn Uhl, and Kristy Zamagni.

I also would like to thank the reviewers who contributed valuable comments about this book's fifth edition and offered helpful suggestions for the sixth: Christian Blum, Bryant & Stratton College; Bryan Crow, Southern Illinois University; Linda Czuba Brigance, SUNY Fredonia; Jonathan M. Gray, Southern Illinois University, Carbondale; Roxanne Tuscany, Grossmont College; Alex Wang, University of Connecticut, Stamford; and Melinda Williams, Williams Baptist College.

I would also like to thank the reviewers for previous editions of this book. Reviewers for the First Edition were Martha Ann Atkins, Iowa State University; Dennis Beaver, Bakersfield College; Carol Berteotti, University of Wisconsin–La Crosse; Carole Blair, University of California–Davis; Cynthia Brown-El, Macomb Community College; Ferald J. Bryan, Northern Illinois University; Bruce G. Bryski, Buffalo State College; Jacquelyn Buckrop, Ball State University; Michelle Burch, Clark State University; Kathleen Farrell, Saint Louis University; Norma Flores, Golden West College; Franklin L. Gray, Ball State University; Charles Griffin, Kansas State University; Susan Hellweg, San Diego State University; Mark Hickson, University of Alabama–Birmingham; Janet Hoffman, Southern Illinois University at Carbondale; Susan Huxman, Wichita State University; Karla Jensen, Texas Tech University; Tina Kistler, Santa Barbara City College; Shelley D. Lane, Collin County Community College; Jo Ann Lawlor, West Valley College; Steven March, Pima County Community College; Victoria O'Donnell, Montana State University; Sean Patrick O'Rourke, Vanderbilt University; Patricia Palm McGillen, Mankato State University; Mark Morman, Johnson County Community College; Teresa Nance, Villanova University; Patricia O'Keefe, College of Marin; Mary Pelias, Southern Illinois University; Mark Stoner, California State University–Sacramento; Patricia Sullivan, State University of New York at New Paltz; Marsha Vanderford, University of South Florida; Donald E. Williams, University of Florida; Lee Winet, State University of New York–Oswego; and Anne Zach Ferguson, University of California–Davis. Reviewers for the Second Edition were Thomas E. Diamond, Montana State University; Kevin E. McClearey, Southern Illinois University at Edwardsville; Susan Messman, Arizona State University; Karla D. Scott, Saint Louis University; Jessica Stowell, Tulsa Community College; and Lori Wisdom-Whitley, Western Washington University. Reviewers for the Third Edition were Clifton Adams, Central Missouri State University; Linda Anthon, Valencia Community College; Jay Baglia, University of South Florida; Carol Barnum, Southern Polytechnic State University; Lori Basden Arnold, Rowan University; Julie Benson-Rosston, University of Montana; John Bourhis, Missouri State University; Cheri Campbell, Keene State College; Faye Clark, Georgia Perimeter College; Risa Dickson, California State University at San Bernardino; Hal Fulmer, Georgia Southern University; Matthew Girton, Florida State University; Sherrie L. Guerrero, San Bernardino Valley College; Robert Gwynne, University of Tennessee–Knoxville; Fred Jandt, California State University at San Bernardino; Laura Nelson, University of Wisconsin–La Crosse; Jean E. Perry, Glendale Community College; Susie Richardson, Prince George's Community College; Paula Rodriguez, Hinds Community College; Scott Rodriguez, California State University at San Bernardino; Cathy Sargent Mester, Pennsylvania State University; Kristi A. Schaller, University of Hawaii; Ann M. Scroggie, Santa Fe Community College; Karni Spain Tiernan, Bradley University; David Walker, Middle Tennessee State University; June D. Wells, Indian River Community College; Nancy J. Wendt, Oregon State University; L. Keith Williamson, Wichita State University; and Marianne Worthington,

Cumberland College. Reviewers for the Fourth Edition were James E. Bruce, University of Tennessee at Martin; Ferald J. Bryan, Northern Illinois University; Nanci Burk, Glendale Community College; Helen Chester, Milwaukee Area Technical College; Omar Guevara, California State University at Bakersfield; Janice D. Hamlet, Northern Illinois University; Jeff Przybylo, William Rainey Harper Community College; Diana D. Roberts, Community College of Southern Nevada; Amy R. Slagell, Iowa State University; Lisa Waite, Kent State University; and Diane E. Waryas, Community College of Southern Nevada; and Kathryn Wylie-Marques, John Jay College, City University of New York.

Writing takes a toll on an author's family. I am grateful for Jack, Sara, Josh, J. C., and all the little ones who make a difference in my life. Wadsworth Cengage Learning has provided a series of editors who have guided this text throughout the five editions. Monica Eckman and Greer Lleuad were consistently patient and supportive.

Clella Jaffe, Ph.D.

1

INTRODUCTION TO PUBLIC SPEAKING AND CULTURE

© Tim Timmerman

THIS CHAPTER WILL HELP YOU

▶ **Explain why public speaking courses are valuable**

▶ **Define culture in the context of public speaking**

▶ **Give reasons for studying public speaking from a cultural perspective**

▶ **Identify three ways culture affects public speaking**

▶ **Explain how public speaking influences culture**

▶ **Understand aspects of the dialogical theory of communication**

▶ **Identify elements of the transactional model of communication**

WHAT DO THE WORDS *public speaker* mean to you? Do you first think of a politician? A business leader? A member of the clergy? A teacher? True, public speaking is common in these professions, but public speakers give talks in many other contexts. A coach giving a locker-room pep talk, a concerned citizen speaking before the city council, or a camp counselor telling a campfire story are just a few examples of people who educate, inspire, persuade, or entertain audiences. By definition, **public speaking** occurs when one person prepares and delivers a speech for a group that listens, generally without interrupting the speaker's flow of ideas.

Although you may not associate the words "public speaker" with yourself, chances are you bring some experience to this course. Even if you've never spoken at "Show and Tell", presented a report, or given an announcement, you've heard many speeches, and you have formed some ideas about what makes a presentation effective or ineffective. Your experiences provide a foundation on which you can build additional competencies. Throughout this term, you will learn strategies for thinking through the process of planning, presenting, and evaluating effective speeches. You will assess your current skills, identify areas for improvement, and plan ways to deal with the challenges of speaking and listening in a free

public speaking when a person delivers a presentation to a group that listens, generally without interrupting the speaker's flow of ideas

www.americanrhetoric.com features clips from movies such as "Rudy" and "Friday Night Lights" (football), "Miracle" (hockey) and "Hoosiers" (basketball) that show impassioned coaches inspiring their teams to victory. None of the coaches are "professional speakers"; they are like thousands of ordinary people who regularly give talks as part of their occupational duties.

society. As you create first one speech and then another, you will improve your skills by adding competencies and by refining those you already have.[1]

Although this text has *speaking* in the title, speech-*making* is only one element of the course. More often than not, you will be in the audience, listening to speeches as a member of a population that is increasingly diverse. Consequently, learning to better understand and evaluate the messages you hear daily is another major course goal. The competencies needed for these two roles—speaker and listener—are the focus of this text.

Why Do People Take a Public Speaking Course?

Most universities not only offer courses in public speaking, they require them. Why? What competencies do curriculum designers believe these courses offer? Stop a minute and think of what you hope to get out of this course:

▶ Why am I taking this course?
▶ What do I already bring to this subject?
▶ What competencies do I want to develop during the term?
▶ What skills do I want to improve?
▶ What role does public speaking and listening play in my life now?
▶ What role will good speaking and listening skills play in my future?

There are at least two good reasons for requiring public speaking courses: they emphasize critical thinking, and they provide instruction and practice in communication skills that are important in your professional and personal life.

An Emphasis on Critical Thinking Skills

Throughout history, the ability to present one's own ideas and to understand and weigh the ideas of others has proven valuable; this ability is even more essential in a world flooded with messages of all kinds. (The Diversity in Practice box on the next page describes the historical importance of speaking skills in ancient Egypt.) From classical Greek and Roman academies to modern English and communication departments, the study of **rhetoric** or "the art, practice, and study of human communication"[2] has played a central role. In fact, rhetoric is one of the original seven liberal arts.

This emphasis may seem surprising, given the generally negative feeling people today have about the word rhetoric. For instance, during the last presidential election campaign, one candidate issued a press release titled, "Rhetoric vs. Results:"[3] " . . . this election doesn't come down to change versus experience, but words versus deeds, talk versus action, rhetoric versus reality." Clearly, she considered words, talk, and rhetoric to be less important than deeds, action, and reality. This mindset, coupled with phrases such as "empty rhetoric," helps explain why this term is so misunderstood. But is rhetoric just words? Here are three additional definitions:[4]

rhetoric the study of persuasion in its various forms, a term often used negatively

▶ . . . the faculty of discovering in any particular case all of the available means of persuasion (Aristotle).
▶ . . . the study of misunderstandings and their remedies (I. A. Richards).

▶ . . . an instrumental use of language. One person engages another person in an exchange of symbols to accomplish some goal. It is not communication for communication's sake. Rhetoric is communication that attempts to coordinate social action. For this reason, rhetorical communication is explicitly pragmatic. Its goal is to influence human choices on specific matters that require immediate attention (G. Hauser).

As you can see, most definitions associate rhetoric with persuasion in its many forms, whether it be public speaking or writing, advertising campaigns, or film and art. Because persuasion has been important in every culture and every generation, this text covers both ancient and modern principles of rhetoric. Studying these principles will help you develop critical thinking competencies that you can use to analyze information, sort through persuasive appeals, discriminate faulty arguments from valid reasoning, and follow ideas to logical conclusions.[5] In the process you will learn to appreciate a diversity of opinions and presentation styles.

DIVERSITY IN PRACTICE

PUBLIC SPEAKING IN ANCIENT CULTURES

PUBLIC SPEAKING has its place in every society. For example, fragments of the oldest book in existence, *The Precepts of Ke'gemni and Ptah-hotep* (ca. 2100 BCE), provided young Egyptians with guidelines for both speaking and listening:[6]

- ▶ Speak with exactness, and recognize the value of silence.
- ▶ Listeners who have "good fellowship" can be influenced by the speeches of others.
- ▶ Do not be proud of your learning.
- ▶ Keep silent in the face of a better debater; refute the false arguments of an equal, but let a weaker speaker's arguments confound themselves.
- ▶ Do not pervert the truth.
- ▶ Avoid speech subjects about which you know nothing.
- ▶ Remember that a covetous person is not a persuasive speaker.

It was good advice then, and it's good advice now!

An Emphasis on Professional and Personal Skills

A second reason to take a speech course is to improve your presentational skills while decreasing your anxiety about public speaking.[7] Because employers typically assume that job applicants have job-related expertise, they look for an additional something in job candidates. Most employers want individuals who can listen effectively, present their ideas clearly, think critically, and exude enthusiasm. In one survey, 98 percent of personnel interviewers said that both verbal and nonverbal communication skills are important, and they overwhelmingly agreed that these skills are vital for higher-level positions.[8] Many of the competencies you develop in this course are used daily in occupations as diverse as law, medicine, engineering,[9] teaching, and accounting.[10]

In addition to job success, the ability to present your thoughts clearly and persuasively enables you to voice your ideas about important issues. You can probably identify many individuals whose communication has made a difference in some way. Students hold peace rallies, set up environmental workshops, and rally audiences to take part in community service activities. People call in to radio talk shows and send feedback to newspaper editors.[11] On blogs, listservs, online social network pages, and other discussion forums, millions of people share ideas about everything from sport controversies to movies to politics. The more skillful communicators influence thinking and actions about local, national, and international issues.

Finally, public speaking skills are valuable in a variety of social situations. Narrating a "cousins' story" at a family reunion, telling a joke to a group of friends, and giving a wedding toast or a funeral eulogy are examples of situations where short, often impromptu speeches create and maintain strong, personal connections.

Although there are many good reasons for taking a public speaking course, many students still dread the thought of giving a public speech. The good news? Most people feel both more competent and more confident after gaining experience in such a course.

In summary, studying public speaking allows you to add to your communication abilities within a culture that values them. You can develop critical thinking skills that enable you to sort through the ideas and persuasive appeals that surround you daily. You can develop skills that serve you well in almost any profession, and you can also sharpen your ability to participate in the broader cultural conversation that can make a difference in the world. On top of these benefits, you can gain confidence as you face your fears and meet the challenge of preparing and giving speeches.

Why Take a Cultural Perspective?

Every day, news reports describe cultural celebrations, natural disasters, wars, and other stories that remind us that we live in a rapidly shrinking world where members of distinctly different cultures regularly come into contact. Not all diversity is global in scope; in various regions of the United States and in local communities you also encounter people with diverse ethnic backgrounds, faiths, political affiliations, economic circumstances, views about sexuality, and so on. Although your community or school may not seem especially diverse, you will better understand our nation and our world if you understand how diversity affects communication. That is why this text presents both the public speaking norms most common in the United States and the speaking traditions of other cultures in this country and abroad.

What exactly is a culture? **Cultures** are integrated systems of learned beliefs, values, attitudes, and behaviors that a group accepts and passes along from older to newer members. Professor Charles Conrad[12] defines the term this way:

> . . . cultures are communicative creations. They emerge through communication, are maintained through communication, and change through the communicative acts of their members. Simultaneously communication is a cultural creation. Persons' perceptions of the cultures in which they live . . . form the situations that guide and constrain their communication.

Don Smith,[13] founder of Daystar University in Kenya, compares a culture to an onion: It has visible outer layers (clothing, art, food, language, and so on) and embedded perceptual filters that influence how we view the world (ideologies, folk beliefs, attitudes, values, and so on).[14] Put another way, culture exists at a conscious as well as at an unconscious level; cultures include relatively stable elements, but they can and do change.

Although members of a society share many commonalities, culture is not spelled with a capital "C."[15] That is, we do not belong to a single "U.S. Culture"; instead, our

cultures integrated systems of learned beliefs, values, behaviors, and norms that include visible (clothing, food) and underlying (core beliefs, worldview) characteristics of a society

Devan Marchbanks

A culture can be compared to an onion with many integrated layers surrounding an inner core of beliefs, values, and attitudes.

nation contains many subgroups, or **co-cultures**, made up of people who diverge in some way from one another. If you log on to **www.myspace.com**, go to "groups," and click on Cultures and Community, you will find thousands of groups. Seeing the extensive list of links and visiting some of the interesting sites they lead to will help you better understand why this text integrates diverse perspectives throughout.

Finally, taking a cultural approach increases your communication competence. Because you perform each speech within a specific situation to an audience that holds expectations regarding its length, appropriate delivery, and so on, you succeed best when you understand and adapt to cultural and co-cultural norms. This also increases your **rhetorical sensitivity** and marks you as a person who "can adapt to diverse social situations and perform reasonably well in most of them."[16]

Culture Affects Public Speaking

Some cultural influences on public speaking are obvious. For example, street protesters are common in U.S. cities but rare in rural areas of China. Whiteboards and overhead projectors are widely used in businesses and schoolrooms but almost never found at funerals. However, cultures also influence speaking in less obvious ways by providing core resources, technological aids, and cultural norms.

Cultures Provide Core Resources

According to communication professor W. Barnett Pearce,[17] each culture offers a pool of **core cultural resources**, or "logics of meaning and action," that define our obligations as well as our taboos. These systems of intertwined beliefs, attitudes, and values (BAV) underlie our behaviors in every area of life, including public speaking.

Beliefs are the ideas we mentally accept as true or reject as false. Attitudes are our predispositions to evaluate—either negatively or positively—persons, objects, symbols, and the like. Values are our underlying evaluations of what is important, significant, moral, or right. Finally, behaviors are the actions we consider appropriate or normal. Here are some foundational cultural resources for public speaking in the United States:

▶ A *belief* that we can change society by speaking out and creating public policies instead of giving in to fate.
▶ Positive *attitudes* toward open forums and negative attitudes about suppressing dissent.
▶ A *value* that places individuality over conformity.
▶ Standards for predictable speaking and listening *behaviors* that vary according to context.

co-cultures subgroups of culture, characterized by mild or profound cultural differences, that coexist within the larger culture

rhetorical sensitivity the ability to adapt to a variety of audiences and settings and to perform appropriately in diverse social situations

core cultural resources beliefs, attitudes, and values (BAV) along with behaviors that provide a logical basis for a culture to define what is necessary, right, doubtful, or forbidden

These core resources, and others like them, combine to create public speaking expectations in the United States. Because we typically value freedom and choice, we ideally respect one another's ideas. Our beliefs that individuals are intelligent and reasonable lead us to prefer persuasion to coercion. In contrast, some cultural groups discourage their members from expressing their ideas freely, and many leaders choose force instead of reason as a means of control.[18]

Cultures Provide Technological Aids

The technology available to a culture greatly affects how its members create and exchange messages. A strictly **oral culture** has no technology for recording, storing, or transmitting ideas, so speakers and audiences must of necessity meet face to face. Because everything they know must be memorized, they rely on poems and chants, proverbs and sayings, and stories and genealogies that help them learn and remember their values, beliefs, and traditions.[19]

In contrast, most cultures provide at least some access to literacy and to electronic devices that allow their members to record their ideas and convey them to audiences separated by both distance and time. You have an almost overwhelming amount of available resources for speaking and for disseminating your ideas. There are printed materials, electronically stored databases, the Internet, and audiovisual resources for gathering speech materials. There are additional devices such as microphones, cameras, sophisticated playback machines, and inventions like presentation software that can help you support your ideas. You can write your thoughts out on note cards, which frees you from the limitations of memory. You can record your speeches and post them on YouTube, or another video site. Throughout this text you'll find guidelines for using the most common research and presentation technologies available in this culture.

Cultures Provide Expectations about Speaking and Listening

Cultures vary not only in the value they place on *expressiveness* and explicitness but also in their expectations regarding the *how*, *who*, and *what* of public speaking.

Cultures Vary in Expressiveness

Members of **nonexpressive cultures** value privacy and guard their emotions and ideas rather than express them indiscriminately. For example, Japanese people who choose their words carefully are considered thoughtful, trustworthy, and responsible.[20] In China, where feeling, emotion, and personal opinion are considered private, people hesitate to express personal opinions for fear of losing face; instead, they typically choose unassertive and indirect speech.[21] Finnish culture has a high tolerance for silence;[22] similarly, many Native American groups accept silence—even between friends.[23] As you might guess, someone from a comparatively nonexpressive culture can be overwhelmed at the thought of speaking in public.[24]

In contrast, Koreans and Puerto Ricans are considerably more verbal and confident about speaking out.[25] Theirs are **expressive cultures** which encourage people to give their opinions, speak their minds, and let their feelings show. Many African cultures, such as the Anang tribe, also value fluency. In fact, the tribal name *Anang* means "the ability to speak wittily yet meaningfully upon any occasion."[26] Barack Obama is just one example of the many African Americans who are among this country's most skilled speakers.

Of course, differences exist within cultures and among individuals. One cross-cultural study showed that, across nations, southerners are statistically more expressive than northerners, even within the same country.[27] And we all know individuals who are

oral culture culture with no writing and no technology for recording messages apart from face-to-face interactions

nonexpressive cultures cultures that value privacy and encourage members to keep their emotions and ideas to themselves rather than to express them publicly

expressive cultures cultures that encourage members to give their opinions, speak their minds, and let their feelings show

naturally more reserved than others. In addition, rhetorically sensitive people commonly regulate their expressiveness to appear more or less outgoing, depending on the circumstances.[28] For example, the same man who normally creates a dramatic image by expressing his emotions and verbalizing his opinions sometimes withholds his expression to "be cool" and keep his thoughts or feelings from showing.[29]

ETHICS IN PRACTICE

VIR BONUM, DICENDI PERITUS

EVERY CULTURE has maxims or proverbs that capture cultural ideals in short, pithy statements. The Latin phrase *Vir bonum, dicendi peritus*—"The good person, skilled in speaking"—is a slogan that ancient Romans might have put on their chariots, if bumper stickers were then in style. Quintilian, a popular speech teacher who lived in the chaotic days of the notorious Emperor Nero and his successors, instilled it into his students. Roman rhetors knew the power of words and the ethical implications of persuasive speaking. Put simply, speakers then and now can urge others to act out horrors or to make the world better. Today, "good people, communicating skillfully" are even more essential in a world where technology opens the possibilities for millions of people to get a wide hearing.

Questions

1. Make a list of people who were skilled in speaking but were not "good" persons. (Hitler tops many people's list.)
2. Add to this list Internet sites that you think promote negative values or behaviors. (For example, there are many pro-anorexia websites or YouTube videos that demean one religion or another.)
3. How might the principles in the slogan mentioned above apply to the Internet and YouTube generation?
4. Identify situations, real or hypothetical, in which good people want to do something to better their world but lack the skills to present their ideas to those who could support their efforts.

Cultures Influence "Who" Speaks—and "To Whom"

In some cultures, only adult men, and sometimes just those men judged to be the oldest, wisest, or most knowledgeable, speak publicly.[30] This restriction virtually eliminates the voices of children, young people, nonexperts, and women in public arenas. Some cultures silence certain people or groups such as the poor, ethnic minorities, or people with divergent political views, by ridiculing, misunderstanding, or punishing them for speaking out.[31] Moreover, it may be difficult to gain access to a specific speaking venue. For example, could you just walk into the places where decisions are made at your university and ask the president and board to do something about the price of textbooks? Probably not. Could a minimum-wage worker at your local fast food restaurant enter corporate headquarters and ask for better health coverage? Probably not.[32] Fortunately, the Bill of Rights boldly proclaims the ideal of free speech; unfortunately, this ideal is not always realized in practice. However, you can do your best to make public speaking situations safe spaces where everyone can speak and listen.

Cultures Guide the "How-To" of Speaking

A culture's core assumptions and norms work together to produce a preferred **communication style**.[33] In many institutions in the United States, a *problem orientation*

communication style a culture's preferred ways of communicating, given its core assumptions and norms

is common. People assume that the world is rational and that we can create solutions to problems ranging from the global to the personal by acting on them. The style is also *direct*, featuring ideas that are logically organized in a way that gets to the point without "beating around the bush." A related characteristic is *explicitness*, or the use of clear, concise, and precise language instead of indirect or vague statements. The cultural values of equality and individuality result in *informality*, which is characterized by conversational delivery, and in *personal involvement*, which leads speakers to identify with audiences by sharing personal experiences or finding points of common ground. Your competency in many public speaking contexts will be judged against these norms.

The voices of women, children, minorities, or the poor often are ignored or discounted. However, in May 2002, Gabriela Azurduy Arrieta from Bolivia was one of two children who addressed the United Nations General Assembly at a special session devoted to children's issues. UN members, who hear mainly from adults, took their speeches seriously.

Cultures Influence the "What" of Public Speaking

Some cultures discourage the expression of personal feelings and viewpoints; others find this desirable, even at the expense of "objectivity."[34] Controversial topics in the United States are passionately debated; consequently, political candidates can clash one night in a spirited public forum and then work side-by-side the next day in the Senate for a cosponsored piece of legislation. You probably disagree with your friends on many issues but still remain friendly. However, in traditional China and Japan, speakers downplayed personal arguments—a behavior traceable to the Confucian idea of *hsin*, in which speakers and their words are inseparable. In these cultures, challenging speakers in public shames them by casting doubt on their honesty.[35]

Cultural factors such as these can affect how comfortable you feel in a public speaking classroom that teaches Euro-American cultural norms. What is considered competent in a classroom or in a workplace setting may be quite different from your cultural traditions. If so, you can become **bicultural**, knowing the rules for competent speaking in the dominant culture while appreciating and participating in your own ethnic speech community. In the following example, a Nigerian woman living in the United States explains how she accomplishes this:

> At work, . . . I raise my voice as loud as necessary to be heard in meetings. At conferences where I present papers on "Women from the Third World," I make serious arguments about the need for international intervention in countries where women are deprived of all rights. . . . Yet as easily as I switch from speaking English to Ibo [her Nigerian language], . . . I never confuse my two selves.
>
> Hundreds of thousands of women from the Third World and other traditional societies share my experience. We straddle two cultures, cultures that are often in opposition. Mainstream America, the culture we embrace in our professional lives, dictates that we be assertive and independent—like men. Our traditional culture, dictated by religion and years of socialization, demands that we be docile and content in our roles as mothers and wives—careers or not.[36]

bicultural knowing and applying different rules for competent behaviors in two cultures

As you can see, students from many traditions bring contrasting expectations of "how to" speak into the college classroom. If you judge other traditions by your own culture's standards, misunderstandings and negative evaluations can result.

STEPHEN CHERNIN/AP Photo

Public Speaking Influences Culture

Cultures are not static. This means they can and do change, often through the efforts of skillful public speakers. Historically, women and men have spoken out against slavery and for women's suffrage; currently, public speakers debate educational policies, immigration laws, use of technology, and so on. They speak to transmit, reinforce, repair, or transform their cultures.[37]

Montana Historical Society Research Center Photograph Archives, Helena, Montana

Many cultural transformations have come about because people willingly argued for change. Women's suffrage was a major theme 100 years ago; today, the themes are different, but reformers still speak out to create a more just, equitable, and safe society.

▶ Those who *transmit* cultural resources teach cultural beliefs, values, and behaviors. For example, volunteers prepare immigrants to become citizens by explaining the U.S. government and describing voting procedures. Religious leaders hold special classes to teach their religion's beliefs to youth and to converts.

▶ Other speakers *reinforce* or support existing cultural elements by encouraging listeners to "keep on keeping on"—to persist in their behaviors or beliefs. Politicians who urge people to keep voting and inspirational speakers who emphasize the value of tolerance are in this category.

▶ When events threaten to tear apart communities, speakers make public pronouncements that *restore* matters to a healthy state. For example, after a community tragedy, officials host meetings that provide information essential for re-establishing the community's feelings of security.

▶ Speakers *transform* societies by becoming instruments for social change. Prison reform, civil rights legislation, environmental protection—skilled speakers argued for all these changes. Even relatively well-functioning societies can be improved, and people are currently arguing for hundreds of reforms including health care and election reforms.

✔ STOP AND CHECK

RECOGNIZE YOUR CULTURAL SPEAKING TRADITIONS

What public speaking traditions does your cultural heritage provide? How expressive were you encouraged to be? Were you encouraged or discouraged from speaking because of your ethnicity, your age, your socioeconomic class, or your gender? If so, when and how? What topics are sensitive or taboo? How might your cultural traditions affect your participation and your comfort in this course?

To investigate this topic further, log on to InfoTrac College Edition to search for and read Celeste Roseberry-McKibben's article "'Mirror, Mirror on the Wall': Reflections of a 'Third Culture' American." The author was raised in the Philippines, where she was considered a "third-culture" child—not exactly American and not exactly Filipina. She now works as a speech pathologist with a diverse clientele, but her third-culture status follows her. Because she was not raised in the United States, she looks at customs here at least somewhat through the eyes of a Filipina. Compare and contrast her list of "mainstream American" values with the information presented throughout this chapter.

Whether the goal is to transmit, reinforce, repair, or transform culture, we who live in dynamic and changing cultures depend on communicators who are willing and competent enough to speak out and perpetuate positive cultural characteristics or, when necessary, who will resist and change cultural elements that need improvement.

A Theory and a Model of Communication

The word *communication* is so common that you may not think much about what actually happens when people communicate. However, scholars continue to probe the many ways that speakers, messages, listeners, and situations are interrelated. Current theories and models typically emphasize both speakers and listeners who jointly and actively co-create meaning. We'll first look at the dialogical theory and then turn to the transactional model of communication.

The Dialogical Theory of Communication

Theories are explanations by which scholars provide the general or abstract principles of a field of study. The **dialogical theory of communication** is common in communication studies. Think back to how you first learned to talk. Chances are you spent a lot of time listening and then practicing words and phrases with parents and older relatives. According to the dialogical theory, the give-and-take quality of these first conversations form the foundational pattern for all other communication activities, even public speaking.[38] In this theory, conversation and public speaking share many similarities along with some differences:

▶ In both types of communication, nonverbal cues such as facial expressions, gestures, eye contact, and vocal emphasis on specific words add meaning to the message.

▶ In both types, everyone involved actively engages the ideas presented. Helmut Geissner coined the term *respons-ibility*[39] to explain the interactions and mutual responses that co-create meanings. In conversations, the partners must work together to confirm that what is said is being understood. For example, you might hear something like this: "Let's stop at the mall." "You mean Washington Square?" "Yeah, Washington Square." Audiences also engage speakers directly, but they usually wait until the end of the speech to participate in a question-and-answer period.[40]

▶ Conversations and public speeches each have predictable structures, functions, and lengths. The Russian scholar Mikhail Bahktin explained, "We 'pour' our speech into ready-made forms or **speech genres**. These forms are given to us in the same way in which our native language is given."[41] In other words, there are cultural ways to propose marriage or greet a friend (interpersonal genres or forms), and there are cultural norms for giving an award or a eulogy (public speech genres).

▶ Meaning in both contexts depends on factors such as "[w]ho says what, where and when, why and for what, in what manner, with and for whom? . . . and who understands what, where and when, how, why, and for what, in what manner, with or from whom."[42] A conversation with your best friend about a speeding ticket differs from the conversation you have with the police officer about that same incident. A resident assistant's report about specific student concerns given in a walnut-paneled boardroom to the university's board of trustees differs from a similar report by the same RA given in a dorm lounge where students munch snacks and sip drinks as they listen. Each situation affects the multiple meanings in the speech act. In short, meanings lie in people;[43] for instance, you, your best friend,

dialogical theory of communication theory proposing that face-to-face conversation is the prototype that is foundational to all other communication

respons-**ibility** speakers' and listeners' mutual engagement with the ideas, which allows them to jointly forge meanings

speech genres cultural forms we rely upon when we participate in a specific type of communication

and the police officer will probably differ about the meaning of your speeding ticket. The purpose of communication is to get the other person to come to understand and accept your meanings.[44]

▶ As a general rule, the language and organizational structure of public speeches are more formal, and speeches are more carefully prepared than conversations (although conversational delivery is desirable in public speaking).

Theories, in short, explain a phenomenon or process, and the dialogical theory helps explain the communication process. This theory builds on the prototype of dialogue as foundational to all other communication. However, because theories are generally abstract, many people prefer a diagram or model to help them better understand the concept.

The Transactional Model of Communication

The most common model of communication, the **transactional model**[45] shown in Figure 1.1, depicts communication as a process in which the communicators create mutual meanings. The model is one way to think about what happens during communication. It includes the following components, described by showing how they interact when you give a speech:

▶ As a *sender-receiver* (or source), you originate or *encode* a message by selecting words (a verbal code) to represent your ideas. In your preparation, you must consider your audience, reflecting on what you learn about them and their knowledge of and interest in your topic. For instance, you may discover some of their interests, past experiences, their need-to-know, or other pertinent information as you prepare your remarks.

transactional model of communication represents communication as a process in which speakers and listeners work together to create mutual meanings

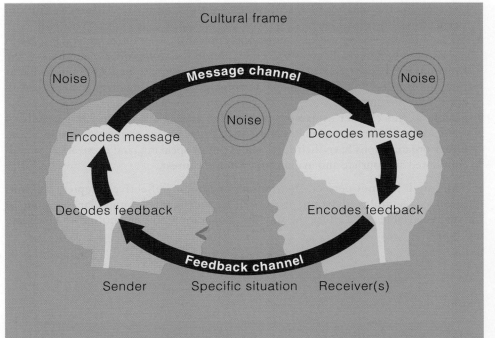

Figure 1.1
Transactional Model of Communication. The transactional model depicts communication as a dialogical process in which communicators co-create messages in culturally appropriate situations.

- Your *messages* are intentional. In your speech classroom, you might be assigned to inform or persuade. In other settings, you might give a report, honor another person's achievements, or try to make your audience laugh. You intentionally choose language your audience will understand, reasoning they accept, and illustrations that relate to their lives.

- In classroom speeches you use the face-to-face, voice-to-ear *channel* along with nonverbal channels such as gestures or tone of voice to convey your message. In other settings you might speak in a video conference or record your message digitally and upload it to a fileserver or Internet site where your audience can listen at their leisure.

- *Receivers-senders* hear your words and *decode* or interpret them. They create meanings out of their personal backgrounds and heritages, plus their individual beliefs, values, worries, and judgments. Each listener filters your words through his or her personal perceptions, thoughts, and feelings, and sometimes through the influence of other listeners.

- Your audience sends you messages called *feedback*. With face-to-face audiences, some may ask questions; some may nod, frown, smile, or clap. Some may even heckle you. You decode this feedback and adapt to it. For example, if you see confused faces, you might add details to clarify your point. If your listeners seem bored, you might regain attention with an interesting example. Were you to use another channel, such as YouTube or a personal blog, feedback would come in the form of written remarks below your video. In this transactional process of mutual sending-receiving-responding, you and your listeners cooperate in creating meaning.

- *Noise*, or static, can interfere with both the message and its reception. So if you have a sore throat and must speak softly, your words might be difficult to hear. If a leafblower is roaring outside the window (*external noise*) as you speak, the message might be lost. *Internal noise*, such as listeners' worries over being overdrawn at the bank or their hunger pangs, can also disrupt the process. Finally, *cultural noise* occurs when cultural differences make the message irrelevant or offensive, as when the topic or the manner of the presentation run counter to a listener's cultural norms.[46]

- Your speech takes place within a situational context. During the term, you'll speak in a classroom within a college or university. But in the workplace or community, the situations will be more varied. Regardless of the situation, things like room temperature, lighting, room decor, available technology, and seating arrangements can all affect your presentation.

- Finally, as this chapter explained, each speech takes place within a larger cultural framework. Classroom speeches come with expectations about higher education. Other organizations have their ideas about public speaking, and these affect what is considered appropriate and inappropriate in the context.

Although it is not perfect, the transactional model effectively depicts communication as a complex, dynamic process. It further identifies and clarifies some of the many variables that affect the way we cooperate with one another to co-create meanings.

PRACTICALLY SPEAKING

LIINA TEOSE, PIANO TEACHER

Sara Reamy

On a sunny winter afternoon in Portland, Oregon, about forty of Liina Teose's piano students crowded into a small performance hall to overcome their anxiety and play their carefully rehearsed pieces before a supportive crowd of relatives and friends. Liina, who never thought of her occupation as one that would require public speaking, found herself addressing the crowd twice. First, she welcomed the audience and the performers with this short, encouraging speech:

> There are two types of people at this recital: musicians and nonmusicians. All of the musicians here have been in your shoes— every musician gets nervous from time to time. Therefore, the musicians TOTALLY sympathize with you. The non-musicians? They totally admire you, because you can do something they cannot do. They are in awe that you have the courage to get up there and play! So now, I'd like to introduce the first musician . . .

After the recital, she congratulated the performers for their fine work and added remarks that informed the audience about a professional milestone she recently attained. Her goal was to explain the nature of her newly granted certification, which, in turn, bolstered her credibility as a music teacher:

> You may have noticed the letters NCTM after my name on the program today. Those letters are an abbreviation for "Nationally Certified Teacher of Music." I belong to the Music Teachers' National Association, which is the professional association for music teachers throughout the United States. I am excited to let you know that, at the beginning of this month, I became a *nationally certified* teacher of music.
>
> Earning MTNA certification means that my qualifications as an independent music teacher have been evaluated and approved by a board of leaders in the field.
>
> It has been a year-and-a-half process for me to fulfill the requirements and study for the certification examination, and I know that I am now a much better teacher than I was before. Certification also demonstrates my commitment to the profession of piano teaching. It *reflects* achievement and *establishes* professional credentials.
>
> It also demonstrates my commitment to you, my students, as well as to my continuing professional development.

She closed the formal part of the recital by thanking the audience for coming and then announcing the location of refreshments.

Questions for Discussion

▶ Identify at least five occupations in which public speaking is essential.
▶ Identify at least five occupations in which a person might not expect to speak. Then identify some situations in which a person in each of these occupations might speak in job-related venues.

Summary

This chapter introduced some of the benefits you can gain by studying public speaking from a perspective of cultural diversity. The study of rhetoric, a cornerstone of a liberal arts education, can equip you with critical thinking skills useful in everyday interactions. Along the way, you will learn skills that are personally and professionally valuable in a culture that relies on skilled speakers and listeners.

By definition, cultures emerge, maintain themselves, and change through communication. Cultures include both the visible and the underlying (embedded) aspects of a society; they are complex, containing many co-cultural groups which often have different norms for speaking and listening. Our cultures affect our public speaking in a number of ways. They provide us with core resources that include beliefs, values, attitudes, and behaviors that shape our own speeches and our responses to others' messages. In addition, our technologically advanced society provides a variety of resources we can use to research topics and present our speeches. Finally, our cultural heritages provide expectations regarding the *how*, the *who*, and the *what* of public speaking. Of course, within each culture, individual personalities and preferences also shape the ways we communicate.

Culture affects public speaking, and public speaking affects culture. Through public speaking, we transmit core cultural beliefs, values, and attitudes to newcomers who must learn appropriate behaviors in specific contexts. Public speeches reinforce or support culture as it is, and through speaking we repair or restore community when it is threatened. We also change or transform cultural elements that are outmoded or dysfunctional.

The chapter closed with the dialogical theory and the transactional model of communication. Dialogical theory assumes that face-to-face conversations form the prototype for other types of speech, including public speaking. Although public speaking shares similarities with conversations, it also differs in significant ways. The communication model depicts in visual form the transactional nature of communication. It emphasizes that both the originator of the message and the receiver must cooperate if they are to *transact* or negotiate meaning. Although public speakers originate messages, they should remember that meanings lie in people, so they must adapt to feedback both as they prepare and as they speak. Listeners participate by actively decoding information and encoding feedback. All this communication, which can be negatively affected by both internal and external noise, takes place within a specific situation and cultural frame.

STUDY AND REVIEW

Your online resources for *Public Speaking: Concepts and Skills for a Diverse Society* offers a broad range of tools that will help you better understand the material in this chapter, complete assignments, and succeed on tests. Your online resources feature

- Speech videos with critical viewing questions, speech outlines, and transcripts
- Interactive versions of this chapter's Stop and Check activities and Application and Critical Thinking Exercises
- Speech Builder Express and InfoTrac College Edition
- Weblinks related to chapter content
- Study and review tools such as self-quizzes, an interactive glossary, and downloadable audio summaries

You can access your online resources at http://www.cengage.com/login, using the access code that came with your book or that you bought online at http://www.iChapters.com.

KEY TERMS

The terms below are defined in the margins throughout this chapter.

bicultural 8
co-cultures 4
communication style 7
core cultural resources 6
cultures 4
dialogical theory of communication 10
expressive cultures 6
nonexpressive cultures 6

oral culture 6
public speaking 1
respons-ibility 10
rhetoric 2
rhetorical sensitivity 5
speech genres 10
transactional model of communication 11

APPLICATION AND CRITICAL THINKING EXERCISES

1. Sometimes people do not see themselves as public speakers because they define the word *public* too narrowly. They think of public speakers as politicians speaking at conventions but not as a concerned citizen testifying before the city council. Write your definition of "public." Then, make a list of specific publics you have already addressed and those you may address someday.

2. To gain experience in speaking publicly, prepare an announcement using the guidelines in Appendix B, and deliver it to your classmates. Look for upcoming campus or community events that would interest the audience.

3. To understand the importance of critical thinking skills, work with a group to select a short video on YouTube, a news report, or an ad to analyze. Begin by giving your first impressions. What does the piece you've selected say or suggest? Then probe deeper and identify the assumptions on which it relies. Next, ask question about those assumptions. Finally, compare your first impressions with your impressions about the selection after you've examined it more carefully. Discuss with your classmates the value of critical analysis.

4. What stereotypes do you hold about the word *rhetoric?* The Internet has many sources of information on this topic. Visit **www.americanrhetoric.com** and do some of the "Cool Exercises" or watch a couple of speeches. This will help you understand the value of rhetoric.

5. Throughout the term, listen for the word *rhetoric* as it is used in public discourse. Each time you encounter the word, decide whether it's being used negatively, positively, or neutrally. Note if any of the sources speak of rhetoric as essential in a free society.

6. Interview a person working in the career you hope to enter after you graduate. Ask what opportunities exist for public speaking within that occupation. Ask if and how public speaking is related to the higher-paying, more prestigious jobs within that career.

7. Work with a group to evaluate the role of public speaking in creating and maintaining your college or university.
   ▶ What role did public speaking play during the founding years?
   ▶ How does your school currently use public speaking to recruit new students and donors?
   ▶ What role does ceremonial speaking, such as convocations or commencement addresses, have in maintaining the vision and the values of your institution?
   ▶ When issues threaten to divide your campus, how do groups and individuals use public speaking to negotiate differences?

8. Many online speeches can help you see the relationship between public speaking and culture. One such example is Barack Obama's speech on race, "A More Perfect Union," given in response to widely disseminated video clips of controversial statements by his pastor. It's available at **www.americanrhetoric.com**. Watch it outside of class and then come to class prepared to discuss how it might function to transmit, reinforce, restore, and/or transform culture.

9. In a small group, give examples to show how public speaking is similar to everyday conversation and how it differs. Use the dialogical theory and the communication model to guide your thinking.

10. Elaborate on the transactional model of communication by selecting a communication event from your own life and analyze it by identifying and explaining each element of the model.

SPEECH VIDEO

Short speeches are common at commemorative events such as graduation parties, retirement or award dinners, weddings, and funerals. Here is a speech that Alexandria Reed gave at her twin brothers' graduation party. Go to your online resources to watch and critique her speech.

Sample Speech

GRADUATION PARTY SPEECH
Alexandria Reed

Think about the last time someone gave you directions. They may have included the phrase "a fork in the road." Today, Jeffrey and Michael have come to that fork in the road. But first, let me share with you the journey that has brought them to this fork in the road.

Courtesy of Alexandria Reed

Their journey began, not on different paths, but as one single cell: Jeffrey was born first, and Michael followed just 57 minutes later. They were close as babies. They even spoke their own "twin language" before they spoke English. The doctors almost had my parents separate them because they would only say the words they used to communicate with each other; they didn't even say "Mommy" or "Daddy." When they were toddlers they also liked to bite (particularly their older sister). Their word when they got mad must have been "nony" because they always yelled it before they bit someone. My mom learned to come running to my safety when she heard that from one of the twins.

They remained a "single unit." In fact, through elementary school, they were always in the same classroom. I have always referred to them as "the boys."

Their journey began to take them on different paths during middle school, and high school became a time for them to grow. Michael became involved with band and later with drama. He even became drum major his senior year. Jeffrey grew to love sports (especially basketball) and fell in love with cars. He is now restoring his own truck. "The boys" still hold a close bond and support each other's activities.

Now their journey brings them to a fork in the road. Next year Jeffrey will join me at Hope College, while Michael will attend the University of Michigan. Jeffrey will try out for the basketball team and Michael for the marching band. You can bet you will see Michael at some of Jeffrey's games and Jeffrey at the Michigan football games cheering on his brother.

Michael and Jeffrey, I am proud of each of your accomplishments. As you take this fork in the road, may the directions in your life always be clear. I look forward to seeing you succeed in all of your future endeavors.

GIVING YOUR FIRST SPEECH: DEVELOPING CONFIDENCE

THIS CHAPTER WILL HELP YOU

▶ **Develop skills to overcome process anxiety**

▶ **Explain the five canons of rhetoric: invention, disposition, style, memory, and delivery**

▶ **Develop strategies to deal with performance anxiety**

▶ **Develop strategies to deal with physiological anxiety**

▶ **Develop strategies to deal with psychological anxiety**

▶ **Learn skills for effective rehearsal**

© Tim Timmerman

communication apprehension (CA) the fear or dread of negative responses you might experience because you speak out

I N A MEMORABLE SCENE from the 1998 movie *Elizabeth*, Cate Blanchett portrays the young English queen rehearsing an important speech that she will later deliver to an imposing audience of older male leaders who are largely hostile toward her ideas. In the privacy of her room, she stammers; she thinks of the men whose eyes will be fixed on her; she pauses; she repeats her phrases, searching for just the right words; at several points, she covers her face with her hands as she thinks of how best to persuade the men. Dissolve. Next scene: Elizabeth I sits regally on her throne, clearly stating her case and expertly fielding questions from the audience. (Watch the movie clip at **www.americanrhetoric .com** under "Movie Speeches.")

We don't know whether or not Queen Elizabeth I actually suffered from stage fright, but we might expect that she was no different from other mortals who experience anxiety in at least some situations. We don't always know what to say, and we can't always predict how others will react to our speeches. Sometimes our messages are important, but our listeners are intimidating. In short, communication can be scary. Because so many people express at least some anxiety in some contexts, communication researchers have conducted thousands of studies looking for causes and cures of **communication apprehension (CA)**, which is commonly defined as "the fear or anxiety associated with either real or anticipated communication with another person or persons."[1] It is the dread of possible negative reactions you might experience when you communicate.[2] CA is linked to learning style preferences[3] and to inborn temperament traits such as shyness.[4]

One context that strikes fear into many hearts is public speaking. Call it stage fright or **public speaking anxiety (PSA)**—whatever name you prefer, the term refers to the common feelings of dread many people have at the thought of giving a speech. For example, one student confessed:

> Nothing scares me worse than public speaking. I would rather shoot myself in the foot or go bungee jumping than speak in front of people. I spend days with my stomach in knots and when I get up to speak, I feel like I can't breathe. My hands shake and my legs feel like jelly.
>
> ANNA

Other students gave specific reasons for their PSA:

> Standing in front of people, knowing that they are judging you
>
> CLAIRE

> Knowing what to speak about
>
> JONATHAN

> I am very shy, and I don't like to talk much to a single person, let alone a group.
>
> REESE

Their comments reveal two types of anxiety: **process anxiety** (not knowing how to create a speech) and **performance anxiety** (nervousness about actually giving the speech). The goal of this chapter is to help you decrease both types by demystifying the speechmaking process and by giving you strategies for dealing with nervousness. Putting this information into practice will increase your overall speaking competence.

Polygram / The Kobal Collection / Bailey, Alex /Picture Desk

One scene in the movie *Elizabeth* shows the young queen, who is nervous about addressing a hostile audience of powerful men, rehearsing in the quiet of her room. Careful planning and practice helped her successfully present her ideas.

public speaking anxiety (PSA) fear or dread specifically related to speaking in public

process anxiety fear due to lack of confidence in knowing how to prepare a speech

performance anxiety fear of forgetting or of poorly presenting a speech

Develop Skills to Overcome Process Anxiety

"I'm counting on you to give a speech next week, so let me tell you what I'm expecting . . ." When you first hear these words—whether the setting be work, school, or an organization you belong to—you may begin to experience tension. In fact, Paul Witt and Ralph Behnke[5] found that **anticipatory speech anxiety** is highest just after the speech is announced. Why? Perhaps it's fear of the unknown—you may feel like you're in unfamiliar territory without a map.[6] Fortunately, studying speech principles, observing others speak, and actually speaking yourself, can remove some of the mystery from the process. As speechmaking becomes more familiar, most people experience less process anxiety and the panicky feelings that accompany it.

Think of it this way: When you learn any new skill, you follow the guidelines quite closely at first. Only after you have mastered the basics do you feel confident enough to take liberties. Remember when you first learned to drive? You concentrated on every move; later, the process of steering, shifting, and braking became automatic. Public speaking is similar. Early on, the guidelines are more structured and specific. However, after you gain experience, you can be more creative in your preparation.

As Chapter 1 pointed out, rhetoric has a 2,500-year tradition in the West, rooted in classical Greek and Roman academies. As a result of closely studying the "how-to" of speechmaking, early speech educators divided the process into five major elements or categories: (1) invention—creating the speech; (2) disposition or arrangement—organizing speech materials; (3) style—choosing effective language; (4) memory—learning the major ideas; and (5) delivery—actually performing the speech. (See Figure 2.1.) In each category they identified a **canon** (a set of principles, standards, norms, or guidelines) that students should master to become effective orators. They called these five categories, and the principles within them, the five **canons of rhetoric**.[7] When you know the principles in the canons you will understand the process of speech creation.

Create Your Speech: The Canon of Invention

The **canon of invention** provides guidelines for creating the content of your speech. Just as an inventor designs a product that solves a particular problem, you must design a speech that meets a need for a specific audience in a specific situation. Principles in the canon of invention help you analyze your audience, select an appropriate topic and purpose, gather evidence, and develop reasonable and logical arguments and explanations. This text devotes nine chapters to this vital canon, but as a general introduction and to help you prepare your first speech, each principle is briefly summarized here.

Consider the Audience and the Setting

Your first task is to think about your audience and the individuals within it. Look around and notice any details that might influence your speaking choices. Of course, gender and age may be obvious, but look for additional features such as wedding rings, religious jewelry, or clothing that suggests particular interests or affiliations. Strike up conversations with people as a way to learn more about them. It may help if you think of your entire class as a miniculture that develops unique ways of interacting. (See the Diversity in Practice box for more on this point.) These strategies will help you think of each audience as individuals who make up a larger group.

Consider also the situation in which your speech takes place. Elements such as lighting, ventilation, acoustics, and room layout make a difference. Other factors, such as time of day, matter as well. Is your audience typically hungry or sleepy during the time you're scheduled to speak? Being mindful of details such as these will help you move to the next task—choosing your subject and purpose.

anticipatory speech anxiety tension experienced at the mere thought of giving a speech

canon a set of principles, standards, norms, or guidelines

canons of rhetoric principles, standards, norms, or guidelines for creating and delivering a speech

canon of invention principles for designing a speech that meets a need of a specific audience

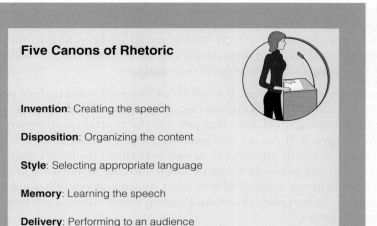

Figure 2.1
The Romans identified five canons of rhetoric. Each canon contains principles, standards, norms, or guidelines for one aspect of speechmaking.

⬤ DIVERSITY IN PRACTICE

YOUR CLASSROOM CULTURE

Cultures are not always national or regional in scope. Groups—even those as small as your class—develop distinct ways of doing things, which means that each becomes a miniculture with its own set of beliefs, values, and norms or rituals.[8] If this seems confusing, consider the differences between a speech class and a biology class. Or contrast three business classes: In one, a professor lectures every period; in another, an instructor uses discussions and small group exercises to present course concepts; the third is a hybrid course, with some face-to-face and some online interactions.

Similarly, one speech class may develop a warm, open, supportive climate in which class members believe in each other's ability to succeed. They value one another's feelings, and they create rituals, such as learning the names of their classmates and chatting as they gather. In contrast, another class might develop a closed, hostile, or competitive culture whose members ignore one another and sleep, study, or text message during other students' speeches.

Instructors generally identify their beliefs, values, and behavioral norms during the first class session. They typically state that public speaking is important, and they affirm openness, honesty, and diversity as fundamental values. They also provide expectations about respectful listening and speaking behaviors. Throughout the term, everyone contributes to the classroom culture by the way they accept and live out the norms.

Choose a Topic

"What will I talk about?" This may be your first question for a classroom assignment. (In other contexts, such as in an organization or workplace, the topic will be more obvious.) The first class assignment is often either a self-introduction or the introduction of a classmate. If so, topic choice is partly done for you, but finding an interesting focus is still a challenge. If you must introduce a classmate, set up an interview that will uncover one or more unusual facts about the person, and focus your speech around these details. A self-introduction may create more anxiety because *you* are in the spotlight. You must reveal something personal, and you must decide just what details you are willing to share. With any speech assignment, consider these guidelines:

▶ *Be sure you understand the expectations.* You will be embarrassed—and perhaps penalized—if you prepare carefully only to discover that you've misunderstood the assignment. So pay special attention to guidelines that describe the general requirements and time limits for the speech. If you are confused, ask questions. Look at the examples at the end of chapters and in Appendix C, as well as those on the book's online resources, where you'll find numerous videos of sample speeches to watch and critique. The examples will help you understand how other students successfully completed similar assignments. In workplace situations, knowing what's expected will help you avoid unpleasant surprises.

▶ *Reveal something unusual.* Avoid boring your audience with something everyone has experienced; instead, search for a unique focus. Students have described unusual jobs (working as a pyrotechnician, setting off firework displays), vacations (a trip to New Zealand), and volunteerism (helping residents recover after a natural disaster).

▶ *Select a significant topic.* Have you had life-changing experiences? Have you learned important lessons that others could also learn? Consider incorporating your personal adventures or insights into a speech. For her first class assignment, Mona described her decision to return to school after a divorce, and Enrique described his experiences with AnyTown USA.

▶ *Consider a story format.* Sharing a story is often a good way to connect with your audience. In fact, Chapter 15 describes narrative speaking in detail; there, you'll find a pattern that is especially effective for introductory speeches.

▶ *Consider your listeners' sensibilities.* Your purpose is not to shock your audience by revealing highly personal information or potentially embarrassing details. This is an opportunity to be rhetorically sensitive in your preparation; try to think from the diverse perspectives of audience members.

▶ *Try out your ideas on people you trust.* Discuss your audience and your assignment with close friends or associates. If you have two or three ideas, elicit opinions about each one.

If you have been considering your audience all along, you should have a pretty good sense of what are and are not appropriate topics.

Identify Your Purpose

After you have selected your topic, identify your reason for speaking, given your specific audience. What response do you want from them? Your answer to this question determines your general purpose. Most speeches focus on one of the following four goals:

▶ Do you want your audience to learn something? If so, your general purpose is *to inform*.
▶ Do you want them to respond by believing or doing something? Are you trying to reinforce their beliefs or behaviors? Then your general purpose is *to persuade*.
▶ Do you want them simply to laugh and enjoy themselves? If so, your purpose is *to entertain*.
▶ Do you want to highlight and reinforce a particular cultural ideal? If so, your general purpose is *to commemorate*.

Of course, these purposes often overlap. In a speech of introduction, your major goal is to inform the class about either yourself or another classmate, but you should also be at least somewhat entertaining. And, Enrique Ruiz's speech, printed at the end of this chapter, shows that it's often effective to highlight a cultural ideal such as the importance of diversity and tolerance.

Roshan Begay

Interesting and unusual personal experiences often make good speech topics. Enrique spoke about his experiences at Anytown USA, a camp that teaches diversity skills. He supplemented his personal experiences with research on the history and mission of the camp.

Gather Speech Materials

Although you are probably familiar with many of the topics you choose, you can fill the gaps in your knowledge by consulting outside resources. Go to the library or log onto its website to search for information in databases, on CD-ROMs, DVDs, video or audiotapes, or in books, journals, newspapers, and magazines. Television and radio shows can also provide useful information. And of course, the Internet is a major source of information if you think critically about what you find there. Finally, remember to take advantage of materials on this text's online resources for help in doing your research.

Although an introductory speech generally relies less on outside research and more on personal experiences or on an interview with the subject, you may need to consult some sources. For example, before Brent introduced himself by talking about the most interesting job he ever had (working at the Oregon Garden), he read brochures from the garden and studied its website for information. His basic outline included three major points:

▶ Working at the Oregon Garden was one of the most interesting jobs I've ever had because the garden was still being developed, so it changed all the time.
▶ I met people from all over the world who visited the garden.
▶ Major concerts were held there and I helped set up the sound stage for some famous entertainers.

If your assignment is to introduce a classmate, schedule an interview for an uninterrupted time in a quiet place—and then be on time. Bring a list of questions and record your conversation (with permission only) or take notes as you talk. Be sure you understand what you are told by asking questions such as, "Could you explain in more detail the different types of fireworks you set off?" To avoid any misunderstandings, summarize the major ideas as you conclude.

Organize Your Ideas: The Canon of Disposition or Arrangement

After you've gathered your information, you must then arrange your ideas so that they make sense. The principles of speech organization make up the **canon of disposition** or **arrangement**.

canon of disposition or **arrangement** guidelines for organizing a speech

Most speeches in the Western speaking tradition have three major parts: the introduction, the body, and the conclusion. An introduction orients your audience toward the subject. The body of the speech, which generally takes up most of your speaking time, follows; here, you explain and develop your major ideas. Finally, a memorable conclusion rounds out the speech. Taken as a whole, the outline looks like this:

I. **INTRODUCTION** In general, introductions have these four major functions which were identified by the first-century Roman educator Quintilian:[9]
    A. Draw audience attention to the topic.
    B. Relate the topic to their concerns.
    C. Link yourself to the subject.
    D. Preview the major points.
II. **SPEECH BODY** Here, you present and develop your major ideas, using enough evidence to clarify and support each point. There are many ways to organize speeches, and patterns such as topical, problem-solution, and chronological will be discussed in more detail in Chapter 9. These patterns result in a linear arrangement, as shown by this speech outline:
    A. First main point
        1. Support
        2. Support
    B. Second main point
        1. Support
        2. Support
III. **CONCLUSION** Good speakers don't stop abruptly. Instead, they provide a sense of closure that ties the ideas together and leaves the audience with something to take away with them. Conclusions typically have these elements:
    A. A transition to the conclusion
    B. A reference to the introduction
    C. A summary of the major ideas
    D. A final memorable statement

Connect Your Ideas

Your major work is done, and it's time to weave your ideas together so that your speech flows smoothly from point to point. Words and phrases that link your ideas with one another are called **connectives**. Simple connectives include words such as *first, next,* and *finally*. More complex connectives, such as "Not only did I watch the Oregon Garden develop and meet international visitors, I also helped set up sound stages for some nationally known performers," summarize where your speech has been and where it is going. Connectives help your listeners keep their place in the speech by linking the various points to one another and to the speech as a whole.

Once you have gathered materials and selected an organizational pattern, you can then choose precise wording and learn your speech well enough to deliver it to an audience. The principles for these aspects of speechmaking are found in the final three canons of rhetoric: style, memory, and delivery.

Choose Suitable Language: The Canon of Style

When asked "What do you think it means when someone says, 'I like your style?'" two students responded:

> You would most likely mean that you like the way I carry myself or the way I act.
>
> MATT

---

connectives words and phrases used to tie the ideas together

It would probably mean that you like something about my personality or the way I handle things and people.

Josh

A dictionary would say they're right. Style can mean your individuality as expressed in your actions and tastes.[10] However, in rhetoric, **style** means language. Because the **canon of style** contains the principles for using language effectively in both speaking and writing, you may have used a style manual in a writing class.

Put the finishing touches on your ideas by polishing the words of the speech, always with an ear tuned to your listeners. Here are a few general guidelines for effective use of language in public speaking:

▶ Choose vocabulary and grammar that fit both the occasion and the audience. This means adapting to audience characteristics such as occupation, age, or educational level.
▶ Omit offensive language such as swear words or demeaning language.
▶ Choose understandable words. Either define technical jargon or replace it with more familiar terminology.
▶ Minimize slang expressions. Language used in public speeches is generally more formal than language used in everyday conversation.

More detailed information on the canon of style is provided in Chapter 12.

Learn and Present Your Speech: The Canons of Memory and Delivery

Because they lacked index cards, teleprompters, and other memory aids, Roman educators taught their students elaborate techniques for learning a speech by heart. However, the **canon of memory** is often called *the lost canon* because so few people in this culture rely on memory alone and because **memorized delivery** can be risky. Forgetting even a few simple words can lead to public embarrassment—something you definitely want to avoid. **Manuscript delivery**, in which you write out your entire speech and then read it to your audience, helps you remember your ideas, but it is generally more useful for formal talks than for classroom or workplace speeches where reading might mean you lose important eye contact with listeners. Also, spur-of-the-moment **impromptu delivery**, where you stand up and speak with little advanced preparation is not recommended for most classroom assignments, although it's not uncommon in workplace settings or social events, where you might be asked to "say a few words" on a familiar topic.

Mary Kate Denny/PhotoEdit

Rehearse before your speech. Learn your main ideas and give the speech differently each time instead of trying to memorize it word for word. When possible, practice on friends who are willing to listen and give feedback.

style in rhetoric, style refers to language

canon of style principles for choosing effective language

canon of memory guidelines to help you remember your ideas

memorized delivery learning the speech by heart, then reciting it

manuscript delivery reading a speech

impromptu delivery speaking with little advanced preparation

Instead, **extemporaneous delivery**, in which you carefully prepare your remarks in advance but choose the exact wording as you speak, is preferable in most classroom and work situations. Gather your materials, organize them carefully, and then jot down key ideas, single words, phrases, and statistics on note cards that you later use to jog your memory during the talk itself. Your main ideas are in place, but you choose the exact wording as you go. Chapter 14 elaborates on these four delivery methods, and Chapter 11 gives you additional information on content outlines and speaking outlines.

Rehearsal is a vital part of the preparation process. Find a quiet place where you can deliver your speech out loud, using your note cards. If possible, practice in the room where you'll actually speak. Recruit friends or family—basically anyone who can act as an audience, provide feedback, troubleshoot problems, and let you practice speaking in front of a group. Go through the speech several times, each time selecting slightly different words. Focus on looking away from your notes and communicating conversationally. Although practice may not make perfect, the more prepared you are, the better you will feel about your presentation.

Principles found in the **canon of delivery** provide guidelines on the four delivery methods described earlier and on nonverbal behaviors, such as gestures and eye contact. In brief, you will be more skillful if you do the following during your speech:

▶ Make eye contact with your listeners.
▶ Maintain pleasant facial expressions.
▶ Avoid speaking in a monotone voice.
▶ Smile at appropriate times.
▶ Assume a posture of confidence.
▶ Incorporate appropriate gestures.
▶ Speak conversationally.
▶ Stay within the time limits.

Focus throughout, not on giving something *to* your audience, but on creating something *with* them.

The guidelines found in the five canons of rhetoric build process competence. You learn to analyze your audience, select a topic and purpose, and gather materials (invention). Then you organize or arrange your ideas into meaningful patterns (disposition), choose appropriate language (style), and learn your major points (memory), so that you can present them effectively (delivery). Afterwards, you must deal with performance anxiety.

For additional information on the canons of rhetoric, follow links on the website The Forest of Rhetoric at **http://humanities.byu.edu/rhetoric/silva.htm**.

BUILD YOUR SPEECH
YOUR FIRST SPEECH

Using the five canons of rhetoric, prepare a self-introduction or the introduction of a classmate. Throughout your preparation, consider the following questions:

1. Do I understand the assignment?
2. Is my topic somewhat unusual? If not, do I have a unique or novel approach?
3. How will I adapt this speech to this audience?
4. Which friends can I ask to listen to my ideas?

For additional help building your first and subsequent speeches, use your online resources to access Speech Builder Express.

---

extemporaneous delivery
preparing a speech carefully in advance but choosing the exact wording during the speech itself

canon of delivery rules or standards for presenting a speech

Develop Strategies to Overcome Performance Anxiety

Performance anxiety comes in two forms: physiological and psychological. **Physiological anxiety** is your bodily response to the feared event. **Psychological anxiety** manifests itself in worry, dread, and feelings of inadequacy about the performance itself. This student describes both types:

> I was anxious about my speech from the first moment I knew about it. I became most worried the night before and the day of the speech. I worry about how I present my speech, and I'm not very confident in my abilities. Once I stand in front of the class, I become rigid and my stomach is in knots. I generally turn red (shades) and talk differently (due to nerves).
>
> EILEEN

This section discusses a number of specific skills you can use in combination to overcome both kinds of nervousness.

Develop Strategies to Deal with Physiological Responses

You know from experience how your body responds to dangerous situations. You might have a "deer-in-the-headlights" response in which you **freeze** or become rigid in the face of danger. Or you might experience the **fight-or-flight mechanism** that takes over when adrenalin rushes in to help you race away from the danger or stay to fight the threat. Unfortunately, your body doesn't distinguish between physically threatening situations (where you actually need the extra physical energy to make your escape) and psychologically threatening experiences (where your increased heart rate, butterfiies, and adrenaline rush only add to your stress). Ralph Behnke and Chris Sawyer[11] identify four milestones of anxiety-producing events: (1) *anticipation*, the prespeaking period; (2) *confrontation*, beginning the speech; (3) *adaptation*, completing the speech; (4) *release*, after the speech. Anxiety peaks in the anticipation period and steadily decreases, virtually disappearing in the release milestone, although some symptoms may linger.[12] (See Figure 2.2).

Here's how a beginning speech student described the process:

> As I sit in class, my anxiety level increases by the minute. Right before and as I walk to the front of the room, I use all my power to hide how nervous I am. I take a deep breath and start talking. During the beginning of my speech, anxiety is the worst. My nervous habits show through most in the beginning. As I continue my speech, it gets easier and I become more comfortable. By the conclusion, I'm usually cool, calm, and collected!
>
> EMILY

To counteract physical tension, engage in some form of physical exercise beforehand, such as lifting weights, brisk walking, or running. Listen to soothing music. Don't skip breakfast or lunch, and limit sugar and caffeine if these substances make you feel wired. Focus on relaxing your major muscle groups and breathe slowly and deeply just before you speak.

These additional tactics may ease your anxiety:

▶ Plan a compelling introduction to help carry you through the anxiety peak at the beginning of the speech. Just before you speak, silently repeat the goal of the speech, the main ideas, and your introduction so you will start well.

▶ Volunteer to go first. This decreases the length of the anticipation period.

▶ Use appropriate visual aids, especially at the start of your speech. They can ease your tension because they give the audience something to look at besides you.

▶ Deliver your introduction from notes, rather than reading it or reciting a memorized text. When you read, you risk disengaging your audience, and a memorized introduction is hazardous at such a high-anxiety point in your speech.

physiological anxiety bodily responses to a perceived threat (increased heart rate, adrenaline rush)

psychological anxiety mental stress about a perceived threat

freeze become rigid or unable to function in the presence of threat

fight-or-flight mechanism physiological mechanism your body automatically activates when threatened; helps you fight or flee

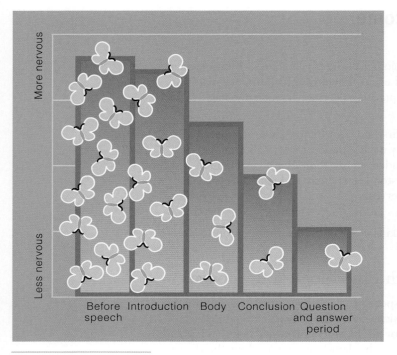

More nervous

Less nervous

Before speech   Introduction   Body   Conclusion   Question and answer period

Figure 2.2
Performance Anxiety
Knowing that anxiety is greater at certain periods can help you control your nervousness by planning strategies that enable you to get through these periods.

Develop Strategies to Deal with Psychological Anxiety

Although you may know better, you might hear an internal voice saying, "I don't know what I'm doing. I'll forget halfway through. I probably won't get my ideas across. They'll see my knees shake." Self-talk is called **internal monologue** (I-M).[13] Negative I-M contributes to negative stress, which, according to Mt. Sinai Medical Center, occurs when you believe the demands of the situation exceed your ability to cope.[14] Although negative self-talk adds to your discomfort, it's not fatal. Researchers have identified two areas of vulnerability: your level of confidence (I've never done this before; I'm embarrassed about my looks; I'll flunk) and your expectations regarding the audience's reactions (they'll make fun of me; they don't want to hear what I have to say; they won't pay attention; they'd rather be somewhere else).[15]

Control Your Internal Monologue

Mt. Sinai experts suggest one way to manage stress is to change your perceptions. That is, learn to control your I-M by a process called **cognitive modification**. Identify negative thoughts and replace them with positive ones[16] in four areas: the message, the audience, yourself, and the assignment:

▶ To think positively about the message, select a topic that interests you and is relevant to your audience. Know your goal for the speech. Give yourself enough time for research and organization. Check the dictionary to make sure you know how to pronounce unfamiliar words.

▶ To promote positive thoughts about the audience, think of each listener as an individual with personal quirks. Each person alone would not be threatening, so why should several be intimidating?[17] Remember that your listeners are probably just as nervous when they speak and that they are not experts in your subject. Assume that they want you to succeed, and focus on the purpose of your speech. (If your first language is not English, think of how your audience would feel if they had to give a speech in *your* native language.)

▶ Maintain a positive self-image by concentrating on things you do well. Remind yourself that your worth as a person is unrelated to your skill as a novice public speaker and that competence develops with experience.

▶ Finally, think realistically about the assignment.[18] Don't take a world-class orator as a model of what your classroom speech should look and sound like. Instead, watch examples of beginning public speaking students fulfilling an assignment. This book and its accompanying materials provide many sample speeches that will give you reasonable expectations for student speeches.

Remember, too, that being nervous does not mean you're doing a bad job. The fact is that some nervousness can energize you and make you appear more vital and enthusiastic.[19]

internal monologue (I-M)
self-talk

cognitive modification
identifying negative thoughts and replacing them with positive ones

STOP AND CHECK

ASSESS YOUR PUBLIC SPEAKING ANXIETY

Take this test to self-assess your anxiety regarding public speaking. In the blank beside the statement, write the number of the response that best reflects your feelings.

0 = Rarely
1 = Sometimes
2 = Usually
3 = Almost always

_____ 1. I begin to get nervous the moment the speech is assigned.
_____ 2. I feel panicky because I don't know how to create a speech.
_____ 3. I usually feel nervous the day before I have to speak.
_____ 4. The night before the speech I can't sleep well.
_____ 5. I'm afraid people will think I'm dumb or boring or weird in some way.
_____ 6. On the morning of the speech, I am really tense.
_____ 7. I find it difficult to think positively about giving a speech.
_____ 8. I think my physical reactions are greater than those that other people experience.
_____ 9. During my speech I actually think I'll faint.
_____ 10. I continue to worry even after the speech is over.

Add Your Scores

_____ Total score
0–5   You are virtually fearless.
6–15   Your level of anxiety is quite normal.
16–25   Your level of anxiety may give you problems.
26–30   Consider making an appointment with your professor. Go back and look at the areas that bother you the most, and develop specific strategies from this chapter to help you with your unique stresses.

Use Visualization

Another helpful strategy, often used by athletes and musicians, is called **visualization**. This is a form of positive self-talk or mental strategizing in which you see yourself successfully performing a complex task. Professors Joel Ayres, Theodore Hopf, and their associates have taught thousands of students how to use visualization techniques to ease their anxiety. They found that those who use these techniques during their preparation are less apprehensive and report fewer negative thoughts during their speeches.[20] This is true even for speakers who tend to freeze under stress.[21] The suggested process goes like this:

1. In a quiet place, picture all the details from the beginning to the end of your speech.
2. Mentally place yourself in the audience and pretend you are watching as you give your speech.
3. Imagine yourself as a competent, well-prepared performer who stands confidently, stresses important words, pauses effectively, and makes appropriate gestures.
4. Think about the audience responding positively with nods, smiles, and interest.
5. Continue to visualize yourself completing your speech, gathering your notes, making final eye contact with the audience, and returning to your seat.
6. Finally, imagine yourself back in the audience, delighted to be through!

visualization rehearsing by using your imagination to envision your speech from start to finish

Two key elements accompany successful visualization: You must create vivid images, and you must control the images you generate.[22]

Believe it or not, research shows that most highly anxious students finish their speech class feeling less anxious[23] because of the process of **habituation**. This means that anxiety lessens when an experience is repeated over time and the anticipated negative outcomes are not as bad as expected.[24] Jennifer's comments support this idea:

> I think it was really good that we did so many speeches because when we did it so many times, I was less nervous each time.

PRACTICALLY SPEAKING

MANFRED TSCHAN, HEALTH PROFESSOR AND SOCCER COACH

Traci Flitcraft

Manfred Tschan, an assistant professor and soccer coach, teaches health and human performance classes. In his stress management class where they study sports psychology, students write journals about personally stressful situations, and public speaking always comes up—regularly—by many, many students. Tschan says students can't think of anything harder to do than to give speeches in other classes.

What do you teach them about dealing with their anxiety? I use a model from Rainer Martens, a sports psychologist from Michigan State, who says stress derives from the relationship between your uncertainty about the outcome and the importance of that outcome. I use four points:

Perception of an imbalance

between an *objective demand*

and your perceived *response capability*,

where failure is perceived to have *serious consequences*.

This gives students four areas to manage, change, or improve:

1. Sometimes they can change the *objective demand*; sometimes they can't. Some people put themselves in situations above their response capability. In life, we sometimes set goals that *should* stress us out because they are above our ability to handle. This may not very useful in speech class because students don't make the assignment. But it might happen if they put themselves in the position of starting to prepare the speech the night before it's due.
2. They can increase their *response capability* for whatever tasks they must do. So they can study harder, prepare better, and improve their ability or capability for giving speeches. I draw a little old-fashioned scale where we pile the demand on one side and on the other side we pile the response capability. One way of balancing is to add to the response capability. Study harder, practice harder.
3. Changing *perceptions* is the third strategy. Sometimes students exaggerate the objective demands or they don't give themselves enough credit for their response capability. There are all kinds of techniques for changing perceptions such as using positive language and not thinking in black and white (10: I'm great, or 0: I'm terrible—with nothing in between). Not using magnification and not making mountains out of molehills also helps. If they think, "I must not

habituation lessening anxiety by successfully repeating an experience over time

make mistakes, and if I do it's terrible," they should remember it's human to err. If they mess up, it's not desirable, but it's normal. We don't perfect everything.

4. *Reevaluate the consequences* and see if they really are that serious. There's a difference between not succeeding and not succeeding completely. In the big scheme of things, doing poorly on a speech probably won't change their life or make them have to drop out school or change their major or send troops to the border. Some students tend to overestimate every assignment or every grade—at least those who care enough to get nervous.

Does this help conquer public speaking anxiety? Often students will come to me and say, "I gave my speech, and it went great, so I shouldn't have been so nervous."

Questions for Discussion

▶ If Professor Tschan wanted to incorporate material from this chapter into his presentation, where might he put the idea that it's important to learn the process of public speaking by understanding the guidelines in the five canons of rhetoric?
▶ Where would he talk about cognitive modification?
▶ Where might he include the guidelines relating to visualization?

Summary

It is not enough simply to get up in front of an audience and talk; good speaking requires thought and preparation. The Greeks and Romans identified a set of principles or standards in five areas of speechmaking (the five canons of rhetoric): invention, disposition, style, memory, and delivery. Use guidelines from the canon of invention to consider your audience's characteristics and interests, and take into account their responses to the specific situation. After that, select a unique, significant, and appropriate topic and focus. Decide whether your major purpose is to inform, persuade, or entertain; then gather information from oral, print, or electronic sources that will support your topic adequately.

Organize your ideas to create an introduction, body, and conclusion using norms from the canon of disposition. Choose appropriate wording (canon of style) and learn your major ideas (canon of memory) so that you can extemporaneously deliver your speech (canon of delivery).

Finally, plan strategies for dealing with your nerves. Know when to expect the highest levels of physical symptoms, and prepare accordingly. Plan specific activities to counteract the physical tension brought on by the fight-or-flight mechanism. Then work on your psychological stress. Control your internal monologue by cognitive modification, substituting positive thoughts for negative ones. Visualize yourself performing your speech successfully from beginning to end. This is especially useful if you tend to freeze during a speech. Use vivid images and control your imaginary scenario.

Doing these steps thoughtfully and thoroughly can give you confidence on speech day, and they equip you with the necessary knowledge and skills to be a more competent public speaker.

STUDY AND REVIEW

Your online resources for *Public Speaking: Concepts and Skills for a Diverse Society* offers a broad range of resources that will help you better understand the material in this chapter, complete assignments, and succeed on tests. Your online resources feature

- Speech videos with critical viewing questions, speech outlines, and transcripts
- Interactive versions of this chapter's Stop and Check activities and Application and Critical Thinking Exercises
- Speech Builder Express and InfoTrac College Edition
- Weblinks related to chapter content
- Study and review tools such as self-quizzes, an interactive glossary, and downloadable audio summaries

You can access your online resources at **http://www.cengage.com/login**, using the access code that came with your book or that you bought online at **http://www.iChapters.com**.

KEY TERMS

The terms below are defined in the margins throughout this chapter.

anticipatory speech anxiety 20	freeze 27
canon 20	habituation 29
canon of delivery 26	impromptu delivery 25
canon of disposition or arrangement 23	internal monologue (I-M) 28
canon of invention 20	manuscript delivery 25
canon of memory 25	memorized delivery 25
canon of style 24	performance anxiety 19
canons of rhetoric 20	process anxiety 19
cognitive modification 28	physiological anxiety 27
communication apprehension 19	psychological anxiety 27
connectives 24	public speaking anxiety 19
extemporaneous delivery 26	style 24
fight-or-flight mechanism 27	visualization 29

APPLICATION AND CRITICAL THINKING EXERCISES

1. Many factors affect communication apprehension (CA). An interesting study found that athletes have less CA than nonathletes, and those who play team sports have less CA than individual athletes.[25] From your own experiences, does this seem true? What factors might contribute to these differences?
2. Rank from 1 to 5 (easiest to hardest) the five canons of rhetoric in order of difficulty for you personally.

   ____ Invention: audience analysis, topic selection, purpose, research
   ____ Disposition: organization or arrangement and connection of ideas
   ____ Style: choice of appropriate language
   ____ Memory: remembering what you want to say
   ____ Delivery: actually presenting your speech

   Why did you rank them in this order? Identify some strategies you can use to work on the areas that challenge you most.

3. Work with a group to analyze your classroom audience, using the suggestions on page XXX. In light of material from Chapter 1 and from your own experiences, discuss some adaptations you might make to speak successfully to your class. For instance, how might your classmates

influence your choice of topics? How might you adapt to diversity? How might the classroom itself, the time of day of the class, and other outside factors affect your speaking?

4. At the top of a sheet of paper, write down an occupation that interests you. Then, along the left side of the page, list the five canons of rhetoric, leaving several spaces between each one. Beside each canon, identify ways that the skills developed within that canon will be useful in the job you named. For example, how will identifying a purpose or doing research help in a career such as nursing or engineering? How might organizing ideas help in teaching or computer programming?

5. Log on to **www.whitehouse.gov** and explore the site. How could you use the links found on this site to apply principles of invention such as topic selection and research?

6. Often persuasive speeches require informing, and informational speeches have persuasive effects. Think about the goals of two speeches about the same general topic of study abroad programs. An informative goal could be to describe the various study abroad opportunities on campus; a persuasive goal could be to urge audience members to study abroad. With a small group of your classmates, identify at least three other topics and write down an informative goal and a persuasive goal for each.

7. Classroom speakers generally use extemporaneous delivery; however, the other modes of delivery are sometimes more appropriate. With a group of classmates, write down the four modes: memorized, manuscript, impromptu, and extemporaneous. Beside each, identify specific instances in which that mode would probably be the most effective. For instance: impromptu delivery goes with most wedding toasts; manuscript delivery works with commencement addresses. After you have identified several examples, discuss with your group some guidelines that you think speakers should follow for each type of delivery.

8. Memory is often considered the "lost" rhetorical canon because so little emphasis is placed on memorization in our digital age. Discuss these questions in your class: Is there any value to learning how to memorize information? If so, when and where might memorization be useful?

9. Consider the ways that preparation and rehearsal contribute to your speaking competence. What effect does last-minute preparation have on competence? What effect does it have on anxiety? Knowing this, how do you plan to prepare for your next speech?

SPEECH VIDEO

Go to your online resources to watch and critique Enrique Ruiz delivering a speech about a significant event in his life. The transcript of Enrique's speech appears below.

Student Speech with Commentary

ANYTOWN USA
By Enrique Ruiz

Roshan Begay

I would not be the person I am today if I had not experienced Anytown. In fact, I would not be here right now if it were not for this camp.

You are probably wondering what I'm talking about. What could so dramatically change someone's life? Anytown is a summer leadership camp. Now, there are thousands of camps out there—Young Life camps, science camps, Boys & Girls Club camps. There are a plethora of camps we could put on the list of "great camps." Camps that change our lives in different ways.

The summer before my junior year in high school, I attended Anytown. Before this camp, I was a teen going down the wrong road; after camp, I was never the same.

So what exactly is Anytown? What is its history? And what goes on at camp that's so power-ful? Today, I'll discuss these three things.

According to its website, Anytown Arizona is a youth development program that focuses on "diversity awareness, social justice, and personal empowerment." Its mission is to be "a catalyst and facilitator of social change." This camp brings together a diverse group of young people with leadership ability from grades 9–12. They spend a week at a campground in Prescott, Arizona, where they explore issues of personal identity, diversity, and inclusion.

The Anytown USA organization sponsors several other types of camps and programs:

- Anytown, Jr. is for students in grades 7–8. It is similar to the high school program, but it is adapted for younger students.
- UniTowns are usually based at high schools. They feature weekend programs that teach the same values taught in other Anytown programs.
- Beyond Anytown is for young adults who have attended Anytown camps and who want to continue developing their leadership abilities and work for social justice.
- Powertown focuses on parents and community members, teaching them intergenerational communication skills.

The week-long Anytown camp is filled with activities geared towards understanding diversity through a great deal of educational activities that have an emotional impact. One activity that had a big impact on me was called Five Levels of Violence. This activity consisted of the camp counselors putting on a skit. Typically, the counselors act out the different levels of violence that are seen everywhere.

- They start with verbal violence; maybe someone says something aggressive to someone.
- They continue to physical violence by ganging up on and pummeling one of the counselors simply because she was a different skin color.
- And they finish with genocide, where about six counselors who act out Jewish roles get killed one after another by two other counselors who act out Nazi roles.

This is only one activity; there are many others.

So where did Anytown come from? According to Anytown Arizona's website, the program was started in 1957 by the National Conference for Christians and Jews (NCCJ), now known as National Conference for Community and Justice. The goals, then as now, were to bring together a group of diverse youth from a variety of backgrounds and empower them to overcome their isolation, segregation and discriminatory treatment of others. Anytown Arizona eventually in-corporated into an independent nonprofit organization. You can see that the Anytown camps and programs have been around for more than fifty years helping strengthen our youth.

What is this power that the delegates walk away with? The leaders carefully set up experi-ences to make the most of each day. Each delegate is assigned to room with people of a dif-ferent ethnicity or religion. Each day has a different theme such as know yourself, know your family, know your friends. Throughout the week there are lots of activities like Five Levels. We also do activities such as gender night and sexual orientation night. Usually, by the fourth or fifth day, the delegates understand one another better and began to build strong relation-ships where they learn to understand their differences. The rich boy in the cabin who has never heard a foul word in his life and his gangster thug roommate who has had a very dysfunctional upbringing come together, learn from each other, and create a lifelong bond. Toward the end

Enrique describes an organization that helped him better deal with cultural diversity in his personal interactions.

He briefly summarizes the organization, but he adds more details when he describes the actual activities. This helps listen-ers understand his opening statement declaring Any-town to be a life-changing experience.

Enrique's topic taps into strong cultural values on the value of diversity and the importance of understanding and tolerance.

of camp, the whole camp is again segregated into groups. In other words, there is a test. Each camp reacts differently to the segregation. Some break it and integrate the camp; others continue it until one delegate finally speaks up. Campers never fail the test, and counselors find the change to be truly amazing.

I hope you have learned a thing or two about this great organization that has been around for five decades. Anytown Arizona, I am sure, will be around for years to come to help young minds overcome their prejudices and lead the world to deal better with diversity.

Jared Cohen, an Anytown alumni and counselor, says "One person can achieve wonders in the world with an individual. Then they pass those beliefs on to another who can pass them on to more. I have impacted the world just by having an effect on one person."

This is the power Anytown has. Changing the world one person at a time.

SOURCE: Speech given Spring 2008, George Fox University (adapted)

ETHICS AND DIVERSITY

THIS CHAPTER WILL HELP YOU

▶ Define ethical communication

▶ Describe three responses to diversity

▶ Identify characteristics of dialogical speaking and listening

▶ Explain three democratic principles for public speaking

▶ Discuss ethical responsibilities of listeners

▶ Define two kinds of academic dishonesty: plagiarism and fabrication

▶ Explain three types of plagiarism

▶ Paraphrase and cite sources correctly

© Tim Timmerman

■■■"DEMOCRACY IS organized conflict . . . disagreement and different points of view are actually the very foundation of democracy."[1] Pam Plumb, former city councilor and mayor of Portland, Maine, made this startling statement. Put another way, democracy is a means of bringing together people with divergent points of view and allowing them to fashion solutions that bring about positive results for the greatest number of people. However, forging a civil society is often messy and unpleasant, and people with differing viewpoints frequently encounter ethical challenges when they interact.

In our diverse society, you are regularly called to make communication choices that have ethical implications. When you defend your beliefs or remain silent, when you respectfully listen or refuse to hear someone with a different perspective, when you check facts or knowingly pass on faulty information, when you credit your sources or plagiarize speech materials, you are making ethical choices.

Professor Vernon Jensen describes **ethical communication** as the conscious decision to speak and listen in ways that you, in light of your cultural ideals, consider right, fair, honest, and helpful to others as well as yourself.[2] Because the U.S. Constitution guarantees freedom of speech, you have the right to express your ideas even if others find them disgusting or offensive—but you must balance your rights with your

ethical communication the conscious decision to speak and listen in ways that you, in light of your cultural ideals, consider right, fair, honest, and helpful to all parties involved

responsibilities. You can't legally yell "FIRE!" in a crowded theater, for example, nor can you legally damage another person's reputation by spreading information you know to be false. Professor Jensen recommends a focus on both rights and responsibilities, which he calls **rightsabilities**.[3]

Maintaining this dual focus can be challenging. Think of the many individuals and groups whose beliefs and behaviors differ dramatically from yours. Some differences seem irreconcilable, and this can lead to tensions that overshadow the many things you might otherwise have in common.[4] These tensions give rise to a number of ethical questions. On what basis should we determine right and wrong in public discourse? Should you leave some things unsaid? When? Who decides? What responsibilities do you have as a listener or as a researcher? This chapter presents some principles that have emerged out of discussions about these ethically challenging questions. We will first examine common responses to diversity and then discuss guidelines for ethical speaking, listening, and researching in a complex culture.

Responses to Diversity

Diversity, even at minimal levels, can divide people and result in discussions, public hearings, open disputes, or marches. More substantial differences can lead to boycotts, sanctions, even wars. However, people from different backgrounds can and do come together in productive ways. Common responses to diversity include resistance, assimilation, and accommodation.

Groups or individuals who choose **resistance** defend their beliefs and traditions against change. Some withdraw from situations that challenge their cherished ways of thinking and behaving. Others attack their opponents[5] with an intensity ranging from mild challenges that ignore, discount, or ridicule divergent ideas to physical assaults, death threats, terrorism, or armed conflict. In public arenas, we commonly attack with words. In fact, dispute and contention are so pervasive that Deborah Tannen, a professor of linguistics, calls our culture an "argument culture."[6] Tannen is especially sensitive to the war metaphors that frame much of our public discourse. To illustrate, think about all the battle terminology you hear: culture wars, fighting for your ideas, battles between the sexes, battles over Supreme Court nominees. We arm ourselves for arguments; we shoot down ideas. There are hundreds of additional examples. In many cases, however, resistance has positive outcomes. Resisting groups and individuals often confront social, environmental, and global injustices and bring about necessary reforms. (For more information about resistance, do an Internet search for "protest movement," and read about two or three movements that interest you.)

A second response, **assimilation**, contrasts with resistance. Instead of defending their views or attacking others, assimilating groups or individuals reject or surrender their own ways of believing and acting and embrace different perspectives and behaviors.[7] At the turn of the twentieth century, the United States was often called a "melting pot," and a major societal goal was to "Americanize" immigrants. A century later, however, we've found that assimilation is rarely total, so we use updated metaphors such as "tossed salad" (a whole comprising distinct entities) or "stew" (distinguishable entities, but changed and merged into a whole) to describe this country's multiethnic reality. In the United States where choice is a dominant value, people are free to change their ideas and lifestyles, but ethical implications arise when individuals allow themselves to be coerced or manipulated into changing without critically examining good reasons for the change.

"rightsabilities" phrase coined by Professor Vernon Jensen to highlight the tension between our right to free speech and our responsibility for our speech

resistance response to diversity in which you refuse to change and you defend your own positions or attack others

assimilation response to diversity in which you surrender some or most of your ways and adopt cultural patterns of another group

In an "argument culture," a war of words is a common form of resistance by those who are unwilling to assimilate or to accommodate diverse ideas.

Finally, groups or individuals who approach diversity through **accommodation** show a willingness to hear diverse ideas and evaluate them with an open mind. (To *accommodate* means to adjust or adapt.) Accommodating individuals allow themselves to rethink their ideas and surrender some, modify others, but hold still others relatively intact. Accommodation helps create a **multivocal society** in which a variety of ideas, opinions, and visions are sought out and voiced openly and formally. Henry Louis Gates, Jr., Director of the W. E. B. Du Bois Institute for African and African American Research at Harvard University, believes that an ideal society should consist of co-cultural groups that diverge from the mainstream and recognize their diversity of opinions yet work together to forge a civic culture that accommodates both differences and commonalities.[8] Barnett Pearce and Kimberly Pearce[9] describe the challenges of accommodation:

> Participating in this form of communication requires a set of abilities, the most important of which is remaining in the tension between holding your own perspective, being profoundly open to others who are unlike you, and enabling others to act similarly.

Barnett Pearce[10] uses the term **cosmopolitan communicator** to describe someone who can comfortably interact with people from diverse backgrounds and perspectives and who can judge those people and groups based on their standards, not on his or hers.

Resistance, assimilation, and accommodation all have ethical implications. It's easy to label extreme forms of resistance (terrorist attacks, for example) or even taunting as unethical, but what about simply ignoring people who differ from you? What about cruel remarks in anonymous posts on Internet sites? Your decision to resist new ideas or to embrace them with relatively few questions, to block voices from being heard or to invite dialogue—all these have ethical implications for both speaking and listening in a diverse society. Let's now turn to specific cultural resources that can help you be a more ethical speaker.

accommodation response to diversity in which you listen and evaluate the views of others; both sides adapt, modify, and bargain to reach mutual agreements

multivocal society society that actively seeks expression of a variety of voices or viewpoints

cosmopolitan communicators communicators who accept and judge others on their own terms

STOP AND CHECK

YOUR RESPONSES TO DIVERSITY

Examine your personal responses to diversity. Where do you resist diverse ways of believing and behaving? When, if ever, do you march or openly protest differences? What perspectives, if any, do you ignore or put down? What *wars* or *battles* do you wage? In what areas, if any, have you changed your beliefs or behaviors and assimilated diverse perspectives into your personal life? When and how have you made an effort to be accommodating? What tensions have you experienced between holding your own positions and being open to the perspectives of others?

Speaking Ethically

Your concern with ethics should begin as soon as you receive your speech assignment, because you have responsibilities to your audience, your topic, and yourself. So it's important to consider some guidelines that scholars have proposed for ethical speaking. These principles fall into two major categories: dialogical and democratic.

Use Dialogical Principles

Chapter 1 pointed out how foundational dialogue is for all other communication activities, including public speaking. **Dialogue** is not a set of communication "rules," but rather, a dialogical perspective is a mindset that is linked to cultural values of honesty, openness, and freedom of choice.[11] In *The Magic of Dialogue: Transforming Conflict into Cooperation*, Daniel Yankelovich[12] identifies three essential components: equality, empathy, and examination.

- *Equality* means you and your listeners respect one other and regard each other's opinions as important enough for consideration. This mindset contrasts with the belief that your opinions are the most important and that you have the right or the obligation to impose them on others, even if this requires trickery or manipulation.
- *Empathy* means you attempt to understand other perspectives by showing compassion and a willingness to identify emotionally with others. Empathy contrasts with self-centered absorption with your personal needs and perspectives.
- *Examination* means you put aside a know-it-all attitude and willingly scrutinize both your assumptions and those of others with an open mind. Examination doesn't mean you must abandon your personal biases or strong beliefs; in fact, you may *never* agree with some people, or they might eventually be persuaded to adopt your views. But, in the process, you've challenged your own ideas.

Barnett Pearce and Kimberly Pearce summarize three skills required for a dialogical perspective: (1) the ability to engage in dialogue in response to another's invitation; (2) the ability to invite others into dialogue; and (3) the ability to create contexts that facilitate dialogue.[13] Chapter 18 summarizes "invitational rhetoric," a concept developed by communication professors Sonja Foss and Cindy Griffin that applies dialogical principles to methods of reasoning.[14]

What does dialogue look like in practice? Amitai Etzioni[15] has set up several rules of engagement to make dialogue more productive when people have major differences:

1. Don't demonize the other side or depict it as completely negative.
2. Don't insult or offend the deepest moral commitments of other people or groups; don't bring up dark moments from a group's history.
3. Talk less about nonnegotiable "rights" and more about negotiable needs, wants, and interests.

dialogue perspective or mindset, linked to honesty, openness, and choice, that invites examination of ideas in a spirit of equality and empathy

4. Don't feel you must deal with every issue; it is okay to let some things drop.
5. Don't abandon your convictions, but balance your beliefs and passions against those strongly held by others.

Dialogue is considered so important globally that the United Nations designated the year 2001 as the Year of Dialogue Among Civilizations. Former UN Secretary General Kofi Annan[16] explained:

> The United Nations itself was created in the belief that dialogue can triumph over discord, that diversity is a universal virtue, and that peoples of the world are far more united by their common fate than they are divided by their separate identities.

In the past, dialogue has been credited with bringing about international changes. For instance, Mikhail Gorbachev, head of the former Soviet Union, said the turning point in the Cold War came during a conversation in which he and President Reagan respectfully discussed their values and aspirations for their respective countries.[17] The Seeds of Peace project described in the Diversity in Practice box or the Anytown Camps described in the speech at the end of Chapter 2 are examples of programs that bring together people with very divergent opinions for honest discussions of their prejudices and conflicts. Leaders aim to give participants the tools they need to live with diversity without settling for stereotyping, name-calling, or violence.

Not all solutions are national or international in scope; dialogue also helps resolve campus-level problems. For example, Bruce Mallory and Nancy Thomas facilitate campus dialogues by developing "intentionally designed, permanent spaces on campuses for identifying, studying, deliberating, and planning action regarding pressing issues with ethical or social implications."[18]

DIVERSITY IN PRACTICE
SEEDS OF PEACE

Seeds of Peace is dedicated to dialogue among young people from mutually hostile groups.

Courtesy of Seeds of Peace Organization/www.seedsofpeace.org/Seeds of Peace

FOUNDED IN 1993, Seeds of Peace's mission statement says, "Treaties are negotiated by governments. Peace is made by people."[19] Organizers first brought together forty-three young people from Egypt, Palestine, and Israel to communicate in face-to-face dialogues held at a three-week international camp in Maine. Since then, its mission has expanded to include young leaders from three additional regions of conflict: South Asia, Cyprus, and the Balkans. The goal remains the same: to empower future leaders with the communication, negotiation, and leadership skills they need to advance coexistence and reconciliation between combative groups in their home regions. Empathy and respect are fundamental aspects of the program, which aims to reach youth "before fear, mistrust, and prejudice blind them from seeing the human face of the enemy."[20]

The Maine-based organization developed two additional programs: Maine Seeds focuses on ethnic and racial issues within the state of Maine, and Beyond Borders brings students from Arab countries such as Kuwait and Iraq to interact with students from the United States.

Whether or not they knew it, Seeds of Peace founders built upon Arab customs relating to dialogue. Traditionally, Arabs met in tents to discuss socially important issues; participants were required to respect other's opinions, to listen carefully, to speak their minds, and to negotiate divisive social issues. Thus, these contemporary dialogues perpetuate longstanding cultural traditions.[21]

To learn more about this organization, visit its website at **www.seedsofpeace.org**.

Practice Democratic Principles

Whereas dialogical principles focus more on your relationship with your audience, **democratic principles** focus more on the ethical issues you face when you create the speech itself. Events over the last several decades have highlighted tensions in the United States between free expression and responsible expression. McCarthyism in the 1950s, antiwar and civil rights protests in the 1960s, "shock jocks" in the 1990s, rancorous political campaigns and the rise of Internet users spouting widely varying opinions in the 2000s—all these events continue to bring First Amendment issues into focus. The National Communication Association (NCA) has responded with a credo that summarizes widely accepted principles for ethical communication; you'll find the latest version in the Diversity in Practice box.

Develop a Habit of Research

During your speech, you are your listeners' primary source of information. Consequently, you owe it to them to know what you're talking about, and it's important to do your homework beforehand. Let's say you decide to discuss a complicated issue such as school vouchers. Don't just settle for a surface understanding; instead, examine a variety of sources and search for diverse viewpoints. Find the positions taken by major political parties and by typical parents. Seek out representative public and private school perspectives, and identify relevant social class issues. Although you may end up arguing for one position over another, make sure it is well-reasoned. Presenting your listeners with a wide variety of perspectives gives them the breadth of information they need to form their own reasoned conclusions. This approach contrasts with what Deborah Tannen calls an argumentative mentality that "obscures the complexity of research"[22] and creates oversimplification, disinformation, and distortion of issues.

Be Honest and Fair

Speaking honestly means that you present your information as truthfully as you can. Don't exaggerate a problem and make it seem greater than it actually is. Don't distort or twist evidence. Statistics can be particularly misleading, so find out as much as you can about the numbers you present. For instance, you might discover statistics showing a decline in identity theft, but the research was partially funded by credit card companies and banks. Does this mean the numbers are inaccurate? Not necessarily, but probe

democratic principles focus on rights and responsibilities for creating ethical speeches in a free society

> DIVERSITY IN PRACTICE
> ## NCA CREDO FOR ETHICAL COMMUNICATION
>
> QUESTIONS OF RIGHT AND WRONG arise whenever people communicate. Ethical communication is fundamental to responsible thinking, decision making, and the development of relationships and communities within and across contexts, cultures, channels, and media. Moreover, ethical communication enhances human worth and dignity by fostering truthfulness, fairness, responsibility, personal integrity, and respect for self and others. We believe that unethical communication threatens the quality of all communication and consequently the well-being of individuals and the society in which we live. Therefore we, the members of the National Communication Association, endorse and are committed to practicing the following principles of ethical communication:
>
> ▶ We advocate truthfulness, accuracy, honesty, and reason as essential to the integrity of communication.
> ▶ We endorse freedom of expression, diversity of perspective, and tolerance of dissent to achieve the informed and responsible decision making fundamental to a civil society.
> ▶ We strive to understand and respect other communicators before evaluating and responding to their messages.
> ▶ We promote access to communication resources and opportunities as necessary to fulfill human potential and contribute to the well-being of families, communities, and society.
> ▶ We promote communication climates of caring and mutual understanding that respect the unique needs and characteristics of individual communicators.
> ▶ We condemn communication that degrades individuals and humanity through distortion, intimidation, coercion, and violence, and through the expression of intolerance and hatred.
> ▶ We are committed to the courageous expression of personal convictions in pursuit of fairness and justice.
> ▶ We advocate sharing information, opinions, and feelings when facing significant choices while also respecting privacy and confidentiality.
> ▶ We accept responsibility for the short- and long-term consequences for our own communication and expect the same of others.
>
> For more on the NCA's position on ethical communication, visit the organization's website at **www.natcom.org**.
>
> ----
> Source: Endorsed by the National Communication Association, November 1999. Reprinted by permission of the National Communication Association.

further and see if sources with nothing to gain from the data, financially or otherwise, come up with similar findings.

Strive for fairness, balance, and evenhandedness rather than presenting one side—the one that favors your position. Don't give in to the slanted, unfair approach of various talk show hosts, political spinmeisters, and Internet sites or blogs that only provide a lopsided view of their topics. For example, compare and contrast the methods used by the Brady Campaign to Prevent Gun Violence (**www.bradycampaign.org**), the Second Amendment Sisters, Inc., (**www.2asisters.org**), the National Rifle Association (**www.nra.org/home.aspx**), and the federal government's Center for Disease Control (**www.cdc.gov/mmwR/preview/mmwrhtml/rr5214a2.htm**) to present issues related to gun control.

✓ STOP AND CHECK

WOULD YOU USE QUESTIONABLE STATISTICS?

KILOLO is researching the topic of breast cancer. She finds many sources such as breastcancer.org, the American Cancer Society, and MedLine Plus that give women a 1 in 8 chance of developing the disease. However, the government's Center for Disease Control (CDC) and other sources call this figure a "lifetime risk," meaning that a woman who lives to be 110 has a cumulative 1 in 8 chance of contracting the disease. Even then, the woman risks dying from some cause other than cancer. The incidence of breast cancer rose in the 1980s (probably because of increased awareness and testing), but it decreased by more than 3 percent per year during the early 2000s. So if the 1 in 8 figure is misleading, why is it so common? According to a *New York Times* article, an American Cancer Society spokesperson admitted the ratio is more metaphor than fact but said it's used for good ends: It increases awareness of the disease and makes women concerned enough to seek early detection. Some physicians disagree; they point to an "epidemic of fear" that the inflated numbers create.[23] Furthermore, many women focus on detecting and preventing breast cancer but remain in the dark about their much higher risks of heart and lung diseases.[24]

Questions

1. Should Kilolo use the 1 in 8 figure because she's seen it in so many sources and because it is technically true? Why or why not?
2. What do you think of the American Cancer Society's decision to continue using the figure when they know it could be misleading? Is this ethical?
3. How might hyped information about one disease contribute to women's overall health?

Practice Civility

Talking heads on all-news cable channels interrupt their guests who are noisily talking over one another; politicians dig for dirt and create negative ads to use against their opponents. Rowdy audiences sometimes loudly boo or heckle speakers with whom they disagree. This all-too-common lack of civility in public discourse led one commentator to coin the term *drive-by debating* to describe this rudeness.[25]

Civility is a social virtue that involves self-control or moderation instead of pride, insolence, and arrogance. Civil speakers and listeners are more than simply polite; they *choose* persuasion, consultation, advising, bargaining, compromising, and coalition building. Civility is related to the accommodation response to diversity and to dialogical public speaking. Both approaches require communicators to strive for understanding, appreciate opposing perspectives, and accept the outcome when their own position loses. Cultures from the ancient Greeks to modern Asian societies have promoted civility as an ethical principle.[26]

An example of civility comes after each election in the United States. At local, state, and national levels both the winning and the losing candidates deliver a civil public speech. The loser concedes; the winner thanks voters for their ballots. Both winners and losers pledge to support the democratic process, even as they promise to continue working for the causes they hold dear.

Habits of research, honesty and fairness, civility—these are by no means all of the democratic principles related to public speaking. However, this list gives you a starting point for thinking about ethical speaking in a pluralistic culture. Since diversity is pervasive, you must create your own way to best respect (and live comfortably with) cultural differences.[27]

civility self-control or moderation, contrasts with arrogance; civil speakers persuade, consult, and compromise rather than coerce and manipulate

> ✓ **STOP AND CHECK**
>
> CIVILITY IN PUBLIC LIFE
>
> To learn more about civility, go to InfoTrac College Edition and search for the article "In Legislating and in Life, Long May Civility Reign." It describes the 2004 inauguration ceremony that installed Bart Peterson as mayor of Indianapolis. Discuss with your classmates the recommendations for both dialogical and democratic principles that you find in this article.

Listening Ethically

The dialogical attitude applies to listening as well as speaking. Obviously, you can't listen to everyone. You simply don't have time. But polite listening affirms the right to speak, and giving others your respectful attention is one way to empower them. Think about how positive you feel when someone who disagrees with you still takes time to ask how you came to your conclusions. Sincere questions that are not meant as personal attacks show that the listener is really trying to understand your viewpoint.

In contrast, it is easy to silence others. Someone who won't give you a hearing, who walks away while you're talking and says, "I don't want to hear this," leaves you frustrated. And someone who talks while you're talking or argues loudly with everything you say makes you give up trying to say anything at all. A similar thing can happen in public speaking settings. **Hecklers** disrupt speeches and confront speakers during their speeches, trying to embarrass them and making it difficult for others to hear what they have to say. Leaving in the middle of a speech or whispering and laughing while someone is talking show disrespect for the speaker, the ideas, and other listeners who want to hear the speech.

This is not to say that you should listen to just anything, and you might find yourself facing ethical dilemmas as a listener. When you hear someone saying something you know is false or arguing for a viewpoint that does not seem well-reasoned, what should you do? Should you confront the speaker in front of others? Should you prepare a

heckler listener who disrupts a speech or confronts a speaker during a speech

Open forum sessions provide the public with opportunities to deliberate about important issues. Speakers should enact dialogical and democratic principles; participants should be mindful of their ethical responsibilities to each speaker, to other audience members, and to themselves.

Jennifer Durepo/University of Maine at Fort Kent

PRACTICALLY SPEAKING

HECKLING

Buena Vista/Courtesy Everett Collection

In the movie, "O Brother, Where Art Thou?" the politician, Homer Stokes, gives an impromptu speech full of racist comments. His audience heckles him and cuts him off mid-speech. Are their actions justifiable? Why or why not? (Watch the movie clip at **www.americanrhetoric.com** under "Movie Speeches".)

Heckling is common at comedy clubs, sports events, and political speeches. During the 2008 presidential campaign, for example, antiwar hecklers interrupted many talks, shouting war-related questions while candidates or their supporters were speaking on another topic:

▶ During a speech about women leaders given by Hillary Clinton at Brown University, one heckler stood on a chair, interrupted the speech, and shouted, "Is it leadership to oppose the war?" Soon two others joined him, unfurling an antiwar banner and chanting antiwar slogans in a demonstration that lasted four minutes before they eventually quieted down.[28]

▶ During a campaign speech in Denver promoting his wife's candidacy, Bill Clinton was interrupted by several sign-waving protestors who shouted that the 9/11 incident leading up to the Iraq War should be re-investigated. Clinton stopped his remarks and addressed the hecklers directly. After even more interruptions, Clinton said, "We heard you the first ten times," and the heckling stopped.[29]

▶ Protestors from Code Pink, an antiwar organization, interrupted John McCain four times during an address at the National Association of Latino Elected Officials. One of the protestors followed the candidate from event to event throughout the campaign season, heckling him on numerous occasions.[30]

Questions for Discussion

▶ What ethical responsibilities do audience members have toward a speaker, in general? Toward other listeners? Toward their own political opinions? Which should assume the most importance in settings such as these? Explain your choice.

▶ After one heckling incident John McCain appealed to his audience by saying, "One of the things Americans are tired of . . . is people yelling at each other in America. Have you noticed that? They want us to respect each other's opinions. . . . Americans want a dialogue."[31] Is this a good way to respond to heckling? Why or why not?

▶ To control hecklers, many politicians today speak before carefully selected audiences, comprised of people chosen to prevent unwanted interruptions. What do you think of this practice?

▶ Have you ever been in a situation where a speaker was heckled? If so, discuss the situation and your responses to it with your classmates.

speech to present more accurate information or provide a different perspective? Should you ask questions that help other listeners detect the misinformation or bias? These are all possible responses. To think about your ethical responsibilities as a listener, ask yourself these questions:

▶ Do I keep myself informed about significant issues by exposing myself to a number of arguments, or do I listen only to the side with which I already agree? In short, do I listen with an open mind?
▶ Do I fulfill my ethical responsibilities to other listeners by not distracting them?
▶ Do I fulfill my responsibilities to speakers by letting them know they are being heard?
▶ Do I encourage speakers to meet ethical standards? This may mean that I ask for further information about their sources or that I point out relevant information they omit.

Academic Honesty

Tom's speech started dramatically:

How would you react if I told you that inside this box there was a snake? Would you frantically jump up on top of your desk? Would you panic and let out a shrill scream? Would you run hysterically from the room? If you answered yes to one or more of these questions, chances are you have a phobia of snakes.

Students listened intently, but the professor frowned. This scenario sounded too familiar, and a quick check of department speech files turned up an identical outline submitted in a previous term. Tom's speech was plagiarized. Plagiarism is a specific ethical breach. In a speech about drug cartels, Aaron made up a statistic—an act of fabrication, a second type of ethical breech. To avoid ethical problems such as plagiarism and fabrication, it is important to understand just what they are.

Avoid Plagiarism

After you walk across the platform at commencement and receive your college or university degree, you'll have in hand your school's official recognition and certification that you have personally grappled with important ideas and learned the practical skills associated with your degree.[32] Consequently, colleges and universities crack down hard on **plagiarism**. They reason that, when you plagiarize, you don't personally do the work; instead, you present other people's ideas, words, or works as your own, without giving credit to the originators. It's somewhat like sending your roommate to the weight room to do your weight training; you don't benefit from the exercise.[33] (Not every culture shares these concepts. See Diversity in Practice: Plagiarism and Culture for other cultural notions about intellectual property.)

According to **www.plagiarism.org**,[34] plagiarism is easier today than ever before because of the Internet, which makes it simple to download textual material, pictures, diagrams, and other information without citing it. For instance, a student, who would never consider ripping a paragraph out of a *Washington Post* column and cutting a sentence out of a *Newsweek* article and then gluing the two onto a piece of paper and turning it in, would find it easy to cut and paste the same paragraphs from **www.washingtonpost.com** or **www.newsweek.com** into a paper written with a word processor. And because the material is electronically stored, it might be easy to conceptualize as somehow different in kind from hard copies of the same material.[35]

To avoid plagiarism, you should understand its various forms:[36]

▶ **Deliberate fraud.** This happens when students borrow, buy, or steal someone else's speech or written outline and present it as if it were their own work; it is knowingly

plagiarism presenting the words, images, or ideas of others as if they were your own

deliberate fraud knowing, intentional plagiarism

and intentionally done. Because Tom's speech on phobias, mentioned above, was deliberately copied, he would be subject to his university's penalties for plagiarism.

▶ **Cut-and-paste plagiarism.** Here, plagiarists copy entire paragraphs word-for-word from various articles and piece them together into a paper or speech without using quotation marks or naming the sources next to the material, even though they might supply a list of resources at the end of the paper.

▶ **Improper paraphrase.** This type of plagiarism occurs when the plagiarist changes or translates a few words but keeps the basic structure and ideas of the original intact, and fails to credit the source next to the material. For example, a professor at MIT made national news for his book about the poet E. E. Cummings; a literary magazine argued that the following paraphrase was actually plagiarism:[37]

> *From a 1980 biography of Cummings:* "Esther Lanman organized a cocktail party for Cummings with as many of the old Cambridge crowd as she could locate. Amy Gozzaldi was there, her jet-black hair now grey. She and [Cummings] looked at each other and grinned self-consciously, feeling what the years had done to them. He raised his hand to his bald head."[38]

> *From the professor's 2004 biography about Cummings:* "Lanman even organized a cocktail party for Cummings, inviting every member of the 'old gang' she could round up, including Cummings's first crush, Amy de Gozzaldi. Her hair, once jet black, was now gray and Cummings, now fifty-eight, had finally gone bald. They looked at each other self-consciously, then grinned."[39]

The professor didn't realize he plagiarized, because he credited the 1980 biography throughout. However, he failed to cite the original source for this specific section.

Plagiarism can be intentional or accidental. **Accidental plagiarists** don't know the rules about plagiarism, so they innocently fail to properly paraphrase or give credit to their sources. For example, Allison created a series of PowerPoint slides with pictures of Mia Hamm that she'd cut and pasted from the Internet. She omitted the URLs of the websites where she found the pictures. However, it never occurred to her that she was supposed to credit the source of a photograph. Intentional or not, this was plagiarism.

Because your school's policies are easily available in student handbooks and in library and writing lab resources, you are held responsible for knowing the rules relating to plagiarism, so you have no basis for pleading ignorance.

Here are some guidelines for citing sources, according to Purdue University's Online Writing Lab:[40]

▶ Give credit whenever you use somebody else's words, ideas, or creative works—whether taken from library resources, the Internet, films or television shows, audio recordings, advertisements, letters from friends, or elsewhere.

▶ Provide sources for information taken from interviews, conversations, or email.

▶ Tell your audience the source of the unique words and phrases that were not your own.

▶ Identify the sources of diagrams, illustrations, charts, photographs, and figures.

You do not need to document:

▶ Personal experiences, observations, conclusions, or insights.

▶ Common knowledge, such as folklore or traditions within your cultural group. References to Cinderella or Robin Hood are examples.

▶ Generally accepted facts—the kind of information you find in five or more sources or information you think your audience already knows or could easily find in reference material. For example, Presidents John Adams and Thomas Jefferson both died on the fourth of July, 1826.

▶ Results of experiments you personally conduct.

cut-and-paste plagiarism copying material word-for-word and then patching it together without quotation marks or citations

improper paraphrase changing some words of a source but keeping the basic structure and ideas intact without citing the source

accidental plagiarist plagiarist who lacks knowledge about the rules

Yoruba drum with stick, n.d., Wood, string, and hide./The Trout Gallery/Dickinson College, Carlisle, Pennsylvania

Some students accidentally plagiarize because they don't know they must include the source of a downloaded image on the slide itself.

Sources can be either published or unpublished. Books, magazines, newspapers, paintings, journal articles, websites, films, or sound recordings are considered published. Lecture notes, handouts, papers you've submitted for another class, sermons, most speeches, personal interviews, personal photographs, and letters are unpublished.[41]

To avoid plagiarism, name your sources within your speech. For example, when you use a direct quotation, introduce it as such. When you paraphrase someone else's ideas, cite the originator. When you present a diagram or chart on a PowerPoint slide or an overhead transparency, write the source somewhere on the slide. Here are some specific examples:

▶ *Published source, book.* In *The No-Nonsense Guide to Fair Trade*, David Ransom states that more and more consumers are not only asking "Is this good for me?" but also "Is this good for others and the environment?"[42]

▶ *Published source, Internet.* Citation in small font at the bottom of the PowerPoint slide showing a photograph of *dun dun* drummers and featuring a sound clip downloaded from the Internet: Source: Yoruba drums from Benin, West Africa: The world's musical traditions 8. [online]. Accessed April 25, 2002. **www.eyeneer.com/Labels/ Smithsonian/Sounds/yoruba.aiff** [43]

▶ *Unpublished source, personal interview.* Today I checked in with the hospital's chief of staff, Dr. Callari. He said the situation has worsened. Though he has never been sued, his liability insurance has doubled. He couldn't afford it and had to drop it.[44]

Chapter 11 describes ways to document sources on your outline. Be sure to list your references at the end using a standard format such as MLA (Modern Language Association) style or APA (American Psychological Association) style. These style manuals and others are available on the Internet or in the reference section of the library, and they show you how to cite just about any source, from a book to a personal letter, from a CD to a website. Because these manuals are often updated, look for the latest version.

Plagiarists, accidental or intentional, are subject to severe penalties. Typically, those guilty of intentional fraud receive an "F" for the assignment. More serious breaches may result in temporary suspension, permanent expulsion, and/or a notation on the student's permanent record, which can seriously affect that person's life. Accidental plagiarists may be asked to redo the assignment, or they may lose points.

DIVERSITY IN PRACTICE
PLAGIARISM AND CULTURE

IN THE UNITED STATES, plagiarism is considered a serious intellectual breach because of three important cultural notions.[45] Here, writing something down is thought to be a concrete way to demonstrate your knowledge and skills; consequently, instructors expect you to do your own assignments. Turning in someone else's work does not show what *you* know.

A second concept is linked to the cultural value of individuality. You should develop yourself to your highest potential and do creative, original thinking. Turning in someone else's work does not demonstrate your originality.

Third is the cultural notion that ownership of personal property includes ownership of intellectual property. You can patent, copyright, or sell your ideas, creations, musical works, unique words, and writings. They are legally yours. Consequently, if someone else uses your original work or even a portion thereof without crediting you, you can charge them with "stealing" your intellectual property.

However, many cultures view intellectual property differently. Consider a society that values the group over the individual, one in which words and ideas belong to the culture as a whole, not to any one person. Would stealing or pirating works be viewed with the same perspective? What might happen when U.S. businesses move into such a culture? Also, consider the impact of the Internet on notions of "ownership" of words and ideas. For example, hypertext allows people to "write collaboratively and use nonlinear connections to create products that show few indications of who said what."[46] Wikipedia is just one example of a jointly created resource. Who "owns" a Wikipedia entry?

For more information about academic honesty and culture, read the speech, "Confessions of an Academic Honesty Lady," by Judy Hunter. It is available online at **www.grinnell.edu/academic/writinglab/faculty/forum/con_hj.pdf**

Avoid Fabrication

Plagiarism is but one form of academic dishonesty. Another is **fabrication**, which happens if you make up information or guess at numbers but present them as factual. Citing a reference you did not actually read or passing along rumors or other unsubstantiated information are additional types of fabrication. For example, when Barack Obama began his bid for the U.S. presidency, facts competed with exaggerations and misinformation regarding his background. Here are just a few: His middle name is Hussein (correct); therefore, he is a Muslim (incorrect; he's a Christian); during his childhood, he attended a radical Muslim school (his biography says he went to a Muslim school in Indonesia; but it was not radical; he also attended a Catholic school, but he is not a Catholic); he refuses to recite the Pledge of Allegiance (false, although one photographer once caught him without his hand over his heart during the playing of the national anthem). These rumors, and others like them, swept across Internet blogs, emails, talk radio, and whispered conversations. However, accurate information was always available to those willing to search for it, and people who passed along unsubstantiated rumors were guilty of fabrication. (Hypothetical examples, described in Chapter 8, are in a different category because the audience understands that these examples are not real.)

The best ways to avoid fabrication are to use a number of sources and be alert for conflicting data. Thoroughly check any discrepancies before you present information as factual. If something seems suspicious, check it out. For example, **www.snopes.com** is a site that uncovers hoaxes and false claims and exposes urban legends of all kinds, from food to computers, holidays to weddings.

> **STOP AND CHECK**
> GOOD VERSUS BAD PARAPHRASING
>
> Many students think that changing a few words of the original equals a paraphrase, but according to the *Academic Integrity Handbook* published by the Journalism Department of the University of Arizona,[47] it's unacceptable to directly use even three to eight words of a source. They cite Judy Hunter, director of the writing lab at Grinnell College, who says this about paraphrasing:
>
> In a bad paraphrase, you merely substitute words, borrowing the sentence structure of the organization directly from the source. In a good paraphrase you offer your reader a wholesale revision, a new way of seeing the text you are paraphrasing. You summarize, you reconstruct, you tell your reader about what the source has said, but you do so entirely in your own words, your own voice, your own sentence structure, your own organization.[48]

fabrication making up information or repeating information without sufficiently checking its accuracy

Here is an example:

Original (from an article about a worldwide survey assessing corporate social responsibility): "U.S. companies are by far bigger givers than their global counterparts. . . . When [a recent] survey asked businesses why they give back, both U.S. and non-U.S. companies responded that their main motivation was to promote recruitment and retention. But U.S. companies stood apart on one critical point. Given a list of reasons for engaging in corporate social responsibility, Americans were by far the least likely to cite "saving the earth" as a motivator. In fact, only 21 percent said their efforts were motivated by this sort of idealism, compared with 40 percent worldwide."

Inappropriate Paraphrase: U.S. companies give a lot more than foreign companies. A recent survey asked businesses why they contribute to social causes; both U.S. and foreign companies said their main motivation was for recruitment and retention. However, U.S. companies differed in a basic way. When asked to choose from a list of reasons to participate in corporate social responsibility, U.S. companies were the least likely to say they did it to "save the earth." Only 21 percent said this sort of idealism motivated them, compared to 40 percent of foreign companies. [Analysis: Although many words are changed, the sentence structure and organizational pattern is similar.]

Appropriate Paraphrase: American companies seem far less motivated than their foreign counterparts to engage in socially responsible policies because of environmental concerns, although they give far more overall to social causes. A recent survey, summarized in *Inc. Magazine*, June 2008, found that all companies worldwide chose responsible social policies mainly as a way to recruit and retain workers and customers. However, foreign companies checked off a box marked "saving the planet" 40 percent of the time whereas U.S. companies chose that motivation about half as often. [Analysis: This version summarizes the ideas in the speaker's words; it also cites the source.]

Source: Hofman, M. (2008, June). The best cause of all. *Inc. Magazine, 30(6)*, 23–24. Retrieved June 4, 2008, from the Business Source Complete database.

Now try your hand at it. Here's a quotation about the same general topic of corporate social responsibility. First, write an inappropriate paraphrase by making a few substitutions and changing around a few phrases. Then write an appropriate paraphrase by summarizing the material into your own words.

[Radiohead's album,] "All I Need," which debuted earlier this month on MTV properties worldwide . . . was created for MTV Exit (End Exploitation and Trafficking), a multimedia initiative launched in Europe in 2004 by Viacom's MTV Europe Foundation, an independent charity based in London. The effort includes the distribution of anti-human trafficking information at Radiohead's concert tour in North America, Europe and Asia . . . The network's efforts illustrate the growing use of branded-entertainment as a way to distribute corporate-responsibility campaigns, which are geared to creating deeper relationships with do-gooder consumers.

Source: Shanhaz, M. (2008, May 12). Good vibrations. *Adweek, 49(16)*, Retrieved June 4, 2008, from the Business Source Complete database.

Summary

People in pluralistic cultures differ in beliefs, values, attitudes, and behaviors to degrees that range from superficial to fundamental, and responses to diversity vary. If you choose to defy or resist, you defend or bolster your position and (perhaps) attack or ignore diverse perspectives. If you assimilate, you surrender some aspect of your own beliefs or cultural traditions and replace it with something new. Finally, if you choose accommodation, you accept differences and work with others to create a society in which all can live together.

Our culture provides both dialogical and democratic resources that you can use to speak and listen ethically. When you choose a dialogical relationship with your listeners, you respect them as equals, have empathy with their perspectives, and examine both your own and your listeners' assumptions in an honest, open manner. Democratic principles remind you to develop a habit of research, to present your materials honestly and fairly, and to respond to diversity with civility.

Listening also calls for ethically responsible actions. Allowing people to speak empowers them, giving them a voice and enabling others to hear their ideas. However, when speakers present incorrect or misleading information, you face an ethical decision, in which you must balance your rights and responsibilities against the rights and responsibilities of the speaker and other listeners. Vernon Jensen coined the term *rightsabilities* to highlight this tension.

As you present your materials, be sure to cite your references and check a variety of sources to avoid the ethical problems of plagiarism or fabrication. Plagiarism occurs when you present the ideas, words, organizational pattern, or images created by another person as your own without giving credit to the original source. Fabrication occurs when you make up material or present something as factual when it is not.

STUDY AND REVIEW

Your online resources for *Public Speaking: Concepts and Skills for a Diverse Society* offer a broad range of resources that will help you better understand the material in this chapter, complete assignments, and succeed on tests. Your online resources feature

- Speech videos with critical viewing questions, speech outlines, and transcripts
- Interactive versions of this chapter's Stop and Check activities and Application and Critical Thinking Exercises
- Speech Builder Express and InfoTrac College Edition
- Weblinks related to chapter content
- Study and review tools such as self-quizzes, an interactive glossary, and downloadable audio summaries

You can access your online resources at **http://www.cengage.com/login**, using the access code that came with your book or that you bought online at **http://www.iChapters.com**.

KEY TERMS

The terms below are defined in the margins throughout this chapter.

accidental plagiarist 47	ethical communication 36
accommodation 38	fabrication 49
assimilation 37	heckler 44
civility 43	improper paraphrase 47
cosmopolitan communicators 38	multivocal society 38
cut-and-paste plagiarism 47	plagiarism 46
deliberate fraud 46	resistance 37
democratic principles 41	"rightsabilities" 37
dialogue 39	

APPLICATION AND CRITICAL THINKING EXERCISES

1. Draw a minimum-maximum scale that represents diversity on your campus. Identify differences at the minimum end of the range. Work your way up the scale, identifying increasingly greater areas of diversity that create conflicts. When and how do campus speakers address this diversity?

2. With a small group of your classmates, choose a specific international, national, or local situation in which conflicting beliefs, attitudes, values, or behaviors caused a conflict. Identify which of the three ways of dealing with differences—resistance, assimilation, or accommodation—the various participants used to respond. Assess the ethicality of their responses.

3. With a small group in your classroom, discuss ways that people who hold diverse perspectives on a controversial topic might engage in dialogue (for example, pro-choice advocates meeting with pro-life activists; born-again Christians talking with committed Muslims; animal rights activists meeting with research scientists; leaders of NATO meeting with leaders of the African Union). How can each group listen to the other and explore their perspectives with an open mind?

4. Conduct an Internet search for the phrase "hate speech," and come to class prepared to share an example you found. With your classmates, discuss the importance of First Amendment rights to free speech, balanced against the ethical responsibilities described in this chapter.

5. Using the NCA credo as a guide, work with a small group of your classmates to create a class code of conduct.

6. Form small groups and choose a controversial issue about which you have moderate to strong disagreement. Discuss the topic within the group, and put into practice the principles for speaking and listening in this chapter.

7. For an example of a famous speech that addresses religious diversity, read or listen to streaming video of John F. Kennedy's Address to the Greater Houston Ministerial Association in June, 1960, available at **www.americanrhetoric.com**. Kennedy became the first Catholic president in November 1960, but five months before the election, some voters worried that his allegiance might be to the Pope, not the American people. Notice how JFK lays out his views on religious diversity and how he affirms core American values.

8. Use your own values and beliefs as well as the guidelines described in this chapter to write an ethical code that states the principles by which you want to speak and listen.

9. Evaluate yourself as a responsible listener. How do you avoid silencing speakers? Use the questions in the section on Listening Ethically on page 45 to guide your self-evaluation.

10. Look up your campus's guidelines regarding academic honesty. What guidelines do they provide to help students learn and practice ethical research procedures? What are the penalties for plagiarism?

SPEECH VIDEO

Go to your online resources to watch and critique a commencement address by Edwin J. Feulner, president of the Heritage Foundation. The transcript of Feulner's speech appears below.

Professional Speaker's Speech with Commentary

LAY YOUR HAMMER DOWN: DEFEND YOUR CONVICTIONS
Edwin J. Feulner

In 1969 a Stanford University psychologist named Philip Zimbardo set up an experiment. He arranged for two cars to be abandoned—one on the mean streets of the Bronx, New York; the other in an affluent neighborhood near Stanford in Palo Alto, California. The license plates had been removed, and the hoods were left open. Zimbardo wanted to see what would happen to the cars.

In the Bronx, he soon found out. Ten minutes after the car was abandoned, people began stealing parts from it. Within three days the car was stripped. When there was nothing useful left to take, people smashed windows and ripped out upholstery, until the car was trashed.

In Palo Alto, something quite different happened: nothing. For more than a week the car sat there unmolested. Zimbardo was puzzled, but he had a hunch about human nature. To test it, he went out and, in full view of everyone, took a sledgehammer and smashed part of the car.

Soon, passersby were taking turns with the hammer, delivering blow after satisfying blow. Within a few hours, the vehicle was resting on its roof, demolished. . . .

Among the scholars who took note of Zimbardo's experiment were two criminologists, James Q. Wilson . . . and George Kelling. The experiment gave rise to their "broken windows" theory of crime, which is illustrated by a common experience: When a broken window in a building is left unrepaired, the rest of the windows are soon broken by vandals. But why . . . does the broken window invite further vandalism? . . . The broken window is their metaphor for a whole host of ways that behavioral norms can break down in a community. If one person scrawls graffiti on a wall, others will soon be at it with their spray cans. If one aggressive panhandler begins working a block, others will soon follow.

> Feulner opens with a story that leads into the metaphor he will use throughout the speech.
>
> Feulner explains the metaphor; throughout, he will compare incivility to a hammer.

In short, once people begin disregarding the norms that keep order in a community, both order and community unravel, sometimes with astonishing speed. . . . Now all this is a preface. My topic is not crime on city streets; rather, I want to speak about incivility in the marketplace of ideas. The broken windows theory is what links the two.

As the head of a think tank in Washington, I work exclusively in the marketplace of ideas. . . . What we're seeing . . . today is a disturbing growth of incivility that follows and confirms the broken windows theory. Alas, this breakdown of civil norms is not a failing of either the political left or the right exclusively. It spreads across the political spectrum from one end to the other.

A few examples:

- A liberal writes a book calling Rush Limbaugh a "big fat idiot." A conservative writes a book calling liberals "useful idiots."
- A liberal writes a book titled *The Lies of George W. Bush*. A conservative writes a book subtitled *Liberal Lies about the American Right*. . . .

> He works in politics, so he uses politics as an example, but he could be talking about other controversial subjects such as music lyrics or workplace policies toward gays and lesbians.
>
> This speech was given during the Bush presidency. What examples might he use today?

Those few examples—and unfortunately there are many, many more—come from elites in the marketplace of ideas. All are highly educated people who write nationally syndicated columns, publish best-selling books, and are hot tickets on radio and television talk shows.

Further down the food chain, lesser lights take up smaller hammers, but they commit even more degrading incivilities. The Internet, with its easy access and worldwide reach, is a breeding ground for websites with names like Bushbodycount.com or Toostupidtobepresident.com.

This is how the broken windows theory plays out in the marketplace of ideas. If you want to see it working in real time, try the following: Log on to AOL, and go to one of the live chat rooms reserved for political chat. Someone will post a civil comment on some political topic. Almost immediately, someone else will swing the verbal hammer of incivility, and from there the chat degrades into a food fight, with invective and insult as the main course.

> Here, the examples move closer to home—to personal computers and the Internet where people hammer one another in chat rooms.

This illustrates the first aspect of the broken windows theory, which we saw with the car in Palo Alto. Once someone wields the hammer—once the incivility starts—others will take it as an invitation to join in, and pretty soon there's no limit to the incivility.

Now if you watch closely in that chat room, you'll see something else happening. Watch the screen names of people who make civil comments. Some—a few—will join in the food fight. But most will log off. Their screen names just disappear. They leave because the atmosphere has turned hostile to anything approaching a civil exchange or a real dialogue.

This illustrates the second aspect of the broken windows theory: Once the insults begin flying, many will opt out. Wilson and Kelling describe this response when the visible signs of order deteriorate in a neighborhood: "Many residents will think that crime, especially violent crime, is on

> The consequences of incivility are that good people drop out.

the rise, and they will modify their behavior accordingly. They will use the streets less often, and when on the streets will stay apart from their fellows, moving with averted eyes, silent lips, and hurried steps. Don't get involved. . . ."

The chat room shows us that a similar response occurs when civility breaks down in the marketplace of ideas. Many people withdraw and tune out . . . This is the real danger of incivility. Our free, self-governing society requires an open exchange of ideas, which in turn requires a certain level of civility rooted in mutual respect for each other's opinions and viewpoints. . . .

Incivility is not a social blunder to be compared with using the wrong fork. Rather, it betrays a defect of character. Incivility is dangerous graffiti, regardless of whether it is spray-painted on a subway car, or embossed on the title page of a book. The broken windows theory shows us the dangers in both cases.

But those cases aren't parallel in every way, and in closing I want to call your attention to an important difference. When behavioral norms break down in a community, police can restore order. But when civility breaks down in the marketplace of ideas, the law is powerless to set things right.

And properly so. Our right to speak freely—and to speak with incivility, if we choose—is guaranteed by those five glorious words in the First Amendment: "Congress shall make no law. . . ."

And yet, the need for civility has never been greater. Our nation is divided as never before between the left and the right. We are at loggerheads on profoundly important political and social questions. . . . Sadly, too many of us are not rising to these challenges as a democratic people. . . .

Rather than helping to reverse this decline, the rising chorus of incivility is driving out citizens of honest intent and encouraging those who trade in jeering and mockery. . . .

If we are to prevail as a free, self-governing people, we must first govern our tongues and our pens. Restoring civility to public discourse is not an option. It is a necessity.

Who will begin the restoration of civility?

I hope you will. Your graduation today is proof that you're up to the job, and I urge you to take it on as a serious, lifelong commitment. . . . After four years of study [here], you know the difference between attacking a person's argument and attacking a person's character.

Respect that difference.

Your education here has taught you how to engage in rational debate and either hold your own or lose with grace and civility.

Take that lesson with you.

Your professors . . . have shown you, by their example, that you don't need the hammer of incivility to make your point.

Follow their example.

Defend your convictions—those virtues—with all the spirit you can. But do it with all the civility that you ought. . . . So, as you leave this special place,

Lay your hammer down . . . .

Thank you and congratulations to the Class of 2004.

Feulner emphasizes the cultural value of and necessity for open dialogue.

Here's another metaphor. It is not table manners that show a lack of polish; it's a deeper flaw.

Here he uses a contrast to show how incivility differs from vandalism or other crimes, and he praises free speech.

He has pointed out the *why* of civility; now he points to the *who*. In the rest of the speech he challenges his listeners to apply their educational learning to contribute to civil dialogues in society.

Feulner, E. J. (2004, July 15). Lay Your Hammer Down. *Vital Speeches of the Day, 70 (19)*, 595–598 (adapted)

CHAPTER **4**

EFFECTIVE LISTENING

© Tim Timmerman

THIS CHAPTER WILL HELP YOU

▶ **Appreciate the importance of listening skills**

▶ **Describe linguistic, cultural, and personal barriers that affect your listening**

▶ **Draw and explain four thought patterns that are common during listening**

▶ **Use cultural schema to improve your listening**

▶ **Discuss diverse cultural listening styles**

▶ **Identify strategies to improve your comprehensive listening**

▶ **Improve your critical listening skills**

▶ **Practice dialogical listening through nonverbal feedback**

▶ **Give appropriate verbal feedback using the D-R-E method**

TAKE A MINUTE AND THINK about all your communication activities during a typical week. Then rank the following activities in order according to the amount of waking time you normally spend doing each one:

_____ reading _____ writing _____ listening _____ speaking

If you ranked listening first, you're like the average person, who spends about 50 percent of his or her communication time listening. An ancient proverb, attributed to Zeno of Citium, emphasizes the comparative importance of this skill: "We have been given two ears and but a single mouth in order that we may hear more and talk less."

If we listen so much, we should be pretty good at it. Right? Unfortunately, we often fail to focus on developing this vital skill as much as we focus on improving our other communication skills. Compare the number of reading, writing, and speaking courses to the number of listening courses your college or university offers. Most schools offer many writing, literature, and speech courses, but few offer even one course in listening

Listening is the communication skill we use most, and good listening skills are valuable in a variety of contexts. Your listening can be more productive if you think about your personal stake in each listening situation.

Devan Marchbanks

to comprehend or in critical listening. Instead, instructors typically incorporate listening into other courses or ignore it entirely.

Because listening is so vital, this chapter begins by stressing its importance. Then it looks at several factors that typically hinder effective listening. Finally, it presents some strategies you can use to become a more effective listener.

Listening Skills Are Valuable

If you do an Internet search for "listening skills," you will get more than 2.3 million hits. Obviously, many people think good listening is important, and Internet sites typically promote workshops or listening quizzes, give advice, or suggest activities aimed at improving listening in the workplace, in classrooms, or in relationships. So there definitely seems to be room for improvement. Some people don't think much about how they listen, and many others are overly confident, thinking that they remember 75 to 80 percent of what they've heard, when, in fact, two days later, the average listener can recall only about 25 percent.[1] It's worth developing good listening skills because they are essential for many reasons:

▶ *Listening takes up much of our time.* Listening is the most commonly used skill in the workplace; understanding and following instructions (skills linked to listening) come in second.[2] And, according to the student handbook of the University of Minnesota, Duluth,[3] the average student spends fourteen hours each week in class listening; this is over and above the hours spent listening to friends and to media.

▶ *Good listening skills are good job skills.* The most successful people are effective listeners. For example, one study reports that 80 percent of executives rank listening as the most important work skill.[4] Another reported that physicians with good listening skills have fewer malpractice claims.[5] And Madelyn Burley-Allen, author of *Listening: The Forgotten Skill*, says the most common comment about well-liked bosses is: "he or she really listens to me."[6] Barbers, interior designers, journalists, automobile service advisers—even politicians—understand the need to listen;[7] in fact, "listening tours" are now indispensable in political campaigns. President Calvin Coolidge once said, "No one ever listened himself out of a job."[8]

▶ *Good listening skills are good academic skills.* Researchers administered a listening test to all incoming students at one university. At the end of the first year, 49 percent of low-scoring students were on academic probation, compared to less than 5 percent of high-scorers. On the other hand, 68.5 percent of high-scorers were earning honors, compared to just over 4 percent of low-scorers.[9]

▶ *Listening and being heard empowers people and aids personal relationships.* Sheila Bentley, past president of the International Listening Association, says, "Most people would agree that having someone listen to you makes you feel better—mentally and physically. In fact, according to Ralph G. Nichols, . . . 'The most basic of all human needs is to understand and to be understood. . . . The best way to understand people is to listen to them.' Thus, being listened to is one of our most basic needs."[10]

▶ *You have an investment in the listening situation.* The Student Counseling Services team at Texas A & M University advises students to develop a positive, consumer-wise attitude toward listening. Because you are in the situation for one reason or another, you have something at stake. Choosing to listen well and benefit from what you hear will help you gain the most from your investment.[11]

These are only a few reasons that listening is important; you can probably think of many other ways that good listening makes life easier. Pause now, and ask yourself how your listening habits help or hinder your comprehension of course work. What personal relationships benefit or suffer as a result of your listening behaviors? How are listening skills used in a job you currently hold or plan to hold someday? Keep these questions in mind as you study the remainder of the chapter.

Barriers to Listening

The Chinese character for listening (Figure 4.1) combines the symbols for ears, eyes, and heart; it reinforces the idea that good listeners are wholly involved in listening. Most of us don't begin our days thinking, "I'm going to be a terrible listener today." We intend to listen well, but we face linguistic, cultural, and personal barriers that hinder our effectiveness. Understanding these barriers and planning strategies to deal with them will build your listening skills.

Linguistic Barriers

Sometimes the speaker's language is a barrier, and a diverse culture includes many language variations. Visit a large city in the United States, and the number of languages and accents multiplies; for example, more than one hundred languages are spoken in New York City alone. Add to these the slang that teenagers invent and the phrases their grandparents use, or the terminology that skateboarders use and the legalese that only lawyers understand. Clearly, the potential for linguistic misunderstandings is great. Linguistic barriers show up in both language and vocabulary differences.

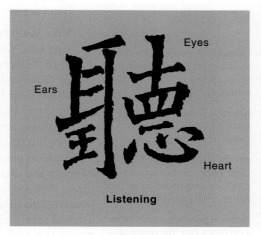

Figure 4.1
The Chinese character that translates as "listening" emphasizes its holistic nature by combining the symbols for ears, eyes, and heart.

▶ *Language differences.* When you don't share a speaker's language, you need an interpreter to translate the ideas. Even then, you'll probably miss some concepts or nuances of meaning, because languages and the ideas they embody are so different. In addition, you may have a hard time understanding a person who speaks with a heavy accent, whether it is a regional or ethnic accent, or an accent influenced by a first language.

▶ *Vocabulary differences.* Speakers whose vocabulary is more extensive than yours will most likely talk over your head at times. In addition, speakers who use the technical jargon associated with a specific topic such as medicine or engineering will lose lay audiences unless they translate the jargon. And speakers who use slang or other specialized linguistic codes will reach some people but talk past others.

To overcome linguistic barriers, listen very carefully and see if you can gain meaning from the general context of the speech. Take notes; jot down words to study later. Speakers can help by translating jargon terms and by displaying words in a visual form (such as a PowerPoint slide) when possible so that listeners can see as well as hear them. (Chapter 12 provides more information on language differences and comprehension.)

Cultural Barriers

Comprehension also depends upon your ability to understand **cultural allusions**, or references to culturally specific historical, literary, and religious sources. You can probably think of many things that are familiar in your culture or co-cultures that would confuse someone from a different group. Here are a few examples:

- A highly educated person whose major interest is opera will be more familiar with Wagner's Ring Cycle than with Elliott Yamin or Los Lonely Boys.
- Allusions to the classic Japanese novel *The Tale of Genji* would need to be explained to most people outside of Japan.
- Although he is one of the most famous sufi poets, Jalāl ad-Din ar-Rūmi would have to be introduced to many audiences.

In our pluralistic society and multicultural world, each group draws from different resources in their various backgrounds. In pluralistic settings, you may be unfamiliar with these culture-specific references. It is up to each speaker to be sensitive to differences and explain allusions or choose areas of common knowledge. Listeners can also play their part by jotting down unfamiliar allusions and doing research about them later.

Personal Barriers

Personal distractions can obstruct your listening. For example, William identified a number of common listening problems:

> Sometimes I become aggressive; sometimes I get defensive when I feel attacked. I have attention deficit disorder; at times I am easily distracted by others around me. I let my feelings for people get in the way.

Like William, many personal factors can hinder your listening. **Physical factors** (hearing loss, sleep deprivation, hunger pangs, the flu) can affect your ability or your desire to focus on a speech. **Psychological factors** can also keep you from listening closely: You just had an argument with a friend; you have a huge test coming up in your next class; your bank account is overdrawn. The worries that accompany psychological stressors can take your energy away from listening. You may also feel defensive and anxious about messages that you feel will challenge or threaten you in some way. And, if you lack interest in the topic, you may struggle to remain focused.

Stereotypes and prejudices can also hinder listening. When you put people into a category and then assume they will fit the characteristics of the category, you **stereotype** them. When you listen with preformed judgments about the speaker, either negative or positive, you show **prejudice** or bias. To illustrate, several supporters of abortion rights listened approvingly to a speaker from Planned Parenthood, but they yawned through a speech that took a right to life position, and vice versa.

Because attention constantly fluctuates, maintaining focus is another major listening skill. Here Gail discusses some of her struggles to pay attention:

> I'm easily distracted. . . . It's easy for me to either focus on one particular thing that has been said, and then sort of drift off, exploring it further in my

---

cultural allusions references to historical, literary, and religious sources that are culturally specific

physical factors bodily conditions that can limit your desire or ability to listen

psychological factors mental stressors or distractions that take away from your desire or ability to focus

stereotype place someone in a category and then assume the person fits the characteristics of that category

prejudice preformed biases or judgments, whether negative or positive

own mind, or—and this applies more specifically to someone whose speaking style or subject does not impress me—float off on unrelated topics ("I wonder where she gets her hair cut?"). Also, depending on the subject, I can get easily bored.

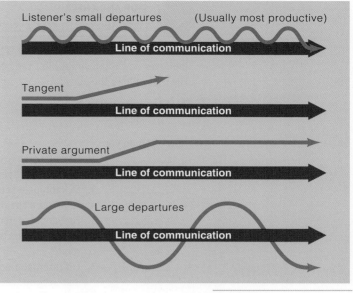

Paying attention is often hard work. For one thing, you can think far more rapidly (about 500 words per minute) than the fastest speaker can talk (about 300 words per minute). Most speakers average about 150 words per minute, leaving you with 350 words per minute of a **speech-thought differential**, also called **"leftover thinking space."**[12] The following four thought patterns, illustrated in Figure 4.2, are common during listening:[13]

▶ *Taking small departures from the communication line.* Small departures can hinder your comprehension, but they can also help you follow a message if you produce your own examples, relate the material to your personal experiences, answer the speakers' rhetorical questions, and otherwise interact with the ideas during the departure.

▶ *Going off on a tangent.* When you leave the speakers' line of thinking and seize on one of their ideas, taking it in your own direction, you stop listening. One idea leads to another, and before you know it, you're in a daydream, several subjects removed from the topic at hand.

▶ *Engaging in a private argument.* When you carry on a running debate or mental argument that parallels the speech, you close your mind and stop trying to understand the speaker's reasoning. In contrast, effective critical listeners identify arguments that don't make sense, but they withhold final judgment until they have heard the entire speech.

▶ *Taking large departures from the communication line.* Your attention wanders off into unrelated areas; you bring it back and focus on the speech for a while; then, off it goes again, and you find yourself thinking about a totally unrelated topic. This cycle repeats indefinitely.

As you can see, linguistic, cultural, and personal factors can challenge your listening abilities. To assess your skills in this area, complete the test in the Stop and Check box on the following page. In the remainder of the chapter, you will discover some strategies you can use to become a better listener.

Figure 4.2
Listening Thought Patterns
These four thought patterns are typical during listening. The first can be productive, but the rest characterize poor listening.

Strategies to Improve Listening

Margarete Imhof, past president of the International Listening Association, found that most students do not think of listening as an active process that they can control. Instead, they find it easier to criticize the speaker's mannerisms and characteristics rather than critically analyze the message. She researched several approaches such as asking pre-questions, interest management, and elaboration strategies that students could choose to help them listen better. Some of her suggestions are discussed in this section which explains several ways to become a more effective listener.[14]

Use Cultural Schemas

Listening schemas are sets of cultural expectations that can help you organize and understand messages (Figure 4.3). **Schemas** are mental plans, blueprints, or models you

speech-thought differential the difference between the rate you think (about 500 words per minute) and the average speaking rate (about 150 words per minute)

leftover thinking space another term for the difference between your thinking rate and the speaking rate

schemas mental models that guide your perception, interpretation, storage, and recollection of a speech

STOP AND CHECK

LISTENING SKILLS SELF-ASSESSMENT

Evaluate your listening by taking this test. First, write the letter that most accurately indicates how often you exhibit the behavior; then tabulate your listening score using the key that follows the questions.

A = Almost always   B = Usually   C = Sometimes
D = Rarely   E = Almost never

How often do you:

_____ 1. Give up trying to understand a speaker's accent and tune the speaker out?
_____ 2. Get lost in a speech because of your small vocabulary?
_____ 3. Stereotype a speaker and let that affect how you listen?
_____ 4. Tune out a speaker whose position is different from one you hold?
_____ 5. Feel angry, defensive, or fearful when you disagree with the speaker?
_____ 6. Become distracted by external factors, such as noises outside the room?
_____ 7. Let internal preoccupations, such as personal worries or stresses, distract you?
_____ 8. Carry on a running argument with a speaker instead of hearing him or her out?
_____ 9. Go off on a tangent?
_____ 10. Give in to your short attention span and lose your place in a long speech?

Key

For every A give yourself 2 points.
For every B give yourself 4 points.
For every C give yourself 6 points.
For every D give yourself 8 points.
For every E give yourself 10 points.

Total score _____

More than 90	Your listening skills are exceptional.
Between 76 and 90	You are above average.
Between 60 and 75	Your skills are about average.
Below 60	You are probably not as effective a listener as you could be.

If you scored below 80, identify specific strategies from the rest of this chapter to improve your listening.

use to perceive information and then interpret, store, and recall it.[15] Think of how you listen to a story. You have a mental model of what a good story is like, and you use this model to interpret a specific story—your schema tells you whether to take it seriously, how to draw lessons from it, what parts are worth remembering, and so on.

You formulate schemas through listening to many speeches of various types. For instance, you've heard lots of announcements, and you have a pretty good idea of what they are like, because they follow a fairly predictable pattern. Similarly, you've learned what to expect from a how-to speech, a news report, a funeral eulogy, or an award presentation because you've heard many speeches in each category. (The Diversity in Practice box about Cultural Listening Styles identifies some listening expectations that are common in other cultural and co-cultural groups.)

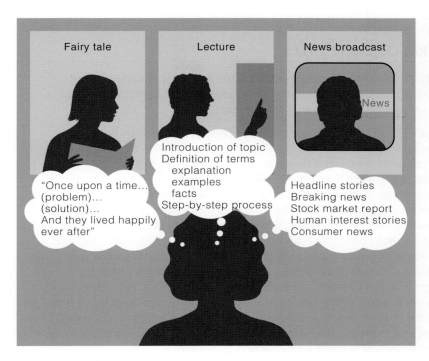

Figure 4.3
Listening Schemas Our minds contain a number of schemas or models that help us listen and respond to specific types of speeches.

Know Your Listening Purpose

Just as you have speaking goals, you also have listening goals. You turn on the radio for entertainment but when a commercial comes on, you tune out, or you critically evaluate the claims, deciding whether or not the product interests you. You listen to a lecture for information, and then you eat lunch with friends and listen empathetically to their frustrations. For each type of listening, you shift strategies to meet your listening goals. This section focuses on listening to comprehend and listening to evaluate messages.

Improve Your Comprehension

Think of all the times you listen for information: Your professor clarifies a complex process; your boss gives directions for your next project; your physician explains your medical condition; a friend directs you to the financial aid office; a radio reporter tells where an accident blocks traffic. Listening to learn, or **comprehensive listening**, is a vital skill in many areas of life, and there are several strategies you can employ to increase your comprehension.[21]

▶ *Prepare in advance.* Before the session, prepare by asking some pre-questions such as "What do I already know about this topic? What do I *want* to know? and What do I *need* to know?" Answers to these questions can help you set a learning goal for the session.

  • Tips for classroom listening include reviewing notes from previous sessions and reading related material in the text or looking up background information before the upcoming session. Also, study the list of concepts found at the chapter opening; skim the chapter, and notice headings and boldfaced terminology; read the summary. Look at the pictures and diagrams, or search for supplementary information on the Internet.

  • In the workplace, do your homework before an important session by asking pre-questions and brushing up on background information. This will help you ask more thoughtful questions and better participate in co-creating meaning.

DIVERSITY IN PRACTICE
CULTURAL LISTENING STYLES

THE WAYS LISTENERS APPROACH public speeches reflect differences in worldviews and behaviors among cultural groups. Knowing some cultural variations will make you more mindful of listening diversity. Here are a few examples:

▶ *A Javanese listening schema:* On the Indonesian island of Java, listeners turn to their neighbors and repeat phrases they like. The resulting buzz of voices throughout the speech signals the speaker that the audience is receiving it well.[16]

▶ *Additional listening traditions found in several Asian cultures:* In cultures that emphasize unity, listeners often expect speakers to develop oneness with them rather than present divisive ideas. Both the speakers and their audiences share responsibility for making the speech successful.[17] In some groups, audiences listen in silence, thinking that noise breaks their concentration and diverts their attention. Applause signals suspicion, similar to booing by United States audiences; some cultures do not applaud at the end of the speech so that the speaker can remain modest.[18]

▶ *An African American schema:* The entire audience participates in a "call and response" pattern which reflects African traditions. The speaker's statements (calls) are punctuated by the listeners' reactions to them (response), and in a real sense, the audience is talking back to the speaker. No sharp line distinguishes speakers and listeners, and everyone cooperates to create the message.[19]

▶ *Various student preferences:* A cross-cultural study of student listening preferences[20] showed that American students like short, to-the-point messages. They tend to prefer speakers with whom they can identify (women more so than men). German students prefer precise, error-free messages; disorganized presentations frustrate and annoy them. They are much less concerned about identifying personally with the speaker. Israeli students prefer complex and challenging information that they can ponder and evaluate before they form judgments and opinions. The length of the speech is relatively unimportant.

For more on this topic, log on to InfoTrac College Edition and read Christian Kiewitz's study of cross-cultural student listening preferences, "Cultural Differences in Listening Style Preferences: A Comparison of Young Adults in Germany, Israel, and the United States."

▶ *Use attention-directing strategies.* Watch for times your attention wanders to that movie you saw recently or the phone call you received just before the session, and develop strategies to bring the speaker back into focus. A common strategy is to take notes. Direct your attention to particular areas of the message; for example, listen for and write down the main ideas, focus on practical "things I must remember," or listen for examples that will help you remember concepts.

▶ *Think about why you're listening.* It's easier to pay attention when you understand your investment in the topic. For instance, a lecture on anatomy may seem boring at the time, but learning the information is essential to a pre-med student's success. So try to reframe your attitude about uninteresting material. Think of positive things about the topic and how that particular information will help you. In the classroom, try to anticipate what might be on a test; in the workplace, look for the main things your boss wants you to remember.

▶ *Enhance the meaning through elaboration strategies.* Use small departures productively by linking the material to your personal experiences and ideas. For example, you

comprehensive listening listening to learn, understand, or get information

might ask: "Who do I know who is like that?" "What comes next?" "Does this match what I learned in another context?" "How does this relate to tasks I'm doing now?" Elaborate on the ideas by creating mental images or by referring to what you already know or have experienced.

▶ *Look for organizational patterns.* Use what you know about speech organization to help you remember material. For instance, identify the main points and watch for signals such as "first," "next," or "finally" that will help you understand a series of steps. Be alert for words like "therefore" or "in contrast" that connect ideas.[22]

▶ *Use strategies that complement your personal learning style.* For instance, if you are an auditory learner, get permission to record the speech and replay it later. If you are a linear learner, outline the main points and the important supporting information. If you are more graphically oriented, make a mind map and draw connections between ideas, or sketch useful illustrations in the margins of your notes. I personally include the speaker's examples in my notes, because I learn and remember abstract ideas better when I tie them to real-life situations.

▶ *Take note of the speaker's manner but don't get hung up on delivery.* A speaker's confident enthusiasm about the subject adds a dimension that says "this is important, pay attention" or "I care about this topic and so should you." In contrast, a tentative, apologetic, or apathetic manner suggests "this is not very important material" or "this speaker seems unsure about this message, so how can I trust it?" However, some speakers with important things to say have annoying delivery habits that can take your focus off the main idea.

Devorah Overby

Effective note taking is one way you can improve your comprehensive listening skills.

In summary, comprehensive listening requires you to understand words and ideas, to identify major ideas and supporting materials, to connect new material with old, and to recall information. Comprehensive listening corresponds with the general speech purpose of informing. We now turn to critical listening skills that you should put into practice when you hear a persuasive speaker.

Improve Your Critical Listening Skills

Persuasive messages surround you, urging you to buy a product, sign a petition, donate time or money, accept a religious belief, and so on. Consequently, you need to develop **critical listening** skills to sort out competing claims for your allegiance, your beliefs, your money, and your time. Taking a critical approach does not mean that you find fault in everything, but it does mean that you analyze the evidence, ponder the implications, and evaluate the merits of various appeals rather than accepting them without reflection. Critical listening skills build on comprehensive listening skills but add questions such as these:

▶ What is this speaker's goal?
▶ Should I trust him or her?
▶ Is this speaker knowledgeable about *this* topic?
▶ Does this message make sense?
▶ Where does the supporting information come from? Are those sources reliable?

ETHICS IN PRACTICE

LAPTOPS IN LECTURES[23]

You've probably seen them: students who sit facing the professor with laptops open. In one window they take notes, glancing up at the professor occasionally. In other windows they email friends, play solitaire, or surf the Net.

Back in 2006 law professor June Entman decided that students in her civil procedures class should take notes the old-fashioned way—with paper and pencil. Laptops, she declared, created a "picket fence" between professors and students, discouraging interaction and promoting a mere transcription of her words. She called activities other than note taking "dishonest and inconsiderate . . . annoying and distracting to other students."[24] So she banned laptops from her classroom. Students protested that they could type faster than they could write, but Entman argued that the class required active participation in discussion. Administrators backed her ban.

Professor Entman is not alone. Many professors write paragraphs in their syllabi Curtailing the use of laptops in their courses.

Questions

1. What has been your experience with laptops in class?
2. Do you agree with Professor Entman that surfing the Web instead of taking notes is "dishonest"? Why or why not?
3. Are there ethical implications in "annoying and distracting" other students who are paying tuition to learn the information?
4. What is your response to this statement: "A student has the right NOT to listen in class"?

▶ What will I gain or lose if I adopt these ideas?
▶ What problems, if any, go along with this position?
▶ Am I being unduly swayed by my emotions?

Critical listening is one way to live out the cultural saying "Don't believe everything you hear." Sharpening these skills will guide you as you sift through all the persuasive appeals each day brings. Chapters 8 and 18 provide tests you can use to evaluate evidence and reasoning.

In a diverse culture, it's psychologically rewarding to seek out those speakers who bolster and affirm your ideas, especially if the dominant society challenges them. The following examples may clarify this concept.

▶ People who give money to support needy children attend a banquet where they hear narratives describing how their gift literally saved lives. They want to know that their money is not being wasted, and these stories convince them to continue their donations.
▶ Members of religious groups gather regularly in their churches, synagogues, mosques, and temples to reaffirm their spiritual beliefs.
▶ Members of neo-Nazi groups organize gatherings in which speakers passionately argue for the merits of white supremacy.
▶ Every January 22, the anniversary of the Supreme Court decision of *Roe v. Wade*, supporters on both sides of the abortion issue attend rallies to hear speakers reaffirm their respective positions.

critical listening listening that requires you to reflect and weigh the merits of messages before you accept them

In this type of context, you might find yourself enthusiastically clapping, nodding, or verbally encouraging the speaker. Because of your biases, you might accept questionable arguments or emotional appeals that support your cause. However, a listener from a

Office of the Governor of Texas

Rallies often attract people whose views are similar. However, even if you basically agree with a speaker's ideas, you should apply critical thinking skills whenever you listen.

different perspective would probably reject out of hand much of what's said there. Thus, you should test these messages just as you would any other persuasive speech.[25]

To practice the skills described here, listen to two political convention speeches from the 2008 Republican and Democratic national conventions. Go to **www .americanrhetoric.com** and do a site search for speech videos archived from each convention. If you prefer the Republican Party, practice your comprehensive listening skills on a Democrat's speech. Be able to summarize it and show that you understand it. Then listen to a Republican's speech critically and analytically, using the guidelines described above. If you prefer the Democratic Party, do the opposite: Make sure you understand what the Republican is saying and then critically evaluate a speech given by a Democrat.

✓ STOP AND CHECK

DEVELOP STRATEGIES TO LISTEN MORE EFFECTIVELY

Return to the Listening Skills Self-Assessment (pages 59–60 or on your online resources), and note each question you answered with an "A" or a "B." Using materials from this section, develop a Listening Skills Development Plan that will help you overcome the listening barrier implied in each question.

For additional effective listening tips, log on to InfoTrac College Edition and read Arleen Richman's article "Listen Up!"

Practice Dialogical Listening

Remember the communication model and the dialogical theory described in Chapter 1? Because dialogue involves active participation from listeners and speakers alike, your feedback helps co-create the meanings that ultimately come out of the presentation. Feedback comes in combinations of nonverbal, verbal, or written messages. As you read the suggestions that follow, remember that cultural expectations influence appropriate feedback behaviors.

Give Appropriate Nonverbal Feedback

Your posture, your movements, even the distance you sit from the speaker are all ways to provide meaningful feedback.

▶ *Posture.* Posture communicates involvement and helps focus your attention. Face the speaker squarely and lean forward slightly. When you are thoroughly engrossed, being "on the edge of your seat" is natural. Even if you sit in a corner or off to the side, you can still turn in the direction of the speaker, and let your body assume a relaxed, open position.

▶ *Distance.* Think about the difference in your attentiveness when you sit far away from the speaker where people are passing by an open door versus when you sit closer to the presenter where fewer outside distractions disrupt your focus. Which seat contributes more to good listening? Choose a place where the speaker can readily make eye contact with you; this puts more pressure on you to pay attention and give nonverbal feedback, because the speaker is more likely to look at you more often.[26]

▶ *Movements.* Avoid distracting behaviors such as fidgeting, shuffling papers, or playing with your pen. Instead, look at the speaker, which helps focus your attention. Obviously, opening your computer and checking your email or texting a message to your best friend are distracting. Give nonverbal feedback in the form of smiles at amusing anecdotes, nods in support of a major point, or applause when appropriate to further increase your involvement and provide additional interactions with the presenter.

When listeners are attentive, the speaker may actually become more interesting. One campus legend relates that a boring professor always stood at the lectern and read from his notes. His students decided to act *as if* he were fascinating. Whenever he moved away from his notes, ever so slightly, they all leaned forward a bit, made eye contact, and used supportive motions. According to the legend, the professor eventually was walking back and forth across the front of the room, lecturing animatedly.

Give Verbal Feedback

"Where can I get more information?" "One article I read presented very different information." "How is he defining that word?" Questions and comments such as these arise as you listen. Question-and-answer periods provide opportunities to co-create meanings. Here are a few of the most common types of questions:[27]

▶ When you are confused, ask **clarification questions** to gain more information, such as: Could you explain the difference between the Russian Old Believers and the Molokan Russians? How are you defining the word "generous"?

▶ **Closed questions** ask for brief, specific answers such as "yes" or "no". Use them to gain precise information or to verify your understanding. Here are some examples: Are you a member of the NRA? Would you buy coffee from a company that did not purchase fair trade coffee beans? Which search engine do you use most? Was this the same person who directed the movie, *Time for Drunken Horses?*

▶ **Open questions** invite longer answers that could be developed in a variety of ways, as these examples show: What do you think is the best way to bring down the price of gas? What suggestions do you have for getting rid of unwanted email? How will your spending habits change now that you've destroyed your credit cards?

▶ **Loaded questions** put a speaker on the defensive because of what they imply. Try to avoid them. When will you begin to look at both sides of the issue? implies that the speaker was one-sided, and *when* is not really asking for a time. In other words, you wouldn't expect to hear, "I am going to research the other side tomorrow afternoon at 3:00."

---

clarification questions requests to clear up confusing ideas

closed questions requests for brief, specific answers

open questions requests for more lengthy responses

loaded questions questions containing implications intended to put the speaker on the defensive

▶ To get a speaker to expand on an idea, make a **request for elaboration**: You said the Electoral College was modeled on the system used in the Roman Republic; could you elaborate? Can you provide more information about the cost and availability of the eye chip?

▶ Instead of questions, you can add **comments** or information from your own experience and research. For instance, after a speech on bullying, Tiffany shared statistics she had heard on a television show. Jon told a story about a coach who bullied his team. If you know that data in the speech is incorrect (for example, the statistics are outdated), you could provide supplementary information.

Although question-and-answer periods are common in the United States, not all cultures participate equally in a co-creation of meaning process, as the Diversity in Practice box titled Saving Face explains.

DIVERSITY IN PRACTICE
SAVING FACE

QUESTION-AND-ANSWER PERIODS are rare in some cultural groups. For instance, in the context of traditional Chinese or Japanese public speaking, listeners are supposed to understand the speaker. Asking a question is an admission that they lack the intelligence to unravel the speaker's shades of meaning. Furthermore, a question reflects on the speaker's communication abilities; in other words, if listeners are left confused, the speaker failed to communicate. Finally, to preserve the speaker's "face," it's considered inappropriate to publicly question a speaker's information and, thus, his or her character.[28]

Give Written Feedback

Your instructor will probably ask you to respond in writing to some of your classmates' speeches. The most effective comments focus on two or three specific elements of the presentation, using the **D-R-E method**: Describe-Respond-Evaluate.[29] *Describe* what you heard; *respond* with your personal interpretations and reactions; and *evaluate* by critiquing what you found effective and what could be improved. Phrase your comments objectively and positively. Here are some examples:

▶ Description: "I noticed that you quoted a variety of sources with diverse viewpoints, including *Newsweek*, the *Jerusalem Post*, and *National Review*." (content) Or, "You looked out the window during your introduction, but you looked more directly at us as the speech progressed." (delivery)

▶ Response: "I really connected emotionally with the story about the grandfather and the little boy." (content) Or, "Because your tone was so conversational, I found myself wanting to hear what you had to say." (delivery)

▶ Evaluation: "Using a variety of sources was good, because it showed you sought out opinions from national, international, conservative, and less conservative sources. Your use of examples balanced the statistics well. I think your speech would be even stronger if you added a map to your PowerPoint slides." (content) Or, "Your ability to remember your ideas was impressive, but try to eliminate the phrase 'you know.' It became distracting." (delivery)

Comments such as these are both specific and beneficial because they give the speaker an idea of the overall impression the speech made on you and why. On the other hand, writing "good job" is not helpful at all because it is so vague. In general, write out as many positive things as you can, and then evaluate the performance by identifying a few things that could be improved.

requests for elaboration questions asking for more information

comments information from personal experience or research

D-R-E method a feedback method that describes content, shares personal responses, and gives evaluation

STOP AND CHECK

WRITE A CRITIQUE

Log on to your online resources or **www.americanrhetoric.com** to watch a speech video of your choice. As you listen, take notes on the speech content and jot down some personal responses and observations on the effectiveness of the speech. Then write a critique that (1) describes, (2) responds to, and (3) evaluates the speech. Discuss this critique with a group of classmates.

PRACTICALLY SPEAKING

RECEIVER APPREHENSION (RA)

Receiver apprehension (RA) refers to the anxiety people experience during listening. Specifically, RA occurs when listeners fear they'll misinterpret, inadequately process, or fail to adjust psychologically to a particular message.[30] Professor Kaidren Winiecki Sergienko first became interested in RA when she was a graduate student, studying with Dr. Joe Ayres and Dr. Tim Hopf whose extensive research in communication apprehension is discussed Chapter 2. Sergienko finds RA interesting because so many of us experience it so often, and it can have a variety of significant impacts in our lives, but it is less visible and less studied than CA in general.

Is RA a widespread phenomenon? I certainly believe so. If asked, I'm sure most people could recall a situation in which they experienced listening apprehension. Of course, different people experience different levels of RA and in different situations.

Can you give some examples of RA? I sometimes experience RA at work. I feel a level of RA when a student comes to my office upset with a grade, an assignment, or another student in class. I may also feel RA during a class discussion in which students disagree with each other or are giving each other negative feedback and critiques.

When or where do you see RA in college life? RA is experienced in virtually every part of college life, because students are coming to a new place with new people and new norms. Attending orientation, listening to financial aid guidelines, attending the first day of class, hearing a complex or abstract lecture and knowing there will be a test on the material, learning the guidelines for a mid-quarter project, listening to a classmate discuss an opposing opinion, and meeting with a teacher—all of these can result in a low or high level of RA. And these are only a few of the experiences students have.

Faculty, staff, and administrators feel its effects as well. Meeting with colleagues to discuss controversial policy or action plans and attending workshops to learn new technologies are just a few examples of situations that can create RA.

Why did your research focus on RA in the workplace? The workplace is a kind of shared experience that virtually everyone will have. It is where we spend the majority of our waking hours. Many people closely identify with their work. Finally, I believe that our workplace communication can affect our lives outside of work, such as our degree of fulfillment, our self-esteem, and our ability to provide for ourselves and our families. So, if RA is affecting our happiness or our ability for upward mobility within an organization, it is important to acknowledge it and respond to it.

receiver apprehension (RA) anxiety that people experience while listening

Questions for Discussion:

‣ When, if ever, do you fear you'll misinterpret a confusing message?

‣ When, if ever, are you afraid you won't understand an abstract or complex message?

‣ When, if ever, do you avoid listening to a topic that you find psychologically or emotionally upsetting? (For example, it may directly challenge your beliefs or may be otherwise very disturbing.)

‣ How might you overcome your RA in a specific situation where listening fears could have a negative effect on your life?

Summary

Listening is the communication activity that we do most and study least. Listening is important in your personal and work life. However, listeners often face cultural as well as personal barriers that impede effective listening. Different languages, vocabularies, and cultural allusions all make comprehension difficult. In addition, personal and psychological factors—such as fatigue, stresses and worries, stereotypes and prejudices, and wandering attention—can hinder listening.

Fortunately, you can devise strategies to listen more effectively. Use cultural schemas or mental blueprints to guide your perception, interpretation, storage, and recollection of what you hear. Know your listening purpose, and identify strategies to help you comprehend information or critically evaluate persuasive messages.

Finally, practice dialogical listening by contributing appropriate nonverbal, verbal, and written feedback. Nonverbal actions communicate that you are interested in the speech; they also help you pay attention. Useful nonverbal elements include a posture that communicates involvement, a distance that helps focus your attention, and movements that support rather than disrupt the speech. When you have an opportunity to interact verbally with a speaker, ask questions or provide comments that elaborate on the topic. However, be aware that after-speech questions and comments are inappropriate in some cultures. Finally, write out comments using the D-R-E method to describe what you heard, respond personally, and evaluate the overall presentation.

STUDY AND REVIEW

Your online resources for *Public Speaking: Concepts and Skills for a Diverse Society* offer a broad range of study tools that will help you better understand the material in this chapter, complete assignments, and succeed on tests. Your online resources feature

- Speech videos with critical viewing questions, speech outlines, and transcripts
- Interactive versions of this chapter's Stop and Check activities and Application and Critical Thinking Exercises
- Speech Builder Express and InfoTrac College Edition
- Weblinks related to chapter content
- Study and review tools such as self-quizzes, an interactive glossary, and downloadable audio summaries

You can access your online resources at **http://www.cengage.com/login**, using the access code that came with your book or that you bought online at **http://www.iChapters.com**.

KEY TERMS

The terms below are defined in the margins throughout this chapter.

clarification questions 66	open questions 66
closed questions 66	physical factors 58
comments 67	prejudice 58
comprehensive listening 62	psychological factors 58
critical listening 64	receiver apprehension (RA) 68
cultural allusions 58	requests for elaboration 67
D-R-E method 67	schemas 60
leftover thinking space 59	speech-thought differential 59
loaded questions 66	stereotype 58

APPLICATION AND CRITICAL THINKING EXERCISES

1. Listening skills are important in thousands of jobs, ranging from academic advisors or financial aid officers on campus to haircutters and real estate agents. Tell of a time when someone really listened to you while performing his or her job, and then tell of a time when someone failed to listen well. What was the outcome in each case?

2. Think about the Chinese symbol that stands for listening (see Figure 4.1). In what way do you use your ears, eyes, and heart when you listen to your classmates? Your professors? People at work? A speaker whose ideas support your own opinions? A speaker with whom you fundamentally disagree?

3. Using the diagrams in Figure 4.2 as models, draw a diagram that depicts your listening pattern during the most recent lecture you heard. Next, draw a diagram that depicts your listening pattern during the last conversation you had with your best friend. Draw a third diagram that shows your listening pattern during your last major conversation with a family member. Compare the three. What conclusions can you draw about your listening patterns in various contexts?

4. In the Internet article "The Listener Wins," career consultant Michael Purdy discusses the importance to professional success of listening effectively. He also summarizes a study listing the traits of good versus poor listeners. Find this article at **http://featuredreports .monster.com/listen/overview/** and identify two things you learned about listening in the workplace from this article.

5. Randall Davis has collected a number of listening assessment exercises that you can complete outside of class to evaluate your listening effectiveness. His Cyber Listening Lab is available at **www.esl-lab.com**. To see what a good listener you are (or not) take at least one test from each listening level. What does this tell you about your listening abilities?

6. Go to **www.usu.edu/arc**, a Utah State University Web site that provides many student aids. Link to "Idea Sheets," where you'll find two especially helpful worksheets: (1) "Note taking: Cornell method," and (2) "Listening skills for lectures." Use the suggestions in these handouts to create your Listening Skills Development Plan under your online resources for Chapter 4.

7. Practice the nonverbal skills of active listening in one of your courses. That is, use posture, space, and movement to help focus your attention on the lecture. Afterward, evaluate how much your nonverbal behaviors helped you pay attention and recall the class material.

8. Verbally interact with one of the speakers in the next round of classroom speeches. During the speech, jot down several comments or questions to ask during the question-and-answer period.

9. Use the Describe-Respond-Evaluate method to give written feedback after one of your classmates' speeches.

10. To face receiver apprehension head on, listen to a speaker who makes you anxious because he or she takes a position that differs dramatically from your views. You may find the person on radio, television, or the Internet (for example, a person whose lifestyle differs from yours, one whose views on a social issue such as capital punishment diverge from yours, or a person with different religious beliefs). Describe, respond to, and evaluate the content and delivery, and then assess how your apprehension affected your listening.

SPEECH VIDEO

Go to your online resources to watch and critique speeches of your choice, or link to other sites that offer speech videos, such as **www.c-span.org**, **www.americanrhetoric.com**, or **www.you-tube.com**.

5

SELECTING YOUR TOPIC AND PURPOSE

THIS CHAPTER WILL HELP YOU

▶ Choose your speech topic

▶ Narrow your topic to fit the situation

▶ Identify a general purpose and a specific purpose for your speech

▶ Write a thesis statement that states your subject and its importance to the audience

▶ Write a preview that summarizes your main points

© Tim Timmerman

I N WORKPLACES and other public settings, your speech topic is often obvious. You're scheduled to present a report at work? The topic is the project you've been working on. You're asked to give a toast at a wedding? The topic is the happy couple.

However, for a classroom speech, your task is not quite so easy, because the topic is not generally assigned, and there are literally millions of topics in the world. In fact, there are so many possible subjects that selecting just one that's appropriate for your class may feel daunting. The subject can't be too broad or too complex (after all, most classroom speech assignments are limited to ten minutes at the most); it should be interesting to your audience, as well as to you; it should be relevant; it should be novel... there are many factors to consider.

Is there a surefire method for selecting a topic that suits you, your audience, and the occasion? Probably not, but here are some techniques that students have found helpful:

> When given the assignment, my brain becomes engaged immediately, flipping through various experiences, analyzing them to see if they're shareable and if they're actually significant. Typically, I look for a subject I feel strongly about. Sometimes an idea is triggered by a conversation or something I've read. (I read a lot.)

> GAIL

When I choose a topic, I analyze the parameters first: time limit, any given topic area, audience... then I think of something I'm interested in. If nothing comes to mind, I file the assignment in my thoughts—and often something during the day sparks an interest.

Joy

I spend a lot of time on the Internet, so I naturally go online and browse for topics. Google and Yahoo provide links to newspapers and magazines that include international and national topics, as well as business and entertainment news. I always find several interesting topics.

Terrence

Regardless of method, eventually you will come up with a number of possible subjects. The key—as Gail, Joy, and Terrence point out—is to find something you are comfortable with, something that is significant enough to discuss publicly. This chapter will give you guidelines for choosing your topic, narrowing it to a manageable size, and then selecting your purpose and focus.

Choose Your Topic

Because most instructors don't assign specific subjects, topic choice for classroom speeches is up to you. To avoid being overwhelmed at the open-endedness of this challenge, first consider the topic's significance to your audience. Does it need to be discussed? How and why is it relevant? Then look for subjects in four places: your personal interests and experiences, other courses you're taking, current events, and international and cultural subjects.

Assess Your Audience's Need to Know

Topics are everywhere. Do you have credit cards? Why, or why not? What historical memorials are in your area? What's the traffic like where you live? What are the causes and the effects of a price increase on a product everyone uses? Everyday topics such as these can result in interesting speeches.[1] The key is to find something significant—a subject that *needs* to be discussed because it will increase your audience's knowledge, bring about change, or highlight important cultural values and beliefs.[2] Evaluate topic possibilities from your audience's perspective (see Figure 5.1). How familiar are they with the subject? What more do they need to know? Does the subject affect their finances? Their future? Their health? Will it appeal to their curiosity?

Another general principle is to provide a measure of novelty, which is a basic

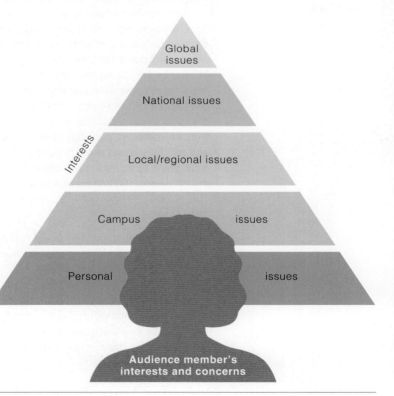

Figure 5.1

Topic Pyramid Topics range from personal to global in scope. Most listeners are more interested in subjects that are closer to home, although their interest increases when you link the topic to their lives. Think about why your audience needs to hear about your subject, and develop your speech in a novel way that connects to their concerns.

element of maintaining interest. Speak about something unfamiliar, or present a familiar topic in a different way.[3] Don't demonstrate how to make coffee (plug in a coffee maker; put in a filter and scoop in some coffee; add water; press the "on" button). Going over such a common procedure wastes your listeners' time. But is this topic completely out of line? Not necessarily. One student presented research that showed the effects of coffee on the body; another talked about the coffee industry and the importance of buying only Fair Trade certified coffee; a third discussed a major coffee corporation that employs millions of workers the world over. Many of these facts were novel and potentially valuable, even to non-coffee drinkers.

In short, choosing a topic that meets some need in your audience and presenting your subject in a novel way are two fundamental principles in speech making. When audience members already know a lot about your subject, you'll be more successful if you dig for supplementary information or select another topic. (Chapter 16 discusses this in more detail.) For additional ideas, the Web site developed by librarians at the University of Louisville provides an alphabetized list of topics, all linked to resources you can use to develop that topic: **http://library.louisville.edu/government/news/otherlinks/otherlinks.html**.

ETHICS IN PRACTICE

ARE ANY TOPICS TABOO?

In a January 15, 2008, article in *BusinessWeek*, "The Ethics of Talking Politics at Work," Bruce Weinstein argues that there are ethical reasons to avoid four topics at work: politics, religion, sex, and money. Discussing them won't help workers be more productive because they cause disagreement and raise strong passions. Weinstein identifies five ethical principles that underlie his position: do no harm, make things better, respect others, be fair, be loving.[4] While this may be good advice for the workplace, do some topics that cause disagreement, raise strong passions, or make people uncomfortable *need* be addressed in other contexts? For example, some people feel very anxious about the topic of race, but *should* race or religion, with their potential for creating discomfort, be addressed publicly? Several politicians thought so when they confronted racial and religious issues directly during the 2008 presidential campaign. Their speeches were given to increase understanding of diverse perspectives, invite respect for a variety of viewpoints, and make American society better overall.

Questions

1. Should student speakers avoid topics such as abortion, which often have political and religious underpinnings and which arouse emotional responses? If so, what topics should be avoided and why?
2. How should students balance First Amendment rights to speak freely against their responsibilities as outlined in the five principles Weinstein proposes or the dialogical and democratic principles described in Chapter 3?
3. Describe how discussion of a political, religious, sex-related, or money-related topic of your choice could actually enhance the five ethical principles Weinstein identifies.

Consider Your Personal Interests

Talk about what you know and what you care about. Use your natural curiosity and personal interests to generate possible topics.[5] What is your major? Your occupational goals? What pets do you own? Which famous people have you seen in person? What irritates you? What changes would you like to see in society? What ideas would you like to explore further? Unique life experiences also make good topics. You are who you are because of what you know and what you've experienced. Think about things in your family background, jobs, hobbies, or recreational interests that might interest others.[6] Here are some ways students created speeches around their interests and experiences:

▶ Chris saw an article in a magazine about making diamonds from cremated human remains. His curiosity was sparked, and he created a speech on the topic. The text of his speech is printed in Appendix C.

▶ Because Josh is a drummer, he chose the African *dun dun* drum for his topic. His outline is included at the end of Chapter 16.

▶ Emily had a liver transplant when she was a baby, so she discussed the disease "bilary atresia" and the liver transplant that saved her life. You can read her outline in Chapter 11.

▶ Carrie's father died during her sophomore year, so she was forced to work through her devastating grief while maintaining her studies. She argued for a grief support system on her university campus. The text of her speech is printed at the end of Chapter 8. Videos of all these speeches are available on the book's online resources.

Speaking on a topic that is personally compelling has obvious advantages. When you are truly interested in your subject, you can be more enthusiastic about it. Your enthusiasm can then help you concentrate on your message rather than focusing on yourself and your insecurities. Your enthusiasm will also energize your audience—after all, what is more boring than a bored speaker? For additional ideas on how to find a topic out of your personal experiences, check out Professor Ron St. John's Web site: **www .hawaii.edu/mauispeech/html/infotopichelp.html**.

Look for Topics from Other Courses

Look for speech topics in your academic major or in other courses you are taking. For example, if you're taking anthropology, study your textbook's table of contents for possible topics, such as marriage customs, kinship patterns, or gender differences among cultures. Dustin, a history major, spoke on the history of Iraq; Jenn, whose major is cognitive science, discussed neuroimaging. (The text of her speech appears at the end of Chapter 7 and on the book's online resources, where you'll also find a video of the speech.) Preparing a speech on an interesting topic from another class has the added advantage of helping you learn the material for that course. The librarians at Old Dominion University generated lists of hundreds of topics, organized by majors such as business and public administration, health sciences, or psychology: **www.lib.odu .edu/libassist/idea**.

Don't hesitate to use research you have done for a paper in another course if the subject is appropriate. For example, as part of a nursing course, Jack wrote a paper on Cherokee beliefs and practices. He used information from that paper in his classroom speech on Native American medicine. Remember, however, if you adapt a paper, you must organize the material differently and tailor it to a listening audience, not a reader.

Investigate Current Events

Newspapers, news magazines, and television shows are other good topic sources. Skim headlines or surf Internet news sites and blogs, jotting down current issues that interest you. Major newspapers and news magazines, as well as trade and other specialized periodicals, are available on InfoTrac College Edition and on sites such as **www.refdesk.com**. Here are some topics from a single day's news:

ricin	plagiarism leads to resignation
polar bear cubs	high school brawl
pennies	text messaging while driving
perjury	performance-enhancing drugs

PRACTICALLY SPEAKING

BRAD LAU, UNIVERSITY ADMINISTRATOR, STUDENT LIFE

Brian Rurik

In his job, Brad Lau's topics range from pleasant welcomes to new students to unpleasant briefings about campus tragedies.

Brad's career requires him to speak to a variety of audiences on a variety of topics. He answered a few questions about the challenges he faces.

Who are your major audiences? I speak to several types of audiences in a given year, and they often come from very different perspectives and backgrounds with diverse interests and needs. My most common audiences include college students in general, student leaders, community audiences, student life professionals (through workshop presentations, and so on), and the press.

How do you find your topics? This happens in a number of different ways:

▶ Asking people who will be in my audience what they perceive the felt need to be
▶ Reading books and articles that deal with the needs and interests of a given audience
▶ Asking others who speak to those audiences what the key issues are and if they have suggestions about specific things that should be addressed
▶ Keeping a file of articles dealing with relevant issues and topics for the various audiences
▶ Emailing people I trust and who are credible for that audience for suggestions about topics that need to be addressed
▶ Looking at publications (online and in print) that seek to reach that particular audience

What are your most stressful topics? It is difficult to speak about very emotional topics. For example, I am the person who must speak with the press when there is a campus controversy or tragedy involving students such as a fatal traffic accident. Student audiences can also be stressful. Students often hear a lot of speeches and I feel the pressure of making a topic relevant and timely while also saying what I think they need to hear (sometimes whether they want to or not). In other words, in my job, I don't always give an audience what they like to hear; sometimes I must speak to what I think they need to hear, or I must present and defend unpopular administrative policies.

Questions for Discussion

▶ Count the number of times Brad uses the words *need* or *should* to discuss topic selection. How could you use the strategies he lists to find a topic your audience needs to know about?
▶ Give examples of topics that student audiences might *need* to hear about but might not *want* to hear about.

Topics from current events usually address a need in society. The fact that they are important enough to discuss in the print or broadcast media means that they are significant to many people. And, because they are publicly covered, you should be able to locate information easily. For example, Google provided hundreds of thousands of links related to text messaging while driving, many from credible sources such as news

DIVERSITY IN PRACTICE

DOES REQUIRING ONE SPEECH ON "COMMUNICATION AND CULTURE" INCREASE STUDENTS' EMPATHY?

PROFESSOR LORI CARRELL[7] reported the results of research done in a medium-sized Midwestern university. The goal of the study was to determine if students increased in *empathy*, the ability to understand diverse perspectives, when diversity issues were incorporated into the course. An underlying assumption was that competent communicators can view issues from multiple perspectives. Four groups participated in the study: The control group had no special treatment; the second group took an entire course in intercultural communication; the third discussed concepts related to diversity at several points during the term; and the fourth group had a one-shot assignment to give a public speech on a "communication and diversity" topic.

Results indicated that students who studied intercultural communication for an entire term significantly increased in empathy. Those who often discussed diversity issues throughout the semester also showed increases. However, students who gave only one diversity speech made no significant gains.

What does this mean to you? How might an increase in empathy make you a more competent communicator? What connections can you see between the ability to understand a variety of perspectives and the diversity concepts presented in this text and in your classroom? How might your topic choices make you more sensitive to issues of diversity?

outlets and government agencies. Information includes potentially useful survey results, examples of accidents, laws, and so on.

Consider International and Cultural Topics

You may find it easier to come up with personal or national topics that are closer to our lives and that regularly appear in the news. However, don't overlook international subjects. Explore your cultural heritage and experiences; for example, Namky, who emigrated from Vietnam, talked about how to write and pronounce the Vietnamese alphabet. (See his outline in Appendix C.) Ryan, whose ancestors were Basque, spoke about the Basque artist, Jorge Oteiza. Another possibility is to consider global aspects of your major. Film studies majors might investigate a director or film genre from another country or a different cultural group. Your job can also be a starting point. For instance, a restaurant worker might give a speech about American fast food franchises overseas. Other sources include newspapers, magazines, and television broadcasts, which regularly report on trade, global investments, and international crime—all topics of increasing importance in the twenty-first century.

Cultural topics are easily found on the Internet. Go to sites such as BBC News World Edition (**http://news.bbc.co.uk/**) or the *Christian Science Monitor* (**www.csmonitor.com**), or go to **http://lamp.georgetown.edu/asw/about.php**, which is maintained by Georgetown University. Select the "Ethnicity, Race, and Religious Cultures" link, and follow additional links that interest you.

A word of caution: Whatever your topic, be sure to make connections to your listeners' here-and-now concerns. For example, the subject of land mines in another country a continent away might seem pretty far removed from your campus world. How could your classmates identify with the topic? Would they empathize with children and other civilians who lose limbs when they step on a mine? Do any listeners have friends or relatives in the military who might encounter these weapons? Do you have ancestors who emigrated from countries that are heavily mined? What about tax dollars that pay for specialists who detonate the mines? Could you link the topic to fundamental values, such as the desire for a world at peace or for freedom and justice for all? Your challenge is to help your audience understand the significance of the topic.

Narrow Your Topic

Once you have chosen a broad topic, you must then narrow it enough to discuss it within a designated time frame. This principle applies across all speaking contexts, from workplace project reports, sales presentations, and announcements to civic and ceremonial contexts. Here's how one professional speaker narrowed his topic in his introduction:

> I'm going to talk about technology and an introduction of technology into developing markets. I'm going to focus on agriculture. I'm going to focus particularly in Africa and particularly in Sub-Saharan Africa . . . in Malawi . . . with a woman named Sabina Xhosa.[8]

As a classroom topic, let's consider the general subject of workplace issues. Obviously, you can't discuss "The World of Work" in seven minutes, but you can focus on a specific topic such as how to negotiate a salary, on a controversy such as drug testing, or on a trend such as corporate social responsibility. Consider using a mind map as a way to let your ideas flow. Figure 5.2 illustrates how to use a mind map to start with a broad subject and narrow it to a series of more realistic classroom topics. Use your creativity to approach the topic from a personal, national, or international level.

Careful work early in the term will produce several subjects you can use throughout the term. Let's say Figure 5.2 is Erica's mind map.

▶ Her first presentation, a self-introductory narrative, relates a challenging experience with a coworker.

▶ Her informative speech describes corporate social responsibility. (Read her outline at the end of this chapter, and watch a video of her speech on the book's online resources.)

Figure 5.2
Mind Map This mind map shows several work-related topics.

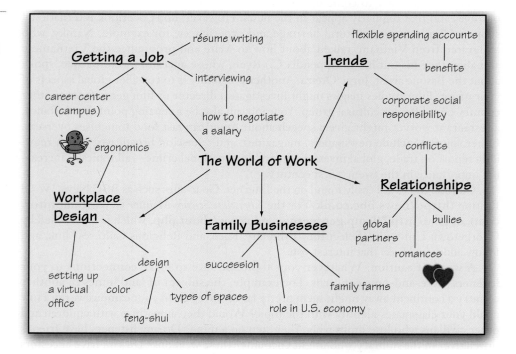

Later, she reports on feng shui design in the workplace.

▶ Finally, she urges her audience to take advantage of resources in the campus career center.

As you can see, the broad topic of workplace issues provides a wealth of subtopics for specific speech purposes.

STOP AND CHECK

IDENTIFY SEVERAL USABLE TOPICS

List about ten major topic areas that interest you (such as sports, animals, food). Then narrow your list to two or three, and make a mind map for each of those topics.

By selecting these general areas early in the term, you can be alert for information to use in your speeches. Let's say you are looking for material on workplace bullies; you might take advantage of the "news alerts" feature at Internet sources such as Google (news) or Yahoo (news) that provide updates on relevant stories. For different perspectives, consider blogs related to your topic, and use a blog tracker service that lets you know when a particular blog is updated. You could also set up interviews with human resource professionals as well as with people who have experienced bullying. Because you have the topic clearly in mind, you should have plenty of time to gather materials.

You can also create a file for each subject, photocopying or clipping articles from newspapers or magazines, downloading Internet stories, taking notes on lectures, or video recording related television programs. At speech time, you should have many resources available for a good presentation, including a number of audiovisual aids that a last-minute scramble might not produce.

Choose Your Purpose and Focus

You don't just "accidentally" give a public speech; instead, you speak to accomplish specific goals or purposes.[9] Consequently, at the outset of each speech, carefully clarify what you want to achieve by identifying your general purpose and tentatively formulating a specific purpose for that particular speech. Continue to refine your specific purpose as you work on the speech. Writing out a thesis statement helps both you and your listeners understand your central idea, and a preview lays out the major points you will develop.

Identify Your General Purpose

Almost 2,000 years ago, St. Augustine, who taught rhetoric long before he became a bishop, identified three public speaking purposes: to teach, to please, and to move.[10] In the eighteenth century, George Campbell[11] identified four purposes that reflected the psychology of his era:[12] to enlighten the understanding, to please the imagination, to move the passions, and to influence the will. In the mid-twentieth century, Alan Monroe[13] said we attempt to inform, to entertain, to stimulate through emotion, or to convince through reasoning. Today, speech instructors commonly identify four **general purposes:**

▶ *To inform.* Here your goal is to explain, teach, describe, announce, introduce, or provide a basis for your audience to have a greater understanding of your topic. Within the broad subject of work, you might explain a mentoring program or tell how to prepare for an interview.

general purpose four general purposes are: to inform, to persuade, to entertain, or to commemorate

▶ *To persuade.* Persuaders hope to convince, motivate, nominate, and reinforce cultural ideals. You might gather evidence that will convince your audience to buy a product or to continue giving to a cause.

▶ *To entertain.* Sometimes you just want listeners to laugh at your humorous portrayal of a subject. There are thousands of humorous workplace incidents; funny coworkers, crazy memos, weird customer requests—all would make entertaining speeches.

▶ *To commemorate.* On special occasions, your purpose is to highlight and reinforce cultural ideals. These speeches take the form of tributes, toasts, awards ceremonies, and other special occasion speeches. A farewell speech for a departing coworker is an example.

Speech purposes often overlap. Take the case of a university recruiter who attempts to persuade her listeners to attend the school she represents by both informing them about its distinctive advantages and providing entertaining accounts of campus life. She has several purposes, because she has several potential audiences: One goal is to persuade prospective students to fill out application forms; another is to inform their families about financial aid; and a third is to entertain alumni (while encouraging donations). Although her talk is not specifically commemorative, she reinforces cultural values on education throughout her speech.

Your instructor will probably assign the general purpose for each of your classroom speeches. Consequently, when you are assigned an informative speech, focus your research on discovering and presenting factual material that will increase your audience's knowledge or understanding of your topic. When you must persuade, select convincing and motivating materials that will influence your listeners to believe and act in the ways you advocate. If you're asked to be entertaining, choose a ridiculous event or situation and use strategies such as exaggeration and wordplay to highlight humorous aspects of the topic. Although giving a speech to entertain is less common in the classroom, you should always strive to be interesting—not boring—no matter what kind of speech you give; this will help you accomplish your other speech purposes. For a commemorative speech assignment, choose a worthy subject and develop it around cultural values. Keisha Walkes's tribute to Barbara Jordan in Appendix C and on the text's online resources shows how to do this. Figure 5.3 shows how to come up with a variety of speech purposes for a broad topic such as the workplace.

✓ **STOP AND CHECK**

NARROW YOUR PURPOSE

Practice narrowing your purpose by making a diagram similar to the one in Figure 5.3, using one of the subject-area mind maps you made for the Stop and Check exercise on page 79.

Identify Your Specific Purpose

Linnea has become convinced that her morning cup of coffee may mean that a worker in a coffee-producing company is being exploited, so she chooses "Fair Trade certified coffee" as her topic. Her next step is to decide exactly what she wants the audience to know or do as a result of her speech. Does she want them to know more about the production of coffee? How it affects workers in the coffee industry? Where their coffee dollar goes? Does she want them to stop purchasing coffee that is not Fair Trade certified? Does she want to use coffee as an example of Fair Trade products in general, in

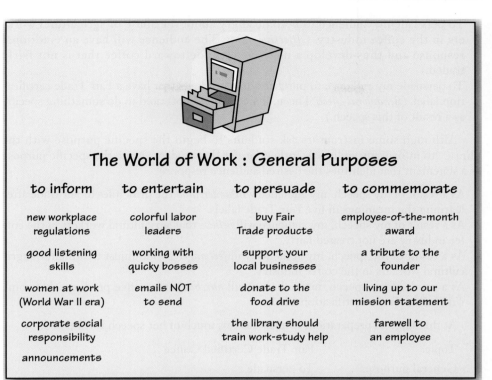

The World of Work : General Purposes

to inform	to entertain	to persuade	to commemorate
new workplace regulations	colorful labor leaders	buy Fair Trade products	employee-of-the-month award
good listening skills	working with quicky bosses	support your local businesses	a tribute to the founder
women at work (World War II era)	emails NOT to send	donate to the food drive	living up to our mission statement
corporate social responsibility		the library should train work-study help	farewell to an employee
announcements			

Figure 5.3
General Purposes
A broad topic such as the world of work can generate informative, entertaining, persuasive, and commemorative speeches.

case some listeners are not coffee consumers? How she answers these questions leads her to her **specific purpose** statement, which identifies her desired audience response or her speaking goal.[14] She could concentrate on influencing her listeners' thoughts, their emotions, or their actions.

▸ **Cognitive effects** are influences on the audience's beliefs, thoughts, or understandings. If she chooses this specific purpose, Linnea will focus more narrowly on providing information or on changing her listeners' beliefs about coffee production.

▸ **Affective effects** are the feelings or emotions aroused in the listeners. This is a potentially emotional topic, and Linnea might hope to instill anger and maybe even guilt feelings over the treatment of workers in the coffee industry.

▸ **Behavioral effects** are the actions audience members perform as a result of a speech. She might ask them to sign a pledge to change their purchasing habits and buy only Fair Trade certified products.

In short, Linnea must clarify what she wants her audience to know, feel, or do and then combine her topic and goal into a specific purpose statement. One way to keep her desired response in mind is to begin with an infinitive phrase and use the words "my audience" within the statement. Here are some specific purpose statements that illustrate a variety of general speech purposes.

▸ To inform my audience about the meaning of Fair Trade by decoding the meanings in five Fair Trade certification labels. (*Cognitive effect:* The audience will learn to interpret Fair Trade labels.)

▸ To convince my audience that agricultural workers in the coffee industry often labor in unfair working conditions. (*Cognitive effect:* The audience will believe that there is a labor problem at the production level of the coffee industry.)

specific purpose the cognitive, affective, or behavioral responses a speaker desires

cognitive effects influences on beliefs, understandings, and other mental processes

affective effects influences on listeners' feelings

behavioral effects influences on audience actions

▶ To persuade my audience to become angry about the abuse of agricultural workers in the coffee industry. (*Affective effect:* The audience will have an emotional response and thus develop a negative attitude toward coffee that is not fairly traded.)

▶ To persuade my audience to purchase only products that have a Fair Trade certification label. (*Behavioral effect:* The audience will be motivated to do something specific as a result of this speech.)

Although some instructors ask students to begin the specific purpose with the phrase "to inform my audience," others prefer that students write the specific purpose as a statement that identifies the desired audience response:

▶ As a result of my speech, my audience will *understand* the principles of fair trade after learning the meanings in five Fair Trade labels.

▶ As a result of my speech, my audience will *believe* that agricultural workers in the coffee industry are not treated fairly.

▶ As a result of my speech, my audience will *feel anger* about unjust treatment of agricultural workers in the coffee industry.

▶ As a result of my speech, my audience will *purchase* only coffee products that come with a Fair Trade certification label.

At this stage of preparation, Linnea has this much of her speech formulated:

Topic:	Fair Trade Certified Coffee
General purpose:	To persuade
Specific purpose:	As a result of my speech, my audience will purchase only coffee products that come with a Fair Trade certification label.

By formulating her general and specific purpose early on, she can focus her additional research more effectively. She needs facts, descriptions, and explanations for all her speeches, but especially for informative ones. If she wants to prove links between coffee consumption and mistreatment of laborers on coffee plantations, she should look for opinions from experts in global economics. She should search out examples of exploited workers if her goal is to motivate listeners to care or to act. If her goal is to have listeners purchase only Fair Trade certified coffee (or fairly traded products, in general), she should present specific information that will help listeners see this goal as a realistic possibility.

After selecting the general purpose and writing out a specific purpose statement, the next step is to begin formulating a statement known as the *central idea* or *thesis statement* that captures the major idea of the speech.

Write Your Thesis Statement

The **thesis statement** is the most important sentence in your speech because it tells your audience your subject and your purpose for the speech.[15] It's as if someone asked, "Tell me in one sentence what you're going to speak about. No details, just the bottom line. A complete declarative sentence, not a question." The sentence you come up with is your thesis statement, sometimes called the **central idea.** In contrast to the specific purpose, which you write with your own goals in mind, write this sentence from the audience's point of view.[16] Richard Engnell of George Fox University gives his students the following guidelines:[17]

Write a single declarative sentence
    that makes a statement about the subject matter and
        summarizes the content of the speech

A topic such as Fair Trade can be developed several ways. A speaker could focus on influencing the audience's knowledge or beliefs, their attitudes, or their behaviors related to Fair Trade certified products.

Mark Richards/PhotoEdit

in a reasonable, simple manner
that is precise enough to guide you and your audience.

Notice, for example, the contrast between these correctly and incorrectly written thesis statements:

Correct:	Workers in many countries are exploited by unfair labor conditions, but we can help improve their lives by buying only Fair Trade certified products.
Incorrect:	Why should we buy Fair Trade certified coffee? (This is a question, not a declarative sentence.)
Incorrect:	Workers are exploited in many countries. This is unfair, but we can help by insisting on Fair Trade certified products. (Use one sentence, not two.)
Incorrect:	Why you should care about coffee production. (This is a fragment, not a complete sentence.)

Begin to formulate your thesis statement as soon as you select your topic and decide on your general and specific purposes. Then allow yourself plenty of time to explore and develop your ideas, narrowing the approach, the slant, the point of view you'll develop, and the general direction you'll take.[18] The process of invention takes time and energy. New ideas will emerge and others will seem less important, so don't be afraid to revise your direction as you do additional research, preparation, and organization. As this student explains:

> I tend to have running dialogues in my head, sometimes even out loud. While I talk to myself, I work out particulars. I answer questions I've posed to myself ("Well, really, Gail, if you argue that, where will you go? It's too huge!" or "Now does that really make sense?"). My answers often lead me to modify my central idea as I continue my preparation.
>
> GAIL

When you actually give your speech, incorporate your thesis statement into your introduction, and follow it with a **preview,** or short summary of the major points you'll use to develop your thesis. Linnea previewed her speech like this:

> I will explain some problems associated with coffee production, show how Fair Trade certified coffee provides a solution, and challenge you to take action to promote and consume only fairly traded coffee.

Linnea's outline appears at the end of Chapter 17 and on the book's online resources where you can watch it on video. Here are two additional examples from student speeches that show the relationship between topic, general purpose, specific purpose, thesis statement, and preview.

Topic:	Corporate Social Responsibility (CSR)
General purpose:	To inform
Specific purpose:	To inform my audience about the arguments for and against corporate social responsibility
Thesis statement:	There are arguments both for and against the level of social responsibility a business should have and we, as participants in corporate America, have influence on how a company responds.
Preview:	I will explain the concept of CSR, give illustrations of how it plays out, and provide arguments both for and against CSR.

thesis statement a single sentence that names the subject and establishes its significance

central idea a synonym for thesis statement

preview short summary of the major points you'll develop in the speech

(A complete outline of this speech is included at the end of this chapter.)

Topic:	Driving While Tired
General purpose:	To persuade
Specific purpose:	As a result of my speech, my audience will choose not to drive while drowsy.
Thesis statement:	Driving while tired is dangerous and potentially affects not only your own life but the lives of others on the road as well.
Preview:	Tired drivers are responsible for many road accidents and deaths, and the only real solution lies within our hands, but the benefits of avoiding driving while tired greatly outweigh any sacrifices you make.

(An outline of this speech appears at the end of Chapter 10 and on the book's online resources which include a video of the speech.)

In summary, topic and purpose selection are important aspects of speech making. Focus your preparation by selecting a subject that interests you, narrowing it to a manageable subtopic, formulating general and specific speech purposes, and then synthesizing your main ideas into a thesis statement or central idea that names the subject and alerts the audience to its significance. When you give your speech, state your thesis in the introduction, and add a preview of the main points you will use to develop your central idea.

BUILD YOUR SPEECH
GENERAL PURPOSE, SPECIFIC PURPOSE, AND THESIS STATEMENT

Choose three topics from the list below (or select three topics that you could talk about without doing much research). Then quickly write out a general purpose statement, a specific purpose statement, and a thesis statement for an impromptu speech about each topic.

- Online shopping
- Stress relievers for college students
- Simple breakfasts
- Free things to do in this community
- Going to a live concert
- Garage sales
- Study tips

Summary

As you begin the process of choosing a speech topic, look for something your audience needs to know. Then, examine your personal experiences, other courses, current events, and international or cultural possibilities for significant subjects. Be sure to find a topic that interests you. If you do careful work early in the term, you can produce a list or develop a series of files on topics that will interest both you and your listeners.

After selecting your topic, decide on your general intention or purpose for the speech. Will you inform, persuade, entertain, or commemorate? Then write the specific purpose that names the cognitive, affective, or behavioral response you want from your listeners. Focus on the speech's content by writing out the thesis statement, a single sentence that summarizes your major ideas in a way that guides both you and your listeners. Begin to formulate your thesis early in the speech, but revise it if necessary as you proceed in your research and preparation. Finally, write a preview of the major ideas you will develop in the speech.

STUDY AND REVIEW

Your online resources for *Public Speaking: Concepts and Skills for a Diverse Society* offer a broad range of study tools that will help you better understand the material in this chapter, complete assignments, and succeed on tests. Your online resources feature

- Speech videos with critical viewing questions, speech outlines, and transcripts
- Interactive versions of this chapter's Stop and Check activities and Application and Critical Thinking Exercises
- Speech Builder Express and InfoTrac College Edition
- Weblinks related to chapter content
- Study and review tools such as self-quizzes, an interactive glossary, and downloadable audio summaries

You can access your online resources at **http://www.cengage.com/login**, using the access code that came with your book or that you bought online at **http://www.iChapters.com**.

KEY TERMS

The terms below are defined in the margins throughout this chapter.

affective effects 81	general purpose 79
behavioral effects 81	preview 83
central idea 83	specific purpose 81
cognitive effects 81	thesis statement 83

APPLICATION AND CRITICAL THINKING EXERCISES

1. Discuss in a small group some ways you could add the element of novelty to the following common topics: seatbelts, making a sandwich, television violence, writing a résumé.
2. Design a mind map on the general topic of education after high school. Identify two or three topics that would be significant to your audience.
3. Work with a small group of your classmates to create a mind map based on a very general international topic such as China, global diseases, ethnic conflicts, or global natural disasters. Record your ideas on a blank transparency or a large piece of paper and then display it and explain it to the entire class.
4. For additional information on St. Augustine, one of the great figures of rhetoric, go to **http://ccat.sas.upenn.edu/jod/augustine/ddc4.html** and read Chapters 12 and 13 of his treatise on rhetoric. He gave this advice seventeen centuries ago. Which principles still apply?
5. For each of the following topics, tell how you could create one speech to inform, one to persuade, and one to entertain: negotiating a raise at work, attending an opera, cable news programs, spring break, recreational hiking.
6. Choose one of the topics above and write a general purpose statement, specific purpose statement, central idea or thesis statement, and preview that match the ideas you had for informative, persuasive, and entertaining speeches.

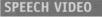

SPEECH VIDEO

Mike McNamara/Cengage Learning

Go to your online resources to watch and critique Erica Nelson delivering her speech, "Corporate Social Responsibility."

Student Speech Outline with Commentary

CORPORATE SOCIAL RESPONSIBILITY (CSR)
By Erica Nelson

General purpose: *To inform*

Specific goal: To inform my audience about perspectives on appropriate levels of corporate social responsibility (CSR)

Thesis statement: There are arguments for and against the level of social responsibility a business should have, and we, as partipants in corporate America, have an influence on how a company should respond.

Preview: I will explain the concept of CSR, give examples of how it plays out, and provide arguments about the level of responsibility a corporation should take.

Introduction

   I. Imagine that you manage a corporation that is struggling to make ends meet.
      A. Would you seek employees who would work for less money or use cheaper materials that might harm the environment?
      B. Managers face such questions all the time—questions of corporate social responsibility (CSR).
  II. Even if you never manage a corporation, we are all part of corporate America and face CSR issues.
 III. I learned about this topic in my marketing class and realized the importance of understanding and bettering our economy.
 IV. I will explain the concept of CSR, show how it plays out in different businesses, and give arguments regarding various levels of responsibilities.

Body

   I. CSR includes the responsibilities a business has other than to increase its stakeholders' income—to the environment, suppliers, customers, employees, competitors, and the community.
      A. *Environmental* responsibility means pollution reduction, conservation, recycling, and waste disposal.

Erica found her topic in a course she took in her major.

Her preview lets the audience know how she'll develop her ideas.

In this main point she explains what CSR is.

B. The success of businesses and *suppliers* depend on one another, which involves trust and honor.

C. *Employees* keep the business going, so they should be compensated, rewarded, and listened to.

D. Responsibility to *competitors* means to operate legally and not hinder a competitor's success.

E. *Community* involvement means sponsoring events and making donations as a way to give back.

II. To understand this better, let's look at three corporations: Wal-Mart, Nike, and Ben & Jerry's.

A. Wal-Mart's corporate actions have critics as well as loyal customers.

  1. As the #1 retailer in the world, it can name its prices.

    a. To meet its low prices, some suppliers must lay off employees, close U.S. plants, and outsource work (Fishman, 2003).

      i. Outsourcing to other countries has benefits and hazards.

      ii. *Social Policy* describes mistreatment of workers in a supplier located in southern China (Judd & Levine-Sabol, 2005).

        (a) The company employs 70% women, some 15–16 years old, who average 12–14 hours a day, often with no overtime pay and for wages equivalent to $54–58 U.S. monthly.

        (b) Factory conditions are substandard and injuries are common.

    b. On the other hand, the obvious benefit for the consumer is low prices.

      i. The company mission is "Saving people money so they can live better" (walmartstores.com, 2008).

      ii. The company contributed to low inflation during the 1990s (Fishman, 2003).

      iii. It contributed about 12% to national economic productivity that decade (Fishman, 2003).

      iv. Wal-Mart's Web site (2008) says forty-nine million customers shop weekly in stores located in thirteen countries outside the U.S.; Mexico has more than 1000 stores.

    c. However, these low prices have caused many competitors in small towns to close.

      i. Steve Dobbins, CEO of Carolina Mills, a company that supplies thread to apparel makers, says Wal-Mart is in a Catch-22 situation (Fishman, 2003).

      ii. His customers cannot compete against Wal-Mart's prices, and his business has shrunk.

      iii. He says, "People ask, 'How can it be bad for things to come into the U.S. cheaply? How can it be bad to have a bargain at Wal-Mart?' Sure it's held inflation down, and it's great to have bargains, but you can't buy anything if you're not employed. We are shopping ourselves out of jobs."

  2. In its favor, however, Wal-Mart is socially responsible in many areas.

    a. It donates millions of dollars and workers volunteer thousands of hours to charities and community organizations.

      i. Walmartstores.com (2008) says it gave $295 million to charities.

      ii. *Chronicle of Philanthropy* named it the largest cash donor in America (Wal-Mart Stores, Inc., Fact sheet, 2008).

    b. It employs 1.3 million workers locally and more than 600,000 internationally.

B. One publicized mistake, like what happened to Nike, can stain a company's reputation for years.

  1. In the early 1990s, protestors targeted Nike for low wages and child laborers overseas.

She gives examples of two well-known corporations that were criticized widely in the press for CSR violations, but she also shows positive aspects of those same corporations.

Erica includes sources in her outline. She can work them in as she delivers her speech.

2. Today, many still remember this, although the corporation has cleaned up its act.
3. In fact, Nike ranked number three on the 100 Best Corporate Citizens for 2008 list (Schaal, 2008).
   a. It changed its overseas employment practices.
   b. It rid its production of toxic waste materials and byproducts (Raths, 2006).

Here she gives an example of a corporation known for its socially responsible practices.

C. In contrast, socially responsible businesses such as Ben & Jerry's have a good reputation, based on great ice cream plus safety for the environment, workers, and customers (Ben & Jerry's, 2008).
1. They limit waste, deal with it responsibly, and use recyclable packaging and materials.
2. They stood up to their parent company and refused to use a genetically modified ingredient (Dairy Foods, 2006).

It's important to choose a topic that meets some audience need, and here Erica makes a strong link with her audience.

III. Now that you know more about CSR, you might ask if the public even cares about these issues.
A. Environics International conducted a global survey in 2004.
1. Over half of those surveyed in the U.S. had read about or heard of a corporate social or environmental report.
2. Over half of them bought the company's product, spoke favorably, or improved their impression of the company.
B. My class survey produced interesting results.
1. Of twenty responses, ten of you were at least somewhat familiar with Wal-Mart's issues.
2. Nine out of the ten changed their attitude toward shopping at Wal-Mart.
IV. Although CSR seems like good policy, there are legitimate arguments about appropriate levels of social responsibility.
A. In 1972, Nobel Prize winning economist, Milton Friedman, wrote a widely cited article, "The Social Responsibility of Business Is to Increase Its Profits.".
1. He argued that businesses are not people, and they can't be held responsible.
   a. Only people have moral and ethical convictions and duties.
   b. One person or board cannot make a decision for all the others.
   c. Giving away corporate money for social purposes is unfair to stockholders and employees.
B. Requiring CSR also raises the questions of limits.
1. Should regulations or laws require social responsibility to customers, for example, limiting tasty foods with low nutritional value such as fast food?
2. Should individual wrapping used in packaging be limited by law to protect the environment?
3. Should companies contribute to charities that some employees would *never* support?
C. Who should decide in these matters?

Conclusion

The brief conclusion restates her thesis and reviews her points.

I. Today we have looked at the concept of CSR.
II. By looking at Wal-Mart, Nike, and Ben & Jerry's, we can gain a better understanding of how CSR can positively or negatively affect a business.
III. We also looked at another view that says individuals, not corporations, have social responsibility, and there are questions about limits.
IV. Are you willing to sacrifice a few dollars to make a better society?

Sources

Ben & Jerry's. (2008). Our mission statement. Retrieved June 2, 2008, from www/benandjerrys.com/our_company/our_mission/

Dairy Foods. (2006, August 1). Ben & Jerry's avoids new GM ingredient. *Business News Publishing Company*. Retrieved June 2, 2008, from Business Source Premier database.

Fishman, C. (2003, December). The Wal-Mart you don't know. *Fast Company*, 77, 68. Retrieved June 2, 2008, from Business Source Premier database.

Raths, D. (2006, Spring). 100 best corporate citizens 2006. *Business Ethics Magazine*, 20, 1. Retrieved June 2, 2008, from Business Source Premier database.

Schall, D. (2008). 100 best corporate citizens 2008. The CRO blog. Retrieved September 3, 2008, from www.thecro.com/node/615

Wal-Mart Stores, Inc. (2008). Corporate facts: Wal-Mart by the numbers. Fact Sheets. Retrieved June 2, 2008, from http://walmartstores.com/media/factsheets/fs_2230.pdf

Wal-Mart Stores, Inc., (2008, May). International operational data sheet—May 2008. News Room. Retrieved June 2, 2008, from http://walmartstores.com/FactsNews/NewsRoom/8304.aspx

6

AUDIENCE ANALYSIS

THIS CHAPTER WILL HELP YOU

▶ Describe various audience motivations

▶ Tell how demographic audience analysis helps you adapt your topic to a particular audience

▶ Develop a questionnaire to assess your listeners' psychological profile

▶ Explain how the situation, including time and place, affect your audience

▶ Analyze your audience's perception of your credibility

© Tim Timmerman

---

audience analysis identifying audience characteristics to communicate more effectively

listening speaker dialogical speaker who hears audience interests and concerns before, during, and after a speech

EVERY YEAR, colleges and universities recognize and honor outstanding instructors who are especially effective in communicating complex academic material to students from a variety of backgrounds. One such honoree, Dawn Wright, professor of geosciences (marine and coastal geography) at Oregon State University, was recently named Oregon Professor of the Year for her ability to make a potentially difficult subject "personal and accessible" to a wide variety of students. Affectionately called "Deepsea Dawn," she is legendary for sharing experiences from her twenty-five scientific voyages across the globe and for her many illustrations that are particularly relevant to Oregonians—on topics such as wave-generated electricity, fisheries management, coastal erosion, and tsunami preparedness.

University science majors are but one audience. Deepsea Dawn also loves to talk to young people, especially to girls and members of underserved groups who aspire to science careers.[1] Professor Wright's effectiveness is linked to her sensitivity to each audience at every step of preparation. Using **audience analysis** skills, she thinks carefully about each speaking situation and then finds resources that will best communicate her ideas, given that group. In doing so, she embodies the dialogical perspective and becomes a **listening speaker**,[2] who takes notice of audience interests and concerns before, during, and after her presentation.

Oregon State University

Professor "Deepsea Dawn" Wright makes complex science topics personal and accessible to her many audiences—whether they are graduate students, undergraduates, community members, or grade schoolers.

Because your relationship with each audience will be complex, this chapter describes some ways to think about the relationships among your audience, your topic, the situation, and yourself. It might help you to visualize a rhetorical triangle with three sides—audience, speaker, and situation—that come together around a message.[3] (See Figure 6.1.) The previous chapter discussed the center of the triangle, the topic; however, a great topic, a specific goal, and significant content alone won't make a speech successful. That's why this chapter focuses on the three sides of the triangle—the audience's motivations and perspectives on you and your topic as well as some aspects of the speaking situation that affect the effectiveness of your presentation.[4]

Analyze Your Audience

A good speech is prepared for a particular group at a particular time. Although some careers such as politics or sales require speakers to present similar material repeatedly, those who give an identical speech (sometimes called a "canned" speech or a "stump" speech) to different audiences are generally less effective than those who adapt their material to each audience and each setting. This section explores a number of ways to think about audiences and situations.

Consider Audience Motivations

Why do audiences gather? What attracts them? What holds them? Answering these questions provides clues about your listeners' motivations and helps you prepare each message more effectively.[5] You can classify audiences into two general categories: unmotivated and motivated.

1. **Unmotivated audiences** are characterized by their lack of a purposeful listening goal. Some are **random**—meaning that the participants are initially involved in another activity, but they decide to pause and listen for awhile because something attracts their attention. A salesman's flashy demonstration of a food processor, the impassioned voice of an activist in an outdoor forum, a creative television commercial, or the humorous stories of a sidewalk entertainer might lure them.

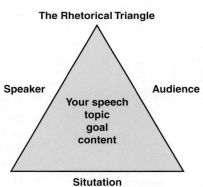

The Rhetorical Triangle

Speaker — Audience

Your speech topic goal content

Situtation

Figure 6.1
The Rhetorical Triangle
The audience, the speaking situation, and the speaker come together around the message.

unmotivated audiences lack a listening purpose or goal

random audience attracted by a message that catches their attention; initially doing something else

They may be browsing the radio dial or surfing YouTube when a speaker or topic temporarily captures their interest. Your challenge with a random audience? To attract and maintain attention long enough to present your message. (If you communicate through a form of media, remember that your audience can easily change channels or tune you out.) So focus on being interesting and relevant, and use conversational delivery as if you were addressing one listener at a time.

2. **Passive audiences** are made up of unmotivated listeners who are in the audience for a variety of reasons, but *not* because they want to hear a particular speaker or a particular topic. For example, the staff in the sitcom *The Office* sat through "Diversity Day" because their job required it, not out of felt need or real interest. Some people show up to hear a speech because a parent or a friend they want to impress drags them there. Most speech classes consist of at least some passive listeners who come to class to receive academic credit, not just to hear you or to learn about your topic. Because their motivation is minimal, you must make a special effort in three areas: (1) select a relevant, interesting topic; (2) gain and maintain interest; and (3) help your listeners understand the significance of the topic to their lives.

3. In contrast, **motivated audiences** have a listening goal. They want to know more about a topic, or they want to hear a particular speaker. Consequently, they are **self-selected** in that they voluntarily and intentionally seek out an opportunity to hear a particular speech. Here are some examples:

   - Sports-minded listeners pay to hear a world-renowned windsurfer talk about her sport, because they are interested in both the topic and the speaker.
   - A graduating senior attends a workshop by an unfamiliar speaker on how to get into graduate school because he needs the information.
   - Following a major natural disaster in a neighboring state, students flock to a campus rally where they know they'll get specific information about relief efforts their university is planning.
   - Huge audiences turn out to hear a politician, not necessarily because they like politics, but because they want to hear the candidate personally.
   - Students read about John F. Kennedy's Inaugural speech in a text, and they seek it out on YouTube so they can capture some of the experience of that historic inauguration.

   A special type of audience, such as a campus governance board, a city council, corporate board, or legislative committee, actually invites speakers to voice opinions on issues because these boards have been granted power or authority to act on a situation. Sometimes these meetings are open to ordinary citizens; at other times, only invited experts can gain access to this type of decision-making group.

4. **Homogeneous audiences** share an attitude, whether positive or negative, toward the speaker, the topic, or both. Speaking to an audience with a positive attitude toward you and your topic can be fun, but you must still develop your ideas clearly so that listeners can understand and accept them. **Hostile audiences**, in contrast, come with a negative attitude toward a speaker or toward that speaker's opinions. Chances are, your audiences won't be hostile toward you as a person—that sort of hostility is generally directed toward public figures such as Ann Coulter, an intentionally controversial conservative "firebrand" whose "inflammatory rhetoric"[6] raises eyebrows. More commonly listeners may be hostile to your conclusions about your topic, especially if they are controversial or if audience members are committed to other perspectives. Here are two examples: How would a gay-marriage advocate get her ideas accepted by a marriage-is-between-one-man-and-one-woman audience, and vice versa? How would a Slow Food advocate get his positions to be taken seriously by listeners who daily rely

passive audiences unmotivated listeners who listen to accomplish other goals

motivated audiences listen for a reason

self-selected audiences choose to listen to a selected subject or speaker

homogeneous audiences listeners who are similar in attitude

hostile audiences listeners who are negative toward the topic or the speaker

on prepared dinners and take-out meals? Hostile audiences present a unique set of challenges. Your best strategy is to find as much common ground as you can with those who hold disparate views and to emphasize commonalities before you address areas of divergence. (Chapter 17 discusses additional ways to design speeches for hostile audiences.)

As you might imagine, audience motivations are not entirely homogeneous. For instance, a mostly passive audience such as your class may include several students who select both the course and the instructor, or a mostly self-selected audience may also include passive listeners who are just tagging along with friends. And passive audience members may become engaged when the topic or speaker is particularly interesting. All things considered, you'll be more effective if you consider the fundamental motivation of most people in the audience and design speeches that are sensitive to their listening goals.

Analyze Audience Demographics

If someone were to ask "Who are you?" how would you reply? Would you tell your age? Your occupation? The ethnic group or religion you most closely identify with? Would you describe character traits such as creativity or curiosity? Would you list musical or artistic talents? Consider also how you stand in relationship to others. Put another way, who is above you? Who looks up to you? Whom do you consider an equal? These are all overlapping elements of your identity—elements that exist in complex relationships.

Just as your identity is multilayered, so is your audience's. One way to think about audiences is to do a **demographic analysis** by considering some basic categories such as age or ethnicity. Awareness of demographic factors will help you plan your remarks; however, to avoid classifying listeners into categories and then stereotyping them, keep in mind that no one has a single, fixed cultural or social identity.[7] Membership in a specific group is more **salient** (significant or relevant) in some situations than in others.[8] Rothenberg[9] summarizes the complexity of demographic analysis:

> When we engage in [demographic analysis], we should never lose sight of the fact that (1) any particular woman or man has an ethnic background, class location, age, sexual orientation, religious orientation, gender, and so forth, and (2) all these characteristics are inseparable from the person and from each other. . . . It is also true that . . . we may have to make generalizations about the experience of different groups of people, even as we affirm that each individual is unique.

In short, no one is simply a "lawyer" or a "Latina" or a "senior citizen," but being a lawyer, senior citizen, or Latina can be an inseparable part of the person's identity. The best advice is to analyze your listeners' identification with various groups *in light of the topic and your specific speaking situation.* That is, think about their possible responses to your topic and your goal, given the situation in which you speak. The following categories are common in demographic analysis: ethnicity, race, religion, gender, marital status, age, group affiliation, education, occupation and socioeconomic status, and region. Let's briefly look at each of these.

Ethnicity refers to a group's common heritage and cultural traditions, usually national or religious in origin.[10] Language and dialects are often linked to ethnicity, as is **race**; however, race is a **social category,** meaning that racial categories are culturally constructed around such physical traits as skin color or facial features. Races and ethnicities are not clearly distinct, and millions of people have mixed backgrounds that further blur the lines between groups.[11] Faulty as racial or ethnic categories may be, being classified into one category or another can have real consequences on the life experiences and the opportunities available to an individual.[12]

---

demographic analysis identifying audiences by populations they represent, such as age or ethnicity

salient relevant or significant

ethnicity heritage and cultural traditions, usually stemming from national and religious backgrounds

race categories, often associated with stereotypes, based on physical characteristics

social category culturally constructed category such as race or gender

Religion is a particularly sensitive topic because of the deep emotions religious issues can evoke. Consequently, disparaging or dismissing a group's sacred texts, heroes, or rituals will likely create intense reactions—even among people who hold them loosely. As you might expect, a single audience can hold a range and intensity of religious beliefs. Some may be nonreligious; others may claim a particular faith, but their religion is peripheral to their identity. To still others, religion is a central factor that guides their daily decisions. Be aware of ways that your listeners' religious commitments can make a difference in how they respond to your topic.

Sex, gender, sexual orientation, marital status and sexual expression extend beyond the simple "M for male" and "F for female" or the "single, married, divorced, or widowed" boxes that show up in demographic surveys. Whereas sex refers to biological categories, **gender** refers to culturally constructed concepts about what is feminine, masculine, or androgynous (not specifically masculine or feminine). Audience members also vary in their sexual orientation and their sexual expression. Some are sexually active; others are not. Some are heterosexual; others are not. For some topics and in some contexts, categories relating to sexuality become highly salient.

Not surprisingly, *age* affects listeners' motivations and concerns. Demographers identify four general groups: mature Americans, baby boomers, Generation Xers, and millenials, sometimes called the "I-generation" (Internet generation). Because the generational cohorts were raised differently and lived through distinctive historical, cultural, and technological eras, they have different goals and interests.[13] Most traditional college students are millennials; most professors are baby boomers who grew up on television but not YouTube, on typewriters but not word processing.[14] Although generational gaps can obviously be large, even minor age differences sometimes play out differently in audience concerns. For example, college seniors and first-year students may have varying interest in a topic as seemingly simple as résumé writing. In the workplace, millenials and baby boomers will look at retirement plans differently.

Group affiliation is another category to consider. Demographers note political affiliations, but people also join interest groups to share experiences and hobbies. These are as varied as Wheelchair Athletes, Alcoholics Anonymous, fraternities or sororities, and professional business organizations. Obviously, the common interests or concerns of group members determine the topics and appeals that are appropriate in the group's meetings.

Differences in *education* and *occupation* are salient in particular contexts. For example, a university education inculcates certain values and patterns of thought; this means that MBAs from around the world can interact around business topics because they have learned to share a world view with certain values. Scientists, similarly, have learned specific ways of doing research that allow them to collaborate across major cultural barriers.[15]

Socioeconomic status is related to educational and occupational opportunities. Comfortably middle-class individuals and those who struggle in minimum wage jobs differ in many important ways. The very wealthy live in a culture very different from the culture of poverty.

You know that audiences in different countries require different speaking strategies, but what if you move from one state or *region* to another, or even from area to area within a single state? Although people in the United States share many things in common, people in different regions or areas tend to have somewhat varied characteristics due to climate, history, language, economic base, politics, and so on. These differences help shape their interests and perspectives.[16] In the state of Oregon, for example, residents along the Pacific Ocean, those who live in the middle "wine country," and inhabitants of the eastern semiarid ranch lands all have different issues, interests, and concerns.

gender clusters of traits culturally labeled as masculine, feminine, or androgynous

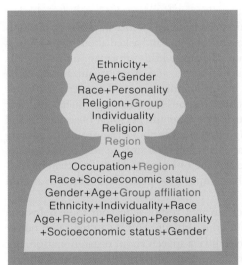

Figure 6.2
Demographic Silhouettes
These silhouettes represent a single audience member who is influenced by many demographic factors that are interwoven with individual traits and personality characteristics. In one situation, her age is the salient factor; in another, her region and group affiliation matter more.

In summary, demographic audience analysis provides insights into your listeners' ethnicity, religion, gender concerns, age, occupational, socioeconomic status, group membership, and regional identity. Keep these factors in mind when you select a topic and goal, choose supporting materials, and organize your speeches. However, instead of stereotyping your listeners, try to use the more inclusive model depicted in Figure 6.2. Your major challenge will be to determine which demographic characteristics are most significant to your topic.

 STOP AND CHECK

ANALYZE YOURSELF USING DEMOGRAPHIC CATEGORIES

How would a demographer describe you? Write a self-analysis using the demographic categories just discussed. From what you observe about your classmates, how are you like others in the class? How are you different?

Then identify which aspect(s) of your identity, if any, would be most salient if you were listening to a speech with the following central ideas that came from actual classroom speeches? What should a speaker to do to make the topic appeal to you?

- To inform my audience about the historical development of the guitar from the early versions to our modern electric guitars.
- As a result of my speech, my audience will know the history of the foster care system and how it evolved into what it is today.
- To persuade my audience to broaden their cultural experiences by attending a ballet.
- To persuade my audience to buy a houseplant to decorate their living space.
- As a result of my speech, my audience will be convinced that the $10.5 billion allotted to NASA is essential.

The Audience and the Topic

How do you figure out your audience's approach to your topic? One way is to identify their **psychological profile,** which means you identify their beliefs, attitudes, values and behaviors related to your subject. There are two basic strategies for doing this: direct and indirect.

Using **direct methods** means you ask the audience what they think and do, whether by an interview, a focus group, or a questionnaire. For instance, before his address, one university commencement speaker interviewed several students and asked about their campus experiences and their expectations for the future. He worked this information into his talk. Focus group consultants, especially in politics, businesses, and other organizations, often invite a small number of people to participate in a group interview and answer a few questions that help them assess a larger target audience's response to various products or ideas.

Indirect methods are less straightforward. They include personal observation and consulting secondhand sources such as asking other people about the group, or getting printed information such as brochures or material from Web sites related to the group. The commencement speaker could have accessed the university's Web site, read its mission statement, looked at online editions of the campus newspaper, and talked to alumni to get a feel for the makeup of the school.

Creating a psychological profile of your classmates' response to your topic helps you assess their beliefs, values, and attitudes about your subject. And it can help you better focus your speech. For example, Terah wanted to give a speech about organ donation, but after she analyzed the results of a questionnaire she'd distributed to her classmates, she realized that they already knew quite a bit about organ donation and they were very positive about donating their own organs. They just hadn't registered as donors yet, so she focused on motivating them to sign up to donate their organs by showing how easy it was.

Direct Method: Use a Questionnaire

Amara, a pre-med student, wanted to inform her audience about the biological makeup of food, but she didn't want to repeat widely known information. So the week before she spoke, she created a questionnaire to assess what they knew or believed about her topic, what attitudes they'd formed, what they valued, and how they actually ate.

As Chapter 1 briefly pointed out, a **belief** is a mental acceptance of something as true or false, correct or incorrect, valid or invalid.[17] Beliefs are based on study or investigation, as well as on convictions developed without much factual information or knowledge; consequently, misconceptions are common. A series of open questions such as these allowed Amara's audience to express their beliefs in a variety of ways:

▶ What are the benefits of a healthy diet?
▶ What are your reasons for eating a healthy diet, if you do? If not, why not?
▶ How do fats function in our bodies?

psychological profile assessment of an audience's beliefs, values, and attitudes

direct methods asking audience members directly for their opinion by questionnaires or interviews, for example

indirect methods assessing audiences by observation or secondhand sources

A focus group assembles a representative group for the purpose of assessing their beliefs, attitudes, and behaviors regarding a particular topic. These students are giving their opinion about a new musical group.

She added some closed questions such as these:

Are fats essential to health?

_____ yes

_____ no

_____ I'm not sure

List the four kinds of macromolecules that make up our food:

_____, _____,

_____, _____

She discovered that all her classmates knew that fats were essential in a healthy diet, but half of them did not understand why. Most couldn't name all four types of macromolecules. Overall, a few had a fairly good understanding of macromolecules and the biology of food, but most had knowledge gaps, and several considered their diets to be unhealthy. Some acted on their beliefs by eating well; others did not.

Attitudes are our tendencies to like or dislike something or to have positive or negative feelings about it. Attitudes include an emotional component that involves feelings and values, a mental component that involves beliefs, and a behavioral component that involves actions. For instance, Americans tend to *feel* positively about nutritious foods because they *believe* good nutrition is linked to good health, which they *value*, so they *act* by choosing healthy meals—at least some of the time. **Scaled questions** typically measure attitudes along a range or continuum, from highly positive to neutral to highly negative. Listeners with neutral attitudes probably have not thought enough about the subject to form an opinion. Here are typical scaled questions related to healthy eating:

scaled questions asking for responses along a continuum; used to assess attitudes

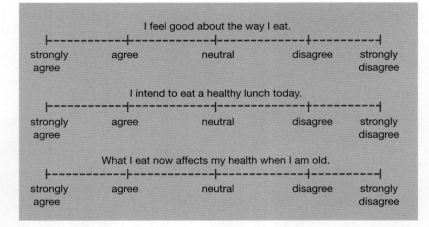

Notice that the first statement is about feelings; the second, about actions; and the third, about beliefs. When listeners share your attitude toward your topic, whether it's negative or positive, your speaking task is usually easier than when audience attitudes are diverse. Amara found that most classmates were positive about healthy eating.

ETHICS IN PRACTICE

PANDERING: TELLING AUDIENCES WHAT THEY WANT TO HEAR

During the political campaign of 2008, one editorial writer lamented what he called Congress's "Pander-monium."[18] He chided politicians for sidestepping difficult issues and speaking, instead, about "hot button" topics that energized their base or by playing to voters' unrealistic hopes and ideas. "Pander-Bear" is a nickname for leaders who tell one crowd one thing and another crowd something different.

Politicians are not the only ones who pander. In the preface to his book, *Our Culture of Pandering*, retired Illinois senator, Paul Simon, wrote, "In too many areas [including politics, media, religion, and education] we have spawned 'leadership' that does not lead, that panders to our whims rather than telling us the truth, that follows the crowd rather than challenging us, that weakens us rather than strengthening us. . . . Pandering is not illegal, but it is immoral. It is doing the convenient when the right course demands inconvenience and courage."[19]

Many politicians and others like them have a negative image.

In contrast, a recent book, *The Word of the Lord Is Upon Me: The Righteous Performance of Martin Luther King, Jr.*[20], told of King's willingness to speak unpopular sentiments. The famous civil rights leader's decision to speak out against the Vietnam War shocked and upset many civil rights leaders who believed that King's stance could undermine President Johnson, "the president who's done more for Black rights, how can you take him on?" Even the NAACP came out in opposition to his position. However, Dr. King's core values, "the power of his faith, his love of humanity, and an irrepressible resolve to free black people, and other people too,"[21] led him to tell the truth as he saw it.

Martin Luther King, Jr., has a holiday named after him.

Questions

1. It's easy to see how politicians pander, but to better understand how the media, religious leaders, and educators pander, read excerpts from Simon's book at **www.siu .edu/~siupress/titles/s03_titles/simon_excerpts.htm**

2. In what instances, if any, have you heard a speaker pander to an audience? How did you respond?

3. Do you agree with Simon that pandering is immoral? Explain your answer.

Several were neutral, but no one was downright hostile toward her topic. Knowing her audience's range of attitudes helped her plan an effective speech.

Values are the standards we use to make judgments such as good or bad, beautiful or ugly, kind or cruel, appropriate or inappropriate. U.S. core cultural values include choice, individualism, fair play, progress, freedom, and equality. Almost all your topics touch on your values in some way, because you at least consider the subject significant enough to discuss. However, when you use words such as *right* or *wrong, moral* or *immoral, important* or *insignificant*, you are directly addressing value questions. Scaled questions such as this work well for value questions:

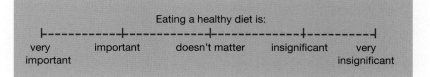

Amara found that most classmates recognized the importance of nutritious diets, so she built her speech around the fundamental value of health. Because values are our assumptions about what is good, people usually respond positively when their values are supported.

Throughout her speech, Amara wove together the insights she gleaned from her questionnaire, which increased her overall sensitivity to her audience. (Read her outline at the end of this chapter or on your online resources, where you can also watch her deliver the speech.)

Your listeners' psychological profiles affect their interest in your topic. Take a listener who doesn't know what a credit rating is, can't explain why it is important, and has no idea how he can create and maintain a good one. Once he understands the importance of the topic to him personally, he has a motivation for listening. Contrast him to a listener who understands the need to wear seat belts, who values safety, and who buckles up automatically. Her interest in a "why you should wear a seat belt" speech will be minimal.

STOP AND CHECK

CONSTRUCT A QUESTIONNAIRE

With your topic in mind, construct a questionnaire you can use to examine your classmates' psychological profile. You may also use the sample Combination Questionnaire here as an example; it shows how to combine closed questions, open questions, and scaled questions on the topic of road rage.

A Combination Questionnaire

Name (optional) _____

Age _____   Sex _____   Major _____

Have you experienced road rage?   _____ yes _____ no _____ not sure

Have you been the object of road rage?   _____ yes _____ no _____ not sure

Place an X on the point of the scale that best indicates your response to the sentence. Use the following codes:

SA	=	strongly agree
A	=	agree
MA	=	mildly agree
N	=	no opinion
MD	=	mildly disagree
D	=	disagree
SD	=	strongly disagree

Sometimes I get so angry at other drivers that I feel
I could do something that might endanger their safety.

```
+-------+---------+-------+-------+-------+-------+------+
SA      A         MA      N       MD      D       SD
```

(continued)

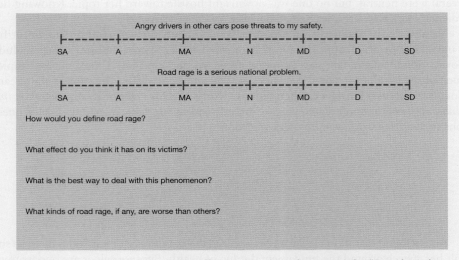

Angry drivers in other cars pose threats to my safety.

SA   A   MA   N   MD   D   SD

Road rage is a serious national problem.

SA   A   MA   N   MD   D   SD

How would you define road rage?

What effect do you think it has on its victims?

What is the best way to deal with this phenomenon?

What kinds of road rage, if any, are worse than others?

To learn more about how to design effective questionnaires, go to the "Questionnaire Design" page at **www.quickmba.com/marketing/research/qdesign**. Pay particular attention to the advice on content, wording, and sequencing of questions.

Assess the Situation

After you consider your listeners' demographic categories and their psychological profiles, assess situational features such as time and the environment that can affect an audience.

Consider the Time

Three aspects of time affect public speaking: the time of day, cultural time norms, and the timeliness of the topic. First, consider when your speech will be given and the effect this may have on this audience. For instance, what problems might listeners face in an early morning session? What about an audience just before lunch when everyone is hungry? Or a group just after lunch when they're sleepy? What challenges might an evening session pose? Evaluate these questions, and adapt your talk appropriately. For instance, you might be more animated when listeners are sleepy, or you might shorten your speech when it's very late.

Also, consider the *cultural* time system. In the United States, time is commonly seen as a line divided into segments, each lasting a specific duration, with distinct activities assigned to each segment.[22] Take your speech class, for example. You chose it partly because it filled a time slot you had available. The clock tells you when class starts and when it ends. In this setting, both the date and length of your speech are important. Your listeners expect you to work within this time pattern. You may be graded down if you don't appear on the assigned date or give a speech of the assigned length, partly because timing is important in work situations. If you're assigned to give a 10-minute briefing at an 11:00 meeting on a Wednesday in mid-March, you could get a lower appraisal or even lose your job if you show up on a Friday prepared with an hour speech—even if the speech is wonderful.

In contrast, listeners from a culture or co-culture with a more relaxed sense of time often focus less on starting precisely on time or on fitting their remarks into a rigid time frame. Professor Robert Levine, who grew up in fast-paced Brooklyn, tells of his experiences in slower-paced Brazil where he went to teach a psychology class that was scheduled from 10:00 a.m. to noon.[23] His cultural expectations traveled with him, so he assumed the class would begin at 10:00 and end at 12:00. To his surprise, students unapologetically arrived as late as 11:00. At noon he was ready to quit, but almost everyone else was still hanging around. At 12:15 they were still asking questions. Finally, at 12:30, Levine himself ended the class and left. The students, however, seemed willing to stay even longer.

Third, consider how events at the time may affect the topic and the audience's response. For example, on January 28, 1986, President Ronald Reagan was scheduled to deliver the annual State of the Union address. However, early in the day, the space shuttle *Challenger* spectacularly disintegrated before a horrified television audience who were watching the launch of the first teacher into space. That night, he delivered a tribute to the crew instead. (You can view it at **www.americanrhetoric.com/speeches/ronaldreaganchallenger.htm**.) Reagan made reference to a historical event that occurred on the same date:

> There's a coincidence today. On this day three hundred and ninety years ago, the great explorer Sir Francis Drake died aboard ship off the coast of Panama. In his lifetime the great frontiers were the oceans, and a historian later said, "He lived by the sea, died on it, and was buried in it." Well, today, we can say of the *Challenger* crew: Their dedication was, like Drake's, complete.

Consider the Environment

Instructors tell horror stories about difficult rooms:

▶ One class was held in a basement classroom with no windows and three large drain pipes that segmented the room in such a way that not all the students could see one another.

▶ Another was assigned to a small college theatre that was painted black. Floor, ceiling, chairs—everything was black. The few tiny windows all had heavy black shades. Although it was small for a theatre, the class only took up about 20 percent of the space.

▶ A third taught in a room that was wider than it was deep. A grand piano sat in the center, and the blackboards were all covered with five-lined staffs for musical notations.

Rooms such as these—windowless spaces, those with awkward arrangements, or other unpleasant places—may all affect your audience, whether or not they realize it. Change the location if you can. If not, consider changing the seating, and always make sure everyone can see you and any visual aid you might use.

In addition, other environmental considerations such as the temperature inside (too hot, too cold), the weather outside (sunny and beautiful, stormy and icy), or noise (an air conditioner or radiator) can also affect audience comfort or distract their attention. You'll be a better speaker if you recognize potential effects on your audience and do what you can to make your listeners comfortable and focused on your speech.

✓ **STOP AND CHECK**

DO A SITUATIONAL ANALYSIS

Log on to your online resources to complete an interactive situational analysis of your audience. For more information on situational analysis, read the article "One Speaker's Pet Peeves" on InfoTrac College Edition. What similarities and differences do you find when analyzing a classroom versus a business situation?

Jack Jaffe

This speaker is trying to attract an audience of random passersby. Because she is a stranger to them, they initially assess her credibility based on what she is wearing.

Consider Your Audience's Perception of You

While you are forming impressions of your listeners by considering demographic, psychological, and situational factors that relate to them, they are busily forming perceptions about your **credibility** or believability. They evaluate your knowledge and intelligence regarding the topic, and they make judgments about your motivations and intentions regarding them. Their impressions affect their interpretation of your message. Their evaluation begins before your speech, it's modified while you speak, and it leads to a lasting impression after you finish.[24]

Be Aware of Prior Credibility

Let's say a former senator comes to your campus to speak on foreign policy. You attend the speech assuming that she will know her subject well. Or let's say you know that one of your classmates is on the fencing team, so when he arrives on his speech day with fencing equipment in hand, you expect him to have an insider's perspective on the topic. Or a coworker in a business gives a report on a project that has occupied her time for six months. You expect her to know what she is talking about. This type of credibility—the speakers' reputation or expertise that makes them believable even before they say a word—is called **prior** or **extrinsic credibility**. Practically speaking, you will probably lack prior credibility in your classroom, unless your classmates already know something about you that links you to the topic. Therefore, you should establish some connection between yourself and your topic in the introduction. On the job, this will be a different story. There, you will speak because you have some knowledge and expertise on a particular topic. (The Diversity in Practice box provides some cross-cultural information on prior credibility.)

To further your understanding of prior credibility, log on to InfoTrac College Edition and read the article titled "Marquee Speaker Adds Prestige to Engagement." Work with several classmates to identify a campus event such as a commencement ceremony, an alcohol abuse workshop for dormitory residents, or a sports recognition banquet for athletes and their parents. Using information from this article, identify a local, regional, or nationally known figure who would make a good speaker for the event.

credibility listeners' impressions of your character, intentions, and abilities that make you more or less believable

prior or **extrinsic credibility** credibility that speakers bring to the speech because of their experience and reputation

DIVERSITY IN PRACTICE
PRIOR CREDIBILITY IN OTHER CULTURES

CULTURES VARY in their evaluations of prior credibility. Age and gender loom large in some Native American cultures. When the occasion calls for "saying a few words," younger males and women will seek out older men to speak for them. Weider and Pratt relate the story of a young woman who spoke for herself and her husband on a public occasion. Her elders scolded her for not knowing how to act.[25]

In Kenya, credibility is linked to wealth, social status, education, age, and ethnicity. Wealth comes in the form of wives, children, cattle, or money, but wealth in itself is not the only criterion for respect. The more credible speakers are those who have used their wealth to help others. Furthermore, unmarried men or men with few children or no sons lack authority, especially in rural areas. In a country made up of forty distinct groups, members of certain ethnic groups have higher overall credibility.[26]

Your age may affect your audience, either positively or negatively. Because U.S. culture celebrates youth and actively looks for fresh ideas, young people often receive as much or more attention than older speakers. In contrast, listeners in cultures that respect the wisdom and experience that come with age may pay less attention to youth and more attention to their elders. Be aware of this potential difference whenever you adapt to a culturally diverse audience.

Demonstrate Credibility in Your Speech

Regardless of your reputation, you must demonstrate credibility as you speak. Not surprisingly, this is called **demonstrated** or **intrinsic credibility**. Think back to the student on the fencing team. If he couldn't name pieces of equipment or describe a fencing match, you would decide he was no expert. Or consider what would happen if a coworker were unable to answer questions about the material in her report. Her overall credibility would suffer.

What does your audience look for as they decide whether you are credible? They look for evidence that you are knowledgeable about your subject. Consequently, it is important to do careful research and cite your sources. Define unfamiliar terminology, give examples, tell your personal experiences with the subject, and otherwise show your thorough understanding of the subject. Finally, be prepared to answer questions afterward.

Your listeners also expect you to be calm and poised. Think of it this way: If you're agitated during a classroom presentation, your audience will wonder why you can't control yourself. In contrast, if you appear confident, they will perceive you more favorably.

Take Terminal Credibility into Account

Relief! Your speech is over and you're through. But wait. Your listeners will continue to evaluate you. The overall impression you leave, your **terminal credibility**, is a balance between the reputation you brought to your speech, the expertise you demonstrated as you spoke, and the overall information your audience has about you and your topic. Thus, terminal credibility is not set permanently. If your listeners eventually discover that some of your information was incorrect, they will lose confidence in you. For example, suppose one of your classmates praises the pharmaceutical product Ritalin, commonly used to treat attention deficit disorder (ADD). In a previous speech, she mentioned that her little brother had ADD, which gives her some prior credibility for this speech. In the speech itself, she provides facts and figures that describe the prescription drug: what it is, what it does, what doctors say about it. You're impressed for a month. Then your cousin's physician suggests that he take Ritalin. As you do further research, you learn that your classmate's speech was clearly one-sided; she presented only the positive side of the medication. Unfortunately, your final impression of her credibility plummets.

demonstrated or **intrinsic credibility** obvious knowledge the speaker shows during the speech

terminal credibility final impression listeners have of a speaker

PRACTICALLY SPEAKING

WHAT AUDIENCES DO NURSES ADDRESS?

Ron Mitchell

Ron Mitchell, B.S.N., Ph.D., is a nurse educator and director of a nursing program at a university. He answered a number of questions about the value of public speaking skills in the nursing profession.

Do nurses speak in public very often? Nurses have many opportunities to speak to a variety of groups.

What types of audiences do they typically address? Overall, nurses speak to a variety of audiences.

▶ At the hospital level, there are in-house workshops; for example a nurse who specializes in informatics educates other nurses on the use of new technology for recording patient data. Nurse educators also instruct groups of patients on how to manage a particular medical condition.

▶ At the professional level, nurses attend conferences, and they always include break-out sessions on specific topic areas.

▶ At the community and civic level, public speaking is also common—especially to interest groups such as diabetes or arthritis support groups; a nurse might talk to the American Association of Retired Persons about home care or other topics of interest. Another big area is prenatal parenting classes. Nurses sometimes speak to teens or to senior citizens in houses of worship.

▶ Nurses work in many specialized fields. For example, there are school nurses and nurses who work in large corporations that have their own clinics. The school nurse might speak to parents at P.T.A.-type events; she might also talk to the school board if it were considering cutting funding for school health programs. Occupational health nurses address company employees about preventative health care and safety needs.

▶ At the government level, we also address local, state, and national decision makers on overall health policies. For example, a city council might be considering a development that would impact the water quality—and thus the health—of nearby residents, or the county might be considering closing a clinic, and we would speak out on how that would affect underserved people in the area. At the state level, I just went to the last legislative session and testified about the need to fund nursing education.

How can good public speaking skills help a nurse? In any occupation, if you are able to clearly communicate the needs of the profession, the community, or society, you can get the ear and attention of those people who can support what you are advocating, and you assure the survivability of your cause.

Questions for Discussion

▶ Choose at least four of the audiences that Professor Mitchell describes and analyze each audience's major motivation for listening. Which are self-selected? Which are homogeneous? Which are passive? And so on.

▶ Identify a specific audience and subject (such as a city council considering a development), and discuss how a nurse might do a psychological profile on that audience.

Summary

You and your audiences are involved in an interactive process in which you form impressions of one another. You assess your listeners' motivations as well as their demographic characteristics such as age, ethnicity, race, religion, gender, marital status, group affiliation, occupation and socioeconomic status, and region; however, you also realize that these characteristics are only salient at specific times and in specific circumstances.

Just as focus group leaders analyze a group's psychological profile, you can analyze your audience's opinions about your topic. What do they already know or believe? How do they feel about your subject? What attitudes and underlying values influence their interest? Developing a questionnaire with various types of questions will help you identify their responses to specific aspects of your subject.

Finally, situational characteristics affect your audience. The time of day, the length of your speech, and the noise level or temperature in the room all influence an audience's interest and attention. Do what you can to minimize environmental distractions.

Your listeners actively evaluate you as well. Before your speech, they assess your reputation. During your speech, they form impressions of your credibility and your overall trustworthiness based on cultural criteria such as sound evidence, source citation, overall knowledge, and composure. After you've finished, your listeners continue to assess your credibility, either positively or negatively.

This is one of the most important chapters in this text. As award-winning teachers and other good speakers know, sensitivity to a specific audience is not an option. It is essential to good speechmaking.

STUDY AND REVIEW

Your online resources for *Public Speaking: Concepts and Skills for a Diverse Society* offer a broad range of study tools that will help you better understand the material in this chapter, complete assignments, and succeed on tests. Your online resources feature

- Speech videos with critical viewing questions, speech outlines, and transcripts
- Interactive versions of this chapter's Stop and Check activities and Application and Critical Thinking Exercises
- Speech Builder Express and InfoTrac College Edition
- Weblinks related to chapter content
- Study and review tools such as self-quizzes, an interactive glossary, and downloadable audio summaries

You can access your online resources at **http://www.cengage.com/login**, using the access code that came with your book or that you bought online at **http://www.iChapters.com**.

KEY TERMS

The terms below are defined in the margins throughout this chapter.

audience analysis 90	hostile audiences 92
credibility 102	indirect methods 96
demographic analysis 93	listening speaker 90
demonstrated or intrinsic	motivated audiences 92
credibility 103	passive audiences 92
direct methods 96	prior or extrinsic credibility 102
ethnicity 93	psychological profile 96
gender 94	race 93
homogeneous audiences 92	random audience 91

APPLICATION AND CRITICAL THINKING EXERCISES

1. Identify times when you have been a member of each type of audience: unmotivated, random, passive, motivated, self-selected, homogeneous, and hostile. Select one situation and describe how your motivation affected the way you listened.

2. What occupation(s) most interest you? Think of opportunities you might have to address each type of audience listed in Exercise 1 within your chosen occupational field. Which type of audience is most common in that occupation? Which is least common?

3. To understand race and ethnicity better, read the first-person account of one woman's ethnic and racial identity at **http://dardel.info/Textes/Race.html.** Identify the various labels the author has been tagged with. What conclusions has she drawn?

4. Choose one of the topics below, and talk with a small group of your classmates about the different ways you would use demographic factors in your audience to develop a speech for each of the following groups or audiences.

   Topic: Your school's administrators are discussing a policy that will abolish all competitive sports on campus.

   Audiences
   ▶ Your classmates
   ▶ A group of prospective students
   ▶ Alumni who are consistent donors to the school
   ▶ Basketball team members

   Topic: The United States should double its foreign aid budget.

   Audiences
   ▶ Senior citizens
   ▶ A high school government class
   ▶ The local chapter of the League of Women Voters
   ▶ Your classmates

5. Select a topic that you might use for a speech and then try to see yourself as your classmates might see you speaking on that subject. At this point in the term, what credibility would you bring to this speech? How could you demonstrate credibility in the speech? How do you think your audience would see you after you're finished?

6. In 1981 *Washington Post* reporter Joel Garreau wrote *The Nine Nations of North America*. You can find a summary of his ideas online at **www.harpercollege.edu/~mhealy/g101ilec/namer/ nac/nacnine/na9intro/nacninfr.htm**. Follow the link to your region and see if you agree with his description of the area in which you live. Then link to another region. Do you think the regions have changed in the last twenty-five years? If so, how? How might a speaker from your region adapt to an audience in the second region?

7. With a small group of students list the physical characteristics of your classroom. Include size, acoustics, lighting, temperature, ambient noise, placement of seats, and distance between speaker and listeners. Then discuss how these physical characteristics might affect the audience's ability to listen effectively. What can you do as a speaker to overcome potential barriers to listening in your classroom setting?

8. Experienced speakers always try to check out the physical setting for a speech in advance. Work with a group of your classmates to develop a checklist of what to look for in any physical setting and then discuss how specific obstacles might be handled.

9. For a somewhat different perspective on audience analysis, read artist Dan Brady's essay describing the characteristics he considers when he shows a piece of artwork, hoping for a positive audience response. The essay can be found at **www.creativeideasforyou.com/essofprf.html**.

SPEECH VIDEO

Go to your online resources to watch and critique Amara Sheppard's speech. An outline of her speech appears below and also is available on your online resources.

Josh Nauman / Cengage Learning

Student Speech with Commentary

THE BIOLOGY OF YOUR LUNCH: YOU ARE WHAT YOU EAT
Amara Sheppard

General Purpose: To inform

Specific Purpose: To inform my audience about the biological explanation of the phrase "you are what you eat."

Thesis Statement: The human body breaks down four major macromolecules in food to provide many bodily functions.

Introduction

   I. In a short skit, I will discuss lunch and take a phone call from my body calling to remind me that "you are what you eat."

  II. By understanding how it is that you are what you eat, you can make more informed choices about the food you eat.

 III. As a biology/pre-med major, I have studied the human body for five of the last six years, and I am interested in how it works on a daily basis.

 IV. The human body breaks down four major macromolecules in food to provide many bodily functions.

     A. Today, we will see how our bodies use carbohydrates, lipids, proteins, and nucleic acids, the four molecules I asked you about on the questionnaire you filled out.

     B. You can remember these components by learning the acronym: Can Lucy Play Now?

Body

   I. First, carbohydrates are complex sugars that are found in a variety of foods.

     A. Carbohydrates are found in a variety of foods.

       1. They are in breads and fruits.

       2. The majority of you claimed to include carbohydrates in your lunches in the forms of fruits and sandwiches.

(Commentary, right margin:)

In a late-morning class, Amara gains attention by referring to lunch.

She has no prior credibility, so she shows her qualification to speak on the topic.

She states her thesis and previews her points.

Here, she incorporates specific results from the questionnaire her audience previously completed.

Each person has a small cup with a grape, a Goldfish cracker, and a small carrot.

B. You may eat the grape, which symbolizes carbohydrates.
   1. Even now, the carbs are breaking down to become the simple sugars your body uses for energy.
   2. Carbs give you the energy you need to provide energy to stay awake in class.
II. Lipids, better known as fats, are the second category.
   A. All twenty-two of you correctly answered on the questionnaire that some fat is needed, but only eleven could tell why.

Again, she refers to the questionnaire results and invites them to eat the fish cracker. In this point, she cites several credible sources.

   B. Like carbohydrates, lipids are found in many foods, including dairy products, meats, nuts, oils, and dressings.
      1. You can eat the fish as an example of lipids because it's made of cheese.
      2. About.com's online biology resource explains that fats store energy, help insulate the body, and cushion and protect organs.
      3. In an article entitled "Human Nutrition," Encyclopedia.com adds that fats form important portions of cell membranes and aid in the absorption of important fat-soluble vitamins.
III. Third are proteins, which are probably the most familiar.
   A. Proteins, made of twenty building blocks called amino acids, exist in several types of lunch food.
      1. Associate professor of biology Dwight Kimberly said that eight proteins cannot be made by the body.
      2. They must all come from our foods, such as the fish you previously ate.

She continues to build intrinsic credibility by citing credible sources.

      3. A 1997 issue of the *Harvard Health Newsletter* says that complete proteins are found in seafood, meat, eggs, and soy.
   B. Proteins are all over your body, skin, hair, and nails.
      1. Proteins provide structural support and aid in muscle contraction.
      2. Proteins do most of the work in your body.
IV. The final component are the nucleic acids DNA and RNA.
   A. They are found in the vegetables you say you include in your lunch, such as the carrot (which you may now eat).
   B. Raven and Jones's 6th edition of *Biology says* nucleic acids are information-storage devices.
      1. *Biology* uses an analogy, comparing nucleic acids to blueprints.
      2. These acids instruct the body's cells on how to build proteins.

She displays their questionnaire responses on a pie graph on an overhead transparency.

V. According to the questionnaire, 62 percent of you said you were healthy eaters; 24 percent said you were not; 14 percent were neutral; perhaps after this speech, you will all be better eaters.

Conclusion

I. In conclusion, the foods we eat can largely be placed into four categories of substances our bodies can use.
   A. Carbohydrates are the energy providers.
   B. Lipids or fats repair damaged tissue, keep you warm, and absorb vitamins.
   C. Proteins made up of amino acids are the body's "workers."
   D. Nucleic acids are the "blueprints" or instructions for the body's cells.

After a brief review, Amara concludes with "you" words that reinforce the importance of the topic to the audience.

II. So as you head off to lunch, be kind to your body and choose foods that will keep your body functioning at its best.
III. Before your body gives you a call, remember, you are what you eat.

7

RESEARCHING YOUR SPEECH IN AN ELECTRONIC CULTURE

© Tim Timmerman

THIS CHAPTER WILL HELP YOU

▶ Plan your research

▶ Distinguish between primary and secondary sources

▶ Gather materials from personal experience, interviews, and lectures

▶ Use the Internet critically

▶ Find library resources and electronically stored resources

▶ Include diverse perspectives in your research

▶ Record your information in a way that suits your learning style and avoids plagiarism

J AKE'S TOPIC WAS TITLE IX; Krista chose the Electoral College; Diamond decided to speak about organ transplants for prisoners. However, none of these students was an "expert" on the topic. They all faced the challenge you face: once you have selected and narrowed your topic, you must find appropriate information to support your ideas.

Coming up with speech materials should be easier than ever nowadays—with library consortiums that share their holdings, media resources, and new information and communication technologies (ICT). However, the Educational Testing Service research found that students are typically skilled at using technology but don't always know what to do with the materials they come up with. Alexius Macklin, associate professor of Library Science at Purdue University, summarizes a major concern:[1]

> . . . [W]hen you give students a research assignment, they go straight to Google™ without any thought to their actual research question or the information need. They draw information from questionable resources because they don't know the difference between information they find from an ad or a biased source, and that which they find on an authoritative, timely, objective site. . . . A majority of our students are not ICT literate enough to succeed academically . . . they do not currently have the skills to analyze and synthesize information into something manageable and useful for their needs.

Gathering effective supporting materials is part of the canon the ancient Romans called *invention* (see Chapter 2). Choosing the best material and discarding less relevant information combines several skills that add to your developing competence in speech making. These skills, which contribute to academic and workplace success, include

◗ Knowing how to locate the data you need to support your ideas
◗ Formulating a research plan
◗ Critically evaluating sources and choosing the best materials available
◗ Recording your findings in a systematic way that steers clear of plagiarism
◗ This chapter overviews the research process, with the goal of helping you effectively accomplish these four major tasks.

Gather Materials for Your Speech

So that you can learn about your subject from a variety of perspectives, your instructor will probably ask you to consult from three to seven sources. You should be able to easily come up with enormous amounts of information; however, selecting the *best* information requires critical thinking on your part. This section discusses effective ways to plan, conduct, and evaluate your research.

Plan Your Research

Reference librarian Laurie Lieggi says students often wait until the last minute to do research, thinking they can pop into the library once, spend a couple of hours in attack mode, get speech materials that are easy to find, and leave—satisfied with whatever they come up with.[2] Or they go directly to the Internet, and, because it's so fast and convenient, use it exclusively. Lieggi likens this type of research to only eating at fast-food restaurants. Fast food alone fails to provide the nutrients, variety, and quality of meals you carefully prepare at home.

If you're a typical student, you already have a busy schedule, so you don't want to waste your energy ineffectively searching for speech materials. Taking time to plan a search strategy at the outset will help you focus your research and save you time in the long run. The following tips will help you:

◗ *Budget enough time.* Set aside on your calendar more than one block of time for research. Good research is time consuming, and if you think you'll get wonderful, usable information in one short session, you will be disappointed. The word *research* combines the Latin prefix *re* (meaning "back" or "again") with the root word *search*. Re + search implies that you come again and again, seeking new information about a subject.
◗ *Get to know your library.* Because each library is different, visit or tour the one you will use the most. Become acquainted with its online services. Most libraries now subscribe to a variety of academic databases that you can access on your computer. Look for how-to pamphlets and brochures your campus librarians have prepared to explain the features available in your library. Even a fairly small campus library is usually part of a consortium of regional academic libraries, and when a book is not available in one library, it is generally available from another. If you request a book through an interlibrary loan, be sure to factor in the time it takes to get the book.[3]
◗ *Include a librarian in your research plan.* Part of your tuition money pays your librarians' salaries, so be sure to consult them whenever you need help. Lieggi said, "I'm a reference librarian because I want to be available to students. That's what I enjoy. Every question is a puzzle, and I get to help a student solve a puzzle." Besides, who knows a library better than the people who work there daily? In large academic

---

reference librarian library specialist whose job is to help you find research information

Devan Marchbanks

This student used a variety of sources for her speech about the raku pottery technique. First, she read magazine articles and Web sites that told the history of the process (secondary sources); she then examined several pots and interviewed the potter who made them (primary sources).

libraries, **subject librarians** have an advanced degree in another discipline as well as a library degree.

▶ *Let your topic guide your research.* This chapter suggests a number of research sources, but you won't need them all for a single speech. Instead, identify the best sources for your particular subject. For instance, if your topic is a current event, search the Internet for network and cable news channels, which routinely post video clips of their stories on their Web sites. Or visit a site such as **www.google.com/news** for regularly updated information. For a speech on pet overpopulation, write an interview with a humane society worker into your plan. For whitewater rafting, look to personal experiences, books, articles in sports magazines, and Internet sites.

▶ *Identify key terms for your searches in computerized catalogs, databases, or the Internet.* Think creatively, consult a librarian, or find the Library of Congress subject headings in the reference section of the library. For example, Marcus searched for "disabled" and "housing" with little success until his librarian suggested he use the word "handicapped." Then he found all the information he needed. (Headings do not always reflect current usage.) Many online databases have thesaurus, index, or browse features you can use to identify key terms.

▶ *Identify experts in the field (if possible).* You'll save research time if you know the names of recognized experts on your topic.

▶ *Make critical evaluation a part of your plan from the outset.* So many resources are available that you might think you're drowning in data—some are highly credible; others are very questionable. Find out as much as you can about every source you use, whether it be a book, article, Web site, or personal interview. Then compare sources. Some will be OK, some pretty good, and some excellent. Choose the best.

▶ *Keep a running list of all your sources as you search.* This way, you can easily assemble your final bibliography and return to a source if necessary. If you are using the Internet, bookmark each site you use. Carefully noting each source also helps you avoid plagiarism and credit your sources appropriately.

▶ *Use a variety of sources.* Remember the fast-food analogy? You wouldn't eat only Big Macs, so don't expect to use only the Internet or newspapers or encyclopedias or any other single type of source. Also, look for diverse perspectives so you can approach the topic from various viewpoints.

This is not an exhaustive list, but these tips will help you focus your search more effectively.

subject librarian librarian who also has an advanced degree in a particular subject such as law or medicine

Log on to your online resources for Chapter 7 and begin your research plan by completing steps 1–6 on the electronic form. You'll be guided through the following steps:

1. Identify your topic, general purpose, specific purpose, and central idea.
2. Make a list of the days and the time periods you plan to set aside to do research.
3. Identify questions to ask a research librarian.

   After you complete sections 1 to 6 of the form, read the rest of this chapter to identify and evaluate the best type of material to use, given your topic and purpose. Additional Stop and Check activities help you refine your research strategies.

Distinguish Between Primary and Secondary Sources

Primary sources are original materials created by individuals and groups who are directly involved in events as they take place. These sources fall into several categories. **Original documents** are resources such as diaries, emails, public opinion polls, news footage, autobiographies, and minutes of meetings produced by participants in the events. **Creative works** include books, paintings, poems, and dance performances. **Relics** or **artifacts** are cultural objects such as jewelry, tools, buildings, clothing, and other created items.

    Secondary sources are a step away from the actual events. These works are produced by nonparticipants who summarize or interpret original reports. Some, such as a critical review of an artistic performance, are created at the time the events occurred; others, such as a biography or a history book, are created months, decades, even centuries later. Generally, magazine articles, dictionaries or encyclopedias, Web sites that summarize information from a variety of sources, and textbooks are considered secondary sources.

    The distinction between primary and secondary sources is not always easy to make. For example, an audio recording of the NASA control room made during the *Phoenix* Mars Lander's final touchdown on Mars and a photograph of that planet transmitted from the spacecraft are primary sources, but a news article about the landing is a secondary source that summarizes the historical event and the events leading up to it. However, the news article *could* be a primary source if your topic were media coverage of the *Phoenix* Mars Mission.[4]

    As you do research, think about how primary and secondary sources work together to flesh out a topic. Let's say you decide to watch the *News Hour* on PBS for information on a nationally discussed current event such as the price of gasoline. A segment typically begins with factual information about the subject and then the host assembles several guests, who continue the discussion for up to fifteen minutes. Some guests, such as a representative of the oil industry, are primary sources who give a participant's perspective. Others, such as a university professor of economics who interprets what is happening in the industry, are secondary sources who provide reasoned opinions and explanations. Both can be useful, but there is a difference between a participant's account and an outsider's summary or interpretation.

    Now that we've reviewed the distinction between primary and secondary materials, let's look at the variety of forms they take, including personal experiences, interviews and lectures, print materials, and recorded and electronically stored data.

primary sources information from people actually involved in the event

original documents evidence recorded by a primary source such as letters or autobiographies

creative works poems, dances, paintings, writings, and other aesthetic creations

relics or **artifacts** culturally significant creations such as buildings, jewelry, or tools

secondary sources summaries or interpretations of an event or a person provided by nonparticipants

Draw from Your Personal Experiences

You probably chose your topic because it relates in some way to your interests and experiences; therefore, your past experiences can provide useable speech material. In fact, personal expertise is almost essential for some types of demonstration or how-to speeches. Think how unusual it would be to hear a speaker, who never personally took a photograph, describe picture-taking techniques. Why would you believe her? Personal experiences with subjects such as cartooning, fighting forest fires, immigration, or diabetes add a dimension that increases the speaker's credibility.

In the workplace, most speakers are expected to draw from personal experiences when they speak about products or people or processes. Because Beth plans to be a teacher, she gave an informative classroom speech on learning styles, and she mentioned her personal experiences as a kinesthetic learner. She could someday modify this speech and give it at a Parent Teacher Association meeting. There, she would need to add her experiences of working with students with a variety of learning styles.

Interview a Knowledgeable Person

If you don't have personal experience with a topic, you can talk with someone who does. In a well-planned interview you can gain information and clarify confusing ideas by questioning someone with firsthand knowledge. **Experts** are people whose studies, experiences, or occupations make them knowledgeable. For example, I interviewed two reference librarians when I wrote this chapter. Students have talked with chiropractors, police officers, construction workers, and other professionals when gathering materials for their speeches. **Laypeople** or **peers** are individuals who have gained insights and formulated opinions about a topic through ordinary living. By interviewing several students who use library research tools effectively, for example, I gained practical tips about what works and what doesn't work for them.

Because most people have full schedules, and potential interviewees are doing you a favor when they agree to be interviewed, keep these factors in mind:

▶ *Give the person an idea of your topic and the kind of information you need.* This is especially important if you interview nonnative English speakers. In order to think through and prepare their answers, they may request written questions before the interview.

▶ *Be conscious of the time.* When you make the appointment, estimate the length of time your questions will take, and then respect those limits! Although different cultural groups have different norms regarding punctuality, be on time. If anyone is late, let it be your interviewee. If you absolutely cannot keep your appointment, give the person as much advanced notice as possible.

▶ *Prepare in advance.* Write out your questions so you will remember everything you want to ask. (Written questions also keep the interview focused.)

▶ *Take careful notes.* Make sure you've understood correctly by reading your notes back to the interviewee, who can then make corrections or additions. Ask questions such as "Is this what you mean?" or "Did I understand you correctly when you said . . . ?"

▶ *Aim to understand your topic from your interviewee's perspective.* If your interviewees' ideas and actions clash with yours, practice civility. Listen politely, and try to understand how they came to believe or behave the way they do.

▶ *If you want to record the interview, ask permission* in advance, and place the recorder in full view.

When you cannot meet in person, consider a telephone interview, following the same guidelines regarding questions, advance preparation, and punctuality. Or use email to write back and forth, using a question-and-answer format. In fact, thousands of

experts people whose knowledge is based on research, experience, or occupation

laypeople or **peers** ordinary people whose knowledge comes from everyday experience

Information for speeches can come from experts such as tour guides, whose mini-lectures about the sites where they are knowledgeable, are often interspersed with questions from the listeners.

Devan Marchbanks

experts in hundreds of subjects allow Web sites such as **www.askanexpert.com** to list their email addresses because they want to share their knowledge.[5] In addition, television and radio programs regularly feature interviews. Some shows allow you to call in, email, or fax your questions for the interviewee to answer on the air.

To investigate this topic further, search InfoTrac College Edition for the article "10 Tips for Top-Notch Interviews," by Lynn Alfino. Read the author's tips and identify additional pointers you could incorporate into your interviews.

Attend Lectures and Performances

College and university communities typically sponsor well-known speakers and outstanding performances of various kinds. Take advantage of lectures, recitals, tours, theatre productions, and book or poetry readings that relate to your topic. Many universities record significant campus events and podcast them on the university Web site for students to download and watch at their convenience. Important national addresses are often televised; C-SPAN broadcasts live deliberations in the House of Representatives as well as a variety of speakers on topics of national concern. Cable news channels carry many speeches live, including political speeches and eulogies for significant public figures. *Great Performances* on PBS stations show outstanding theatrical and musical presentations. Check your library's video collection for recordings of lectures and performances that are available in its holdings.

✓ STOP AND CHECK

REVISIT YOUR RESEARCH PLAN

Return to your online resources for Chapter 7 to continue your research plan by completing 7 to 12 of the form. You'll be guided through the following steps:

1. Identify personal experiences that can support your ideas. Or list places such as museums, hospitals, or schools that you might visit.
2. Identify experts or laypeople who could provide helpful information, and plan an interview.
3. Think back on classes you've taken, and identify lecture notes you could use.
4. Look for usable recorded interviews. Public libraries, campus libraries, and media centers usually have taped interviews or lectures on common topics, such as eating disorders. For current topics, look for interviews on television or radio news broadcasts, or search online news outlets such as **www.bbc.com** or **www.c-spanvideo.org** for videos of interviews.

Computer Aided Research

When you begin to research a topic your first impulse may be to find a computer and log onto the Internet. But where do you go online? That should depend on what kind of research you're doing. If you need to know today's news, a site such as **www.refdesk .com** can be a good first choice. But if you need to know more about a topic such as learning styles or neuroimaging, you'd be better off doing library research, and fortunately, most university libraries have made a great deal of information available online. This section describes Internet research and library research via computer.

Internet Research

As the introduction to this chapter pointed out, many students lack the skills they need to use technology to do academic research. So, if academic research on the Internet is new to you, you would probably profit from taking an online tutorial. Check at your campus library or writing lab or do a tutorial at a credible, award-winning site such as the University of California Berkeley's Learning Library.[6] Tutorials introduce you to the concepts and skills you need to navigate the Net efficiently. Revisit them whenever you run into a problem.

Of course, effective Internet searches require some strategies that are similar to traditional research strategies. The Berkeley Learning Library suggests five general search steps:

1. *Analyze your topic to decide exactly what you need.* Do you want an overview of a subject? Are you looking for specific, specialized words or phrases? Is your topic narrowed and focused?
2. *Decide where to start.* The Internet provides subject directories (good for overviews), search engines (good for unique words and phrases), and specialized databases (good for specialized facts or statistics). Learn the distinctive features of each tool, and plan out where you'll search first. (Each tool is described below.)
3. *Jump in.* Learn from your successes and your mistakes, and then vary your strategies accordingly.
4. *Don't get bogged down or frustrated.* When your attempts are ineffective, just try something else.
5. *Use what you learn by trial and error.* This will help you be more effective the next time.

The three general categories of search tools include subject directories, search engines, and searchable databases. A **subject directory** is somewhat like the *Yellow Pages*, where your fingers "walk" to a general category (health), find a more narrowed designation (diseases and conditions), and zero in specifically (liver diseases). The Web pages on these directories are hand-picked by humans, classified by subject, and often annotated. You can browse or use fairly broad search terms, because you are searching for categories and descriptions, not for specific words. Here are some recommended subject directories:

▶ *Librarians' Index to the Internet* (**www.lii.org**) links you to Web sites that librarians carefully select and annotate.
▶ *Academic Info* (**www.academicinfo.net**) gives you sites chosen primarily for academic research at the undergraduate level.
▶ *Yahoo!*® directory (**www.dir.yahoo.com**), the biggest and best-known subject directory, differs from the first two in that page authors often supply the annotations themselves.

In contrast to human-built subject directories, **search engines** are built by computer robot programs called *spiders*, which create a database of pages linked to one

subject directory created by humans; searches the Internet by subject categories

search engine created by computer robots (spiders), matches search terms to words in its database

Figure 7.1
Content Differences by Domain Although a search for "neuroimaging" might turn up both of these Web pages, the .com site is sponsored by a commercial enterprise that sells imaging products; the .edu site is sponsored by a lab at UCLA that does scientific research on brain mapping.

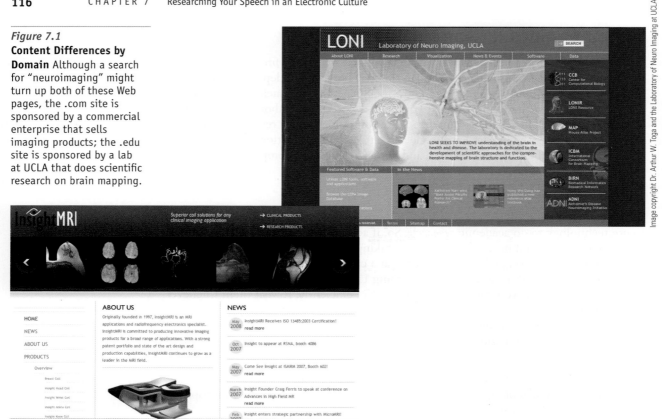

Image copyright Dr. Arthur W. Toga and the Laboratory of Neuro Imaging at UCLA

another. Thus, when you type in a keyword, the search engine produces a list of Web pages containing terms that match your search term. Here are three recommended search engines:

▶ *Google*™ (**www.google.com**) dominates the field with its enormous database that yields documents according to a popularity ranking. This means that the Web pages it lists are ranked by the number of other sites linked to a particular page. Because Google is so widely used, it's to your advantage to learn to use it well.

▶ *Yahoo!Search* (**http://search.yahoo.com**) compares favorably to Google in size and has an especially good spam blocker.[7]

▶ *Ask* (**www.ask.com**) has a smaller database, but it ranks a site's popularity based on the number of links from same-subject pages, not just the number of total links. Consequently, it claims to yield more finely tuned, more precise hits. It also suggests ways to expand or to limit your search.

Although search engines find billions of documents, less than half of the Internet's total documents are searchable on them. The remaining documents lie in **specialized databases** that are not linked to other Web pages, so the spiders fail to "see" them. For this reason, they are sometimes called the **Invisible Web** or **Deep Web**. Many specialized databases are free, but others charge a fee or require you to register before you can access their information. Librarians are developing resources to help you find material on what they call the **Academic Invisible Web** or **AIW**, which are more scholarly databases. One such resource is **http://infomine.ucr.edu**, a site supported by the government and maintained by the University of California, Riverside. Check out its search tips and then explore a few of the databases in the areas that interest you most.[8] Say, for example, that you are interested in media history. Typically, universities house media departments in the humanities. So on the Infomine subject categories, go to SocSci &

specialized databases databases on thousands of topics, can be accessed by searching specifically for them

Invisible Web or **Deep Web** the vast number of Web pages that are not seen by computer spiders

Academic Invisible Web (AIW) scholarly databases in the Invisible Web that librarians are identifying

Humanities and search for |*media history*|. You'll get two academic hits: one free, one for a fee. Check out the free site.

Evaluating Internet Resources

Because search tools can provide so much information, you'll have a better speech if you exercise critical judgment about each source and its content.[9]

Source

Before you even open a document, carefully examine its URL (uniform resource locator). The **domain** suffixes indicate the provider's primary purpose and tax status. The most common are educational (.edu), commercial (.com), government (.gov), military (.mil), nonprofit organization (.org), and foreign (.ca for Canada, .jp for Japan, and so on). Ask yourself which domain is most reliable for your particular topic. Ask who or what entity published the page. A source that provides educational information (.edu) or one set up to make money (.com)? A government agency (.gov) or a nonprofit (.org) that may rely on donations? (For example, www.cdc.gov means the entity is a government Web site; it is hosted by the CDC or Centers for Disease Control.) Decide if the entity supports your subject well, and choose links that seem the most appropriate, given your topic.

After you open the Web page, look for information about the author, institution, organization, or agency that accepts responsibility for the material on the site. If this is not immediately apparent, look for a home page or follow links such as "about us," "philosophy," or "background" that provide information about the site's creators, distinguishing between primary or secondary, expert or peer sources.

Content

Look for a site rating. Outside teams often evaluate a site to determine how complete, current, and thorough its coverage of a topic is. They also look at how the material is organized to assess whether or not the site is user friendly. However, a rating, although helpful, does not guarantee that the site provides accurate or high-quality materials, and lack of a rating doesn't automatically mean the site is not useful or authoritative. Do your own rating based on these tips:

1. *Determine the intent or purpose of the site.* Pages don't just spring up on the Internet. People put them there intentionally. So ask if the page is designed to inform, to entertain, or to sway opinion. Who is its intended audience?
2. *Look for bias.* Does the material emphasize a particular perspective, or is it relatively objective? Is it free of gender or ethnic stereotyping? Does the creator or sponsor have a personal or commercial goal? Does the source have an established position on the topic?
3. *Check timeliness.* Is the information (especially factual or statistical data) up to date? Are the pages maintained regularly? Look for the latest update.
4. *Assess accuracy.* Is the material similar to what you find in other credible sources? Would reputable sources accept the ideas as plausible and accurate? Look for links. Do linked sites appear to be reputable? Does the document list its sources? Its methodology?
5. *Assess originality.* Many sites use material from other sources, and they sometimes plagiarize. For instance, exactly the same material about the painter John Everett Millais appears on childingstone.net and on myweb.tiscali.co.uk, but neither site credits the source.
6. *Finally, consider organization.* If you must decide between two sites that appear to be equal in accuracy and quality of information, choose the one that is better organized and easier to use.[10]

domain the type of site such as .com, .edu, or .org that tells the site's purpose and tax status

For example, Jenn's speech on applications of brainimaging, found at the end of this chapter, required a number of sources. A search for the topic "neuromarketing" turned up more than 400,000 Web pages, including the following:

▶ "Neuromarketing: Is It Coming to a Lab Near You?" by Mary Carmichael. It's on a PBS (Public Broadcasting System) site under the program, *Frontline: The Persuaders*. PBS is generally considered to be a source of carefully researched educational information. The article was written in 2004, so some of the information may be outdated.

▶ "Neuromarketing: Understanding the Buy Buttons in the Brain" is a blog that summarizes studies and provides links to companies, articles, and books related to neuromarketing. If Jenn couldn't find any information about the author, she should look for more reputable sites.

▶ CCLE: Center for Cognitive Liberty & Ethics. This Web page reprints an article from the *New York Times*, April 20, 2004, "Using M.R.I.s to See Politics on the Brain," which describes research on Democratic and Republican voters' responses to political ads. The *Times* is generally considered reputable, and the mission statement of the CCLE states their guiding principles as privacy, autonomy, and choice. She might use the *Times* article, but not follow other links.

▶ "NeuroMarketing: Top 7 Insights to Unlocking Your Customers' Brains for Instant Sales," by Denise Corcoran. The Web page is full of advertisements, and when it first opened up, an ad came floating down, blocking the initial view of the article. The text is broken up by ads throughout. Ms. Corcoran says she is a "business and leadership coach" and a former CEO. The article is definitely from a .com domain. Jenn shouldn't waste any time on it.

Because the search term you choose can influence the type of Web pages you receive, it's a good idea to try more than one term. For example, a study about search terms used to locate information about childhood immunizations or vaccinations discovered that the term "vaccination" resulted in 40 percent provaccination hits and 60 percent antivaccination hits. However, a search for "immunization" resulted in 98 percent provaccination hits and only 2 percent antivaccination hits. Using both terms gave a spread of opinions.[11]

In summary, Internet research is potentially satisfying but frustrating as well, so it's vital to use your critical thinking abilities whenever you log on.

STOP AND CHECK

CRITICAL THINKING AND THE INTERNET

1. Use the guidelines provided above to assess the reliability of the following sites about brainimaging. That is, evaluate the source and the content (the purpose, bias, timeliness, accuracy, and organization) of information you find on an .edu site for neuroimaging, available at **www.loni.ucla.edu,** and on a .com site such as **www.insightmri .com** (follow some of its links to relevant research).

2. Then go to **www.whitehouse.gov** and read the biographical information about the president of the United States. Assess the content. What is the purpose, the bias, the timeliness, and the accuracy of this biographical information? Use a subject directory such as **www.yahoo.com** and search for the president by name. Follow at least one link and, using the same tests for site content, compare the biographical information you read there with the information the White House presents.

3. Of these sites, which materials are more apt to be verifiable? Which features more expert contributions? Which materials were probably not screened or edited? What are the strengths and limitations of each type of material? That is, when could you use each source effectively?

Sometimes you will discover hoax sites that look legitimate, but are really prank Web pages that mimic and poke fun at the real thing. For example, for a prank site set up to look official, type .net instead of .gov in the White House Internet address.

You can access these links and answer these questions via your online resources for Chapter 7.

Use Library Resources

As you already know, libraries contain a great variety of materials, from printed matter to pictures, maps, video and audio recordings in various formats, from research works such as indexes to specialized databases. Library resources have academic credibility because of the many screenings the materials undergo before they are acquired. For example, book publishers employ editors and reviewers to validate each manuscript. Magazine and newspaper editors screen articles and use fact checkers to catch and correct errors. However, library materials still require critical evaluation. Publications often have a bias, which they sometimes state forthrightly: The *New Republic* proclaims its liberal bias, for example, and the *National Review* proudly labels itself conservative. Other publications and books have an unstated bias that you must discern. This is one reason your instructor has you consult several sources.

Almost all college libraries have converted to Online Public Access Catalogs (**OPACs**).[12] Although the catalogs are computerized, they reflect a mind-set carried over from the days of card catalogs. For example, the average librarian is a baby boomer, but the average OPAC user comes from the "Google generation."[13] Googlers tend to approach OPACs with the tools they use for Web surfing,[14] where they type in a few terms and expect the search engine to come up with numerous results. Google also suggests spelling alternatives, and it adjusts to abbreviations.

Online catalogs, however, are less flexible. They use controlled vocabulary, not natural language. Consequently, a keyword or author search is usually more effective than a subject search, because subject terms are often highly specific.[15] For example, to find material on the Civil War, it would seem logical to search for "civil war," but if you do, you'll end up with data about civil conflicts in ancient Greece, nineteenth-century Bolivia, and twenty-first-century Sudan. Instead, look for "United States—History—1861—1865—battles." OPACs require correct spelling and typing with no abbreviations.

If you have not done so already, spend some time becoming familiar with your library's cataloging system; however, the research principles discussed next are applicable to many systems.

Books

It goes without saying that libraries contain books, but an academic library's collection differs in kind from the books for sale in commercial bookstores. Bookstores carry **trade books**, the kind of books aimed at a general audience, such as a John Grisham bestseller. In contrast, campus libraries focus on **scholarly books**, the kind of books that advance knowledge in a given field. Experts write them based on research; they are peer reviewed before publication, and they are aimed at specialized audiences of professionals and researchers. Scholarly books also include reference books and works of literature.

Library books are cataloged by subject, author, title, and key words. For example, Denise Von Herrmann's book about lotteries is found under the author (Von Herrmann, Denise), the title (*The Big Gamble: The Politics of Lottery and Casino Expansion*), and the

OPACs online public access catalogs

trade books books aimed at a general audience

scholarly books books based on research that advances knowledge in an academic field

> DIVERSITY IN PRACTICE
> ## RESEARCH IN KENYA
>
> Different cultural groups have different traditions regarding research. For instance, a study compared the public speaking norms in Kenya to the guidelines commonly taught in the United States. Three Kenyan students described typical speech preparation in their culture:
>
> ▶ "Audiences in the African context do not expect researched and memorized speeches, but speeches compiled spontaneously and using the speaker's wisdom."
> ▶ "Public speaking in Africa is not . . . something that someone will spend a week researching."
> ▶ "In the African context there are less rules to follow, or at least the emphasis is not as much as it is in the West."[16]
>
> Kenyan students, however, noted that research and preparation is becoming more common in their country.
>
> Even within the United States, the type of research described in this chapter is not required for every speech. Examples include the narrative speeches described in Chapter 15 and some of the special occasion speeches described in Appendix B.

subject (Gambling—Government policy—United States or Casinos—United States). Key words include *lottery* and *casino* and *gambling*.

Look carefully at the copyright date in the front of the book and in the catalog information. For topics such as bicycle helmets or AIDS medications, up-to-date materials are essential. However, a subject such as *honesty* draws from philosophical, religious, and cultural traditions that go back thousands of years, and books written in ancient Greece may still be useful.

Many free full-text books, especially classics or books in the public domain, are available online. To access them, browse through sites such as **http://onlinebooks.library .upenn.edu/, www.gutenberg.org**, or **www.bartleby.com**.

The Reference Section

What was the murder rate in New York City in 2008? Whose faces are on Mount Rushmore? When was the Taj Mahal built? How do you define "trade books"? To find specific information quickly, there are hundreds of reference works such as encyclopedias, dictionaries, and sources for statistics.

Encyclopedias

General encyclopedias, such as the *Encyclopedia Americana* and *Collier's Encyclopedia*, review and summarize information on thousands of topics. Although they should not be your only source for information, encyclopedias provide a helpful overview early in your research.[17] The *Encyclopedia Britannica* is especially useful for international topics. The index will guide you to related subjects, and bibliographies at the end of each article suggest other sources of information. Many encyclopedias are available online, some for a fee; however, libraries often pay the fees so that you can freely access the information via your library's Web site.

In addition to general encyclopedias, hundreds of **specialized encyclopedias** provide information about more narrowed subjects. If you want to know about a particular bird, look in the *Encyclopedia of Birds*. Psychological depression? There is a whole encyclopedia on the topic. How about the *Encyclopedia of American Indian Costume*, or one on world pop music? Use your judgment to evaluate the publication date for specialized

specialized encyclopedias texts that summarize information in specific subject areas

Emily Wornell

Library materials have
a measure of academic
respectability because the
books, magazines, and
other resources found there
undergo a several-step
selection process before
they appear on the shelves.

encyclopedias. One about world pop music will be rapidly outdated, but one about birds can remain useful for decades.

Dictionaries

The most familiar type of dictionary provides definitions, historical sources, synonyms, and antonyms for words. If your computer's software program has a built-in dictionary, simply type in a word and the definition and pronunciation will appear. Libraries contain many specialized dictionaries in the reference section, including ones devoted only to pianists, psychotherapy, or American slang.

Sources for Statistics

Consult the *Statistical Abstracts of the United States* (a government document) for U.S. statistics on a wide variety of topics, including population, health, education, crime, employment, elections, the environment, and defense. The *Abstract* shows historical trends as well as current statistics. Almanacs, such as the *World Almanac*, also provide statistical information.

Reference Materials on the Web

Millions of reference materials are available online. Here are some suggestions for using these resources:

▶ Look for materials from .edu sources such as *The Encyclopedia of Educational Technology* (San Diego State University) or the extremely specialized *Encyclopedia of Revolutions of 1848* (Ohio University). The *Dictionary of the History of Ideas* comes from the University of Virginia. In contrast, the *Illustrated Dictionary of Jewelry* is from a .com source, and its information is less reliable overall.

▶ Check out **www.refdesk.com.** Calling itself "the fact checker for the Internet," it is one of the most comprehensive sources for reference materials online. It has everything, including Soduku puzzles and Letterman's Top Ten.

▶ Bartleby.com has links to easy-to-access reference works including a gazetteer (geographical information), a thesaurus (synonyms and antonyms), a style book (grammar), and sources for quotations. It even has the medical textbook, *Gray's Anatomy*.

▶ For statistics, try the site that makes statistics "from more than 100 agencies available to citizens everywhere," **www.fedstats.gov.**

▶ The U.S. Census Bureau's Web page is located at **www.census.gov.** This user-friendly, reliable site records each new birth automatically; consequently, population figures are updated regularly.[18]

◗ **Wikipedia** was launched in 2001 to provide free, easily accessible articles. Currently, it's available in more than 250 languages and has more than a million entries, many on topics not found in other encyclopedias.[19] Its major innovation was "community-generated knowledge,"[20] which means that anyone (you included) can contribute an original article or correct or add to someone else's entry. **Wiktionary** is its dictionary counterpart. The *Wall Street Journal* called this concept a "free-for-all approach to editing";[21] and, although it is often reliable, accuracy is not guaranteed. As a result, your instructor may insist that you choose other sources with established credibility.

Periodicals

Periodicals are issued once per time period—weekly, monthly, quarterly, or annually. They range from popular or general interest magazines like *U.S. News & World Report* or *Sports Illustrated* to more specialized periodicals such as *Hiker's World* or *Vital Speeches of the Day*. Popular magazines are generally easy to understand, with their contemporary examples, up-to-date statistics, illustrations, and quotations from both experts and laypeople.

Libraries also house **trade journals**, such as the *American Journal of Nursing* or *Architecture and Design*, which contain topics of interest to people in specific occupations, and **academic journals**, such as the *Quarterly Journal of Speech* or the *Journal of Nonverbal Behavior*, which contain the research findings of scholars writing in academic areas. Some journal articles may be too technical for classroom speeches; others, however, can provide excellent materials.

The *Congressional Digest: The Pro-and-Con Monthly* is especially helpful for researching controversial topics. Each issue presents multiple viewpoints on a single issue like overtime pay, global warming, or crack cocaine. For example, an issue on highway funding provides a timeline of federal highway legislation, explains the Highway Trust Fund, and assesses the status of U.S. highways and transit systems. It then identifies relevant subtopics and summarizes the proposed highway funding bill. Finally, it presents pro and con arguments about the bill made by members of Congress. When you need to understand both sides of a complex issue, you can save valuable time by consulting this source early.

Current issues of periodicals are kept on file and older issues are archived. Nowadays, most campus libraries purchase electronic databases that contain thousands of periodicals, so you can log on to your library Web site and easily find these materials in databases such as EBSCO or Academic Search Premier. Currently, most major magazines and many scholarly journals are also on the Internet. They're easy to find by typing the magazine's name into a search engine. The InfoTrac College Edition database, one of the online resources available with this text, also provides articles from thousands of popular, trade, and academic magazines and journals.

For the speech found at the end of the chapter, Jenn searched her library's databases for "neuroimaging" and "neuromarketing"; she found dozens of usable articles. Study the bibliography at the end of her speech, and you will see information retrieved from the Academic Search Premier database and the ScienceDirect College Edition database.

Newspapers

Newspapers generally cover current events in greater depth than radio or television news broadcasts. You'll find articles on current issues and events, along with opinion pieces by editors, syndicated columnists, and readers who submit letters to the editor. Newspapers typically print humorous articles, obituaries, human interest pieces, and critical evaluations of movies, plays, books, art exhibits, and musical performances.

Wikipedia the online encyclopedia created by Internet users

Wiktionary the online dictionary created by Internet users

trade journals journals that pertain to specific occupations

academic journals journals that pertain to specific areas of academic research

Daily, weekly, and monthly newspapers range in size from metropolitan papers with international circulation to small student papers. Some are targeted toward various cultural and ethnic groups (see the Diversity in Practice box for more on this). A few are dubbed the "elite media" because of their reputation for high-quality, detailed reporting and because many smaller papers reprint their articles; "elite" papers include the *New York Times*, the *Washington Post*, and the *Los Angeles Times*. Most school libraries carry at least one elite paper, and they are all available on the Internet. Log onto **www.refdesk .com/paper.html** for links to thousands of local, national, and international papers; see if your hometown paper is there.

The *New York Times* often reprints primary documents, such as the president's State of the Union address, in part or in whole. Look there for excerpts of testimony given at Senate hearings, presidential remarks made at press conferences, and majority and dissenting opinions on significant Supreme Court decisions. The *Times*, along with many other major newspapers, is included in the InfoTrac College Edition database.

DIVERSITY IN PRACTICE

INTERNATIONAL AND ETHNIC PRESSES

Most libraries carry newspapers from around the world, and many more are available online. Foreign papers allow you to gain different perspectives and to hear voices other than those found in local or national sources. Check out *World Press Review,* a monthly magazine that prints excerpts of translated materials from international papers; its editors identify the bias of each source as conservative, liberal, or moderate. Also look for diverse perspectives within the United States—such as papers published by labor unions, African Americans, gays and lesbians, Catholics, and Muslims, which all produce periodicals from their perspectives.

If your library doesn't subscribe to the periodicals you need, go to InfoTrac College Edition and check its list of journal names; you'll find a wide variety of diverse perspectives there. Or check out the international and ethnic resources on **www.refdesk.com**.

Indexes

An easy way to locate articles from scholarly journals, popular magazines, and newspapers is to use indexes. They're found in books and in computerized databases, such as the *ERIC* index for the field of education. The *Readers' Guide to Periodical Literature* is invaluable for locating articles in popular magazines from 1900 to the present; its editors list each article in alphabetical order by subject, author, and title. Also indexed are broad topics with a number of subheadings, as this sample entry found under *Golf* demonstrates:

> Tournaments—Ethical aspects
> Quiet, Please [Heckling at golf tournaments] J. Dodson, il Golf Magazine v46 no10 p143–4 O 2004.

Each entry gives the title, author's name, magazine, volume, page number, and date. The "il" indicates that the story is illustrated.

Use keywords to search a computerized index. Many of the resulting hits come with an abstract, a brief summary that helps you decide which articles are worth looking up. For example, while researching her speech on learning styles, Beth typed in both "learning" and "styles." She skimmed abstracts from more than twenty articles, marked those that seemed suitable, printed the references she'd marked, and then went to the magazines and journals to read the articles.

Major newspapers also provide tools for locating articles. The *New York Times Index*, for example, provides the date, page, and column location of almost every news article that has appeared in its pages since 1851. Each annual index lists articles alphabetically under one of four types of headings: subject, geographic name, organization, and personal name. Since 1962, the foreword has summarized each year's important events. The index itself is a source of information for brief answers to questions such as "Is the teenage birth rate rising or falling?" or "How many rhinoceroses are left in the wild?"

Record Your Information

Obviously you won't remember everything you discover during your search, so you need a strategy for recording your findings, avoiding plagiarism, and citing sources properly. Then, when you sit down to organize your speech, you will have the necessary information at your fingertips, and you can easily classify your ideas into themes and patterns. There are three common methods for recording information: note cards, photocopies or printouts, and mind maps. Choose the one that matches your learning style or your topic, but always list your sources at the end of your outline, using a standard bibliographic format.

Write Note Cards

With all the technology now available to copy and print materials, why would anyone write information on index cards or note cards? Actually, this method has several advantages: It is probably the most structured way to do research; the cards are small enough to handle easily; you can cite your sources directly on each card; and you can easily classify the information into points and subpoints. Better yet, cards can help you avoid cut-and-paste plagiarism because it's easier to jot down key ideas and summarize the material than to copy long paragraphs. For these reasons, we'll look at this method first. There are two basic kinds of note cards: source cards and information cards.

Source Cards

Begin by making a separate **source card** for each reference, using a standard bibliographic format. Include the author, date, article or chapter title, book or periodical title, place of publication (for books), followed by the page number(s). For online information, add the title of the Web site, the sponsoring organization, the date you retrieved the material, and the site's URL. It is helpful to **annotate** your bibliography, meaning that you write a brief description of the information you found in the book, article, or Web site. Make source cards for materials gathered from interviews and films as well. See Figure 7.2 for an example.

Information Cards

Next, write down important data, using a separate **information card** for each idea, statistic, quotation, example, and so on. Use quotation marks around every direct quotation and each uniquely worded phrase, and write down the page number each piece of information is from, whether directly quoted or not. This practice will help you avoid plagiarism.

On the top of each card, create a heading that classifies the information into a category you might later use as a main point. Also, label the card with an abbreviated source citation so that when you use the material in the speech, you can cite its source. Figure 7.3 shows examples of information cards.

The advantage of this method is that you can separate your cards into piles and move them around, placing your major point at the top and arranging your supporting information below. You can easily change the order of your points and your relevant supporting materials before writing your outline.

source cards cards used to record bibliographic information

annotate to summarize a book or article's contents on a source card

information card card for recording and categorizing important data

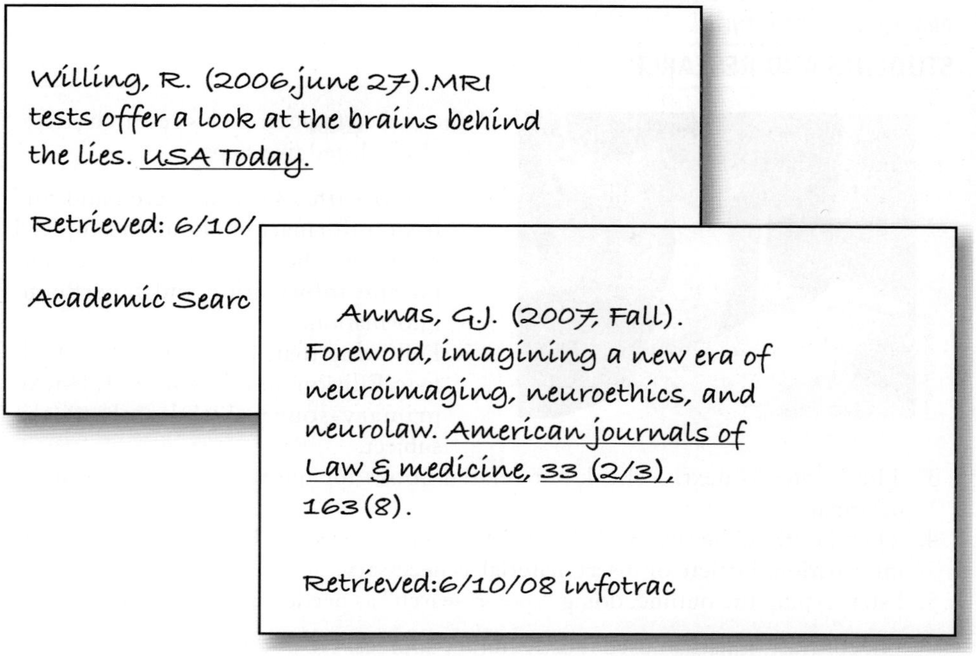

Willing, R. (2006, june 27). MRI
tests offer a look at the brains behind
the lies. USA Today.

Retrieved: 6/10/

Academic Searc

        Annas, G.J. (2007, Fall).
Foreword, imagining a new era of
neuroimaging, neuroethics, and
neurolaw. American journals of
Law & medicine, 33 (2/3),
163(8).

    Retrieved: 6/10/08 infotrac

Figure 7.2
Source Cards
Source cards contain bibliographic information. Annotated cards also include a brief summary of the material found in the source.

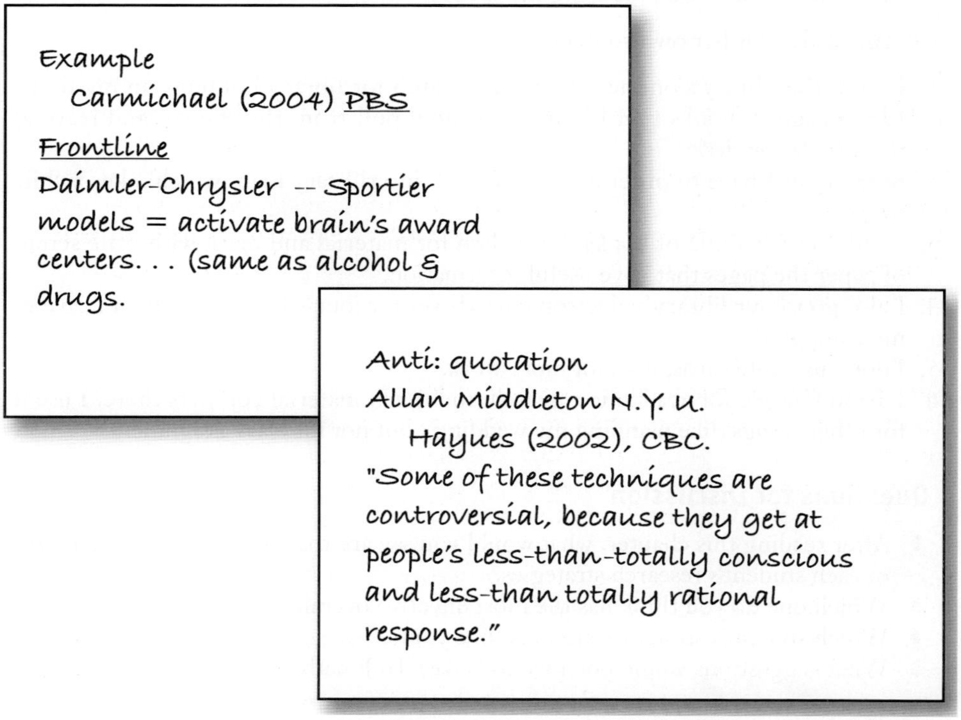

Example
  Carmichael (2004) PBS

Frontline
Daimler-Chrysler -- Sportier
models = activate brain's award
centers. . . (same as alcohol &
drugs.

    Anti: quotation
    Allan Middleton N.Y. U.
        Hayues (2002), CBC.
    "Some of these techniques are
    controversial, because they get at
    people's less-than-totally conscious
    and less-than totally rational
    response."

Figure 7.3
Information Cards
Use a different information card for each source, and classify each card according to the major idea the information supports. Include an abbreviated source citation, including the page number, on each card.

PRACTICALLY SPEAKING

STUDENTS AND RESEARCH

When asked to describe his research strategies, Luke listed five steps:

1. I start with a Google search and find basic information about the topic. I figure out the difference between important information and superfluous information.
2. Following that, I go to InfoTrac College Edition and find some full-text, primary-source articles about the subject.
3. The library is next. I check out related books for quotations and additional information.
4. Then I outline the speech with information I've collected, looking for gaps in the information. I delete or insert material as necessary.
5. I start typing the outline, doing "spot-research" as needed to fill in gaps.

In contrast, Jonathan used mostly library sources. He described his strategies:

1. First I figure out how much I already know about the subject and try to outline what I might want to write or speak about.
2. Second, I go to the university library or the city library and find credible books on my topic.
3. I flip through and check to see if they will be useful.
4. Usually I check them out or at least take notes and photocopy important pages.
5. I look through and grab the important information for my subject and outline, then start writing and practicing my speech.

Alicia also has her own strategies:

1. I go to the library's online catalog and search for library holdings on my topic. I then request books that library personnel pull from the shelves and leave at the circulation desk.
2. Sometimes I have to order a book through interlibrary loan, which takes awhile to get.
3. I end up with a pile of books that I skim for material and mark with little scraps of paper the pages that have useful information.
4. I also go to our library's electronic databases for journal articles, which I save to my computer.
5. I don't use note cards; it's a lot more work.
6. I avoid Google for academic research; too much material conflicts there. I use it for other things (like planning my wedding), but not for class assignments.

Questions for Discussion

▶ After reading this chapter, what would you say are the strengths and weaknesses of each student's research strategies?
▶ Which one do you think has the most effective overall strategies? Why?
▶ Which student's strategies are most like yours?
▶ What suggestions would you give to Luke? To Jonathan? To Alicia?

Photocopy or Print Out Your Materials

There are many advantages to photocopying material or downloading and printing an article directly from the Internet.

▶ When you print out an article instead of downloading it to an electronic file, you can more easily avoid cut-and-paste plagiarism.

▶ Having hard copies of your research can protect you against plagiarism charges and provide materials for future research.

▶ Many Web sites are updated daily, and what you find one day might be gone the next. The only proof you have that it was ever there is your printed copy.

▶ Both photocopying and printing out copies are quick, easy, and available, and you can have the entire resource in front of you when you sit down to write your outline.

▶ Downloaded materials usually have source information on the printout, but also make sure the source (in standard bibliographic form) is on your photocopies. And write the date you retrieved it. Then, use highlighters to mark major ideas and salient information.

For example, for her topic "neuroimaging," Jenn might photocopy pages from books and newspapers and supplement them with articles downloaded and printed off from the Internet. She would next write the entire reference on each page. Then, using one color for major points and a second color for examples and quotations, she would highlight relevant material. When she is finally ready to organize and outline her ideas, she would spread out her photocopied and highlighted articles and weave the materials together into a coherent speech.

When you copy materials, you are using the intellectual property of another person who has a right to profit from its use, so you are obligated to credit your sources. Fortunately, the **Fair Use provision** in the federal Copyright Act allows you to print and use materials for nonprofit educational purposes; therefore, photocopying materials for one-time speech research is within your legal rights as a student.[22]

Create a Mind Map

If your learning style is more holistic, consider making a mind map. Chapter 5 showed how to create mind maps to generate speech topics, and you can use a similar process to record, subdivide, and categorize information. Although there is no single "right" way to create a mind map, there are some general principles. First, identify your subject in the center of the page, using a diagram or drawing. Write your major points around the subject and then draw a line from each main point to the center. Identify further subtopics and connect each one to the main point it supports. For example, a mind map of Jenn's speech on neuroimaging, might have a brain drawn in the middle of the page, with lines radiating out to her three major points: neuromarketing, brainimage based lie detection, and brainimage based trait prediction. Each point would then have supporting material linked to it. If you have a lot of material, you can make a separate page for each major point. But always list your sources. If there is room, write references directly onto your mind map; however, if space is limited, make source cards or list your references on a separate piece of paper.

Use a Standard Format to Cite Your Sources

To avoid plagiarism and build and maintain credibility, list each source in a bibliography at the end of your outline. Alphabetize your sources, and use the standard bibliographic format found in the style or publication manual your instructor recommends.

Fair Use provision the provision in the federal Copyright Act that allows free use of materials for educational and research purposes

The basic elements of any source citation include the author(s), date, title, publisher or source, and place of publication or location in a database or Internet site. Here are some examples in the American Psychological Association (APA) Style:

Book

Granger, R. H. (2007). *The 7 triggers to yes: the new science behind influencing people's decisions.* New York: McGraw-Hill.

Magazine article

Mucha, T. (2005, September 5). In the mind of the shopper. *Advertising Age, 76(36),* 16.

Online article

Carmichael, M. (2004, November 9). Neuromarketing: Is it coming to a lab near you? PBS: *Frontline.* Retrieved June 10, 2008, from www.pbs.org/wgbh/pages/frontline/shows/persuaders/etc/neuro.html

Academic article, database

Lee, N. J. (2007, February). What is "neuromarketing"? A discussion and agenda for future research. *Journal of International Psychophysiology, 63(2),* 199-204. Retrieved June 10, 2008, from Academic Search Premier database.

Movie

Berman, B. (Producer), & Wachowski, A. & Wachowski, L. (Director). (1999). *The matrix.* [Motion Picture]. United States: Warner Brothers Pictures.

Incorrect

www.pbs.org/wgbh/pages/frontline/shows/persuaders/etc/neuro.html

Incorrect

Neuromarketing. PBS *Frontline.* www.pbs.org/wgbh/pages/frontline/shows/persuaders/etc/neuro.html

Incorrect APA Style

Mucha, T. (2005, September 5). In the Mind of the Shopper. *Advertising Age, 76(36),* 16. (This is not standard APA formatting; although other formats capitalize all the words in the title, APA does not.)

The reference section of your library contains many style manuals, and your campus librarians have also created citation guidelines. In addition, many online sites, such as the Writing Center for the University of Wisconsin-Madison (www.wisc.edu/writetest/Handbook/Documentation.html), give guidelines for most of the common styles, including APA, MLA (Modern Language Association), Chicago/Turabian, APSA (American Political Science Association), and CBE (Council of Biology Editors). Whichever style you use, there are two good rules to follow: (1) Use the style your instructor recommends, and (2) use it consistently.

You can see that a vital aspect of research is recording information so that it is readily available when you need it. If you prefer a structured, linear method, note cards may be your best choice. If you approach the research task holistically, you might download or photocopy your materials and use highlighters to identify important information. If you are a visual thinker, you could make mind maps, using images as well as words to record your findings. Whatever method you choose, always use a standard bibliographic format to list your sources alphabetically.

STOP AND CHECK

COMPLETE YOUR RESEARCH PLAN

Return to your online resources for Chapter 7 and complete sections 13 to 16 of your research plan. You will be asked to:

1. List usable library and online sources.
2. Tell how you will incorporate sources that provide diverse perspectives.
3. Describe how you will evaluate your sources.
4. Tell how you will record your information.

   Make any other alterations that seem justified in light of what you have learned in this chapter.

Summary

Part of your competence in speechmaking is your ability to gather information. To be more effective, set aside plenty of time to explore your topic, and use a research plan that is appropriate for the subject. Distinguish between primary sources—original documents and other firsthand information—and secondary sources, which interpret, explain, and evaluate the subject. You can find both primary and secondary materials in interviews and in print sources such as books, periodicals, and newspapers, both in traditional libraries and online. Consider also the wide variety of visual and recorded materials that are available. Throughout your research, seek out diverse perspectives from a variety of viewpoints.

Through the Internet, you can access literally millions of documents from local, national, and global sources—some highly credible, others quite useless. Use a subject directory to find human-selected materials on general topics. If you want information on unusual topics or if you're looking for specific phrases, use a search engine. Or look for academic materials on specialized databases located on the Invisible Web. Sift through the online materials by evaluating each source, the site's purpose, and the bias, timeliness, accuracy, originality, and organization of content.

In the library, look for materials in books, periodicals, newspapers, and indexes. Consult the reference section for specific information in encyclopedias, dictionaries, sources for statistics, and so on. Many reference resources are now available online, and online books are increasingly available. Currently, most campus libraries have vast amounts of electronically stored materials, which give you around-the-clock access to their data.

Consistently record your findings, using a method that meets your learning style preferences, such as source and information cards, photocopying, and making a mind map. Whatever your method, avoid plagiarism by crediting your sources in your notes, in your speech, and on the bibliography that accompanies your outline. Finally, choose a standard source citation format and then use it correctly and consistently throughout your work.

STUDY AND REVIEW

Your online resources for *Public Speaking: Concepts and Skills for a Diverse Society* offer a broad range of study tools that will help you better understand the material in this chapter, complete assignments, and succeed on tests. Your online resources feature

- Speech videos with critical viewing questions, speech outlines, and transcripts
- Interactive versions of this chapter's Stop and Check activities and Application and Critical Thinking Exercises

- Speech Builder Express and InfoTrac College Edition
- Weblinks related to chapter content
- Study and review tools such as self-quizzes, an interactive glossary, and downloadable audio summaries

You can access your online resources at **http://www.cengage.com/login**, using the access code that came with your book or that you bought online at **http://www.iChapters.com**.

KEY TERMS

The terms below are defined in the margins throughout this chapter.

academic journals 122	relics or artifacts 112
Academic Invisible Web (AIW) 116	scholarly books 120
annotate 124	search engine 115
creative works 112	secondary sources 112
domain 117	source card 124
experts 113	specialized databases 116
Fair Use provision 127	specialized encyclopedias 120
information card 124	subject directory 115
Invisible Web or Deep Web 116	subject librarian 111
laypeople or peers 113	trade books 120
OPAC 119	trade journals 122
original documents 112	Wikipedia 122
primary sources 112	Wiktionary 122
reference librarian 110	

APPLICATION AND CRITICAL THINKING EXERCISES

1. Read the cover story from a current magazine like *Time* or *Newsweek*. Make a list of all the experts and laypeople quoted in the article. Compare and contrast the type of information, primary or secondary, given by each type of source.

3. To learn more about finding credible information on the Internet, do a Google search for "Internet tutorial." Read the material on at least two of the Web sites. Compare and contrast the two sites in terms of source and content, following the guidelines on pages 117–119. Which site would you recommend to others in your class?

5. Have you heard of the "Mozart Effect" (the idea that babies who listen to Mozart are smarter)?[23] Do an Internet search for this topic. How many Web pages do you get? What kind of domains (.com, .edu, for example) sponsor the sites? Use note cards to summarize the information on at least three sites. Afterward, search for the topic in your campus online databases such as Academic Search Premier. How many Web pages come up there? Summarize the findings in at least two articles there. Bring your findings to class and discuss how you would compare what you find on the Internet with what you find in the library databases. Overall, what would you tell a friend who was playing Mozart to her baby in order to improve the child's IQ?

6. If you have not already done so, visit your campus library. Locate and browse the reference books, the newspapers and periodicals, and the indexes and the guides to their use.

7. If your library provides handouts with instructions for using your campus library, make a file containing the ones you'll use most often, and consult these during your research. Or search your library's online resources for information about research and recording information. (Examples: HOW TO: Locate U.S. Government Documents; HOW TO: Cite References According to the APA Manual; Periodicals Collection: A Service Guide.)

8. Not all librarians dislike Wikipedia. In fact, an article by a librarian called "Head for the Edge: Evaluating Collectively Created Information", commends Wikipedia for "the breadth of its scope, its timeliness, and its clear notification of controversial or undocumented sources."

Read his article on InfoTrac College Edition, and come to class prepared to discuss the good as well as the bad things about this online encyclopedia.

9. Discover the international, ethnic, and alternative newspapers and magazines in your library by making a list of available sources that provide diverse perspectives. Read an article in at least one of the resources.

10. To understand the variety and number of specialized encyclopedias and dictionaries online, do a search for "encyclopedia of" and "dictionary of" and list at least ten titles in each category that may someday be useful to you. Note the source of each. Are they from .com or .edu or another domain's sites? Why does this matter? Bring your lists to class and discuss your findings with a small group of your classmates.

11. Set aside an hour to explore news outlets on the Internet. Try **www.refdesk.com/paper.html**, or check Google news for information about current events, noting the variety of papers and television news sources linked there. With your classmates, select an interesting, significant current event and surf around, clicking on relevant news links. Then, discuss the value as well as the drawbacks of using the Internet to do research into current events.

12. Browse several weblogs (**www.blogarama.com** links you to thousands) on a subject related to your topic. Assess the quality and bias of each blog. Why or when might you use a blog as a source? Why or when might you avoid them?

13. As a class, research a current event or an issue. Go to the library and find and photocopy a print article, or download information from a Web site. If possible, interview an expert or layperson. Assign some students to consult mainstream sources and others to seek out diverse perspectives. Bring your information to the next class meeting, and discuss and evaluate the various sources and data by determining the purpose, the source bias, the timeliness, the accuracy, and the organization of the material.

14. Of the three ways to record information presented in this chapter, which method—note cards, photocopies or downloaded material, or a mind map—will you most likely use? Which are you least likely to use? When might you combine methods? Discuss your research style with a classmate.

SPEECH VIDEO

Go to your online resources to watch and evaluate the sample speeches that are research-based. Also, read the text of Jenn's speech and the accompanying commentary.

Student Outline with Commentary

APPLICATIONS OF NEUROIMAGING
Jennifer Salame

Mike McNamara/Cengage Learning

Jenn gains attention with thought-provoking statements. She then involves the audience by using "you" words.

You will purchase a 1969 Ford Mustang GT hatchback, candy apple red.

You were lying about the information on your income taxes.

You will not be hired because you brain scan shows an abnormally larger amygdala that may lead to excessive aggression.

The common theme here is that all of these activities are, in one way or another, dependent upon brain function. As humans, we have been given certain mental capacities such as choice and the ability to form opinions. Some of these activities can be monitored in the brain through new imaging technologies.

The ability to influence you to purchase something, to predict your truthfulness with a 90 percent accuracy, or to make a judgment about you based on your brain image are all possibilities lying just around the corner. Welcome to the hot'n'now world of brainimaging and neuroethics!

This topic interests me because I am a cognitive psychology major, and I'm fascinated by how the brain works.

Here she previews the three main ideas she'll develop in the speech.

Today, we will discuss three controversial uses for the recent advances in brainimaging and then discuss some of the ethical questions associated with them. First, we will look at the field of neuromarketing and its potential to influence purchases. Second, we will discuss brainimage-based lie detection. Finally, we will come to terms with the possibility of brainimage based trait prediction.

This section explains neuromarketing and gives some examples. This is the longest point, because there is more information about it than about the other two applications of neuroimaging.

Let us begin with a definition of neuromarketing. If a company uses a young male model to show off a product, how will their target demographic respond? Will the model encourage or discourage a purchase? What more could be done to stimulate neural activity that could lead to a purchase? These questions are a few that someone in the field of neuromarketing might try to answer. The February 2007 issue of the *International Journal of Psychophysiology* defines neuromarketing as the application of neuroimaging to market research. For decades, scientists have mapped the brain through MRI machines. Now, *Newsweek International*, June 30, 2003, reports they are using fMRI (functional-MRI) machines to pinpoint areas of the brain that are brought into play during a given thought or behavior. For example, PBS's *Frontline*, November 9, 2004, explained that researchers use fMRI machines to identify which areas of the brain light up when the subject is presented with an ad or a brand name like "Daimler-Chrysler". *Reward centers* in the brain lit up when sportier models were shown (interestingly, alcohol and drugs also light up those same centers).

Throughout she demonstrates credibility by citing respectable sources.

A January 2007 article in *Neuron Magazine* called "Neural Predictors of Purchases" provides another example of this technology. Researchers at Stanford University gave participants $20 to spend. When presented with some desirable products, a part of the brain associated with the anticipation of pleasure was activated; however, when shown excessive prices for those products, a different part—the insula—was activated and the medial frontal cortex, the region associated with balancing gains vs. losses, was deactivated. Through imaging which brain regions were activated or deactivated, researchers were able to predict which products would be purchased. This is the general idea behind the services being sold to corporate marketers by up-and-coming companies such as BrightHouse, Neurosense, and SalesBrain.

What companies are buying into this method of research into the mind of the consumer? Adam Koval of the Brighthouse Institute of Thought Sciences, a provider of neuromarketing research, told CBC News on February 2, 2002, "We can't actually talk about the specific names of the companies, but they are global consumer product companies. Right now, they would rather not be exposed. We have been kind of running under the radar with a lot of the breakthrough technology." Obviously, there is some controversy surrounding the use of neuromarketing if companies have been reluctant to confirm that they use it.

Is it ethical? Neuroscientists and marketers have lined up on both sides of this debate. From a neuromarketing perspective, selling this new technology to corporations as a resource to boost marketing is similar to using focus groups, surveys, and other marketing tests of days gone by.

Although neuroscientists began the movement, they are also the ones who most vehemently oppose it. A February 2004 article in the *Lancet Neurology* responded to the advent of neuromarketing by stating, "Although many independent experts doubt that fMRI can be meaningfully used [to predict whether a person will respond favorably to a product or brand], this is unlikely to concern marketers wanting to dazzle potential clients with snazzy imaging technology."

Some neuroscientists who have become very passionate about this issue have ethical concerns for the privacy of the brain. A 2005 article in the *Brain Research Bulletin* says that ethical questions are always present when the inner workings of the mind are revealed. The question then becomes, is this research an infringement on the private confines of the brain? Or is it simply a continuation of techniques marketing experts have been using for years? The previously cited *Lancet Neurology* article says that regulations and further discussions must take place to ensure that no one's right to a free choice is endangered. There is a fine line between influencing a decision and manipulating people to do something they wouldn't do on their own, and critics are concerned that neuromarketing could cross that line.

Gary Ruskin, retired executive director of Commercial Alert, a nonprofit organization that monitors advertising, is very concerned that governments, not just marketers, could use this technology to manipulate citizens through highly sophisticated propaganda. Researchers at UCLA have already compared brain responses of Republicans and Democrats. Interestingly, one study showed that areas related to fear lit up more in Democrats than Republicans who were viewing ads with images of the September 11 attacks. The scans don't tell why.

Now that we have discussed neuromarketing, we can venture into yet another use of brain-imaging, that is, its use as a lie detector. If you were a prisoner of the government, do you think they should have the ability to force you to tell the truth? We debate methods such as waterboarding, but brainimaging may be much simpler than nearly drowning a detainee to obtain the truth. How about spouses under suspicion? Or candidates for a job? It would be nice to know if they were lying or not. A June 27, 2006 article in *USA Today* reports on an fMRI machine being marketed by companies such as Cephos as a lie detector that is 90 percent accurate. It functions by actually watching your brain as you speak and noticing certain "hot spots" that become more active when you lie.

[Display poster with images.] Cephos says that it appeals only to a specific target audience. According to their Web site, they target the government, "which currently uses a variety of techniques such as the polygraph as part of the process of granting national security clearances to individuals in government and industry." Second, they target the legal system "where truth, integrity, and trust form the foundation".

As you might imagine, neuroethicists see the potential for abuse. Hank Greely and Judy Illes, authors of the article, "Neuroscience-Based Lie Detection: The Urgent Need for Regulating," from the 2007 *Journal of Law and Medicine*, call for better regulations on these tests as well as a demonstration of safety and efficacy. How much of someone's thoughts should be open to search by, say, the U.S. government, and how much is private? Is a forceable brain scan ever warranted? (By the way, much of the research is funded by federal funds, meaning that your tax dollars and mine are supporting this research.) These questions ought to continue to encourage you to take an interest in following the progression of this technology and how it is being used. According to neuroethicists, that may be the difference between maintaining the privacy of your mind and falling into a 1984 scenario where nothing is sacred, not even your mind.

Remember at the beginning of my speech how I presented the possibility of a job applicant not being hired for a job because of the results from his or her brain scan? The use of brain imaging as a trait predictor is our third point of discussion. Here's an example: *Time Magazine*, on January 29, 2007, reported on research done at New York University where neuroscientists studied responses of the amygdale (the part of the brain that is aroused when emotions are stimulated) in a search for racism. Armed with fMRI machines, they scanned subjects' brains as they looked at pictures of unfamiliar White and Black faces. They found that some participants had heightened activity in the amygdala when they viewed unfamiliar Black or White faces. Martha Farah, a University of Pennsylvania neuroscientist, foresees a day when employers, such as police departments, might want to eliminate racist candidates from their applicant pools. However, she cautions, 'If we could, in fact, define racism, this would be a potentially useful tool—but with very serious issues of privacy and informed consent.' The *Time* article quotes Stanford psychologist, Judy Illes, who says, "It's not so

She emphasizes ethics. True, scientists might be able to map the brain and use information for marketing or other purposes, but should they? Is this an invasion of privacy? She uses many questions for listeners to contemplate.

The third point arouses emotions in listeners. Who wants someone else to be able to read their thoughts and then use that against them?

futuristic to imagine an employer able to test for who is a good team player, who is a good leader or a follower."

What do neuroethicists have to say about this issue? Does heightened brain activity in response to a different-colored face state definitively that someone is a racist? We are reminded to ask ourselves where the line is between what your brain image says you are predisposed for and what you willfully do. How much of what you do is controlled by the size of your cerebral cortex or the activation of a neural pathway and how much is will, intellect, soul? Neuroethicists are concerned with the neglect of the self-will factor in the use of brain-imaging to predict personality traits or tendencies such as racism. Secondly, neuroscientists admit that any judgment based on an image involves many levels of interpretation, signal processing, and statistical analysis. These separate the imaged brain activity from the psychological traits and states inferred from it. While an image seems authoritative, it may not say what it seems to. This concern is well put by George Annas, author of the "Foreword to Imagining a New Era of Neuroimaging, Neuroethics, and Neurolaw." He says, "[The images'] potential to provide vivid and compelling, but simultaneously misleading, information is at the heart of many of the articles on neuroimaging in this issue."

Today, we discussed neuromarketing, brainimage-based lie detection, brainimage-based trait predictions and how researchers are striving to maintain high ethical standards amidst the technological advancements brainimage brings. We discussed how companies may use brain imaging to gain further insight into the consumer's mind, how the next frontier of lie detectors may be based on brain imaging, and finally how certain traits may be assessed through these same brainimaging technologies. Will you be persuaded to purchase that Mustang? Will a brain scan prevent you from evading your taxes? Will your brain activity disqualify you from getting that new job? These brainimaging technologies are real, current, and potent. Only through knowledge can we begin to have a true understanding of and a true perspective on these technologies.

Her conclusion summarizes her main points. Because this is an informative speech, she calls for understanding and increased awareness, not action.

Sources

Annas, G. J. (2007, Fall). Foreward, imagining a new era of neuroimaging, neuroethics, and neurolaw. *American Journal of Law & Medicine, 33*(2/3), 163(8). Retrieved June 10, 2008, from InfoTrac College Edition.

Carmichael, M. (2004, November 9). Neuromarketing: is it coming to a lab near you? PBS: *Frontline*. Retrieved June 10, 2008, from www.pbs.org/wgbh/pages/frontline/shows/persuaders/etc/neuro.html

Greely, H. T. & Illes, J. (2007). Neuroscience-based lie detection: the urgent need for regulation. *American Journal of Law & Medicine, 33*(2/3), 377–431. Retrieved June 10, 2008, from Academic Search Premier database.

Kelly, M. (2002, December 2). "Troubling science" worries some. CBC News. Retrieved June 10, 2008, from www.cbc.ca/consumers/market/files/money/science_shopping/index2.html

Knutson, B., Rick, S., Wimmer, G. E., Prelec, D., & Lowenstein, G. (2007, January). Neural predictors of purchases. *Neuron, 53*(1), 147–156. Retrieved June 10, 2008, from Academic Search Premier database.

Lee, N. J. (2007, February). What is "neuromarketing"? A discussion and agenda for future research. *Journal of International Psychophysiology, 63*(2), 199–204. Retrieved June 10, 2008, from Academic Search Premier database.

Russo, R. (2007, January 29). Who should read your mind? *Time*. Retrieved June 10, 2008, from http://bioethics.stanford.edu/news/2007/documents/Time1.7.doc

Walter, H., Abler, B., Ciaramidaro, A., & Erk, S. (2005). Motivating forces of human actions: neuroimaging reward and social interaction. *Brain Research Bulletin, 67*, 368–381. Retrieved June 10, 2008, from ScienceDirect College Edition database.

Willing, R. (2006, June 27). MRI tests offer a look at the brains behind the lies. *USA Today*. Retrieved June 10, 2008, from Academic Search Premier database.

Her bibliography is formatted in APA style.

CHAPTER **8**

CHOOSING SUPPORTING MATERIALS

© Tim Timmerman

THIS CHAPTER WILL HELP YOU

▶ Identify types of facts and learn how to test factual data

▶ Use examples effectively

▶ Quote authoritative sources

▶ Select numerical data carefully

▶ Distinguish between literal and figurative analogies

THINK ABOUT SOME OF TODAY'S CONTROVERSIES. How can intelligent, well-meaning people come to such different conclusions that they polarize into opposing camps? Take, for instance, the issue of global warming. Former vice president Al Gore, along with hundreds of environmental groups and individual activists, regularly warn audiences that, unless we—individually and globally—act quickly to save the environment, human-created global warming will change the planet so much that the future will be bleak indeed.[1] They support their claims with data from seemingly reputable sources such as the National Academy of Sciences and the Intergovernmental Panel on Climate Change.

On the other hand, Bjorn Lomborg,[2] author of *Cool It: The Skeptical Environmentalist's Guide to Global Warming*, is one of an opposing group of distinguished scientists and other knowledgeable persons who've studied the issue in depth. A statistician formerly with a university in Denmark and now director of the Copenhagen Consensus Center, Lomborg once set out to prove the dangers of global warming. But as he pored over statistical data from the World Bank, the United Nations, and other credible sources, he eventually concluded that changes are indeed taking place, but that "eco-fundamentalists" are overstating the problem. He argues that dangers such as the global need for pure drinking water pose far more urgent concerns.

Lomborg's critics say that he manipulates data, discards inconvenient statistics, plagiarizes, is motivated by money, and so on. Gore's critics say his data is flawed, exaggerated, and conducted by people or groups who stand to gain financially by creating a crisis. (Truth be told, both men receive recognition and make a lot of money by promoting their respective positions.)

This example illustrates the importance of evidence, because it illustrates how different evidence can lead to different conclusions about important topics. Each culture has its own rules for what counts as credible evidence. So rather than taking all information at face value, we follow our cultural standards for weighing evidence, accepting some as valid and rejecting other data as inaccurate, inadequate, or irrelevant. Speakers in the United States commonly use facts, examples, quotations, statistics, and analogies to support their ideas. Listeners judge this evidence, based on guidelines they've learned. This chapter examines the typical types of evidence used in public speaking situations nationwide. Following the presentation of each type of evidence, you will find a Stop and Check section to help you think critically about the quality of the data or evidence, both when you're selecting materials for your own speeches and when you are listening to the speeches of others.

Provide Facts

Much of the information you present will probably be factual, because audiences typically demand facts before they accept an idea or proposal. **Empirical facts** are data that can be verified by observation, and **established facts** are data that are consistently validated by many observers. Facts derive from a variety of sources, as these examples show:

▶ Each U.S. President gets to design a rug for the Oval Office to be used during that president's term; each rug must have the Great Seal of the United States in the center. [source: the White House Web site]

▶ The program, Puppies Behind Bars, gives prisoners young dogs to train as guide dogs; some of these dogs go to returning Iraq vets who suffer from traumatic stress syndrome. [source: newspaper article]

▶ High blood sugar levels are linked to some types of cancer in women. [source: empirical research reported in a scientific journal]

empirical facts data verifiable by observation

established facts data verified consistently by many observers

Generally accepted definitions and descriptions are also considered facts. Factual information is judged as being true or false, accurate or inaccurate.

In the spirit of democratic debate, Bjorn Lomborg and Al Gore shake hands before they present their opposing conclusions at a Congressional hearing on global warming.

MANNIE GARCIA /AFP/Getty Images

Use Definitions

Definitions are the meanings of terms generally accepted in common usage; most people look up definitions in dictionaries or thesauruses. However, speakers also define terms derived from traditions, philosophers, and so on. In a commencement address, communication professor James E. Sayer gave the dictionary definition of "character":[3]

> *Webster's* will give you many different definitions for the word character—all the way from symbols used in writing and printing to a person in a play or novel—and lots of other definitions in between. Today I am concerned exclusively with the notion of character as it pertains to our moral and ethical natures, the very core of who we are.

Sayer then added a cultural definition:

> Perhaps you have heard the old axiom that "reputation" is what people think you are, but "character" is really what you are.

He continued with definitions from classical teachers of rhetoric:

> In the fourth century B. C., the great Greek philosopher and rhetorician Aristotle . . . [noted] that character was one of the most important elements in human existence, and that "character is manifested in choice." That is, decisions we make about what to do and what not to do reveal our character, for our character controls those decisions. Other ancient theorists like Cicero and Quintilian also emphasized the importance of character, for they understood that our real being would be demonstrated in everything that we did.

Provide Vivid Descriptions

Descriptions provide details about a subject, such as its size, shape, sound, and color. This description of an earthquake in China was given by a foreign correspondent covering the story:[4]

> We are standing on a pile of rubble. Bricks and wooden rafters are strewn across the ground and much of the roof now lies on the floor of what was [a] restaurant. It is a scene of complete devastation. One bedroom is still standing. Inside there are children's books scattered over the bed and floor.

The details (bricks, wooden rafters, children's books) give facts; the choice of words (*rubble, strewn, scattered*) makes these facts easy to visualize.

The danger in using factual material is that it is easy to pass along unverified or inaccurate material. If something looks suspicious, double-check it. For example, hundreds of inaccuracies are passed along as fact, including the following:

▶ Chief Seattle gave the speech "Brother Earth, Sister Sky" to warn against desecrating the environment. [False: A screenwriter named Ted Parry wrote it in 1972 for a film about ecology.]

▶ When a park statue features a horse rearing so that both front legs are in the air, the rider died in battle; if one foot is raised, the rider died of battle wounds; four feet on the ground means the rider died of natural causes. [This is mostly true for statues honoring those who fought at Gettysburg, but it is not true in general.]

▶ You should drink eight glasses of water a day. [**Snopes.com** says no one knows where this number comes from. We should take in as much water as we lose, but that amount varies from person to person and from day to day. As much as four cups of water can come from food.]

With the current explosion of available information, especially through the Internet and other electronic sources, verifying facts is now more important than ever.

Snopes.com and **breakthechain.org** are two good Web sites that exist to investigate bogus "facts"; **www.factcheck.org** checks political information.

✓ STOP AND CHECK
THINK CRITICALLY ABOUT FACTS

Many Arab Americans say they are stereotyped and subject to simplistic or just plain incorrect information that circulates widely about them. A fact sheet from the *Detroit Free Press* explains, "Although the Arab culture is one of the oldest on Earth, it is, in many parts of the United States, misunderstood. There are no easy, one-size-fits-all answers. Culture, language and religion are distinct qualities that act in different ways to connect Arabs, and to distinguish them from one another."[5] To avoid passing along misinformation on this or any topic, apply the following three tests:

1. *Check for accuracy or validity.* By definition, Arab Americans have ancestors in Arabic-speaking countries in the Middle East (including northern Africa). This definition excludes Iranians, who originate from the Farsi-speaking Persian Empire. The Arabic language is a unifying factor among Arabs; however, Arabic has many dialects, and third- or fourth-generation Arab Americans often only speak English.

2. *Are the facts up to date?* Recently, the Associated Press began substituting *Quran* for *Koran. Muslim* designates a follower of Islam; the term *Mohammedan* is outdated. In the U.S. Census 2000, about 1.25 million people identified themselves as Arab Americans. However, the Arab American Institute puts the number as at least 3.5 million, based on Zogby Poll data showing that people of Arab descent often fail to self-identify. The Arab American Institute reports that the majority of Arabs in the United States are Christians.[6]

3. *Consider the source.* The *Detroit Free Press* prepared a fact sheet for journalists called "100 Questions and Answers about Arab Americans." It is available online at **www.freep.com/legacy/jobspage/arabs/**. What credibility does a major newspaper have? How would you assess the credibility of sources such as the U.S. Census, the Zogby Poll, and the Arab American Institute **(www.aaiusa.org/about)**? What other sources might provide credible factual information?

In short, test facts by asking three questions: Is this true? Is this true now? Who says so? Log onto the *Detroit Free Press* site or another source mentioned here and identify some common misconceptions about Arab Americans that are debunked there.

Use Examples

Have you ever listened to a speech that seemed abstract and irrelevant until the speaker used an example that illustrated how the topic affected someone like you? If you're typical, your interest increased, because examples attract and maintain attention. Narrative theorists argue that we listen for examples and stories because they make abstract concepts and ideas more concrete and relevant.[7] Illustrations also help us identify emotionally with the subject. David explains his responses to examples:

> The speeches that are interesting usually start with an example—often from that person's life. It shows the communicator is human. The story adds credibility . . . and leads the audience into the speech, almost like a conversation; this lets the speaker earn the audience's trust.

When an example rings true, a listener's internal dialogue runs something like this: "Yes, I've known someone like that" or "I've seen that happen—this seems real." And, as David points out, examples can enhance your personal credibility. They let listeners know that you understand real-world experiences and the practical implications of your theories and ideas. Examples, or specific illustrations, can be short or long, real or hypothetical.

Use Real Examples

Real examples, those that actually happened, provide concrete, true-life illustrations of your concepts. For instance, John's topic was culture shock. He began by defining the term and explaining the first stage, the honeymoon stage. His audience listened politely, but their attention really perked up and they more clearly understood the emotional impact of this stage when he described Sara's experiences during her first few weeks as a nanny in Belgium. As you gather materials, look for people's experiences and actual events as ways to illustrate your ideas, and provide names, dates, and places to make your examples more vivid. For instance:

▌ To illustrate a speech about the downside of winning the lottery, Maria told about William, a lottery winner whose brother hired a hit man to kill him; about Daisy, whose friend sued for half her winnings (because he had prayed that she'd win and she did); and about Debbie, whose sisters no longer spoke to her after she won because she refused to pay their bills. (An outline of this speech is featured at the end of Chapter 9, and your book's online resources include a video, a transcript, and outlines of this speech.)

▌ For her speech on organ transplants for prisoners, Diamond told of a 31-year-old two-time California felon who received a million-dollar heart transplant while still serving his sentence. (About five hundred Californians were waiting for an available heart at the time.) The prisoner, whose name was never released, died a year later, because he failed to consistently take the medications that would keep his body from rejecting the heart. His last eighteen days at the Stanford University hospital cost taxpayers $12,500 a day.[8]

Personal examples can bolster your credibility. Carrie gave a speech on the importance of making a grief support specialist available to students on her campus, based on her own experience. (You can read her speech at the end of this chapter.) Here's how she began:

> The phone rings. You answer it, and suddenly the world stops. You have just become one of the hundred of thousands of college students experiencing the grief of losing a loved one. September 13th, 2006, my life changed forever when it was my phone that rang. My dad was gone. I was 18.

Personal stories are indispensable in some cultures. Ann Miller's 2002 study of Kenyan public speaking found that focus group participants rated personal stories as the *most* convincing type of example. One Kenyan said, "We believe you only really know about something if you've experienced it."[9] In fact, some Kenyans thought personal narratives should be placed in a separate category because their impact is so different from other types of narratives.

Consider Hypothetical Examples for Sensitive Topics

A **hypothetical example**, one that did not actually occur but seems plausible, usually contains elements of several different stories woven together to create a typical person who has experiences relevant to the topic. So in a speech about teens who injure themselves, instead of revealing details about a specific person you knew, you might combine elements from the experiences of various teenagers to create a typical self-mutilator. To

hypothetical example not a real incident or person, but true-to-life

In the closing argument of the movie *A Time to Kill,* a young lawyer tells a hypothetical story that makes his point more powerfully than the actual story would have made it.

Everett Collection

distinguish hypothetical examples from fabricated stories, introduce them something like this: "Let's say there's a 16-year-old girl named Carly; let's put her in a close-knit family in rural Oregon. . . ."

Our cultural value on privacy makes hypothetical examples more appropriate than real ones for sensitive topics like mental illness or sexual behaviors, so speakers whose work involves confidentiality, such as physicians, members of the clergy, counselors, and teachers, often use them. Family counselors who present parenting workshops, for instance, might tell hypothetical stories of bad parenting skills, stories that do not reveal confidential information about identifiable clients.

Creating an imaginary scenario that invites your listeners to personalize your topic can also attract attention and help audience members become emotionally involved. Here's the opening illustration that Maria used for her speech on the problems that lottery winners face:

> Imagine that you just won the lottery. You can't sleep; you're so excited! You call everyone you know, and for a few days you bask in the joy of being an instant millionaire. Notice I said a few days. A week after you win, relatives you've never seen start asking for loans. A few days later, a friend sues for half the money, arguing that she encouraged you to buy the ticket, and without her urging, you'd still be poor. . . . The demands and the expectations pile up—so much so that you may almost wish you'd never bought that ticket!

Although hypothetical examples and imaginary scenarios can work well in informative speeches, real examples are better for persuasive speeches. Think of it this way: Your listeners are probably more persuaded by something that *did* happen than by something that *might* plausibly happen.

ETHICS IN PRACTICE

HYPOTHETICAL EXAMPLE OR FABRICATION?

Margaret B. Jones's 2008 memoir, *Love and Consequences*, told of growing up in Los Angeles foster homes and participating in gangs as a racially mixed adolescent. Turns out, Margaret is not "Jones;" she's Margaret Seltzer, well-to-do, white, private school-educated, and raised by her biological parents. Selzer eventually admitted the account was hypothetical, based on experiences of people she'd met while working in antigang outreach. But, she explained, "For whatever reason, I was really torn, and I thought it was my opportunity to put a voice to people who people don't listen to."[10]

Selzer is not alone. Best-selling author, Monica Defonseca confessed that her book (which was made into a movie) about surviving the Holocaust was fabricated. And James Frey's book about overcoming addiction, *A Million Little Lies*, was promoted by Oprah Winfrey's Book Club; it turned out to be a "fiction addiction."[11] Didn't happen. Or at least didn't happen the way he said it did.

Questions for Discussion:

1. What's the difference between a hypothetical example and a fabricated story?
2. What, if any, ethical concerns should a speaker have when using hypothetical examples?

Combine Brief Examples

Examples don't have to be long; in fact, you may prefer shorter illustrations. However, a single, short example is easily missed or disregarded, so it's better to string together two or three. Layering them one upon another gives your listeners a number of images they can use to visualize and personalize your subject. The following brief examples of women in prison who are training puppies as guide dogs or companions for returning Iraq veterans could be effectively used to introduce the topic:

> Jayme Powers, a convicted murderer, is teaching Devon, a Labrador retriever puppy, to take a box of cereal from a counter and put it into her grocery bag; inmate Sheron Thomas is training a black Lab, Peter, to "speak"; Bliss Edwards, in prison for assault, is working on the "watch me" command with her Lab, Athena.[12]

Create Emotional Connections with Extended Examples

Extended examples include many details; each one gives your listeners an opportunity to identify emotionally with the subject of the story. Use longer illustrations to clarify, to explain in depth, and to motivate your listeners. Look at how each detail in this example makes the story more engaging. The subject is gastric bypass surgery for teens:

> At 7, Nikki weighed 160 pounds. At 9, she was a veteran dieter whose weight was 250 pounds. By 14, she was up to 363 pounds; her heart was enlarged, her liver inflamed, and her face turned blue when she exercised. Finally, her mother agreed to let her have gastric-bypass surgery—an extreme procedure that costs about $30,000 and sometimes has deadly consequences. Today, Nikki feels "like a whole other person;" she is 6-foot-1, and she is down to 207 pounds.[13]

Listeners can identify with one or more of the details: health issues and money concerns; self-esteem issues during childhood and the teen years. These facts help them become interested in Nikki and the medical procedure she underwent. Because extended examples provide multiple points that engage listeners, they are generally more compelling. In fact, narratives or well-developed stories can function as the entire speech. (Chapter 15 gives detailed information about organizing and evaluating narrative speeches.)

STOP AND CHECK

THINK CRITICALLY ABOUT EXAMPLES

Let's say you're researching a speech about social anxiety and you come across the example of Grace Daily, who experienced panic attacks so severe that she often had to leave college lectures. To help her complete her college degree, her professors agreed to leave the classroom door open during lectures, and they let her take tests alone.[14] To evaluate the usefulness of such an example, ask yourself the following questions:

- *Is this example representative or typical?* That is, does Grace represent a typical college student with social anxiety? Or does her case seem extreme? This test relates to the probability of occurrence.
- *Do you have a sufficient number of examples?* Are enough cases presented to support the major idea adequately? How many people like Grace are attending college? Your listeners should be able to see that the issue affects a significant number of people.
- *Is the example true?* Did Grace actually leave lectures? How often? How did such a shy woman convince her professors to work with her? If Grace is a hypothetical character, does her experience ring true with what you know about the world and how it operates?

Use Visual Evidence

In a culture where visuals are everywhere, speakers and audiences often use evidence contained in pictures, images, and symbols as support for their ideas. Images tell a story or put forth an analysis of a topic—or both. In short, visuals allow us to gain information and "see reasons."[15] How bad is the hurricane's damage? A few photographs tell a lot. What's your university like? Pictures on its Web site show people, events, and places that capture the school's ambiance. Why should I donate to your organization? A photograph of a hungry child provides a reason.

Some images are **literal** in that they show the actual subject under discussion.[16] For instance, a speaker promoting gastric bypass surgery might show before-and-after photographs of a patient who underwent the procedure successfully. But an informative speech on the topic would probably feature a diagram of the procedure. Images can help you fulfill your cognitive, affective, and behavioral goals for a speech. In her classroom speech on the importance of sanitary procedures for body piercings, Katrina displayed graphic pictures of piercings-gone-wrong to support her goals of increasing her listeners' understanding ("I see what you mean!"), getting them emotionally engaged ("That's repulsive!") and motivating them to act. ("I will never get a piercing unless the conditions are sanitary!")[17]

Metaphorical images are also common, especially in advertising where a fluffy kitten posing beside a box of tissues implies "softness" or a flower beside a skin care product implies "beauty." Metaphorical visuals are often displayed during speeches to evoke emotional responses. For example, in a talk about marriage, the speaker might display metaphorical images of hearts and flowers that suggest love and happiness—images that support positive attitudes toward marriage.

Margaret LaWare[18] examined the messages conveyed in Chicano/a murals in Chicago. She says murals—like those reproduced in this text—make statements or arguments about ethnic pride, community activism, and cultural revitalization. Study some of the murals used as chapter openings. Look for images such as mythical beasts or a pink rose (associated with the Virgin of Guadalupe); find possible portraits of community members. Then think of ways these images combine to define identity, reflect

literal image shows the actual subject

metaphorical image implies the subject

Sarah Reamy

To increase her listeners' understandings of a project that helps Ugandan families raise farm animals, Kate showed literal images of African children with pigs. These images engaged listeners' emotions, and motivated them to donate to the project.

people's needs, and celebrate their histories. LaWare believes "the murals argue that Mexican American people need not assimilate or give up their culture to survive in an urban center that is both geographically and socially distant from Mexico and from the Southwest." (LaWare's article is available on InfoTrac College Edition.)

STOP AND CHECK

THINK CRITICALLY ABOUT VISUAL EVIDENCE

Images tell a story, but not necessarily the whole story, and sometimes the story they tell is misleading, because PhotoShop and similar programs allow images to be manipulated or cropped in a way that promotes a particular point of view. For example, someone with a negative attitude toward an issue might show a wide shot of a sparse crowd at a rally to indicate how few attended; however, someone else with a positive attitude toward that same issue might choose a close-up of a single, particularly intense participant to emphasize the importance of the topic.

Analyze the photographs on your college or university's Web site. Your school uses them to imply messages such as, "you will make lifelong friendships if you come here," or "professors are accessible to students," or "the campus is lovely." Typically, the photographs are true, but they don't tell the entire story. Compare the photographs to your personal experiences by answering the following questions:

- What kind of weather is shown in the photographs? Is that weather typical of the climate where the school is located?
- What students are most typical of the student body? What types of students are shown in the photographs? What types are missing from the promotional materials?
- Which buildings or interiors, if any, are shown? Why do you think they were selected?
- What's left out? Why?

Quote Culturally Acceptable Authorities

Remember this childhood challenge?

You make a statement.

Your friend responds, "Who says?"

"My dad says!"

"Your dad? What does he know?"

Mentally reactivate this question-and-answer scenario as you gather speech materials. Whatever your subject, think of your audience as asking, "Who says?" Then support your ideas by citing the sources you think your listeners would respect and believe, given your topic and purpose. Would they accept opinions of scholars or scientists? Laypeople? Medical practitioners? Literary or scriptural texts? Each culture has its own recognized authorities, and these vary among cultures and co-cultural groups. Authoritative sources differ in degree (some have little credibility, others have a lot), and their sphere of influence varies (an authority in one subject may be uninformed in another).

Citing culturally accepted sources is valuable, especially when your personal expertise on the topic is limited. Integrating the ideas of experts or credible laypeople into your speeches shows that knowledgeable, experienced people support your conclusions. But quoting authorities bolsters your ideas if, and only if, your audience views them as credible on the topic. Therefore, it's up to you to provide pertinent information about the persons you cite, why you believe their testimony, and why your audience should believe them.

Quote Culturally Accepted Experts

As Chapter 7 pointed out, we look to people whose occupational or educational expertise, career success, and reputation in their field make them experts. Thus, testimony from scholars, elected officials, practitioners such as doctors or other professionals, and so on generally provides good supporting materials. (Keep in mind, however, that experts are often biased. In fact, as a person's expertise increases, his or her bias may also increase. To understand this better, think of political figures; the longer they're in office, the more partisan they tend to be.)

Here is an example of expert testimony that would fit well in a speech about puppies in prison, taken from an article published in the *Independent Tribune*, Concord, North Carolina:[19]

▶ "It's a win-win situation for me, the inmates and the dogs. If everyone does what they're supposed to, everyone gets something valuable out of the program." [Jacqueline Bankhead, Cabarrus Correctional Center case manager and program coordinator]

▶ The constant interaction with the prisoner trainers gives the dogs almost ten weeks of training in just eight weeks, which would cost about $500 outside the prison. [Tonya Hess, professional dog trainer and prison volunteer]

Notice that the first example directly quotes the expert, but the second example paraphrases or summarizes the person's main point. Because most listeners will be unfamiliar with either of these sources, the speaker should state each woman's institutional affiliation or explain her credentials.

We commonly expect people to agree with the general beliefs of others who are similar to them in some notable way. However, well-known people sometimes hold surprising opinions. Consider these examples:

▶ William F. Buckley, Jr., a well-known conservative writer and journalist, supported legalization of drugs, a position not generally associated with conservatives.

▶ Nat Hentoff, a writer and editor associated for many years with the liberal New York newspaper *The Village Voice*, held a pro-life position, which many readers of the *Voice* disagreed with.

Using unexpected testimony like this can be especially powerful in persuasive speeches. Why? Because your listeners will reason that someone willing to go against his peers has probably thought through his opinions carefully.

Quote Credible Peers or Laypeople

Often "regular people" who have firsthand knowledge about a subject provide good supporting information. These peer or lay sources may not know scientific facts and related theories, but they can tell you how it feels to be involved as a participant. What do lay people report about prisoners training puppies? For that, you need the prisoners' perspective:[20]

▶ "It's not all puppy, puppy, lovey, lovey. When I first got Ices [my dog] he did not want to get up. We didn't go for walks. We went for drags. It took a good 2 ½ months before he got the idea. I kept saying, 'Is it me? Am I doing something wrong?' this is the first puppy in my whole life. It was like we were being trained at the same time." [Caridad Kelly, convicted on cocaine, heroin, money laundering charges]

▶ "The more time you spend with them, the more you get to see their personalities. I guess it's like kids. Each one is different." [Jennifer Jaramillo, convicted on cocaine and heroin charges]

▶ "I like the satisfaction of seeing [my pup, Heather,] grow from a rowdy little puppy. She's already showing the signs of being a good guide dog." [Pat Johnson, convicted of Medicare fraud charges]

Each participant's perspective adds important details about the Puppies in Prison program.

Quote Sayings, Proverbs, and Words of Wisdom

Every culture provides a store of sayings, proverbs, phrases, and other words of wisdom that encapsulates culturally important ideas, beliefs, and values. Words of wisdom come from literary and oral traditions, from well-known and anonymous sources, from philosophical and political treatises. Here are a few examples:

▶ Love looks not with the eyes but with the mind. (literature)
▶ Examine what is said, not the one who speaks. (proverb)
▶ You shall know the truth, and the truth shall set you free. (religious text)
▶ The ignorance of one voter in a democracy impairs the security of all. (political speech)
▶ I know nothing except the fact of my ignorance. (philosophy)

Sayings do not always originate in well-known sources. You can quote your personal authority figures, as long as your audience respects the source. Farah Walters' speech illustrates this:

> My parents—and especially my father—taught me to draw an invisible line. He said to me, "Farah, you decide how you want other people to treat you, and if somebody crosses that line and it's unacceptable to you, just walk away from it. Don't let people treat you the way that they feel you should be treated. Have people treat you the way *you* feel you should be treated." That was good advice then. It is good advice now.[21]

Walters expects her audience to accept her father as a credible source of wisdom because this culture respects (although we sometimes reject) parental advice.

Religious writings also provide rich sources of material when the audience accepts the text as valid. The Pope, for example, uses the Bible and Catholic teachings in his speeches; by doing so he affirms the authoritative sources of his church. However, listeners who are not Christians, or Christians who are not Catholics, might question one or both of these sources.

To find usable sayings, proverbs, and wise words, go to **www.bartleby.com/100**. (The Diversity in Practice box on page 146 provides additional details about the importance of proverbs in some African cultures.)

DIVERSITY IN PRACTICE

PROVERBS IN A WEST AFRICAN CULTURE

AN ARTICLE ENTITLED, "YOUR MOTHER IS STILL YOUR MOTHER"[22] describes the importance of proverb usage among the Igbo people of Nigeria, where proverbs both contain and transmit cultural wisdom. Chinua Achebe, a famous Nigerian author, calls them the Igbo's "horse of conversation." Adults who are considered wise conversationalists invari-

ably use proverbs effectively, and every functioning adult in the village community learned to use them properly during childhood. Each competent user understands each proverb's meaning and discerns the situations in which a specific proverb fits.

You can find the full article on InfoTrac College Edition.

STOP AND CHECK

THINK CRITICALLY ABOUT QUOTING AUTHORITIES

Look back at the quotations from experts and laypeople relating to inmates training puppies in prison, and ask yourself these questions about each source cited.

1. *What is the person's expertise?* For example, what is Jacqueline Bankhead's or Tonya Hess's expertise? Is it relevant to the subject under discussion?
2. *Is the person recognized as an expert by others?* How could you determine the reputation of each woman?
3. *Is the layperson stating an opinion commonly held by others like him or her?* In other words, is it a typical or representative view? Is each prisoner's experience typical? Or is one or more of the situations extreme?
4. *Are the words taken out of context?* Because you don't have the entire article, you cannot assess the context for each person's words. However, whenever possible, ask if the words fairly represent the speaker's intended meaning. Words can be distorted so that the quoted person appears to hold a position not actually held.
5. *Is the quotation accurate?* One speaker said, "I was reminded of DeTocqueville, who wrote about [America] in the late eighteenth century, 'America is great because America is good, and when America ceases to be good, America will cease to be great.'[23]
   Although hundreds of speakers and writers have used this quotation, including Bill Clinton and Pat Buchanan, it is, unfortunately, nowhere to be found in any of DeTocqueville's writings—although he did say nice things about America.

To investigate quotations further, do an Internet search for the exact words "taken out of context," and read several of the Web pages to identify the effect of misleading quotations.

Use Statistics Carefully

People in U.S. society tend to like numbers. We begin measuring and counting in pre-school. We study opinion polls and statistical research. Numbers and measurements are typically thought to be hard facts that are credible and trustworthy. Consequently, using numerical support well may increase your credibility and cause you to appear more competent and knowledgeable. Numerical information commonly helps us understand the extent of an issue or predict the probability of some future happening.

Although numerical data can be useful, it has unique drawbacks. In general, statistics are short on emotional appeal because they don't involve listeners' feelings, and too many in a speech may bore your audience. In fact, better speakers typically balance statistics with examples in order to both clarify and personalize a topic. Furthermore, numerical information is often misleading, and if you present biased information, your listeners may distrust you. So take extra care to use enumeration and statistics both accurately and sparingly.

Provide a Count

Enumeration means counting. A count helps your listeners understand the extent of a problem or issue: the number of people injured in accidents annually, those diagnosed with a particular disease, the number of older child adoptions, and so on. Two tips will help you use enumeration more effectively.

1. *Round your numbers up or down.* There are two good reasons for doing this. First, listeners find it hard to remember exact numbers. In addition, numbers related to current topics can change rapidly. By the time they're published, they're probably outdated. Consequently, instead of hearing that "New Yorkers spend 16 hours, 43 minutes, and 38 seconds online weekly compared to Clevelander's 11 hours, 57 minutes, 16 minutes," an audience would better understand, "New Yorkers spend more than 16.7 hours online weekly compared to about 12 hours for Clevelanders."[24]

2. *Make numbers come alive by comparing them to something already in your listeners' experience.* Let's take hot dogs. In 2000, baseball stadiums sold about 26.5 million hot dogs during the season, but just how many *is* that? If you were to lay that many hot dogs end-to-end, they'd stretch from Dodger Stadium in Los Angeles to the Baseball Hall of Fame in Cooperstown, New York.[25]

A reporter on *The Early Show* (CBS) used specific details to explain the amount of information available on Google's database:

> Within two seconds, the search engine Google provides you with enough information that, if it were printed out, would create a stack of paper 140 miles high.[26]

enumeration a count

Courtesy Deirdre Steinberg

Presenting numerical information creatively helps audiences understand it better. Instead of simply stating the number of victims in a natural disaster, Elizabeth Winslea, Portland State University campus pastor, poured water from a pitcher—nine quarts' worth. Each drop of water represented a life lost.

These specific, meaningful details helped clarify her numbers.

Unfortunately, numerical information can be misleading, as almost every political campaign demonstrates. For example, one unsuccessful candidate for the presidency said insurance companies make $600 billion a year that ought to go into health care. However, **www.factcheck.org** (September 10, 2007) reported that people paid about $694.4 billion on premiums, *but* $596.7 went back to them in benefits. Of the $97.7 difference, profits would come after administrative costs, taxes, marketing, sales and so on were taken out. Clearly, the candidate exaggerated the numbers.

Choose Statistics with a Critical Eye

The statistics most commonly used in speeches include means, medians, modes, percentages, and ratios.

Mean

The **mean** is the *average* of a group of numbers. To calculate the mean, add up the individual measurements and divide by the total number of units measured. Here are some examples:

▶ Mean age in 2000 for a Massachusetts woman having her first child was 27.8 (up from 22.5 in 1970); for a woman in Utah it was 23.3 (up from 21.4 in 1970).[27]

▶ Average cost of a private college (2007–2008) was $23,712 (up 6.3%); average cost of a public two-year college was $2,361 (up 4.2%).[28]

▶ Mean number of hours of television viewing per week is 19 (U.S.), 13.3 (India), and 11.6 (Mexico); mean number of hours spent reading is 5.7 (U.S.), 10.7 (India), and 5.5 (Mexico).[29]

The mean is skewed when extreme figures at either end of the range make the comparison less useful. Just average the annual incomes of nine people who work for minimum wage and one billionaire to understand the limitations of the mean.

Median

The **median** is the middle number in a set of numbers that have been arranged into a ranked order: half the numbers are above and half below. For example, home prices in a particular area are typically stated as a median, which balances the very expensive mansions against the less expensive fixer-uppers.

Mode

The **mode** is the number that appears most commonly. For instance, on some college campuses, a few first-year students may be 16 years old, more are 17, some are in their twenties, thirties, or forties, but most are 18—the mode. A few nurses in one hospital might earn $30 an hour; a few might earn only $18; but the mode for nurses' pay in that particular hospital is $23 per hour.

Percentages

Percentages show the relationship of a part to the whole; the whole is represented by the number 100. Public speakers might use this type of information about credit card debt:[30]

▶ About 48% of credit card holders owed less than $1,000.

▶ About 10% of cardholders had total card balances in excess of $10,000.

▶ More than half of all people with credit cards use less than 30% of their total credit card limit.

mean average of a group of numbers

median middle number in a set of numbers arranged in a ranked order

mode most frequently occurring number

percentage figure that shows the relationship of the part to the whole, which is represented by the number 100

rate of increase or decrease percentage that uses an earlier baseline figure to compare growth or decline

Often you'll find percentages stated as **rates of increase or decrease**, which compare growth or decline during a specific period of time to a baseline figure from an earlier period. Treat these rates cautiously, for unless you know the baseline number, the rate of increase or decrease is almost meaningless. Think of it this way: A company that employs two people in the year 2008 and adds an additional employee in 2000 increases its hiring at a rate of 50 percent. However, a company that employs 100 people in 2008 and adds one additional employee in 2009 increases hiring by 1 percent. The actual number of additional employees hired for the two companies is the same, but the rates of increase are dramatically different. The reverse is also true: The two-person company that loses one employee decreases by half or 50 percent; there's barely a blip when the larger company loses one worker. As you can see, when baseline numbers are initially very low, the rate of increase is potentially astounding.

Ratios

Relationships between numbers are often shown as a **ratio**, instead of a percentage because 10% and 1 in 10 are interchangeable, as are 25% and 1 in 4. Ratios are especially helpful when the percentage is very small; for example, .000001 percent equals 1 case in 100,000. You can see that it's more effective to say, "18 out of 100,000 teens died of gunshot injuries in 1989, up from the 12 per 100,000 recorded in 1979," than to say "eighteen-hundred-thousandth of one percent of teens. . . ."[31]

Use Visual Aids to Clarify Numerical Data

Because numerical data are sometimes complex, present them in visual form whenever you can. Elizabeth Winslea, shown in the photograph on page 147, used drops of water to illustrate her point. Figure 8.1 shows the value of a table to help your audience visualize complex numbers. Imagine trying to understand a speaker who simply says:

> Child care workers are underpaid. Men who graduate from college average more than $59,400 annually; female graduates average about $44,700. Men who have some college earn an average of $39,000 versus women in the same category, who average $28,800. Even men with a high school diploma average $33,500, and women who have graduated from high school earn on the average $25,400. Compare all these salaries to the median of $17,600 that child care workers earn.[32]

ratio relationship shown by numbers, such as 1 in 10

Comparative Salaries of Child Care Workers

	Average for all men	Average for all women
College graduates	$51,804	$33,615
Some college	$33,161	$22,445
High school diploma	$27,865	$19,309
Highest paid child care worker	$15,488	

Figure 8.1
Tables
A table, such as this one presenting salary information, effectively depicts complex numerical data in a format that listeners can easily grasp.

Is your head spinning? Do you remember any of this data? Now, imagine that the speaker either gives you a handout or projects a transparency with Figure 8.1 on it. How is your response different? In what ways does the visual help you grasp the material more easily?

You can see that different types of data call for different types of visual aids. The Practically Speaking feature in this chapter points out that visuals are essential in speeches that engineers give on technical topics. Because visual aids are vital in American culture, this text devotes Chapter 13 to the topic of creating and displaying visual materials.

STOP AND CHECK

CRITICALLY ANALYZE NUMERICAL DATA

Because numbers are easy to manipulate, evaluate them carefully with these questions before you use them.

1. *What is the source of the numbers?* Does the source have an interest such as a possibility of financial gain that would make high or low numbers more desirable?
2. *Are the numbers up to date?* Using a count or a percentage that is old is generally not applicable to current conditions.
3. *Before you use startling rates of increase, look at the baseline figures of the percentages.* Note any other relevant factors that might affect this rate. For example, one source said the rate of U.S. children and teens killed by gunfire is 120 percent higher than in the other twenty-five industrialized countries combined. (Any deaths are lamentable, but what if the other countries only have 10 such deaths? What if they have 20,000?)[33]
4. *Be careful of combined statistics.* The same source said that males experience violent crime at rates 28 percent greater than females; however, females are raped and sexually assaulted at 7.5 times the rate of males. Why do you think the authors reported the figure relating to males as a percentage but the figure relating to females as a multiple? What is 7.5 when stated as a percentage?

Find Compelling Comparisons

A **comparison** or **analogy** points out similarities between things. We understand new information or unfamiliar ideas better when we find points of comparison to something that's already in our experience. Comparisons can be literal or figurative.

Use Literal Analogies

comparison or **analogy** stating similarities between two things

literal analogies comparisons between two actual things that are alike in important ways

Literal analogies compare actual things that are similar in important ways. For example, a Pakistani speaker, Liaquat Ali Khan,[34] explained to the U.S. Senate the similarities between his country's founding and the founding of the United States:

Pakistan was founded so that millions of Muslims should be enabled to live according to their opinions and to worship God in freedom. . . . Like some of the earlier founders of your great country, these Muslims, though not Pilgrims, nevertheless embarked upon an undertaking, which, in aim and achievement, represented the triumph of an idea. That idea was the idea of liberty, which has had its ardent followers in all climates and all countries. When our time came, its call summoned us, too, and we could not hold back.

By showing the similarities and by linking both countries in their shared values, Khan helped his listeners understand why Muslims broke away from India's majority Hindu population to create Pakistan.

Sometimes pointing out *differences*, or showing **contrasts** between a new concept and a more familiar one, is a good strategy. For example, Andres explained lacrosse by contrasting it with the more familiar games of baseball and football. You can read the text of his speech in Appendix C.

Create Vivid Figurative Analogies

When you highlight similarities between otherwise *dissimilar* things, you're using **figurative analogies**. These analogies require your listeners to apply their imagination and integrate likenesses between two otherwise different things or ideas. In a convocation speech at Queens College in North Carolina, a music professor compared personalities to various melodies:

> . . . each of us has a unique melody. . . . Some of you are quiet, soft, and lyrical. Others are rhythmic and energetic. Some are majestic and somber. Yet others may be whimsical and funny. Still others are cool and mellow. And truthfully, some of you are like the new styles of music, you are just way out there. Regardless, your melody is your own sound, your own style, your essence, your identity.[35]

In short, figurative analogies connect familiar images with those less known. Many of the students in the audience could identify characteristics of musical genres—hip-hop, soft rock, jazz, heavy metal—that resemble different people.

contrasts stating differences between two things

figurative analogies stated similarities between two otherwise dissimilar things; requires an imaginative connection

---

✓ STOP AND CHECK

THINK CRITICALLY ABOUT ANALOGIES

Evaluate your use of comparisons and contrasts. To test literal analogies, make sure the two items are alike in essential details. For instance, you could mislead your audience by comparing the work of a police officer in Houston, Texas, with one in Sioux Falls, South Dakota. Although their duties are alike in many ways, they have significant differences. Comparing the Houston officer to one in Los Angeles or Miami is more appropriate because all three operate in large metropolitan settings with diverse populations. Sioux Falls officers, on the other hand, have more in common with police officers in smaller cities in Michigan or Washington state.

To test figurative analogies, be sure the comparison is clear and makes sense. Can your listeners make the necessary connection of ideas?

To learn more about both literal and figurative analogies, log on to InfoTrac College Edition and do a subject search for "analogies."

PRACTICALLY SPEAKING

ENGINEERS AND EVIDENCE

Devan Marchbanks

Good communication skills are vital in engineering, because the majority of an engineer's workday is spent writing or speaking. An Engineering Curriculum Task Force identified "effectiveness in communicating ideas" as second in importance to problem recognition and solution skills and above math, science, and technical skills in importance in the career. Good communication is linked to good performance ratings and to career advancement.[36]

Engineers typically speak to two types of audience: technical (such as other engineers and scientists) and nontechnical (such as project managers, public relations personnel, customers, and government regulators).[37]

Let's say a team has designed a handheld device that could tell a blind person what denomination of bill he'd just received in change from a store clerk. The team would present different evidence to different audiences. Engineering audiences respond to numerical evidence and calculations, so using numbers with them is key. They are also visually sophisticated. Show them a visual of the product and they "get it."[38] One engineering professor advised his students, "If you're running out of time the last thing you should give up is the visual—cut other things because having the visual there will make it or break it."[39]

On the other hand, a nontechnical audience might respond better to other types of evidence. Marketers could better develop sales strategies if they knew the number of legally blind people who need a product that would tell them whether they're holding a $20 bill or a $1 bill. And customers would more likely respond to examples of a legally blind person who was ripped off at a garage sale because he was unable to count his change.

Question for Discussion:

▶ Identify an occupation that interests you and then list two or three audiences that someone in that occupation might address. What types of evidence would work best with each audience?

Summary

It is vital to support your ideas with evidence that listeners can understand so they can see reasons for your major ideas. Select facts including definitions and descriptions that you can verify in a number of sources. In addition, select up-to-date facts and take care to not pass on distorted or incorrect information.

Almost all listeners respond to examples, and using specific incidents as supporting material helps make abstract concepts more concrete and relevant. Whether real or hypothetical, brief or extended, illustrations also help listeners identify emotionally with your topic. To be effective, examples should be representative, sufficient in number, and plausible.

Visual evidence in the form of pictures, images or symbols can help your audience "see reasons," which can lead to increased understandings and engaged emotions and can provide a motivation for behaviors.

The use of quotations or testimony can enhance your credibility if you are not considered an expert on the topic. Directly quote or paraphrase the opinions of experts and lay or peer sources. In addition, quote cultural proverbs, written texts, and even words of wisdom from relatively unknown sources that your audience will accept as credible.

In a society that tends to place value on quantification, the judicious use of enumeration and statistics can increase your audience's acceptance of your ideas. However, be sure that your numerical support is understandable, up to date, and used in ways that do not create misleading impressions. Visual aids are often helpful in clarifying complex numerical data.

Finally, comparisons or analogies are an additional means of support. Literal analogies compare or contrast two actual things; figurative analogies compare two things that are generally considered different but share one likeness. Both types add vividness to your speeches.

As you interweave facts, examples, numbers, visuals, testimony, and analogies, you give your listeners more reasons to accept the conclusions you present.

STUDY AND REVIEW

Your online resources for *Public Speaking: Concepts and Skills for a Diverse Society* offer a broad range of study tools that will help you better understand the material in this chapter, complete assignments, and succeed on tests. Your online resources feature

- Speech videos with critical viewing questions, speech outlines, and transcripts
- Interactive versions of this chapter's Stop and Check activities and Application and Critical Thinking Exercises
- Speech Builder Express and InfoTrac College Edition
- Weblinks related to chapter content
- Study and review tools such as self-quizzes, an interactive glossary, and downloadable audio summaries

You can access your online resources at **http://www.cengage.com/login**, using the access code that came with your book or that you bought online at **http://www.iChapters.com**.

KEY TERMS

The terms below are defined in the margins throughout this chapter.

comparison or analogy 150
contrasts 151
empirical facts 136
enumeration 147
established facts 136
figurative analogies 151
hypothetical example 139
literal analogies 150

literal image 142
mean 148
median 148
metaphorical image 142
mode 148
percentage 148
rate of increase or decrease 148
ratio 149

APPLICATION AND CRITICAL THINKING EXERCISES

1. What do you personally believe about global warming? Why? What actual research have you done on the subject? What kind of information would you trust on an issue such as this? When you find conflicting data on a topic, how do you judge which makes more

sense? How would you go about forming a reasoned opinion on this topic? Does it matter if you do? Why or why not?

2. Construct a hypothetical example that would be appropriate in your next speech. Come to class prepared to share your example and explain why you chose the details you included in it.

3. Make a list of topics that almost require visual evidence. (Examples: purchasing a diamond or *feng shui*.) Discuss your list with a group of your classmates and explain why a visual would be so essential.

4. Discuss with your classmates the criteria that determine whether or not someone is an expert on a particular topic. Can students be experts on their speech subjects? How can they communicate their expertise to their classmates?

5. Stalin is alleged to have said, "A million deaths is a statistic; a single death is a tragedy." Examples are the primary tool for eliciting emotional identification with the story. They add drama, emotion, and vividness to any topic. Statistics appeal to the mind; examples appeal to the heart. Be prepared to discuss the differences and how to use each in speeches.

6. Bring to class a current edition of a newsmagazine or newspaper. With your classmates, choose a topic from the week's news. Collect and display information by dividing the board into five sections, one for each kind of evidence: facts, examples, quotations, numerical data, and analogies. Contribute information from your magazine or paper, cooperating with your classmates to fill the board. Evaluate the evidence using the tests presented in this chapter.

7. Go to the online edition of *Time* Magazine (**www.time.com**) or *U.S. News & World Report* (**www.usnews.com**). Read the cover story and find examples of a fact, expert and peer testimony, a statistic, and an analogy.

8. With a small group of your classmates, evaluate the effectiveness of the following pieces of evidence taken from student speeches. What kind(s) of evidence does each excerpt represent? Is the evidence specific or vague? Does the speaker cite the source of the evidence adequately? Does it meet the tests for the type of evidence it represents?

   ▶ According to the *Natural History of Whales and Dolphins,* dolphins communicate through a system of whistles, clicks, rattles, and squeaks. These clicking sounds are not only used for navigation in the deep waters but they may also be used to convey messages. Pulsed squeaks can indicate distress, while buzzing clicks may indicate aggression.

   ▶ As far as deaths from killer bees are concerned, Mexican officials report that only sixteen people have died in the last three years as a result of their stings. That number is similar to the number who die of shark bite. As one Texan put it, "The killer bee will be no more a threat to us than the rattlesnake."

   ▶ According to New Jersey congressman Frank Guarini, "American families play amusement ride roulette every time they go on an outing to an amusement park."

   ▶ As reported by the *World Press Review Magazine,* the Japanese use of disposable chopsticks has resulted in the destruction of half of the hardwood forests in the Philippines and one-third of the forests in Indonesia. This trend will likely continue as long as the Japanese use twelve billion pairs of throwaway chopsticks a year, which is enough wood to build 12,000 average-sized family homes.

   ▶ Fetal brain cells were implanted deep into the brain of a 52-year-old Parkinson's victim. Traditional treatments all failed this person. Later, he reported that his voice is much stronger, his mind is sharper and not confused, and he can walk without cane or crutches.

SPEECH VIDEO

Go to your online resources to watch and critique Carrie Weichbrodt's use of supporting materials in her classroom speech. Identify the types of support she uses. Then, using the tests in the text, evaluate the effectiveness of her support. (Your online resources also include the transcript and outline of the speech.)

Student Speech with Questions

NEEDED: A GRIEF SUPPORT SYSTEM ON CAMPUS
Carrie Weichbrodt

Mike McNamara/Cengage Learning

The phone rings. You answer it, and suddenly the world stops. You have just become one of the thousands of college students experiencing the grief of losing a loved one.

On September 13th, 2006, my life changed forever when it was my phone that rang. My dad was gone. I was 18.

As a student and Resident Assistant, I know many other people on our campus who are grieving. Somehow we find each other.

To deal with my grief, I went to the Health and Counseling Center and asked for a grief specialist. There were no resources for me. I got a doctoral student in psychology who told me I was fine.

Freud did not believe that normal bereavement is a pathological disturbance requiring professional intervention. In his 1917 essay "Mourning and Melancholia," he argued that mourning is our reaction to a loss, but we eventually form new attachments and move on without professional help. But I believe he was wrong, and today, I will prove it. I will show that there is a significant and compelling need for grief specialists in the campus Health and Counseling Center. Then I'll outline a plan that will solve this problem.

How extensive is the problem? The number of undergraduates dealing with grief is substantial. In a Spring 2008 article in the journal *New Directions for Student Services*, David Balk, the leading researcher in the field of college student bereavement, asserts that at any given time, 20–30 percent of college undergraduates are in the first twelve months of grieving the death of a family member or friend. The National Students of Ailing Mothers and Fathers (AMF) Support Network, initiated at Georgetown University, says that between 35 and 48 percent of college students are dealing with a death that occurred within the previous two years. Counselors at Kansas State University, Oklahoma State University, City University of New York, and the University of Arizona estimate that grief is a defining issue in the lives of no fewer than 50 percent of the students on their respective campuses.

What impact did her opening story have on you?

Obviously, her personal experience gives her credibility. How else does she establish credibility on the topic?

She relies mainly on statistics in the first point where she establishes the problem. Would you advise her to add examples? Why or why not?

One reason is the mortality rates on college campuses. The numbers are somewhat difficult to assess, but 5,000 to 18,750 students nationwide die annually. That's about 4 to 15 per 10,000. Most deaths are vehicle accidents. Our own small campus has had two traffic fatalities, plus one drowning in recent years. And last year, a popular professor died of cancer. In addition, many students have parents or other close relatives and friends who are struggling against terminal illnesses.

In an often-cited article, "College Student Loss and Response, Coping with Death on Campus," Louis E. LaGrand, professor of health science at the State University of Arts and Science, Potsdam, New York, argues that colleges and student communities too often dismiss the serious and continuing impact of unresolved grief among young adults.

My goal today is not to depress you with staggering statistics, but to assure you that there *is* a need that we should address. Irreparable loss can devastate any young adult.

Now that we know some of the numbers, let's look at five areas affected by grief: physical, behavioral, interpersonal, cognitive, and spiritual.

Physical effects include insomnia and exhaustion. Insomnia is especially significant during the first twenty-four months of bereavement. That's the first two years! Grieving students also suffer from exhaustion as a result of the emotional struggle they are going through.

There are *behavioral* effects as well. Students struggle to stay organized, manage their time, and meet deadlines. They lose their typical patterns of conduct as they try to absorb the loss of the loved one.

Interpersonal effects result when friends dismiss the intensity and duration of the grief cycle and begin to shun the griever. Let's face it, ongoing grief is uncomfortable to be around.

There are also *cognitive* effects. Grieving students have problems concentrating, studying, and remembering what they've studied, which has obvious effects on grades and test taking. They typically experience a drop in test scores in the first six months of bereavement, and a timely response by institutions is warranted.

Finally, there are *spiritual* effects. Bereaved students ask "why?" and begin to question their assumptions about reality, fairness, and goodness.

Now that we understand the extent of the problem and its effect on students, let's discuss what can be done.

First, I propose that the university hire a bereavement specialist who would work with campus personnel to design a program for educating professors, Residence Life personnel, and Resident Assistants in ways they can assist grieving students. This would include annual professional workshops on grief and grieving.

Second, many students feel more comfortable expressing their grief in an informal environment with someone who has had a similar experience. The bereavement specialist would recruit students who have skillfully walked through grief to be peer counselors; these students can further process their own experience when they mentor fellow students.

There is a model for this. Georgetown University is the home of the National Students of Ailing Mothers and Fathers (AMF) Support Network. It was started by David Fajgenbaum, whose phone call came July 17, 2003. His mother had stage four brain cancer, and she died while he was still a student. The group's name Ailing Mothers and Fathers (AMF) includes his mother's (Anne Marie Fajgenbaum) initials: A.M.F. The group's Web site says its mission is to support all grieving college students, to empower them to fight back against terminal illnesses, and to raise awareness about the needs of grieving college students.

Our university's Health and Counseling Center's Web page states its goal as, "Helping students stay healthy so they may achieve the highest personal growth and intellectual success." Providing effective resources for grieving students, allows these students to achieve their highest personal growth and intellectual success. David Balk says:

> Rather than deciding that bereaved college students are on their own and merely wish them good luck, we should make the effort to determine whether appropriate institu-

Her second point presents mostly factual information. Would you advise her to add other supporting evidence? If so, which type(s) and why?

Does she give enough information about her sources for you to consider them credible? Why or why not?

tional responses can be put in place to help students get beyond a life event that can obstruct their best academic performance and may ultimately affect a school's retention and graduation rates.

So we have the opportunity to make a difference in the lives of hundreds of students on our campus. This number may be as high as 720 undergraduates each year. Creating a grief support program would further the university's commitment to holistic health for all students.

Today we've seen there is a significant need and that grief affects a student's ability to be a competent scholar. However, specialists can make a difference, and it's been done before.

I hope that none of you get that devastating, life-changing phone call during your college career. But I hope that if you do, a program will be in place to help you work through the grief that inevitably follows.

Overall, what were the strongest areas of this speech? What might she improve and how?

Sources

National Students of AMF. (n.d.) AMF mission statement. Retrieved March 12, 2008, from **www .studentsofamf.org/**

Balk, D. (2008, Spring). Grieving: 22 to 30 percent of all college students. *New Directions for Student Services, 121,* 5–14. Retrieved March 12, 2008, from Academic Search Premier database.

Balk, D. (2001). College student bereavement, scholarship and the university: a call for university engagement. *Death Studies, 25,* 67–84. Retrieved March 12, 2008, from Academic Search Premier database.

Berson, R. (1988). A bereavement group for college students. *Journal of American College Health, 37.*

Cusick, A. (2007). Death response plans in universities: a structural approach. Unpublished Manuscript.

Floerschinger, D. (1991). Bereavement in late adolescence: interventions on college campuses. *Journal of Adolescent Research, 6.*

Freud, S. (1957). Mourning and melancholia. *The complete psychological works of Sigmund Freud, Vol. 14.* London: Hogarth Press.

McGowan, K. (2008, March 7). OPTIMISM: Make the road by walking. Retrieved March 12, 2008, from **www .studentsofamf.org/National_Students_of_AMF_featured_in_Psychology_Today_Magazine!-nid-39.html**

LaGrand, L. (1986). College student loss and response: coping with death on campus. *New Directions for Student Services, No. 31.* San Francisco: Jossey-Bass.

ORGANIZING YOUR SPEECH

THIS CHAPTER WILL HELP YOU

▶ Organize your main points

▶ Identify and use a number of linear patterns, including chronological, spatial, causal, problem-solution, pro-con, and topical

▶ Identify and use alternative patterns—including the wave, the spiral, and the star—when they are appropriate

© Tim Timmerman

BY NOW, you have chosen and carefully focused your topic. You've done research and found a variety of supporting evidence. Now you must sort through it all and make an understandable speech—one that hangs together with distinct main points that have some sort of logical connection. Good speakers find ways to organize their material and present their ideas in *patterns* that audiences can follow and remember. Otherwise, they frustrate their listeners, as Heidi and Gail point out:

> If an audience is confused or overwhelmed with disarrayed information, not only is the speech difficult to understand but the whole underlying credibility of the rhetor is diminished. HEIDI

> Organization is everything. . . . I consider it being kind to your audience as well as yourself. GAIL

Guidelines for organization fall into what the Romans called the *canon of disposition*. (See Chapter 2.) This chapter begins with general tips for identifying and organizing main points, moves on to explain some linear organizational patterns, and concludes with alternative methods of arranging the body of your speech.

Organize Your Main Points

Although the *body* is the middle part of your speech, you should plan it before you plan the introduction. Throughout your research, you probably have identified several sub-categories of information such as the sequence in which events occurred, causes of a problem, or proposed solutions. Identifying these patterns can help you organize your major points and the supporting materials under each one. Here are a few general organizational tips.

Limit the Number of Points

Cognitive psychologists say we learn better when we portion blocks of information into three to seven major units (which explains why your telephone number is divided into three- and four-digit segments).[1] Consequently, listeners will remember your speech better if you develop a limited number of main points—generally, three to five.

At this point in your preparation, return to the thesis statement you developed in Chapter 5. There you clearly identified the goal and direction of your speech; now you can start fleshing it out. For instance, Maria wants to convince her classmates that lottery winners are often unhappy, and people who want to be wealthy should spend their money elsewhere. So she initially sets out this thesis:

> The lottery is a form of gambling that should be avoided because it often leads to unhappiness.

During her research, she decides that she can cluster her material into three major points: (1) the history of lotteries, (2) the problems that winners encounter, and (3) alternatives to buying lottery tickets. She then revises her thesis statement to read like this:

> Although lotteries have a long history, participants can avoid the financial and personal problems that often accompany lottery winnings by finding alternatives to this form of gambling.

Her major points are now easy to identify:

> I. Lotteries are a form of gambling that have a long history.
> II. Lottery winners often have financial and personal problems as a result of winning.
> III. Most people would be happier if they found an alternative to playing the lottery.

She can now refine the preview of her major points:

> The lottery is a form of gambling that raises money for good causes; however, winning often creates financial and personal problems for winners, who would be better off spending their money elsewhere.

Support Each Point with Evidence

Chapter 8 describes numerous ways to support the major ideas of a speech, among them facts, examples, quotations, numerical information, and analogies. At this stage, Maria sits down with her articles about lottery winners and arranges specific pieces of data under each main point. Here's an example of her first major point:

> I. Lotteries are a form of gambling that raise money for good causes.
>   A. *Webster's Dictionary* identifies the lottery as a popular form of gambling.
>   1. Winners pay to participate, generally by purchasing tickets at a uniform price.
>   2. Winners are determined by chance.

  B. Lotteries generate revenues for good causes.
   1. The earliest lottery, organized in London in 1680, raised money for a municipal water supply.
   2. A French lottery helped pay for the Statue of Liberty.
   3. Early lotteries helped support the Jamestown colony and the American Revolution.
   4. They provided funds for Harvard, Princeton, and Dartmouth colleges.
   5. Current lotteries in New Hampshire and Oregon, among other states, provide educational funding.

(Maria's entire outline can be found at the end of the chapter and on your online resources, where you can also watch a video of the speech being delivered.)

Order Your Points Effectively

For some topics, the ordering of points flows logically. Obviously, explaining lotteries in general before moving to the problems that winners encounter and suggesting alternatives is more logically satisfying than if Maria were to suggest alternatives, discuss the problems, then explain what lotteries are. For other speeches, the natural flow is less obvious. A topic such as recreational opportunities available in your state might have the following organization:

  I. Bungee jumping
  II. Hang gliding
  III. Hot air ballooning
  IV. Windsurfing

No logical reason dictates that bungee jumping should come first and windsurfing last. In fact, the speaker might start with windsurfing, which happens on a river, and then describe the airborne sports. Or he might move from the least expensive to the most costly, depending on the audience. If these sports are centered in specific places, he could move from the nearest to the most distant options.

With these principles in mind, we now turn to a number of common organizational patterns.

Traditional Patterns

From listening to speakers throughout the years, you have internalized some schema for organizational patterns. Some patterns work especially well for presenting facts and information; others are better for persuasive messages; additional persuasive patterns will be covered in Chapter 17. Here, we look at six common patterns that are useful for a wide variety of topics: chronological, spatial, causal, problem-solution, pro-con, and topical.

Chronological Organization

In a **chronological pattern**, the sequencing—what comes first and what follows—must occur in a given order. This pattern is useful for biographical and historical speeches and for those that explain processes, stages, or cycles. It stands to reason that biographical speeches are often developed chronologically, because an individual's life unfolds across a period of years. Here is a sketch of the main points of a speech about a person's life:

Gustave Eiffel never intended to become an engineer.
  I. He planned to work in his uncle's vinegar factory, but there was a family falling out.
  II. He gained engineering skills in an entry-level job in a bridge building factory.

chronological pattern presents points in a sequential or time order

III. He began his own company and gained a good reputation.
IV. He got a major contract for the Statue of Liberty.
V. The Eiffel Tower is his crowning achievement.

Chronological organizational patterns also function effectively for describing historical happenings:

Horse racing, one of the most widely attended spectator sports in the United States, has a long history.
I. The ancients, including Greeks and Romans, raced horses.
II. In the twelfth century, returning Crusaders brought swift Arabian horses to Europe.
III. Racing became a professional English sport during Queen Anne's reign (1702–1714).
IV. British settlers brought thoroughbreds to America, where a racetrack was built in 1665.
V. Today there are 119 race tracks in 33 states.

Process speeches generally feature a chronological pattern, in which several steps or stages follow one another in fairly predictable sequences. You can speak about natural as well as social processes. This outline shows the chronological organization of a natural process:

Tsunamis are enormous waves that have destructive potential.
I. They are triggered by landslides, volcanic actions, or, most commonly, undersea earthquakes.
II. The trigger generates enormous waves that can move at speeds of 500 miles per hour.
III. As they approach land, the waves slow down and become higher.
IV. They hit land in an enormous wall of water.[2]

Many social, psychological, or personal processes also occur in patterned sequences or cycles. Norma summarized Professor Steve Duck's "theory of relational dissolution" in this brief outline:

Four phases are typical when a relationship dissolves.
I. Intrapsychic phase: one or both partners ponder what to do about the relationship.
II. Dyadic phase: they discuss the possibility of breaking up.
III. Social phase: they tell other people about their breakup.
IV. Grave-dressing phase: they rationalize the breakup.

The key with chronological speeches is that events *must* occur in a sequence and follow a clear "first, next, finally" pattern. Occasionally, however, speakers vary the pattern by beginning with the final point before showing the events that led up to it. For instance, the speaker could first describe a divorced person rationalizing the divorce ("grave-dressing phase"), then flash back and provide details about the first three phases.

Spatial Organization

A less common way to organize points is spatially—by location or place. The **spatial pattern** is useful for speeches about places or things made up of several parts. For example, a campus guide leading a tour of the library usually provides a map and describes what is located on each floor. Beginning on the ground floor, she works her way up to higher floors. The order in which you present your points doesn't matter

Sue O'Donnell

The chronological pattern is useful for biographical topics (such as Gustave Eiffel's life) and for processes that can be described in stages or cycles (such as the various stages of constructing the Eiffel Tower).

process speech describes a sequence of steps or stages that follow one another in a fairly predictable pattern

spatial pattern presents points by place or location

with some topics, as this speech outline (with points describing geographic regions) demonstrates:

> The Pacific islands, more than 25,000 in all, are divided into three groups.
>   I. Melanesia, lying north and east of Australia, includes New Guinea and Fiji and is named for the amount of melanin in its native population.
> II. Micronesia, scattered across a vast territory north of Melanesia, is named for the tiny islands that comprise it.
> III. Polynesia, extending from New Zealand to Easter Island to Hawaii, is named for the many islands in its territory.

Objects described from top to bottom, bottom to top, or side to side are suitable for this pattern. For example, a brick pathway in a garden is constructed in four layers: gravel, heavy-duty weed-barrier fabric, sand, and bricks. A speech on the effects of alcohol on the human body could move from the brain down to the heart and other organs. Similarly, an exercise instructor might begin at the top with the head and neck and then work his or her way down the body spatially.

DIVERSITY IN PRACTICE
SOME AFRICAN ORGANIZATIONAL PATTERNS

IN MANY AREAS OF THE WORLD, speakers choose patterns markedly different from those presented in this text. Two such examples come from Africa.

Madagascar

Elders in the Merina tribe use a four-part organizational pattern when they speak:[3]

1. First is a period of excuses in which the speaker expresses his humility and reluctance to speak. He uses standard phrases such as "I am a child, a younger brother." He sometimes relates well-known stories and proverbs.
2. He follows this by thanking the authorities for letting him speak at all. He uses a formula that thanks God, the president of the republic, government ministers, the village headman, major elders, and finally the people in the audience.
3. In the third section, he uses proverbs, illustrations, and short poems as he makes his proposal.
4. He closes by thanking and blessing his listeners.

Kenya

The body of the speech is not necessarily linear. In fact, a circular pattern, somewhat like a bicycle wheel, is more typical. The hub or center of the wheel is the single main point that ties the entire speech together. The speaker then wanders out repeatedly from the central point, telling stories and providing other supporting materials and stories that tie back to the main idea. To an outsider, the speech might seem boring or illogical, but Kenyan listeners are able to follow the logic that ties the points together.[4]

Causal Organization

Because Euro-American thought patterns emphasize causes and effects, we typically look for reasons behind events. Consequently, **cause-effect patterns** are useful for organizing speeches on problems. First, examine both the reasons underlying the problem (the causes) and then the implications of the problem for individuals or for society

cause-effect pattern presents reasons (causes) and implications (effects) of a topic at large (the effects). There are two basic causal patterns: cause to effect and effect to cause. Here is a cause-to-effect outline for a speech on amusement park tragedies:

Amusement park tragedies injure thousands of people annually.
I. Tragedies have three major causes.
   A. Equipment sometimes fails.
   B. Operators make mistakes.
   C. Riders' behaviors cause accidents.
II. The effects are both personal and corporate.
   A. Riders suffer death or dismemberment.
   B. The industry becomes defensive and stonewalls the problem.

For some topics, you might decide it is more effective to examine the problem's effects on an individual or group before you explore its causes. This is an effects-to-cause organization pattern.

As many as 2 million Americans are addicted to gambling, and another 408 million are problem gamblers.
I. Effects include the gamblers themselves, their families, their employers, and their community.
   A. The person may lose his job, go into great debt, or even commit suicide.
   B. Families get less time, lose their savings, and sometimes lose their mortgages.
   C. Employers lose when employees are undependable.
   D. Gamblers sometimes commit crimes or resort to insurance-related fraud.
II. There are several causes of gambling addiction.
   A. Legalization of gambling has led to more gambling and to pathological gambling.
   B. There are inadequate treatment programs.
   B. The government is addicted to gambling revenues.

Problem-Solution Organization

In line with our core cultural beliefs that life presents many challenges we can solve through knowledge and effort, we often approach global, national, local, and personal issues as problems that require solutions. (In contrast, some cultures believe it is futile to fight fate.) Thus, you may find that your material lends itself to a **problem-solution pattern**. Not surprisingly, this pattern requires that you first look at the problem—sometimes examining its causes and effects—and then you propose solutions. Here is an outline for a persuasive speech on the global problem of blood diamonds:

Blood diamonds, or conflict diamonds, are mined in war zones in Africa.
I. Diamonds are mined to finance civil wars.
   A. The nations where they are mined have corrupt governments that oppress the people.
   B. The diamond trade helps fund rebel groups.
   C. Innocent people are maimed and killed by diamond traders.
II. The solutions are international and personal.
   A. The UN mandated the Kimberley Process, which certifies diamonds that are from free sources.
   B. We can refuse to buy any diamonds that are not certified.

Some speakers present problem-solution approaches to personal as well as national or global topics. This outline shows the major points in a speech about a personal issue:

Hair loss affects millions of people.
I. Women as well as men experience hair loss.
   A. Hair loss is triggered by hormones, genetic factors, disease, drugs, or stressors.
   B. Hair loss effects are both psychological and social.

problem-solution pattern describes a problem and a possible solution to it

Stephen Finn / Used under license from Shuttershock

The major points of a speech on sovereignty for the Hawaiian Islands can be organized in a number of ways, including pro-con, topical, chronological, and spatial.

II. There are several solutions on the market.
   A. Hairpieces or "rugs" vary in price and quality.
   B. Bonding requires glue that fixes hair fibers to the scalp.
   C. Certain medications have proved effective in hair regrowth.
   D. Transplanting is a surgical process done by a doctor.

When your purpose is to inform, introduce your listeners to a variety of solutions. In persuasive speeches, however, propose several solutions and then focus on the one solution you believe should be implemented. Chapter 17 gives more information on the problem-solution pattern and explains additional organizational plans commonly used for persuasive speeches.

Pro-Con Organization

In the United States, we commonly explore arguments on both sides of controversial issues. Consequently, for speeches that summarize both sides of an issue, the **pro-con arrangement** is very useful. Classify all the arguments in favor of the issue under the *pro* label, and then list the arguments against it under the *con* label. Here is an example of pro-con organization. The topic: Should Hawaii be a sovereign nation instead of a state?

The Hawaiian sovereignty movement has both proponents and opponents.
   I. There are four major arguments for an independent nation of Hawaii.
      A. The 1898 annexation was illegal because the Senate never approved it.
      B. Promises to return lands to Native Hawaiians made in the 1920s are still unkept.
      C. The 1959 statehood vote is meaningless because independence was not a ballot option.
      D. In 1993, President Clinton apologized for the illegal overthrow of 1898.
   II. There are three basic arguments against an independent nation of Hawaii.
      A. Most residents of Hawaii are not native Hawaiians.
      B. Changing the current legal, economic, and political systems would be difficult.
      C. Other less drastic solutions would solve the problems.

This organizational pattern is like an investigative report that works best for informative speeches, when your goal is to explain the nature of an issue. By hearing both sides, your listeners can weigh the evidence and evaluate the arguments for themselves. When your purpose is persuasive and you intend to advocate one set of arguments over another, a different pattern is usually more appropriate.

pro-con arrangement presents arguments in favor of and arguments against an issue

topical arrangement divides a subject into subtopics, each of which is part of the whole

Topical Organization

When your material doesn't really fit into any of these patterns, arrange your points with the most common pattern: **topical organization**. This arrangement classifies the major points into subdivisions, each of which is part of the whole. Although every point contributes to an overall understanding of the subject, the points themselves can be ordered in different ways. For instance, Deborah Gandy, vice president of U.S. Trust used the following topical arrangement for her 2007commencement address at St. Leo University (Florida):[5]

There are four simple secrets to becoming very wealthy:
I. Save.
II. Know the difference between needs and wants.
III. Make smart choices.
IV. Give back.

Ms. Gandy could have changed the order in several ways. For example, she could have started with knowing the difference between needs and wants and then moved to making smart choices, saving, and giving back.

PRACTICALLY SPEAKING
CAREER ADVICE

Thousands of people make their living by giving career advice, including advice on how to develop more effective public speaking skills. One such consultant wrote a book titled *101 Secrets of Highly Effective Speakers*, but Secret #24 is really not all that "secret": Organized ideas are easier to understand.[6] Not surprisingly, audiences are more likely to pay attention, understand, accept, and remember your speech if it's well organized. Put yourself in the listener's place: "Are you apt to be interested in something you don't understand? How hard will you work to make sense out of a speech that is hard to follow? If you don't see the speaker's point, you will probably soon take a mental exit." The "secret" concludes, "Some speeches are nothing more than a lot of thoughts on a given topic strung together. These 'stream of consciousness' presentations are an affront to the audience."

Questions for Discussion

- What is the relationship between speech organization and your ability to remember ideas?
- How hard do you work to understand a speech that is disorganized?
- Do you consider a "stream of consciousness" speech to be an affront or insult when you are an audience member?
- Think back to Chapter 6 on audience analysis. How might your organization, or lack thereof, contribute to your credibility with an audience?

Choose the Best Pattern

Because you can organize the same topic in a number of ways, choose the pattern that works best given your purposes and your supporting materials. For instance, the topic of Hawaiian sovereignty could be effectively developed by using three other patterns:

Chronological: The Hawaiian sovereignty movement has made rapid gains in recent years.

I. In 1993, President Clinton apologized for the U.S. treatment of Hawaii.
II. In 1994, the Ohana Council members, led by "Bumpy" Kanahele, declared Hawaiian independence.
III. In 1998 and 1999, sovereignty supporters led an Aloha March in Washington, D.C. and held a sovereignty convention.
IV. In 2003, Hawaiian politicians submitted the Native Hawaiian Federal Recognition Bill.
V. In 2005, the U.S. Senate voted on the Native Hawaiian Government Reorganization Act, which gives legal recognition to and a governing body for native Hawaiians.

Spatial: Four Hawaiian regions are so different that each one would experience sovereignty uniquely.

   I. Ceded lands include 1.5 million acres of crown lands.
  II. Homesteaded lands comprise 200,000 acres promised to homesteaders in the 1920s.
III. Privately owned islands were purchased and developed by individuals such as Bill Gates.
 IV. Developed islands are used for tourism and other industries.

Topical: Supporters of sovereignty have three general demands.

  I. Independence: desires international recognition as a sovereign nation.
 II. Nation-within-a-nation status: makes Hawaiians similar to Native American tribes in the United States.
III. Status quo: asks for reparations and full control of Hawaiian trust assets granted to Native Hawaiians.

Remember that you can combine patterns within your speech. For instance, in a speech on the history of gambling in the United States, you could order your main points chronologically and use a topical pattern for your subpoints.

BUILD YOUR SPEECH
DEVELOPING YOUR MAIN POINTS

Write your topic here: _____

Begin the process of organizing your material into main points. Study the evidence you found in your research, and then check all that apply.

____ The topic unfolds in *stages*.
____ The topic unfolds in *steps*.
____ *Ordered dates* are important to this topic.
____ There is a *before, during,* and *after* pattern.
____ The topic takes place in *distinct locations* or *places*.
____ Several *causes* are mentioned.
____ Several *effects* are present.
____ The topic describes a *problem*.
____ There is a *solution* or *solutions* to a problem.
____ There are *pro arguments* for a particular position.
____ There are *con arguments* against a particular position.
____ There are several *topical points* that don't really fit into one of these patterns.

Write your tentative thesis statement here: _____

_____
_____
_____

In light of the boxes you checked and your tentative central idea, select the organizational pattern that would work best with your speech:

_____
_____

Revise your thesis statement, if necessary: _____

_____
_____

Once you know which organizational pattern will work best for your speech and have confirmed your central idea, log on to Speech Builder Express for help developing the main points of your speech.

Alternative Patterns

In addition to the traditional patterns we've just examined, researchers have identified several alternative organizational patterns that allow speakers to visualize their speeches in a less linear way. For example, Cheryl Jorgensen-Earp[7] points out a number of alternative patterns that women have used historically. She believes that many speakers, because of their cultural backgrounds or personal inclinations, are uncomfortable with the standard organizational patterns. As alternatives, she proposes several less direct and more **organic patterns** that provide a clear structure for a speech but have a less linear form. Jorgensen-Earp uses visual images to describe these patterns, comparing them to a wave, a spiral, and a star.[8]

The Wave Pattern

This pattern, illustrated in Figure 9.1, consists of repetitions and variations of themes and ideas. Major points come at the crests of the waves, which are developed with a variety of examples leading up to another crest, which repeats the theme or makes another major point. Conclusions wind down and lead the audience gradually from your topic; or they begin with a transition and then rebuild, so that the final statement is a dramatic peak. Professor Karen Zediker says that women and members of various ethnic groups often choose the **wave pattern**.[9] This pattern is common in ceremonial speaking.

Perhaps the most famous wave pattern speech is Martin Luther King, Jr.'s "I Have a Dream." Throughout the speech you'll hear a number of "crests" including "One hundred years later . . ." "Now is the time . . ." and the memorable line "I have a dream . . ." that King repeats, each repetition followed with examples of what he dreamed. His conclusion is a dramatic peak that emerges from the final wave in the speech—the repetition and variation of the phrase "Let freedom ring." (Dr. King's entire speech is reprinted at the end of Chapter 12.)

The wave pattern shows up in other famous speeches including Sojourner Truth's "Ain't I a Woman?"[10] and Nikki Giovanni's speech, "We Are Virginia Tech,"[11] delivered at the memorial ceremony for the victims of a campus shooter in April 2007. (Truth's speech is in Appendix C; you can read the text and watch the video of Giovanni's speech in your online resources.)

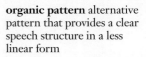

organic pattern alternative pattern that provides a clear speech structure in a less linear form

wave pattern repetitive pattern that presents variations of themes and ideas, with major points presented at the crests

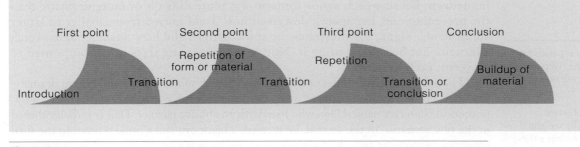

Figure 9.1
The Wave Pattern A wave pattern speech is built around a repetitive theme such as "I have a dream" or "one question."

Dr. E. Ratcliffe Anderson, Jr., used a wave pattern in a section of his keynote address at a leadership conference for physicians:[11]

> But of all the questions we have ever asked—there's one that more than any other, must be asked in every area of health care today.
>
> One question—so simple. So obvious. So necessary—that if it didn't exist—we'd have to invent it.
>
> One question. That ultimately drives the entire health care debate and our response to it.
>
> A question that gives voice to our purpose and to our professionalism. . . .
>
> Is it good medicine?
>
> This question is a simple diagnostic for a complicated world. It speaks to the very foundations of medicine itself.
>
> When deciding on the course of treatment for your patients—how many times a day do you ask yourself—is it good medicine?
>
> When prescribing a new drug for your patients—how many times a day do you ask yourself—is it good medicine? . . .
>
> When our American health care system is the patient—the question shouldn't be any different.
>
> We are here as physician leaders—the doctors that our members and colleagues and patients—and even Washington and our state houses—look to for answers. But before we can provide the answers—we have to get the question right. Is it—good medicine? . . .

In summary, between the major points or crests of your speech, provide specific and general examples to illustrate and support them. As you can see, repetition and variation can be a powerful strategy to stir audience emotions.

The Spiral Pattern

When Shanna was asked to talk to high school students about selecting a college, she created a hypothetical student, Todd, and had him appear in three scenarios, each one costing more money and taking him further from home. She visualized a **spiral pattern** as she framed the three scenarios. In the first loop of the spiral, she described Todd's experiences at a local community college. In the next loop, she sent Todd out of town but kept him at a public institution within the state. In the third and final loop, Todd was at a private university across the continent from his hometown. Because each major scenario was more difficult or more dramatic than the preceding one, her speech described how Todd moved from smaller to larger adjustments. Figure 9.2 illustrates the spiral pattern and how Shanna might sketch and write out her points using it. Notice the increasing sizes of the loops used to represent each scenario.

The spiral pattern is often useful for speeches on subjects that can build in dramatic intensity. For the topic of battered men, a series of narratives might revolve around a hypothetical character named Dan who lives with an abusive partner. Dan is verbally abused in the first scenario. In the second, he receives a black eye and a broken nose. In the final scenario, his partner rams him with her car and he is hospitalized with life-threatening injuries. Each scene builds in tension, with the most controversial scenario reserved for the final spiral.

spiral pattern repetitive pattern with a series of points that increase in drama or intensity

star pattern presents relatively equally weighted speech points within a thematic circle that binds them together; order of points may vary

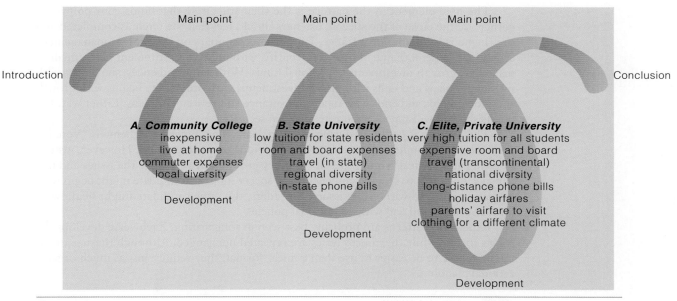

Main point   Main point   Main point

Introduction   Conclusion

A. Community College   **B. State University**   **C. Elite, Private University**
inexpensive   low tuition for state residents   very high tuition for all students
live at home   room and board expenses   expensive room and board
commuter expenses   travel (in state)   travel (transcontinental)
local diversity   regional diversity   national diversity
    in-state phone bills   long-distance phone bills
Development   holiday airfares
        parents' airfare to visit
        clothing for a different climate

Development

Development

Figure 9.2
The Spiral Pattern Spiral pattern speeches are useful for speeches based on points that build in dramatic intensity.

The Star Pattern

Each point in a **star pattern** speech, illustrated in Figure 9.3, is more or less equally weighted within a theme that ties the whole together. This variation on the topical pattern is useful if you present the same basic speech to a number of audiences. By visualizing your major points as a star, you have the flexibility of choosing where to start and what to emphasize, depending on what's relevant for a specific audience. For example, you could begin with a point your audience understands or agrees with and then progressively move to points that challenge their understanding and agreement. For inattentive audiences, begin with your most dramatic point. For hostile audiences, begin with your most conciliatory point. This gives you the advantage of quickly making audience adaptations and still having your speech work effectively.

There are two ways to develop the points of the speech. One way is to state the point, support or develop it, and then provide a transition to the next point. Alternatively, you could develop each point fully and then state it. Base your decisions on the type of audience and the nature of your message.

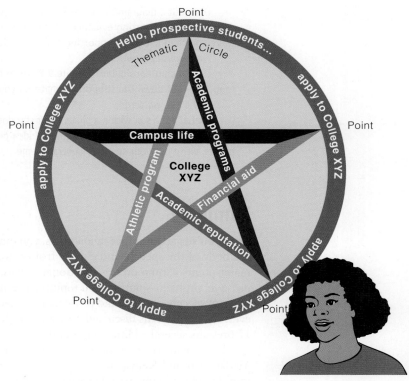

Figure 9.3
The Star Pattern This college recruiter visualizes her speech as points of a star enclosed within the general theme "Apply to this college." Sometimes she starts with academics, sometimes with campus life, depending on the specific audience's interests.

The final element in the pattern is the thematic circle that binds your points together. By the close of the speech, listeners should feel that the circle is completed and the theme is fulfilled. For instance, Jan presents seminars on investment management around the general theme of financial security, with points on retirement plans, medical insurance, growth investments, and global funds. With some audiences, she begins with retirement plans and ends with global investments; with others, she begins with growth and global funds and ends with medical insurance and retirement plans. Either way, her points show how listeners can create financial security.

This pattern is common during election years. The underlying theme is "Vote for me!" Then the candidates stake out their positions on various issues. However, instead of giving an identical "stump speech" to every group, they rearrange the issues and target specific points to specific audiences. For soccer moms, a candidate might begin with education and end with crime issues; for elders, the same candidate might begin with Social Security and end with educational policies.

Repetition patterns are probably best seen in songwriting. Each verse develops the song's theme, while the chorus lyrics are repeated unchanged. Although these patterns might appear to be easier to use than a linear format, they require just as much organizational planning.

STOP AND CHECK

DEVELOP YOUR SPEECH USING AN ALTERNATIVE PATTERN

Write your topic here: _____

For a wave pattern:
Draw out a diagram similar to Figure 9.1, and then identify each wave crest that you will develop with supporting evidence. Write the repetitive phrase or idea at the crest of the wave and then list your supporting material below it.

For a spiral pattern:
Draw a diagram similar to Figure 9.2. Write out the main point at the bottom of each loop. Then jot down the supporting material you will use to develop each loop.

For a star pattern:
Sketch out a star within a circle. (Your star does not have to have five points.) Write your major ideas on the points of the star, one idea per point. In the circle that connects your points, write out your speech's central theme.

Summary

After you've gathered speech materials, you must organize them into a pattern. Begin with the body of the speech, and choose from among several *linear* patterns to organize your major points. Common organizational frameworks include chronological, spatial, causal, pro-con, problem-solution, and topical patterns. These patterns are appropriate for many types of speeches; causal and pro-con are especially good for informative purposes. However, the six patterns discussed here are not the only ways to organize materials; Chapter 17 presents several additional methods typically used in persuasive speeches.

Furthermore, *nonlinear* are typical in diverse settings, as the examples from Madagascar and Kenya and the alternative patterns show. Some speakers, for example, might prefer organic patterns such as the repetitive wave or the spiral. The wave is especially suited to ceremonial speaking. Speakers who want flexible points within a major theme pattern can visualize their ideas in the form of a star. Regardless of the pattern, traditional or alternative, you must carefully identify your main points and then develop them with appropriate supporting materials.

STUDY AND REVIEW

Your online resources for *Public Speaking: Concepts and Skills for a Diverse Society* offer a broad range of study tools that will help you better understand the material in this chapter, complete assignments, and succeed on tests. Your online resources feature

- Speech videos with critical viewing questions, speech outlines, and transcripts
- Interactive versions of this chapter's Stop and Check activities and Application and Critical Thinking Exercises
- Speech Builder Express and InfoTrac College Edition
- Weblinks related to chapter content
- Study and review tools such as self-quizzes, an interactive glossary, and downloadable audio summaries

You can access your online resources at **http://www.cengage.com/login**, using the access code that came with your book or that you bought online at **http://www.iChapters.com.**

KEY TERMS

The terms below are defined in the margins throughout this chapter.

cause-effect pattern 162
chronological pattern 160
organic pattern 167
problem-solution pattern 163
process speech 161
pro-con arrangement 164

spatial pattern 161
spiral pattern 168
star pattern 169
topical arrangement 165
wave pattern 167

APPLICATION AND CRITICAL THINKING EXERCISES

1. Work with a group of your classmates to make a list of ways that organization helps speakers be more effective.
2. Outline one of the speeches available on your online resources. (Don't use a Speech of Introduction; they usually have a slightly different organizational pattern.) Is the organizational pattern easy to discern? What suggestions, if any, could you give the speaker about arranging the points of the speech?
3. With a small group of your classmates, take a topic such as credit cards, divorce, alcohol on campus, or immigration, and organize major points in as many of the following patterns as you can: topical, chronological, spatial, cause-effect, pro-con, problem-solution, spiral.
4. Read or listen to a recording of a speech by an African American such as Vernon Jordan, Barack Obama, or Martin Luther King, Jr. You can find several good examples on **www.AmericanRhetoric.com**. What basic organizational pattern does the speaker use? Can you find examples of alternative patterns within the speech?
5. Do an Internet search for "I Have a Dream" or "Ain't I a Woman?" How many hits do you get? Both of these speeches have inspired groups as well as individuals, which shows the power of rhetoric to influence a culture. Follow one of the links and read more about King's or Truth's vision.
6. Take the theme of creativity or the theme of perseverance. Then work with two or three classmates and discuss how you might create a speech organized around the wave, the spiral, or the star pattern. For example, think of three famous people who persevered . . . each one in a more dramatic way. Or use examples from your school's sports teams, your personal lives, lives of entertainers, and so on.
7. Read Dr. Martin Luther King, Jr.'s Nobel Prize acceptance speech at **http://nobelprize .org/nobel_prizes/peace/laureates/1964/king-lecture.html** Try to outline his speech, using the star pattern. List his main points as well as the thematic circle. Notice, also, the way he uses the wave pattern.

After reading and analyzing Maria DiMaggio's speech outline below, go to your online resources to watch and critique a video of her speech. In addition to the video of Maria's speech, your online resources include the transcript of the speech.

Josh Nauman / Cengage Learning

Student Outline with Commentary

YOU HAVE MY DEEPEST SYMPATHY: YOU JUST WON THE LOTTERY
Maria DiMaggio

General Purpose: To persuade
Specific Purpose: To persuade my audience that winning the lottery is not as great as it's perceived to be and that they should invest their money in alternative ways.
Thesis statement: Although lotteries have a long history, participants could avoid the financial and personal problems that often accompany lottery winnings by finding alternatives to this form of gambling.
Preview: The lottery is a form of gambling that raises money for good causes; however, winning often creates financial and personal problems for the winners, and participants are better off spending their money elsewhere.

Introduction

Maria's introduction starts dramatically. She follows with her thesis statement and previews the major points she'll develop.

   I. You have my deepest sympathy; you just won the lottery.
  II. Most of us would be shocked if someone said we'd won $20 million and then offered us condolences; however, hundreds of lottery winners have discovered the downside of winning big.
 III. I used to think I'd be the happiest person in Brooklyn if I could just win a million dollars, but my research about lottery winners convinced me to spend my money elsewhere—and I hope you'll follow my example.

Maria uses a problem-solution organizational pattern.

 IV. Lottery participants can avoid problems that often accompany lottery winnings by finding alternatives to this form of gambling.
  V. Today, I'll explain that the lottery is a form of gambling that raises money for good causes; however, winners often end up with financial and personal problems, and you are better off spending your money elsewhere.

Body

The problem section will come in two main points, but first she gives some background information.

   I. Lotteries are a form of gambling that raise money for good causes.
    A. *The World Book Encyclopedia* (Chuman, 2000) identifies lotteries as a popular form of gambling.
      1. Winners pay to participate, generally by purchasing tickets at a uniform price.
      2. Winners are determined by random drawings; unfortunately, you are 16 times more likely to get killed driving to buy the ticket than you are to win a record amount (Associated Press, 2002).

3. Lotteries were popular in the United States in the 1700s.

4. However, several states made them unconstitutional in the 1880s due to fraud by lottery companies and pressure from social reformers (von Herrmann, 2002).

5. New Hampshire reinstated the lottery in 1963; now, more than half the states have state-run lotteries.

B. Lotteries generate revenues for good causes.

  1. The earliest lottery, organized in London in 1680, raised money for a municipal water supply.

  2. A French lottery helped pay for the Statue of Liberty.

  3. Closer to home, a national lottery helped support the American Revolutionary War (Findlay, 1986).

  4. In 1772, one lottery's proceeds were divided among a Presbyterian church, a German Lutheran church, the Newark Academy, and three Philadelphia schoolmasters (Findlay, 1986).

  5. Current lotteries in New Hampshire and Oregon, among other states, provide educational funding.

Transition: Now that we know a bit about the history of lotteries, you'd think your life would be great if you could only win big. Right? Well, there can be major problems for winners and their heirs.

II. Unexpected problems arise for lottery winners.

A. First, their dreams of instant riches are not always fulfilled.

  1. Unless winners take a much lower lump sum, funds are distributed over twenty to twenty-five years.

  2. A lottery "millionaire" is really a "thousandair" who gets about $50,000 annually before taxes, delinquent taxes, past-due child support, and student loans are taken out (Sanford, 1996).

  3. Winners cannot draw cash from winnings, use them as collateral for loans, or liquidate future payments.

B. In addition, many suffer personal loss and rejection.

  1. William "Bud" Post won $16.2 million but watched his brother go to jail, convicted of hiring a hit man to kill him (Goodman, 2004).

  2. Debbie won $6.85 million but lost contact with her sisters, who stopped speaking to her when she declined to pay their debts.

  3. Bernice took a day off work to claim her $1 million; her job was given to someone else.

  4. Daisy won $2.8 million but went through a painful lawsuit.

    a. Her son's friend sued for half the winnings because she asked the friend to pray that she'd win.

    b. He prayed, she won, so he thought he was entitled to some of her money.

    c. The court ruled against him, saying he couldn't prove his prayers caused her to win.

C. Lottery winnings don't necessarily bring happiness.

  1. A study of people with the best of luck and those with the worst of luck supported this conclusion (Brickman, Coates, and Janoff-Bulman, 1978).

  2. Accident victims weren't as unhappy as expected; however, lottery winners were more unhappy and took less pleasure in life than expected.

D. Finally, heaven help the heirs if a lottery-winning relative dies and leaves them a fortune.

  1. They must immediately pay estate taxes on the unpaid total, with monthly penalties added after nine months.

  2. Johnny Ray Brewster won $12.8 million, taking it in annual payments. His sister Peggy inherited the payments, but upon inheritance she immediately owed $3.5 million in taxes (Beyer and Petrini, 2000).

Given the low probability of winning and the many problems winners face, there surely must be other solutions if you have money to burn.

The transition tells where she's been and where she's going.

In this, her second major subpoint in the problem section, Maria describes problems not only for the winners but also for their heirs.

The solution section is relatively brief. Maria focuses on personal solutions, not top-down regulations.

III. Use your extra money in far more profitable expenditures.
   A. Invest in the stock market; investing just $10 to $20 monthly can pay off immensely by the time you retire.
   B. Donate your extra money to a charitable organization and claim a tax deduction.
   C. Indulge yourself: buy cable, eat lobster occasionally, buy season tickets to a sporting or a cultural event, or get an exotic pet.
   D. Finally, if you like to think your lottery money supports education, you can donate to my college fund!

Her final suggestion adds humor.

Conclusion

   I. I hope I've convinced you that playing the lottery is not all it's advertised to be.
   II. I've explained what the lottery is, the problems it can cause, and some alternative ways to get rid of money.
   III. So the next time you see a new lottery multimillionaire, consider sending your sympathies rather than your congratulations.

References

Associated Press. (2002). Compare the odds. *The Detroit News*. [Electronic version]. Retrieved June 2, 2005, from www.detnews.com/2002/metro/0204/16/b01-446437.htm

Beyer, G. W. & Petrini, J. (2000). Lottery players and winners: estate planning for the optimistic and the lucky. Retrieved June 2, 2005, from www.professorbeyer.com/Articles/Lottery.htm

Brickman, P., Coates, D. & Janoff-Bulman, R. (1978). Lottery winners and accident victims: is happiness relative? *Journal of Personality and Social Psychology, 36*(8), 917–927.

Findlay, J. M. (1986). *People of chance*. New York: Oxford University Press.

Goodman, E. (2004, November 18). *8 lottery winners who lost their millions*. Retrieved June 2, 2005, from http://moneycentral.msn.com/content/Savinganddebt/Savemoney/P99649.asp

Sanford, R. (1996). *Jackpot! What to do before and after you win the lottery*. Retrieved June 2, 2005, from www.note.com/note/pp.jackpot.html

Von Herrmann, D. (2002). *The big gamble: the politics of lottery and casino expansion*. Westport, CT: Praeger.

CHAPTER **10**

COMPLETING YOUR SPEECH

© Tim Timmerman

THIS CHAPTER WILL HELP YOU

▶ Develop an introduction for your speech that gains attention, motivates the audience to listen, establishes your credibility, and previews the speech

▶ Develop a conclusion that signals the end, summarizes, provides psychological closure, and ends with impact

▶ Link the parts of the speech to one another through skillful use of connectives such as signposts and transitions, internal previews and internal summaries

FOR SOME TIME NOW, you've immersed yourself in your topic. You've worked hard to gather material and organize it into major points, and you've selected interesting supporting data. But your audience is so far unaware of all the interesting information you have discovered. Your task now is to create an introduction that functions to take listeners from their everyday concerns into the carefully crafted world of your speech. Then you finish up with a brief conclusion that brings your audience back to the here-and-now of the classroom but leaves them with something to remember.

Effective introductions and conclusions are carefully researched, planned, written, and practiced. Speakers who start strong are more likely to be forgiven for minor slips later. Speakers who begin poorly have trouble regaining the audience's confidence. The old saying, you rarely get a second chance to make a positive first impression, is true here. Also, speakers who have otherwise good speeches but trail off or lose focus at the end miss the chance to drive home their point.

This chapter will help you skillfully draw your listeners into your subject and, at the end, conclude in a way that summarizes your thoughts and leaves a memorable impression. You will also learn how to connect your ideas to one another and to the speech as a whole.

Plan Your Introduction

The time to design your introduction is after you have planned the body of the speech and after you have your material firmly in mind. Chapter 2 points out that the Roman educator Quintilian identified four purposes for an introduction[1]:

1. To draw the listeners' attention to the topic
2. To motivate the audience to listen
3. To establish yourself as knowledgeable about the topic
4. To preview the major ideas of the speech

Here, also, is your opportunity to present definitions or background information your listeners must know if they are to understand your subject. By including Quintilian's four elements in your introduction, you'll answer the four basic questions that listeners ask up front: What's this all about? Why should I listen? Why should I listen to you? What will you cover? Figure 10.1 depicts the four introductory functions that this section covers.

Gain Attention

Gaining attention is the first step in the listening process, so it's important to answer immediately your audience's question, What's this speech about? Avoid the temptation to simply announce: "Today, my speech is about blood diamonds, also known as conflict diamonds." True, this introduces your subject, but it's not very creative, and you may find that you have "leftover" material from your research that didn't quite fit under a main point but that would introduce your topic more dramatically. This section discusses several effective attention-gaining strategies.

Ask a Question

Questions can be either rhetorical or participatory. **Rhetorical questions** are the kind that listeners answer in their mind; **participatory questions**, in contrast, ask for an overt response, such as a show of hands or a verbal answer. In a speech given at the Louisville School of Medicine, Dr. Edward C. Halperin used two similar rhetorical questions to gain attention:[2]

> Why have the entering medical students been given white coats? If you were to look at a painting or a photograph of physicians from one hundred years ago, the overwhelmingly male crowd would be dressed in frock coats. Business attire, similar to the modern day suit that I am wearing, was the standard appearance for a physician. Why, nowadays, do doctors wear white coats?

rhetorical questions questions that listeners answer in their minds

participatory questions questions that listeners answer overtly

Figure 10.1
The Audience's Four Questions
Your introduction functions to answer these four questions that your listeners have.

The occasion was a ceremony in which his audience of medical students had just been given their coveted white coats; these questions readied the students for his speech about the history of the coats and the challenges they would face as doctors.

In contrast, when you ask a participatory question, let the audience know the response you want. For instance, ask for a show of hands or call on a member of the audience to answer a specific question you pose. One professional speaker[3] asked listeners to take out a pen or pencil and write down the age to which they expected to live; he then asked these questions:

> By a show of hands please, how many put in at least age 70? Just about everyone in the room. How many put in at least age 80? How many put at least age 90? Still a healthy number, isn't there? And how many put at least age 100? How about 105? . . . The people who raised their hands for 90 or 100 are likely to be accurate . . . but the paradox of living to 100 or 105 is that it's wasted if each day flies by quickly.

To capture attention, the question must be sufficiently intriguing to engage listeners. How would you respond to these three questions from student speeches?

> How many of you have ever used the Internet?

> Have you ever had your finger almost sliced off and left hanging by a small piece of skin?

> Have you ever visited a nudist colony?

Each one has a flaw. The first is too broad. Who hasn't used the Internet? The second is too specific. It's the rare individual who slices off a finger. The third is too remote for most people to relate to. The number of nudist colonies open to college-aged students is minimal. In contrast, good rhetorical and participatory questions can help establish dialogue between you and your listeners at the very outset of the speech because they invite audience responses, whether mental or physical.

Provide a Vivid Description

Draw attention to your subject by describing a scene so vividly that your listeners are compelled to visualize it. The scene can be either real or imaginary. Danae's opening for her classroom speech on arachnophobia (fear of spiders) is a good example:

> Imagine yourself just hanging out one morning, minding your own business, when a large, monstrous body, fifty times your size, casually approaches you, then, suddenly, lets out a blood-curdling scream, hurls a giant bowl your way, and takes off running. Sound familiar? It would if you were the spider that had the misfortune of getting just a little too close to Little Miss Muffet of nursery rhyme fame. I venture to say that we all have had to deal with spiders at some time in our lives. They seem to be everywhere, especially at this time of year. What causes this Muffet-type reaction? It just may be arachnophobia—the irrational fear of spiders.[4]

> DIVERSITY IN PRACTICE
> ## A NAVAJO (DINÉ) SPEECH INTRODUCTION
>
> NOT EVERY CULTURAL GROUP assumes speakers will gain attention first, relate to audience interests next, and establish credibility after that. Audiences at Diné College (formerly Navajo Community College) expect speakers to first answer the question, "Who are you and what is your clan affiliation?" This information discloses the roots of the speaker's identity, and only after these personal, identifying facts are shared do speakers and listeners feel comfortable discussing a topic.[5]

Begin with a Quotation

Beginning with a quotation or a familiar cultural proverb, either *about* a subject or, for a biographical speech, *by* the subject, is a good way to gain attention. Choose a short saying that captures your overall theme—preferably a quotation that is familiar or from a familiar source—and cite that source. For example, in a speech to the National Press Club, a professional speaker[6] used a quotation in his introduction:

> Fifty-nine years ago today, with the enormity of the Holocaust haunting the world's collective conscience, the United Nations adopted the Universal Declaration of Human Rights. It stated that "recognition of the inherent dignity and . . . inalienable rights of all members of the human family is the foundation of freedom, justice and peace in the world." It was the first global proclamation of human rights—an occasion we observe every December 10, International Human Rights Day.

In a speech given on Flag Day, June 14, 2007, a political figure[7] envisioned a world free of nuclear weapons:

> On Veterans Day in 1948—at the dawn of the nuclear age after the devastation of Hiroshima and Nagasaki—General Omar Bradley said in a speech:
>
> > "The world has achieved brilliance without wisdom, power without conscience. Ours is a world of nuclear giants and ethical infants. We know more about war than we know about peace, more about killing than we know about living."
>
> It might surprise General Bradley, if he were alive today, to know that we have made it 60 years without a nuclear catastrophe. . . .

Quotations from song lyrics, poems, and scriptural or literary texts are common. Family sayings or memorable words spoken by someone such as a coach or teacher also work well. For instance, a speech on perseverance might open with "My immigrant grandmother used to say, 'It's a great life if you don't weaken.'" As Chapter 7 pointed out, the Internet contains sources for thousands of quotations on sites like **www.quoteland.com**, **www.bartleby.com/100/**, or **www.quotesandsayings.com**.

Use an Audio or Visual Aid

Posters, charts, tape recordings, and other visual and audio materials can successfully draw attention to your topic. For example, Tom displayed a large poster of an automobile as he began his speech explaining how to buy a car overseas. Denise began her speech on artist Dale Chihuly with a photograph of one of his blown glass pieces. Yesenia, who spoke about the composer Hector Berlioz, played a short cut from a Berlioz symphony as a background for her opening words:

> [Play a 20-second clip of Berlioz's music during points I & II of the introduction.] (Voice over, pausing between words) unearthly sounds . . . nighttime . . . distant horn calls . . . summoning . . .

Tell a Joke or Funny Story

Professional speakers often begin with a joke that immediately creates an informal, humorous atmosphere. If you have good comedic skills, you might try this strategy; however, you can easily embarrass yourself and make your listeners uncomfortable if the joke flops. To avoid humiliation, test your attempt at humor in advance, on some friends and let them decide if it's really funny. Also, make sure your joke relates to your topic. Otherwise, you might gain attention, but it won't focus on your subject. Here is a humorous experience that Cal Ripken, Jr., used at his Baseball Hall of Fame induction ceremony:[8]

I've really appreciated all the people who have congratulated me in the months since my election to the Hall of Fame. It sure helped me get over a conversation I had recently with a 10-year-old boy I was instructing. I was teaching him hitting and he was starting to have success and feeling quite proud of himself.

And he asked me, "So, did you play baseball?"

I said, "Yes, I played professionally."

And he goes, "Oh, yeah, for what team?"

I said, "I played with the Baltimore Orioles for 21 years."

And he said, "What position?"

And I said, "Mostly shortstop but a little third base at the end."

And he began to walk away and he looked back and said, "Should I know you?

That certainly puts all this in perspective.

You can include humor by displaying a relevant cartoon that you have transferred to a transparency or scanned into a PowerPoint presentation (giving proper credit to the source, of course).

Refer to a Current Event

One way to identify with your listeners and establish common ground is to begin with well-known current happenings—airplane crashes, campus controversies, weather disasters, well-publicized trials, elections, and the like. Here's how the CEO of Adidas opened his talk just before Super Bowl 2007:[9]

> As I mentioned to a few of you before, I'm heading right afterwards to the Super Bowl in Arizona, because [my company's] brand is the official uniform supplier of the NFL.
>
> Now before coming here, I was told that a few CEOs who've spoken in the past have brought gifts—so I'd like to put at least one topic to rest: . . . no, I did not bring you any Super Bowl tickets. . . . With the Patriots playing for another Super Bowl ring, however, it is certainly great to be here in Boston. I feel quite lucky. Regardless of the outcome on Sunday, I'm the one person I know who'll be leaving Arizona happy. Because the Giants and the Patriots will be playing in front of a television audience estimated at over 1 billion viewers worldwide . . . and both teams will be wearing [our brand]!
>
> Well, I might not know as much about American football as some of you but, as a CEO, I do know that means my team can't lose!

Source: Sara Reamy

Search InfoTrac College Edition for the journal *Vital Speeches*, and look for examples of other speakers who have used current events in their speech openings.

Begin with an Example

As Chapter 8 pointed out, examples give your listeners an opportunity to become emotionally involved with your topic. Everyone

Beginning with an example immediately gains listener attention. For her speech on teaching young children to swim, Megan used Pete as an example of a child she taught while he was still a preschooler.

likes a good story, and stories of real people involved in real situations generally make us more attentive. Bonita began her speech on the dangers of driving drowsy with this example:

> On July 3, 2003, a man and his family are driving their van down the road as it is getting light. An oncoming driver has been driving since midnight; he tries to pass a bus, but fails to see the van coming toward him. Because he is tired, the would-be passer cannot react quickly enough to slide back into his own lane, and his car collides head-on with the van, killing the woman in the passenger seat.

(This entire speech is found at the end of this chapter, and your book's online resources include a video, an outline, and a transcript.) The following example introduced a speech about the process of marriage annulment:

> After twenty-three years of marriage, four children, a year of separation, and fifteen years of divorce, a man tells his ex-wife that he has decided to get an annulment in the Catholic Church.

Start with Startling Numbers

Numbers and statistics can be dry; however, they can also capture and hold your listeners' attention if they are shocking enough or if they are put into an understandable context, as this example illustrates:

> According to the Centers for Disease Control, 72 percent of young adults eat too much fat, and fewer than one in five follow recommended dietary guidelines. That means that, in this classroom with twenty-five students enrolled, we might predict that eighteen people indulge in too many hamburgers and milkshakes and that twenty people routinely ignore their physicians' nutritional recommendations. I confess, I'm talking about myself here.

Although this is not an exhaustive list of successful opening strategies, it gives you examples of common means used in a variety of settings. Remember that your opening should not simply gain attention; it must also draw attention to your topic.

> DIVERSITY IN PRACTICE
> ## CONSIDERING ORGANIZATIONAL CULTURE
>
> CHAPTER 1 POINTS OUT THAT culture includes the visible, stated aspects of a group's way of life as well as the more embedded beliefs and assumptions that guide group members. The concept of **organizational culture** extends this definition by recognizing that organizations and institutions also have histories, traditions, hierarchies, rituals, folklore, and so on, which makes them function as small cultures within the larger society. Insiders know the group's culture; newcomers must learn it. For example, Microsoft differs from IBM; St. John's University (Catholic sponsored) is unlike George Fox University (Quaker sponsored) or the University of Washington (state sponsored) in many ways.
>
> Before you speak within an organization, learn whatever you can about its culture—even expectations for speech introductions change from setting to setting. For example, a community leader recently addressed graduates at my university. She introduced her remarks by referring to the occasion, congratulating the graduates, expressing respect for the university, and acknowledging the cultural event (commencement exercises). The graduates and their families would think it abrupt and strange if she immediately launched into her speech on this special occasion.
>
> To see how speakers adapt their introductions to specific organizations, look at several issues of *Vital Speeches of the Day* at your campus library or through InfoTrac College Edition. Read the introductions of three or four talks given at ritual events, and analyze how the guest speakers recognize elements of the organization's culture in their opening remarks.

organizational culture the way of life of a specific organization, which includes its history, traditions, heroes, folklore, vocabulary, rituals, and ways of doing things

© Brendan McKeon

Audiences relate to some topics easily. But it takes more creativity to link other subjects to your listeners' lives and interests. The cost in time or money, the impact of national or international issues on their lives and future, and an appeal to curiosity are just a few strategies you can use to make connections.

Give Your Audience a Reason to Listen

After you gain attention, answer your listeners' second question, Why should I listen to this speech? You may consider your topic important and interesting, but your listeners may think it boring or irrelevant. Jill, from Hawaii, faced this challenge when she spoke about Hawaiian sovereignty for one of her classes at Oregon State University. Most OSU students had never heard of the controversy about returning Hawaii to Hawaiian rule, and the issue seemed pretty remote. Jill related the topic to her Oregon audience as follows:

> Although you may not be aware of the issue of Hawaiian sovereignty, your senators are voting on the issue soon, and you may someday vote on whether or not to allow Hawaiians to again be a sovereign nation instead of a state.

You can frame your topic within a larger issue; for instance, childhood obesity is health related, and elder abuse is part of a nationwide problem of violence. A speech on polar bears does not directly relate to listeners in most classrooms; however, the treatment of polar bears is linked to larger issues such as animal rights and animal overpopulation. Here's one way to relate this topic to an urban audience:

> At this point, you may be curious about polar bears, but you may not think much about them. After all, the only polar bears in New York are in the zoo. However, the polar bear problem in Canada is similar to problems here on Long Island with a deer population that is getting out of control. What do we do with animals that live close to humans?

Two important human characteristics are curiosity and the ability to learn new things, so you sometimes will speak to increase your audience's knowledge or to satisfy their curiosity. For instance, few people in the classroom will ever annul their marriages, but 58,000 annulments are granted annually to U.S. Catholics—and about 25 percent of the U.S. population claims affiliation with the Catholic Church. Here's how Maureen related her topic, "The Annulment Process," to her audience:

> Since at least two people in this classroom are Catholic, this subject should be of interest to you. For you who are non-Catholics, I hope this information will help you better understand one aspect of the Catholic religion.

Many issues that don't seem to directly concern your listeners may actually affect their pocketbooks, whether or not they know it. National issues that rely on tax dollars for support are in this category; think about funding for public broadcasting, weapons development, and Medicare increases. Chapter 18 provides more details about the needs, wants, emotions, and values that motivate people to listen to speeches.

Establish Your Credibility

After you have the audience's attention and they have a reason to listen to your topic, give them a reason to listen to you by linking yourself to your subject. In the classroom, this is more challenging when you are delving into a topic for the first time; consequently, mentioning the research you've done will be your major source of credibility. Typically, classroom speakers relate subject-related experiences, interests, and research findings. If relevant, you can mention your major, courses you have taken, television shows that sparked your interest in the topic, and so on. Maureen linked herself to the topic of annulment through her personal experiences:

> The annulment process is of particular interest to me since I am a divorced Catholic who is engaged to be married to a Catholic man.

Here are some additional ways students have linked themselves to their topics:

> *Topic: Hector Berlioz, composer.* As a musician trained in piano, clarinet, and guitar, I attended Fiorello H. La Guardia High School of Music and Art, where I was required to study music history and research the lives of musicians and composers.

> *Topic: The Health Benefits of Antioxidants.* I became interested in the topic of antioxidants because of my childhood. I always begged for Cocoa Puffs, but I got oatmeal and bananas instead. So I developed my health consciousness from my mother who fed me fruits and vegetables and other good foods.

Establishing your credibility is optional if another person introduces you and connects you with the topic or if your expertise is well established. And in workplace situations, it's generally assumed that you are speaking about a topic because you have some expertise in it. However, when professionals speak on topics outside their area of expertise, they should link themselves with the topic. An engineer, for instance, who urges her local school board to adopt a district-wide sex education program, would cite her experiences as a parent rather than her engineering expertise.

Preview Your Ideas

You may have heard the old saying, "Tell them what you're going to say; say it; then tell them what you said." The **preview** serves the first of these functions. It is the short statement that provides the transition between the introduction and the body of your speech, in which you state some form of your thesis statement and indicate how you will develop it. Chapter 5 gave details on how to write it. A preview aids listeners who are taking notes or outlining the talk. Heidi explains its importance for listeners:

> It obviously helps to have an idea of where the speaker is headed. The preview provides a brief synopsis of what key points will be expanded upon. The speech then should continue in the order first declared.

Here are three student previews that alert their audiences to the speaker's organizational pattern:

> Today, I will explain the visual, auditory, and kinesthetic learning styles, using each style in the process.

preview the transition from the introduction to the speech body; a summary of what you'll say in the speech

Today, I'll retell the story of the boy who cried "wolf," with a few character changes. The boy who cries "wolf" is the American government, and the wolf we are to fear is industrial hemp.

I will share with you some aspects of Hector Berlioz's fascinating biography and explain the important contributions he made in music composition.

In summary, a good introduction draws attention to your topic, relates the subject to your listeners, links you to the subject, and previews your major ideas.

STOP AND CHECK

CREATE AN INTERESTING INTRODUCTION

Select one or two of the following previews. Then work with a classmate to create an introduction that answers the four questions your listeners ask regarding any subject.

▶ Childhood obesity is an increasing problem in our society, but several solutions have been proposed.
▶ Arachnophobia, the irrational fear of spiders, has three major causes and two basic treatments.
▶ Many women, as well as men, experience hair loss, and they try medications, hairpieces, bonding techniques, and transplants to solve the problem.
▶ You can save money at the market on produce, meat, cereal, and baked goods.
▶ Thousands of students default on federal student loans every year, leaving taxpayers with their school tabs.

The listener's questions are:

1. What's this about? (Identify several strategies to gain attention to the topics you choose. Which do you think are more effective?)
2. Why should I listen? (How could you relate the topics to audience interests or experiences?)
3. Why should I listen to you? (How might a speaker establish credibility on each subject?)
4. What will you cover? (How would you preview the main ideas of each topic?)

To learn more about introductions, do an Internet search for "speech introductions" and skim several results for tips you can incorporate into your speeches. Alternatively, watch the introductions of several speech videos in your online resources. Evaluate how well each one fulfills the criteria described here.

Conclude with Impact

A conclusion leaves listeners with their final impression of both you and your topic. This is the place to provide closure through a summary and a satisfying or challenging closing statement without adding new information. Appearing disorganized at the end can lessen the positive impressions your audience may have gained during the speech. Like the introduction, the conclusion has several important functions: to signal the end, to summarize the main points, to provide psychological closure (often by a reference to the introduction), and to end with impact.

Signal the Ending

Just as your preview provides a transition to the speech body, your ending signal lets the audience know that you're concluding. Both beginning speakers and professionals use common phrases such as in *conclusion* or *finally*. However, the following transitions are more creative:

> Hopefully the information I have shared today about culture shock will allow you to understand better the process of integrating into a new culture.

> Today we've taken a look at our National Debt . . . our national sleep debt, that is.

Nonverbal actions can also be used to signal to your conclusion. For instance, pause and shift your posture, or take a step away from the podium. You can slow down a bit and speak more softly. Combining both verbal and nonverbal transitions generally works well.

Review Your Main Ideas

Briefly summarize or recap your main points to fulfill the "Tell them what you said" axiom, but make the review brief. The audience already heard your speech, so you don't have to repeat any supporting material. The following brief summaries are examples:

> We've explored ways that sleep deprivation affects us in three areas: in our personal lives, in our relationships, and in our workplaces.

> I hope that I have increased your knowledge about oxidation and convinced you that antioxidants help prevent heart disease, arteriosclerosis, strokes, chronic illnesses, and even cancer.

Many speakers combine their transition statement with their summary, as this example shows:

> Now that we have looked at the shark as it really is [transition phrase] I hope you realize that its reputation is really inaccurate and that humans present a greater threat to sharks than sharks present to humans [restatement of the central idea].

Provide Psychological Closure

Looping back to something from your introduction—which some instructors call an "**echo**"—provides your audience with a sense of psychological closure. One writing professor explains:

> The echo is the inside joke of writing. By repeating or suggesting a previous detail— a description, word, question, quote, topic or whatever—you make a point with that which is already familiar to your reader. It's a way of putting your arm around the reader and sharing a bit of information that only the two of you can appreciate.[10]

The echo principle similarly applies to speaking. Look in your introduction for something that you could echo at the end. For instance, if you began with an example, you might return to it in the conclusion. Or you could refer to startling statistics or to quotations you presented in the opening. Here are some examples:

> The woman whose 23-year marriage ended in annulment is more common than you might think. Although she considered an annulment inconceivable, she did not contest her ex-husband's request for one. She realized that the annulment did not erase the existence of her marriage, but it allowed her ex to have good standing within the Catholic Church.

> For those eighteen of us in this classroom who eat too much fat and the twenty of us who regularly ignore our doctor's nutritional advice, there's hope.

---

echo repeating something from the introduction in the conclusion

End Memorably

Finally, plan to leave a positive and memorable impression. During the few minutes you speak, the audience is focusing on your subject. After you finish, however, each listener will return to his or her thoughts, moving away from the mental images you co-created throughout the speech. All of the devices for gaining audience attention are equally effective at achieving impact in the conclusion. In persuasive speeches, you could also issue a challenge; in commemorative speeches, you might reinforce a larger cultural theme or value. Consider using parallel construction. That is, if you began with a story, end with a story; if you began with a rhetorical question, end with a rhetorical question, and so on. This is not only effective, it is another way to provide closure.

Study some of the speeches and outlines throughout the text and notice the different and creative ways that students memorably end their speeches. Here are two effective endings—the first, a student speaker; the second, a professional:

> I myself will avoid driving while tired, because the woman who was killed in the van that July morning was my mom. Next time you drive, consider those in the cars around you and think of whose friend, mother, sister, brother they are. Do you really want others to go through pain and suffering simply so you can get to your destination a little earlier?

> To the Medical Students of the Class of 2011: I welcome you to the company of educated men and women, in white coats, stretching backward and forward in time, who have chosen to make their life's work the amelioration of suffering, the alleviation of pain, and the avoidance, where possible, of premature death. I invite you to take your place in that honorable line. Godspeed on your journey, young doctors.[11]

In summary, a good conclusion provides a transition, summarizes your major points, gains psychological closure, and closes with a thought-provoking statement.

Bettmann /CORBIS

Using humor and using quotations are two memorable ways to end a speech. Quoting a well-known humorist such as Mark Twain is one way to combine the two.

✓ **STOP AND CHECK**

EVALUATING INTRODUCTIONS AND CONCLUSIONS

Here you'll find an introduction and a conclusion for two different speeches. Read through each set and then answer the questions that follow it.

Introduction: Four of the six leading causes of death among Americans are diet related: heart disease, cancer, stroke, and diabetes mellitus, as stated by the *Vegetarian Times* magazine. Everyone here would like to live a healthy life, right? Today, I will explain the advantages of being a vegetarian to your health and to the environment.

Conclusion: Because I have this information, I have reduced my consumption of meat lately, and I ask you to do the same thing. Being a vegetarian is not that bad; you're improving your health and, at the same time, saving the environment. Don't forget, once you're old and suffering from a heart ailment or cancer, it will be too late. Take precautions now.

▶ Does this introduction make you want to hear this speech? Why or why not?

▶ How does the speaker gain attention?

▶ How does he relate to the audience? Is this effective?

▶ Do you think he is credible on the topic?

▶ Could you write a brief outline of his major points from his preview?

▶ Compare his introduction to his conclusion. Which is more effective? Why?

Introduction: What is the easiest way to raise $125,000 for research for multiple sclerosis? That's right. Swim 1,550 miles down the Mississippi River like Nick Irons did. Nick, a 25-year-old, swam the murky waters to raise money for a disease his father has. Many people would think this was crazy, because they don't know about the disease. Only one in ten students who responded to my survey had the slightest idea of what MS was. My dad has had this disease for eight years, and I really didn't know a lot about it until I researched MS and found a lot more than I expected. Because most people are unclear about multiple sclerosis, I will first define the disease, describe some of its effects, and tell you what is known about the cause, the cure, and the current treatments.

Conclusion: In conclusion, little is known about the causes and cures of MS, a disease that attacks the central nervous system, impairing many senses. Next time you question why a person might swim over 1,500 miles down a dirty river, you will have a clearer understanding of the reason. A lot is being done to find a cure for this debilitating disease. It will be found.

▶ What is the most effective part of her introduction?

▶ What's the most effective element of her conclusion?

▶ Which is better: her introduction or her conclusion? Why?

▶ What improvements, if any, should she make?

To learn more about conclusions, do an Internet search for "speech conclusions" and skim several results for tips you can incorporate into your speeches. Alternatively, watch the conclusions of several speech videos in your online resources. Evaluate how well each speaker signals the ending of the speech, reviews main ideas, provides psychological closure, and ends memorably.

Connect Your Ideas

After you plan the body of your speech and formulate your introduction and conclusion, you're ready to add final touches in the form of **connectives**—the words, phrases, and sentences that lead from one idea to another and unify the various elements of the speech. They function somewhat like tendons or ligaments by holding your speech together. You can also think of them as bridges that link one idea to another or relate one major point to the whole. Use them to emphasize significant points, show relationships between ideas, and help your listeners keep their place as you talk. The most common connectives are signposts and transitions, internal previews, and internal summaries.

Signposts and Transitions

Signposts are similar to highway signs, those posted markers that help you know your location as you drive along. Verbal signposts help your listeners orient themselves to their place in your speech. Words such as *first*, *next*, and *finally* introduce new points and help your listeners identify the flow of your ideas. Other words and phrases such

connectives words, phrases, and sentences used to lead from idea to idea and tie the parts of the speech together smoothly

signpost connective such as *first*, *most importantly*, and *consequently* that links ideas, lends emphasis, and helps listeners keep their place in the speech

as *in addition*, *for example*, *therefore*, and *as a result* connect one idea to another. Signposts such as *the main thing to remember* or *most importantly* highlight ideas you want to emphasize. Here are some examples of signposts from student speeches:

▶ The *final step* occurs when the case is submitted to the judge for a decision.
▶ *On the other hand*, the computer does have a lot of things going for it.
▶ *In addition*, brain wave patterns can be measured and analyzed.
▶ *Not surprisingly*, people who carry high sleep debts are also more susceptible to disease and micro-sleep.
▶ *However*, this idea seems a bit far-fetched.

Transitions summarize where you have been and where you are going in the speech. You can use them both between points and within a single point. Here are some simple transitions between major points:

> We have looked at what oxidation is [where we've been]; now let's examine what antioxidants are and what they can do to help prevent oxidation in the arteries [where we're going].

> The problem, as you can see, is complex, because both the people and the polar bears need protection [a summary of the last point]; however, two solutions have been proposed [a preview of the next main idea].

> Although the glass ceiling is widespread [where we've been], it is not shatterproof [where we're going].

Transitions can also lead from subpoint to subpoint *within* a major point. For example, Tamara's major point "There are several causes of amusement park tragedies" has three subpoints: equipment failure, operator failure, and rider behavior. After she describes the first two causes, she could transition to the final one by saying this:

> While both equipment and operator failure cause accidents [first and second subpoint], a number of tragedies are additionally caused by rider behavior [third subpoint].

Here's another example. Jenny's speech about goldenseal root has as one of its major points that people use this herb both internally and externally. She first describes internal uses and then transitions to the second use by saying:

> Not only do people use goldenseal root internally [first use], they also apply the herb externally [lead-in to second use].

Internal Previews and Internal Summaries

Internal previews occur within the body of your speech and briefly summarize the subpoints you will develop under a major point. For instance, Tamara might say:

> Experts agree that there are three main causes of amusement park tragedies: equipment failure, operator failure, and rider behavior.

This internal preview helps her audience see the framework she'll use as she develops her major point, the causes of accidents.

If you summarize subpoints after you've made them but before you move to another major point, you're using an **internal summary**. Thus, this sentence summarizes the causes before moving on to the effects of amusement park accidents:

> In short, we have seen that equipment failure, operator failure, and rider behavior combine to create thousands of tragedies annually.

transition summary of where you've been and where you're going in your speech

internal preview brief in-speech summary that foretells the subpoints you'll develop under a major point

internal summary restatement of the ideas within a subpoint

After she discusses the uses of goldenseal root, Jenny could summarize her entire point by saying:

In summary, people use goldenseal root both internally and externally.

Connectives, then, are the words, phrases, and sentences you use to weave your ideas together and enhance the flow of your speech as a whole. They serve to introduce your points, show the relationship of one point to another, preview and summarize material within a point, and help your listeners keep their place in your speech.

Summary

After you've organized the body of your speech, plan an introduction that will take your listeners from their various internal worlds and move them into the world of your speech. Do this by gaining their attention, relating your topic to their concerns, establishing your credibility on the subject, and previewing your main points. Finally, plan a conclusion that provides a transition from the body, summarizes your major points, gives a sense of closure by referring back to the introduction, and leaves your listeners with a challenge or memorable saying. Throughout your speech, use connectives to link your points and subpoints into a coherent whole.

STUDY AND REVIEW

Your online resources for *Public Speaking: Concepts and Skills for a Diverse Society* offer a broad range of study tools that will help you better understand the material in this chapter, complete assignments, and succeed on tests. Your online resources feature

- Speech videos with critical viewing questions, speech outlines, and transcripts
- Interactive versions of this chapter's Stop and Check activities and Application and Critical Thinking Exercises
- Speech Builder Express and InfoTrac College Edition
- Weblinks related to chapter content
- Study and review tools such as self-quizzes, an interactive glossary, and downloadable audio summaries

You can access your online resources at **http://www.cengage.com/login**, using the access code that came with your book or that you bought online at **http://www.iChapters.com**.

KEY TERMS

The terms below are defined in the margins throughout this chapter.

connectives 186	participatory questions 176
echo 184	preview 182
internal preview 187	rhetorical questions 176
internal summary 187	signpost 186
organizational culture 180	transition 187

APPLICATION AND CRITICAL THINKING EXERCISES

1. Before your next speech, partner with someone in your class. Trade outlines and, using the guidelines in this chapter, evaluate each other's introduction, conclusion, and connectives, and advise your partner on what you think is effective and what could be improved. When you get your own outline and suggestions back, make adjustments that would improve these sections of your speech.

2. Outline a speech given by one of your classmates. Evaluate the effectiveness of the introduction and conclusion. What suggestions, if any, would you give the speaker to improve the beginning or the ending?

3. Review the section on credibility—what your audience thinks of you—in Chapter 6. How and why does a good introduction and conclusion affect your audience's perception of your credibility? How and why does a poor start or finish influence their perception?

4. Read the introductions and conclusions of some speeches you find on **www.americanrhetoric .com**. Evaluate them using the criteria in the text. Does the introduction gain attention, link to the audience, establish credibility, and preview the major points? Does the speaker provide a transition to the conclusion? Review the major points? Provide psychological closure? End memorably? What improvements, if any, would you suggest?

5. Search the Internet for the exact phrase "introductions and conclusions." You should find many sites that were created by both writing and speech instructors. Go to a site for writers, and compare and contrast the guidelines there with those for speakers that you find in this text. What are the similarities? The differences? How do you account for the differences?

SPEECH VIDEO

Go to your online resources to watch and critique a video of Hillary Carter-Liggett's introduction to her informative speech titled "Shakespeare." Then watch Bonita Persons deliver her speech "Driving While Drowsy." To complete her persuasive speech assignment, Bonita chose a topic that she cared deeply about. After she finished, her fellow students commented on the effectiveness of her very personal introduction and conclusion. As you read and watch her speech, evaluate the way she begins and ends it.

Josh Nauman /Cengage Learning

Student Speech with Commentary

DRIVING WHILE DROWSY
Bonita Persons

Introduction

July 3, 2003, a man and his family drive their van down the road as it is getting light. Another driver has been driving since midnight. He tries to pass a bus, but fails to see the van coming toward him. Because he is tired, the driver cannot react quickly enough to slide back into his own lane, and his car collides with the van, killing the woman in the passenger seat.

How well does Bonita fulfill the four major elements of a good introduction? Does her overall introduction make you want to hear more?

Almost everyone will drive while tired at some point in their lives, especially worn out, stressed college students and workers.

I'm guilty of this. I drove tired just last summer when I went to visit my brother in Kansas.

However, drowsy driving is not a good idea. A lot of people are killed because of tired drivers, and the only real solution lies within our hands, but the benefits of avoiding tired driving definitely outweigh the sacrifices one must make.

Body

Underline all the connectives you can find in the body of this outline. Where could she effectively add a transition, internal preview, or internal summary?

Many people have died because of accidents related to tired driving. According to the American Academy of Otolaryngology, driving with sleep apnea is just as bad as driving with an alcohol content of 0.08 percent. In addition, the Pennsylvania Department of Transportation says statistics show that 1,500 people die each year because of drowsy-driving accidents. Finally, the Queensland Transport website on road safety tells us that 1 in 6 fatal crashes in Queensland, Australia, are caused by driving tired. However, these statistics do not include the damage done to cars and other property. All over the world, sleep-related accidents happen.

The consequences for driving while tired can be fatal, so precautions are important. According to David Jamieson, Road Safety Minister in the United Kingdom, most sleep-related accidents happen on Mondays, although most accidents occur on Fridays.

Dr. Mercola, author of *The Total Health Problem*, says that "After 17–19 hours without sleep, performance on some tests was equivalent or worse than that at a blood alcohol content of 0.05%." This may sound like a long time to be up, but consider that if a college student woke up at 7 for this class and did not get to bed until midnight, that is 17 hours without sleep right there. Going to bed at midnight, for many, is early.

Because sleepiness can be a problem, we need to be able to tell when we are getting sleepy. Signs warning that you are tired are fairly obvious and should not be ignored. Queensland's road safety website outlines several signs of fatigue: sore or heavy eyes, dim or fuzzy vision, "seeing" things, droning and humming in the ears, general tiredness, stiffness and cramps, aches and pains, daydreaming, delayed reaction times, unintentional increases or decreases in speed, fumbling for gear changes, and a car that wanders across the road.

Consequently, if you feel yourself getting tired, PULL OFF THE ROAD! The Pennsylvania Department of Transportation says to pull off and take a 15–25 minute nap when you feel tired and to switch drivers every few hours if the drive is going to be long. Make sure the driver has a good night's rest before driving.

Coffee is a stimulant, but the effects, according to PENNDOT, do not come into play for half an hour after you drink it, and the effects do not last long, so it should not be relied on. Interestingly enough, the Driving While Tired Advice and Checklists from the UK states that certain foods such as turkey, warm milk, and bananas induce sleepiness and therefore should NOT be eaten before or during a drive!

Is there a government solution to this problem? According to ABC News, New Jersey is the first state to make driving tired a crime if a deadly accident occurs when there are signs that it is a tired-related accident. But this still does not cure driving while tired. The solution is a decision each person must make as an individual.

The benefits for driving when one is NOT tired are obvious: Lives are saved. The downsides are that one may take a bit longer getting somewhere or may not be able to stay at that place for quite as long. However, when one considers the good versus the bad, the good obviously outweighs the negative.

Conclusion

If we ourselves don't want to become a statistic of tired driving, then we need to take steps to protect ourselves and others. Know when you are tired and do your best to prevent driving then. Longer road trips may be inevitable because you avoid tired driving, but it is worth it if you want to live. I myself will avoid driving while tired, because the woman who was killed in the van that July morning was my mom. So next time you consider driving while tired, consider those in the cars around you and think of whose friend, mother, sister, or brother they are. Do you really want others to go through pain and suffering simply so you can get to your destination a little bit earlier?

Identify the ways this conclusion signals the end and reviews the main points. How effectively does she create psychological closure? What other ending choices could she have made?

11

OUTLINING YOUR SPEECH

THIS CHAPTER WILL HELP YOU

▶ Outline the contents of your speech in a linear form

▶ Create a heading that provides a nutshell look at what you plan to accomplish in your speech

▶ Use standard outlining features including alternation, coordination, indentation, full sentences, and subordination

▶ Prepare note cards or a speaking outline

▶ Know how to record your ideas using an alternative pattern

© Tim Timmerman

NOTICED HER from the very first moment of class. She sat in the front row, arms folded, looking grim. After I took roll, I asked students what they hoped to get out of the class. She said, "Credit." She was a pharmacy major. Why would she ever need public speaking? Every day, there she was, scowling. She even refused to give her first speech.

Then something began to change. She started to relax and turn in outlines and give speeches. One day near the end of the semester, she stayed behind after others left the classroom. "I want to thank you for this class. I was really mad that I was forced to take it, but I found out how useful it turned out to be—especially learning how to outline," she said. "Choosing ideas and supporting materials, organizing my ideas—I have been able to use these skills in many other classes. I just want you to know."

Although it may sometimes seem like "busywork", your instructor has good reasons for requiring you to outline your material. A good outline highlights your speech's framework and displays your ideas and their relationships to one another. And, as the pharmacy student discovered, outlining skills are transferable. Nancy Wood, head of a university study skills and tutorial service, said that many students who come for help have no idea where to start or how to organize their thoughts, but students taking speech classes "confess to us regularly that their speech course is helping them learn to organize and write term papers for their other classes as well."[1]

By now you've done most of the work necessary for creating an outline. In fact, you may have made a **rough draft outline** of your main points and supporting materials. Now it's time to tie everything together and complete a formal content outline.

Experienced speakers know that there's no single way to outline a speech correctly, and there's no set length for an outline. The type of speech, the circumstances, the time limitations—many factors shape your final product. The more speeches you give, the more you'll work out your own method for ordering your ideas, given your individual learning preferences. This chapter presents tips for making full-sentence content outlines, followed by a description of how to prepare speaking notes. It concludes with ideas for alternative, more visual methods of recording your ideas that take into account diversity in individual thinking styles.

How to Prepare a Content Outline

Most instructors require a **content outline**, also called a **preparation outline** or a **full-sentence outline**. This written outline is a record of your major ideas and speech materials and their relationship to one another. It differs from a **script** or a **text**, which includes every word you say. And both differ from the **speaking notes** you actually take to the podium and discard afterwards. Compare and contrast the script at the end of Chapter 7 with the outline in the middle of this chapter and with the speaker's notes presented later in this chapter. Although details may vary, several general guidelines can help you prepare your outlines.

Begin with a Heading

Give your speech a heading which includes your *title*, the *general purpose*, *specific purpose*, finalized *thesis statement*, *preview*, and *organizational pattern* that you've developed using principles found in Chapters 5 and 9. The heading is a nutshell look at what you plan to accomplish. Here is Emily's heading for her speech on biliary atresia:

Topic:	Biliary Atresia
General Purpose:	To inform
Specific Purpose:	To inform my audience about liver function and the disease called biliary atresia.
Central Idea:	Biliary atresia is a rare congenital liver disease that leads to liver failure and death unless treated by the Kasai procedure or a liver transplant.
Preview:	I will inform the audience about liver functions and the rare disease, biliary atresia, that caused me to have a transplant as an infant.
Organizational Pattern:	Topical

Use a Standard Format

Five features—*alternation*, *coordination*, *indentation*, *full sentences*, and *subordination*—make visible the structure and interrelationships of your various speech elements.

Alternate Numbers and Letters

Show the relationships among your ideas by alternating numbers and letters in a consistent pattern. First, identify your major points using one of the patterns described in

rough draft outline preliminary outline that's not yet formatted formally

content, preparation, or **full-sentence outline** formal record of your major ideas and their relationship to one another in your speech

script or **text** writing down every word of the speech

speaking notes key words and phrases you use during your speech and discard afterwards

Chapter 9 and then designate each major point with a Roman numeral (I, II, III, . . .). Under each main point, identify first-level supporting points and give each one a capital letter head (A, B, C, . . .). Give second-level supporting points Arabic numerals (1, 2, 3, . . .), designate third-level points by lowercase letters (a, b, c, . . .), and so on. The following system is typical:

I.   Major point
   A. First-level supporting point
 	
     1. Second-level supporting point
 	
     2. Second-level supporting point
       a. Third-level supporting point
       b. Third-level supporting point
 	
   B. First-level supporting point
 	
II.   Major point
 	
   A. First-level supporting point
 	
   B. First-level supporting point
	I. The visual learning style is common.
	   A. These learners need pictures and words.
	     1. They learn best alone with no noise.
	     2. Bright colors and drawings help.
	       a. Use colored flashcards.
	       b. Make colorful diagrams and charts.
	   B. Visual learners tend to be neat and organized.
	
	II. There are two types of auditory learners.
	   A. *Listening learners* best learn by hearing.
	   B. *Verbal learners* learn from conversation, talking and discussing.

Coordinate Points

The principle of **coordination** means that you give your major points the same basic value or weight, your second-level points are similar in value, and so on. In the following outline, the problem and the solution are major points. First-level points—causes and effects—are coordinated approximately equally. Each first-level point is further supported by coordinated second-level points.

I. Problem
  A. Causes
    1. First Cause
 	
    2. Second Cause
  B. Effects
 	
    1. First Effect
 	
    2. Second Effect
 	
II. Solution
  A. First Solution
  B. Second Solution
	I. People in the U.S. consume too much sugar.
	  A. There are several causes for this.
	    1. Common foods have unrecognized amounts of sugar.
	    2. Carbonated drinks are a major source.
	  B. Obesity is on the increase, even in young children.
	    1. Obesity is linked to several diseases in adults.
	    2. Obesity is linked to Type II diabetes in children.
	II. There are national and personal solutions.
	  A. Nationally, we can increase awareness.
	  B. Personally, we can eat less sugar.

Use Indentation

Indentation involves spacing some lines further to the right in a way that visually separates them from the surrounding text. Indenting various levels of supporting points allows you to show interrelationships between materials. For example, I- and II-level points begin at the left margin, but A and B headings are indented to the right.

---

coordination points arranged into various levels, with the points on a specific level having basically the same value or weight

indentation formatting by spacing inward various levels of points

Third-level supporting points are spaced even further right and so on, as this example illustrates:

I. Sleep deprivation affects safety in our work environments.
  A. Subjects in a sleep-deprivation study did poorly on vigilance, reaction time, and simple arithmetic tasks.
    1. Imagine a truck driver or firefighter with lowered vigilance and reaction time.
    2. Visualize a teacher or bank officer who makes simple math mistakes.
  B. Work accidents related to sleep deprivation include the *Challenger* space shuttle disaster and the Exxon *Valdez* oil spill.

An outline is like a map that helps you plot out where you're going.

Write Your Points in Full Sentences

Complete sentences allow you to see the content you will include in each point. If Emily's introduction to her speech on biliary atresia uses only phrases, it would look like this:

I. Your liver?
II. Not thought much about it
III. My credibility
IV. Function, purpose, biliary atresia, my liver transplant

Obviously, someone reading this outline could not figure out what each point actually covers, and her phrases would function better as a speaking outline. Both Emily and her professor will have a clearer idea of her speech content if she uses full sentences to outline her major points, as this introduction illustrates:

I. Do you think about your liver as much as I do mine?
II. Unless you are a liver transplant recipient, like I am, you may have not thought much about this important organ.
III. Every day I must take medications to stay alive.
IV. Today, I will discuss your liver's function and purpose and the rare liver disease, biliary atresia; then I will describe my liver transplant, the most harrowing adventure of my lifetime.

Another key is to construct **parallel points**. That is, don't write out some points as declarative sentences and others as questions. Avoid mixing phrases and complete sentences, and don't put two sentences in a single point. This student originally made all these mistakes:

I. What is multiple sclerosis (MS)? [a complete sentence in question form]
II. The big mystery! [a sentence fragment or phrase]
III. Who? [a single word in question form]
IV. Effects . . . symptoms of MS. [an incomplete sentence]
V. There are three prominent medications being used right now to treat MS. These are talked about in the magazine *Inside MS*. [two declarative sentences]

Here's how her rewritten points should look:

I. Multiple sclerosis (MS) is a disease of the central nervous system.
II. The causes remain a mystery.
III. Its victims tend to be similar in age, gender, and regional characteristics.
IV. The condition affects eyesight and bodily coordination.
V. Most physicians prescribe one of three major medications.

parallel points making the points similar in construction

PRACTICALLY SPEAKING

OUTLINES AND SPEAKING NOTES

Several people featured in Practically Speaking boxes throughout the text shared practical experiences with outlines.

Brad Lau (Chapter 5): I do background research and gather appropriate materials and then I organize my ideas into a pattern and write them down in outline form. I usually try to speak from a key word outline that I become very familiar with rather than speaking from a manuscript. I occasionally use note cards.

Jim Endicott (Chapter 13): Creating a clear outline is the fulfillment of a silent commitment to the audience.[2] Many professionals use presentation programs such as PowerPoint to help organize ideas. They should first lay out titles (main points) and then ask if the flow of the titles create a crisp and logical path through the content. If not, this is the time to change the order and delete non-essentials. The next level of support material can be outlined in bulleted form under the main point, but presenters should *never* write out their outline on slides and then read the points word-for-word.

Chris McDonald (Chapter 14): Outlining the ideas for my speech topic is helpful because it keeps me on track and ensures that I will get the key message across to my audience. It also enables me to time my speech, which is always a concern in order to run an effective event.

Questions for Discussion

▶ What do you think Jim Endicott means by the statement, "Creating a clear outline is the fulfillment of a silent commitment to the audience?"

▶ Choose an occupation that interests you and interview a person in that career who speaks frequently. What are his or her outlining strategies? Compare and contrast those strategies with the forms of outlining described in this chapter.

Use the Principle of Subordination

The word **subordination** comes from two Latin root words: *sub* (under) and *ordinare* (to place in order). This means you place all first-level points under the major points they support; all second-level points go under the first-level points they support, and so on. Return to the above example and think critically about the speaker's points. Are all her first-level points equal? Don't some seem more logically to follow others? What would happen if she used a problem-solution pattern for first-level points, and then subordinated the other material to the second level of support? Her new outline might look like this:

I. Multiple sclerosis (MS) is a disease of the central nervous system. [problem]
   A. Its causes remain a mystery. [causes of the problem]
   B. Victims tend to be similar in age, gender, and regional characteristics. [extent of the problem]
   C. It affects eyesight and bodily coordination. [effects of the problem]
II. Most physicians prescribe one of three major medications. [solution]

subordination placement of supporting points under major points

Coordinating her major points into a problem-solution pattern is a much more effective way to organize this speech. And subordinating three points—the causes, the extent, and the effects of MS—under the problem section of this speech creates a more logical flow of ideas.

In summary, good content outlines begin with a heading and use a standard format that includes coordinated points arranged by alternating letters and numbers and by indenting material in a way that shows the relationship of ideas to one another. They are written in complete sentences that are parallel in construction, and they contain supporting materials arranged underneath the major ideas.

Emily's complete content outline, shown below with commentary, pulls all these elements together and provides a good model and an explanation of Emily's speech-making strategies. Her professor requires a list of references at the end of the outline. Although she outlines her introduction and conclusion, some instructors ask students to write out these sections of the speech. As you study this outline, notice that it does not read like a speech script. Instead of putting in each word she'll say, she writes one sentence that summarizes the contents of each point.

Student Outline with Commentary

BILIARY ATRESIA
Emily Smith

Topic:	Biliary Atresia
General Purpose:	To inform
Specific Purpose:	To inform my audience about liver function and the disease called biliary atresia.
Central Idea:	Biliary atresia is a rare congenital liver disease that leads to liver failure and death unless treated by the Kasai procedure or a liver transplant.
Preview:	I will inform the audience about liver functions and the rare disease, biliary atresia, that caused me to have a transplant as an infant.
Organizational Pattern:	Topical

Introduction

  I. Do you think about your liver as much as I do mine?
 II. Unless you are a liver transplant recipient, like I am, you may have not thought much about livers.
III. Every day, I take medications to stay alive.
    A. I was born with biliary atresia, a rare congenital disease that leads to liver failure and death unless treated by the Kasai procedure or a liver transplant.
    B. I always wanted to research this topic more, and this was the perfect opportunity to learn fascinating things to share with you.
IV. Today, I will discuss your liver's function and purpose and the rare liver disease, biliary atresia; then I will describe my liver transplant, the most harrowing adventure of my lifetime.

Body

  I. Let's first look at the liver's function and purpose.
    A. *Digestive Health*, updated December 2006, says the liver is one of our most vital organs (Friedel, 2006).
      1. It produces necessary chemicals for digestion.
      2. It breaks down toxic substance and waste and produces bile.

By writing out her heading, Emily makes sure her speech focus is clear and that her outline accomplishes her stated purposes.

Identify your speech introduction, body, and conclusion. This introduction gains attention, relates to the audience, establishes credibility, and previews major points.

Point IV is the preview, the transition between the speech introduction and body. It tells the audience to listen for topically organized information.

Emily labels the body of her speech, and she uses the principle of coordination. Points I, II, and III are first-level points that are made up of second-, third-, and fourth-level supporting materials. Second- and third-level supporting points are subordinated by indentation and alternating numbers and letters.

    B. Bile is a greenish substance with many different functions.
      1. It converts food into energy, makes proteins, and cleanses the body of toxins.
      2. Bile contains bilirubin, which causes the yellow coloring of the skin during jaundice.
        a. Jaundice is caused when red blood cells get old and are destroyed.
          i. A chemical in red blood cells is called bilirubin.
          ii. In a healthy person, bile takes care of this bilirubin.
        b. If bile ducts are hindered, the bile can't destroy bilirubin, and the chemical is turned loose in the body.
        c. The yellow-green skin color and eye color of jaundiced people is caused by the yellow bilirubin.

All points are phrased as declarative sentences, one sentence per point.

II. Jaundice is a leading indicator for many diseases including biliary atresia, a rare disease that appears two to eight weeks after birth.
    A. I was diagnosed when I was two weeks old.
      1. This rare disease, for some unknown reason, affects more girls than boys (Cincinnati Children's Hospital, 2006).
      2. Although the cause is unknown, we were told it is caused by a virus; my mother, a nurse, says that's another way of saying they don't know the cause.
    B. Biliary atresia means the bile ducts are somehow blocked or undeveloped.
      1. The bile can't go into the intestines to perform its usual tasks.
      2. The result is liver failure and eventual death.
      3. The build-up of bilirubin causes symptoms of biliary atresia—jaundice, dark urine, clay-colored stools and weight loss—which show up a couple of weeks after birth.
    C. Infants with biliary atresia are very sick because they can't digest food properly.
      1. None of their waste products get destroyed.
      2. That's why I'm a vegetarian.

This is the separation point between her discussion of the disease and its treatment, so Emily writes out a transition statement.

Transition: Now that you know a little bit about the function of the liver and the condition, biliary atresia, let's look at two treatment options.

III. There were then two options for treatment of biliary atresia: a minor surgery called the Kasai procedure or a complete liver transplant (Cincinnati Children's Hospital, 2008).
    A. The Kasai procedure removes the damaged bile ducts and replaces them with a piece of the baby's own intestine.
      1. This procedure is effective about 1/3 of the time if done during the first eight weeks of life.
      2. Patients generally need a liver transplant before they turn 20 (*Medical Encyclopedia*, 2008).
      3. Doctors performed this procedure on me when I was six weeks old and when I was nine weeks old; both were failures.

Subpoints A and B are first-level points, both with second-level supporting points. B also has third- and fourth-level support.

    B. My only option was a liver transplant.
      1. Doctors didn't expect me to live until my second birthday, but they put me on a waiting list to receive a liver.
        a. This was in the 1980s, and infant transplantation was still fairly new.
        b. They didn't have the latest methods where they transplant a piece of someone else's liver into the patient's body (Chamberlain & Blumgart, 2007).
        c. Babies like me were put on long waiting lists, and many died while waiting.
      2. Liver transplants take between five to about sixteen hours, depending on complications.
        a. My surgery took about six hours with many little miracles during that process.
        b. Transplant patients are hospitalized for 2–3 weeks to take care of any infections and make sure there are no further complications (Stanford University's Liver Transplantation Program, n.d.).
        c. Once released, survivors take many medications to help disguise the liver in the patient's body.

      i. If my body decided that the liver didn't belong to me, it would reject it, and I would have to have another transplant.

     ii. I must take an immunosuppressant for the rest of my life (my magical pills of life) to weaken my immune system so that it won't think my liver is an intruder.

  d. Liver transplant patients usually bounce back quickly, although it takes time to get used to the medications and the weekly blood tests that watch for any negative signs.

Conclusion

I. I could tell many stories of the miracles that surrounded my transplant, but for now I just wanted to inform you about:

  A. The importance of your liver, take care of it!

  B. The signs and causes of jaundice.

  C. An obscure, but deadly liver disease, biliary atresia.

II. I will leave you with this quotation by Robert Byrne (n.d.), which pretty well sums up the conclusion I have come to after asking God why He let me live: "The purpose of life is a life of purpose."

By setting apart the conclusion, she makes sure that she's crafted a memorable ending that summarizes the speech and is both purposeful and brief.

References

Byrne, Robert. (n.d.). *Robert Byrne quotes*. Retrieved June 8, 2008, from http://en.thinkexist.com/quotes/robert_byrne/

Chamberlain, R.S. & Blumgart, L.H. (2007). *Pediatric liver transplantation at UCLA*.

UCLA Health System Transplant Services. Retrieved June 7, 2008, from www2.healthcare.ucla.edu/transplant/liverpeds.html

Cincinnati Children's Hospital Medical Center. (2006, August, last reviewed). Liver Diseases and Treatments. *Biliary Atresia*. Retrieved June 1, 2008, from www.cincinnatichildrens.org/svc/alpha/l/liver/diseases/biliary.htm

Friedel, D. (2006, December 11, last reviewed). Liver & biliary function. *Digestive Health*. Retrieved June 6, 2008, from http://digestive.healthcentersonline.com/liverpancreasbiliary/liverbiliaryfunction.cfm

Medical Encyclopedia. (2008, May 27, last updated). Biliary atresia. MedlinePlus: U.S. National Library of Medicine and the National Institutes of Health. Retrieved June 6, 2008, from www.nlm.nih.gov/medlineplus/ency/article/001145.htm

Stanford University Liver Transplant Program. (n.d.). *Pediatric liver transplantation*. Retrieved June 7, 2008, from http://med.stanford.edu/shs/txp/livertxp/HTML/selection.pediatric.html

Emily formats her references in the American Psychological Association (APA) style. Ask your instructor which format he or she prefers, but always list the references you consulted during your speech preparation.

✓ STOP AND CHECK

EVALUATE YOUR CONTENT OUTLINE

Return to Speech Builder Express and select Completing the Speech Outline to preview your content outline. Using this complete outline, you can easily prepare your speaking outline or note cards. Evaluate your content outline using the checklist shown here. An electronic version of this checklist is available in your online resources.

yes	no	Did I accomplish the following content outline goals?
		1. My heading provides important summary information about my speech.
		2. My introduction, body, and conclusion are clear.
		3. My organizational pattern is clearly identifiable.
		4. My points and subpoints are properly indented.
		5. I have alternated numbers and letters.
		6. I have written out my transition statements.
		7. I have used complete sentences throughout.
		8. My references are in the standard bibliographic form my professor recommends.

How to Create Speaking Notes

Content or full-sentence outlines help you organize your ideas and visualize your points in relationship to one another. They provide a permanent written record that you can file them away after you speak. They are also a good resource to use during rehearsal when you are getting your speech firmly in mind. But content outlines are not *speaking notes*—what you actually use when you deliver the speech. Speaking notes or speaking outlines are temporary; after your speech you can throw them away. They use full sentences in only two places: transition statements and direct quotations. Otherwise, use **key words** for your points, including just enough phrases or words to jog your memory as you speak. This section describes two major formats for speaking notes: note cards and speaking outlines.

Use Note Cards

Writing key words out on note cards and using them in delivery offers several advantages. For one thing, cards are smaller, less noticeable, and easier to handle than standard sheets of paper. They are sturdy enough not to waver if your hand trembles. And if you must deliver your speech without a podium, you can hold your cards in one hand and still use the other to gesture. Here are some tips for creating note cards:

- Use index cards.
- Write legibly; print or type key words in capital letters; double- or triple-space your lines.
- Number your cards so that you can quickly put them in place if they get out of order.
- Write on only one side of each card because turning note cards over can be distracting.
- Delete nonessential words—use only key, or significant, words and short phrases.
- Use no more than five or six lines per card, and space your lines so that you can easily keep your place. For longer speeches, use more cards instead of crowding additional information onto a few cards.
- Highlight important ideas; circle or underline words you want to emphasize during delivery.
- Put delivery advice such as *pause* or *slow down* on your cards.
- Practice in front of a mirror using your note cards. Revise them if they are not as helpful as you would like.
- When you give your speech, use your cards unobtrusively. Place them on the lectern if one is available, and never wave them.
- Don't read from your cards, unless you are reading a direct quotation or giving complicated statistics; then hold up a card and look at it frequently to show your audience that you are being as accurate as possible.[3]

Figure 11.1 shows two note cards for Emily's speech on biliary atresia.

Create a Speaking Outline

A second strategy is to create a speaking outline by writing key terms on a standard sheet of paper. Many of the tips for creating note cards apply to key term outlines, but there are some minor differences:

- Use plenty of space to distinguish between the various sections of your speech.
- Use highlighter pens to distinguish the sections easily. For example, you might underline signposts and transition statements in orange, and use yellow for the introduction, the body, and the conclusion.

key words important words and phrases that will jog the speaker's memory

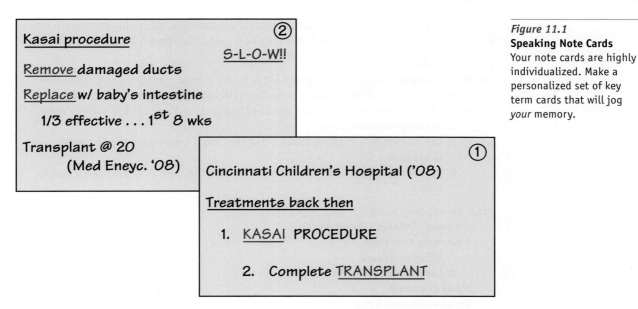

Figure 11.1
Speaking Note Cards
Your note cards are highly
individualized. Make a
personalized set of key
term cards that will jog
your memory.

- Use different font sizes and formatting features to break up visual monotony and to direct your eyes to specific places as you go along. For example, in Figure 11.2, Emily sometimes alternates lowercase and capitalized words.
- If you have several sheets of notes, spread them across the lectern in such a way that you can still see the side edges of the lower pages. Then when you move from one page to another, slip the top sheet off unobtrusively and tuck it at the bottom of the pile.
- If no lectern is available, you can place your pages in a dark-colored notebook or folder that you hold with one hand while gesturing with the other. (Angle the notebook so your audience doesn't see your pages.)

Figure 11.2 shows the first page of a speaking outline for the biliary atresia. If you use brief notes, rather than reading from an outline or trying to memorize your speeches, you can remember your major ideas and supporting materials. Moreover, you can still maintain eye contact with the audience, secure in the knowledge that if you lose your train of thought you can easily glance at these notes to regain your place.

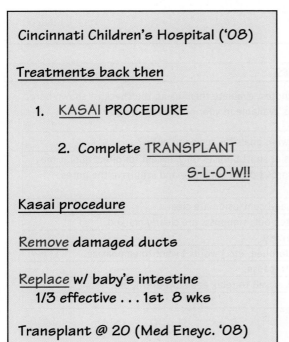

Figure 11.2
Speaking Outline Speaking outlines contain key words to remind you of your ideas plus "advice" words to remind you of your delivery.

To understand the different functions of these outlines, study this section excerpted from Emily's content outline, her speaking notes, and the speech itself:

From her outline:

III. There were then two options for treatment of biliary atresia: a minor surgery called the Kasai procedure or a complete liver transplant (Cincinnati Children's Hospital, 2008).

    B. The Kasai procedure removes the damaged bile ducts and replaces them with a piece of the baby's own intestine.

        1. This procedure is effective about 1/3 of the time if done during the first eight weeks of life.

        2. Patients generally need a liver transplant before they turn 20 (*Medical Encyclopedia*, 2008).

From her speaking notes:

Cincinnati Children's Hospital ('08)

Treatments back then

    1. KASAI procedure

    2. Complete TRANSPLANT

Kasai procedure

<u>Remove</u> damaged ducts

<u>Replace</u> w/ baby's intestine

1/3 effective . . . 1st 8 wks

Transplant @ age 20 (Med Encyc., '08)

From the speech itself: (Note: in extemporaneous delivery, wording varies somewhat each time):

According to the Cincinnati Children's Hospital website (last updated 2008) my parents back then had two options for treating my condition: the Kasai procedure or a complete liver transplant. The Kasai procedure is a comparatively minor surgery where the doctors would remove part of my damaged bile ducts and replace them with a piece of my

✓ STOP AND CHECK

EVALUATE YOUR SPEAKING NOTES

When you have finished your speaking notes, evaluate them using the checklist shown here. An electronic version of this checklist is available in your online resources.

yes	no	Did I accomplish the following goals for speaking notes?
		1. My notes have key words or short phrases only, except for direct quotations.
		2. I can't find any other words I could eliminate and still have the notes remain useful.
		3. My introduction, body, and conclusion are clear.
		4. My transitions are written out; signposts are clearly marked.
		5. I have used color effectively.
		6. I have highlighted (underlined, etc.) words I want to emphasize.
		7. I marked where I want to pause.
		8. I made notes to remind myself to relax and slow down, etc.
		9. I numbered my cards.

own intestine. When done within the first eight weeks of life, the procedure is effective about one-third of the time, although the 2008 *Medical Encyclopedia* says patients like me usually need a liver transplant before their twentieth birthday.

How to Work with an Alternative Pattern

Diversity in Practice: Individual Cognitive Preferences (on page 204) points out that diversity in individual thinking styles has an influence on outlining. If your **cognitive preferences** lean toward more visual or imagistic thinking, you might prefer an alternative pattern, such as the wave, spiral, or star, described in Chapter 9. Although your depiction of your speech's content will be less conventional, you can still design an appropriate representation of your ideas and their relationship to one another by using the tips provided here:[4]

▶ First, select an appropriate pattern and sketch the diagram.
▶ With your pattern in mind, write out your main points.
▶ Then indicate what you'll use for developmental material and subordinate this material under the main point it supports.
▶ Indicate how you plan to begin and end your speech, and then write out key transition statements.
▶ Use standard indentation and numbering only if it's helpful.

Figure 11.3 provides an example of Mark Antony's dramatic speech from Shakespeare's play, *Julius Caesar*, formatted into a wave pattern. You can watch this speech at **www.youtube.com/watch?v=eNRoeMvzMVo**.

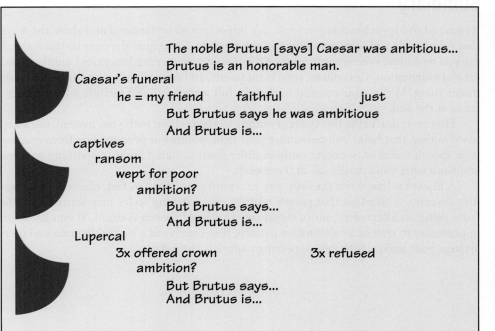

Figure 11.3
Using an Alternate Pattern This figure depicts the points in Mark Antony's speech visualized in a wave form.

cognitive preference comprised of the ways you typically like to perceive, reason, remember, and solve problems; it's influenced by your culture but unique to you

DIVERSITY IN PRACTICE

INDIVIDUAL COGNITIVE PREFERENCES

A DIVERSITY PERSPECTIVE should take into account individual differences in cognitive preferences (sometimes called thinking styles or learning preferences). Because every student's thinking style is unique, every classroom contains "a diverse population of learners."[5] Your thinking style is comprised of the ways you typically prefer to perceive, reason, remember, and solve problems. Our cultures influence our styles to an extent, but your particular way of processing information is unique to you.[6]

In 1981, the cognitive scientist Roger Sperry won the Nobel Prize in Physiology or Medicine for his research in brain hemispheric dominance. His studies revealed that our right brains process information more globally, intuitively, and artistically; in contrast, our left-brain processes are more linear, analytic, logical, and computational.[7] This text obviously will not describe the finer points of cognitive science research; however, diversity of cognitive preferences and the fact that they reflect both a personal and a cultural orientation fit the emphasis of this text.

Why is this topic in a chapter on outlining? Well, the linear form of outlining described in this chapter and in most public speaking texts is a more left-brained way to frame a speech, which may or may not match your learning preferences. Although you are required to produce a linear outline, your personal style may be more holistic, and when you organize speeches in contexts outside the classroom, you may prefer alternative, more visual ways of showing your points.

To learn more about this topic, do an InfoTrac College Edition search for "thinking styles," "cognitive preferences," "learning styles," or other related terms.

Summary

As part of the speechmaking process, it's important to understand and show the ways that your points and subpoints relate to one another. Consequently, your instructor may ask you to outline your ideas in a linear form, using alternating letters and numbers and careful indentation. Coordinate your main points, and subordinate supporting materials under them. Write your content outline in full sentences, and include a list of references at the end.

However, don't take this content outline to the podium with you. Instead, use a key word outline that helps you remember your main points but prevents you from reading your speech verbatim. Content outlines differ from speaking notes or speaking outlines and from what you actually say in the speech.

A linear outline is not the only way to record your ideas; in fact, one way to recognize diversity is to admit that people with various learning styles may actually benefit from using an alternative, more visual way to record speech content. If you have the opportunity to choose an alternative pattern, first sketch out a simple diagram and then arrange your major ideas and supporting materials around it.

STUDY AND REVIEW

Your online resources for *Public Speaking: Concepts and Skills for a Diverse Society* offer a broad range of study tools that will help you better understand the material in this chapter, complete assignments, and succeed on tests. Your online resources feature

- Speech videos with critical viewing questions, speech outlines, and transcripts
- Interactive versions of this chapter's Stop and Check activities and Application and Critical Thinking Exercises
- Speech Builder Express and InfoTrac College Edition
- Weblinks related to chapter content
- Study and review tools such as self-quizzes, an interactive glossary, and downloadable audio summaries

You can access your online resources at **http://www.cengage.com/login**, using the access code that came with your book or that you bought online at **http://www.iChapters.com**.

KEY TERMS

The terms below are defined in the margins throughout this chapter.

cognitive preferences 203
content, preparation, or
full-sentence outline 193
coordination 194
indentation 194
key words 200

parallel points 195
rough draft outline 193
script or text 193
speaking notes 193
subordination 196

APPLICATION AND CRITICAL THINKING EXERCISES

1. Outline an in-class speech while it is being given by one of your classmates. After the speech, give the outline to the speaker, and ask him or her to check its contents for completeness and faithfulness to the speech.
2. Using the same outline, ask another student to evaluate your formatting—use of indentation, alternating numbers and letters, complete sentences, and the like.
3. Work with another person in your class and create speaking notes for one of the speeches or outlines in Appendix C.
4. Before you give your next speech, work from your content outline to prepare a speaking outline. Let a classmate evaluate both outlines and make revisions that would improve either one or both.
5. To understand how outlines are adapted for situations outside the classroom, go to http://sixminutes.dlugan.com/2008/02/29/speech-preparation-3-outline-examples/. The author of this public speaking and presentation skills blog shows the general framework for outlines that could be used in a scientific conference talk, a community association meeting, and a business proposal to investors. How are these outlines like and how are they different from the content outlines described in this chapter?
6. People who are experienced speakers do not always prepare a content outline, complete with heading and references. Ask your instructor how she or he prepares lectures, informal talks, and speeches to groups outside the classroom.

12

CHOOSING EFFECTIVE LANGUAGE

THIS CHAPTER WILL HELP YOU

▶ Explain how words are linked to culture and meaning

▶ Distinguish between the denotative and connotative meanings of words

▶ Define dialect and jargon, and explain when they are appropriate in public speaking

▶ Recognize examples of epithets, euphemisms, and inclusive language

▶ List six guidelines for effective language in public speaking

▶ Understand how alliteration, rhyming, repetition, metaphor, simile, personification, and hyperbole can make a speech more interesting

▶ Give guidelines for listening and speaking in linguistically diverse contexts

© Tim Timmerman

LANGUAGE DOESN'T JUST convey ideas. The word choices you make also provide clues about your region of origin, age, educational level, income level, sex, ethnicity, and occupation, as these examples show:

▶ *Regional distinctions:* Oregonians might purchase a can of pop; New Yorkers would call it soda; in much of the South, it's a coke (meaning any brand of soda pop).

▶ *Occupational distinctions*: Communication professors say things like "the exclusions that characterize the historical practice of the bourgeois public sphere are constitutive of the concept itself. . . ."[1] Stockbrokers, barbers, and dentists don't talk like this.

▶ *Cultural and gender distinctions*: The Setswana language (from Botswana in Africa) has five basic color terms (black, white, red, blue/green, and brown).[2] English has eleven basic terms, plus hundreds of distinctions such as maroon, sage, and periwinkle. In general, women use more extensive and elaborate color terms than men do.[3]

In the study of rhetoric, language falls within the *canon of style*, which is the focus of this chapter. First, it looks at various aspects of language and examines how our vocabularies both reveal and express cultural assumptions. Next, it provides tips for effective language choices in public speeches. Finally, it discusses language issues in linguistically diverse settings.

Languages Reflect Culture

Languages are verbal codes comprised of a system of symbols that a community of speakers uses to share their ideas. **Symbols** represent or stand for objects and concepts within the community. We sometimes use visual symbols, such as a donkey or an elephant to represent political parties. But more commonly we use verbal symbols—**words** that stand for or represent cultural ideas. Each member of the culture must learn the language in order to communicate and interact within the group. Cocultures often use both the larger culture's vocabulary and terminology that is unique to their group.

Devan Marchbanks

Languages name what a culture deems important enough to label. English has many color-related words, but some cultures have as few as five basic terms that denote all hues. Obviously, color distinctions are more significant here than there.

Words and Meaning

In *New Words and a Changing American Culture*, Raymond Gozzi[4] explains that words are the names we give to our "cultural memories." They serve as "markers of cultural attention" or shared experiences that we consider significant enough to name. Put another way, one or more people in a culture notice a phenomenon, formulate a concept about it, and label it, encoding their idea into a word. The process looks something like this.

Long ago humans:

1. *Noticed a phenomenon*—some creatures can fly.
2. *Formed a concept*—all these creatures have two legs, two wings, a beak, and feathers.
3. *Created a label for this category* of flying animals—*bird* (English), *oiseau* (French), *pájaro* or *ave* (Spanish), and so on.

According to this theory, our vocabularies name what our societies identify as significant, and our labels carve out the ways we interpret our world, forming our social realities. The theorist Kenneth Burke explains that when we learn to "name", we assume a perspective on the world.[5] Some examples might help.

How many mustache-related words do you know? One? Two? An Albanian dictionary gives more than twenty possibilities (along with numerous eyebrow-related words).[6]

How about camel-related words? If you lived in Somalia, you'd have words for a male pack camel (*awr*), dairy camels (*irmaan*), a female camel kept away from her young (*kareeb*), a camel loaded with water vessels (*dhaan*), and so on—more than forty different terms. You'd also have dozens of words for camel diseases, things camels do, and things made from camels.[7]

languages verbal codes consisting of symbols that a speech community uses for communication

symbols signs that represent or stand for objects and concepts

words verbal symbols that stand for or represent ideas

English has many time-related words such as hours, minutes, milliseconds, tomorrow, or eternity; the Hopi language has no word for later.[8]

Obviously, vocabulary words show that facial hair or camels aren't as significant in English-speaking cultures as time is and that time in Hopi culture is less rigid than in English-speaking cultures.

It's easy to see how humans create words for visible objects such as birds, camels, buildings, or mustaches, but we also name less tangible experiences, actions, feelings, and ideas. Language is, in Owen Barfield's words, "the storehouse of imagination"[9]. Here are a few examples:

> Imaginary things: unicorn, Martian, elf
> Qualities of objects: soft, generous, wide
> Feelings: anger, envy, love
> States of being: happiness, depression, gratitude
> Abstractions: justice, beauty, conscience
> Actions: exercise, study, clean up

Languages change to reflect cultural changes. Among the thousands of words added to English in the last few decades are *gridlock*, *serial killer*, *microchip*, *junk food*, and *minivan*. Sportscaster Chick Hearn added *slam dunk* and *air ball*. More recent additions include *carb-friendly*, *phish*, and *blue state/red state*. When your grandparents were growing up, there were no microchips or junk food, no carb-friendly foods or slam dunks. They either didn't exist or they weren't important enough to name.[11] English often adopts words from other languages, including *giraffe* (Arabic), *ambiance* (French), and *kamikaze* (Japanese). Meanings also change over time; you notice this every time you read a Renaissance text such as a Shakespearean play. Thankfully, footnotes translate the archaic words into contemporary English.

---

dialect a variant form of a language

Standard English the English dialect most commonly used in public speaking and in U.S. institutions

code switching changing from one dialect to another

> ### DIVERSITY IN PRACTICE
> ## DIALECTS
>
> A DIALECT IS A VARIANT FORM OF A LANGUAGE that differs in pronunciation, vocabulary, and/or grammar. English dialects include British English, American English, Black English (sometimes called ebonics or African American English, AAE), international English, and a variety of other regional and ethnic group variations.[10] **Standard English** is the dialect most common in institutions such as education, business, and broadcasting in the United States; it is the language of print and the version of English generally used in classroom speeches.
>
> Dialects other than Standard English function effectively in many settings, and if you speak one, you may choose to be bidialectical—using Standard English in public contexts and your dialect around family and friends. This is called **code switching**. Bank officer Pauline Jefferson, for instance, uses Standard English to transact business with customers in her bank and to make public presentations for her coworkers. However, in front of a small female audience in her local church, she alternates codes, switching between Standard English and AAE.
>
> For more information, log on to InfoTrac College Edition and read Jeanette Gilsdorf's article "Standard Englishes and World Englishes." The Internet also has many sources of American slang and idioms. One interesting site, set up for English as a Second Language students is **www.schandlbooks.com/AmericanSlang.html**.

Denotative Meaning

A word denotes or "points" to an object or abstract idea. Thus, a word's **denotative meaning**, the meaning you find in a dictionary, is what the word names or identifies. Many words are **ambiguous**; they have more than one meaning, so you must rely on the context to determine which meaning fits the situation. For instance, the word *pot* could denote at least five things:

▶ A rounded container used chiefly for domestic purposes
▶ A sum of money, as in the total amount of bets at stake at one time (the jackpot)
▶ An enclosed frame of wire, wood, or wicker used to catch fish or lobsters
▶ Slang for marijuana
▶ Ruin, as in "her business went to pot"[12]

When you cook in a pot, you think of the first meaning. But when you talk about legalizing pot, you know you're not talking about cooking or poker. The context helps you discern what is meant. As you plan language for your speech, choose the correct word for the correct context to denote your intended meaning. Consult a dictionary or thesaurus if you are unsure.

Increasing your vocabulary and discriminating among shades of meaning between words are valuable skills, because a larger vocabulary gives you more power to communicate your thoughts precisely. Check your vocabulary prowess by searching the Internet for the list of 100 words that every high school graduate should know. (It's very challenging!)

Connotative Meaning

Although words denote objects and concepts, they also carry emotional overtones or **connotative meanings**. That is, words not only stand for ideas; they also represent feelings and associations related to those ideas. For instance, the dictionary says the term *police officer* denotes "a member of a police force" and *principal* denotes "the chief executive officer of an educational institution."[13] But police officer and principal have different connotations for different individuals depending on their experiences. Some people like police officers because they have relatives or friends in that job; others fear or mistrust them because they've had negative experiences

denotative meaning what a word names or identifies

ambiguous word that identifies more than one object or idea; its meaning depends on the context

connotative meaning emotional overtones, related feelings, and associations that cluster around a word

Universal/The Kobal Collection/Grodon, Melinda Sue/Picture Desk

In the movie *Patch Adams*, Robin Williams plays a medical student who tries to treat patients' emotional as well as physical needs. In one key scene, he comes to a dying man, dressed as an angel, and reads him denotative definitions (to expire) and euphemisms (cash in your chips) for death. Eventually, the man begins to contribute his own euphemisms to the list (to check out) and accepts his fate. Watch this clip at **www.youtube.com/ watch?v=jwFxrtpPitU.**

with law enforcement professionals. Similarly, a person's school experiences influence his or her view of principals. Each person's reactions form the connotative meanings of the words for that individual.

Because language can be emotionally charged, people sometimes choose negatively loaded words to demean persons or ideas, or they substitute neutral or positive terms to talk about unpopular ideas. To discuss this further, we now turn to epithets and euphemisms.

Epithets

Epithets are words or phrases, often with negative connotations, that describe some quality of a person or group. For example, one political party calls the other *extremists* because opinion polls show that voters respond negatively to that term. Within hours, the attacked party counters with the term *big government spenders* or another negative term. Words like *nerd* or *pig* (for police officers) are negative epithets that function to frame perceptions about people in these groups. Calling anti-abortion advocates *anti-choice* creates a negative image, whereas the group's self-chosen title, *pro-life*, has positive connotations.

Members of labeled groups often try to lessen the negative power of the epithet by accepting and using the term themselves. Police officers take the letters of the word *pig* and reinterpret them to form the slogan Pride, Integrity, Guts. And *Newsweek* reported on a group of female engineering students who label themselves "Nerd Girls", star in a YouTube video titled "Meet the Nerd Girls", and conduct weekly outreach programs for younger women, where they describe the benefits of being an engineer.[14]

Euphemisms

Euphemisms, in contrast, are words or phrases that substitute an agreeable or inoffensive term for a more embarrassing, unpleasant, or offensive word. Euphemisms are commonly used for things we hesitate to speak about such as bodily functions (*go to the powder room*), religion (*the Man Upstairs*) or weight (*ample proportions*). Euphemisms also mask unpleasant situations such as corporate layoffs. It's supposedly easier to be *dehired* or *downsized* rather than *fired*.

Public speakers, especially politicians, often use euphemisms for controversial actions, ideas, and policies. Their proposals are meant to *protect the rights of the middle class* (in contrast to their opponents, who are obviously *obstructionists*). Their planned tax increases become *revenue enhancements* or *investments in America*. Similarly, *shell shock* (World War I) became *combat fatigue* (World War II), which became *post-traumatic stress syndrome* (Vietnam War). Each subsequent term further removes the condition from its cause.[15] Be alert for connotative language in your research. By carefully choosing their wording, speakers hope to create perceptions that produce their desired spin or interpretation. (Learn more about this subject by doing an Internet search for the word *euphemisms* or *doublespeak*.)

Jargon

Jargon is a specialized, technical vocabulary and style that serves special groups (doctors, lawyers), interests (feminism, education), activities (football, gardening), and so on. For example, football has specialized meanings for *drive*, *down*, and *safety*. When everyone in your audience knows the meaning of the jargon, it's appropriate to use it. However, when you're communicating with nonspecialists, you should define and clarify technical terms, or you will exclude some of your audience. Translating jargon is a good way to demonstrate your rhetorical sensitivity.

In summary, languages are *systems of symbols*—words that denote or stand for ideas and evoke feelings or connotative meanings that differ from person to person. Carefully

epithets words or phrases with powerful negative connotations, used to describe some quality of a person or group

euphemism word or phrase that substitutes an inoffensive term for a potentially offensive, embarrassing, or unpleasant thing

jargon a specialized, technical vocabulary that serves the interests and activities of a particular group

STOP AND CHECK

THINK CRITICALLY ABOUT DENOTATIVE AND CONNOTATIVE WORDS

Test your understanding of meanings with these exercises.

1. Whenever they launch a new product, marketers carefully select terminology that will have positive connotations for consumers. Look up two or three advertisements in your favorite magazines, and then list some of the words found in each ad. What is the denotative meaning of each word on your list? Now jot down some of your personal connotations for each term. Evaluate the overall marketability of the term itself.

2. Work with your classmates to make a list of the car models owned by class members (Mustang, Explorer, Sport, and so on). Within a small group, identify the denotative meaning of each word. Then discuss the connotative associations you think the manufacturers hope will sell the car.

choose your words, making sure you use the correct word in context. Pay attention to connotative meanings, either positive or negative, that listeners might attach to your words. And demonstrate that you are rhetorically sensitive by adapting your dialect and your jargon to your audience and the occasion. As you do this, you take into account the cultural implications of your language choices.

Use Language Ethically: Inclusive Language

Language choices have ethical implications because words and phrases can include or exclude, affirm or dismiss individuals or entire groups.[16] A university publication, *Just Talk: Guide to Inclusive Language*,[17] defines discriminatory language as words that create or reinforce a hierarchy of difference between people. It is both a symptom of and contributor to the unequal social status of women, people with disabilities, people from various ethnic and social backgrounds, and so on. Consequently, it's important to use nondiscriminatory, inclusive language.

Emory University's Statement on **Inclusive Language** recommends, "A recognition of the full humanity of all peoples should prompt an attempt to speak and think in ways which include all human beings and degrade none."[18] Using inclusive language is not only ethical, it's practical because it can increase your credibility. One study[19] found that speakers who put down persons with disabilities or focus on the disability rather than on the individual lose credibility, likeability, and persuasiveness. Here are several guidelines for the sensitive use of language.

▶ *Avoid language that privileges one group over another.* **Sexist language** subtly gives priority to males, their activities, and their interests. One type, **nonparallel language**, talks differently about women and men. *Actress* (setting apart a *woman* actor) is nonparallel language, as is *male nurse* or *female judge*. (Would you ever say *female nurse* or *male judge*?) *Man and wife* are nonparallel, but *husband and wife* are parallel because both words focus on roles. **Ageist language** portrays older people in ways that privilege youthfulness and demean or devalue age. Phrases like *over the hill* or *look ten years younger* subtly reinforce the notion that youth is better than age. **Racist language**, similarly, favors one racial or ethnic group and degrades or devalues others. Nonsensitive language also highlights physical conditions, demeans sexual orientation, puts down a particular religion or social class, and so on.

inclusive language ethical terminology that affirms and includes, rather than excludes, persons or groups of people

sexist language language that negatively influences the way listeners perceive men or women

nonparallel language language that does not treat the two sexes equally

ageist language language that negatively influences the way listeners think about older people

racist language language that privileges one racial group over another

- *Avoid stereotyping.* Recognize and avoid language that perpetuates stereotypes of athletes as stupid, Native Americans as alcoholics, and so on. That Democrats are pro-choice (at least forty states have Democrats for Life chapters), and Chinese Americans are Buddhists (most are Christian) are two additional stereotypes.
- *Avoid creating invisibility.* Language can render people and groups invisible. The "generic *he*" is a good example; forms of *he* once designated a person of either sex. But the statement "Everyone should wash his hands before eating" implies that only men eat. Similarly, the use of the suffix *–man* makes women invisible. So substitute inclusive labels such as *chair* for chairman, *mail carrier* for mailman, and *firefighter* for fireman. Other language assumes that relationships are all heterosexual or that Americans equals U.S. residents. (Canadians, Brazilians, and Guatemalans are also Americans.)

ETHICS IN PRACTICE

THE INTERPLAY OF LEGAL RIGHTS AND HUMAN RIGHTS

At a Congressional hearing on demeaning language in entertainment, committee members quizzed entertainment industry executives about the production and distribution of works with explicit and demeaning lyrics. When asked if they counseled artists about their language choices (the answer was yes) or if they refused to produce works with demeaning language (the answer was no) the producers uniformly invoked the performers' First Amendment rights to free speech.

Most people would agree that free speech is foundational to a democracy, but on the other hand, is there a human right *not* to be a victim of demeaning language or hate speech? Chapter 3 introduced the term *rightsabilities*: rights + responsibilities. How should they be balanced?

Dolores Frida, writing in the *New York Daily News* (Latino), argues that most songs throughout history have been about women,

> But when, with rhyme but without reason, we are called bitches and ho's and *perras* (female dogs) and *potras* (female horses) in songs heard by millions, and that language becomes part of the culture, it is time to say ¡*basta*! (enough). [20]

She does not advocate censorship, but she says women can walk off the dance floor when demeaning songs play. They can stop buying CDs, and they can start producing and buying their own songs.

Questions

1. Is hate speech the same as demeaning language? Why or why not?
2. How might hate speech violate someone's human rights?
3. What limits, if any, should the government put on speech? How about universities or other institutions? What are your personal limitations?
4. Have you heard "horror stories" about "thought police" going too far? How do you respond?

 For more information about Congressional hearings on music lyrics, go to **www .youtube.com/watch?v=JXtk-bw5YZw.**

Delores Frida's article, "Revenge of the muses: could it be that finally women have had it with demeaning language?" is in the *New York Daily News/Latino* at **www.nydailynews .com/latino/2007/05/09/2007-05-09_revenge_of_the_muses.html.**

▶ *Avoid demeaning language.* Epithets are demeaning because they frame negative perceptions of a group. Think about how the negative labels commonly applied to the elderly (*old duffer, little old lady, granny, old hag,* or *dirty old man*) create mental images that demean seniors. Other examples of slurs include *woman driver, sissy, dumb blonde,* and *computer nerd.*

▶ *Avoid dismissive language.* Dismissive language or put-downs are applied to people in ways that discount the importance of their ideas. Phrases like *just a secretary, white trash,* and *typical female* imply that person's ideas are not worth hearing.

▶ *Avoid undue emphasis on differences.* Mention differences only when they matter in the context of the speech. For instance, say "*my professor*" unless it is somehow important to say "my *Latina* professor". Don't mention someone's competency as if it were unusual for that group: Instead of "an *intelligent* welfare recipient," simply say "a welfare recipient." Don't describe the disabled as helpless victims to be pitied and aided, but don't suggest they are more heroic, courageous, patient, or special than others, and avoid contrasting them to *normal* people.[21]

In short, terminology is not neutral. The words you select have the power to influence audience perceptions regarding issues as well as individuals and groups. The fact that some language choices demean or put down others raises ethical questions and colors your listeners' impressions about you. Choosing inclusive language is one way to show respect for diversity and enhance your personal credibility as well.

✓ STOP AND CHECK
AVOIDING DISCRIMINATORY LANGUAGE

With a small group of your classmates, select a group that has been demeaned by language use. This may include women, members of specific ethnic groups, religious groups, or groups with alternative lifestyles.

1. Make a list of some terms that outsiders have used to label group members.
2. Then list some labels the group places on itself.
3. Assess the connotative meanings associated with the words on each list.

   With a few classmates, talk about ways you can select language that respects the group you've chosen. (To investigate this topic further, do an InfoTrac search for an exact term such as "sexist language" or "racist language.")

Use Language Effectively

Language is effective when it fits the context, purpose, subject matter of the speech, and your personal style. Six principles in the canon of style will help you choose language more effectively: accuracy, appropriateness, conciseness, clarity, concreteness, and vividness.

Be Accurate

Accuracy involves three areas: meaning, context, and grammar. Check a word's meaning by looking it up in your dictionary. However, it's also important to know the context in which the word is used. For example, a Japanese student once described a wreck that "distorted" the car door. Her Japanese-English dictionary came up with *distort* to convey the idea that the car was bent, caved in, or dented. Although *distort* does mean crooked or contorted, no native speaker of English would use it in the context of a dented fender.

In addition, use standard grammar when the situation calls for Standard English. Nonstandard forms such as *me and him* (instead of he and I) or *they was* (instead of they were) or *it don't* (for it doesn't) create negative impressions in public presentations. The key is to adapt your grammar to fit the occasion. The grammar-checking feature on your word processor or a style manual can help you check grammatical forms.

Be Appropriate

Generally, language in public settings is more formal, with fewer slang expressions; however, your audience and the situation should have the final influence over your linguistic choices. For example, the language in a lecture differs from the language in a eulogy. Similarly, you'd use different words and different levels of formality when speaking to teenagers gathered in a park than when addressing members of an alumni association at a formal banquet, even for the same topic.

A dialect can be appropriate for some speakers, but not for others. An African American, for instance, might use African American English (AAE) when it's expected and appropriate; however, a Euro-American or an Asian American who used AAE, even in the same setting, would almost certainly be out of line.

Famous speakers such as Martin Luther King, Jr., adapt to various settings, as an excerpt from Jonathan Reider's book explains:

> King was . . . a code switcher who switched in and out of idioms as he moved between black and white audiences. But he also made such moves *within* his black talk and his white talk. . . . [He was] a man who blended all sorts of oppositions. The key crossings were not just between black and white but between raw and refined, sacred and secular, prophetic and pragmatic. This mixing suggests . . . a "postethnic" man . . .[22]

Be Concise

Because directness is valued in the United States, we commonly eliminate unnecessary words or **verbiage**. However, it's easy to clutter a speech with verbiage—especially a demonstration speech, where this form is common: "What you want to do next is you want to take the coffee and pour it over the cake. . . ." It would be more concise to say, "Next, pour the coffee over the cake." This excerpt from a student speech on the value of learning a second language contrasts how he actually gave the speech with how he could have given it:

As he gave it:

> I became interested in this topic upon the constant hounding of my father urging me to take a foreign language, preferably Japanese, the reason being is because my major is business, and the Japanese are dominating the international business scene.

As he might have given it:

> I became interested in this topic because my father constantly hounded me to take a foreign language—preferably Japanese, because my major is business, and the Japanese are dominating the international business scene.

Although brevity or conciseness is valued in the United States, many other cultures value flowery words and language. Consequently, what we may consider verbiage, other groups may regard as essential elements of eloquence.

---

verbiage nonessential language

"SAY, ISN'T THAT THE GUY WHO USED TO DRAFT LEGAL DOCUMENTS AT OUR LAW FIRM?"

Harley Schwadron / www.cartoonstock.com. Used with permission.

Use of specialized language, such as jargon, is appropriate in contexts where everyone knows the terminology. However, be sure to define words or phrases you know your listeners will have trouble understanding.

Be Clear

The purpose of public speaking is to clarify ideas, not make them harder to understand. One of the best ways to be clear is to avoid jargon, but because many topics involve technical terms, you may have to look up jargon words to translate them into understandable English. Jesse failed to do this in his discussion of how AIDS is transmitted:

> We've all been taught that AIDS is perinatal and that it is transmitted through sexual contact.

When asked what *perinatal* meant, Jesse couldn't answer; the word came from an article he had read, and he had not bothered to look it up. (It means "associated with the birth process, the period immediately before, during, or just after the time of birth.") If he'd used his dictionary, he could have said instead:

> We've been taught that AIDS is transmitted from mother to child perinatally—that is, during the birth process—and that it is transmitted through sexual activity.

This brief definition clarifies the word's meaning and makes the speech more understandable.

Be Concrete

Another important aspect of style, one that can help your listeners form precise understandings, is to choose **concrete words** that are specific rather than abstract, particular rather than general. Words range along a scale of abstraction such as this:

abstract/general	animal
	invertebrate
	insect
	butterfly
concrete/particular	Blue Morpho butterfly

When you say, "I photographed a Blue Morpho butterfly," your ideas are much more concrete than when you say, "I photographed an insect." But that is more concrete than "I photographed an animal." The more distinct your word choices, the more vivid your images and the more precise your meanings.

concrete words specific, rather than general or abstract, terms

Here is an excerpt from British author Doris Lessing's lecture to the Nobel Peace Prize Committee[23]; it is exceptional for its use of concrete language:

> [I'm in] northwest Zimbabwe early in the eighties, and I am visiting a friend who was a teacher in a school in London. He is here "to help Africa" as we put it. He is a gently idealistic soul and what he found here in this school shocked him into a depression, from which it was hard to recover. This school . . . consists of four large brick rooms side by side, put straight into the dust, one two three four, with a half room at one end, which is the library. In these classrooms are blackboards, but my friend keeps the chalks in his pocket, as otherwise they would be stolen. There is no atlas, or globe in the school, no textbooks, no exercise books, or biros [ballpoint pens], in the library are no books of the kind the pupils would like to read: they are tomes from American universities, hard even to lift, rejects from white libraries, detective stories, or with titles like *Weekend in Paris* or *Felicity Finds Love*.

Lessing's concrete language presents sensory imagery that helps you place yourself into the sights and the emotions of the setting. The rooms are "put straight into the dust," the books are "tomes . . . hard to lift . . . rejects . . ."; each image is carefully chosen.

Vague words have indefinite boundaries and are consequently imprecise. For example, what is a hill? When does it become a mountain? Who is young? An 80-year-old thinks a 50-year-old is young, but the 50-year-old thinks young is 35. What is large? Small? Compared to what? A large glass of orange juice is not on the same scale as a large barn. You can minimize your use of vague words by choosing specific details to define or illustrate what you mean. For instance, if you talk about a small inheritance, give a dollar figure that shows what you consider small. One listener may think $500 is small whereas another has $50,000 in mind.

✓ STOP AND CHECK

CHOOSING MORE PRECISE WORDING

The purpose of this exercise is to raise your awareness of vague words that we typically use in place of more precise ones. For example, you can often replace *get,* an ambiguous verb, with a more concrete term. In the blank that follows each sentence, replace *get* (or a form thereof) with more precise wording.

Can you *get* the mustard, please? _____

What did you *get* him for his birthday? _____

Why did you *get* angry about that? _____

I'm *getting* ready to outline my speech. _____

He *got* a thousand dollars just for giving one speech! _____

It *got* really hot yesterday afternoon. _____

He *gets* excited just before a big race. _____

After I studied the calculus problem for over an hour, I finally *got* it! _____

You can *get* information 24 hours a day on the Internet. _____

After he *gets* here, we can leave. _____

Be Interesting

A major speaking goal is to enable your audience to understand and remember the information you present. Using colorful, vivid language is one way to support your ideas and keep your listeners' attention and interest. Some linguistic devices that can make

vague words imprecise terms that have indefinite boundaries

your speech more memorable are alliteration, rhyming, repetition, metaphors, similes, personification, and hyperbole.

Alliteration

Alliteration is the use of words that have the same recurring initial sounds. Alliteration can occur within a sentence: an environmental activist wondered what "traits, tenacity, and talents" make a good environmentalist?[24] Another speaker referred to author Harriet Beecher Stowe as "very proper, primly dressed, and precisely spoken."[25] Alliteration is also a good way to help listeners remember your main points. William Brody alliterated both the title and the main points in his speech, "What's Promised, What's Possible":[26]

> I'd like to tell you about the five C's of healthcare. . . . Two of these five C's you already know—cost and coverage. These are the issues we hear about all the time. . . . And while everyone is talking about the costs of health care and the lack of coverage, meaningful change will only come when we address other issues.
>
> These are the other 3 C's—the issues we're not hearing about: consistency, complexity, and chronic illness. . . .

Rhyming

Rhymes—whether single words, longer phrases, or entire lines—are comprised of words that end in the same sounds. Although rap artists rhyme their entire presentations, most people use rhymes in more limited ways. In his speech about electronic drums, Bob rhymed three words within one sentence: "What or who would you rather have in your band, a *mean* and *clean* drum *machine* or a stereotypical rock drummer?"

Rhymes are also effective for wording your main points. Here are two examples:

We are faced with two choices:
    Retreat
    Compete

Workplaces typically have three generations of employees.[27]
    Boomers
    Bloomers
    Zoomers

As you might imagine, rhyming your main points will make them more memorable.

Repetition

Technically, there are two ways to use **repetition**. One is to repeat the same word or phrase at the beginning of clauses or sentences. For example, Ronald Reagan's tribute[28] to the space shuttle *Challenger* astronauts who lost their lives when their spacecraft exploded included these repetitive phrases: "We will cherish each of their stories, stories of triumph and bravery, stories of true American heroes." Another type of repetition restates the same phrase at the end of a clause or a sentence. Lincoln's famous phrase "government of the people, by the people, for the people" is an example. This speech excerpt, which shows two repeated phrases, comes from a talk by a Native American speaker:[29]

> This idea is not original with me. It was taught to us by a great leader of the Lakota people—my people—Chief Sitting Bull. He taught us that Indian children could succeed in modern society and yet retain the values of their culture, values such as respect for the earth, for wildlife, for rivers and streams, for plants and trees; and values such as caring for each other and for family and community. He taught us that we must leave behind more hope than we found.

alliteration words with recurring initial sounds

rhymes words that end in the same sound

repetition saying the same word or phrase at the beginning or at the end of clauses or sentences

Sometimes speakers repeat, but reverse in a second phrase, some words from the first phrase. (The technical term for this is **antimetabole.**) Some examples from **www .americanrhetoric.com** include:

> *The absence of evidence* is not *the evidence of absence.* (Carl Sagan)

> We say *to our children, "Be like grownups,"* but Jesus said *to us grownups, "Be like children."* (Rev. Billy Graham)

> *We do not stop playing because we are old; we grow old because we stop playing.* (George Bernard Shaw)

President Kennedy's inaugural address, printed in Appendix C, includes several famous examples of antimetabole.

Metaphor

A **metaphor** compares two dissimilar things without using the words *like* and *as.* To Professor Michael Osborn,[30] speech students are *builders* who frame and craft their speeches; or they are *weavers* who intertwine verbal and nonverbal elements into a successful performance; or they're *climbers* who scramble over barriers or obstacles such as speech anxiety on their way to a successful speech. Each metaphor provides a different perspective on the subject. Which comparison best describes you as a speech student? Can you come up with a better metaphor for speech making?

One danger in using metaphors is the possibility of beginning with one comparison and ending with another, creating a **mixed metaphor**. To illustrate, a panelist on a news broadcast said:

> We must solve the root problem, or the line will be drawn in the sand, and we'll be back in the soup again.

Unfortunately, he combined three images: *root* compares the problem to a plant; the *line drawn in the sand*, an uncrossable boundary; and *soup*, a food. This left his listeners with no clear image of the problem. Should they dig out the root, avoid the line, or stay out of the kitchen?

Simile

Similes are similar to metaphors in that they compare two items that are unlike in most ways but alike in one essential detail. However, similes use *like* or *as* to explicitly state the connection. Here are some examples:

> When we harbor resentment, it's like drinking poison and hoping the other person dies.[31]

> It is a curious thing, the death of a loved one. It's like walking up the stairs to your bedroom in the dark and thinking that there's one more stair than there is. Your foot falls down through the air and there's a sickly moment of dark surprise.[32]

Similarly, Native American Chief Seattle[33] used vivid similes in the following speech excerpt:

> [The white] people are many. They are like the grass that covers vast prairies. My people are few. They resemble the scattering trees of a storm-swept plain. . . . There was a time when our people covered the land as the waves of a wind-ruffled sea cover its shell-paved floor, but that time long since passed away with the greatness of tribes that are now but a mournful memory.

Some metaphors and similes emerge and reemerge, because they arise from our experiences of being human. For instance, all human groups experience day and night,

antimetabole saying words in one phrase, and reversing them in the next phrase

metaphors comparison of two dissimilar things

mixed metaphor combining metaphors from two or more sources, starting with one comparison and ending with another

similes short comparisons that use the word *like* or *as* to compare two items that are alike in one essential detail

Karen M. Andrews

Archetypal symbols, such as water and the sea, sickness and health, parent and child, are widely used as metaphors by people all over the globe.

sickness and health, seasonal changes, and family relationships. Professor Michael Osborne[34] calls these **archetypal symbols,** because humans the world over understand them. Other common comparisons relate to cultural modes of transportation (the ship of state) and sports (the game of life) and, as the culture changes, new metaphors linked to electronic technology are emerging (experiencing static, feeling wired).

Personification

Personification means giving human characteristics to nonhuman entities such as animals, countries, natural objects and processes, and social processes. Chief Seattle[35] used personification in an 1853 speech, given before the governor of the Washington Territory:

> Yonder sky that has wept tears of compassion upon my people for centuries untold, and which to us appears changeless and eternal, may change.

Hyperbole

Hyperbole (hype) is the use of exaggeration for effect. A politician might say something like "If we don't do something about health care, there will be no more jobs." The exaggeration serves to emphasize that the problems are serious and deserve government attention.

Although hyperbole can be effective, excessive hype in a serious speech can lessen a speaker's credibility. Some exaggerations border on the ridiculous, and listeners think the speaker is overreacting, stretching the truth, or just plain lying. As a result, instead of focusing on the policy, the discussion often focuses on the hyperbole itself. No jobs? Really? Not even subsistence farming? In the classroom, Zack's use of hyperbole created a negative impression:

> Imagine a world where you have no trees, total pollution, and a landfill in every neighborhood. This is where we are heading because of our abuse of the land and lack of concern for ways to replenish the earth and her resources. There is a way where each person . . . could help, maybe even solve the problem. It's called recycling.

His point that recycling will contribute to the preservation of natural resources is a good one. However, *no* trees, *total* pollution, and landfills in *every* neighborhood overstates the case; furthermore, although recycling may help, it will not solve the problem

archetypal symbols recurring metaphors and similes that arise from shared human and natural experiences

personification giving human characteristics to nonhuman entities

hyperbole using exaggeration for effect

of environmental pollution in and of itself. As a result, Zack's exaggerations led some listeners to question his reasoning in general and, because this hype was in his introduction, to discount his ideas from the very beginning.

PRACTICALLY SPEAKING

SPEECHWRITERS

People whose jobs require them to give important speeches often consult gifted wordsmiths to help craft distinctive language when every word matters. Typically, Presidents of the United States work with speechwriters, some of whom become famous in their own right. For example, Franklin Roosevelt worked with a playwright; Dwight Eisenhower used a journalist. Comedian Ben Stein wrote for Richard Nixon. Author and TV news show host, Chris Matthews, wrote for Jimmy Carter. Peggy Noonan became famous for her work on President Reagan's tribute to the crew of the space shuttle *Challenger* and for President George H. W. Bush's speech, known for the phrase "a thousand points of light." Even President Bartlet on *The West Wing* had his team of speechwriters.

While still a candidate, John F. Kennedy discovered his exceptional speechwriter, Theodore "Ted" Sorensen, whom he called his "intellectual blood bank."[36] Then a recent law school graduate, Sorensen is now in his eighties. He is credited with such memorable lines from JFK's Inaugural as "Ask not what your country can do for you . . ." and ". . . the torch has been passed to a new generation of Americans."

Effective presidential speechwriters frame national political issues in memorable images. They also influence world affairs. The movie, *Thirteen Days*, although inaccurate in some details, shows Sorensen's importance as a member of the team that faced down the Soviets during the Cuban Missile Crisis. He also helped pen the speech President Kennedy delivered to a fearful nation, and some historians credit a letter he wrote to the Soviets with saving the world from nuclear destruction during that period.[37] He joined Barack Obama's team of speechwriters in February 2008 and put, as ABC News phrased it, "Kennedy's touch on Obama's words."

Questions for Discussion

- Which, if any, words spoken by a politician do you remember? What was it about the language that was memorable?
- ABC News says political speechwriters "wield untold power over voters." What does the phrase "*untold* power" mean to you?
- Although you don't have a speechwriter, consult with a few classmates as you prepare your next speech. Ask for specific ways to make your language more memorable. How does this consultation improve your speech?

Language and Pluralistic Audiences

Students enter classrooms across the country with many types of linguistic diversity:

- Monolingual (speaking one language only)
- Bidialectical (speaking two dialects)
- Multidialectical (speaking three or more dialects)
- Bilingual (speaking two languages)
- Multilingual (speaking three or more languages).

Communicating in a linguistically diverse setting is often complicated and frustrating, but you can plan ways to adapt to multilingual situations that will be beneficial to everyone involved.

Adapting to Multilingual Situations

When you speak to a linguistically diverse audience, don't assume you'll be instantly understood. Take a hypothetical student, Ryan, whose only language is Standard English. Some of his classmates speak Spanish and English; others speak Japanese and English, AAE and Standard English, or Russian and English. In order to speak effectively, he adapts his language, using a few simple strategies:

- Before preparing his outline, he tries to "hear" the terminology and jargon related to his topic in the way a nonnative speaker of English might hear it.
- When possible, he chooses simple words that most people understand; however, he avoids talking down to his audience.
- He identifies words that might be confusing and puts them on visual aids, which he displays as he talks.
- He defines difficult words and jargon as he goes along.
- He builds in redundancy by saying the same idea in a number of different ways. This way, if listeners are unclear about a concept the first time around, they may grasp it when it's expressed another way.

   When you listen to a nonfluent speaker, you must make a more-than-normal effort to create a satisfying experience, both for the speaker and for yourself. Remember that the major goal of any speech is communication of ideas, not perfection of language skills. So concentrate on the main points rather than on each specific word. Use patience and **perspective taking**; put yourself in the speaker's shoes and try to imagine what it would be like to give a speech in a foreign language to listeners who have spoken that language from birth. Also, remember that nonfluency is linked to inexperience in English, not to a lack of intelligence or education.[38] These additional tips can help you listen more effectively:

- Approach the speech with a positive attitude, expecting to understand.
- Listen all the way through. Make special efforts to keep your mind from wandering in the middle of the speech. It may help to take notes.
- Assume responsibility for co-creating meaning. Give appropriate nonverbal feedback to demonstrate your interest, patience, and support for the speaker.
- Control your negative emotional responses. Let's face it, linguistic barriers are challenging, and people often get frustrated or bored when faced with language differences.
- Don't laugh, even if the speakers do, at their language skills. Often they laugh nervously to relieve tension.[39]

Adapting to an Interpreter

Although using an interpreter may seem remote right now, you may eventually communicate through someone who translates your words into another language, including sign language. If you must use an interpreter, here are a few things to remember:

- Keep your language simple. Avoid overly technical or uncommon words.
- In advance of the speech, give your interpreter an outline or script so he or she can check the meaning of any unfamiliar words. Your interpreter may also refer to it during your speech as a guide to what you will say next.
- Speak in short units, not entire paragraphs. After a sentence or two, allow the interpreter to speak.
- Look at the interpreter while he or she speaks. This encourages the audience to look at the interpreter instead of at you.
- Because it takes two to three times longer to speak this way, shorten your speech accordingly.

perspective taking trying to imagine something from another person's point of view

Kelly Bilinski and Uriel Plascencia teamed up for a classroom speech. He spoke in Spanish; she interpreted into English.

© Josh Nauman/Cengage Learning

Remember that using interpreters is not easy, but without them, you could not communicate effectively. Consequently, work on maintaining a positive attitude throughout the speaking event. (Appendix C provides an example of a classroom speech, delivered in Spanish and interpreted into English by a fellow student. Video of this speech is also available on your book's online resources.) Here is an excerpt:

> *Cuando estaba en mi último año de Preparatoria, yo tuve buenos amigos. Nuestra amistad era muy fuerte que estábamos juntos mucho tiempo.* (When I was a senior in high school, I had some very good friends. Our friendship was so strong that we spent a lot of time together.) *Nosotros éramos como un equipo en todos los aspectos porque estábamos en las mismas clases, hacíamos juntos nuestra tarea, practicábamos deportes y platicábamos mucho. Nosotros nunca tuvimos problemas serios.* (We were like a team in all aspects because we spent time in classes doing our homework, playing sports, and talking. We never seemed to have any serious problems.) . . .

Summary

Language is a tool that humans use to communicate with one another and build complex societies. We create words to name our cultural memories, meaning that we label those things we notice and need to know in order to survive. In short, we name the events, people, and things we find important, and passing on these labels perpetuates our cultural ideas in new generations. Languages are dynamic, and words are added, borrowed, and discontinued in response to social changes.

Words denote or stand for objects, actions, and ideas; jargon, a technical vocabulary common to members of an occupation, can confuse outsiders who don't know its meaning. More importantly, words have connotative meanings that consist of the feelings and associations that they imply. Epithets generally carry negative connotations, whereas euphemisms put negative things more positively. In recent years, people have become concerned about the power of words—especially those used in discriminatory ways—and have worked to eliminate sexist, ageist, racist, and other noninclusive language from acceptable vocabulary.

Your speaking effectiveness depends largely on how well you can put your ideas into words. Thus, there are several guidelines for using language effectively. First, be accurate in both your vocabulary and grammar. Further, use language that is appropriate to the audience and occasion, and to you. Eliminate extra words and phrases that make your speech less concise. Define jargon in an effort to be clear, and select concrete words that enable your listeners to form more precise meanings. In addition, choose interesting strategies, such as alliteration, rhyme, repetition, metaphors, similes, personification, and hyperbole.

Finally, you may someday be in a public speaking situation where you either speak in a second language, necessitating the use of an interpreter, or, more likely, where you listen to a speaker who is not a native speaker of English. In these situations, it is most important to communicate ideas rather than expect linguistic precision. When you listen to a speaker from another linguistic background, take the responsibility of listening with an open mind in a supportive manner.

STUDY AND REVIEW

Your online resources for *Public Speaking: Concepts and Skills for a Diverse Society* offer a broad range of study tools that will help you better understand the material in this chapter, complete assignments, and succeed on tests. Your online resources feature

- Speech videos with critical viewing questions, speech outlines, and transcripts
- Interactive versions of this chapter's Stop and Check activities and Application and Critical Thinking Exercises
- Speech Builder Express and InfoTrac College Edition
- Weblinks related to chapter content
- Study and review tools such as self-quizzes, an interactive glossary, and downloadable audio summaries

You can access your online resources at **http://www.cengage.com/login**, using the access code that came with your book or that you bought online at **http://www.iChapters.com**.

KEY TERMS

The terms below are defined in the margins throughout this chapter.

ageist language 212	euphemism 210	racist language 212
alliteration 217	hyperbole 219	repetition 217
ambiguous 208	inclusive language 211	rhymes 217
antimetabole 218	jargon 210	sexist language 212
archetypal symbols 219	languages 207	similes 218
code switching 208	metaphors 218	Standard English 208
concrete words 215	mixed metaphor 218	symbols 207
connotative meaning 209	nonparallel language 212	vague words 216
denotative meaning 208	personification 219	verbiage 214
dialect 208	perspective taking 221	words 207
epithets 209		

APPLICATION AND CRITICAL THINKING EXERCISES

1. A Web page by Phil Simborg titled "Incredible Facts" (**http://bg-info.com/humor1.html**) claims that the English word with the most dictionary meanings is *set*. First, come up with all the meanings of *set* that you can, and then use a dictionary to look it up. Do you agree with Simborg, or can you prove him wrong? Thumb through a print edition instead of an online dictionary, and look for other ambiguous words with more than ten meanings.
2. Do an Internet search for the word *ebonics* or African American English (AAE). Print out at least two articles and bring them to class. In a small group, discuss one of the following questions; then share your group's conclusions with the entire class.

- Identify some ways that AAE (ebonics) differs from Standard English.
- What controversies swirl around AAE? Why do you think the dialect is controversial?
- What do linguists say about the dialect?
- What are some arguments in favor of instruction in AAE?
- What are some arguments against instruction in AAE?

3. On the Web site The Word Spy (**www.wordspy.com/index/subjects.asp**), technical writer Paul McFedries shares his collection of new words in a variety of subjects, from gadgets and appliances to marriage and relationships. Technology has created many terms. For example, a *tweep* posts a *tweet* on Twitter; the two have a *tweetup* when they meet in the real world. Go to the site and make a list of six new words you know and six that are unfamiliar to you. Bring the list to class and share it.

4. A speech can be informative without being interesting. Make a list of not-so-interesting topics and, working with a small group of your classmates, choose one and then think of alliteration, rhyming, repetition, metaphors, similes, personification, or hyperbole that could make the topic more interesting.

5. The speech archives at **www.americanrhetoric.com** give you the opportunity to listen to the greatest words ever spoken in the English language. Link to "Top 100 Speeches" and you'll find Lou Gehrig's 1939 farewell to baseball, General Douglas McArthur's farewell to Congress, Margaret Chase Smith's "Declaration of Conscience", and 97 more. Listen to a speech of your choice and then write a paragraph explaining how the language choices contribute to the effectiveness of the speech.

6. Interview a member of an occupation that interests you, and make a list of jargon terms associated with the job (for example, carpenters, waiters, foresters, pharmacists, truckers, bankers). Discuss your list with a classmate. How many terms do you know? Which terms are unfamiliar? If you were listening to a speaker from that occupation, what would you want the speaker to do so that you would better understand the speech?

7. Find a speech by a speaker who represents a culture different than your own on **www.americanrhetoric.com**. Locate the metaphors and similes in the speech. Note the similarities and differences between the metaphors of that culture and your own.

8. When (if ever) might you use an interpreter in the future? When might you listen to a speech delivered with the help of an interpreter? (Include televised speeches.) When (if ever) might you give a speech in a second language? When might you listen to a nonnative speaker of English?

9. If you know a second language, prepare a short speech in that language, and then work with an interpreter who will present your speech in English as you give it in your language. For example, Maria prepared and gave her speech in Italian; an Italian-speaking classmate interpreted when she gave it to the class. Paula prepared her speech in Romanian and brought her cousin to class to translate because all her classmates were monolingual.

SPEECH VIDEO

Go to your online resources to watch and critique Uriel Plascencia deliver a speech, which Kelly Bilinski interprets. The transcript is in Appendix C and online where you'll also find an outline and video of the speech. In addition, log onto **www.americanrhetoric.com** or **www.youtube.com** and view Dr. Martin Luther King, Jr.'s "I Have a Dream" speech, focusing especially on his language choices. The transcript of Dr. King's speech is featured here.

Josh Nauman/©Cengage Learning

Professional Speech with Commentary

I HAVE A DREAM
Reverend Martin Luther King, Jr.

This speech was delivered on the steps of the Lincoln Memorial on August 28, 1963, to an audience that numbered about 250,000 people. The occasion was a March on Washington for Jobs and Freedom. It was televised and reprinted in newspapers. The *Seattle Times*, April 4, 1993, calls it "the most famous public address of 20th Century America." King was praised for his skillful use of repetition and metaphor.[40]

I am happy to join with you today in what will go down in history as the greatest demonstration for freedom in the history of our nation.

Five score years ago, a great American in whose symbolic shadow we stand today signed the Emancipation Proclamation. This momentous decree came as a great beacon light of hope to millions of Negro slaves who had been seared in the flames of withering injustice. It came as a joyous daybreak to end the long night of their captivity.

But one hundred years later, the Negro still is not free. One hundred years later, the life of the Negro is still sadly crippled by the manacles of segregation and the chains of discrimination. One hundred years later, the Negro lives on a lonely island of poverty in the midst of a vast ocean of material prosperity. One hundred years later, the Negro is still languished in the corners of American society and finds himself an exile in his own land. So we have come here today to dramatize a shameful condition.

In a sense we have come to our nation's capital to cash a check. When the architects of our republic wrote the magnificent words of the Constitution and the Declaration of Independence, they were signing a promissory note to which every American was to fall heir. This note was a promise that all men, yes, black men as well as white men, would be guaranteed the inalienable rights of life, liberty, and the pursuit of happiness. It is obvious today that America has defaulted on this promissory note insofar as her citizens of color are concerned. Instead of honoring this sacred obligation, America has given the Negro people a bad check, a check which has come back marked "insufficient funds."

But we refuse to believe that the bank of justice is bankrupt. We refuse to believe that there are insufficient funds in the great vaults of opportunity of this nation. So we have come to cash this check—a check that will give us upon demand the riches of freedom and the security of justice. We have also come to this hallowed spot to remind America of the fierce urgency of now. This is no time to engage in the luxury of cooling off or to take the tranquilizing drug of gradualism. Now is the time to make real the promises of democracy. Now is the time to rise from the dark and desolate valley of segregation to the sunlit path of racial justice. Now is the time to lift our nation from the quicksands of racial injustice to the solid rock of brotherhood. Now is the time to make justice a reality for all of God's children.

It would be fatal for the nation to overlook the urgency of the moment. This sweltering summer of the Negro's legitimate discontent will not pass until there is an invigorating autumn of freedom and equality. Nineteen sixty-three is not an end, but a beginning. Those who hope that the Negro needed to blow off steam and will now be content will have a rude awakening if the nation returns to business as usual. There will be neither rest nor tranquility in America until the Negro is granted his citizenship rights. The whirlwinds of revolt will continue to shake the foundations of our nation until the bright day of justice emerges.

But there is something that I must say to my people who stand on the warm threshold which leads into the palace of justice: In the process of gaining our rightful place we must not be guilty of wrongful deeds. Let us not seek to satisfy our thirst for freedom by drinking from the cup of bitterness and hatred. We must forever conduct our struggle on the high plane of dignity and discipline. We must not allow our creative protest to degenerate into physical violence. Again and again, we must rise to the majestic heights of meeting physical force with soul force. The marvelous new militancy which has engulfed the Negro community must not lead us to distrust of all white people, for many of our white brothers, as evidenced

President Abraham Lincoln signed the Emancipation Proclamation on January 1, 1863. In this special occasion speech, King is framed by the giant statue of Lincoln.

King opens with metaphors of light and darkness. Look for these and other archetypal metaphors of seasons, thirst, weather, or mountains, throughout the speech.

Here is the first series of repetitions "one hundred years later . . ." Make a list of all the repetitions in the speech. They illustrate the wave pattern described in Chapter 9.

The *Bank of Justice* is King's second major metaphor.

Language changes over time. In 1963, the term "Negro" was common; today, it is rarely used. King refers to black and white children later in the speech, but he never uses the term "blacks," which came later in the 1960s. Today, "African American" is common. Notice, also, that King uses the "generic he," which was common usage in his day.

by their presence here today, have come to realize that their destiny is tied up with our destiny. And they have come to realize that their freedom is inextricably bound to our freedom. We cannot walk alone.

And as we walk, we must make the pledge that we shall march ahead. We cannot turn back. There are those who are asking the devotees of civil rights, "When will you be satisfied?" We can never be satisfied as long as the Negro is the victim of the unspeakable horrors of police brutality. We can never be satisfied as long as our bodies, heavy with the fatigue of travel, cannot gain lodging in the motels of the highways and the hotels of the cities. We cannot be satisfied as long as the Negro's basic mobility is from a smaller ghetto to a larger one. We can never be satisfied as long as a Negro in Mississippi cannot vote and a Negro in New York believes he has nothing for which to vote. No, no, we are not satisfied, and we will not be satisfied until justice rolls down like waters and righteousness like a mighty stream.

I am not unmindful that some of you have come here out of great trials and tribulations. Some of you have come fresh from narrow jail cells. And some of you have come from areas where your quest—quest for freedom left you battered by the storms of persecution and staggered by the winds of police brutality. You have been the veterans of creative suffering. Continue to work with the faith that unearned suffering is redemptive.

Go back to Mississippi, go back to Alabama, go back to South Carolina, go back to Georgia, go back to Louisiana, go back to the slums and ghettos of our northern cities, knowing that somehow this situation can and will be changed. Let us not wallow in the valley of despair, I say to you today, my friends. And so, even though we face the difficulties of today and tomorrow, I still have a dream. It is a dream deeply rooted in the American dream.

I have a dream that one day this nation will rise up and live out the true meaning of its creed: "We hold these truths to be self-evident, that all men are created equal."

I have a dream that one day on the red hills of Georgia, the sons of former slaves and the sons of former slave owners will be able to sit down together at the table of brotherhood.

I have a dream that one day even the state of Mississippi, a state sweltering with the heat of injustice, sweltering with the heat of oppression, will be transformed into an oasis of freedom and justice.

I have a dream that my four little children will one day live in a nation where they will not be judged by the color of their skin but by the content of their character.

I have a dream today!

I have a dream that one day, down in Alabama, with its vicious racists, with its governor having his lips dripping with the words of "interposition" and "nullification"—one day right there in Alabama little black boys and black girls will be able to join hands with little white boys and white girls as sisters and brothers.

I have a dream today!

I have a dream that one day every valley shall be exalted, and every hill and mountain shall be made low, the rough places will be made plain, and the crooked places will be made straight; "and the glory of the Lord shall be revealed and all flesh shall see it together."

This is our hope, and this is the faith that I go back to the South with.

With this faith, we will be able to hew out of the mountain of despair a stone of hope. With this faith, we will be able to transform the jangling discords of our nation into a beautiful symphony of brotherhood. With this faith, we will be able to work together, to pray together, to struggle together, to go to jail together, to stand up for freedom together, knowing that we will be free one day.

And this will be the day—this will be the day when all of God's children will be able to sing with new meaning: "My country 'tis of thee, sweet land of liberty, of thee I sing. Land where my fathers died, land of the Pilgrim's pride, From every mountainside, let freedom ring!"

King, a clergyman, refers to the Biblical passage of Amos 5:24.

This short repetitive phrase ("Go back to . . .") is almost dwarfed by the more famous phrases in the speech.

This is King's most famous repetitive sequence, the one that gives the speech its title. Notice the two additional repetitions that follow: "with this faith . . ." and "let freedom ring. . . ." Metaphors, alliteration, and other vivid imagery are woven into this final section.

He is quoting from the Bible, Isaiah 40:4-5.

This is a well-known patriotic song.

And if America is to be a great nation, this must become true.

And so let freedom ring from the prodigious hilltops of New Hampshire.

Let freedom ring from the mighty mountains of New York.

Let freedom ring from the heightening Alleghenies of Pennsylvania.

Let freedom ring from the snow-capped Rockies of Colorado.

Let freedom ring from the curvaceous slopes of California.

But not only that:

Let freedom ring from Stone Mountain of Georgia.

Let freedom ring from Lookout Mountain of Tennessee.

Let freedom ring from every hill and molehill of Mississippi.

From every mountainside, let freedom ring.

And when this happens, when we allow freedom ring, when we let it ring from every village and every hamlet, from every state and every city, we will be able to speed up that day when *all* of God's children, black men and white men, Jews and Gentiles, Protestants and Catholics, will be able to join hands and sing in the words of the old Negro spiritual:

Free at last! free at last!

Thank God Almighty, we are free at last!

> This repetitive series, which recognizes geographical diversity but emphasizes the unity that comes with freedom, brought roars of approval from the crowd.

Reprinted by arrangement with the Estate of Martin Luther King, Jr., c/o Writers House as agent for the proprietor, New York, NY. Copyright © 1963 Martin Luther King, Jr., © renewed 1991 Coretta Scott King.

VISUAL AIDS: FROM CHALKBOARD TO COMPUTER

© Tim Timmerman

THIS CHAPTER WILL HELP YOU

▶ Explain the value of visual aids

▶ Create your personal visual presentation plan

▶ Choose specific visual aids, including objects, models, people, lists, charts, graphs, photographs, drawings and maps, and audio resources

▶ Determine the advantages and disadvantages of using various presentation technologies, including overhead projectors, slide projectors, LCD projectors, document cameras, classroom boards, poster boards, flip charts, and handouts

▶ Explain some principles of visual design

▶ Give guidelines for using visual aids

YOU MAY NOT IMMEDIATELY think of a personal trainer as a public speaker who must master the use of visual aids, but Neil Wolkodoff, Ph.D., fitness trainer and owner of Physical Golf, is one trainer who did. In his more than fifteen years of fitness workshops and seminars, he has relied on a variety of visual aids. For example:

▶ *Objects*. Golf clubs and an exercise ball help him demonstrate how to use equipment.
▶ *Himself*. He uses his own body to illustrate how to stretch and strengthen core muscles.
▶ *Transparencies and slides*. Overhead transparencies or PowerPoint slides reinforce his major points.
▶ *Handouts*. Wolkodoff creates handouts with plenty of room for note taking, which helps some listeners learn the material better.

His advice regarding transparencies and slides is, "Keep the visual points very simple, and elaborate verbally."[1] Clearly he understands the value and the limitations of visual aids.

In this era when visual and audio aids are readily available, the most competent speakers know how to create and use these resources well. Because visual aids are a type of support, not a substitute for a carefully designed speech, this chapter falls here in the book—after you've planned and prepared your speech. Most of this chapter focuses on visual support, but it also suggests ways you can use audio resources to enhance your message and create positive impressions about your abilities.

Visual Aids Transcend Culture

Although technology has changed across the millennia, visual aids have a long tradition. In oral cultures, speakers used objects to clarify their ideas, help their listeners better understand abstract concepts, and dramatize their words. For instance, in the sixth century BCE, the Hebrew prophet Jeremiah used a ruined linen belt as an object lesson to symbolize the decay that disobedience to God would bring upon the kingdom of Judah.[2] In the days of the Roman republic, noted orators such as Cicero drew his audience's attention to statues and other landmarks in the Forum.[3] Today, communicators in pluralistic settings, such as international marketers[4] and presenters who must speak in a second language, know that visual aids are invaluable. The Diversity in Practice box explains how they can help nonnative English speakers.

In our image-saturated culture, many audiences expect visual support. Think of your own listening experiences. Don't you learn more and remember more from speakers who use some sort of visual than from those who don't even use the chalkboard? As a result, a good visual aid package is not only a good presentation strategy, it's culturally appropriate in classrooms and workplaces in the United States.

DIVERSITY IN PRACTICE
IF YOUR FIRST LANGUAGE IS NOT ENGLISH

NONNATIVE SPEAKERS of English often worry that their English will not be understood or that they will make mistakes when they address their American classmates. Visuals offer these speakers the following advantages:

- Putting key words on your visual lets your listeners see as well as hear your words. This enables them to understand you more clearly when your English is accented.
- When you provide something for your audience to see, their focus—at least part of the time—is on your visual rather than on you. This may lessen your anxiety.
- Visuals help you remember your speech. Words on a list or figures on a graph, for instance, can function as a cue card to remind you of your main points.

Planning Your Visual or Audio Aids

Visual or audio aids have at least four major functions:

1. Some information is very complex, and the right visual or audio support helps audiences understand it.
2. Visuals can emphasize or reinforce important ideas.
3. They relieve monotony and help keep audience attention.
4. They appeal to a variety of learning preferences.[5]

To use visual aids effectively, you must design them carefully. After you prepare your outline, go over it and look for places where visual or audio support would fulfill one of the four functions stated above. But don't overdo it. In short speeches (six to ten minutes), some consultants suggest a maximum of three visuals, each selected because it shows your speech structure, supports your concepts, or shows relationships between your ideas.[6]

Start with parts of the speech that are difficult to express in words alone.[7] Subpoints within speeches about artists or composers come to mind. For instance, images of Jackson Pollock's paintings were almost essential for Andrea's speech about the artist's career. Ysenia's audience better understood Hector Berlioz's music only because she played clips from his symphonies. Many technical topics also need visual support. A math concept is more easily understood when a formula is written out on a whiteboard; the results of a campus survey make sense when shown on a pie graph; and the facial expressions of gorillas come to life, not just through words, but through supplementary photographs. Demonstrations, similarly, are best understood with visuals. How well could you explain the process of folding a flag or drawing a hand in words alone?

Next, ask where support would illustrate an idea but is not essential because the concept could be easily explained in words.[8] The mullet hairstyle is familiar enough that Philip could probably get by just describing it; however, pictures of mullets throughout history added greatly to his presentation. Consider also, where a visual would emphasize or reinforce an idea. Stephanie used a list to preview the three types of listening she would describe during her speech.

Look for places where supporting materials could gain or maintain attention. A photograph of a pristine mountain scene would nicely illustrate a speech about environmental protection. Or a cartoon that illustrates a point, inserted well into the speech, could break the monotony of words alone. Here's your chance to adapt to diverse learning preferences by incorporating more sensory support into your speech for those who learn best by seeing, hearing, or doing.

In summary, identify the purpose of each visual by asking: Is it necessary? Is it interesting but not essential? Is it chosen because it's memorable? Is it included because it will help maintain attention? Which learning preferences do these visuals support?

STOP AND CHECK

BEGIN YOUR AUDIOVISUAL AID PLAN

Review your speech outline, and decide which ideas must be supplemented by a visual or audio aid.

What elements of your speech are difficult to convey in words alone?

For which ideas would visual support be helpful, but not essential?

What ideas need emphasis?

Where in the speech might the audience's attention lag?

What learning styles could you incorporate into the speech?

You may want to use Speech Builder Express to complete this step of the process, as its prompts include lists of possible visual aids that you can select. Click on "Visual Aids" in the left-hand navigation bar.

Choosing the Right Type of Aid

After you have identified places where support is essential or helpful, look through your many options. Several types of visual or audio aids could potentially make your ideas more understandable, although one type is often better than another. The key is to choose the *best* support, not just the kind that's easiest to create. This section will discuss three basic types of aids:

▶ Three-dimensional visuals
▶ Two-dimensional visuals
▶ Audio- and videotaped resources

Three-dimensional Visuals

A chef who shows how to make a recipe, a science teacher who uses a model of the heart in a lecture, an aerobics instructor whose audience actually makes the moves she describes—these speakers are using three-dimensional visuals in the form of objects, models, or people.

Objects

What soccer coach would even try to convey the finer points of passing without using a ball? What camp counselor would explain a craft without using actual materials? These examples illustrate that some subjects require seeing as well as hearing and that three-dimensional objects are essential, especially in speeches that demonstrate a process.

Your topic and the setting determine whether or not an object is realistic. For example, what object could you use for a speech about bankruptcy reform? The Kyoto Protocol? Grief counseling on campus? It's difficult to think of any thing that would be appropriate. However, a little creative thinking applied to other topics can result in ideas for communicating through objects that can add touch, smell, or taste to a speech. Here are some examples:

▶ Luke brought in samples of melons, asparagus, tomatoes, and avocados for his speech on how to select produce.
▶ Shelly gave each listener a tuft of unprocessed wool and a piece of yarn to touch as she discussed yarn making.
▶ Nutritionist Joanne Lichten uses a big glob of fat and a fast-food bag to gain attention when she speaks.[9]

There are limitations on appropriate objects. For instance, firearms are illegal in classrooms, and it's unwise to use live animals. Furthermore, some objects are impractical. Marko couldn't think of a way to bring his motorcycle into the classroom. (Fortunately, his classmates walked to a nearby parking lot where he spoke from the seat of his bike.) Bottom line: objects must be legal, accessible, and practical. You will use them well if you follow these guidelines:

▶ Be sure the object is large enough for everyone to see, or provide each listener with an individual object.
▶ Don't pass an object around. Some listeners will focus on the visual instead of your speech, and by the time everyone actually holds the object you may be finished speaking.

Models

When an object won't work, look for a **model** or realistic facsimile instead. Scaled-down models depict larger objects, such as buildings, dinosaurs, or cars; enlarged models increase the size of small objects such as atoms, ants, or eyeballs. Teachers often use

model a facsimile of an object you can't easily bring to the speech

them, especially in science classes where models of an enlarged human cell or a scaled-down solar system illustrate the scientific concepts. Architects present scale models to decision-making boards who decide whether or not to approve a proposed building. For your classroom speech, you can make your own model, or you might be able to borrow one from a professional.

One student chose to speak about his summer job as a pyrotechnician (a fireworks display technician). Because federal regulations and common sense prevented him from bringing explosives into the classroom, he made a model of the spherical explosive device, complete with a fuse. He supplemented the model with several objects: the actual cylinder into which he dropped lit explosives while on the job and the jumpsuit and safety helmet he wore at work.

People

Friends, volunteers from the audience, even your own body are often good ways to demonstrate a concept. For example, Jacinda, an Alaskan of Eskimo origin, used two volunteers from the audience to demonstrate a native sport called the "stick pull." In addition, her T-shirt was adorned with the letters W-E-I-O, which stands for "World Eskimo-Indian Olympics." You might incorporate the audience as a whole by asking them to participate in some sort of exercise.

In summary, three-dimensional objects, models, or people are almost indispensable in certain types of speeches, especially demonstration speeches. However, when it's unrealistic to use them, many other types of two-dimensional visuals are available.

text-based visual carry meaning in the written words rather than in visual images

six-by-six rule limit information to six lines, six words per line

Two-Dimensional Visuals

In many cases, two-dimensional visuals are more practical and appropriate than actual objects or models. The type of visuals that you can put on a poster or PowerPoint slide fall into this category: lists, charts, graphs, photographs, drawings, diagrams, and maps.

Devan Marchbanks

Models are good choices for visuals when an actual object is too large or too small or otherwise too difficult to bring into the speaking situation.

Lists

Lists are **text-based visuals** that rely more on written words than on visual images. Although lists can incorporate art in a minor way, their value depends on the words or numerical information they display. Without the art, the message would still come through, but without the words or numbers, it would not.

Lists are popular for chronological speeches because stages or steps lend themselves to listing. Words or phrases on lists can also summarize the key points of topically arranged speeches. For example, a list of the kinds of animal communication, as shown in Figure 13.1(a), helps listeners identify and remember the main subpoints. Lists are most effective when you remember the following guidelines:

▶ Don't put too much information in the list. This confuses listeners who don't know whether to read the material or listen to you.
▶ Follow the **six-by-six rule**: Use no more than six lines, no more than six words per line.[9]
▶ Use words, phrases, or short sentences instead of long sentences or paragraphs.
▶ Never write out your entire speech in a bulleted list and then read it to the audience.
▶ Don't put anything on the list that you do not intend to explain during your talk.

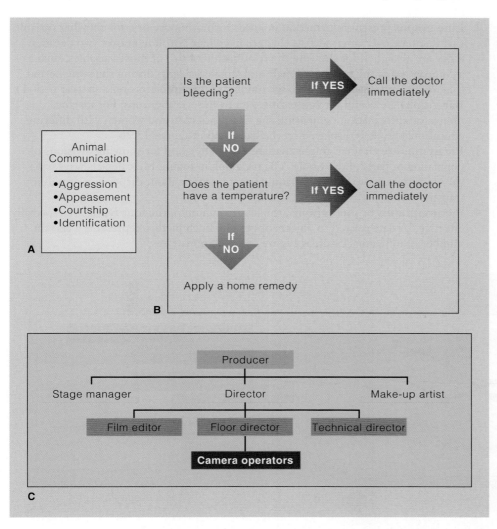

Figure 13.1
Lists and Charts Common visuals include (a) a list, (b) a flowchart, and (c) an organizational chart.

Charts

Charts are a type of **image-based visuals**—visuals that rely on some sort of figure or picture to convey meaning. The two basic types of charts are fiowcharts and organizational charts. **Flowcharts** show the order in which processes occur. You can recognize them by the use of arrows indicating directional movement. Flowcharts can include drawings (pictorial fiowcharts), or they may simply be a series of labeled shapes and arrows. Figure 13.1b illustrates a portion of a flowchart. **Organizational charts** show hierarchies and relationships. A family tree, for example, depicts relationships among family members. The organizational chart in Figure 13.1c shows relationships among various individuals involved in television production.

Graphs

Have you ever felt bombarded with statistics? Speeches full of numerical data are often boring, difficult to follow, and impossible to remember without some sort of graph that represents the numbers in diagram form. Depicting your material in one of four types of graphs allows your listeners to see how your numbers relate to one another.

image-based visual carry meaning in visual images; written words are secondary

flowcharts show the order or directional flow in which processes occur; may simply be a series of labeled shapes and arrows

organizational charts show hierarchies and relationships

line graphs display in a linear form one or more variables that fluctuate over a time period

bar graphs compare data from several groups by using bands of various lengths

pie graphs represent parts of the whole or divisions of a population by circles divided into portions

picture graphs or **pictographs** present data in pictures, each representing a certain number of individual cases

1. **Line graphs** present information in linear form; they are best for showing variables that fluctuate over time, such as changes in college enrollment over two decades. They are also good for showing the relationship of two or more variables, such as a comparison of the number of male and female students during the same period. (Figure 13.2a shows fluctuation in the funding of three projects over a six-year period.)

2. **Bar graphs** are useful for comparing data from several groups. For instance, numerical information comparing the salaries of men and women with differing educational levels is displayed on the bar graph in Figure 13.2b.

3. **Pie graphs** are circular graphs that are especially good for showing divisions of a population or parts of the whole. The pie graph in Figure 13.2c depicts ways typical Americans get to work; you could use it to speak about carpooling or public transportation.

4. **Picture graphs** or **pictographs**, the least common of the four types, are especially effective for data related to objects or people. Each picture represents a certain number of individual cases, as Figure 13.2d demonstrates.

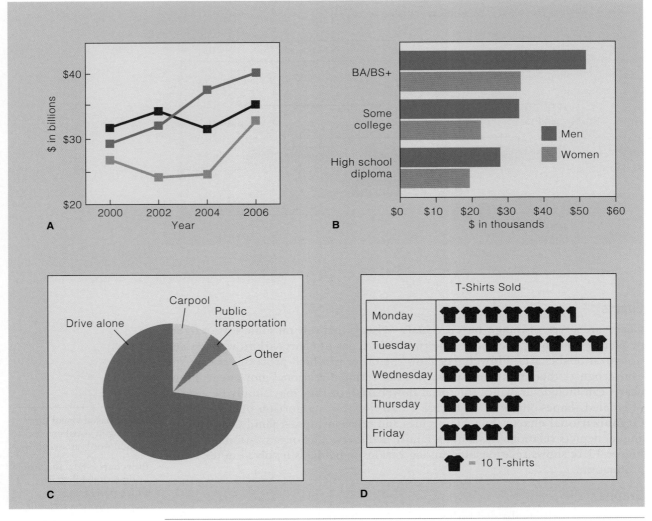

Figure 13.2
Graphs Four major types include (a) a line graph, (b) a bar graph, (c) a pie graph, and (d) a pictograph.

Photographs

Although photographs show objects, people, and scenes, the saying "A picture is worth a thousand words" is not necessarily true. Pictures are of little value if your audience can't see them. Fortunately, many students have successfully used photographs in their speeches, and the next section of this chapter describes several ways you can display them. For her speech on Harry Truman, Tricia showed four pictures of him at various stages of his life. Alene used black-and-white fetal sonograms for her speech on fetal development. NamKy found photographs of Hanoi to illustrate his speech on the capital of his country, Vietnam. To be successful, you should avoid two common mistakes with photographs:

▶ Don't pass them around. As with objects, only the person closest to you sees all the pictures and hears them explained, but the last person sees them long after they have been described.

▶ Don't show pictures from a book. John walked back and forth across the front of the room, displaying several photographs in a book that didn't fully open. Students craned their necks to see the pictures, and John was put into an awkward posture trying to keep the book open. He also wasted time flipping from one page to another. Overall, his visuals were a distraction, not an aid.

Drawings, Diagrams, and Maps

Drawings can stand alone or be added to lists or other visuals as decorative or supplementary support. **Diagrams** are line drawings or graphic designs that explain, rather than realistically depict, an object or a process.

If you can't even draw stick figures, you can at least trace or photocopy a commercial drawing onto a transparency or a handout. Or your computer can come to your rescue. Most software packages have extensive clip art files of drawings, diagrams, and basic maps that you can easily add to your visuals. The Internet also provides thousands of detailed drawings, diagrams, and maps that you can download (with source credits on the visual).

This list gives you some ideas of how to use drawings effectively:

▶ Substitute drawings for illegal firearms, nervous wolf dogs, inaccessible motorcycles, buildings that are too large or insects that are too small to bring into your classroom.

▶ Show a cartoon that perfectly illustrates your point and adds humor to your talk, making sure you read the caption to the audience.

▶ Use a diagram to illustrate the acid rain cycle or the circulatory system.

▶ Maps are drawings that visually represent spaces such as the heavens, the earth, or the weather. There are several kinds of maps:

▶ **Political maps** show borders between nations and states. These maps become outdated with changing political developments. For example, any world map dated before 1990 has obsolete sections, because a number of countries, including the Soviet Union and Yugoslavia, were dissolved during the 1990s when many political boundaries were redrawn.

▶ **Geographic maps** show mountains, deserts, lowlands, and other natural features. They are updated only when remote or previously unexplored territories, such as Antarctica or the ocean floor, are mapped.

▶ Blueprints and floor plans of buildings, maps of routes between two points, city maps, campus maps—the list goes on. Figure 13.3, on the following page, depicts a floor plan of a Native American kiva.

In summary, three-dimensional objects and text- or image-based visuals are useful in visually oriented cultures. However, in some cases, recordings of sounds or images are even more effective support.

diagram drawing or design that explains, rather than realistically depicts, an object or process

political maps show current borders for states and nations; can be outdated in a fast-changing world

geographic maps show mountains, deserts, and other natural features; not easily outdated

Figure 13.3
Map A floor plan of a building, such as this Native American kiva, is a type of map. (Source: Mark Iles)

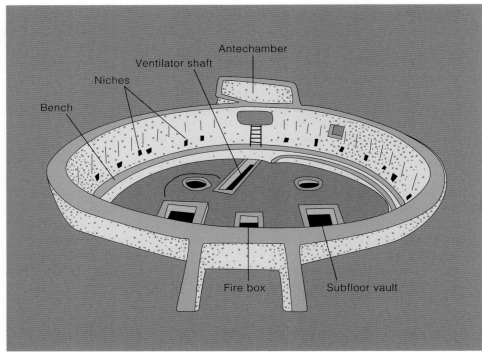

ETHICS IN PRACTICE

CAN A VISUAL BE UNETHICAL?

SPEAKERS have an ethical responsibility to do their listeners no harm. This includes any behavior that could place listeners at risk for physical or psychological injury or harm. Read the following true examples from classroom speeches and then discuss with your classmates some ethical questions they raise:

▶ One student killed, skinned, and cleaned a live fish in front of her stunned classmates.[10]
▶ Another thought it would be creative and dramatic to open his speech on terrorism with a role-play scenario. He arranged for a couple of friends dressed in fatigues and carrying realistic but fake automatic weapons to burst into the classroom and order everyone to hit the floor just as he got up to speak. He didn't anticipate his classmates' reactions: Some screamed, others cried. One began hyperventilating and had to go to the emergency room. (She had immigrated from a country in which terrorist incidents were common.) Someone called 911, and class ended immediately.
▶ Some students have displayed visuals of aborted fetuses.
▶ One student showed pornographic photographs to illustrate her speech about pornography.
▶ Denis brought in a nervous wolf dog that detracted from his speech because wary listeners focused on the animal, not on Denis's words.

Questions

1. Does any example fail to meet the standard of doing no harm, whether physically or psychologically? If so, which one(s)? Why?

2. Try to think from the speakers' point of view. Why might each speaker have chosen that particular visual?
3. What other visual support could each speaker have substituted?
4. How persuasive do you find shocking or offensive visual aids that stir negative emotions?

If you have questions about the appropriateness or safety of any visual aid you intend to use, consult your instructor in advance of your speech.

Video and Audio Recordings

Think of the difference between hearing a speech that only talks about an up-and-coming musical group and listening to a second speech that includes a video clip of that group in concert. Although audio and video support requires extra preparation and planning, these resources can help you better convey certain types of information.

Audio Resources

Audio support is particularly important with music- or sound-related topics. Portable electronic keyboards, other musical instruments, tapes, CDs, MP3 players, and so on can let your audience hear the sounds you are explaining, whether your topic is a musical style, a specific instrument, or a particular composer's works. The speech about *dun dun* drums, outlined at the end of Chapter 16 and available in your online resources, is a good example of the importance of an audio clip.

Although less common, you can effectively use sounds other than music. Before her speech on whales, for instance, Mary Beth played a recording of a whale song and asked her listeners to identify the source of the sound. Use your creativity to think of other ways to incorporate short clips, such as sounds from nature, traffic noises, or conversations, to enhance your presentation.

Video Resources

College recruiters visit high schools, bringing along multimedia presentations showing their institutions, complete with campus images, background music, and interviews with administration, faculty, and students. In many cases, the images themselves provide most of the message. The recruiter simply introduces the video and then fields questions afterward.

In your classroom, however, your goal is to let multimedia resources supplement, not replace, your words. There are massive amounts of recordings available for use, including clips from television shows, feature films, advertisements, and home movies. By carefully selecting short segments to illustrate your points, you can clarify your ideas dramatically and memorably, as these examples demonstrate:

- Lisa made the *Guinness Book of Records* for being part of the largest tap dancing group ever assembled at one time for a performance. As she explained ways to get listed in the famous record book, Lisa used a 15-second video clip that her mother had recorded.
- Mary Beth's whale speech ended with a 10-second clip taken from a television program, showing a number of whales playfully leaping in and out of the water.
- Effie used a scene from the film *The Importance of Being Ernest* to illustrate a particular type of territory violation.
- Andrew discussed the differences between men's and women's gestures. He brought a 15-second commercial showing a male and a female interacting. He played the commercial as he introduced the topic. Then, as he discussed each point, he again played it again, this time with the sound turned off, pausing at various places to illustrate a specific point.

All these students succeeded because they preplanned carefully. The short clips they selected illustrated, rather than substituted for, their words; they cued up their tapes or selected the scene in advance; and they planned exactly when to start and stop the visual. (On the downside, Alex's attempt to use a clip from YouTube showing the damage steroid use can cause backfired because it took forever for the video to load.)

Enabling listeners to see or hear your topic is important in many public speaking settings. Indeed, it's almost essential in some presentations, such as demonstrations. Skillful construction and use of visuals distinguish good speakers from adequate ones, and as you learn to work with visuals, your competence will increase.

STOP AND CHECK

CONTINUE YOUR AUDIOVISUAL AID PLAN

Log on to Speech Builder Express and click on "Visual Aids" in the left-hand navigation bar for prompts that list possible visual aids you can select, or use the form below to continue your plan:

I need this type of VA _____ for this idea _____

I need this type of VA _____ for this idea _____

I need this type of VA _____ for this idea _____

I need this type of VA _____ for this idea _____

Next, using a separate sheet for each visual, make a preliminary sketch of the material you plan to use. Then edit out every unnecessary word or image.

Choosing the Right Type of Presentation Technology

The technology for displaying visuals is big business; in fact, giant corporations exist solely to provide machines and materials for creating and displaying visuals. This section covers a number of common ways to display visual aids, along with their advantages and disadvantages.

Overhead Projectors

Overhead projectors are everywhere; they're in classrooms, businesses, and other organizations, here and abroad. They allow you to enlarge and display an image on a wall or a screen so that everyone can see it, even in a large auditorium. Overhead projectors have many advantages. Transparencies are simple and inexpensive to make; they are easy to store and transport; the film is widely available; and it comes in colors. You can overlap transparencies to show a progression of related content by simply placing one on top of another.

You can draw freehand directly onto the transparency or trace a cartoon, map, or other drawing from any printed copy (giving source credit, of course). For a more professional look, photocopy a printed image onto the transparency. Or insert a transparency into your printer and print directly from your computer.

Skillful use of an overhead projector adds to your audience's perception of your competence. However, poor skills can have the opposite effect. For best results, follow these guidelines:

❱ Before you begin speaking, turn the machine on and adjust the focus. Then turn it off until you're ready to use your visual.

❱ "Build" a list by using a cover sheet and revealing each point as you discuss it.

▶ To draw your listeners' attention to some part of your visual, point to the transparency, not the screen. If your hand trembles, place a pointed object where you want listeners to focus, and then move your hand away from the projector.

▶ If you use a transparency repeatedly but want to highlight or comment on the material each time, place a blank transparency over the material; then underline, mark, or write comments on the blank, using wet erase markers. This ensures that your originals remain clean, and you can easily clean your markings off the top sheet.

Document Cameras

One Web site calls **document cameras** (also known as visual presenters) "the 21st-century overhead projector"[11] because they are like a scanner, microscope, whiteboard, computer, and projector rolled into one. Some units are compact enough to fold into a notebook-sized carrying case.

These high-resolution cameras let you project photographs, slides, three-dimensional objects, a document you've created, photographs from a book, and so on. You can zoom in on a painting or enlarge a small object such as a dime or even a microscopic object, so that small details are visible. Document cameras are becoming more common in classrooms and businesses nationwide.[12]

Slide Projectors

Slide projectors, like overhead projectors, show images on a screen so that fairly large audiences can see them. Because they project high-resolution images with excellent color reproduction, slides are especially useful for talks about artistic works. You can

document cameras
high-resolution cameras
that display documents and
three-dimensional objects

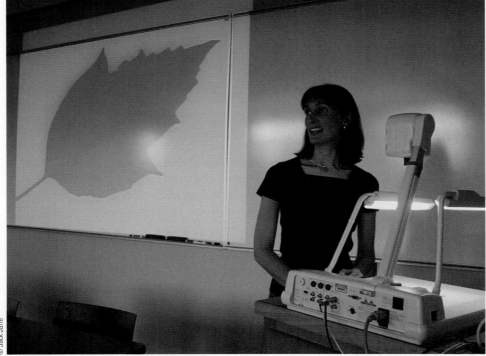

© Jack Jaffe

Document cameras are
more versatile than many
other types of presentation
technology, because they
can easily display written
material, photographs,
drawings, and objects.

make them from photographs or special film. One drawback is that slides are hard to see in well-lit rooms, so you may find yourself speaking in the dark. In addition, many companies no longer manufacture slide projectors; consequently, other presentation technologies may be more readily available.

Common slide projectors have a carousel-type tray in which you place your ordered slides. For each new slide, simply press a button on your handheld control. To enhance your professionalism, put a black slide between sections of content so that you can pause to talk while avoiding a blast of white light or leaving a picture or diagram up so long that it's distracting or boring.[13]

Presentation Software and LCD Projectors

LCD projectors connect directly to your computer and project what appears on your monitor onto a screen. If you create visuals using PowerPoint or another **presentation software program**, you'll need this type of projector. Launch your presentation and move from slide to slide with a click of the mouse. When you discuss material with no visual support, use the "B" key to bring up a blank slide; then return you to your presentation with another click of your mouse.

Unfortunately, this technology is not always used well. For example, an article in *Technical Communication* reports that millions of speakers turn out trillions of slides annually.[14] However, most slides are ineffective and detract from the message—but the problem lies in the creators, not the technology. Think of the presentations you've seen. How many were effective or memorable? To improve your skills with PowerPoint or a similar program, follow these guidelines:

▶ Write out the words you'll use, and sketch the illustrations before you make the slide. Mentally identify the purpose for everything you include on the slide.

▶ While still in the planning stage, go back and remove every unnecessary word or image. In other words: simplify, simplify, simplify.

▶ Avoid the temptation to write out your entire speech and read it to your hapless audience.

presentation software programs computer software to create a package of lists, tables, graphs, and clip art

▶ Develop your slides in black and white, and then add color sparingly to emphasize significant ideas.

▶ Use high resolution images that will display clearly.

▶ Rehearse at least once without the slides to make sure that they don't substitute for your message.

▶ DIVERSITY IN PRACTICE

TRAVELING AND TALKING

TODAY, THOUSANDS of professionals use visuals while abroad. Engineers, marketers, physicians, and computer specialists, who once took a required college speech course, are often surprised to find themselves speaking internationally. Someday you may join their numbers. Many have found that taking along visual aids prepared here presents some challenges.

Business writer Dave Zielinski[15] describes "secrets and strategies of speakers on the go." In the light of post–September-11 security regulations, on-the-road presenters must consider customs agents' or security guards' perspectives on their equipment. Even a collapsible presentation pointer can look suspicious in carry-on luggage. Moreover, expensive equipment tempts thieves in some places. Customs regulations also vary. One sales representative had to post a bond equaling 30 percent of her equipment's cost as a guarantee that she would return with it and not sell it in the country. Overall, Zielinski's advice is: don't assume anything, and have a contingency plan.

Chalkboards or Whiteboards

Chalkboards or whiteboards are standard equipment in most educational settings because of their many advantages. They're widely available. They're great for explaining unfolding processes, such as math problems. They also encourage informality, which is appropriate in some contexts. Finally, they are useful in settings that include speaker-audience interactions, such as brainstorming sessions.[16] Unfortunately, boards have three major drawbacks:

▶ You can't prepare your visual beforehand, and unprepared visuals create additional anxiety if you like to have everything ready and rehearsed in advance.
▶ Most people don't write well on boards, so the visuals look unprofessional.
▶ You must turn your back on your audience while you write on the board. This is probably the major drawback of boards in general.

Boards continue to evolve. Although **interactive whiteboards** are often used in educational settings, businesses are recognizing their advantages. You can connect the board to a document camera or to a computer with markup software. You can then use "electronic markers" or even your finger to overwrite material on the board. Finally, you can save your markups to files and later retrieve, email, or print them out.[17]

Poster Boards and Flip Charts

For convenience and economy **poster board** is a low-tech option. Because it's readily available in a variety of weights and colors at campus bookstores and art supply stores, posters are widely used. Watch C-SPAN and you'll see members of Congress displaying information on poster board. In the workplace, people who deliver the same speech over and over, such as financial planners, also use professionally prepared posters. Posters are effective with relatively small audiences, but at greater distances they're difficult to see, and small details don't show up. In addition, you'll need some sort of easel to hold your posters during your speech. These tips will help you make more professional-looking posters:

▶ Use rulers or yardsticks to ensure straight lines and avoid a "loving-hands-at-home" look.
▶ Use more than one color to attract and hold interest.
▶ For a more professional look, use adhesive letters or computer created text.
▶ To protect your posters from becoming bent or soiled, carry them in a portfolio, or cover them with plastic when you transport them.

Flip charts are oversized tablets, lined or unlined; they are common in businesses and other organizations but rare in college classrooms. Their name reflects the fact that pages can be turned from one to another. The paper they're made of varies from tablet thickness to stiffer weights. Larger charts work well in conference rooms; smaller ones work well for presentations to just a few listeners.

Flip charts can function like a chalkboard or whiteboard, especially in brainstorming-type situations where you interact with your audience. For example, you might ask listeners to contribute ideas that you later incorporate into your talk. Tear off the lists you create together, and pin or tape them to the wall. When you use a flip chart this way, you must overcome disadvantages similar to those you faced with a whiteboard. Your writing may be messy, and writing on the chart causes you to turn your back on the audience. Some presenters overcome this by asking a second person to do the writing.

Use flip charts to "build" a diagram in front of the audience. In advance, lightly draw the entire visual in pencil. Then, during your presentation, trace over the lines for a professional-looking diagram that appears to be done on the spot. This way, you can be sure that all the words are spelled correctly beforehand, and you can use the chart as a giant prompt card.

interactive whiteboards connect to other technology; you can overwrite material and then save your markups

flip charts tablets you prepare in advance or create on the spot; turn to a new page or tear off and display pages as you finish them

If you repeat the same presentation for different audiences, prepare your visuals in advance on heavier-weight tablets. Then use the flip chart much as you would use a series of posters, exposing each new visual as you discuss it. The separate visuals will stay in order. In addition, because the cover is stiff, the tablet can stand alone on a table. This makes it a useful display method when other equipment is unavailable.[18]

Handouts

Brochures, pamphlets, photocopies, or other handouts free audiences from having to take extensive notes and give them details they can study later.[19] Handouts can also provide supplementary information you don't have time to cover in your speech. One student who chose a health-related topic distributed professionally made brochures from his campus health services at the end of his speech; another distributed a photocopied diagram illustrating an origami project. Handouts are common in business settings; for example, sales representatives commonly give brochures to potential customers. Members of important workplace committees often receive an entire book of supplementary handouts.

Your primary challenge with handouts is to make sure they supplement, not replace, your message. You want your audience to listen to you, not just read the handout. To use them more effectively, do the following:

▶ Distribute the handout, face down, before you begin speaking; then, when you discuss the material on it, ask your listeners to turn it over.

▶ Mark the points you want to emphasize with a letter or number so you can easily direct listeners to specific places on the handout. Let's say you distribute a diagram showing how to groom a dog, and you want to highlight three potential trouble spots. Mark the first with an "A," the second with a "B," and the third with a "C." Then, draw your listeners' attention to each place as you discuss it.

▶ Speakers, especially in workplace training sessions, often provide blanks on the handouts for listeners to fill in during the speech; others provide space for notes.

▶ Put identical material onto a transparency and project it as you speak. Highlight on the transparency the information you want them to find on their handout.

▶ If the handout provides supplementary information only, distribute it at the end of the speech.

Read more tips for effective handouts at **www.presentation-pointers.com/showarticle/articleid/20/**.

STOP AND CHECK

CONTINUE YOUR VISUAL PRESENTATION PLAN

With your audiovisual aid plan in mind, assess the equipment that is available for your classroom speech. Try to imagine yourself using the various types of visual display technology during your speech.

• List the presentation technologies available in your classroom: _____

_____

• Which technologies will best display your visuals? _____

_____

Using Proven Design Principles to Create Visuals

Create your visuals by hand, or use a presentation program, such as Microsoft's Power-Point. Invented in 1984 and sold for $14 million to Microsoft in 1987, PowerPoint has revolutionized business, education, science, and communication.[20] PowerPoint slides show up at weddings, in sermons, in grade school show and tell presentations, and so on, partly because it is so simple to vary slide backgrounds, fonts, colors, bullets, and other features. Add clip art or images scanned into the program or downloaded from Internet sources; throw in a video clip, some animation or music, and in a few moments you have a multimedia presentation that your grandparents could only dream about. Transfer your creations to slides, transparencies, or computer disks, and you are off to a successful presentation. Or are you? Perhaps—but only if you remember that the best package is helpful only if it helps listeners understand your ideas, and only if you create your visuals with some design principles in mind.

A plethora of design features may tempt you to overdo things—and impress (one way or another) but fail to enlighten your audience. You can create transitions between slides and include lines of text flying in from the left, the corner, flashing on and off, one letter appearing at a time with clicking sound effects, and so on, resulting in a mishmash of movement that has nothing to do with your ideas. Experiment with a presentation program for fun, but in the end follow the basic guidelines for simple, well-designed visuals described in the following sections.

Choose a Readable Font

Whether you create your visuals on poster board or rely on a computer to produce your materials, make *readability* your primary concern. One key is to choose a **font** that enables your audience to read it easily. As you consider the hundreds of available fonts, keep in mind some basic readability tips that are illustrated in Figure 13.4.

1. Choose title case or sentence case, and avoid using only capital letters.
   - USING ALL CAPITAL LETTERS IS MORE DIFFICULT TO READ— BESIDES, YOU'RE NOT SHOUTING, SO WHY CAPITALIZE?
   - Title Case (Capitalizing the First Letter of the Major Words) Is Easier to Read.
   - Sentence case (capitalizing only what you'd capitalize in a sentence) is also readable.
2. On handouts, use a **serif font** (with cross lines at the top and bottom of letters) rather than a **sans serif font** (with no cross lines). A serif font is easier to read because the serifs lead your eyes from letter to letter,[21] but sans serif fonts are well suited to smaller chunks of text.
3. Adapt your font to the formality or informality of the topic and the occasion. Generally, serif fonts are more formal than sans serif fonts.[22]
4. Determine whether the visual contains display or content material. If you display only a series of photographs, for instance, a more fancy display font, such as a script or handwriting font, might catch attention.[23] However, for slides containing a lot of content, a simple font such as Bookman, Garamond, or Arial is best. When you handwrite your visuals, use plain, legible lowercase letters.
5. Maintain consistency from one visual to another. That is, if you use Helvetica for your title on the first visual, use it on every visual. Do likewise for the subtitle and text fonts. And limit yourself to just a couple of fonts.
6. It goes without saying that letters should be large enough to be visible and that titles and first-level material should be larger than second-level material.

font a complete set of letters and numbers of a given design

serif font a font with cross lines at the top and bottom of letters

sans serif font a simple font with no cross lines on each letter

Figure 13.4
Fonts Both serif and sans serif fonts have their place, but readability is always your major consideration. Make fonts large enough to be read easily, and avoid hard-to-read fonts. Because they can portray an image, you may want to adopt a signature font.

Credit TK

Serif fonts such as these are easier to read; using boldface makes them even more visible.

Palatino	**Palatino (bold)**
Times New Roman	**Times New Roman (bold)**
Bookman	**Bookman (bold)**

Sans serif fonts are useful for titles and headings.

Helvetica	**Helvetica (bold)**
Optima	**Optima (bold)**
Avant Garde	**Avant Garde (bold)**

Tempting as they may be, you're wise to avoid fancy display fonts that are difficult to read.

Zapf Chancery	*Zapf Chancery (bold)*
COPPERPLATE	COPPERPLATE (BOLD)
Wittenberger Frattur	**Wittenberger Frattur (bold)**

For more information about fonts in general, search InfoTrac College Edition for "fonts." One interesting article described the personality of the font, "Georgia." A British psychologist called it "individual, sophisticated, with a curviness that suggests a little bit of rocker chick."[24] Studies show that fonts with rounded O's and tails are "friendly" but more angular fonts are considered "cold." Many celebrities and politicians have their own fonts, as do some cities. For instance, both Barack Obama and the city of Seattle use "the modern classic" Gotham as their signature font.[25]

Use Formatting Features Wisely

A variety of formatting features add visual appeal. For example, centering the title, underlining the subtitle, and bulleting the points can help your audience better see the relationships among ideas. Formatting your letters in boldfaced type makes them show up better on slides. And attributes such as underlining or italicizing can highlight and emphasize specific ideas, but use these features sparingly, or the impact will be lost.

Don't cram too much information on each visual. Limit yourself to one idea per visual, and leave plenty of white space so that the audience can find their place easily. Also, balance the information by spreading it across the visual rather than bunching the material into the upper left quadrant.

Use Color for Emphasis

Use color to add interest and emphasis and to attract and hold attention. However, carefully plan your color scheme. Colors have a variety of associations that vary culturally. Here's just one example: red can be a good emphasis color when used sparingly, but it is "culturally loaded"; in the United States it symbolizes anger ("seeing red") or danger (being "in the red"); in China, it symbolizes luck and celebration; in India, it is associated with purity. Red is the most common color found on national flags.[26]

For words and images, choose colors that contrast dramatically with the background color. White or ivory-colored posters and clear transparencies are best with text material in high-contrasting black or dark blue, not yellows or oranges. Experiment until you come up with a combination you like. To avoid a cluttered look, use a maximum of three colors on all of your visuals. And never use different colored letters in the same word. To emphasize ideas, use brightly colored bullets to draw attention to a list. Or vary the color of a word or phrase you want to stand out.

The most pleasing visuals follow principles of good design: the fonts, sizing and spacing, and color combinations aim at readability and balance. These principles will help you remember that your aids are just that—aids. They aren't your message, and they aren't a display of your personal artistic or computer skills.

STOP AND CHECK

COMPLETE YOUR VISUAL PRESENTATION PLAN

Return to your audiovisual plan. Make any revisions you'd like; next, sketch out each visual—paying attention to the size and spacing of your words and images. Select appropriate colors and decide which words or phrases you want to emphasize. Then go to work on your text- or image-based visuals. If you plan to use audio or video support, make arrangements now for the equipment you'll need. And have fun!

General Guidelines for Using Visual and Audio Aids

As noted throughout this chapter, each type of visual or audio aid comes with guidelines for successful use, but the following general principles apply pretty much across the board:

◗ Whatever type of audio or visual aid you choose, make sure everyone can hear or see it.

◗ Don't create a visual for its own sake. For example, a presenter who says, "Today, I'll talk about 'character,'" and the word "CHARACTER" zooms up a slide, is not clarifying a complex point or strengthening a bond with the audience. She's created what professional presenter Joan Detz[27] calls a "dreaded" word slide that doesn't really add to the message.

◗ Display visuals only when you discuss them. For example, use a cover sheet on posters when they're not in use, or press the "B" key on your computer to bring up a blank screen between slides.

◗ Talk to your audience, not to your visual.

◗ Rehearse using your aids. If you can't use the actual equipment, you can at least visualize yourself using it—think about where you'll stand in relation to the equipment, how you'll point out specific features, what you'll do when you're not discussing content on the visual.

◗ Don't violate your audience's norms or expectations. When you severely shock or violate expectations, you may never regain attention, and your credibility—especially in the area of good sense—suffers as a result.[28]

◗ Whenever machines are involved, have a Plan B. Think about what you will do if the slide projector jams, the light on the overhead projector burns out, or your YouTube video won't load. An alternate plan, usually in the form of a handout, can save your speech. In the big picture, demonstrating your composure in case of equipment failure enhances your credibility.[29]

Now that you have read the chapter, go back to the introduction. From the information provided, how effective do you think Wolkodoff's visuals were overall? Give a reason for your answer.

CONSULT A CONSULTANT

Distinction Communication

Jim Endicott

Jim Endicott is a nationally recognized consultant, designer, speaker and award-winning author specializing in professional presentation messaging, design, and delivery. He coauthored The Presentation Survival Skills Guide (Distinction Publishing, 2001) with psychologist Dr. Scott Lee.

You specialize in "professional presentation messaging." What is that?

Today, most organizational communicators "give" a presentation. Unfortunately, mechanical, presenter-focused speakers rarely consider something more important—did anyone actually "get" their message? "Giving" presentations is about slides, bullets, clip art, projectors, remote pointing devices. The "getting" piece deals with how the underlying message is shaped to cause an audience to internalize it at a deeper level and take action. When we grasp that distinction, we can communicate messages that resonate more effectively with the hearts and minds of busy people.

What's your background?

Before PowerPoint, computer-generated graphics required large design stations, and for eight years, I managed a stable of computer artists in a corporation. When I started my own business in 1998, we rejected the pressure to simply make presentations look nice and focused on things that created more meaningful human interaction: good messages, shaped in visually meaningful ways and delivered with skills that conveyed confidence, authenticity, and believability.

What's the biggest mistake people make in creating and using visual aids?

Many presenters have one approach. They pound out screen after screen of text-heavy slides supplemented by a few charts and poor-quality images. These slides then become a horrible crutch that changes the nature of communication. Take away their visuals and most presenters tend to communicate more conversationally. Put them in front of a screen of bullet slides and they often become rigid, mechanical, and impersonal. This less-is-more perspective has eluded presenters since the first overhead projector image hit the screen.

What types of visual or audio support could be more effective in many cases?

Audiences reward creativity. They also desire variety. *All* bullets, *all* videos, or *all* charts is a recipe for intellectual and relational disengagement. There are many options: props, video interviews with participants, brief voice-over or audio elements, segments from Hollywood videos (see **www.MPLC.com** for licensing), or on-screen demos of Web sites. Creative presenters also find ways to use the audience as a visual aid. These approaches take more preparation but produce significantly higher results.

What major design principles do you emphasize in your workshops?

Less is always more. Only put on screen what listeners can assimilate in 7–8 seconds. Too many words force them to choose between reading and listening—they can't do both.

Use less text. Text information is processed on the left side of the brain and rarely moves into long-term memory. The left brain is also most defense-intensive. Never wrap the point into a second line on a bulleted slide. Rarely use more than five bullets per screen. Never utilize sub-bullets which are typically too small to be read. Presenters use them to "give" information, but audiences don't "get" anything more.

Use images not words. The presentation medium functions most effectively when used to orchestrate simple graphical elements, video or other visually rich talking points. Presenters need to be better storytellers and less story-readers.

It's not about PowerPoint. Know when to turn PowerPoint off during a presentation. (Use the B key.)

How do you coach people to effectively use their visual aids?

We work on specific strategies. Images should transition on screen without fanfare and unfold as a by-product of the speaker's words. Too many presenters stop and start their delivery either by charging the laptop to press a key or by pointing a remote device from across the room. We try to take the emphasis away from supporting technologies and put it back on the presenter's unfolding story where it belongs.

The presenter, the technology, and the visual information should be a well-orchestrated and seamless dance that beckons audiences to join in.

Questions for Discussion

▶ Describe a presenter you've seen who was so tied to technology that the message was lost on the audience.

▶ Jim says, "Audiences reward creativity." What do you think this means?

▶ Do you think of your visuals more in terms of helping you "give" your presentation or as helping your audience "get" your message? How does this affect your speaking?

▶ Describe how the visuals you are planning for your next speech will help your listeners "get" your message.

▶ Design a visual package that illustrates the "well-orchestrated and seamless dance" between you, your technology, your visual information, and your audience. Share your design with a few classmates.

Summary

As a speaker in a visually oriented culture, it is to your advantage to use visual and audio support effectively. Visuals illustrate your ideas, keep your audience focused on your speech, and make abstract ideas more concrete. Although they are not new, the amount and kind of support available today is unprecedented.

Before you make a single visual, sit down with your outline and determine where support is essential, where it would be useful, where variety is needed, and where audio or visual aids would accommodate for a variety of learning styles. If you can state the purpose for every item of support you use, you will have a meaningful package.

Use three-dimensional objects, models, and people when they are legal, practical, and accessible. Or use two-dimensional objects that can be displayed in a variety of ways. These include lists, charts, graphs, photographs, drawings, diagrams, and maps. Finally, don't overlook the potential of audio- or video-recordings that will help your listeners get your message.

Choose a means of display that suits your topic and the room in which you will speak. Various projectors—overhead, slide, document cameras, and LCDs—chalkboards or whiteboards, and interactive boards combine with poster boards, flip charts, and handouts as high-tech and low-tech ways to present visual aids. All have advantages and disadvantages, but you should always take care to have a Plan B in case your equipment fails.

Emerging technologies have produced a variety of sophisticated presentational packages that you can use to create professional-appearing visuals and multimedia presentations to enhance (not replace) your speech. Use principles of design, including readability, formatting, and color, to their best advantage. And follow a few rules: Display visuals only when you are discussing them, and talk to the audience, not to the visuals. Don't create a visual just to have one. Carefully edit tapes and videos, and make sure they are visible and audible to everyone. Rehearse with your visuals in advance of your speech.

Remember that competent use of visual materials can enhance your credibility. Professional-looking resources create more positive impressions than those that appear to be scribbled out just minutes before your presentation. Further, the disastrous case of equipment failure may actually increase your credibility if your listeners see you handle the stressful situation with composure. And you can demonstrate good sense and ethical awareness by selecting and presenting only visual support that does not violate your listeners' expectations.

STUDY AND REVIEW

Your online resources for *Public Speaking: Concepts and Skills for a Diverse Society* offer a broad range of study tools that will help you better understand the material in this chapter, complete assignments, and succeed on tests. Your online resources feature

- Speech videos with critical viewing questions, speech outlines, and transcripts
- Interactive versions of this chapter's Stop and Check activities and Application and Critical Thinking Exercises
- Speech Builder Express and InfoTrac College Edition
- Weblinks related to chapter content
- Study and review tools such as self-quizzes, an interactive glossary, and downloadable audio summaries

You can access your online resources at **http://www.cengage.com/login**, using the access code that came with your book or that you bought online at **http://www.iChapters.com**.

KEY TERMS

The terms below are defined in the margins throughout this chapter.

bar graphs 234	image-based visual 233	political maps 235
diagram 235	interactive whiteboards 241	presentation software
document cameras 239	line graphs 234	programs 240
flip charts 241	model 232	sans serif font 243
flowcharts 233	organizational charts 233	serif font 243
font 243	picture graphs or pictographs 234	six-by-six rule 232
geographic maps 235	pie graphs 234	text-based visual 232

APPLICATION AND CRITICAL THINKING EXERCISES

1. Think about speeches you've heard during the last week. When would visuals have made it easier for you to understand the material? When would visual or audio support have helped you pay better attention? Which support, if any, was best for your learning style preferences?
2. Think about public speakers you know who use visuals. What kinds of visual support are most common? Which do you see used least? Which presentation technologies are most common? Least common? Do most speakers use visual aids well, or should they follow some tips in this chapter? Explain.
3. Which technology for displaying visuals will you probably use for your classroom speeches? Which would you not consider? In your future employment, what equipment do you think you'll use the most? The least? Why?
4. Do an equipment assessment of the room where you will be speaking. Is there an overhead in the room? An easel? Is there a table or podium? An Ethernet connection? Where are the electrical outlets? Can the lights be dimmed? If you need equipment, how do you order it? What adjustments will you need to make to accommodate different kinds of audio and visual equipment?
5. Discuss with a small group of your classmates how you would best display a drawing in (1) a large auditorium, (2) a classroom, (3) a speech given outdoors, and (4) a presentation in someone's living room. (Several means may be appropriate.)
6. Explain what kind of visuals you think would work most appropriately for a speech on each of these topics:
   - The acid rain cycle
   - The physical effects on the lungs of smoking
   - The Oregon Trail
   - Ozone depletion
   - Changes in mortgage interest rates over two decades
7. Working in a small group, choose a sample speech from Appendix C or at the end of one of the chapters in this text and design at least three visual aids for it. Show your designs to the rest of the class and explain your choices.
8. Make a visual package using a presentation software program such as PowerPoint. First, draw your slides on paper, spacing the information across the slide, and cutting every unnecessary word or image. Then go to your computer and make the slides. Experiment with layout, fonts, and colors. Use the print preview function to look at the overall balance of the visual; adjust line spacing and font size as necessary.
9. Browse the Internet using your favorite search engine for material about visual aids. Analyze the credibility of several sites. Does the URL contain an .edu or a .com? Why might that make a difference? Who wrote the materials? When? What links are there? With this information, assess the overall usefulness of each site. Take notes and bring them to class to discuss within a small group.

10. PowerPoint is not universally loved. Visit the website of Robert Gaskins, one of its originators, at **www.robertgaskins.com**. There find the PRESS stories along the right side of the webpage. Read at least two and make a list of negative and of positive aspects of this PowerPoint. Come to class prepared to discuss your list.

11. For fun, read Lincoln's Gettysburg address, formatted in PowerPoint at **www.norvig.com/ Gettysburg/sld001.htm**, or read some of the many PowerPoint-related cartoons at **www.gbuwizards.com/files/powerpoint-cartoons.pdf**.

SPEECH VIDEO

Go to your online resources to watch Anna Riedl's informative speech, "Pumpkins," answer questions for analysis, and evaluate the speech. Your online resources also include the transcript of Anna's speech, her content outline shown below, her speaking outline, and sample note cards for the speech.

Josh Nauman/Cengage Learning

Student Outline with Visual Aids with Commentary

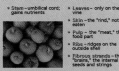

In this speech, Anna uses PowerPoint-generated slides throughout. The LCD display is on standby before she begins. She reactivates it and brings up each slide and each build by clicking the mouse.

Slides act as a transition between points. Each slide has a point-by-point build programmed in.

PUMPKINS
Anna Riedl

General Purpose:	To inform
Specific Purpose:	To inform the audience about characteristics and facts about pumpkins.
Thesis Statement:	Although the pumpkin is well known by name, there are facts that many people may not know about pumpkins.
Preview:	Many facts about pumpkins are not well known, including their anatomy, variety, health benefits, and other interesting trivia.

Introduction

I. Did you know that pumpkins are 90 percent water?
[Display title slide.]

II. Although I've seen pumpkins all my life, I've never really thought much about them, and I'm sure many of you have not as well.

III. After going through pages of information on the Internet about pumpkins, I discovered many things I did not know about this squash.

IV. Today, I will share what I now know about their anatomy, variety, nutrients, and other interesting facts, so that we can all go into the festive October and November months with a little more knowledge of pumpkins.

Body

[Display "Anatomy of the Pumpkin" slide. Throughout this point, click the mouse to build the slide as each point is discussed.]

I. There are several parts of a pumpkin.
  A. The stem is like the umbilical cord of the plant, so when it is attached to the vine, the plant gains nutrients and grows.
  B. Leaves—The leaves are only on the vine, not the stem.
  C. Skin—Also known as the "rind," the skin is not to be eaten.
  D. Pulp—This is the "meat" of the pumpkin, the part commonly made into desserts, ice cream, and so on.
  E. Ribs—These are the ridges on the outside shell of the pumpkin.
  F. Fibrous strands—This part is also known as the "brains," because it is basically composed of strings and seeds.
[Display "Varieties" slide. As each point is discussed, build the slide by clicking the mouse.]
II. These are four major varieties of pumpkins (curcurbita).
  A. Curcurbita moschata—These types of pumpkins are used commercially, such as canned pumpkin, baking, and making other food products.
  B. Curcurbita pepo—These are the teeny pumpkins that we can hold in one hand and that are very difficult to carve!
  C. Curcurbita maxima—These are recognized as the huge pumpkins that are often entered into contests or put on display, such as the one in the cafeteria.
  D. Curcurbita mixta—This group is consists of the genetically modified pumpkins. They can be white, blue, green, or even seedless.
[Display "Pumpkins are Nutritious" slide, and build with each new point.]
III. Health Benefits of Pumpkins
  A. Pumpkins contain no cholesterol and less than one gram of fat; they are a good source of protein.
  B. Pumpkins are high in vitamins A, C, and E.
  C. Calcium, zinc, potassium, and folate are all important nutrients found in pumpkins.
[Display "Interesting facts about pumpkins" and build with each point.]
IV. There are many interesting facts about pumpkins.
  A. Morton, Illinois, is the pumpkin capital of the world: Illinois produces more pumpkins than any other state.
  B. Pumpkins are very versatile; they can be grown on any continent other than Antarctica; their origin is unknown, but they probably originated in Central America.
  C. The largest pumpkin ever grown weighed 1,440 pounds.
[Display "Pumpkins Around the World" slide, and build with each point.]
  D. Pumpkins appear throughout the world.
    1. In South Wales, they are used in pies along with meat, apples, rhubarb, or pears.
    2. French cooks make pumpkin soup and mix pumpkins with other vegetables.
    3. The Jack-o-lantern tradition originated in Ireland.
    4. In Switzerland, pumpkin seeds are mixed with chocolate.

Conclusion

[Press "B" key for a blank slide.]
  I. There is so much more to learn about pumpkins; if only there was more time!
  II. But at least we now know the parts of a pumpkin, the varieties there are, their health benefits, and a few interesting facts.
[Display final slide.]
III. Now we can go into this festive month with a little more knowledge about how great pumpkins truly are.

Each slide has beautiful photographs or clip art with source citations in a small font.

The words and images are artistically balanced.

She includes a photograph of herself on this slide.

Anna uses the "B" key so that a blank screen shows when she is not discussing a particular slide.

References (formatted in MLA style)

The Pumpkin Patch. 1999. **<www.pumpkin-patch.com/facts.html>**
"Pumpkins Around the World." Pumpkin Nook. 1998–2000. **<www.pumpkinnook.com /commune/world.htm>**
Williamson, Joseph F. *Sunset Western Garden Book*. Menlo, CA: Lane, 1988.
Wise, William H. *The Wise Encyclopedia of Cookery*. New York: Grosset and Dunlap, 1978.
Wolford, Ron. "Pumpkins and More." 24 Oct. 2004. University of Illinois Extension, University of Illinois at Urbana-Champaign. **www.urbanext.uiuc.edu/pumpkins/history.html**

14

DELIVERING YOUR SPEECH

© Tim Timmerman

THIS CHAPTER WILL HELP YOU

▶ List four methods of delivery and explain when and how to use each

▶ Describe how you can enhance your use of personal appearance, clothing, and accessories

▶ Plan ways to gesture effectively

▶ Build eye contact skills

▶ Vary your voice effectively in presentations

WHO'S ON YOUR LIST of "Really Good Speakers"? A high school coach? a comedian? a famous politician? a member of the clergy? What do these speakers do that sets them apart from others?

I'll bet they don't do the following:

▶ Read their speeches, looking down all the time.
▶ Read from PowerPoint slides where the entire speech is written out.
▶ Randomly sway back and forth.
▶ Avoid eye contact with the audience.
▶ Say *uh* and *you know* and *like* throughout their speeches.

I'll predict that they are sure to do these things:

▶ Make eye contact with listeners.
▶ Speak conversationally.
▶ Use meaningful gestures.
▶ Act like they are interested in their topics and in the audience.
▶ Control their nervous mannerisms.

Often interesting and intelligent people prepare a well-crafted speech but then deliver it so poorly that the message is lost or ignored. Others could read the phone book and sound impressive. The former have poor delivery of a good message; the latter have good delivery of a poor message.

Delivery—how you perform your speech or how you present your words and ideas—is the topic of this chapter. It first elaborates on the four major types of delivery introduced in Chapter 2, giving tips for developing skills in each one. Next it describes various aspects of nonverbal communication—personal appearance, movements or mannerisms, and vocal variations—that can enhance or detract from your words. The goal throughout is to help you present your speech skillfully and appropriately for the occasion.

Select the Appropriate Type of Delivery

A high-ranking government official reads her prepared address at an Ivy League commencement ceremony, and excerpts of it are reprinted in the *New York Times*. A CEO memorizes her speeches when she speaks in behalf of her nonprofit organization, because she feels more comfortable knowing exactly what she will say. An international consultant is asked to say a few words about her recent trip to Europe for the company; with no advanced preparation she gives an "off-the-cuff" summary of her experiences. A prosecuting attorney prepares his closing arguments carefully, but when he actually faces the jury, he delivers his final appeal using only his legal pad with a few scrawled notes. These speakers illustrate the four major types of delivery, introduced briefly in Chapter 2: manuscript, memorized, impromptu, and extemporaneous.

Manuscript Delivery

Manuscript delivery means you write out your entire speech and read it. In general, this mode is not recommended in the classroom or in most workplace situations because it's the most inactive delivery method.[1] Although it can be information rich, it is interaction poor if you read ineffectively and fail to engage your audience.

Despite its disadvantages, there are many occasions, especially formal situations, where manuscript delivery is appropriate. It is useful when precise wording matters or when the speech is significant. Many ceremonial speeches such as eulogies and awards or important political speeches fall into this category. Manuscripts are also useful for radio or television speeches where exact timing is essential. Finally, speech anxiety is often related to fear of forgetting, and having a manuscript helps minimize that fear.

Consultants give several tips for competent manuscript delivery:

- Write out your speech word-for-word and rehearse by reading each sentence aloud several times, absorbing the meaning of each phrase.[2]
- After that, read the entire manuscript aloud several times and decide which words need emphasis (highlight or underline them) and where you want to pause (use slashes to show this).
- Then read the manuscript again, emphasizing words, pausing, and looking up as much as possible. Think about your audience. How will they hear and respond?
- Rehearse without looking at the script and then go back and change any wording that does not sound like you actually speak.[3]
- Type your final script in a large boldfaced font (20 points). Use double or triple spacing, and be sure to number each page.[4]
- Practice until you can read in a natural, conversational manner; most people don't like to be read to, especially if it sounds "read" and you never pause or look up.
- When you are totally familiar with the speech, practice with a podium and place your manuscript high up on it so that you can see the words without lowering your head too much.[5]
- During the speech, keep two pages visible (like an open book). Read from the page on the right, and when you finish it, slide the page on the left over it and continue without a break.

delivery the verbal and nonverbal behaviors you use to perform your speech

manuscript delivery reading a speech

If you ever speak on television, you'll probably use a **teleprompter** screen, located just beneath the camera lens. Teleprompters project your manuscript line by line so that you can read while looking directly at the camera. It is somewhat like reading the credit lines that unroll on a movie screen at the end of the film. During rehearsal, a technician will work with you to match the speed of the lines to your speaking rate. The technician can circle key words or underline phrases you want to emphasize.

To see manuscript delivery in actual use, go to **www.americanrhetoric.com**, which has outstanding speakers like Barack Obama or Arnold Schwarzenegger using a teleprompter. C-SPAN (**www.cspan.org**) also has a video library of speeches, mostly featuring manuscript delivery.

Memorized Delivery

Memorized delivery used to be the norm. Orators in ancient Rome, for example, often learned their speeches word for word. Orators in oral cultures still memorize their tribe's stories and legends, a tradition that ensures that the exact stories are preserved throughout succeeding generations. Memorized speeches are less common in today's classrooms, workplaces, churches, and clubs, although professional speakers who repeatedly give the same talk often have it memorized after a while. The students who choose this delivery mode are usually competitive speech team members who repeat each speech dozens of times in intercollegiate tournaments.

Some students think that memorizing their classroom speech will help them overcome their fears. Unfortunately, the opposite often happens. Standing in front of an audience, a beginning speaker's mind can easily go blank. Some pause (ineffectively), look toward the ceiling, repeat the last phrase in a whisper, repeat it aloud, and then look hopelessly at the instructor. I once met an elderly lady who vividly remembered her college speech class. She said she was scared to death to give her speech on the topic of spanking, so she decided to memorize it. Unfortunately, memory failed her, and her resulting embarrassment followed her for more than fifty years.

Another drawback is that memorized speeches are often not delivered conversationally. They sound "recited," not natural. And, rather than engaging in a dialogue with the audience, the speaker appears to be centered on the speech. If you must give the same speech repeatedly, the key is to treat each audience and occasion separately so that you don't just recite words.

On the other hand, some speakers trust their memories and feel more comfortable committing their speeches to memory than they do speaking extemporaneously. Chris McDonald, executive director of a nonprofit organization, chooses this type of delivery for formal occasions with large crowds. She confesses that she is a type A personality who likes to control all the elements on important occasions, in this case all the words that come out of her mouth. She gives some tips for memorized delivery:[6]

▶ Speak about key messages and themes that you "own" so that they become second nature.
▶ Write out your talk in its entirety, and then commit it to memory line by line first and then chunk by chunk.
▶ As you rehearse a line, think about its meaning.
▶ Vivid language, such as alliterated main points or parallel wording, can help you remember.[7]
▶ Practice conversationally as if you are talking to audience members individually so that you aren't just reciting words.
▶ Type the speech out onto note cards and take them to the podium in case you find yourself forgetting.

You can read more about Chris's speech preparation and delivery in the Practically Speaking feature in this chapter.

teleprompter screen, located beneath the camera lens, on which the words of the speech scroll up during a filmed speech

memorized delivery giving a speech you've learned word for word

CHRISTINE M. MCDONALD, EXECUTIVE DIRECTOR OF A NONPROFIT ORGANIZATION

Chris McDonald is the Executive Director of the Oregon and SW Washington Susan G. Komen for the Cure nonprofit organization. In an interview, she shared some of the public speaking opportunities she has and some of her strategies for creating and delivering speeches.

Did you take a speech class during your college years?
I took speech class in high school and a formal presentation skills class in the first two years of working after college. At the time, it was part of a nonprofit management certificate I earned from the University of California, Irvine, where I was then working.

I am naturally comfortable speaking in public as long as I have full command of the points I am trying to convey. I tend to get really nervous right before I begin to speak, but I've had people comment that I am a very confident speaker.

How do you prepare when you have to give a speech?
When I begin to write my speech I usually think of it in terms of key messages. When I give a speech in front of a large group (over a few hundred) I write out my speech and memorize it. Generally, I speak to large groups as a representative of our organization in my capacity as Executive Director. The speeches are never longer than 15 minutes, so I am able to memorize them. Also, the longer I am associated with an organization, the more I own the key messages, and the ideas become second nature. However, to be entirely safe, I type my speech out on note cards and have

Impromptu Delivery

Impromptu delivery means you speak with little advanced notice. This mode takes the least amount of preparation and rehearsal, because impromptu speeches are given on the spur of the moment. However, in most cases your life, your knowledge, or your experiences prepare you to make the speech. In fact, people are rarely, if ever, asked to talk about a totally unfamiliar subject.[8] Let's say you attend a farewell reception, and you're asked to say a few words. You don't have time to write out a speech and practice it. Instead, you think quickly and talk about something from your experience with the person who's leaving.

You may shudder at the thought of speaking without preparation and rehearsal, especially if your performance will be rewarded or punished in some way such as a grade or a job evaluation. However, one article in the InfoTrac College Edition says that impromptu speaking is so common in the workplace that "business leaders are eventually going to be asked to give an impromptu speech at some point in their careers,"[9] and top leaders can count on a 99.9 percent chance that they'll be asked to say

impromptu delivery
presenting the speech as you create it

them with me. We often have events where spotlights are used or lighting is bad on the podium so it is hard to "read" a script (or even see it clearly). That's when memorizing saves me!

When I serve as a master of ceremonies I tend to ad lib but follow a general script (which I typically have written so I know it well and it is in my "voice").

Do you use ever speak from an outline?
It depends on the venue. In a training session for under a hundred people where I speak extemporaneously for more than a few hours, my speaking outline is generally the same as my preparation outline, and it is more free flowing.

Are you ever called upon to "say a few words" (to give an impromptu speech)? If so, what kinds of occasions are they? How do you go about giving a talk on very short notice?
This often happens. These occasions occur primarily during fundraising or third-party events that are held for Susan G. Komen for the Cure. Sometimes I arrive at an event and someone in charge asks if I would mind saying a few words. Never one to give up a chance to promote the mission of our wonderful organization, I always say yes. I use the opportunity to string together Komen key messages and explain the mission and purpose of our organization. I usually mention our affiliation with the host organization or some other tidbit of interesting information that I know the audience may appreciate. Of course, it is critical to recognize individuals who are present for all of their efforts on behalf of our organization.

Questions for Discussion

▶ Chris mentions the importance of "key messages" in both memorized and impromptu speeches. If you had to give an impromptu speech right now about your school or your current workplace, what key messages could you build upon?
▶ Compare yourself to Chris. When, if ever, would you feel most comfortable memorizing a speech? Using a manuscript? Speaking extemporaneously from an outline? Giving an impromptu speech?
▶ Why is speaking from an outline the most practical mode for long training sessions?

a few words at banquets, company picnics, farewells, and so on. Here are some tips for impromptu talks:[10]

▶ Always expect to be called on when you are in a key position of some sort (a child of parents celebrating an anniversary, a friend of a graduate, a project manager, and so on).
▶ Listen carefully to what other speakers say at the occasion. Make mental notes of points they are omitting.
▶ If you have a few minutes of advance warning, use the time wisely. Apply what you know about speech structure (gain attention, make a couple of points, support each one briefly, make an ending statement). Decide on a couple of points to develop briefly, and jot down key words when possible. Or think of one good story to tell.
▶ When possible, tie into things others have said.
▶ Conclude with a memorable statement and then sit down instead of rambling on and on.

Of course, "winging it" is a bad strategy when you've been assigned to give a carefully prepared speech.

Martin Luther King, Jr.'s "I Have a Dream" speech is an interesting example of a speech that starts with manuscript delivery but ends with impromptu delivery. In the final section, King departs from his script and draws from his vast knowledge of the Bible, of song lyrics, of previous sermons, and so on, to deliver some of his most inspirational lines.[11]

Extemporaneous Delivery

Extemporaneous delivery is the most common method used in workplaces and classroom in the form of briefings, sales presentations, workshops, lectures, reports, and the like. Here you carefully prepare in advance, but instead of writing out every word, you outline your major ideas and use note cards or a speaking outline with cue words during delivery. (Chapter 11 provided examples of outlines and speaking outlines.) You then memorize the order of ideas, but you choose your exact wording during delivery. There are many tips for effective extemporaneous speaking:

▶ Don't put things off. Give yourself plenty of time to prepare and rehearse.[12]
▶ After making your preparation outline, work on a key word speaking outline or note cards that can prompt you to remember your main points and your supporting evidence. To avoid reading, don't put that much on your cards. Then you'll have nothing to read.
▶ Break up your speech into sections and work on them separately. Create note cards for each section and put the cards in your notebook or bag; pull one out and rehearse the information on it whenever you have a short break.[13]
▶ Rehearse using key word cards to see if your key words actually work. If not, change them or add more.[14]
▶ Memorize the thought patterns, not the exact wording[15] and run through the major ideas in the shower, as you drive, while shopping, and so on.
▶ Practice one thing at a time. For example, in one run-through, concentrate on your visuals; still another time you might focus on the content, on signposts, or on smooth transitions.[16]
▶ Time yourself and make adjustments.
▶ Give yourself at least two full rehearsals: one to find the errors, the second to correct them.[17]
▶ Practice being really good, not just adequate.[18]
▶ On speech day, review your outline and your notes and go with the confidence that comes from thorough preparation.

Following these guidelines will give you the security of knowing where you're headed and knowing the major points you've prepared.[19]

Each of the four types of delivery, manuscript, memorized, impromptu, and extemporaneous—are common in the United States. Each has strengths and weaknesses. The key throughout is to think about your listeners not your delivery. The noted orator Sir Winston Churchill, Prime Minister of Great Britain during World War II, always kept his audience in mind. Once when he was rehearsing in the bathtub, his valet heard him through the door and asked, "Were you speaking to me, sir?" Churchill replied, "No, I was addressing the House of Commons."[20]

Maximize Your Personal Appearance

Erving Goffman[21] develops the concept of **impression management** in his influential book, *The Presentation of Self in Everyday Life*. Goffman compares our self-presentation to a dramatic performance in which we attempt to create and maintain impressions of ourselves as if we were on stage, using a combination of props and

extemporaneous delivery preparing and rehearsing a speech carefully in advance, but choosing the exact wording as you deliver the speech

impression management self-presentation, using the metaphor of a staged drama in which we use props and personal mannerisms to create and maintain impressions of ourselves

personal mannerisms. Part of successful delivery includes management of your physical appearance, your clothing, and your accessories to give your audience a good impression of you.

Make the Most of Your Appearance

Images of physically perfect bodies pervade our media, and by comparison, most people have at least one flaw. Features like less-than-perfect skin, crooked teeth, visible birthmarks, above- or below-average weight or height, or use of a wheelchair can cause reluctance to speak publicly; you may feel as if you're in the limelight, being scrutinized.[22] True, several relatively permanent physical features disclose information about you. For example, others can figure out your general age range, sex, racial background, height, weight, and body type just by looking at you. Unfortunately, some audiences may stereotype you based on your personal appearance. However, audiences don't just see your physical characteristics; they form an overall impression based on your clothing and accessories combined with facial expressions, posture, and gestures. Here are some ways to maximize your appearance.

▶ Control negative thoughts about your looks. Remember that, although people do see your features, they generally don't focus on them throughout your entire speech. If you worry about your appearance, a good strategy is to have an interesting topic and a good opening statement that draws listeners' attention to your subject rather than to you.

▶ Pay special attention to grooming.[23] The proverb "cleanliness is next to godliness" shows that neatness can be even more important than attractiveness. So look as if you think the speech is important.

Make the Most of Your Clothing and Accessories

There's not much you can do to change your basic physical characteristics, but there's a lot you can do with clothing and accessories.

▶ A good general rule is to select clothing that doesn't draw attention to itself. Avoid things like too tight or too loose fitting clothing, low-cut attire, and message T-shirts. For example, Dirk, who normally wore a black T-shirt with an image across the front of a creature whose fangs were dripping blood, changed to a simple black shirt on speech days.

▶ Choose clothing appropriate to the situation. In the classroom, slightly more conservative and formal attire generally works. In other situations, check out expectations for the group and the occasion. For instance, Seana failed to do this when she spoke at a staff retreat at her university. She dressed as if she were going to a job interview, but she did not realize the retreat site was located in the woods and participants would be in casual clothes. She later confessed, "I was overdressed!" If she had asked, she would have known.

▶ Make your accessories matter. **Accessories**—the objects you carry or add to your clothing—include jewelry, glasses, briefcases, notebooks, or folders. Choose appropriate accessories of the best quality you can afford. Avoid accessories that distract or draw attention to themselves. Simple is generally best.

There are ethical implications in impression management. When you try to create an impression that truly reflects who you are or when you try to deceive your audiences to one degree or another, you are making ethical choices. Presenting verbal and nonverbal messages that you actually believe is **sincere**. In contrast, intentionally choosing to create false or misleading impressions is being **cynical**, because you don't believe your own messages.[24]

accessories objects you carry or add to your clothing

sincere speakers presenting verbal and nonverbal messages they themselves believe

cynical speakers presenting verbal or nonverbal messages they don't believe in an attempt to create a false image

ETHICS IN PRACTICE
MANAGING IMPRESSIONS

You can probably think of public personalities who try to appear genuinely interested in people because they want their money, time, or votes. Lawyers hire consultants to advise and coach their clients in selecting clothing, mannerisms, and nonverbal techniques to create an impression of innocence in jury members' minds. Ivy League-educated politicians wear flannel shirts or hard hats to "connect" with the working class. Using the following questions, discuss with a small group of your classmates the ethical appropriateness of these and similar actions.

Questions

1. Is it wrong to imply that a politician, an Ivy League graduate from a wealthy family, is similar to the blue-collar workers in his audience? Why or why not?
2. Are lawyers and consultants acting ethically if they try to create an image of innocence for clients they believe are guilty?
3. What if they believe in their client's innocence?
4. How do sincere lawyers and politicians contribute to the judicial or political process?
5. How do cynical lawyers and politicians contribute to the judicial or political process?

Develop Effective Mannerisms

Although some aspects of your appearance are relatively fixed, to a significant degree you can control your mannerisms. Gestures and eye contact are especially important.

Control Your Gestures

Body movements range from large motions such as posture, walking, and gesturing, to very small movements such as raising one eyebrow. Bodily movements can supplement your words, display emotions, help audiences understand the structure of your speech, or betray nervousness.[25]

It's common to use gestures to emphasize an idea or to supplement your words. For example, you might say, "It's about this wide," and extend your hands to show the distance. Pointing out something is also common. If you say, "Look at this part of the ocean," you'd point to the area on the map.

▶ To be effective, plan where you'll use gestures to make sure they are purposeful. It's easy to wave your arms about randomly or to repeat an annoying or distracting gesture.
▶ During one rehearsal, focus on your gestures and practice them until they seem natural.
▶ Don't hold your elbows close to your body as you gesture.
▶ When possible, videotape a rehearsal and watch yourself with the sound turned off. Analyze when and how you use your hands and arms to make effective points, and when and how your movements are meaningless. Practice what to do with your hands when you are not gesturing.

Some bodily movements show emotions. Facial expressions are especially useful in conveying such emotions as disgust and contempt (appropriate for a topic such as the blood diamond industry) or humor and delight (appropriate for an awards speech). Posture can show confidence and pride or sadness and defeat (just look at the winning and losing benches on a basketball team). Here are some tips for showing emotion:

▶ Maintain pleasant facial expressions. You don't have to smile all the time, but it's important to show a friendly attitude toward your audience throughout your speech.
▶ Even if you don't feel confident, you can look it. Stand tall; relax; hold your head erect and look directly at the audience.

Use movements to emphasize your speech structure. Changing your posture or moving from place to place can give your audience clues about your organizational pattern. One InfoTrac article advises speakers to alert audiences to high points and transitions in the speech because listeners expect such guidance and they want a map to help them listen better.[26] Here are a few ways to do this:

▶ Students on speech teams learn to "walk their points." They begin the introduction in one place and then take a couple of steps to the right to develop their first point. A few steps to the left signal the next point, and so on. The conclusion is given from the starting position. It may seem awkward to walk *every* point, but consider where and how movement could supplement your verbal transitions and signposts.
▶ Step back slightly or drop your hands from the podium to signal a transition.

A final way to maximize your mannerisms is to control nervous gestures. You might be tempted to fidget with your hair, bite your lip, scratch your nose, or rub your hands together during your speech. Or you might jingle keys in your pocket, twist your ring, or tap your note cards against the podium. Finally, you might use a gesture that cuts you off from your audience—like folding your arms across your chest during intense questioning. Gestures such as these suggest that you are subconsciously protecting yourself against the perceived psychological threat of the questioner.

Because these movements indicate anxiety or other stresses, especially when they appear to be nervous mannerisms, here are a few tips for eliminating them:

▶ Video record a rehearsal or elicit feedback from friends. Watch the recording, noting any nervous mannerism you use, and plan specific ways to avoid them. Or ask your friends to list all the movements you do that betray a lack of confidence. Discuss with them how you can improve.
▶ On speech day, do what you can to eliminate temptation. For example, if you typically fidget with a pen, don't take one to the podium with you. If you constantly flip your hair out of your eyes, pin it back or otherwise secure it. On your speaking outline, write cues such as DON'T SCRATCH, if that is your habit.
▶ Be especially aware of your body language, especially during a question-and-answer period. Work to maintain an open body position, and avoid crossing your arms defensively, even if the questioning becomes pointed.

Make Eye Contact

In the United States, direct eye contact communicates honesty and trustworthiness. The phrase "Look me in the eye and say that" is partly premised on the cultural notion that people won't lie if they're looking at you. Here, **eye contact** also communicates

eye contact looking audiences in the eye; communicates friendliness in the United States

Evaluate these speakers on their personal appearance, choice of clothing and accessories, gestures, facial expressions, eye contact, posture, and so on. What impression do you get from each one? What improvements would you suggest for any of them?

friendliness, and a person who purposely avoids another's gaze in interpersonal relationships generally signals a lack of interest. This concept transfers to public speaking where it's also important to look at the audience.

Making eye contact is often difficult at first, because it is tempting to look at your notes, the floor in front of you, the back wall, or out the window—all gazes that communicate your discomfort. However, there are some tips for developing effective eye contact:

- Look in at least three general directions: at the listeners directly in front of you, those to the left, and those to the right. Because of your peripheral vision, you can generally keep most listeners within your vision as your gaze changes direction.

- If your audience is sitting in a rectangular shape, mentally divide the group into a tic-tac-toe–like grid, and make eye contact with a friendly face in each grid.[27] This will help you look at various people within the room, not just at one or two.

- Resist the urge to make more eye contact with listeners you perceive as more powerful. In the classroom, don't just zero in on your instructor; in the workplace, don't focus on your boss's reactions at the expense of other listeners.

- Don't look more at men than women or vice versa. During his presentation to the search committee, one job candidate made noticeably more eye contact with males on the committee, largely ignoring the female department head. Needless to say, he wasn't hired.

Expectations common in the United States are not universally applicable. For instance, Japanese communicators use less direct eye contact. In their country, it is not unusual to see downcast or closed eyes at a meeting or a conference, because within Japanese culture this demonstrates attentiveness and agreement rather than rejection, disinterest, or disagreement. Additionally, Nigerians, Puerto Ricans, and other cultural groups consider it disrespectful to make prolonged eye contact with superiors.[28]

For additional information on gestures and eye contact, search InfoTrac College Edition for the key words *eye contact, nonverbal gestures,* or *body language.* What additional principles can you learn from the articles you read?

Vary Your Vocal Behaviors

When you hear a voice on the radio, you can distinguish between young or old, males or females, Southerners or New Yorkers, native or nonnative speakers of English. Often, you can detect moods such as boredom, hostility, or enthusiasm. This section discusses two important aspects of vocal behaviors that will help you become a better public speaker: pronunciation and vocal variation.

Work on Clear Pronunciation

Pronunciation, the way you actually say words, includes articulation and stress or accent on particular words. **Articulation** is the way you say individual sounds, such as *this* or *dis*, *bird* or *beerd*. Some speakers reverse sounds, saying *aks* instead of *ask*, for example, or *nuculer* for *nuclear*. **Stress** is the way you accent syllables or whole words—*poe*-LEESE (police) or POE-*leese*, for example. Some people alter both articulation and stress, for instance, comparable (COM-*purr-uh-bul*) becomes *come*-PARE-*uh-bul*; potpourri (*poe-per*-EE) becomes *pot*-PORE-*ee*.

How you articulate words can disclose your region of origin, ethnicity, and social status. For example, regional differences include the drawn-out vowels typical of the "southern drawl" and the *r* added by many Bostonians to the end of words. Ethnic dialects such as Appalachian English or African American English have distinctive articulation and stress patterns. And nonnative speakers of English use accents that reflect articulation and stress patterns from their first language. Social status is also linked to pronunciation. This is the premise for the classic musical play and movie *My Fair Lady*. Although Eliza Doolittle says the same words as Professor Higgins, her pronunciation marks her as a member of the lower class. By changing her pronunciation (as well as her dress and grooming), she eventually passes as a Hungarian princess.

In a multilingual world and in pluralistic classrooms and workplaces, there are bound to be accents, and as travel and immigration continue to shrink the world, you'll hear even more in the future. Unfortunately, we tend to judge one another on the basis of accents that reflect ethnicity or social class; however, the letter in Diversity in Practice: Immigrants, Don't Be in Such a Hurry to Shed Your Accents presents a good argument for affirming a variety of accents.

Because clear expression is essential to understanding, here are some tips for improving your pronunciation and articulation:

▶ When you're in doubt about a word's pronunciation, consult a dictionary. Many online dictionaries provide an audio feature so that you can hear the word pronounced. Some words, such as *data* have two acceptable pronunciations—DAY-*tuh* or DATT-*uh*. When the dictionary provides two variations, the first is preferable.
▶ Work on sounds or words that cause you difficulty. Winston Churchill had a lisp, so he carefully rehearsed words that began with /s/.[29] Ralph had trouble saying the word *probably*, so he broke it into syllables (PRAW-buh-blee) and articulated each one slowly and clearly.
▶ During rehearsals, slow down and articulate your words clearly.
▶ In the speech itself, speak slowly enough to avoid slurring your words together or dropping the endings.
▶ If you have a serious articulation problem, a professional speech therapist can help.

articulation the way you enunciate or say specific sounds, an element of pronunciation

stress accenting syllables or words

DIVERSITY IN PRACTICE

IMMIGRANTS, DON'T BE IN SUCH A HURRY TO SHED YOUR ACCENTS

THIS LETTER TO THE EDITOR appeared in the *New York Times*.[30]

To the Editor:

You report that immigrants in New York City are turning to speech classes to reduce the sting of discrimination against them based on accent. . . . I'd like to tell all my fellow immigrants taking accent-reduction classes: As long as you speak fluent and comprehensible English, don't waste your money on artificially removing your accent. . . .

I know I do have an accent. . . . I intend to keep it because it belongs to me. I want to speak and write grammatically flawless English, but I have no desire to equip myself with a perfect American accent. . . .

America is probably the largest place for accents in English because the entire nation is composed of immigrants from different areas of the world. This country is built on accents. Accent is one of the most conspicuous symbols of what makes America the free and prosperous land its own people are proud of and other people long to live in.

I work in an urban institution where accents are an integral part of my job: students, faculty and staff come from ethnically diverse backgrounds. Hearing accents confirms for me every day that the college is fulfilling its goal to offer education to a multicultural population. I wonder what accent my fellow immigrants should obtain after getting rid of their own: a New York accent? a Boston accent? Brooklyn? Texas? California? . . . Fellow immigrants, don't worry about the way you speak. . . .

YanHong Krompacky

Use Vocal Variation

Around 330 BC, Aristotle, in his text on rhetoric,[31] discussed three important vocal components: volume, pitch, rate, and the variations in each.

It is not enough to know what we ought to say; we must also say it as we ought. . . . It is, essentially, a matter of the right management of the voice to express the various emotions—of speaking loudly, softly, or between the two; of high, low, or intermediate pitch; of the various rhythms that suit various subjects. These are the three things—volume of sound, modulation of pitch, and rhythm—that a speaker bears in mind.

What kinds of impressions do **vocal variations** create? Various studies[32] conclude that audiences typically associate vocal characteristics with the following personality traits:

Loud and fast speakers: self-sufficient, resourceful, dynamic

Loud and slow speakers: aggressive, competitive, confident

Soft and fast speakers: enthusiastic, adventuresome, confident, composed

Soft and slow speakers: competitive, enthusiastic, benevolent

vocal variations changes in volume, rate, and pitch that combine to create impressions of the speaker

Is there a relationship between your voice and your credibility? Studies have shown that audiences make a number of associations about trustworthiness based on your voice. Rapid speech is associated with intelligence and objectivity. A moderate rate is associated with composure, honesty, an orientation toward people, and compassion.[33]

Make vocal variations work for you. Here are some specific suggestions for rehearsal:

▶ Get the right emotional attitude toward your material and the occasion. For example, if you want your audience to get excited about an idea, you get excited about it. If you want them to be disgusted, you be disgusted. At a birthday party, be happy; in a serious problem-solving meeting, be serious.

▶ Nick Morgan,[34] a professional trainer, suggests you babble during one rehearsal. That is, give the speech in nonsense syllables but use the vocalics, gestures, and body movements that express its emotional content.

▶ During rehearsal, record your speech and listen to your voice. Notice whether or not your tone of voice, rising or falling inflection, and stress on specific words create the meanings you want. Take notes on specific things you do well and things to improve. Rehearse the parts that could use more energy.

These suggestions apply to your actual performance:

▶ Make sure you're loud enough to be heard throughout the entire room.[35]

▶ Use the lower range of your voice; higher pitches make you sound younger and more excitable.

▶ Intentionally relax your throat before you speak and whenever you feel tense as you speak.

▶ Speak naturally. Don't force enthusiasm.

▶ During the speech, use a slower rate when you're giving key points, and speed up for background material.[36]

▶ Change vocal inflections when your audience appears to be losing interest; add pitch variation and slightly increased volume and rate to communicate enthusiasm.[37]

For additional tips on vocal variation, log on to the Internet site provided by the Birmingham, Alabama, Toastmasters at **www.angelfire.com/tn/bektoastmasters/ Toastmasters5.html**. Practice some of the suggested exercises you find there.

Everett Collection

In the movie, *Meet Joe Black*, William Parrish addressed the board of Parrish Communications. Watch this clip on **www .americanrhetoric.com** under "Movie Speeches." Notice how his initial *um*s and nervous mannerisms give way to meaningful pauses, gestures, and movements that add emphasis to his words.

Pause for Effect

Finally, consider your use of pauses. Pauses can be effective or embarrassing to both you and your listeners. Effective pauses are intentional; that is, you might purposely pause between major ideas or give your audience a few seconds to contemplate a difficult concept. In a speech to corporate executives, Judith Humphrey[38] advised:

> [C]onsider this: when does the audience think? Not while you're speaking, because they can't think about an idea until it's delivered. They think during the pauses. But if there are no pauses, they won't think. They won't be moved. They won't act upon what you say. The degree to which you want to involve the audience is reflected in the length of your pauses.

Humphrey's article is available on InfoTrac College Edition. Look for the title "Executive Eloquence"; step 7 describes effective delivery.

In contrast, ineffective pauses or hesitations disrupt your fluency and signal that you've lost your train of thought or you're searching for words. **Unfilled pauses** are silent; **filled** or **vocalized pauses** include *uh* or *um*, *like*, OK? and *you know*. Many professionals, as well as beginning public speakers, use *um*s. However, too many can be distracting, so work to minimize them. Here are some suggestions for using pauses effectively:

▶ Find places in your manuscript or outline where your audience needs you to pause so they can absorb what you just said. Use double slash marks // to mark these places.
▶ Then rehearse these intentional pauses. What may seem like a very long pause to you may be about right for your listeners.
▶ During a rehearsal, ask a friend to count the number of vocalized pauses you make and then give the speech again, and eliminate as many *um*s or *uh*s as you can.
▶ Use pauses as punctuation marks. For example, at the end of the body of the speech, try pausing, moving one step backward, and then saying, "In conclusion . . ." Your pause functions as a period that signals a separation in your thoughts.

A number of movies on **www.americanrhetoric.com** under "Movie Speeches" provide excellent models of good speakers who aren't afraid of pauses. Queen Gorgo's speech to the Spartan Council in the movie *300* and Coach Gary Gaines's speech on "Being Perfect" in the movie, *Friday Night Lights* are just two examples.

Put It All Together

Communicative competence is defined as the ability to communicate in a personally effective and socially appropriate manner.[39] The key to a competent performance is to find the delivery that works best for you in a given situation. A **confident style** incorporates vocal variety, fluency, good use of gestures, and eye contact to create an impression of dynamism as well as credibility. If you're naturally outgoing, this style may best fit your personality. However, in some situations—somber occasions, for example—you should choose a more **conversational style**, one that's calmer, slower, softer, and less intense, but still maintains good eye contact and gestures.[40] Listeners associate this style with trustworthiness, honesty, sociability, likableness, and professionalism, and it may actually fit you better if your personality is more laid back. But more conversational speakers can adapt for an occasion, such as a rally, where excitement runs high and people expect a more enthusiastic delivery. Both styles are persuasive.

Don't worry if you are not yet dynamic or confident. Instead, begin to develop your personal delivery style, using your appearance, mannerisms, and vocal variations to your advantage.

---

unfilled pauses
silent pauses

filled (vocalized) pauses
saying *um* or *uh* or other sounds during a pause

communicative competence
the ability to communicate in a personally effective and socially appropriate manner

confident style a way of speaking characterized by effective vocal variety, fluency, gestures, and eye contact

conversational style
speaking that's comparatively calmer, slower, and less intense, but maintains good eye contact and gestures

STOP AND CHECK

THINK CRITICALLY ABOUT DELIVERY

Political candidates often illustrate the link between delivery and effectiveness. For example, President Reagan was called the "Great Communicator," and Barack Obama's speaking skills are praised globally. In contrast, however, many politicians fail the "charismatic challenge." One presidential candidate's voice was described as "somewhere between that of a dentist's drill and the hum of a refrigerator. . . ."[41] Another's delivery was wooden, earnest, solemn, and uptight, focused more on content than on delivery. A woman's delivery was called "shrill," but her male opponent's was "smooth." Enter the consultants. Some handlers spun their bland candidate as "authentic." Some sat beside their candidate, watching and rewatching videotaped speeches, analyzing volume, rate, gestures, facial expressions. Their overall advice was to loosen up—leave the podium, gesture widely, smile. Candidates know that no matter how wonderful their ideas, their message will be lost if their delivery annoys the audience or puts them to sleep.

In small groups, discuss the following questions:

1. What qualities are important in a president? How does presidential image matter? What do you think of the handlers' decision to spin unremarkable delivery as "authentic"?
2. Should a candidate undergo a makeover or "be herself," regardless?
3. On MTV's campaign coverage, a young person responded that a specific candidate was, "Uh, uh, old." What difference does it make if a president looks old?
4. President William Taft (1909–1914) weighed around 300 pounds. Would he be elected president today? Why or why not? Is this good or bad?
5. During the 2008 primaries, Hillary Clinton and some of her supporters claimed that media coverage was sexist. Words like "shrill," "strident," and "giggle" appeared in stories about her, but not about her male opponents.[42] Candidate Sarah Palin's wardrobe, hairstyle, and glasses were discussed widely. In your opinion, does this constitute sexism? Why or why not?
6. Could Abraham Lincoln—with his looks and awkward mannerisms—be elected in this television-dominated society? Why or why not?
7. How do you judge your classmates' abilities based on the way they present themselves?

Summary

Of the four major types of delivery, memorization is common in oral cultures and in competitive speech tournaments, but it is less frequently used elsewhere. You may speak spontaneously in the impromptu style, or you may read from a manuscript. But more commonly, you'll join the ranks of extemporaneous speakers—preparing in advance but choosing your exact wording as you actually speak. Each type of delivery has its place, and each is comprised of a number of skills that you can develop through practice.

Delivery also involves nonverbal elements, and you can create a more positive impression of yourself during your delivery. The idea of managing your body and voice to affect listeners' impressions is at least as old as Aristotle—and he surely didn't invent the idea. Modern scholars continue to explore specific aspects of appearance, mannerisms, and vocal variations that create positive or negative impressions in audiences.

How you dress, your grooming, and your accessories communicate your competence. Your mannerisms—gestures, eye contact, and vocal variation—are also important in creating impressions of dynamism, honesty, and other characteristics of credibility. As your nonverbal skills increase, your competence in public speaking will increase correspondingly.

As with all attempts to influence others, the attempt to manage impressions has ethical implications. Speakers who believe in both the verbal and nonverbal messages they are sending are said to be sincere, but those who try to create false or misleading impressions are termed cynical.

STUDY AND REVIEW

Your online resources for *Public Speaking: Concepts and Skills for a Diverse Society* offer a broad range of study tools that will help you better understand the material in this chapter, complete assignments, and succeed on tests. Your online resources feature

- Speech videos with critical viewing questions, speech outlines, and transcripts
- Interactive versions of this chapter's Stop and Check activities and Application and Critical Thinking Exercises
- Speech Builder Express and InfoTrac College Edition
- Weblinks related to chapter content
- Study and review tools such as self-quizzes, an interactive glossary, and downloadable audio summaries

You can access your online resources at **http://www.cengage.com/login**, using the access code that came with your book or that you bought online at **http://www.iChapters.com**.

KEY TERMS

The terms below are defined in the margins throughout this chapter.

articulation 263	extemporaneous delivery 258	sincere 259
communicative competence 266	filled (vocalized) pauses 266	stress 263
confident style 266	impression management 258	teleprompter 255
conversational style 266	impromptu delivery 256	unfilled pauses 266
cynical 259	manuscript delivery 254	vocal variations 264
delivery 254	memorized delivery 255	

APPLICATION AND CRITICAL THINKING EXERCISES

1. With a small group of your classmates, make a set of guidelines for delivery that's appropriate to your classroom's unique culture. For example, would you change the advice about clothing or accessories presented in this chapter? What might you add that's not covered here?
2. According to Erving Goffman, the combination of environment, appearance, and mannerisms forms a "front."[43] Whether intentional or unwitting, this front influences the way observers define and interpret the situation. With this in mind, why do some public speakers appear to be something they're not? That is, why do some speakers appear to be competent or trustworthy, and you later discover they aren't? Now, identify some public speakers who effectively live out their front.[44] What are some ethical implications of fronts?
3. If possible, make a video of one of your rehearsals or speeches and then watch it. Specifically, pay attention to your gestures, noting your use of illustrators or movements that betray nervousness. Plan strategies to improve your gestures, eliminating those that create negative impressions and strengthening those that produce favorable impressions.

4. Watch the recording again. This time, evaluate your eye contact. Throughout your speech, notice the way you use your voice. Check for appropriate rate and volume; be alert for pauses, and count the number of *um*s you use, if any. Discuss with a classmate how you can improve these nonverbal aspects of delivery.

5. If you can't video record a speech, create a worksheet that identifies the elements of delivery mentioned in the chapter. Give it to a classmate just before your speech, and have him or her note nonverbal aspects of your delivery; afterwards, discuss with that person strategies you can use to improve problem areas.

6. Write a script for an ad selling one of these products:
   ▶ Used-car dealership
   ▶ Perfume
   ▶ Vacation to South America
   ▶ Brand of cola

   Bring your script to class and exchange it with a classmate. Demonstrate the type of vocal variation you would use if you were delivering the ad.

7. Some colleges and universities offer public speaking courses online. With a group of your classmates, discuss the pros and cons of this practice. How do the courses work? What are the drawbacks? Would you take one? Why or why not? (Prepare for this discussion by doing an Internet search for the words *public speaking course online*.)

SPEECH VIDEO

Log on to your online resources to watch and critique examples of memorized, extemporaneous, manuscript, and impromptu speeches.

15

TELLING NARRATIVES

THIS CHAPTER WILL HELP YOU

▶ Explain how narratives function to explain, to persuade, and to entertain

▶ List elements of narratives

▶ Give guidelines for using language effectively in narratives

▶ Identify the parts of an exemplum

▶ Apply three tests for narrative reasoning

© Tim Timmerman

"Do you know anything about low-carb diets?"

"Yeah. My mom went on one and she lost 35 pounds. Let me tell you about her lifelong struggle to control her weight . . ."

"I don't see why sleep deprivation is such a big deal."

"Neither did Brent—until one day when he found himself in the hospital because of an on-the-job injury. His story goes like this . . ."

"What happens if I donate to your organization?"

"Let me tell you about Zaur, a little boy in Azerbaijan who attends school because of a donor just like you . . ."

"What does courage mean?"

"Courage can be defined in two words: Dave Dravecky. His life story is a model . . ."

THESE ARE BUT A FEW of the ways we use stories in everyday life. The fact is we live in a "story-shaped world"[1], because storytelling has existed in every culture during every era. Lawyers frame their arguments as narratives, and politicians present their political visions in story form. Coaches, teachers, members of the clergy, and comedians all routinely tell stories. Stories are so much a part of every culture that Professor Walter Fisher[2] refers to us as **homo narrans**, the storytelling animal. The scholar Roland Barthes summarizes the importance of **storytelling**:

> The narratives of the world are numberless. . . . Narrative is present in every age, in every place, in every society; it begins with the very history of [humankind] and there nowhere is nor has been a people without narrative. All classes, all human groups, have their narratives, enjoyment of which is very often shared by [others] with different, even opposing, cultural backgrounds. . . . Narrative is international, transhistorical, transcultural: it is simply there, like life itself.[3]

Psychologists also affirm the importance of narratives. Peer Bundgaard calls the narrative schema the "basic cognitive principle of intelligibility"[4] because of its importance in making meaning. And Jerome Bruner[5] says we reason in two complementary ways: narrative thinking and propositional thinking (which is described in Chapters 17 and 18). Because both are important, this text devotes a chapter to the reasons why we tell stories, how we organize them, and how we judge their merits.

> **homo narrans** a Latin phrase that identifies humans as storytelling animals
>
> **storytelling** an oral art form we use to preserve and transmit commonly held ideas, images, motives, and emotions

Why We Tell Stories

Narrative is a form of speaking we use to meet informative, persuasive, and entertaining goals. Our stories preserve and transmit "ideas, images, motives and emotions with which everyone can identify."[6] They tell about the past, highlight human motivations, illuminate cultural ideals, and illustrate facets of a culture by identifying its themes and showing cultural differences. Stories make audiences more self-aware and more aware of cross-cultural issues.[7]

ETHICS IN PRACTICE

WHO SHOULD TELL NATIVE STORIES?

LENORE KEESHIG-TOBIAS, an Ojibway poet, argues that nonnative writers and filmmakers should not borrow native stories. To do so is to commit "cultural theft, the theft of voice." She reasons:

> Stories, you see, are not just entertainment. Stories are power. They reflect the deepest, the most intimate perceptions, relationships, and attitudes of a people. Stories show how a people, a culture, thinks. Such wonderful offerings are seldom reproduced by outsiders.[8]

Within Ojibway culture, stories are considered so potent that one storyteller must ask permission to tell another's story. Consequently, Keeshig-Tobias believes that someone who wants to use a native story should come live with the storytellers for more just than a few months.

> Hear the voice of the wilderness. Be there with the Labicon, the Inmu. Be there on the Red Squirrel Road. . . . If you want these stories, fight for them. I dare you.[9]

Questions for Discussion

1. What do you think? Should nonnatives tell a native story? Why or why not?
2. Does this apply to other groups? For example, can only Muslims tell stories about Islam or only Christians tell New Testament stories? Can a heterosexual tell the story of someone who's gay or lesbian? Why or why not?
3. What is "cultural theft"? Explain your answer.

Informative Narratives

Stories often provide information or explanations. The scholar Didier Coste[10] says that explanatory narratives provide our cultural understandings of natural, social, and ultimate things.

Explaining Natural Phenomena

Why do cats and dogs fight? The Kaluli tribe from Papua New Guinea explains animal characteristics in a myth. Where do babies come from? Parents dust off the "birds and the bees" story for each new generation. How did the world come into being? Scientists weave facts and ideas into narrative accounts such as the big bang theory combined with evolutionary narratives. Other people and groups counter with alternative explanations because stories of human origin profoundly affect our perceptions of the natural world and our place in it.[11] Narratives are essential in courtrooms. Who killed the victim? How? Prosecutors and defense lawyers offer competing explanations that jury members must weigh and compare before finally accepting the story that makes the most sense to them.

Explaining Society and Institutions

Stories also explain cultural institutions or structures. History texts are peopled with characters who face dramatic choices, overcome hardships, invent useful as well as harmful machines, and make mistakes. Stories explain the country's founding, its wars, blameworthy scenes (slavery), and praiseworthy events (the Constitutional Convention). However, myths often obscure the historical facts, and history books from other countries and other perspectives narrate the same events quite differently.

Organizations and groups have their own unique narratives. Your college has a story as does your family. Because organizations rely on stories to get their messages across, hundreds of corporate trainers emphasize the importance of effective storytelling. Annette Simmons, for example, says when you represent an organization you should have a variety of stories: one to explain who you are, another to tell why you are speaking, a third to describe your vision, a fourth to teach (both positive and negative lessons), and a number of values-in-action narratives that show how your organization operates on its principles.[12]

Explaining Ultimate Things

Philosophical and religious narratives attempt to explain ultimate realities, to answer questions such as "Who are we?" "What is our purpose on Earth?" "What happens after death?" "How should I live a moral life?" Many are found in religious rituals or holidays based in historical events. Jewish people, for instance, narrate the story of Queen Esther as they celebrate Purim. Hindus celebrate the birthday of Ganesha, the deity of good fortune and prosperity during the festival of Ganesha Chaturthi. Christians remember the death and resurrection of Jesus as they celebrate Easter. In short, religious beliefs and practices are grounded in stories that followers have preserved over generations, stories that give ultimate meaning to the lives of adherents.

Persuasive Narratives

Narrative reasoning is so effective that Aristotle classified it as a type of **deliberative speaking**—speaking that provides information and motivates people to make wise decisions.[13] Cognitive psychologists Melanie Green and Timothy Brock argue, "The power of narratives to change beliefs has never been doubted and has always been feared. Consequently, censorship has been ubiquitous for centuries."[14] Far more people absorb public narratives (such as films or news stories) than they do advocacy messages (such as sermons or political speeches). Our stories reinforce and influence our beliefs, actions, and attitudes.

deliberative speaking a form of speaking that gives people the information and motivation they need to make wise decisions regarding future courses of action

Reasons for a Belief, Attitude, or Action

Narratives are especially useful for emphasizing and reinforcing the beliefs, values, attitudes and behaviors that are important to a culture. Consequently, commemorative speeches honoring the lives and achievements of significant individuals often highlight values-in-action stories about those individuals. Many stories are told to provide support for our beliefs:
"Can one person make a difference?"

> Yes. Clara "Mother" Hale opened Hale House in Harlem to care for babies of drug addicts and babies with AIDS. She was an ordinary person who helped a lot of at-risk children by . . .

Stories also provide a rationale for our attitudes and actions. (For example, every war is justified by stories.) The following examples urge listeners toward positive goals:
"Be honest."

> Look at what happened to Pinocchio when he told a lie.

"Peacemaking begins with concerned, committed individuals."

> Israeli storyteller Noa Baum's one-woman show, "A Land Twice Promised," weaves together her personal memories, the memories of a Palestinian woman she met in the United States, and their mothers' stories to provide multiple perspectives on the same places and events.[15]

Sometimes unpleasant stories expose a wrong of some sort. Emotionally moving narratives can motivate listeners to intervene, to make a difference, to improve the lives of people. Here's an example:

> To persuade people to donate time and money to the organization she founded, God's Love, We Deliver, Ganga Stone told about Richard, a dying AIDS patient who desperately needed prepared meals delivered to his home. Originally created to serve AIDS patients, the organization includes other sick people who need regular meals. The organization's story is featured on http://www.godslovewedeliver.org/.

Her goal was to cause listeners to identify with people in need, become concerned, and seek ways to become personally involved in attacking the problem.

Reasons Against an Action, Belief, or Attitude

Some stories give cautionary messages or show what policies not to enact, how not to behave, or what not to believe. Cautionary tales typically use fear, shame, anger, and other strong emotional appeals.
"Practice safe sex."

> Health professionals tell about people who practiced unsafe sex, with dire consequences. . . .

In the movie, *The Great Debaters*, James Farmer, Jr.'s character helps little Wiley College win a debate against mighty Harvard University. His powerful narrative of a lynching supported his persuasive claim that civil disobedience is sometimes justified.

PRACTICALLY SPEAKING

APPLIED STORYTELLERS

©2006/Kent Miles

Applied storytellers use narratives for practical reasons: they want to promote social action or better the world, not just entertain an audience.[16] They show up in prisons, homeless shelters, battered women's shelters, negotiating sessions, and houses of worship. You might find them in hospitals with patients in therapy and recovery.[17]

Laura Simms, pictured here, uses narratives to help children who are trapped in war and conflict situations. She chooses stories from many cultures as "metaphors for redemption, to help children overcome overwhelming feelings of fear or powerlessness."[18] Taking inspiration from centuries-old oral traditions passed on in villages and families across the globe, she reports:

> I have gathered traditional stories from many different cultures that hopefully can provide an internal place of peace and inner nourishment for children who are dealing with tremendously overpowering feelings and images. This is what stories have done through the ages.[19]

Hired to work with delegates at the 1996 UN's International Children's Parliament, Simms met Ishmael Beah, a former child soldier from Sierra Leone. She eventually helped him come to the United States and complete a college education. He tells his own story—and her role in it—in his bestselling book, *A Long Way Gone: Memoirs of a Boy Soldier*.[20]

Other applied storytellers strive to build peace, one story at a time. They believe that conflict arises when our stories don't match the stories of other people or groups. Although we may be tempted to avoid or discount divergent stories, we can actually learn and grow by sharing them, by questioning other narratives and our own as well, and by reconsidering our stories and encouraging others to do likewise. Exchanging competing narratives lets us look for commonalities that can help us understand and examine our differences and together co-create new narratives. Peacemakers use personal stories, as well as folktales about peace and reconciliation from many cultures to offer insights about transforming conflict into peace.[21]

Questions for Discussion

▶ Laura Simms tells stories to heal emotional traumas. Can you give an example of someone who was helped emotionally through a story?

▶ How might storytelling function to help a person heal physically?

▶ Describe a time you resolved a conflict by sharing stories with the person with whom you disagreed.

▶ What conflicts on your campus result from divergent, competing stories? What opportunities, if any, are provided for sharing conflicting stories? How effective are they?

▶ How might storytelling promote civility and dialogue among people who disagree?

applied storytelling using stories for practical purposes, not just for entertainment

"Avoid credit card debt."

> Your personal story about problems that resulted from a credit card spending spree can motivate your listeners to use their credit cards wisely.

Persuasive stories contribute to wider policy changes as well as individual changes. For instance, on the campus level, stories about a series of computer thefts convinced administrators to tighten security policies. National stories about oil spills led to tighter regulations for oil tankers. International tales of earthquake victims led millions across the globe to respond with money and muscle.

Visionary Narratives

Although many stories are told in the past or present tense, some provide a vision of the future. Science fiction writers paint bleak scenarios of out-of-control technology, or they depict a bright future where machines are harnessed and controlled, allowing humans to do superhuman things. Visionary narratives can also suggest ideals by confronting listeners with possibilities and expanding their understandings of themselves and their lives. Through this, the **rhetoric of possibility**,[22] you tell what might be, and you help others envision a future that they can make real. (The Practically Speaking feature on applied storytellers describes some ways that stories are contributing to social change.)

In summary, persuasive stories can influence one person or millions. They provide examples of both wise and unwise behaviors; they provide a rationale for or against a policy, belief, or behavior; and they present a vision of what might be.

Entertaining Narratives

Let's face it: Not all stories are profound, and we tell many a story just to relax or have a good time. Storyteller Jackie Torrence[23] tells "Jump Tales" that end with a "BOO!" because she loves the shivers they give. Children's stories, extended jokes,

---

✓ STOP AND CHECK
YOUR NARRATIVE PURPOSES

Of all the stories you've told within the last twenty-four-hour period, estimate the percentage you told for the following purposes:

____ to inform
____ to persuade
____ to entertain

Will these percentages be similar in your chosen career? If so, what kind(s) of stories will you probably tell more? What kind(s) will you tell less frequently? Discuss with a small group of your classmates how you will probably use narratives to do the following in your choice of career:

- Explain natural things
- Explain organizational or social realities
- Explain ultimate things
- Motivate people to believe or act in specific ways
- Commemorate cultural beliefs, values, attitudes, or behaviors
- Provide a rationale not to believe or do certain things
- Present a vision of the future
- Entertain an audience

---

rhetoric of possibility points out what can be, not what is

situations exaggerated to the extreme, and television sitcoms are just a few examples of narratives that feature unusual or quirky characters in unusual or quirky situations.[24] Search the Internet for silly stories or jokes, for scary stories or campfire tales. The number of links you get in each category should give you some idea of the popularity of entertaining stories. (A Google search turned up more than 100 million links for jokes!)

Kenneth Burke, the great rhetoric scholar, summarizes story categories as "the imaginative, the visionary, the sublime, the ridiculous, . . . the satirical, every detail of every single science or speculation, even every bit of gossip . . ."[25] We are indeed story-telling animals.

How We Organize Stories

Because you have been hearing and telling stories all your life, you are probably quite familiar with the basic elements of narratives. This section describes how to craft your story and choose vivid language.

Weave Narrative Elements Together

The basic elements of a story include your purpose or goal and the setting, characters, and plot you will use to develop that goal.

Identify Your Purpose

Whether you give a narrative speech or tell a story as part of a larger speech, consider your purpose carefully. What function do you want the narrative to fulfill? Do you want to inform, persuade, or entertain? Will you present a vision of possibilities that your audience has not yet considered? Remember that even when a story is mainly told for entertainment purposes, it should convey a lesson or point; otherwise, it's pointless.

Set Up the Story

Identifying the scene or situation provides the foundation for the overall story line. Giving space and time details about where and when the story takes place is a good way to start. (Examples: Before the newfangled invention of the telephone, the family was still living on their farm in Kansas . . . Yesterday afternoon in a downtown business . . .) Background information on the situation or the social conditions at the time can help transport your audience into the world of the story and make them more receptive to its message.[26] (She lived in the days before the printing press, when every book was hand-written, when a single book could cost a half year's salary . . . Before the war, most of the men tended the cattle and most of the women worked in the fields . . .). Additional details also set the mood you want to convey. (Morning broke over another dry, windy day in the desert, the hundredth day without rain . . .)

Mythical stories often begin with the formulaic phrase, "Once upon a time in a faraway land." Listeners immediately pull up their mental "fairy tale schema" and listen to the story through that filter. True-life narrative draws listeners into the world of the story by starting with realistic details, "When I was a junior in high school, I was enrolled in a very small private school in the mountain country of Montana." This opening immediately activates the listeners' "personal experiences" schema. Regardless of the type of story, details about the setting help listeners place themselves psychologically in the story's space.

Develop the Characters

It almost goes without saying that stories contain characters, whether real or imaginary. Fictional characters include animals (like Nemo, a fish) or natural objects (like a talking tree) that are personified or given human traits. Clearly imaginary characters (dragons, talking trains, or other fanciful characters) commonly convey and reinforce important cultural values. For almost 2,500 years, Aesop's fables have used animals to communicate western cultural wisdom. Coyote stories, similarly, communicate the wisdom of various Native American groups.

Depending on your purpose, realistic stories about people who act, move, speak, form relationships, and interact with others are more effective. To be believable, these characters will come with their own perspectives and will be motivated by distinctive personality traits, ethnic and religious backgrounds, educational experiences, and social backgrounds.

Develop the Plot

The **plot** is the challenge or conflict that tests the characters' assumptions, values, or actions. The way they respond to the challenges and the resulting changes in their lives form the plot, or action of the narrative. During this period of change, natural processes, such as growing up, occur. The characters may meet physical, psychological, and economic challenges. They may have accidents, begin and end relationships, lose their possessions in a tragic manner, and so on. How they deal with these challenges provides the point or moral of the story.

Format Your Speech as a Story

Many speeches that are outlined in other common patterns could be presented in a story format. For example, the outline of Emily's speech on biliary atresia appeared in Chapter 11. She used a topical organizational pattern; however, she could have organized her speech as a narrative by creating a plausible story line from the elements of setting, characters, and plot.[27]

▶ Setting: a small town in Oregon in the 1980s when medical breakthroughs were happening but were not as advanced as they are now. [A photograph, displayed on a PowerPoint slide shows the family home.]

▶ Characters: the parents, the very ill newborn, the doctors, the donor's family, family and friends from the community, and so on. [Slides show the major characters she will emphasize.]

▶ Plot: the crisis that was discovered when the tiny child became jaundiced. The villain is biliary atresia. [A diagram of the liver illuminates the concept.]

plot the story's action

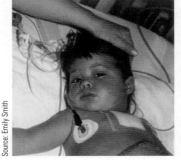

Source: Emily Smith

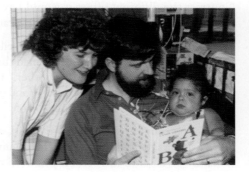

Emily could have presented her speech as a narrative with a series of slides to illustrate the setting, the characters, and the plot. The character or characters chosen to play the role of hero would depend on her purpose.

Presenting the speech as a narrative would give the audience a different perspective from the one outlined in Chapter 11.[28] A narrative format allows Emily to emphasize her purpose by deciding who plays the starring role(s). If her goal is to inform the audience of medical breakthroughs, the doctors are the lead characters. To persuade listeners to become organ donors, the donor and her family play the starring roles. To emphasize the value of working together during a crisis situation, she would highlight the roles of family and community members who raised money for her treatments.

Select Vivid Language

Narrative speaking requires careful attention to language. Vivid word choices and details bring the story to life and let your listeners feel as if they are present as the events unfold. Detailed descriptions convey information, help create the scene, and provide a sense of authenticity by giving specific names, places, and times. Language includes details, constructed dialogue, and listing.

Provide Detailed Descriptions

Details are important in several places. When you first orient the audience to the plot, include enough descriptive material to give your audience a sense of the context. When you come to the key action points, give listeners important details they can use to clearly understand the changes taking place within the characters. Finally, use a cluster of details in the climax of the story to drive home your main point.

Be careful to include just the right amount of detail. Certain details are vital, but others are irrelevant for two major reasons. First, you may have too many details. Just ask a child to describe a movie he saw, and he'll probably get bogged down in details. He might even miss the movie's point entirely, because children don't always separate details that are relevant to the plot from those that merely add color. Details also can be inappropriate when they reveal more than listeners want to know. For instance, disclosing intimate or shocking information might cause listeners to focus on the details and miss the story's point. For these reasons, be rhetorically sensitive and evaluate details carefully in light of your specific audience, then edit out irrelevant or inappropriate material.

Construct Dialogue

Created or **constructed dialogue** between characters adds realism. By using vocal variety that conveys your characters' personalities and emotions, you increase both your involvement and your listener's involvement in the story. For example, here is one way to report a scene:

> He told me to move my car, but I didn't, because I was only going to park for a moment. The next thing I knew, he threatened me.

Contrast the different effect it would have on your audience if you create a dialogue, then use different "voices," volume, and rate for each character, like this:

> He rolled down his car window and yelled, "Hey, kid, move your pile of junk!" I turned down my radio and explained through my open window, "I'll just be here a minute. I'm waiting for my mother." He jerked open his car door, stomped over to my car, leaned into my window and said slowly through clenched teeth, "I said, (pause) 'Move . . . your . . . pile . . . of . . . junk, kid!'"

As you can see, the scene with vivid, memorable dialogue is far more likely to involve listeners, helping them imagine themselves in the scene. By increasing their emotional involvement in the story, you keep their attention and have greater potential for communicating your point.

constructed dialogue
created conversation between characters that adds realism to a story

Create Lists

Lists increase rapport with an audience because they introduce specific areas of commonality with the storyteller. If you said "I packed my bags and checked twice to see if I had forgotten anything" you would get across the message, but adding specific details that are familiar to travelers enliven it, as this example illustrates:

> As I packed for my trip to China, I was afraid I would forget something vital. I looked through my bag for the seventh time. Toothpaste? Check. Toothbrush? Check. Toilet paper? (I like being prepared.) Check. Deodorant? Yep. Yet something seemed to be missing—as I was to discover in an isolated village in Shanxi Province.

Again, the details involve listeners actively, inviting them to create mental images for each item you list. As you can see, the language you choose makes a difference. Because narratives appeal to emotions, it is vital that your audience become involved in the story, and word choices that increase audience involvement make your story more powerful and memorable.

DIVERSITY IN PRACTICE
ANALYZE A FOLKTALE

DO AN INTERNET SEARCH for Folklore and Mythology Electronic Texts, a site sponsored by D. L. Alishman from the University of Pittsburgh. Download a folktale from another culture. Compare the way it's constructed with the guidelines presented here. What is the purpose of the story? Are the characters real or imaginary? What details provide clues to their personality and motivations? What is the plot of the story? How does the storyteller incorporate vivid language, use of details, dialogue, and lists? How is the story similar to one that's typical of narratives from your culture? If it's different, tell how. Jot down your analysis and prepare to discuss your conclusions with a small group of your classmates.

Use a Narrative Pattern

Although the various elements in the speech could be arranged by importance, interest value, or recency,[29] the chronological pattern is probably used most frequently in narrative speeches. Storytellers typically begin at the beginning, lead to the middle section, and wrap up the action in the conclusion, bringing in relevant information that contributes to the overall main point and editing out irrelevant facts. Often, they state the point or moral of the story explicitly at the beginning, at the end, or both.

Another useful pattern, used by speech teachers for hundreds of years, is called the **exemplum**.[30] The five elements of exemplum speeches are organized around a quotation. Paul Lee's personal experience speech about immigrating to the United States is an example:

1. *State a quotation or proverb.* "Ask not what your country can do for you; ask rather what you can do for your country."
2. *Identify and explain the author or source of the proverb or the quotation.* President John Kennedy, the thirty-fifth President of the United States, said this in his Inaugural Address.
3. *Rephrase the proverb in your own words.* In other words, instead of taking for granted the things our country has to offer, we should actively seek opportunities to improve our country.

exemplum an organizational pattern in which a narrative is used to illustrate a quotation

4. *Tell a story that illustrates the quotation or proverb.* Immigrating to the United States from Hong Kong posed many challenges and hardships as my family learned a new language and customs. Eventually, my family members proudly took the oath of citizenship—with all the rights and privileges that it brought—before a presiding judge who welcomed all of us new citizens with Kennedy's challenging words.

5. *Apply the quotation or proverb to the audience.* Everyone—both native-born and immigrants—should reflect on the privilege of being in the United States; each listener should think of some way to make the country better for all.

Select your narrative from personal experiences, from historical events, or from episodes in the life of someone else. Choose one that represents, illustrates, or explains something important to you, perhaps a turning point in your life. Identify a lesson or point to your story and then find a quotation that supports this point. You might use a common saying, such as "silence is golden," or you can consult sources of quotations (listed topically and by author) in the reference section of the library or online. A good place to start is **www.bartleby.com/100/**.

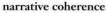

How We Judge Stories

Stories aren't equally valuable, so we should test them to see if they are sensible and worthy of being told. Some are true and honest; others are false, mistaken, or downright lies.[31] But how do we judge narratives? And when faced with competing stories, how do we weigh and decide which is best? To answer these questions, narrative theorists offer three major tests of narrative logic.[32]

1. Does the story have **narrative coherence**? That is, is it understandable? Does it hang together logically? Do the events in the story follow one another in a predictable sequence? Do the characters act and interact in ways that are probable, given their personalities and cultural backgrounds? Or do some things seem out of character or out of order?

2. Does the story truly or faithfully represent what you know about the world and the way it works? In other words, does the story make sense within the larger cultural framework? If it is a myth, folktale, or hypothetical story, does it contain important truths that demonstrate appropriate ways to live? Walter Fisher[33] terms this **narrative fidelity**.

3. Does the **narrative** have **merit**? Should it be told because the message is important or worthwhile? Does it motivate people to behave in ways that result in ethical outcomes for individuals and for society as a whole? Does it serve as a cautionary tale? Does it highlight a cultural value worthy of reinforcement? Before passing along a story, it is important to evaluate the desirability of doing so.

We weigh priorities and make ethical decisions when we choose whether or not to repeat a particular story. A narrative that creates problems for the individuals involved or their families can provide a good cautionary example, but the harm to innocent people may outweigh the benefits. Gossip, such as information about a political candidate's shaky marriage or the suicide attempt of a public figure's child, poses questions of narrative merit. If sensational details of the characters' private lives are merely entertaining, examine your motives. Why disclose them? However, if a story uncovers a public figure's character flaws or tendencies that don't match his or her pronouncements; then it might be appropriate to tell.

Good stories aren't necessarily true—fiction does have its place. But stories that are blatantly false and result in harm are wrong to tell. History provides examples of leaders who spread lies with disastrous consequences. Here's one: In the Middle Ages, people

narrative coherence deciding if a narrative is understandable or sensible

narrative fidelity testing if the narrative faithfully represents how the world works

narrative merit testing whether or not a narrative is worth telling

circulated false narratives about Jews poisoning the water supply of villages, stories that resulted in the murder of many Jewish people and produced irreversible negative consequences on individuals and on society in general.

Summary

In every society, narrative reasoning exists as a form of sense making. Narratives both reflect and shape cultural beliefs and values, and hearing narratives from other cultures highlights commonalities and differences between groups. Narratives in all cultures function to inform, to persuade, to commemorate cultural ideals, and to entertain. Explanatory narratives provide answers for why and how things are the way they are. Persuasive narratives provide reasons for or against a belief or course of action, and they highlight important beliefs, values, attitudes, and behaviors. Visionary narratives help us see possibilities that we had not imagined before. Finally, some narratives are just plain fun, and we tell them for entertainment purposes.

Stories have five major elements: purpose, characters, sequence, plot, and language. Vivid language is especially important because it brings characters to life and makes the action more compelling, causing listeners to identify with more elements of the story.

Organize your story in a chronological pattern or use the exemplum pattern, a pattern with a long history that begins with a quotation, provides information about the source, and paraphrases the saying. An illustrative story forms most of the speech, which concludes with a stated lesson or moral.

Some stories are better than others, but every good story should be coherent, it should have fidelity—meaning that it represents some aspect of the real world—and it should be worthy of being told. To evaluate a story's merit, consider its effect on society, its effect on individuals, and its overall truthfulness about life.

STUDY AND REVIEW

Your online resources for *Public Speaking: Concepts and Skills for a Diverse Society* offer a broad range of study tools that will help you better understand the material in this chapter, complete assignments, and succeed on tests. Your online resources feature

- Speech videos with critical viewing questions, speech outlines, and transcripts
- Interactive versions of this chapter's Stop and Check activities and Application and Critical Thinking Exercises
- Speech Builder Express and InfoTrac College Edition
- Weblinks related to chapter content
- Study and review tools such as self-quizzes, an interactive glossary, and downloadable audio summaries

You can access your online resources at **http://www.cengage.com/login,** using the access code that came with your book or that you bought online at **http://www.iChapters.com.**

KEY TERMS

The terms below are defined in the margins throughout this chapter.

applied storytelling 274	homo narrans 271	plot 277
constructed dialogue 278	narrative coherence 280	rhetoric of possibility 275
deliberative speaking 273	narrative fidelity 280	storytelling 271
exemplum 279	narrative merit 280	

APPLICATION AND CRITICAL THINKING EXERCISES

1. What narratives do you use to explain the world of nature? the social world? your family? other groups to which you belong? the ultimate meanings in life? Do your stories ever clash with the narratives of others? If so, what do you do about these differences?

2. What informative narratives have you heard about your school or about an organization you work for? For example, employees at Wal-Mart hear the story about how founder and billionaire Sam Walton drove his beat-up old pick-up truck to work every day. What kind of values does this type of story teach?

3. To read another culture's explanation of its history, search InfoTrac College Edition for "Stone Camels and Clear Springs" in the journal *Asian Folklore Studies*. This drama features audience participation and feedback in the retelling of the history of the Salar people.

4. Discuss with your classmates how informative narratives help us to prepare for the unknown by sharing your travel stories and the advice you would give to others traveling to the same destinations.

5. Share with a group of classmates a few examples of persuasive narratives you heard while you were growing up. In what ways were they intended to influence your behaviors? How successful were they?

6. To illustrate the power of persuasive narratives, visit the Urban Legends Reference page at **http://www.snopes.com**. Did you find any legends you had heard and believed to be true? What makes urban legends so compelling?

7. In what settings have you heard inspiring life stories that highlight a cultural ideal? Have you ever shared your personal saga of overcoming some challenge? If so, describe the occasion. Where might you give an inspirational personal story in the future? What would be your purpose?

8. To better understand applied storytelling, search InfoTrac College Edition for the words "healing AND storytelling." Read an article and discuss it with a small group of your classmates.

9. Think of stories that you have only heard orally. Who are the "legends" in your family, your sports team, your religious group, living group, or university? What lessons do their stories provide? What values or actions do they help you remember and perpetuate?

10. What functions do classic children's stories play in our culture? What do we teach our children when we tell them the fable of the tortoise and the hare? What is the moral of "The Three Little Pigs"? Does *The Cat in the Hat* simply entertain or does it serve other functions as well?

11. Take one of your speech outlines and reframe the topic into narrative form, weaving setting, characters, and plot into a coherent story line.

12. Children's stories explain, persuade, and entertain. Bring in a copy of your favorite children's book. With a small group of classmates, take turns reading your books and discussing the storyteller's major goals, characters, and use of language.

13. The exemplum pattern is useful in a variety of settings. With a small group of your classmates, sketch out themes and suggest the types of supporting narratives that would be appropriate on each of the following occasions:
    ▶ A sports award banquet
    ▶ A luncheon meeting of a club such as Rotary or Kiwanis
    ▶ A religious youth group meeting
    ▶ A scholarship presentation ceremony
    ▶ A Fourth of July celebration
    ▶ A keynote address to a conference focusing on issues relevant to female physicians

14. Visit the National Storytelling Festival's home page, **www.storytellingfestival.net**, and follow the link to Featured Tellers. Choose the three storytellers you'd most prefer to hear. Why those choices?

SPEECH VIDEO

To watch and critique a narrative speech, go to your online resources and access Gail Grobey's speech about spanking. A transcript of her speech appears in Appendix C. Or read the following historical speech by Chief Joseph, which provides an example of narrative reasoning.

Ciella Jaffe / Cengage Learning

HISTORICAL Speech with Commentary

AN INDIAN'S VIEW OF INDIAN AFFAIRS
Chief Joseph[34]

In-mut-too-yah-lat-lat, also known as Chief Joseph of the *Nez Percé* Indian tribe, told this story on January 14, 1879, before a large gathering of Cabinet officers, congressional representatives, diplomats, and other government officials. His speech argues that Congress should act in behalf of his people for a number of good reasons.

My name is *In-mut-too-yah-lat-lat* (Thunder Traveling Over the Mountains). I am chief of the *Wal-lam-wat-kin* band of *Chute-pa-lu,* or *Nez Percés* (nose-pierced Indians). I was born in eastern Oregon, thirty-eight winters ago. My father was chief before me. When a young man, he was called Joseph by Mr. Spaulding, a missionary. He died a few years ago. There was no stain on his hands of the blood of a white man. He left a good name on the earth. He advised me well for my people.

Our fathers gave us many laws, which they had learned from their fathers. These laws were good. They told us to treat all men as they treated us; that we should never be the first to break a bargain; that it was a disgrace to tell a lie; that we should speak only the truth; that it was a shame for one man to take from another his wife, or his property without paying for it. We were taught to believe that the Great Spirit sees and hears everything, and that he never forgets; that hereafter he will give every man a spirit-home according to his deserts: if he has been a bad man, he will have a bad home. This I believe, and all my people believe the same.

We did not know there were other people besides the Indian until about one hundred winters ago, when some men with white faces came to our country. They brought many things with them to trade for furs and skins. They brought tobacco, which was new to us. They brought guns with flint stones on them, which frightened our women and children. Our people could not talk with these white-faced men, but they used signs which all people understand. These men were Frenchmen, and they called our people *Nez Percés* because they wore rings in their noses for ornaments. Although very few of our people wear them now, we are still called by the same name. These French trappers said a great many things to our fathers, which have been planted in our hearts. Some were good for us, but some were bad. Our people were divided in opinion about these men. Some thought they taught more bad than good. An Indian respects a brave man, but he despises a coward. He loves a straight tongue, but he hates a forked tongue. The French trappers told us some truths and some lies.

Many speeches are given in narrative form; in others, an extended narrative takes up a significant part of the speech. Chief Joseph's speech is an example. Read through it and describe how he sets the story and uses characters and plot to create a story that drives home his point. Then, using the tests for narrative reasoning, explain how the story has coherence, fidelity, and merit.

The first white men of your people who came to our country were named Lewis and Clark. They also brought many things that our people had never seen. They talked straight, and our people gave them a great feast, as a proof that their hearts were friendly. These men were very kind. They made presents to our chiefs and our people made presents to them. We had a great many horses, of which we gave them what they needed, and they gave us guns and tobacco in return. All the *Nez Percés* made friends with Lewis and Clark, and agreed to let them pass through their country, and never to make war on white men. This promise the *Nez Percés* have never broken. No white man can accuse them of bad faith, and speak with a straight tongue. It has always been the pride of the *Nez Percés* that they were the friends of the white men. When my father was a young man there came to our country a white man (Rev. Mr. Spaulding) who talked the spirit law. He won the affections of our people because he spoke good things to them. At first, he did not say anything about white men wanting to settle on our lands. Nothing was said about that until about twenty winters ago, when a number of white people came into our country and built houses and made farms. At first our people made no complaint. They thought there was room enough for all to live in peace, and they were learning many things from the white men that seemed to be good. But we soon found that the white men were growing rich very fast, and were greedy to possess everything the Indian had. My father was the first to see through the schemes of the white men, and he warned his tribe to careful about trading with them. He had suspicion of men who seemed so anxious to make money. I was a boy then, but I remember well my father's caution. He had sharper eyes than the rest of our people.

Next there came a white officer (Governor Stevens), who invited all the *Nez Percés* to a treaty council. After the council was opened he made known his heart. He said there were a great many white people in the country, and many more would come; that he wanted the land marked out so that the Indians and white men could be separated. If they were to live in peace it was necessary, he said, that the Indians should have a country set apart for them, and in that country they must stay. My father, who represented his band, refused to have anything to do with the council, because he wished to be a free man. He claimed that no man owned any part of the earth, and a man could not sell what he did not own.

Mr. Spaulding took hold of my father's arm and said, Come and sign the treaty. My father pushed him away, and said: Why do you ask me to sign away my country? It is your business to talk about spirit matters, and not to talk to us about parting with our land. Governor Stevens urged my father to sign his treaty, but he refused. I will not sign your paper, he said; you go where you please, so do I; you are not a child, I am no child; I can think for myself. No man can think for me. I have no other home than this. I will not give it up to any man. My people would have no home. Take away your paper. I will not touch it with my hand.

My father left the council. Some of the chiefs of the other bands of the *Nez Percés* signed the treaty, and then Governor Stevens gave them presents of blankets. My father cautioned his people to take no presents, for after a while, he said, they will claim that you have accepted pay for your country. Since that time four bands of the *Nez Percés* have received annuities from the United States. My father was invited to many councils, and they tried hard to make him sign the treaty, but he was firm as the rock, and would not sign away his home. His refusal caused a difference among the *Nez Percés*. . . .

Chief Joseph continues the speech, detailing years of treaty negotiations between the Nez Percé and the whites. His conclusion recognizes that the inevitable has happened; his people are powerless against the white settlers. But his final plea is for equal justice under law for the Indian as well as for whites.

CHAPTER 16

INFORMATIVE SPEAKING

© Tim Timmerman

THIS CHAPTER WILL HELP YOU

▶ Describe the global importance of information

▶ Analyze your audience's knowledge of your subject

▶ Create several types of informative speeches including demonstrations and instructions, descriptions, reports, and explanations

▶ Use guidelines to make your informative speeches more effective

WALK INTO A thriving company or organization and you will hear employees or members giving reports, providing instructions, demonstrating techniques and products, and updating others on the latest information related to their organization. Enter a school and you'll hear students and teachers making announcements, discussing facts, defining terms, and explaining complex concepts. Now, take a moment and picture yourself fifteen years down the road. Where are you working? What instructions or directions are vital to your success? What information will you give your coworkers or the public? What information will you need to be healthier, more productive, or happier? Informative speeches, "speeches to teach," are very common, as these examples show:

▶ A leader of a campus club reports on a new fundraising plan.
▶ A forensic nurse informs high school students about unhealthy encounters that resulted from Internet social networking sites.
▶ A teenaged camp counselor explains fire safety to elementary school campers.
▶ An accountant presents the annual audit to a client company's board of directors.

This chapter first examines the global importance of information. It then turns to audience analysis and distinguishes four levels of audience knowledge you should consider before you speak. Next, it describes several types of speeches, including demonstrations and instructions, descriptions, reports, and explanations—with skeletal outlines of speeches in these categories. General guidelines for informative speaking conclude the chapter.

Information Is Important Globally

In this, the **Information Age**, more people, nationally and globally, have access to more information than ever before. Daily uploads of information are added to the Internet and to cable networks by news outlets, government agencies, ordinary citizens, and thousands of other sources. This constant bombardment with fragments of disconnected, irrelevant facts leaves many of us feeling that we are actually in an Over-Information Age,[1] where **information overload** is a burden, not a blessing.

For example, in one five-minute newscast, you might hear about an airplane passenger tussling with a security officer, a politician making a verbal blunder, and a young mother and child missing in Pennsylvania—but do any of these facts affect you personally? What's really important, and what's trivial? What must you know to live better, and what's simply interesting or distracting?

Similarly, your listeners can feel overwhelmed with disparate facts and ideas unless you relate the material to their lives and help them integrate new information with old. This not only helps them make sense of their world but it also provides them with basic information they can use to make wise decisions.[2] A clear description or explanation of new developments in genetically modified foods, effective strategies for studying, or wind power as an renewable energy source can furnish meaningful information for various audiences.

Having access to information has ethical implications and is considered a human right. For example, Article 19 of the Universal Declaration of Human Rights (1948) states:

> Everyone has the right to freedom of opinion and expression; this right includes freedom to hold opinions without interference *and to seek and impart information and ideas through any media and regardless of frontiers* [emphasis added].[3]

You can find the entire UN declaration at **www.un.org/Overview/rights.html**. Article 19 recognizes the potential dangers of an **information imbalance**, where some people and groups have lots of information and others have very little and thus lack fundamental understandings of the world. Democratic countries often try to adjust this imbalance; for example, during the Cold War, Radio Free Europe provided otherwise unavailable information to people living in Communist-controlled countries. Today, a number of Internet providers are attempting to broaden access in countries whose governments have tried to prevent most average citizens from free access to all the available information on the Net.[4]

In summary, information is a valuable resource or commodity. It's abundant in the United States and many other countries; it's more restricted in a number of nations. Some groups and social classes have access to information essential to success and health; others have limited access to the same knowledge, and information imbalance has ethical implications. Finally, some individuals know how to take advantage of the available information; others do not.[5]

Analyze Your Audience's Current Knowledge

Max saw an article about the Romani people (gypsies). His curiosity was piqued because although he'd heard about this group, he didn't know all that much about them, and the article confronted his stereotypes. Max assumed that his classmates were similarly misinformed, so he decided to provide accurate information. First, however, he had to discover what the audience already knew and believed about Romanies so that he could adjust his speech accordingly.[8] Listeners fall into four general categories: some have no information, others have a minimum of information, forgotten or outdated information,

Information Age an era with vast amounts of available information

information overload feeling overwhelmed by the sheer amount of available data

information imbalance some people or groups having very little access to information while others have it in abundance

ETHICS IN PRACTICE
THE RIGHT TO INFORMATION

What are the limits on our rights to know? Not all information is available to all people and "privileged" or "confidential" information is supported by cultural values such as privacy or national security. When you were a little kid, your parents may have kept some information from you "for your own good." In journalism, a staff writer may go to jail rather than name her sources.[6] Politicians or corporations may have strategy secrets that someone eventually "leaks" despite their efforts.

Free access to information is vital to a democracy, so much so that the federal government passed the Freedom of Information Act (FOIA), an act that gives citizens access to federal agency records or information (including your personal FBI file, should you have one). However, its provisions exclude records from Congress, the courts, or state and local government agencies.[7]

Questions for Discussion

▶ Can you think of instances where withholding information is a good thing?
▶ Have you been deprived of information that you think you needed? If so, describe the situation and tell the results.
▶ Is there a difference between "limits on our rights to know" and "censorship"? Explain your answer.

or misinformation (see Figure 16.1). Each level of understanding calls for different strategies. Remember, however, that a single audience can contain listeners from more than one category.

Presenting New Information

When your audience is unfamiliar with your subject, your task is to provide a basic overview of the topic. For instance, what do you know about music thanatology? neuroimaging? Anytown USA? Most people have never heard of them, so your information

Figure 16.1
Early in your planning, analyze what your audience knows about your topic and identify misconceptions or outdated information they have. This will help you design speeches that will make your information more useful to your listeners.

will be novel. I've heard speeches on each of these topics, and they were successful because the speakers followed these guidelines:

▶ Provide basic, introductory facts—"who," "what," "when," "where," and "how" information.
▶ Clearly define unfamiliar terminology and jargon.
▶ Give detailed, vivid explanations and descriptions.
▶ Make as many links as you can to the audience's knowledge by using literal and figurative analogies and by comparing and contrasting the concept with something familiar.
▶ Help audience members understand why they should know about your subject.

Presenting Supplemental Information

The great inventor Thomas Edison said, "We don't know a millionth of one percent about anything."[9] This means that listeners often have vague or superficial knowledge about a topic but lack detailed, in-depth understanding. They don't want a rehash of basic information; they want supplemental information. An audience familiar with running marathons will be more impressed if you provide little-known information about this type of race. Another example: Most people learned in elementary school about choosing foods from different food groups, so presenting the major groups is redundant. However, audiences may lack information about specific nutritional elements such as nucleic acids. Use these guidelines with audiences whose information is limited:

▶ Dig into your research sources to discover less familiar details and facts.
▶ Go beyond the obvious and add in-depth descriptions, details, and explanations.
▶ Narrow a broad topic and provide interesting and novel information about just one aspect of it. For example, talk about a few legendary African marathoners.

Presenting Review or Updated Information

Some listeners were once familiar with your subject, but they've forgotten some or most of what they learned, or they lack current, updated information about it. Your speech can function as a review to refresh their memories, reinforce their knowledge, and keep their information current. Reviews and updates are common in schools or workplace settings. For instance, students may have once studied the five canons of rhetoric, but they need to review them before taking the test; employees may have read or heard about privacy laws a decade ago, but a workshop on new regulations keeps them updated. Peggy Kilburg, featured in the Practically Speaking box, often reviews or updates information. With these audiences, you'll be more effective using these guidelines:

▶ Review material by approaching the subject from different angles and different perspectives.
▶ Be creative; use vivid supporting materials that capture and hold attention.
▶ Use humor when appropriate, and strive to make the review interesting.
▶ For both reviews and updates, present the most recent available information. Educator Dennis Mills[10] reports that our current proliferation of information results in 100 percent new knowledge every five years (at least in high-tech areas); consequently, what we learn can quickly become outdated. Overstated? Perhaps. But people who want to stay current must be lifelong learners.

Countering Misinformation

A third type of audience has misconceptions or misunderstandings that you can clarify by providing definitions and facts and by countering misinformation. For instance, the saying, "A dog is a human's best friend," is widely accepted in the United States. However,

Stephen Budiansky[11] presents scientific evidence suggesting that dogs don't really adore their owners; instead, they fake devotion to manipulate humans. If this is true, many or most people in your audience misunderstand dog behavior.

In other examples, students from different ethnic backgrounds sometimes counter misconceptions about their culture, or politicians sometimes clarify policy positions that their opponents have distorted. When you counter misunderstandings, your material will be inconsistent or contradictory to what listeners "know," so consider the following:

▶ Prepare for emotional responses—often negative. (Think about it. Who wants to hear that her beloved Fido is really a con artist?) Consequently, present the most credible facts you can find, and tone down the emotional aspect.
▶ Look for information derived from scientific studies, especially quantification, when statistical or numerical support would be best.
▶ Define terminology carefully; explaining the origin of specific words or ideas is often a good strategy.
▶ Counter negative prejudices against and stereotypes about a topic (such as a particular culture) by highlighting positive aspects of the subject.

In summary, the amount of information your audience brings to your speech should make a difference in the way you select and present meaningful information, and various listeners can have differing levels of understanding. By assessing listeners' knowledge about your subject in advance, you can more effectively prepare a speech that meets their need to know.

✓ STOP AND CHECK

ANALYZE YOUR AUDIENCE'S KNOWLEDGE

As part of your preparation, analyze your audience's knowledge of your informative speech topic. (Chapter 6 gives guidelines for constructing a questionnaire to determine this.)

____ Most people have probably never heard of it.
____ Most people are familiar with it and need more in-depth information.
____ Most people were once quite familiar with it but need a review.
____ Most people are familiar with it but need updated information.
____ Most people have misconceptions about my topic.

Here's how I plan to show the relevance of the topic to their lives:

_____

These are potentially negative feelings or attitudes they may have toward the topic:

_____

I must take care to:

_____

I can use these strategies if my audience is mixed (some know quite a bit, others know very little or have misconceptions):

_____

Types of Informative Speeches

Informative speeches fall into several categories. Demonstrations and instructions, descriptions, reports, and explanations are some broad categories of informative speaking common in college classrooms and in many careers. This section gives specific guidelines for these types of speeches.

Doing Demonstrations and Providing Instructions

Instructions answer the question, "How do you do that?" Martha Stewart became a billionaire by demonstrating how to do things and creating instructional television shows and magazines. She's just one of thousands of teachers, coaches, and salespeople who both show (demonstrate) and tell (give instructions) how to do a procedure, how to use a specific object, or how to complete a task. Although there's no guarantee you will ever earn millions by providing "how-to" information, several principles can help you give these speeches effectively:

1. First, think through all the required stages or steps by asking the following questions: What's absolutely essential? What comes first? Which step is easiest? Which is hardest? What does the audience already know how to do? Where will the audience most likely be confused? Which step takes the most time? Which take practically no time at all? [12]

2. Next, work on speech content. Organize the essential steps sequentially, and concentrate on clarifying and simplifying difficult or confusing steps. Carefully preplan the environment to facilitate learning—this may mean your audience must move their chairs or stand up and spread out around the room. Or you may have to furnish supplies if you want them to do the project along with you.

3. Plan your visual support. Ask yourself if actual objects are practical (see Chapter 13); if not, plan videotapes or other supplementary visuals. Then practice working with your props so you can use them and still maintain rapport with your audience.[13]
Visual aids are vital during some demonstrations. For example, if Beth simply tried to describe how to draw a hand, she'd have surely failed! However, she drew onto a whiteboard as shown in the photographs below.

Specific Purpose: To inform my audience about six steps in drawing a hand.

Central Idea: It's easier to draw a hand if you follow six steps.

    I. Step 1: block out the outline using simple, geometric shapes.
   II. Step 2: identify the bone structure, including all the knuckles.
  III. Step 3: draw around the basic outline in Step 1.
  IV. Step 4: add details of knuckles, fingernails, creases, rings and so on.
   V. Step 5: shade, using dark, medium, or light shades.
  VI. Step 6: erase excess lines.

Before she started, she had each student take out a pencil (not a pen) and a blank sheet of paper. (She'd brought along some blank paper and extra pencils, just in case.) Then, as she spoke, each student completed each step with her.

4. Time the entire process. If it takes more than the allotted time, you'd be better off demonstrating the process and then distributing handouts with step-by-step instructions for listeners to do later. One student tried to teach her classmates to fold an origami crane in a seven-minute speech; twenty-two minutes later, everyone had half-folded cranes and the class period ran out! Demonstrating the crane and providing each student with an instructional handout and a piece of origami paper would have been a better plan. Another strategy for a lengthy process is to prepare several versions of the item, stopping each at a different point of completion. Cooking and art instructors

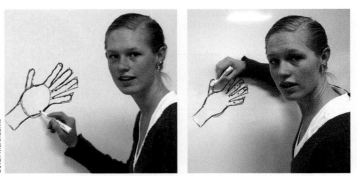

Devan Marchbanks

For her how-to speech on drawing a hand, Beth drew on the board as she explained the process. Her audience drew along with her, following her instructions step-by-step.

commonly do this. The cook, for example, begins a complicated dish, but instead of waiting twenty minutes for it to bake, he sets aside a partly finished pan, reaches for a second pan that contains a baked version of the dish and then proceeds to add finishing touches. Similarly, a sculptor shows an essential step in creating a pot; then she leaves it to dry and takes up a pot she prepared in advance that's ready for the next step.

Not all "how-to" speeches require a demonstration. You can give tips on topics like how to resolve conflict, listen more effectively, select a caterer for a major celebration, or manage time effectively. In these cases, you focus on instructions or pointers that will help audience members accomplish the goal.

Giving Descriptions

Descriptions answer the question, "What's it like?" Before you can describe an object, place, or event to someone else, you must first observe it carefully. Look for details and then select vivid imagery and sensory words that help people understand the look, taste, smell, or feel of your subject. An art museum guide, for example, walks her group from painting to painting, pointing out details of color, form, and texture within each painting that her audience might miss at first glance. Descriptions of places, objects, and events range from personal to global. Because listeners are generally more interested in topics close to their daily lives in location, time, and relevance, explicitly relate each topic to their perceived interests and needs.

Describing Places

People often seek information about places. A prospective student visiting a campus, for example, wants to know how it is laid out, so a college guide will describe campus sites as he shows the visitor around. Descriptions of different countries or places such as national parks or tourist attractions similarly attract audiences, and travel agents or park rangers are just two types of professionals who describe places.

In these speeches, provide vivid details so your listeners can form precise images. Take advantage of visual aids including maps, drawings, slides, brochures, or enlarged photographs, and consider spatial or topical organizational patterns. Here are the main points of a speech about *Ha Noi*, given by a student from Vietnam:

Specific Purpose: To inform my audience about *Ha Noi* and how it communicates.

Central Idea: *Ha Noi* is a thousand-year-old city, and its many scenic attractions reveal a lot about Vietnamese culture.

   I. *Ho Hoan Kiem*, Sword Lake, reminds us of the holy sword the gods gave to protect our country.
  II. *Van Mieu — Quoc Tu Giam*, the Temple of Literature, is Vietnam's first university, which was built in 1076.
 III. *Lang Bac*, Ho Chi Minh's Mausoleum, honors "Uncle Ho," who brought independence to Vietnam.
  IV. *Chua Mot Cot*, the One Pillar Pagoda, which honors the Buddhist goddess of mercy, was built in 1049.

If you are searching for an international topic, consider places such as buildings (the Taj Mahal), geographical features (the Sahara desert), or sites (Vatican City).

Describing Objects

Descriptions of objects, including natural objects (glaciers), human constructions (the Vietnam War Memorial), huge things (the planet Jupiter), or microscopic matter (carbohydrates), are common. Students have described inanimate (wind generators) or animate

PRACTICALLY SPEAKING

INFORMATIVE SPEAKING ON THE JOB

Joel Kelley

Peggy Kilburg

Peggy Kilburg has been in HR for twenty-eight years, working for twelve years in a profit corporation and fourteen years in a nonprofit organization. Most of her presentations are informative.

In your job, what types of informative topics do you speak about?

Topics range from explaining policies, procedures, and benefits to prospective and/or new employees, sharing and explaining policy to (mostly) current employees, making proposals to the executive team (infrequently), making announcements at employee meetings to doing nine hours of training with new supervisors.

This past year we had a new personnel review process (PRP) proposal that links pay to performance, so I did several informative presentations: to the operations and budget team, the executive team, supervisors, and all the employees. Most of the presentations were formal, with PowerPoint slides followed by a question-and-answer session. I also prepared a handout they could take away. Workshops that trained supervisors in implementing the program lasted three hours and included discussion and group exercises.

My favorite presentations take place at the annual service award event. I prepare and present 30- or 60-second service award commentaries. These are commemorative speeches, but they include information about the honorees' job history with the organization.

How excited are your audiences about attending your speeches?

I think employees are interested and curious about new processes. Some probably have a level of skepticism as well. New hires are pretty enthusiastic about listening to talks about benefits and procedures.

What are the three most important things to remember about informative presentations?

1. Know your audience in terms of their interest level, how they will use or apply the information, so that you will know what level of detail to share.
2. Organize your ideas and thoughts in advance. You may still take sidebar trips due to questions, but this ensures the basics are not skipped.
3. Make it interesting—no reading of information/notes/Power Point. Use humor if possible; use examples and stories to make points when possible. People love stories! Be enthusiastic and appropriately engaging. I have a fairly informal style, so I think I present as if I were sharing with just a few people.
4. I know you asked for three, but above everything else is this cardinal rule: Know your information—be prepared. People have often asked me if I'm nervous about presentations. Early on I was, but experience taught me that as long as I know my stuff I can control my nerves.

Questions for Discussion

▶ Select two different audiences and topics that Peggy addresses (for example, supervisors about the PRP or new hires about procedures and benefits), and try to classify the majority of listeners in each situation into one of the categories of

> knowledge presented earlier. Would most of them know nothing? Need additional
> information? Need a review? Or have misconceptions that she must counter?
> ▶ What evidence does Peggy provide that illustrates the importance of understanding an audience and adapting accordingly?
> ▶ Give examples of informative speaking in the career(s) that most interest you.

(brown recluse spiders) objects by providing information such as their origin, how they are made, their identifying characteristics, how they work, how they're used, and so on.

Topic choices range from personal to international. On the personal level, students have described body features such as skin or fingernails. They've talk about campus objects like a historical tree or a memorial plaque and explained cultural artifacts such as the Golden Gate Bridge and guitars. International topics have included the Great Wall of China and London's Big Ben.

Describing Events

Events or occurrences range from personal (birthday customs), community (local festivals), national (holidays), to international (the bombing of Hiroshima). Chronological, narrative, and topical organizational patterns are most common. The first two patterns work well for step-by-step events such as the bombing of Hiroshima. The topical pattern is useful for happenings that consist of several different components. Here is an example of major subtopics for a speech describing a sporting event.

Specific Purpose: To inform my audience about different rodeo events.

Central Idea: Rodeos are athletic contests with people and animals competing in a variety of events.

> I. Bull riding
> II. Barrel racing
> III. Bronco busting
> IV. Calf roping

When you describe events in concrete detail and vivid language, your listeners can place themselves at the happening, and your speech lets them participate vicariously.

Presenting Reports

Reports answer the question, "What have we learned about this subject?" Reporting is a global business that employs millions; around the clock, reporters collect and organize news and information about people and issues of public interest. For example, investigative reporters search for answers to questions such as "What are scientists learning about the causes of autism?" Campus reporters pass along conclusions reached by university task forces. In classrooms and workplaces, here and abroad, people give reports. This section discusses two common topic areas: people and issues.

Reporting about People

What individuals have shaped our world? What did they accomplish? How did they live? You can answer such questions by providing sketches of influential historical or contemporary characters. Biographical reports can be about influential thinkers (Plato), military men and women (Mongol warriors, Bodiecia), artists (Mary Cassatt), writers (Ngugi wa Thiongo), and so on. Don't overlook villains (Machiavelli) as well as heroes (Harriet Tubman) for biographical subjects.

Generally, chronological, topical, or narrative patterns best fit a biographical report. Fei Fei's topical outline has two major points: (1) Confucius's (K'ung-fu-tzu) life and (2) his influence. She then uses chronological subpoints to develop her first section—Confucius's life.

Specific Purpose: To inform my audience of the life and ideas of the Chinese philosopher whose teachings influence more than a billion people globally.

Central Idea: Confucius, who lived in China about 2,500 years ago, developed a life-affirming philosophy that has influenced many Asian cultures.

   I. The evidence for his life is scanty, based mostly on the Analects (sayings) of Confucius.
     A. He was probably born in the feudal state of Lu, in northern China.
     B. He was concerned about war and bad rulers, and he began to gather disciples.
     C. He journeyed as a wandering scholar.
     D. He may have been a minister of state at one time.
  II. Confucius's influence is widespread.
     A. His teaching method focused on growth in moral judgment and self-realization as well as skills.
     B. The concepts of *li* (maintaining proper relationships and rituals) and *jen* (benevolent, humanitarian attitudes) permeate many Asian cultures.
     C. The five vital relationships include: king-subject, father-son, husband-wife, older-younger brother, and friend-friend.

Speeches about groups such as thugs, Indigenous Australians, or medieval knights are also interesting. Here are subtopics from a student speech on the Amish that is organized topically:

Specific Purpose: To inform my audience about the Amish by describing their beliefs and explaining challenges facing their group.

Central Idea: The Amish are a religious group with written and unwritten rules for living that are being challenged by education and tourism.

   I. The Amish people
     A. Number and location
     B. Historical information
  II. Amish beliefs
     A. Written ordinances—Dortrecht Confession of Faith (1632)
     B. Unwritten rules of local congregations—Ordnung
  III. Challenges to Amish culture
     A. Education and teacher certification
     B. Tourism attention

As you develop your major points, keep in mind your audience's questions: "Why should I listen to a speech about this person or group?" "What impact has this subject had on society?" "How is knowing about this individual or group linked to my concerns?" Answering these questions will help your listeners better understand the relevance of the person or group. For links to biographical information on thousands of individuals, both contemporary and historical, visit **www.libraryspot.com/biographies/**.

Reporting about Issues

Newspapers and magazines are good sources for issues currently being discussed in our communities, our nation, and our world. We deliberate about international, national, local, and campus issues that are complex and controversial. Here are a few examples:

- What have we learned about the effectiveness of alternate energy sources?
- What do we know about the various treatments for Alzheimer's disease?
- What issues does each side emphasize in their support of or opposition to taxing sales over the Internet?

Think of your speech as an investigative report, where you research the facts surrounding an issue and then present your findings. Your goal here is to help people to think clearly about a topic, so your major purpose is to provide listeners with a factual foundation they can use in formulating their own conclusions. Consequently, reports do not advocate one position or another, although you may decide to follow up a report with a persuasive speech on the same topic.

Periodicals databases like InfoTrac College Edition or Internet sites like **www .refdesk.com** can help you access up-to-date newspapers and magazines. Look for answers to questions like these: What exactly is the issue? What current beliefs or theories are commonly held about the issue? What is the extent of the problem (how many people does it affect)? How did this situation develop? What solutions are proposed? What are the arguments on both sides of the issue? Generally, pro-con, cause-effect, problem-solution(s), narrative, and topical patterns are effective for investigative reports. The following is the pro-con outline for a speech on wind energy. Most of the articles came from InfoTrac and Academic Search Premier databases.

Specific purpose: To inform my audience about the pros and cons of wind energy.

Central idea: There are several arguments both for and against the widespread use of wind energy.

I. There are advantages to using wind turbines to produce electricity worldwide.
   A. Wind is a clean source of renewable energy that emits no greenhouse gases.
   B. Wind power can help minimize dependency on foreign oil.
   C. The technology is constantly being improved so that electricity produced during peak wind hours can be "banked" and used during peak demand hours.
II. There are a number of problems related to wind turbines.
   A. The blade/wind friction of the wind turbines emits noise and a light flicker that disturbs people who live by wind farms.
   B. Many people think wind farms destroy the beauty of the landscape.
   C. Wind farms can interfere with the habitats of wild bird populations.
   D. There are environmental impacts during the manufacturing, set up, maintenance, and dismantling of the turbines after they wear out.

Issues can be personal (eating disorders), campus (parking problems), local (potholes), national (teens and guns), or global (free trade) in scope. Many global decisions, such as what to do with nuclear waste, have broad implications. Others, although less significant, are related to larger problems. For example, cosmetic surgery on teenaged women is linked to issues of women's rights and stereotypes of female beauty.

Explaining Concepts

The explanatory or **expository speech** is more simply called the "speech to teach."[15] Expository speakers set forth, disclose, unmask, or explain an idea in detail. Science and history teachers regularly define terms and explain concepts; parents also answer the endless "whys" of 4-year-olds with explanations. Good expository speakers can identify the hurdles listeners are likely to encounter in their attempt to comprehend the concept. They then plan ways to overcome those barriers and make meanings clear.

Defining Terms

Definitions answer the questions "What is it?" or "What does it mean?" Definition speeches are common in classrooms and workplaces—for example, a philosophy professor defines justice, a speech professor clarifies the concept of confirmation as it's used in that academic discipline, and an employer defines sexual harassment for new employees.

expository speaking the "speech to teach" that explains an idea in detail

DIVERSITY IN PRACTICE

INFORMATIVE SPEAKING IN AFRICA

"Knowledge is power" could be the motto of these educators who provide health and child care information to women in Kenya.

THROUGHOUT PARTS OF AFRICA, public health educators give people information that may save their lives. They know the problems of information imbalance where some people fail to receive the information they need to live happy, productive lives. For example, women in central Africa empower one another with facts they can use to protect themselves against sexually transmitted diseases. In remote areas of Kenya, where less than 10 percent of tribal people can read and televisions and radios are not available, a few individuals travel from their villages to larger urban centers, where they learn news of the world and bring it back to their villages. In other settings, community members come together to advise newlyweds by giving the young couple practical "how-to" information they need to build an effective marriage.[14]

Inspirational speakers also define words: a priest defines peace making; a commencement speaker defines character; a coach defines commitment. In short, we see people act in ways we classify as just or as sexual harassment, but we can neither see nor touch justice or harassment; defining those terms helps us as a society to discriminate between appropriate and inappropriate behaviors.

One effective organizational pattern for a speech of definition[16] presents first the denotative and then the connotative meaning of a word. (Chapter 12 discusses denotation and connotation in detail.)

1. **Denotative Meaning:** Focus on the definition of the word as found in reference books such as thesauruses or etymological dictionaries. The *Oxford English Dictionary* or another unabridged dictionary provides the most thorough definitions. Books in an academic discipline show how scholars in that field define the term; for example, the definition of *confirmation* found in a dictionary is not identical to the definition you'd find in a book on interpersonal communication. Develop the denotative point of your speech by selecting some of the following ideas:

    ▶ Provide synonyms and antonyms that are familiar to your audience.
    ▶ Explain the use or function of what you're defining.
    ▶ Give the etymology of the word. What's its historical source? How has the concept developed over time?
    ▶ Compare an unknown concept or item to one your audience already knows.

    For example, "an Allen wrench" might be unfamiliar to some listeners, but "a wrench that looks like a hockey stick" or "an L-shaped wrench" helps them select the specific tool, given a line-up of wrenches.[17]

2. **Connotative Meaning:** Focus on connotative meanings, the emotional associations of words, by using realistic life experiences as creatively as possible. Here, draw from whatever you can think of that will add emotional elements to your explanation.

▶ Relate a personal experience that demonstrates the idea.

▶ Quote other people telling what the term means to them.

▶ Tell a narrative or give a series of short examples that illustrate the concept.

▶ Refer to an exemplar—a person or thing that exemplifies the term.

▶ Connect the term to a familiar political, social, or moral issue.

For example, in the denotative section of her student speech on destiny, Terez Czapp first provided the dictionary definition and then explained the etymology of the word like this:

> The Roman saying *Destinatum est mihi* meant "I have made up my mind." In Rome, destiny meant a decision was fixed or determined. Later the word reappeared in both Old and Middle French in the feminine form *destiné*. Finally, from the Middle English word *destinee*, we get the modern form of the word.

Next, a transition led to her connotative section, which consisted of an extended example of a near-fatal car wreck that devastated her family.

> However, it isn't the word's etymological history that is meaningful to me. You see, destiny is a depressing reminder of a car accident. . . .

Terez concluded with the following quotation by William Jennings Bryan:

> Destiny is not a matter of chance; it is a matter of choice. It is not a thing to be waited for; it is a thing to be achieved.

Including both denotative definitions and connotative associations provided a fuller picture of the concept of destiny.

Giving Explanations

Think of explanations as translations: You take a complex or information-dense concept and put it into common words and images that make it understandable. Explanations commonly answer questions about processes ("How does it work?") or about concepts ("What's the theory behind that?" or "Why?"). To answer such questions, you should describe stages, ordered sequences, or procedures involved in processes, both natural and cultural. You can explain how something is done (bungee jumping, international negotiations), how things work (elevators, cuckoo clocks, microwave ovens), or how they're made (mountain bikes, a pair of shoes). Not surprisingly, chronological patterns are common, as this outline of Marietta's speech about international adoption demonstrates.

> Specific Purpose: To inform my audience about the process of international adoption.
>
> Central Idea: The four parts of the adoption process are application, selection, child arrival, and postplacement.
>
> I. Application: the family and a social worker evaluate the adoptive home.
> II. Selection: the agency provides pictures and histories of available children.
> III. Child arrival: the child arrives with an "Orphan Visa."
> IV. Postplacement: for up to a year, the family and a social worker evaluate the placement, after which time the adoption is finalized.

Concepts also provide good, but challenging, topics. What do we know about intelligence? What's in the mind of a serial killer? What is Johari's Window? These questions relate to concepts or abstractions—the mental principles, theories, and ideas we form to explain both natural and social realities. For instance, although we may not know for certain what causes some people to kill repeatedly, we formulate theories or explanations for serial killers' behaviors.

Because concepts are sometimes difficult to define and explain, you must make the complex ideas and theories understandable and relevant to your listeners. Here are some guidelines for speeches about concepts:

▶ Simplify complex ideas by breaking them down into their component parts. For example, subdivide intelligence into categories that include social intelligence, spatial intelligence, and musical intelligence.[18]

▶ Carefully define your terminology, avoiding technical jargon. Exactly what falls into the category of spatial intelligence? Use examples that clarify this component of intelligence, or show the items from the tests that measure spatial intelligence.

▶ Clarify confusing details by using analogies, both figurative and literal, to compare the concept to something that listeners already understand. In this case, you might compare spatial intelligence to running a maze.

▶ Use detailed examples of concrete situations that illustrate the actions of people who test high in various kinds of intelligence.

The following example demonstrates major points for an explanatory outline about African music:

Specific Purpose: To inform my audience about important characteristics of sub-Saharan African music.[19]

Central Idea: Sub-Saharan African music features several major variations in pitch and rhythm.

    I. The music is interlocking; pitches and beats fit into the spaces between other parts.
    II. It features dense, overlapping textures and buzz sounds.
    III. It is cyclical and open-ended, with repeated melodies and patterns.
    IV. Complex rhythms may feature double and triple patterns.
    V. The music features a core foundation, often rhythmic, with improvised elaborations.

We sometimes clash over theories, concepts, and ideas. For instance, exactly what is universal healthcare? People's ideas differ. What caused the dinosaurs to become extinct? Theories vary. What constitutes a date rape? Not everyone gives the same

In the first part of the 1941 movie *Meet John Doe,* actor Gary Cooper delivers a manuscript speech explaining the concept of "John Doe," the average person. You can watch it on **www.americanrhetoric .com** under "Movie Speeches." Notice the many examples he uses to develop his definition.

Everett Collection

answer. The purpose of explanatory speaking is not to argue for one definition or another but to clarify the concept, sometimes by comparing and contrasting differing definitions and theories regarding it.

Guidelines for Informative Speaking

A common complaint about informational speaking is that it's boring.[20] To keep your audience's attention and to be both understandable and relevant, remember these guidelines for producing comprehensible messages:[21]

- **Do an "obstacle analysis" of the audience.** Think from your audience's perspective. Identify the parts of the message that are hard to understand and then work on specific ways to make those sections clear. Next, identify internal barriers that would prevent your audience from learning your material. You might face psychological resistance if you choose a scientific topic for an audience who thinks science is difficult and boring or if you challenge an audience's current misconceptions about a subject they hold dear. Plan ways to deal with each obstacle.[22]

- **Organize the material carefully.** Be kind to your listeners by stating your major points clearly and building in transition statements and signposts such as *next* and *in addition* that enable them to identify the flow of ideas. Use structures such as lists, comparisons-contrasts, or cause-effect patterns. Provide internal previews and summaries along with connectives that show how your material is linked—words and phrases such as *because, therefore,* and *as a result* (see Chapter 10). **Discourse consistency** also helps; for example, you might begin every section with a question or alliterate your main points throughout the entire speech.[23]

- **Personalize your material for your audience.** Help listeners see the connection between your topic and their experiences, goals, beliefs, and actions. When they see the information as personally relevant, they're more likely to listen and learn effectively.

- **Compare the known to the unknown.** Be audience centered. Start with the familiar and then build on this foundation, showing similarities and differences between your topic and what listeners already know.

- **Choose your vocabulary carefully.** You have probably heard lectures or reports so full of technical information and incomprehensible jargon that you left more confused than before. To avoid bewildering listeners, define your terms and explain them in everyday, concrete images. Avoid trigger words with negative connotations that might set off negative reactions in audience members.

- **Build in repetition and redundancy. Repetition** means that you say the same thing more than once. **Redundancy** means that you repeat the same idea several times, but you develop it somewhat differently each time. Phrases such as in *other words* or *put simply* are ways to build in redundancy. Repeat and redefine the critical parts of the message to reinforce these crucial points in your listeners' minds.[24]

- **Strive to be interesting.** In your preparation, occasionally try to distance yourself from the speech and hear it as if it were being delivered by someone else. Do you find yourself drifting off? If so, where? Search for ways to enliven your factual material. Providing examples or detailed descriptions, for instance, engages your audience dialogically, because descriptions and examples invite your listeners to form mental images as you talk.

If you follow these guidelines, you will increase your listeners' motivation and interest in the topic. And your careful attention to details will help them understand the material more clearly.

discourse consistency using a repetitive style such as alliteration of main points throughout the speech

repetition saying the same thing more than once

redundancy repeating the same idea more than once, but developing it differently each time

---

✓ **STOP AND CHECK**

DO AN OBSTACLE ANALYSIS AND STRATEGIC PLAN

As you prepare your speech, ask yourself the following questions:

- What concepts or steps may be obstacles for this audience?
- What psychological barriers are likely?
- What is the best way to overcome these obstacles?
- Are the steps in order? Are my main ideas clear?
- Where might I use alliteration, rhyming, or another form of discourse consistency?
- Where are my signposts and transitions? Should I use more?
- How, specifically, have I connected this material to the lives of my classmates?
- What does my audience already know that I'm building upon?
- Is my language clear?
- Where should I repeat an idea verbatim?
- Which ideas have I presented in a number of different ways?

Summary

The ability to give and receive information has always been empowering; this is especially so in the Information Age. Those who lack information do not have the basic knowledge they need to perform competently in complex societies. As a result, a variety of people in a variety of settings give informative speeches. Their goals are to present new information, to supplement what's already known, to review or update material, or to correct misinformation.

There are several categories for informative speaking that answer listeners' questions such as "How do you do that?" or "What does that mean?" These include demonstrations and instructions, descriptions, reports, and explanations.

Finally, remember seven keys to informative speaking. Do an obstacle analysis that identifies elements within the topic or within the listeners that might prove to be barriers, and then work to overcome those obstacles. Organize the speech carefully, and provide links that connect the material. Relate your topic to your listeners, and make vocabulary choices that clarify your ideas. Think of creative ways to present your information, and throughout your talk, tie abstract concepts to concrete experiences that are familiar to your listeners. Finally, include repetition and redundancy to reinforce the critical points of the message.

STUDY AND REVIEW

Your online resources for *Public Speaking: Concepts and Skills for a Diverse Society* offer a broad range of study tools that will help you better understand the material in this chapter, complete assignments, and succeed on tests. Your online resources feature

- Speech videos with critical viewing questions, speech outlines, and transcripts
- Interactive versions of this chapter's Stop and Check activities and Application and Critical Thinking Exercises
- Speech Builder Express and InfoTrac College Edition
- Weblinks related to chapter content
- Study and review tools such as self-quizzes, an interactive glossary, and downloadable audio summaries

You can access your online resources at **http://www.cengage.com/login**, using the access code that came with your book or that you bought online at **http://www.iChapters.com**.

KEY TERMS

The terms below are defined in the margins throughout this chapter.

discourse consistency 299	information overload 286
expository speaking 295	redundancy 299
Information Age 286	repetition 299
information imbalance 286	

APPLICATION AND CRITICAL THINKING EXERCISES

1. Within a small group in your classroom, discuss implications of the unequal distribution of information. For example: What if only some societies knew how to make sophisticated weaponry? What if only some individuals or groups knew their cultural history? What if only women had access to health information and men were excluded? What if only people under 35 years of age, with incomes over $80,000 a year, knew how to use computers to advantage?

2. For your classroom speech, consider a topic from the field of communication. Look for information that could help your classmates communicate better. For example, topics such as how to work through conflict, how to become independent from parents, or how to successfully navigate the early stages of a romantic relationship are useful in interpersonal communication. Speeches about makeovers or the types of touch address nonverbal communication. For mass communication, you could explain how camera angles communicate meaning or how other countries regulate the Internet.

3. Working with a small group, generate a list of speech topics for each of these categories. The audience:
   ▶ Is totally unfamiliar with the topic (examples: biliary atresia, *dun dun* drums).
   ▶ Has some knowledge of the topic, but not all the details (driving while texting, pumpkins).
   ▶ Has studied the topic, but needs a review (the five canons of rhetoric, D-Day).
   ▶ Has outdated information (an updated computer program).
   ▶ Has major misconceptions regarding the topic (cheerleading, tarantulas).
   Select a subject in two different categories and discuss how you would modify your speech plans to accomplish your general purpose with each topic.

4. In a small group, think of creative ways to present an informative speech that reviews audience knowledge about one of these familiar topics:
   ▶ Good nutrition
   ▶ What to do in case of fire
   ▶ How to read a textbook

5. Descriptions can be speeches in themselves, or good descriptions can be elements of larger speeches. To improve your descriptive skills, identify a place, an object, or an event and then make a list of vivid words that provide information about the look, the feel, the smell, the taste, or the sound of the item or place. Share your description with a small group of your classmates.

6. Search the Internet for the exact term "informative speaking." Read the material on a site from either a speech team (also called a forensics team) or from a university professor who provides additional information about speaking to inform.

SPEECH VIDEO

Log on to your book's on-line resources to watch and critique Josh Valentine's speech "The *Dun Dun* Drum." An outline of the speech is available both here and in your online resources, which also provide a transcript of Josh's speech.

Josh Nauman / Cengage Learning

Student Outline with Commentary

Josh's assignment was to research, outline, and deliver an informative speech using a visual aid. He chose the *dun dun* drum, and created a multimedia presentation that showed pictures of the drum and played actual recordings downloaded from the Internet for this one-time use. Everyone in his audience was previously unfamiliar with the topic.

Josh, a drummer, takes his topic from his interest in music. He chooses to develop a cultural topic.

THE *DUN DUN* DRUM
Joshua Valentine

General Purpose:	To inform
Specific Purpose:	To inform my audience about the *dun dun* (which most will not have heard of), and to describe how and why it is used.
Central Idea:	The *dun dun* is an African drum with an interesting history that is used both musically and linguistically.

Introduction

Because Josh's audience is unfamiliar with the topic, he must provide basic, introductory information about the drums.

I. Imagine that your friend asks you what you did over the weekend, but instead of using words, your friend beats a drum.
II. You will probably never have such an encounter, but in some cultures, music is used for purposes that are different from those we are accustomed to.
   A. *Webster's Dictionary* defines language as "any system of symbols, sounds, or gestures used for communication."
   B. Our culture does not have instrumental sounds that represent English words, but in other cultures around the world, sounds have meaning.
III. I have been playing percussion since junior high, and I first learned about the *dun dun* (pronounced doon doon) drum while attending a percussion workshop two years ago.
IV. Today, I will explain the history of the *dun dun* as well as its linguistic use and its musical use.

Body

The visual helps his listeners "see" what he is talking about.

I. The Nigerian talking drum actually does talk in the Yoruba language.
   [Display photograph of *dun dun* drum, downloaded and used with permission from http://media.dickinson.edu/gallery/Sect5.html]

A. This drum originated during the Oyo Empire of Yoruba-land in the fifteenth century AD for the purpose of worship.

B. Drums are constructed from trees located near roads where many people pass, which allows the tree to hear human speech (DeSilva).

C. The Yoruba language is easily communicated on the *dun dun*.

   1. Yoruba is a tonal language.

   2. Yoruba speakers use three basic pitches or tones, connected by glides, as an essential element of pronunciation (How bata drums talk . . .).

     a. Listen to this sound clip and try to identify the three main tones.

     [Play a sound clip downloaded for one-time use from the Internet.]

     b. If you have a sharp ear, you may also be able to pick out some slides essential to the Yoruba language.

   3. Melody is the basis for the Yoruba language since the same word pronounced with a different melody means something different.

D. The *dun dun* functions by changing the tension of two skin heads using the leather straps that hold the heads in place.

   [Point out the straps on the PowerPoint slide]

II. The *dun dun* was originally created to communicate.

A. The Yoruba from southwestern Nigeria have used drums for spiritual communication throughout their history.

   [Show carved drum downloaded from www.hamillgallery.com . . . YorubaDrum01.html]

   1. The *dun dun* was originally created as a tool for worship of the gods.

   2. Songs and hymns of praise were created entirely on *dun dun* drums and are still recited today.

   3. Listen to the intensity of this spiritual worship song played on talking drums.

   [Play example, downloaded for one-time use from the Internet from www.world-beats.com /instruments/dundun.htm]

B. The Yoruba also use drums for social communication.

   1. The *dun dun* has been a part of day-to-day casual conversation.

     a. "A master drummer can maintain a regular monologue on a talking drum, saying 'hi' to different people, cracking jokes, and telling stories" (Plunkett).

     b. *Dun dun* drummers often speak the names of friends and family on their drums as a greeting and sign of respect.

     c. The *dun dun*'s secondary, yet most obvious, use is as a musical instrument.

   2. It became a musical instrument because of its use in worship.

     a. At first it was used mainly to communicate ideas, but since worship in the Yoruba culture is a corporate activity, people began coming together and music on the *dun dun* was born.

     b. Religious songs are still recited today, although often only for their musical value.

   3. Even everyday speech becomes song when the Yoruba use the *dun dun*.

     a. The word *kabo*, which means welcome, is only a two-syllable word, so a more common phrase "spoken" on a *dun dun* is, "Welcome, we are happy that you arrived safely" (Drum Talk, Ltd.).

     b. "Speech" on the *dun dun* is always made rhythmic, even when the spoken word would not be rhythmic.

   4. The *dun dun*'s use as a musical instrument has spread far beyond Nigeria.

     a. After the *djembe*, the *dun dun* is the most well-known and recognizable African drum used in America.

     b. "[It] fares well in jazz blues, R&B, rock and roll, reggae, classical music, even choral music" (Awe).

     c. This clip comes from a song by African American musician Francis Awe.

     [Play sample clip downloaded from the Internet from www.nitade.com/html/cd1.html]

Margin annotations:

Audio support lets audience members "hear" what is complicated to explain in words alone.

The photograph of the carving on a drum suggests its use in worship.

Point II.B provides details that listeners can relate to.

Josh continues to provide factual information in this, his expository speech.

A final sound clip acts as a summary of the speech body.

Conclusion

I. Whether in language or in song, the *dun* dun's sound is always unusually beautiful.
II. Today, we have seen the origins of the Nigerian talking drum (*dun dun*), its uses as a linguistic tool, and its uses as a musical instrument.
III. So next time you hear music as simple as a beating drum, you might remember that the drummer may be communicating much more than you think.

Josh formats his references in APA style.

References

___

Awe, Francis. (1999). Talking drum drum clinic by Francis Awe. Retrieved March 20, 2002, from **www.after-science.com/awe/clinic.html**

BataDrum.com. (2002). How Bata drums talk and what they say. In Understanding the purpose and meaning behind the rhythms. Retrieved March 21, 2002, from **www.batadrums.com/understanding_rhythms/talk.htm**

DeSilva, Tamara. (1997). Lying at the crossroads of everything: Towards a social history of the African drum. Research, writing, and culture: The best undergraduate thesis essays, 1998–2000 (2). Retrieved March-20, 2002, from **www.artic.edu/saic/programs/depts/undergrad/Best_Thesis_Essay.pdf**

Drum Talk Ltd. (2000). Background information. Retrieved March 20, 2002, from **www.drumtalk.co.uk/drum_background.html**

Plunkett, A. (2002). Nigeria (Africa) Dun dun. World Beats. Retrieved March 21, 2002, from **www.world-beats.com/instruments/dundun.htm**

CHAPTER 17

PERSUASIVE SPEAKING

© Tim Timmerman

THIS CHAPTER WILL HELP YOU

▶ Find a subject for a persuasive speech

▶ Decide on a claim of fact, definition, value, or policy

▶ Narrow the focus of your speech in light of your audience's beliefs, attitudes, actions, and values

▶ Identify organizational patterns for your speeches, including problem-solution, Monroe's Motivated Sequence direct method, comparative advantages, criteria satisfaction, and negative method

N ANCIENT GREECE, Aristotle identified three areas of a healthy democracy in which rhetoric, the art of persuasion, functioned: law courts, governing assemblies, and ceremonial and ritual occasions that reinforce cultural beliefs and values.[1]

Today, speakers in the United States continue to present divergent viewpoints in courtrooms and legislatures, and ceremonial speakers still reinforce and emphasize cultural values on ritual occasions. Fortunately, we live in a culture that places value on citizen participation and free speech. (However, the role of persuasive speaking varies cross-culturally, as the Diversity in Practice feature illustrates.)

This chapter focuses specifically on persuasive purposes and types of speeches. It provides information about selecting a topic and narrowing your speaking purpose, building on your listeners' resources of belief and behavior, values, and attitudes. It closes with several organizational patterns that are especially effective for persuasive speeches.

Select Your Persuasive Topic

Choosing a persuasive topic can be challenging. Even if you have ideas for subjects, you may not know how to focus clearly on one specific purpose and one central idea. This section will describe ways to find a subject. Then, it will explain how you can select your claim and formulate your central idea.

Finding Your Subject

It is important to find a topic that is significant to others and matters to you. It is especially hard to influence others if you yourself are neutral or apathetic. Begin by considering your strong beliefs and feelings and then ask yourself what would improve society in general or people's lives in particular. Here are several categories of questions you can ask yourself as you search for an appropriate topic.[4]

▶ *My strong beliefs*: What ideas and issues would I argue for? What ideas and issues would I argue against?

▶ *My strong feelings*: What makes me angry? What are my pet peeves? What arouses my pity? What makes me sad? What do I fear?

▶ *My social ideals*: What changes would I like to see in society? What current problems or conditions could improve if we believed there is a problem, that there are

---

DIVERSITY IN PRACTICE
PERSUASION IN OTHER CULTURES

DIFFERENT CULTURES place different emphasis on persuasion as a means of publicly discussing issues and coming to reasoned conclusions. Here are a few historical and contemporary examples.

Rome

When Rome was a republic, orators publicly debated issues that affected the entire community. However, after emperors such as Nero and Caligula gained power, they made binding decisions and pronouncements regardless of Senate disapproval; dissenters often met with torture or death. In one notorious incident, Caligula mocked the Senate's power by making his horse a senator.

The Soviet Union

When the Communists ruled the Soviet Union, party leaders made decisions and spoke for the people. They strongly discouraged citizens from dissenting from the "party line," often by using coercive force that could land a nonconformist in a Siberian work camp.

Athabaskan Speakers

Speakers in this oral-based society of native Alaskans think it rude to explicitly state the conclusions they want the audience to accept. They consider it enough to present facts as they understand them and to let listeners draw their own conclusions. This emphasis on information instead of persuasion distinguishes their norms from those found in this chapter.[2]

International Negotiation

Many international cultures recognize the benefits of argumentation in their dealings with the West. Because of trade negotiations, United Nations deliberations, peace talks, and other international exchanges, speakers with different persuasive traditions often adopt aspects of Western rhetoric to communicate with international audiences. For example, Takakazu Kuriyama, former Japanese Ambassador to the United States, studied at Amherst College (Massachusetts) and Lawrence University (Wisconsin). He intentionally incorporated various Western rhetorical strategies when speaking with members of Congress and U.S. media representatives.[3]

solutions, and that we can be part of those solutions? Are there any causes for which I would sign a petition or join a protest?

▶ *My personal ideals*: What can make life more meaningful for others and for me? What activities will expand our horizons? What improves our health? What leads to more fulfilling personal relationships?

Classroom topics have included censorship, high insurance rates, international child sponsorship programs, the joys of skydiving, learning another language, and so on. Carrie's speech about grief counseling on campuses, found at the end of Chapter 8, is just one example of a classroom topic that reflects strong beliefs about issues related to personal or social concerns.

✓ STOP AND CHECK

SELECT YOUR TOPIC

Fold a piece of paper into fourths, and label each quarter with one of the following categories:

• My strong beliefs
• My strong feelings
• My social ideals
• My personal ideals

Next, make a list of possible topics within each section.

Now consider your audience. Circle the topics in each section that would be most appropriate for this particular group.

Analyze the circled topics, and put an X by those you could discuss within the allotted time.

Finally, select the best topic, given your audience and the time constraints.

Making Persuasive Claims

Selecting your subject is just the first step. Next, decide on the claim you want to make. A **claim** is an assertion that is disputable or open to challenge—a conclusion or generalization that some people don't accept, a statement that requires some sort of evidence or backing to be believed. Four types of claims are common: fact, definition, value, and policy.

Factual Claims

Claims of fact argue about what exists or does not exist, what has led to a current situation, or what will or will not happen in the future; we assess the validity of these claims using terms such as *true* or *false*, *correct* or *incorrect*, *yes* or *no*. Three types of **factual claims** are common:

1. *Debatable points* are about statements that either are or are not true, or things that did or did not happen For example, there is life on other planets; Lee Harvey Oswald acted alone to assassinate President Kennedy; the number of children who have Attention Deficit Disorder is greatly exaggerated.

2. *Causal relationships* argue that a particular phenomenon is the result of something that came before it and led to it. For example, pets of smokers have health problems caused by secondhand smoke; underage drinking is influenced alcohol ads; crop circles are caused by aliens.

claim an assertion that's disputable or open to challenge

factual claim argument about existence, causation, or predictions

3. *Predictions* contend that something will happen in the future. For example, a particular stock will lose value; a deadly strain of flu is inevitable; the Mariners will win the World Series this year.

All these claims generate differences of opinion. Is there life on other planets? Science fiction writers may think so, but no one really knows for sure. If there are space aliens, did they create crop circles? Nobody can prove they did. What, if anything, links smoking to diseases in pets? Or alcohol ads to teenage drinking? Studies often find correlations between two things, but correlation is not synonymous with causation. That is, two things may appear together, but this does not necessarily mean that one leads to the other.

Finally, claims about the future are open to debate. People lose huge sums of money in the stock market when their predictions prove wrong. Epidemics may be prevented. And, of course, arguments about sports teams fuel many a conversation.

Definition or Classification Claims

A woman shoots and kills a man. How should she be tried? The answer depends on the category that prosecutors decide best fits the crime: Was the killing premeditated murder? Was it unpremeditated homicide? Was it self-defense? Was she insane, incapable of making responsible decisions? The classification of the crime leads to different charges and different sentencing possibilities.

Claims of **definition** or **classification** are necessary when we must decide what kind of entity or phenomenon we are dealing with, in other words, when we must categorize it. For example, people argue over definitions of pornography, of anti-Semitic, of family, of cruel and unusual punishment. Because the definitions they decide on influence the policies they propose, it is important to define terminology early in the discussion of issues. First, set the parameters of the category and then show why the specific entity fits into that category. The abortion issue is a good example. It is so contentious partly because people classify or categorize the fetus differently. Someone who defines an embryo as a person (deserving the rights accorded to persons) from the point of conception will think of an eight-celled embryo differently than one who believes a fetus is a person only after brain waves are present (usually about six weeks into a pregnancy). Still others classify the fetus as a person only when it is capable of living outside the womb. The accepted definition of personhood influences the kinds of decisions considered proper regarding abortion, frozen embryos, and related concerns.

definition or **classification** claim determining which category an item belongs in

A single topic such as votes for prisoners can be developed by focusing on a variety of claims: Prisoner voting helps in rehabilitation (factual), prison would not be prison if voting were allowed (definition); it's wrong to punish by depriving votes (value), or we should let prisoners vote (policy).

Fabricius & Taylor/Jupiter Images

Value Claims

When you judge or evaluate something using terms such as *right* or *wrong* (it's morally wrong for children to be homeless in the United States), *good* or *better* or *best* (Restaurant X serves the city's best chili), *beautiful* or *ugly* (hybrid cars are ugly), you're making a **value claim**. Here is a value claim (with the evaluative term in italics): "It's *unfair* for airlines to charge obese persons for two seats instead of one." Other examples include "It's *better* to have loved and lost than never to have loved at all" and "Environmental protection is *more important* than economic development." Value conflicts are hard to resolve without agreement on the **criteria** or standards for deciding whether something is right or wrong, fair or unfair, humane or inhumane. That's why it's vital to state the criteria on which you base your judgment. If you can convince listeners to accept your standards, they'll more readily accept your judgment; even if they do not agree, they can at least understand the reasonableness of your argument.

Consider a movie you liked and your friend thought was a waste of time. Why did you reach different conclusions about its merit? Because you each had different criteria for judging a movie. Let's say your friend's criteria include romance, beginning-to-end action, and stunning visual effects, which this movie lacked. However, you like movies only when the characters are realistic and the plot is unpredictable, and this one met your standards. You can argue for hours about the merits of the movie, but unless one (or both) of you adjusts your criteria, you can understand one another's conclusions, but you'll never agree.

Policy Claims

These claims consider whether individuals or groups should act, and, if so, how they should proceed. In short, **policy claims** deal with problems and solutions, assessed by terms such as *should* and *would*. Two major types of policy arguments are common:

▶ Arguments against the **status quo** (a Latin phrase that means the existing state of affairs) are arguments for change, whether in policies or individual behaviors. (Congress should adopt a flat tax system; you should write your senator and urge a vote on the flat tax.)
▶ Arguments supporting the status quo are arguments for the current situation and against change. (The university should not raise tuition; the current tax rate is adequate.)

Take an example from the field of education: many reformers believe that education within the United States needs improvement, and they argue against the status quo by first identifying problem areas and then proposing solutions that will truly improve schools and be workable. Some argue for smaller classes. Others advocate for alternative schools; still others think vouchers are the way to solve specific problems.

Although we separate claims of fact, definition, value, and policy for analysis purposes, in reality a persuasive speech often includes a combination of claims. For example, persuading an audience to change a policy often requires supporting claims of fact, definition, and value. Effective speakers skillfully blend various types of claims in order to successfully persuade an audience.

Let's say you decide to speak about ocean pollution—specifically, dumping garbage in the ocean. You can blend facts, definitions, values, or policies surrounding the issue, but you should formulate your thesis statement more specifically around one, as this table illustrates.

In summary, select your speech subject from topics and issues that concern you, at the personal to the international level. Then, tentatively formulate your central idea by deciding if you want to focus on a factual claim, a definition or classification claim, a value claim, or a policy claim.

value claim argument about right or wrong, moral or immoral, beautiful or ugly

criteria the standards used for making evaluations or judgments

policy claim argument about the need or the plan for taking action

status quo Latin phrase that means "the existing state of affairs"

Claim	Goal	Tentative Thesis Statement
Fact	Argue a debatable point	The amount of garbage dumped in our oceans is not excessive.
	Attempt to prove a cause-effect relationship	Dumping garbage in the ocean poses health risks to seaboard residents.
	Make a prediction	If we do not stop dumping garbage in the ocean, our beaches will become too contaminated to use.
Definition	Clarify the denotative meaning or classification of a term	Garbage should be defined as Non-Point Source (NPS) pollution or "people pollution."
Value	Argue something is right or wrong, good or bad, beautiful or ugly	It is wrong to pollute the ocean with our garbage.
Policy	Propose a policy change	The United States should ban garbage dumping in ocean waters.
	Propose a behavioral change	Write your senator and voice your concern about garbage being dumped in ocean waters.
	Argue against a policy change	There is no good reason to stop disposing of garbage in oceans.

STOP AND CHECK

MAKE FACT, DEFINITION, VALUE, AND POLICY CLAIMS

To better understand that discussions surrounding a controversial topic contain a mixture of factual, value, and policy claims, work alone or with a small group of classmates and choose a controversial topic such as doctor assisted suicide, gay marriage, Internet privacy, environmental protection, or sex education. Then write out a factual claim, a value claim, a definition, and a policy claim relating to your topic. Afterward, share your claims with the class as a whole.

- Write a factual claim dealing with a debatable fact, causation, or prediction.
- Define an essential term.
- Assess questions of good or bad, and develop criteria for a decision.
- Decide whether or not the status quo needs to be changed, and frame your policy claim accordingly.

Narrow Your Persuasive Purpose

Although your general purpose is to persuade, you will narrow it more specifically in light of what your listeners already know and do, how they feel, and what they value, remembering that a single speech will probably touch on multiple claims. For instance, while you try to convince your listeners that there are hazards caused by dumping garbage in the ocean—focusing on factual claims—you may also be reinforcing their health-related values and their current attitudes against pollution.

This section will present a number of ideas you can use when you concentrate on beliefs and actions, values, or attitudes. (Chapter 18 provides additional information on creating persuasive appeals.)

Focusing on Beliefs and Actions

What we accept as true affects how we act. Our beliefs and actions, in turn, spring out of our values and attitudes. To illustrate, you spend time studying because you believe your hard work increases your learning and improves your grades. You value education and dislike wasting your tuition dollars, and you have a positive attitude toward getting a college degree. Your combination of beliefs, values, and attitudes leads you to schedule time for reading textbooks, working on class projects, and joining study groups. Figure 17.1 shows some possible combinations of belief and action that you should consider as you narrow your speech focus.

Unconvinced

Unconvinced audience members neither believe your claim nor act on it. Take a topic like acupuncture. Some listeners know nothing about it; others have some information, but they don't believe it will help them. Still others have misconceptions about this Chinese medical treatment. They all need enough evidence **to convince** them to believe your factual claims before you ask them to act. The following general guidelines are useful with unconvinced listeners:

◗ Begin with logical appeals. Build a factual case carefully, using only evidence that passes the tests for credible supporting material.
◗ Prove your competence by being knowledgeable about the facts, and show respect for your listeners' intelligence and divergent beliefs.
◗ Use comparatively fewer emotional appeals.

Unmotivated or Unfocused

Some audiences are already convinced by what they know about your subject. However, they fail to act on their beliefs due to **apathy** or indifference (unmotivated listeners) or their lack of specific know-how (unfocused listeners). Topics such as improving cardiovascular fitness fall into this category. Your purpose here is to actuate, or move listeners to behave in ways consistent with their beliefs, using two different persuasive strategies.

◗ When your audience is unmotivated, provide good reasons to act. Use emotional appeals to show that what you propose will fulfill their needs and satisfy them emotionally. Liz's audience survey revealed that her listeners knew about the security features on social networking sites, but most had not activated them, so she argued that their physical, psychological, and job security would be enhanced if they utilized the safety features.
◗ When listeners lack focus, provide a detailed plan that spells out specific steps they can take to implement your proposals. Matthew discovered that his audience knew about study abroad opportunities and that they wanted to participate in these programs, but they weren't quite sure how, so he spelled out exactly what they should do to apply.

In both instances, show listeners that you have their best interests in mind as you appeal for action.

to convince a persuasive purpose that targets audience beliefs

apathy indifference due to lack of motivation

	Don't Believe	**Believe**
Don't Act	unconvinced	unmotivated, unfocused
Act	inconsistent	consistent

Figure 17.1
Sample Belief and Action Combinations
Your audience members approach your topic with various combinations of beliefs and actions.

Inconsistent

Often we hold contradictory beliefs, or we behave in ways that are inconsistent with our ideals. Leon Festinger[5] developed the **cognitive dissonance theory** to explain the resulting inconsistency or **dissonance** we experience. Humans, like other living organisms, seek balance or equilibrium. When challenged with inconsistency, we seek to return to a balanced psychological state. If our behaviors don't match our beliefs or if our deeply held beliefs are directly challenged, we typically experience discomfort until we either change our behaviors or reinforce our faltering beliefs by making adjustments to accommodate the challenge. (Festinger originally studied smokers who continued to smoke, even though they knew smoking was harmful to the body.) Inconsistency between actions and beliefs is one of the best motivators for change. For example, if you become disillusioned with your job, it is easier to persuade you to consult an employment counselor than if you love everything about your current workplace.

With inconsistent audiences, either strengthen or reinforce wavering beliefs or persuade listeners to modify their actions to match their beliefs. Here are a few specific things to do when your listeners' actions and beliefs are out of sync.

▶ Support faltering beliefs by concentrating on logical appeals, using as much persuasive evidence as you can muster to help them resolve their doubts. Include emotional appeals as well, giving listeners reasons to want to strengthen their wavering beliefs. For instance, in election years, political party loyalists attempt to dissuade members of their party from switching their votes by extolling the virtues of their candidates and the negatives of the opposition.

▶ When you hope behaviors will change, appeal to emotions such as honesty and sincerity. Use narratives or testimonials that exemplify how you or someone else changed in a similar situation. An example is an intervention with a substance abuser. Close friends and family confront the person with evidence of the problem, with appeals to his or her better self, and with stories of how other people's lives were turned around through detox programs.

For additional information, do an Internet search for "cognitive dissonance theory" and follow a couple of links that have .edu in their URL.

Consistent

Even when people act consistently with their beliefs, they may need encouragement to "keep on keeping on." This type of audience is common in service clubs, religious organizations, and at political rallies where speakers hope the listeners will continue to donate money, give time, and support a particular cause. Here, your narrowed purpose is to reinforce both their beliefs and actions by following these guidelines.

▶ Help listeners maintain a positive attitude about their accomplishments. Use examples and testimony that illustrate how their efforts are making a difference in the world.

▶ Relate personally to their fundamental beliefs and values.

Throughout this section, we have explored ways that audience beliefs and actions influence both your persuasive purposes and the methods you use to present your ideas. Although you will use a variety of appeals in every speech, each type of audience requires somewhat different emphases and strategies.

Focusing on Values

As noted earlier, value claims contend that something should be judged or evaluated as moral or immoral, beautiful or ugly, right or wrong, important or insignificant, and so on. Here are two value claims: (1) embryonic stem cell research is wrong; (2) finding cures for people who are now living is more important than preserving an embryo. The first

cognitive dissonance theory says that humans seek stability or equilibrium; when faced with inconsistency they seek psychological balance; this may motivate them to change in order to be consistent

dissonance inconsistency or clash

comes to a judgment about the issue; the second argues that both values are important, but one supersedes the other.

To make an evaluation, first establish the criteria or standards on which to judge the issue by answering questions such as these:

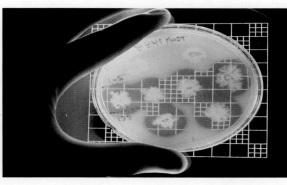

Bill Varie/Jupiter Images

▶ How do we make and apply judgments regarding this issue?
▶ What criteria do we use?
▶ Where do these criteria come from?
▶ Why should we accept these sources?

When listeners accept your criteria, it's easier for them to accept your evaluation. However, value questions are often conflict laden, for the standards used to make value judgments are often contested.

For a variety of reasons, value judgments within a single audience may vary so widely that some judge a topic as unethical whereas others consider it highly ethical. Furthermore, because values are assumptions about what is good, value questions often generate deeply held emotional responses. It is nearly impossible to move listeners from judging a topic as unethical to evaluating it as highly ethical because of a single speech, but here are some tips for arguing value claims:

▶ Establish the criteria you are using to make your evaluation.
▶ Use emotional appeals such as examples that help listeners identify with the issue and link it to related values that you can agree on, such as fairness or freedom.
▶ Appeal to authority if your audience accepts your source as authoritative. (See Chapter 8.) Some audiences will be moved by appeals to cultural traditions, words of poets, philosophers, scientists, or scriptural texts; others will discount those same authorities.

Keisha Walkes's speech, outlined in Appendix C and available in your online resources, argues that Barbara Jordan is worthy of being named "Woman of the Century." Some criteria she identifies are authenticity, integrity, initiative, courage, and the ability to motivate others.

> Within a single audience, listeners often vary widely in their views on issues such as embryonic stem cell research. Some know little about it. Others think it holds potential cures for dozens of diseases; still others believe that destroying embryonic life is immoral and unnecessary— they offer adult stem cell research as an alternative.

Focusing on Attitudes

Generations of scholars have explored how we become persuaded to believe or behave in certain ways. Many recent persuasion-related studies focus on **attitudes**, which, according to the Princeton University Cognitive Science website, are complex mental states "involving beliefs and feelings and values and dispositions to act in certain ways."[6]

According to the **Theory of Reasoned Action** (TRA), we intentionally behave in ways that give us favorable outcomes while allowing us to meet the expectations of others.[7] This theory links our behavioral intentions with attitudes, subjective norms, and perceived behavioral control.[8] It assumes that we are rational and that we systematically weigh the costs and benefits of acting on the information we have, given an opportunity to do so.[9] According to TRA:

▶ Attitudes are our positive or negative evaluations of the behavior in question; they include both a mental (what we believe about it) and an emotional (how we feel about it) component. Typically, attitudes are measured along a scale ranging from strong agreement to strong disagreement. (See Chapter 6.)
▶ Subjective norms are our perceptions of what the people who are important to us think we should do.
▶ Perceived behavioral control is our opinion about our ability to accomplish the behavior in question.

These three factors influence our intentions to act, although our attitudes generally carry more weight. For instance, let's say a speaker urges listeners to purchase energy

attitudes complex mental states that involve beliefs, emotions, and actions

Theory of Reasoned Action links behavioral intentions with attitudes, subjective norms, and perceived behavioral control; assumes we rationally weigh costs and benefits of our actions

efficient light bulbs, and she wants them to perceive that this is something they can easily do. So, in addition to motivational appeals, she includes information about where and how to buy these products. One audience member reasons like this:

> I think I'll buy energy efficient light bulbs (intention) at a local store (opportunity). I dislike having to read labels on packages (negative attitude/cost), but I like the overall idea of saving energy (positive attitude/benefits). My friends and family think energy conservation is a good thing (subjective norms), and they'd admire me for taking steps to save energy (benefits). Therefore, I'll do it.

In contrast, some listeners might respond another way:

> I don't intend to buy these light bulbs any time in the near future (intention). I hate reading labels (negative attitude/cost) and I do a lot of other things to help the environment. None of my friends or family cares about the minimal environmental impacts that might result (subjective norms) if I buy these bulbs (opportunity). So don't ask again.

(You can read more about TRA by searching the Internet or looking on InfoTrac College Edition for "theory AND reasoned AND action.")

In general, the following guidelines will help you plan effective speeches to influence attitudes:

▶ Strengthen positive attitudes about your topic by using examples, connotative words, and appeals to needs and values that evoke emotional responses. Establish common ground throughout (see Chapter 18).

▶ When you face listeners who are neutral toward your claim, ask why. Do they lack information? Are they apathetic? With uninformed audiences, present factual information early so listeners have enough knowledge form an opinion. Then use emotional appeals to create either a positive or negative attitude toward the topic. With apathetic audiences, use emotional appeals by linking the topic to listeners in as many ways as you can, and appeal to values such as fairness and justice.

▶ When your differences are mild, approach your audience directly. Use objective data to make a clear case; present the positive facets of your subject; and make links to personal and community values your audience accepts. This way, although they might still disagree with you, they can understand why you hold your position.

▶ When your listeners are negative toward your proposal because they are attached to the status quo, rethink your options. With mildly or moderately negative audiences, try to lessen the negative so listeners can see positive aspects of your proposal. If they're strongly opposed, you face a hostile audience. So set modest goals and aim for small attitudinal changes. Present your points clearly so that they will at least understand how you came to your conclusions.

▶ With audiences that reject your proposals, approach the subject indirectly by establishing common ground on which you can all agree. For instance, begin with a statement with which everyone agrees, and explain why there is agreement. Then make a statement that most would accept, and explain why this is so. Move gradually to the point about which they disagree. By this time, they will have already seen that they agree with you on many points, and as a result, they may be less negative toward your ideas.[10]

Generally, attitudes change incrementally, so expect change to be gradual. Each new encounter with the subject may bring about only a slight change, but eventually, the small changes can add up.

Perhaps the most distressing speaking situation arises when your audience is hostile toward you personally. Then, it's important to emphasize common ground between yourself and your listeners. Former First Lady Barbara Bush faced hostility at Wellesley College's commencement ceremonies where graduates were vocal about their desire for a different speaker. Mrs. Bush used humor and common ground to turn a negative situation into a positive one. (The script and audio of her address is available in the **www.americanrhetoric.com** speech bank.)

Although we have discussed beliefs and actions, attitudes, and values separately, they are intertwined. Keep this in mind as you analyze your audience, select the specific purpose for your speech, and choose supporting material that will be persuasive.

STOP AND CHECK

ADAPT TO THE AUDIENCE'S ATTITUDE

Analyze the following public speaking situation: An anthropology major prepares a speech on government funding for archaeological digs. Her claim is that the study of archaeology is important enough to receive government funding because knowledge of other human cultures helps us to better understand our own.

Divide into three groups within the classroom. Each group will discuss how the speaker should prepare for one of the following audiences:

1. A group of anthropology majors who agree with her and are highly positive toward her topic.
2. An audience that knows nothing about anthropology but expresses concern about how their tax money is spent.
3. Listeners who consider archaeology to be a waste of time.

Questions

1. How will the speaker analyze the particular audience?
2. What purpose should she select for that group?
3. What specific strategies will she use to make her points?
4. What kinds of reasoning and evidence should she use?
5. What should she emphasize, and why?

Choose a Persuasive Pattern

After you analyze your audience's positions regarding your issue, look for an organizational pattern that will best communicate your ideas. This section presents several common persuasive patterns.

Problem-Solution Pattern

The problem-solution pattern (Chapter 9) is common for both informative and persuasive speaking. Informative speakers try to increase the audience's understanding of the issue and the proposed solution or solutions. Persuasive speakers aim to convince or to advocate for a specific solution. When the intent is to convince listeners that there is indeed a problem, the outline looks like this:

Specific Purpose: To persuade my audience that there are too many air disasters but the problem can be solved by concentrating efforts in three areas.

Thesis Statement: Global air traffic has too many disasters and near-disasters that could be minimized by working to eliminate the sources of the problems.

I. There are too many air disasters and near-disasters around the globe.
    A. The problem involves near-misses and crashes.
        1. The problem is extensive (statistics).
        2. This has negative implications for travelers.
    B. There are several causes of this problem.
        1. There are communication problems between crews and air traffic controllers.
        2. Weather is a consideration.
        3. Mechanical and maintenance failures cause disasters.
II. The problem can be minimized.
    A. Airplanes should be more carefully inspected and maintained.
    B. Both crew members and air traffic controllers should continue to receive on-the-job training in communication and in understanding the effects of weather.
    C. Engineers and researchers should continue to develop state-of-the-art equipment to prevent some of these disasters.

When you argue for a particular solution, a good method is to present several possible solutions first and then advocate or argue for the best one. This adds a third point to the outline.

I. Problem and need
II. Possible solutions
III. The one best solution

This is how a more complete outline looks:

Specific Purpose: To persuade my audience that incineration is the best solution to the problem of medical waste.

Thesis Statement: Of the three methods of medical waste disposal—steam sterilization, ocean dumping, and incineration—incineration is the best.

I. So much medical waste is being generated that we need a safe method of disposal.
    A. Several waste products result from medical procedures.
    B. The problem is extensive (statistics).
    C. Some waste products pose risks.
II. There are three ways to dispose of medical waste.
    A. One is the steam-sterilization process.
    B. The second is ocean dumping.
    C. The third is incineration.
III. Incineration is the best solution.
    A. It completely destroys the product.
    B. Fire purifies.

Monroe's Motivated Sequence

Alan Monroe, legendary speech professor at Purdue University, developed and refined a commonly used persuasive pattern, especially good for speeches intended to actuate behavior. **Monroe's Motivated Sequence** is a modified problem-solution format.

Before people act, they must be motivated to do what they know they should do. Consequently, it's important to provide emotional as well as logical reasons. This pattern includes the word motivated, because it has several built-in steps to increase motivational appeals. (Note that this pattern is not a formula in the sense that you must include each element. Rather, Monroe suggests various ways to develop your points.) Here are the five easily remembered steps in the sequence, as explained by Monroe himself.[11]

Monroe's Motivated Sequence a call to action in five steps: attention, need, satisfaction, visualization, and action

1. **Attention Step:** As with any other speech, you begin by gaining the audience's attention and drawing it to your topic.
2. **Need Step:** This step is similar to the problem part of a problem-solution speech. Monroe suggests four elements: (a) *statement*—tell the nature of the problem; (b) *illustration*—give a relevant detailed example or examples; (c) *ramifications*—provide additional support such as statistics or testimony that show the extent of the problem; and (d) *pointing*—show the direct relationship between the audience and the problem.
3. **Satisfaction Step:** After you demonstrate the problem or need, show its extent and its effects on the audience, and then propose a solution that will satisfy the need. This step can have as many as five parts: (a) *statement*—briefly state the attitude, belief, or action you want the audience to adopt; (b) *explanation*—make your proposal understandable (visual aids may help at this point); (c) *theoretical demonstration*—show the logical connection between the need and its satisfaction; (d) *practicality*—use facts, figures, and testimony to show that the proposal has worked effectively or that the belief has been proved correct; and (e) *meeting objections*—show that your proposal can overcome your listeners' potential objections.
4. **Visualization Step:** This step is unique. Here, you ask listeners to imagine the future, both if they enact the proposal and if they fail to do so. (a) *Positive*—describe a positive future if your plan is put into action. Create a realistic scenario showing good things your solution provides. Appeal to emotions such as safety needs, pride, and pleasure. (b) *Negative*—have listeners imagine themselves in an unpleasant situation if they fail to put your solution into effect. (c) *Contrast*—compare the negative results of not enacting your plan with the positive results your plan will produce.
5. **Action:** In the final step, call for a specific action: (a) *name* the specific, overt action, attitude, or belief you are advocating; (b) *state* your personal intention to act; and (c) *end* with impact.

As you might imagine, this pattern is good for sales speeches. It is also effective in policy speeches that include a "should" or an "ought." Terah, a nursing major, wanted to do an organ donor speech, but when she surveyed her classmates, she found that they already had a lot of information and a good attitude toward donation, so she focused on motivating them to put their good intentions into action. Here are her major points:

Attention: My survey showed that you want to be organ donors but have not yet signed up.

    I. It's easy and accessible.
    II. From my research, I will give you specific steps to take to become an organ donor.

Need: My survey showed that I don't need to convince you of a need or clear up any misconceptions.

Satisfaction: My survey told me you need how-to information about signing up.

    I. For $34 and proof of identity, the Department of Motor Vehicles can mark your driver's license.
    II. You can get a free donor card from www.organdonor.gov/donor/index.htm.
    III. You can sign up for free at www.donatelifenw.org or on the online donor registry at www.organdonor.gov/donor/registry.shtm.
    IV. Tell your family your wishes because they may have to tell doctors who ask about donating.

PRACTICALLY SPEAKING

A MENTAL HEALTH AMBASSADOR

Gayathri Ramprasad

Gayathri Ramprasad answered some questions about her persuasive goals when she speaks about mental illness.

I was born and raised in Bangalore, India, into a loving family. But by age 18, I was debilitated by anxiety and panic attacks. At 23, as a young mother in America, I struggled with deadly depression and found myself in a university hospital's psychiatric ward. While there, I promised to become a harbinger of hope and healing—to fight for myself and others like me. Today, I've spoken to more than 25,000 people nationally and internationally.

The stigma surrounding mental illness once deterred me from seeking treatment. However, I eventually started sharing my journey one-on-one. Many people who had been touched in some way by mental illness thanked me for bringing hope. However, some people within my Indian community found it hard to imagine why a woman with a loving husband, beautiful children, and a fabulous future could be depressed.

My first public speech was as a graduate MBA student, when I delivered a five-minute exemplum and told my story based on the quotation, "Courage is fear that has said its prayers." The response was very positive. I later became associated with the local affiliate of the National Alliance on Mental Illness, and I urged people all over our state to join a statewide walk to promote mental health. It was, however, as keynote speaker at the walk's kickoff luncheon that I decided to become a professional speaker. After I spoke, a girl about 18 years old was among the many listeners who thanked me. "Tonight was going to be the night," she whispered. "I was going to kill myself tonight. But now, I have hope that I too shall recover and reclaim my life like you. Thank you for saving my life." I vowed then to share my story for the rest of my life.

I have presented in prisons, mental hospitals, graduate classes, and conferences. Most memorable was at the Oregon Health and Science University. It was triumphant to return to the same hospital where I was once locked up. Now I promote global mental health awareness through speaking engagements, the *Rally for Recovery World Tour*, and *Culture Counts*, a local event to promote mental health among cultural minorities and cultural competency in mental health.

Visualization:

    I. Imagine you don't follow up, a tragedy happens, and eight people can't benefit from your organs.

    II. Now imagine you sign up, a tragedy happens, and Josh in New Mexico gets your heart; Mary in Colorado has a new kidney, Glen in North Dakota receives your liver, and many more have improved lives from other tissues.

    III. Which choice is ideal?

What are your basic themes or arguments?
There are five: (1) mental illnesses are brain disorders; (2) treatment works; (3) recovery is possible; (4) have hope; and (5) seek help. My ultimate speaking goal is to promote mental health awareness, stop stigma, and save lives. Monroe's Motivated Sequence works well for me.

What must you overcome with listeners?
There is wide cultural variance in beliefs, attitudes, values, and behaviors pertaining to mental illness, and cultural stigma is one of the greatest barriers to overcome. Many think mental illness is a sign of personal weakness or a character flaw. Others believe that medications and hospitalizations are the only treatment options. Still others believe electroshock therapy is barbaric and dangerous—I must dispel all these myths to present my arguments. My program integrates three approaches developed at the UCLA School of Medicine to reduce stigma:

1. *Educate* about the neurobiological nature of mental disorders. This changes **knowledge**.
2. *Give cases* of citizens who recovered and lived normally. This changes **attitudes**.
3. *Have people actually interact* with recovered and functional mentally ill persons. This is an anti-stigma impact at the **behavioral level**.

What already supports your topic in listeners' minds?
There is a growing awareness of mental health issues, locally and globally. More people like me are sharing their testimonials of hope and recovery. Tremendous scientific breakthroughs in understanding and treating mental illness support my arguments. Finally, my greatest advantage is my personal testimonial, which I have found is far more powerful in changing people than any number of papers in scientific journals. (You can find more information about Gayathri's work at **www.mindbeautiful.com** and **www.myasha.org**.)

Questions for Discussion

▶ How does Gayathri's story show the importance of strong beliefs, strong feelings, personal ideals, and social ideals in finding a topic?
▶ What would be her biggest challenge if she were to present her story on your campus or in your community?
▶ Think of another topic that is surrounded by stigma. Discuss within a small group how you might apply the principles from UCLA for reducing that stigma.

Action

I. Follow one of the easy procedures and sign up to be a donor.
II. I did this last year, and I'm very glad I did.
III. No more procrastination; do it today!

STOP AND CHECK
USE MONROE'S MOTIVATED SEQUENCE

Working alone or with a small group, plan a short outline for a speech intended to motivate your audience to action. Choose one of these general topic categories:

• **Sales:** Convince your classmates to buy a specific product.
• **Public service:** Ask your listeners to donate time or money to a worthy cause.

Direct Method Pattern

In the **direct method**, also called the statement of reasons pattern, you make a claim and then state several reasons to support it. Each point provides an additional rationale for accepting your views. It's a good pattern to use when listeners are apathetic or neutral, or when they mildly favor or mildly oppose your claim. Consider it when your goal is to convince, although you can also use it to organize a speech to **actuate** (or motivate the audience to do something).

This outline for a speech on therapy dogs states four reasons these animals are helpful in health facilities, prisons, and shelter homes.[12]

Specific Purpose: To persuade my listeners that therapy dogs provide psychological and physical benefits to people in distressing circumstances.

Thesis Statement: Therapy dogs promote well-being, affection, communication, and movement.

   I. They promote a general feeling of well-being (children, the elderly).
  II. They provide unconditional affection to those who lack it (prisoners, people in shelters).
 III. They interact with those who have trouble communicating (Alzheimer's patients, some psychiatric patients, stroke patients).
 IV. They motivate simple activities (patting, brushing) for patients with physical limitations.

As you can see, this pattern is a variant of the topical pattern. It's easy to use, both in speeches to convince and speeches to actuate.

Comparative Advantages Pattern

The **comparative advantages pattern** is good for value claims that judge the relative merits of one thing by comparing its advantages to those of the competition. These speeches typically combine information with persuasion. For example, you if you compare policies (health care proposals), products or services (local stores), processes (a superior method of learning to play an instrument), candidates for office, cable news channels, and so on, your audience must have information about the things you compare.[14] Study the following outline from a speech evaluating the merits of osteopathic doctors compared to chiropractors:

Specific Purpose: To persuade my audience that a Doctor of Osteopathic Medicine (D.O.) is superior to a chiropractor for many reasons.

Thesis Statement: D.O.s are better than chiropractors because of their training and their ability to do surgery.

   I. They can do everything chiropractors do, and more.
  II. Their training is superior because it includes courses comparable to those in medical schools.
 III. Many D.O.s perform surgeries in hospitals with which they are affiliated.

This method is also useful when you want your listeners to act, and this pattern is common in advertisements, sales speeches, and campaign speeches. For instance, a recruiter from a small private college compares the advantages of her institution over larger state schools. The following outline also urges listeners to do something:

Specific Purpose: To persuade my audience to shop at the local coffee shop, not the giant chain.

direct method or **statement of reasons pattern** makes a claim and then states reasons that provide a rationale for the ideas

actuate motivate the audience to do something

comparative advantages pattern shows the superiority of a proposal by comparing its advantages to those of the competition; useful for value speeches

Thesis Statement: You should patronize Coffee Cottage because it is superior to the large chain in cost, taste, and ambiance.

I. The average cost per item is lower.
II. Its coffee is better because it is roasted daily in the shop.
III. The décor is unique and incorporates local community memorabilia.

It's easy to see that this pattern is related to reasoning by comparison and contrast, for you continually compare and contrast your proposal or product to other proposals and products the audience already knows.

Criteria Satisfaction Pattern

This is another pattern widely used for value claims because it sets forth the criteria or standards for evaluation at the outset and then shows how the solution, candidate, or product meets or exceeds these standards.

Workplace search committees go through this process whenever they select a new hire. They first identify specific qualities the new employee should have and then they look for candidates who have those qualities. Whenever you apply for a job, you first read the criteria spelled out in the job announcement and then you must show how you fit those criteria.

This **criteria satisfaction pattern** works for classification speeches. Here, Kristine argues that cheerleading should be considered a sport, not just an activity:[15]

Specific Purpose: To persuade my audience that cheerleading should be classified as a sport.

Thesis Statement: By considering the definition of a sport, you can agree that cheerleading fits into this category.

What is the definition of a sport?

I. Sports involve physical exertion.
II. Sports are a set of skills governed by rules.
III. A sport is often done competitively.

Cheerleading meets these criteria.

I. Physical exertion includes jumping, tumbling, and stunting.
II. Routines consist of precise movements, are limited to 2.5 minutes, and come with many rules.
III. Cheerleading competitions, both national and international, are televised on ESPN, Fox Sports Net, CBS Sports, and so on.

The following outline demonstrates the criteria satisfaction pattern for the argument that community service is a workable punishment for some criminals.

Specific Purpose: To persuade my audience that community service meets all the criteria for a good punishment for nonviolent criminals.

Thesis Statement: Community service is a punishment that fits the crime, reduces recidivism, and is cost effective.

What does a good punishment for nonviolent felons look like?

I. The punishment fits the crime.
II. It reduces recidivism.
III. It is cost effective.

Community service is the best punishment for nonviolent crimes.

criteria satisfaction pattern good for value or definition speeches; sets forth standards for judgment or for inclusion in a category and then shows how the proposal meets or exceeds these standards or fits into the category

    I. The punishment can be tailored to fit the crime.
   II. It keeps felons out of prison where they can be influenced by career criminals.
 III. It is far less costly than incarceration.

The criteria satisfaction pattern is especially useful for controversial issues, because you initially establish common ground with your audience by setting up criteria on which you all agree. As in the direct methods pattern, it is effective to build to a climax and develop your most persuasive criteria last.

Negative Method Pattern

The **negative method pattern** lets you concentrate on the shortcomings of every other proposal before you show why your proposal is the one logical solution. In other words, you point out the negative aspects in competing proposals; then, after you've dismantled or undermined the other plans, you propose your own. This pattern is often used when a policy claim is just one among many.

Specific Purpose: To persuade my audience that global legalization of drugs is the only way to control the supply and demand of illicit drugs.

Thesis Statement: Because of the failures of drug enforcement agencies and education, we should regulate drugs through legalization.

    I. More drug enforcement agencies are not the answer.
   II. Better education is not the answer.
 III. Global legalization of drugs is the only way we will regulate supply and demand.

As you can see, there are many useful persuasive patterns. Plan your speech using the one that is most appropriate for both your material and your audience. These patterns are not exhaustive, but they are among the most common ways to organize public speeches, advertisements, and other persuasive messages.

Summary

The best subjects for persuasive speeches come from the things that matter most to you personally. For this reason, ask yourself questions such as "What do I believe strongly?" "What arouses my strong feelings?" "What would I like to see changed?" "What enriches my life?" Your answers will generally provide you with topics that you're willing to defend. Choosing your subject is only the first part of topic selection. You must then decide whether you will focus on developing a claim of fact, value, definition, or policy.

We consistently argue for our ideas in an attempt to influence one another's beliefs, actions, values, and attitudes, and we strategically organize our speeches and adapt our ideas to different types of audiences. However, assumptions and actions are always interwoven because, while you are motivating listeners to act, you are also trying to reinforce their positive attitudes and beliefs. Throughout the entire time, you rely on underlying values to support your calls to action.

Several common persuasive patterns are available. The problem-solution pattern and its variant, Monroe's Motivated Sequence, both define a problem and identify a solution. The direct method, also called the statement of reasons pattern, directly lists arguments that support your claim. The criteria satisfaction pattern is good for value speeches because you first set up criteria or standards for judgment before you show how your proposal meets these standards. The comparative advantages method gives the advantage of your proposal over similar proposals; the negative method, in contrast, shows the disadvantages of every proposal but your own.

negative method pattern points out shortcomings of other proposals and then demonstrates why your proposal is the one logical solution remaining

STUDY AND REVIEW

Your online resources for *Public Speaking: Concepts and Skills for a Diverse Society* offer a broad range of study tools that will help you better understand the material in this chapter, complete assignments, and succeed on tests. Your online resources feature

- Speech videos with critical viewing questions, speech outlines, and transcripts
- Interactive versions of this chapter's Stop and Check activities and Application and Critical Thinking Exercises
- Speech Builder Express and InfoTrac College Edition
- Weblinks related to chapter content
- Study and review tools such as self-quizzes, an interactive glossary, and downloadable audio summaries

You can access your online resources at **http://www.cengage.com/login**, using the access code that came with your book or that you bought online at **http://www.iChapters.com**.

KEY TERMS

The terms below are defined in the margins throughout this chapter.

actuate 320	criteria 309	negative method
apathy 311	definition or classification	pattern 322
attitudes 313	claim 308	policy claim 309
claim 307	direct method or statement	status quo 309
cognitive dissonance	of reasons pattern 320	Theory of Reasoned
theory 312	dissonance 312	Action 313
comparative advantages	factual claim 307	to convince 311
pattern 320	Monroe's Motivated	value claim 309
criteria satisfaction	Sequence 316	
pattern 321		

APPLICATION AND CRITICAL THINKING EXERCISES

1. Consider the relationship between beliefs and actions, and identify topics that might fall into each category. For instance, in the "unfocused" category, people often believe they should learn to study more effectively, but they don't know how to proceed. In the "unconvinced" category, people don't know much about the importance of investing while they're still young, so they don't invest at all.

2. Listen to at least one persuasive speech on television, taking notes on the speaker's arguments. (C-SPAN is a good source for such speeches.) What kinds of claims does the speaker make? How does she or he support the claims? Who are the intended audiences? How effectively does the speaker adapt to audience beliefs, actions, attitudes, and values?

3. To explore hostile speaking in greater depth, go to **www.richspeaking.com/articles/ Difficult_Audience.html**. Compare the author's list of ten typical ways to respond to hostile audiences with his six positive alternative strategies.

4. With a small group in your classroom, identify areas in which national attitudes have changed, or areas in which your personal attitudes have changed. How did persuasive public speaking contribute to those changes?

SPEECH VIDEO

Critique Linnea Strandy's speech "Fair Trade Coffee," which is organized according to Monroe's Motivated Sequence. The text of her speech is provided next. Also see Bonita Persons' policy speech, "Don't Drive Drowsy" (featured at the end of Chapter 10), or watch the video of Paul Southwick's value speech, "Embryo Adoption." The videos, transcripts, and outlines of all these speeches are available in your online resources.

Student Speech with Commentary

FAIR TRADE COFFEE
By Linnea Strandy

Mike McNamara / Cengage Learning

Attention Step

The first step in Monroe's Motivated Sequence is similar to other speeches; it requires Linnea to draw attention to the topic and show its relevance to the audience. She has a fairly easy task with this topic, because almost all her listeners are coffee drinkers, and her town has many coffee venues. However, she should be aware that some people avoid coffee for religious, dietary, or personal reasons.

Fair . . . Trade . . . Coffee. These three words are not hard to understand, yet fair trade is a complex issue of which we are all a part. Did you purchase some sort of coffee this week? Or did someone you know purchase coffee last week? Whenever you purchase a product, it's a sign of support——a vote, if you will. We should all be voting Fair Trade.

Catherine Dolan, author of *Ethical Sourcing in the Global Food System,* says that fair trade is a social movement and model of international trade. It promotes paying a fair price to the farmer for his goods all the while maintaining social and environmental standards related to the production of those goods.

OK. So you're not a coffee drinker. Bananas, flowers, and sugar—these should also be fair traded, but I will use coffee as the example in this speech, because, according to www .blackgoldmovie.com, it is an $88 billion industry, second only to oil as the most highly traded commodity globally. According to Global Exchange, it was the first product to become Fair Trade Certified.

Need Step

This section shows that information often precedes persuasion. Before people are motivated to act, they need to know about a problem.

Clearly there is a need for fair trade in the global marketplace. Global Exchange, an organization for fair trade worldwide, reports that local coffee growers rely on middlemen who purchase coffee beans for about 50 cents per pound. Compare that to the world price of about $1 per pound and the consumer price of $3 to $5 per *cup*. This means that coffee bean farmers barely scrape by while large corporations and importers take millions in profits.

According to Tim Harford, from *The Undercover Economist*, this is how it works. Small family farmers grow 50 percent or more of the world's coffee. Most of these farmers are unorganized, so middlemen or estate owners buy their beans at merely 2 — 4 percent of the retail price.

Beans are initially processed at farms and estates where the local middlemen take advantage of the growers' lack of information, transportation, and access to credit, and force them to sell at low prices, while demanding high interest rates on loans.

Exporters then buy from these middlemen who try to buy low and sell high. Brokers sell to importers who sell to roasters who sell to distributors or retailers.

Retailers sell to consumers, who enjoy their daily beverage, oblivious to the injustice currently in the system. According to the coffee calculator at blackgoldmovie.com, a person who drinks one medium latte daily for a year pays the growers between $14 and $40; the traders get $91. And the coffee shops, roasters and importers in our country? About $1200.

Clearly there is a need for economic justice in this, and other products like it.

Satisfaction Step

A proposed solution is Fair Trade Certified™ (FTC) coffee that meets the following international criteria as given by Trans Fair USA:

- Pay enough to sustain farmers.
- Provide credit and technical assistance.
- Use organic farming practices (no harmful chemicals, protection of land and habitat, water conservation).
- Maintain fair labor conditions (safety rules, no child labor).
- Empower through direct trading.
- Develop the community businesses, healthcare, and education.

You can have a part by choosing to buy only FTC coffee. If you're not a coffee drinker, urge your friends to buy certified coffee or you can buy other FTC products. As a result there will be higher living standards for farmers, thriving communities, and more sustainable farming practices.

Visualization Step

Imagine that fair trade certified coffee becomes the norm:

Tim Harford in *The Undercover Economist* envisions small farmers working in trade cooperatives where they earn three to five times as much on their coffee.

The co-ops help farmers to sell directly to importers. Because they are democratically organized, they invest a portion of the premium into community development and environmental protection programs, and they offer credit to farmers at reasonable rates.

Importers buy directly from cooperatives and pay fair trade prices.

Roasters roast coffee with fair trade labels.

Distributors sell this coffee to their accounts.

Retailers sell fair trade coffee in their establishments.

Consumers would still enjoy their coffee, but this time they would feel safe knowing that they've helped people like Edgar's. Edgar's story is featured in *Brewing Justice: Fair Trade Coffee, Sustainability and Survival*, by Daniel Jaffee. Edward is quoted: "All my life, all I have ever done is work, work, work—only work. I had no choice. I wanted my children to have an education so that they could choose what they want to do."

Today all his children have completed secondary school. One son is finishing medical school, helped by Edgar's living wage and a scholarship from the coffee cooperative. Two other children have also received scholarships through the cooperative. Edgar clearly hopes you and your friends will drink more fair trade certified coffee.

Imagine if you don't insist on FTC coffee. People like Edgar continue to receive low wages, and their children continue to be trapped in low paying jobs with no incentive to help their environment or the community.

Action Step

You can do a lot to support economic justice in the coffee industry and other FTC commodities. Spread the word; tell your friends; read materials, and be aware. Think before you drink and patronize companies that only use fair trade certified products. Even if you don't drink coffee, you can pressure politicians to change the trade rules. You can also join an organization like OXFAM America, the FAIRTRADE foundation, Trade Justice Movement, or World Development Movement.

Citing her sources bolsters her credibility and keeps her from plagiarizing material.

The satisfaction step describes the solution. In this case, it's a policy that consumers don't have much control over, but listeners can decide whether or not to support it through their "vote."

The visualization step is a good place to include emotional appeals such as stories of real people and how their lives are affected.

In the conclusion, Linnea gives her audience a number of things they can do, and she briefly states her own intentions to act before ending with the "vote" metaphor she introduced in the beginning section.

Personally, I seek out FTC coffee.

David Ransom states in *The No-Nonsense Guide to Fair Trade* that more and more consumers are like me—and hopefully you. They are not only asking "Is this good for me?" but also "Is this good for others and the environment?" The growth of Fair Trade products proves that many of us are voting for a better world with our purchases.

CHAPTER 18

PERSUASIVE REASONING METHODS

© Tim Timmerman

THIS CHAPTER WILL HELP YOU

▶ Describe the elements of Toulmin's model of reasoning

▶ Explain four basic types of *logos*, or rational proofs, and know how to test each one

▶ Recognize several kinds of fallacious reasoning

▶ Explain the role of *pathos*, or emotional proofs, in reasoning

▶ Identify ways that *ethos*, or speaker credibility, functions as an element of reasoning

▶ Explain how reasoning strategies vary across cultural groups

▶ Identify elements of invitational rhetoric

Is that true? Maybe there's something to what she just said. Let me think about it. That's interesting. Maybe I should change my mind.

WITH THESE WORDS, Columbia University's president, Lee Bollinger, challenged graduating students to continue to deliberate about important issues[1] as they went out into a society, where contentious issues are often reduced to bumper sticker slogans or talking points. Deliberation involves making arguments and weighing the arguments of others. However, if we define argument as a "war of words" or a verbal fight, we only add to the problems, but if we consider an **argument** to be "an intentional, purposeful activity involving reason and judgment,"[2] we can work toward mutually productive decisions.

Every day you use reasoning to make sense of the world and to make decisions that affect your life. Based on your observations, you form conclusions that seem sensible. You may not think much about how you reason; you just "know" if something makes sense or not. However, you sooner or later find that not everyone shares your conclusions, and you often feel compelled to explain them.[3] So you build a case or create an argument to support your ideas.

argument intentional, purposeful speaking that involves reason and judgment

This chapter will help you think about several elements of reasoning that fall into the canon of invention. It first describes three types of reasoning that Aristotle identified centuries ago:[4]

Of the modes of persuasion furnished by the spoken word there are three kinds. The first kind depends on the personal character of the speaker [*ethos*]; the second on putting the audience into a certain frame of mind [*pathos*]; the third on the proof, or apparent proof, provided by the words of the speech itself [*logos*].

Ethos, pathos, and logos work together to form a totality of "good reasons." In other words, emotion is often very reasonable; reason has emotional underpinnings; and it is both reasonable and emotionally satisfying to hear a credible speaker. In specific situations, however, you may emphasize one reasoning type over the others. For instance, when you propose a campus policy change, you'll focus on different kinds of proofs than when you must explain to middle school students the accidental death of a classmate.

Creating and evaluating arguments by using logos, pathos, and ethos effectively will empower you to be a more effective speaker and listener. However, "winning" an argument is neither desirable nor possible in many cases, and this chapter concludes with principles and forms of invitational rhetoric.

Use Toulmin's Reasoning Model

Professor Stephen Toulmin[5] diagrammed six elements of an argument, based on the type of reasoning most commonly found in courtrooms. His linear model, shown in Figure 18.1, illustrates important aspects of reasoning and clarifies the relationships among claims, evidence or data, warrants, backing, qualifiers, and conditions for rebuttal characteristic of traditional reasoning in U.S. culture. Learning to qualify your claim, justifying it with evidence, and planning ways to deal with counterarguments will make your speeches more persuasive.

Claims

claim debatable point or proposal you want listeners to accept

A **claim** is the debatable point or proposal you want your audience to accept. As Chapter 17 points out, claims require evidence or backing to be accepted. Factual claims argue about what exists, what causes a phenomenon, or what the future will bring. Definition or

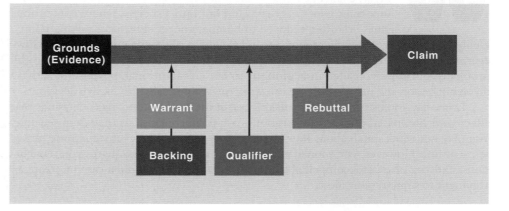

Figure 18.1
Toulmin's Model of Reasoning Stephen Toulmin developed this model as a way to visualize the elements of reasoning.

classification claims determine in which category a phenomenon belongs. Value claims deal with the rightness, the goodness, or the worth of a thing. Finally, policy claims argue over actions or proposals for change.

Grounds, Data, or Evidence

To support your claims you need **grounds** (also called **data** or **evidence**) on which your claim rests. Grounds come in the form of facts, examples, narratives, quotations, statistics, and literal and figurative comparisons, as described in Chapter 8. Use data from a variety of sources to be most effective. Evidence enables your listeners to weigh your argument and decide whether or not your conclusions make sense. Without sufficient and credible data, your claims are simply unsupported **assertions**.

Warrants

The justification or reasoning that you and your listeners use to connect your evidence with your claim is called a **warrant**. Switch your TV on to a police drama and watch how officers justify an arrest. They produce a warrant, which they can only get if they have sufficient data or grounds to connect the suspect to the crime. So, if the fingerprint on the gun (evidence) matches the suspect's print (additional evidence), it is logical to conclude that the suspect fired the gun (claim of fact), because our fingerprints are all unique (the warrant that connects or links the evidence to the claim).

Backing

When a warrant is not broadly understood or broadly accepted, you can give additional reasons, called **backing**, to support or defend it. For example, think of a trial in which blood was found on a defendant's jacket (evidence). In case the jury doesn't understand the link between the blood evidence and the perpetrator (warrant), the prosecution brings in several experts who explain the science of DNA (backing) and testify that the blood must belong to the victim (backing).

Qualifiers

Avoid words such as *always* or *never* when you make claims. Instead, use **qualifiers**, which are words and phrases that limit or narrow the scope of your claim. Here are some examples: *in most cases, in males between the ages of 7 and 9, usually,* and *among voters with a college degree.*

Rebuttal

Because most issues are complex and have many possible solutions, not all listeners will agree with your conclusions. So, as a "listening speaker," you should try to hear their potential arguments and then prepare to deal with them directly. This is the **rebuttal** part of the model. It might help if you think of rebuttals as your listeners' questions that begin with the word *But . . .* or the phrase *But what about . . . ?* Demonstrating that you've considered arguments both for and against your conclusions and that you still have good reasons for your claim enhances your persuasiveness.

In summary, if you learn to recognize the type of claim you are making, qualify it, provide evidence and backing to warrant it, and then confront potential audience rebuttals, you will be more effective in presenting your ideas to others and having them recognize your views as reasonable.

grounds, data, or **evidence** evidence offered to support a claim

assertions claims put forth without any supporting evidence

warrant justification or reasoning that connects the claim and the evidence

backing reasons given to support the warrant

qualifiers words and phrases that limit or narrow the scope of a claim

rebuttal arguments that counter or disagree with a claim

THE INFLUENCE OF CULTURE ON REASONING

CULTURE INFLUENCES OUR REASONING RESOURCES in a number of ways that can easily lead to misunderstandings between cultural groups.[6]

▶ **Topics considered appropriate for discussion vary across cultures.** Some groups, for instance, would not debate such issues as gay rights, day care, or euthanasia. Openly speaking about sex is unthinkable in some cultures.

▶ **Cultures conceptualize issues differently.** It's common in the United States to think of issues as problems and solutions we can define, propose, test and then eliminate or enact; others believe problems result from fate, a bad relationship with the deity or deities, or being out of harmony with one another or the universe.[7]

▶ **The norms for structuring and framing a discussion vary.** Rather than seek causes and effects or pro and con arguments, then making claims and counterclaims, some cultures deplore arguments that present one position as superior to another and draw attention to the rhetor.[8] Still others ground their discussions in the historical perspectives of the various participants or rely on narrative structures to frame their speeches. In the United States, we typically ask, "Who won the argument?" But various other cultures see themselves as a community of equals who must cooperate to reach consensus.

▶ **Levels of explicitness differ across cultures.** In the United States, we commonly hear conclusions stated explicitly and concretely. However, other cultures tolerate much more ambiguity; their speakers exert influence through subtlety and indirectness.

▶ **Forms of proof are often dissimilar.** What's considered rational or irrational, what counts as evidence, and what constitutes a good reason varies across cultures. As Chapter 8 pointed out, facts, statistics, and studies by experts are typically used here, but elsewhere, cultures find good reasons in narratives, analogies, authoritative texts, and the sayings of wise, experienced elders.

▶ **Communication styles vary.** Mainstream U.S. culture is biased toward linear, analytical models of reasoning, as depicted in the Toulmin model. Other cultural groups reason more holistically through drama, intuition, and emotional expressiveness.

Question for Discussion

An article on InfoTrac College Edition has the formidable title, "Microcultural analysis of variation in sharing of causal reasoning about behavior." It describes a study done in a natural foods cooperative store that compares and contrasts the ways a "health food guru" and an animal rights activist make reasonable decisions about foods. Read the introduction and other parts of the article that interest you. Which type of reasoning makes more sense to you?

Use Logos or Rational Proofs

Logos, often called rational proofs, refers to the verbal arguments you make relating to your subject—arguments such as analogy, inductive, deductive, and causal reasoning. (Of course, there are other methods of sense making, as the Diversity in Practice feature on cultural reasoning explains.)

logos verbal arguments; arguments from the words of the speech itself

Reasoning by Analogy: Figurative and Literal

Chapter 8 defines an **analogy** as a comparison between one item that is unknown or less familiar and something already familiar to the audience. Analogies can be either *figurative* (metaphor) or *literal* (parallel case).

Figurative Analogies (Metaphors)

When **reasoning by metaphor**, you figuratively compare two things that are generally different but share a recognizable similarity. Metaphors are fundamentally dialogical in that they require your listeners to participate actively and make sensible connections between the two things you compare. For example, what images do these metaphors evoke in you?

- Good news is music to our ears; insecurity causes us to play it by ear; when we are getting along, we are in harmony or in tune with one another.[9]
- The separation between church and state is a wall or a dance or a two-way street.[10]
- A teacher can see herself as a police officer or a gardener or a ship's captain in the classroom.[11]

Our metaphors often guide our actions. For example, what is the role of the United States in the world? Is it more like a police officer, a kindly big brother, a bystander, or an onlooker? The metaphor we embrace affects U.S. global policies. If we choose "police," our foreign policy is different than if we embrace "onlooker."

Use of analogy is a fundamental, universal form of reasoning. Brian Wicker,[12] author of *A Story-Shaped World*, explains that metaphor is an older, more poetic way of seeing the world, related to the modes of thinking of poets and storytellers. It is a continuation of our oral heritage. Aristotle associated metaphor with mental brilliance, as seen in this quotation from *Poetics*.[13]

> . . . the greatest thing by far is to be a master of metaphor. It is the one thing that cannot be learnt from others, and it is also a sign of genius, since a good metaphor implies an intuitive perception of the similarity in dissimilars.

Asa Hilliard[14] claims that metaphorical reasoning is typical of African and African American speakers.

> Early use was made of proverbs, song, and stories. Direct or symbolic lessons were taught through these. . . . Parenthetically, it is interesting that racist psychologists claim that Black people are not capable of "Level II Thinking," the kind of abstract thinking which is reflected in proverbs and analogies. To the contrary, this is our strong suit. . . . Psychologists . . . miss the extensive use of proverbs and analogies among us.

The images inherent in metaphors have emotional overtones. Contrast your feelings about a *harvest* of justice or the *moneyed scales* of justice; a *flood* of compassion or a *trickle* of compassion; a *turkey* of a deal or a *gem* of a deal.

Literal Analogies (Parallel Cases)

Whereas metaphors highlight similarities between two different things, reasoning by **parallel case** or **literal analogy** points out likenesses between two similar things. We often use this type of reasoning to formulate policies by asking what another person or group decided to do when faced with a problem similar to our own. Here are some examples.

- How should your school deal with campus parking needs? Look at case studies of schools similar to yours that solved similar parking problems, and then infer whether the other schools' experiences will be a good predictor of what might or might not work for yours.
- How should a local hospital keep health care costs under control? Look at cost-saving measures instituted by a similar-sized hospital in a similar location.
- How should the United States solve health care problems? Identify which countries are most like ours. What do they do? How well do those programs work?

analogy comparison of one item that's less familiar or unknown to something concrete and familiar

reasoning by metaphor comparing two things that are generally different but share a recognizable similarity

parallel case or **literal analogy** comparing likenesses between two similar things; arguing that what happened in a known case will likely happen in a similar case

In summary, we commonly use actual cases based on real experiences to formulate policies and make predictions about the future. Then we predict that what happened in a known case will happen in a similar case that we project.

Testing Analogies

Reasoning by metaphor is not generally considered a "hard" proof that can be easily tested. The best test is to make sure your listeners can sensibly connect your concept with the comparison so that the comparison does, in fact, illuminate, clarify, and illustrate your idea.

Parallel case reasoning is different; you should test it more directly by considering the following two questions.

1. Are the cases really alike? Or are you "comparing apples to oranges"?
2. Are they alike in essential details?

PRACTICALLY SPEAKING

JEANNE M. EDWARDS, ACCOUNTANT

Jeanne M. Edwards/KPMG

Jeanne M. Edwards is a partner with KPMG, a major international accounting and consulting firm based in New York City. While she was earning her university degree in business administration with an emphasis in accounting and economics, she was a member of her university's debate team for three years. She now travels all over the world helping clients solve problems.

Of what value was your training in debate?
I apply skills from debating every day. In debating, I learned to look at a broad issue or problem and break it into sections or smaller pieces that I could then sort through and analyze. Debating also taught me to listen to other perspectives on the same issue. By listening carefully, I learned which types of evidence would be most persuasive to different audiences.

In consulting, I generally find that there is an organizational position on the problem and there is a mandate for change—which can be either negative or positive. I help clients identify the various elements of the issue and then find compelling, unique reasons to support the decisions they must make.

Having to debate both sides of issues taught me that there are a variety of perspectives on any issue. With each new problem, I look for the weaknesses and the strengths of the various positions. The issues that keep coming up again and again are the most important, and identifying them allows the common threads to eventually become evident. Clients can then come to a solution based on common interests that makes sense for their organization.

Questions for Discussion

▶ How does the ability to look at an issue from a variety of perspectives make a person more persuasive?
▶ Jeanne doesn't tell clients what to do, she helps them reason their way through difficult issues and find conclusions that work for them. In what other occupations are consulting skills vital?

Reasoning Inductively

In **inductive reasoning**, you begin with specific instances or examples and formulate a reasonable generalization or conclusion from them. In other words, inductive reasoning moves from the particular to the general; it is characteristic of women, many ethnic speakers, and others who ground their knowing and reasoning in personal experiences that arise out of their relationship with others. Patricia Sullivan,[15] for instance, explains that African American leaders typically tie knowledge to human experiences, human actions, and the human life world. Knowledge is grounded in human experience; it does not exist for its own sake or in the abstract. What is relevant is considered relevant because it makes a difference in people's lives.

Here is an example of induction from a *U.S. News and World Report* feature about inner-city debate teams:[16]

▶ Darinka Maldonado got so involved in debate in her Bronx high school that she avoided negative peer pressure and earned a full scholarship to the University of Pittsburgh.
▶ Reena Rani, an immigrant from India who debates in the South Bronx, uses skills she's learned to counter her father's and brother's arguments that, as a female, she shouldn't aspire to a job.
▶ Urban debaters, who are predominately poor, minority, and female, are excelling against opponents from wealthier schools with longer-established debate programs.
▶ LaTonya Starks, a former Chicago urban school debater who went on to Northwestern University, says that successful debate competition improves the self-images of urban debaters.
▶ Angelo Brooks, who coaches a Baltimore high school team, seeks students who are struggling academically, not overachievers. Debate tools (research, listening, outlining arguments) have helped many debaters improve their grades an average of 10 to 15 points.

Generalization: Urban debate has had remarkable success in diverting at-risk kids from poverty, drugs, and violence.

Because you can only be sure of a conclusion only if you can observe 100 percent of a population, it is ideal to look at every example before you form a conclusion. However, 100 percent samples are rare. (Imagine trying to survey every student who's participated in an urban debate league!) Instead, select a representative sample, survey the characteristics of that sample, formulate conclusions and then generalize your findings to the larger population it represents. But take care: If you only study inner-city debate programs on the East coast, don't assume that your conclusions apply to all urban debaters. Other factors may affect outcomes in different regions of the country.

Testing Inductive Reasoning

The three major tests for inductive reasoning are all linked to the tests you used to evaluate examples (see guidelines in Chapter 8 for evaluating examples).

1. Are enough cases represented to justify the conclusion? Or are you forming a conclusion based on too few cases?
2. Are the cases typical? That is, do they represent the average members of the population to which the generalizations are applied? Or are they extreme cases that may show what could happen, but not what usually happens?
3. Are the examples from the time period under discussion, or are they out of date?

Reasoning Deductively

Inductive reasoning moves from specific examples to conclusions or generalizations, but **deductive reasoning** goes the other direction. It begins with a generalization or principle, called the *premise*, and moves logically to an application in a specific case.

inductive reasoning starting with specific instances or examples then formulating a reasonable conclusion

deductive reasoning starting with a principle (the premise) and applying it to a specific case

(See Figure 18.2 for an example of the relationship between inductive and deductive reasoning.) In formal logic, the deductive reasoning process is often shown in the form of a *syllogism* such as this:

> Major premise: All Catholic bishops are unmarried.
>
> Minor premise: He is a Catholic bishop.
>
> Conclusion: Therefore, he is not married.

When you're sure of the major premise, you can state your conclusion with confidence. Because it is a rule that members of the Catholic clergy cannot marry and stay in the priesthood, you can be fairly sure that a Catholic priest who has risen to the level of bishop is unmarried. In contrast, many premises are less certain. Although some, such as "all men are mortal," are 100 percent true, others, such as "urban high school debaters get better grades," are not valid in every case. So it's wise to qualify both your premises and your conclusions. Here is one example:

> Major premise: Many students who participate in urban debate leagues get better grades.
>
> Minor premise: Yolanda Baylor is a debater at an inner-city high school in the South Bronx.
>
> Conclusion: She has probably improved her grades.

When you reason deductively, you rarely state the entire syllogism, so your listeners must fill in the unstated premises. Aristotle called this an **enthymeme**. For example, you might say, "Married? No, he's a Catholic bishop!" and let your audience make the necessary connections. Or (talking with friends about a student's decision to join the urban debate team), "What a great opportunity! Her grade point could use a boost!" Your friends then use their generalizations about urban debating to make sense of what you've just said.

enthymeme omitting part of the syllogism in an argument and letting listeners supply what's missing; inherently dialogical

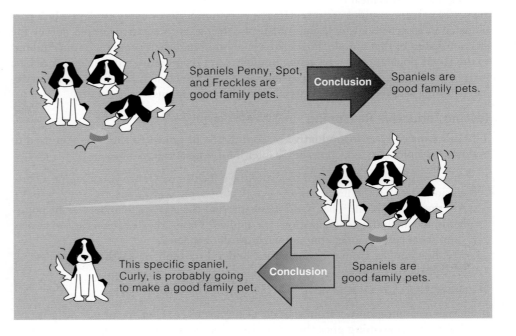

Figure 18.2
Inductive and Deductive Reasoning You observe a number of spaniels and inductively reason that they make good pets. Using that premise, you deduce that Curly, the specific spaniel you've chosen, will be a good family dog.

Using enthymemes is inherently dialogical, for your listeners must form conclusions based on their knowledge of what you *don't* say. However, if they know nothing about your subject (the rules regarding the Catholic clergy or the connection between debating and grades, for example), they'll miss your meaning.

Testing Deductive Reasoning

There are two major tests for deductive reasoning:

1. For the conclusion to be valid, the premises must be true or highly probable.
2. To be reasonable, the conclusion must follow from the premise.

Reasoning Causally

Causal reasoning links two events or occurrences in such a way that one comes first and regularly leads to the second. Because the belief in cause-and-effect is a fundamental element of the Euro-American belief system, causal reasoning is common. Example: It is evident that the lack of oxygen to the brain (first event) causes death (second event)—this link is observed time after time.

Cause-and-effect links are less evident in complex situations where many variables precede a condition and could be linked to it. For example, one speaker stated: "There were nine million immigrants last year, and there were nine million Americans out of work." Both facts can be verified by counting. However, if the speaker blames immigration for causing unemployment his statement might sound like this: "There were nine million Americans out of work last year *because* there were nine million immigrants." In his original statement, the two conditions exist together in time, perhaps by chance. In the second statement, the second phenomenon (unemployment) results from the first (immigration) and would not exist without it. However, most people agree that the causes of unemployment are much more complex than an influx of immigrants. When reasoning by cause, the key is to produce enough reasons to warrant the connection between the two factors.

Here are just a few of the causal claims currently being debated: Smoking causes diabetes. Immunizations cause autism. Man-made processes cause climate change. A vegan diet is linked to longevity.

Testing Causal Reasoning

Test causation by asking a series of questions to assess whether the reasoning is valid.

1. Is there a real connection? Does one follow as a result of the first, or do the two events simply exist together in time? (Is it correlation or causation?)
2. Is this the only cause? The most important cause? Or are there other factors?
3. Is the cause strong enough for the effect?

In summary, you have at your disposal a variety of reasoning strategies you can use to warrant your claims, including figurative and literal analogies, inductive and deductive reasoning, and causal links. All of these reasoning types fall under the category of logos, or rational proofs. (The Diversity in Practice feature provides additional information on men's and women's patterns in reasoning.)

Recognizing Logical Fallacies

A **fallacy** is a failure in logical reasoning that leads to unsound or misleading arguments. Fallacies have been around for thousands of years, as you can tell by the Latin names given to some of them. As a speaker or critical listener, you should examine arguments carefully to avoid being taken in by the following common fallacies.

causal reasoning linking two factors in such as way that the first occurs before the second and regularly leads to the second as a matter of rule

fallacy failure in logical reasoning that leads to unsound or misleading arguments

> ◗ DIVERSITY IN PRACTICE
>
> ## REASONING AND THE SEXES
>
> ALTHOUGH both men and women reason inductively, some feminist philosophers argue that inductive reasoning is a *major* way that women draw conclusions. They say that women typically describe specific experiences of real people, such as the rape survivor, the family without medical insurance, the student athlete whose sport was eliminated, and then generalize from these examples. This means that women's reasoning is characteristically grounded in personal experiences that arise out of their interpersonal relationships.[17]
>
> Women are commonly stereotyped as reasoning with their hearts rather than their heads—an overgeneralization that may have some basis in fact. Studies of women's patterns of thinking show the importance of emotion in their reasoning process.[18] Although obviously different from "dispassionate investigation," emotions complement logic and intertwine with rational proofs. Feelings are not inferior to reason, and they are not something women must overcome if they are to think clearly. Instead, emotions can be a source of knowledge, and "truth" or "knowledge" without emotion is distorted.[19]
>
> Some scholars argue against fundamental differences between men and women. They believe that use of evidence, linear thinking, and deductive logic are not inherently masculine, and that both men and women use them. Further, use of intuitive and emotional arguments are not inherently feminine; men often reason through experiences, emotions, and empathy.[20]
>
> The Laboratory for Complex Thinking and Scientific Reasoning at McGill University,[21] studied male and female scientists. They found no major differences in use of inductive, deductive, or causal reasoning processes. However, they discovered that, given an unexpected finding, men tended to assume they knew the cause, whereas women tracked it down.
>
> Whatever differences there may be, the "difference must be viewed as a resource for—not an impediment to—meaningful dialogue."[22]

Unsupported Assertion

In the **unsupported assertion** fallacy, the claim is offered without supporting evidence. Have you ever argued for a grade change ("I deserve an A, so why did I get a B?")? If you really want to achieve a change, you'll have to produce some pretty convincing data to show that you earned the A. Otherwise, your record will stay the same.

Ad Populum or Bandwagon

The Latin phrase **ad populum** literally translates "to the people." It's an appeal to popular reason, another failure of evidence. Instead of providing sound rational arguments, the speaker justifies a proposal by phrases such as "Everyone's doing it" or "We all agree that. . . ." But ask yourself: How often is the majority wrong?

Ad Hominem (Personal Attack)

Rather than evaluate the claim, the evidence, and the warrant or reasoning behind it, an **ad hominem** (literally, "against the person") attacks, discounts or demeans the messenger. For instance, one person might present good reasons against physician-assisted suicide, to which the listener replies, "You're just a fundamentalist Christian." This focuses not on the arguments but on the speaker's characteristics. Similarly, a woman who presents good reasons to report an incident of sexual harassment in the workplace might be dismissed as a "frustrated feminist."

unsupported assertion a claim presented without evidence

ad populum an appeal to popular opinion

ad hominem an attack on the messenger rather than the message

Post Hoc

Also called ***post hoc***, *ergo propter hoc* (literally: "after this, therefore because of this"), this fallacy of cause-and-effect argues that because one event follows the other, the first must be the cause of the second. For instance, Maria's speech on lottery winners (Chapter 9) describes Daisy, who was sued for half of her $2.8 million winnings because, prior to buying the ticket, Daisy asked for prayers that she'd win. Her son's friend prayed; she won. The teen sued, saying his prayer had caused her fortune. (The judge, however, ruled that there is no way to prove such a link.)

Overgeneralization

This is a fallacy of inductive reasoning that extends the conclusion further than the evidence warrants. For example, you might have a bad experience with a specific brand of computer and you judge the whole line of computers (or worse, the entire company) negatively based on your one bad experience. People overgeneralize about blind dates, crooked politicians, student cheating, members of ethnic groups, and so on. Jumping to a conclusion based on minimal evidence is **overgeneralization**.

Red Herring Argument

Any time you think "That's beside the point" or "That's irrelevant," you're probably hearing a **red herring** argument. In this fallacy, the speaker dodges the real argument and intentionally digresses and introduces an unrelated side issue in an attempt to divert attention. The term derives from the days of fox hunting when a dead fish was dragged across the trail of a fox to set the dogs off in a different direction.[23]

False Analogy

A **false analogy** occurs when the two things compared are not similar enough to warrant the comparison. Particularly common are inappropriate World War II analogies to Hitler's Nazi regime.[24] For example, the Internet has more than 800,000 hits for the analogy "animal Auschwitz," which compares the treatment of animals to the treatment of Jews, gays, and other groups during the Nazi era. Arguably, the treatment of animals is terrible in some cases, but it is arguably different in degree and kind from what happened in Nazi Germany.

False Dichotomy

The **false dichotomy** fallacy states the issue as an either-or choice, overlooking other reasonable possibilities. So you might hear "Either graduate from college, or work in a low-paying job" or "Either you are for us, or you are against us" or (in an election year) "Vote for experience not just change!" Such false dichotomies overlook the range of possibilities between the two extremes.

In summary, arguments are fallacious when they fail to provide evidence or present faulty evidence for the claim. Fallacies also attack the messenger instead of countering

post hoc a fallacy of causation; a false cause

overgeneralization a fallacy of induction; generalizing too broadly, given the evidence

red herring introducing a side issue with the intent of drawing attention from the real issue

false analogy comparing two things too dissimilar to warrant the conclusion drawn

false dichotomy an either-or fallacy that ignores other reasonable options

---

✓ STOP AND CHECK
IDENTIFYING FALLACIES

Working alone or with a group of classmates, copy the list of common fallacies, and come up with an example of each. Use material from television shows or movies, personal experiences, letters to the editor, talk-show callers, current events, and the like. Share your examples with other class members.

For additional information, go to **http://commfaculty.fullerton.edu/rgass/ fallacy31.htm**, a site sponsored by Dr. Robert Gass, University of California, Fullerton. He provides definitions and humorous examples of these and other common fallacies.

the message. Fallacies of analogy, causation, and induction are common. Learning to recognize irrelevant digressions and false choices will help you think more critically about the arguments you make and those you hear every day.

Include Pathos or Emotional Proofs

Contrast the following situations:

- You're listening to a speaker who has all her facts and figures straight, and she provides evidence that passes all the tests: Her examples are representative, her statistics come from reputable sources, and she cites knowledgeable experts. However, you feel no good reason to act. In other words, you're unmotivated—you are neither interested nor concerned.
- You're listening to a second speaker (same topic) who similarly provides excellent evidence and sound reasoning. However, she links the subject to your core beliefs, values, personal goals, and emotions. You find yourself caring about it and wanting to believe and act as she proposes.

The second speaker realizes what good speakers have always known: **Motivation** is an internal, individualistic, or subjective factor that results when listeners understand how topics affect their lives in a personal way. That is, we look for emotional and psychological reasons to support our decisions. And in the end, our subjective reasons may be as influential as our logical ones. This demonstrates the power of emotions, which Aristotle called **pathos**, in reasoning.

Although you often respond subconsciously to emotional appeals, responses can be conscious, and your thoughts may run something like this:

"She's right, that's exactly how it feels to go to bed hungry; we shouldn't let that happen!"

"Writing my résumé carefully will help me get a better job."

"I have to protest over such a fundamental issue as freedom of speech."

"I've experienced frustration just like that! I can relate!"

Pathos relies on appeals to emotions and to needs.

Appeals to Positive Emotions

Aristotle defined emotions as all the feelings people have that change them in ways that affect their judgment. Psychologists say we "approach" pleasurable emotions such as love, peace, pride, approval, hope, generosity, courage, and loyalty. We also feel good about our core beliefs and values, such as freedom and individualism. By appealing to positive feelings and values, you can often motivate your listeners to accept and act on your claims.

Narratives and examples are good ways to highlight emotional appeals. In this speech excerpt, Marieta talks about international adoption. She was originally from the Philippines, but was adopted into an American home when she was a teenager.[25]

> You might be thinking that adopting an international child is a lot of work. Well, it is, but I believe it is worth it. My parents say that bringing me into their family is one of the most gratifying things they have ever done. And their generosity has obviously benefited me. If it were not for my parents, I would not be able to continue my college education. I wouldn't have any parents or sisters to call my own. As far as I know, I would probably still be in an orphanage because I wouldn't have a place to go.

motivation internal, individualized factor that results when we understand how topics affect our lives in a personal way

pathos appeals or reasons directed toward audience emotions

Her personal story emphasizes generosity and hope as well as the underlying values of education, family, belonging, and self-sacrifice for the good of others. It provides a powerful argument for international adoption.

Appeals to Negative Emotions

Because negative emotions are unpleasant, we try to avoid feelings such as guilt, shame, hatred, fear, insecurity, anger, and anxiety. Appeals to negative emotions can be forceful, with sometimes disastrous results. Consider how effectively hate groups appeal to their audiences' weaknesses, rages, fears, and insecurities.

However, negative emotions are often useful. Fear, anger, and guilt, for instance, can motivate us to avoid real dangers—a fact that the campaign against drunk driving uses effectively. Think of a story you've heard or a television ad you've seen that shows adorable children killed by drivers who "just this once" drove while intoxicated. Don't they make you want to prevent the problem?

One way to arouse listener emotion is to use analogies. In this case, Mike Suzuki evoked anger in his speech against the use of Native American symbols as sports mascots.[26] He wanted fellow students at a Catholic university to identify with the Native American perspective, so he used the following analogy:

> Opponents feel that non-Indian people do not have the right to use sacred Indian symbols. Phil St. John, a Sioux Indian and founder of the Concerned American Indian Parents group, said the behaviors of Indian mascots at sporting events were comparable to a Native American tearing apart a rosary in front of a Catholic church. Can you imagine someone dressing up as the Pope and swinging a cross wildly in the air at one of our football games? This is how some Native Americans feel when their sacred symbols are used in sports.

As you might imagine, a speaker can easily overdo negative appeals. For instance, excessive appeals to guilt or fear may turn off an audience. One listener responded to a famous environmentalist activist's speech in this way:[27]

> [Her] presentation is meant to instill unease. In my case, she is succeeding, though not in the way she intends. She is making me worry . . . for the fate of this movement on which so much depends. As much as I want to endorse what I hear, [her] effort to shock and shame just isn't taking. . . . I find myself going numb.

He advises environmentalist speakers to evaluate the psychological impact of their appeals to fear and guilt and to present instead a "politics of vision" that connects environmental goals to positive emotions—to what is "generous, joyous, freely given, and noble" in the audience.

Appealing to Needs

One of the most widely cited systems of classifying needs follows the work of Abraham Maslow,[28] who ranked needs into five levels, each building on the others—generally in the same order. Everyone must satisfy basic physical needs for water, air, food, and shelter. After these needs are met, we need security and a feeling of safety, then love and belonging, followed by esteem, and topped off by self-actualization or the need to reach our potential. Although he described five levels, Maslow himself believed that "most behavior is multi-motivated"[29] and that a combination of levels is active in each situation. Here is a list of each level and some suggestions for ways to address each one:

> ▶ **Basic needs:** Link your topic to your listeners' basic survival needs.
> ▶ **Security and safety:** Explain how to gain peace of mind, job security, safety, and comfort, better health, physical safety, and so on.
> ▶ **Love and belonging:** Show how your topic helps your listeners be better friends, creates a stronger community, or builds ties between people.
> ▶ **Esteem:** Demonstrate that you respect your listeners, and mention their accomplishments when appropriate. Find ways to make them feel competent to carry out your proposals. Let them know that their ideas , opinions, and concerns are significant.
> ▶ **Self-actualization:** Challenge your listeners to look beyond themselves and reach out to others. Encourage them to dream big dreams and accomplish unique things. The Army slogan "Be all that you can be" is an example of an appeal to self-actualization.

Marieta's speech on international adoption touched on many needs. Her adoptive parents provided a secure home where her physical needs were met. Being adopted gave her a sense of love, belonging, and esteem. In addition, she esteemed her parents for their generosity and kindness. And they reached outside themselves and did something significant for another human.

(To learn more about Maslow's hierarchy, do an Internet search for "Abraham Maslow." Look for additional levels that other scholars have added to his hierarchy.)

Understanding Complex Motivations

As you can see, using pathos is complex, because needs, wants, emotions, and values overlap. As you create emotional appeals, keep in mind four important factors that result in motivational variation from individual to individual.[30]

1. *Sometimes you must choose between two desirable goals or feelings*, such as job security or the ability to reach your potential. At other times, you may have to choose between two undesirable things, or "the lesser of two evils."
2. *Motives vary according to our circumstances.* Someone who's just ended a significant relationship may worry more about belonging and self-esteem than someone in a long-term relationship. What motivates you is different from what motivates your parents, and your parents, in turn, respond to different appeals than do your grandparents.
3. *Our responses often come out of mixed motives.* The person who donates out of loyalty to her school may also like the pride she feels when a building is named in her honor. An angry blogger may be writing out of underlying anxiety, fear, or frustration.
4. *Motivations are often group centered.* What we want for ourselves, we want for others, including our family, friends, members of our clubs, religious groups, schools, towns, states, society, and world. Consequently, a speech about child abuse in other countries can motivate listeners who want security for themselves and their own families, as well as for strangers.

Testing Emotional Appeals

Emotions, although essential, are not always trustworthy, so it is important to examine them to see if they make sense. For example, if you use fear to motivate your audience, ask yourself if you are creating or playing on irrational fears or if the fear is justified? Excessive use of emotional appeals can cloud logical reasoning.

When you're listening to emotional appeals, ask questions such as these: "Why am I feeling guilty?" "Is my guilt reasonable?" "Is this speaker trying to manipulate me

ETHICS IN PRACTICE

DEMAGOGUERY

Bettmann/CORBIS

Huey P. Long, also known as
"Kingfish"

Ideally, good speakers blend elements of logos, ethos, and pathos, and the term **demagogue** is typically reserved for speakers who bypass or minimize logos and focus mostly on ethos and pathos. Although not easily defined, a common list of historical examples includes the ancient Athenian Cleon, Hitler, Senator Joseph McCarthy, and the Louisiana politician Huey P. Long, who reportedly said, "The time has come for all good men to rise above principle." In a scholarly article about Long, Joshua Gunn identifies a demagogue as:

> . . . an obsessional neurotic, righteously complete, frequently obscuring or erasing audiences as mere objects at the exact moment of professing his or her love for them. [The demagogue claims] to bring order to chaos, thereby representing strength, resolve, and absolute autonomy . . . [by placing] much more emphasis on the feelings inspired by ethos and pathos, and largely at the expense of logos and reasoned argument.[31]

To Patricia Roberts-Miller, the defining characteristic of a demagogue is "polarizing propaganda that motivates members of an ingroup to hate and scapegoat some outgroup(s)"[32] by promising a coming era of stability and control; the result is an "us" and "them" mentality. Demagogues are often dynamic, dramatic, passionate speakers who inspire devotion among followers. Often they characterize themselves as just a common person fighting for the people.[33] This category includes opportunists who work for their own gain, politicians who inflame passions to gain or maintain power, and doomsayers who create a heightened sense of crisis in order to reveal their novel solutions.[34]

To his credit, Huey P. Long used his persuasive powers to benefit people in the lower economic classes. He embraced many populist causes including free textbooks in school, new buildings and roads, construction of Louisiana State University (including a great football team), and redistribution of wealth. He is classified as a demagogue partly because of the intensity of his supporters and the harshness of his critics. He was eventually assassinated.

The book and the movie *All the King's Men* are based on Long's career. You can also watch a newsreel summarizing his life at **www.youtube.com/watch?v= AbyMeMApC3U&feature=related** or view excerpts from his speeches at **www .youtube.com/watch?v=bwdqeeuGc6g&NR=1**.

Questions for Discussion

▶ Do an Internet search for "demagoguery" and make a list of people who've been called a demagogue. Tell why each person was labeled this way. Do you think the label is appropriate? Why or why not?

▶ The word "demagogue" has very negative connotations. Why is demagoguery considered to be one of the most unethical forms of speaking?

demagogue a polarizing speaker who appeals to audiences more on the basis of emotion and personal charisma than on reasoned arguments

through my feelings?" "Although he is causing me to feel angry, is anger my primary emotion? Could my underlying emotion be fear? Does this challenge to my cherished beliefs create anxiety that I am masking with anger?"[35]

Further, make sure emotion is used ethically. Generally, it is unethical to use emotional appeals in an attempt to bypass logical reasoning. For example, an appeal to national pride may create an argument for going to war in a way that clouds more rational arguments against military involvement. A speaker may use fear to motivate listeners to act for his or her personal profit rather than for their own good.

Develop Ethos or Speaker Credibility

A third type of **proof**, or reason to believe, comes from your personal qualities, as Chapter 5 points out. In fact, Aristotle[36] believed that your character—a proof the Greeks called **ethos**—is the most effective means of persuasion you possess. Here is his explanation of speaker credibility:

> Persuasion is achieved by the speaker's personal character [*ethos*] when the speech is so spoken as to make us think him [or her] credible. We believe good [people] more fully and more readily than others: this is true generally whatever the question is, and absolutely true where exact certainty is impossible and opinions are divided.

This means that people will place their confidence in you if they see you as personally believable, trustworthy, and of good character. Their inner dialogue or reasoning might look something like this:

> She really knows what she's talking about—she's obviously done her homework! And she seems to have good intentions towards me; I trust her. So, I believe her when she says that . . .

In contrast, audiences frequently use the speakers' **ethos** as a reason *not* to believe their claims. The reasoning may run something like this:

> He has no clue as to what he is talking about. I feel he isn't being entirely up-front.

> He seems so arrogant, like he really doesn't care about us. He just wants us to sign up for his pet project. I don't trust him. Therefore, I don't really trust his information about . . .

Because ethos is the perception listeners have of you as a speaker, you can shape a positive impression by paying attention to your personal appearance, showing confidence, making eye contact, using appropriate gestures, and avoiding vocalized pauses as described in Chapter 14. There are four additional components of ethos: good sense, good character, goodwill, and dynamism.

Demonstrating Good Sense

Good sense is a cluster of characteristics, made up of several components.

▶ **Intelligence:** Show that you have a broad understanding of your subject, complete with up-to-date information. Be able to discuss related historical developments, and link your topic to contemporary national and international issues. Then, listeners will recognize that you're not just bluffing your way through your speech.

▶ **Sound reasoning:** Support your claims with trustworthy evidence and logical connections between ideas. Avoid fallacies and unwarranted or excessive appeals to emotions.

proof a reason to believe

ethos personal credibility or character traits that make a speaker believable and worthy of the audience's confidence

⬤ **Composure:** Demonstrate composure by maintaining your poise in a stressful situation. For example, if you become overly agitated, your audience may wonder why you can't control yourself. On the other hand, if you remain composed and controlled, they'll perceive you more favorably. However, note the differences in cultural expectations about composure described in the Diversity in Practice feature.

⬤ DIVERSITY IN PRACTICE

COMPOSURE IN OTHER CULTURES

CONCEPTS OF ETHOS depend on the cultural context. Thomas Kochman, author of *Black and White Styles in Conflict*, explained that credible speakers in the African American tradition are often forceful and emotional rather than calm and composed.[37] Good speakers are genuinely intense in their expression, and sometimes their emotional expressiveness contrasts greatly with the order and procedure common in the Euro-American style of public speaking. For this reason, listeners brought up in the Euro-American culture may consider them loud.

Similarly, Janice Walker Anderson[38] found that Arabs traditionally expected effective speakers to show their emotion and to heighten the audience's emotions through the rhythm and sounds of words. In these cultures, overstating a case indicates the speaker's sincerity, not a distortion of facts; in contrast, a soft tone indicates that the speaker is weak or perhaps dishonest.

Exhibiting Good Character

Remember the Latin phrase introduced in Chapter 1? *Vir bonum; dicendi peritus.* Character counts. Your listeners will believe you more readily if they trust you, so demonstrate honesty, integrity, and trustworthiness by documenting your sources and giving facts that square with what they know to be true. Choose topics that matter to you, and stick by your convictions, even when they are unpopular. Politicians get into trouble when they appear to be poll driven and pander to different audiences, waffling from position to position according to what's popular instead of holding to their core beliefs.

Expressing Goodwill

Your listeners want to know you have them in mind, that you understand "their language." Kenneth Burke,[39] one of the twentieth century's most respected rhetoricians, stressed the importance of "identification." He argued that a variety of "divisions" separate us, but **identification**, sometimes called **co-orientation**, can bring people with diverse beliefs and behaviors together.

But how do you identify with your audience? One way is to find areas of **common ground**—to emphasize similarities between you and your listeners. When you share beliefs, values, attitudes, and behaviors, it's easy to find common ground. However, diversity makes identification more challenging. With a very diverse audience, you may have to search for commonalities on which to build. For instance, every audience shares with you the needs for safety and self-esteem. Here, Susan Au Allen,[40] president of the U.S. Pan Asian American Chamber of Commerce, emphasized common ground with her largely African American audience.

> So I salute you, a cherished ally. . . . We are Japanese, Filipinos, Chinese, Asian Indians, Koreans, Vietnamese, Laos, Thais, Cambodians, Hmongs, Pakistanis,

identification or **co-orientation** concerns shared among speakers and listeners that help overcome divisions and bring diverse people together

common ground specific areas or concerns that both speaker and audience consider important

and Indonesians. Each has a distinct beautiful ethnic cultural heritage, but our goals are the same as yours. We want to remove racial barriers, we want equal opportunity for our members, and we want to create greater horizons for those who follow.

Although you typically rely on commonalities, in some cases your differences will make you more credible, depending on the topic. For example, Gary suffered a stroke when he was 17 years old; consequently, when he spoke about strokes and stroke victims, his words were much more persuasive because of his disability. Patricia spoke credibly about Liberia because she was born and raised in that African nation.

ETHICS IN PRACTICE

DEVELOPING GOOD CHARACTER

© Scala/Art Resource, NY

Quintilian

As chief educator of Rome, Quintilian wrote a treatise on the education of orators (males, in those days).[41] He argued that evil persons cannot be effective persuasive speakers, because they are so bound up in greed, misdeeds, and concerns over being caught in their deceits that they neglect the tools of invention, and audiences will reject them.

In contrast, he urged orators to cultivate justice, honor, and truth seeking before they take to the public stage. To form moral and intellectual character, they should study philosophy, seek wisdom, and pursue sincerity and goodness. Only after they had developed character, should they study oratory. Quintilian was realistic enough to recognize that no orator could be perfect, but he urged each one to be both good and sensible.

Quintilian distinguished rhetoric from oratory. He viewed rhetoric as an amoral activity, meaning that it can function for both good and bad ends. However, he considered oratory to be a moral activity—a means to defend the innocent, repress crime, support truth over falsehood, persuade listeners toward right actions, and promote positive civic action.

Questions for Discussion

▶ What is your response to Quintilian's claim: "I do not merely assert that the ideal orator should be a good man [or woman], but I affirm that no [one] can be a good orator unless he [or she] is a good [person]"?[42]

▶ Do the same high standards hold for people like Peggy Kilburg (Practically Speaking: Chapter 16) whose speaking is mostly informative? Why or why not?

▶ How might our culture be changed if the study of public speaking came during the last semester of every college student's senior year—as the culmination of his or her education—and all other studies were considered foundational?

▶ How might your community be different if every speaker met Quintilian's ideals of being both good and sensible, speaking only to promote moral ends? How might our nation be different? Our world?

Showing Dynamism

Dynamism, or forcefulness, is a fourth trait that influences credibility. It is linked to extroversion, energy, and enthusiasm. (See Chapter 14.) This doesn't mean that you can't be credible if you are introverted; however, your visible enjoyment of your topic, your enthusiasm, and your overall liveliness contribute to your ethos. Think of it this way: Aren't you more likely to believe someone who states ideas forcefully rather than apologetically?

In conclusion, other cultures may not name these proofs in Aristotle's terminology, but that does not mean they don't have them in some form. Across the globe, speakers address their listeners' rationality and their emotional responses, and they follow cultural ideas about what makes a speaker trustworthy.

✓ STOP AND CHECK
EVALUATING ETHOS

Log on to **www.americanrhetoric.com** and read or listen to two of the top 100 speeches. Identify some ways the speaker demonstrates good sense, good character, goodwill, and dynamism.

Incorporate Principles and Forms of Invitational Rhetoric

In many cases, marshaling your best arguments will not resolve disagreements, especially on divisive issues like gay rights and religion. When others disagree heartily with your viewpoints, you may find it more satisfying to practice **invitational rhetoric**, a form of "sense making" identified by Sonia Foss and Cindy Griffin.[43] Rather than focus on winning an argument, you invite your audiences into your world, to understand it as you do, and you then invite them to present their own perspectives. Change may or may not result, but mutual understanding can be enhanced. Foss and Griffin identify three principles and two forms associated with invitational rhetoric.

Combining Three Principles

It is typical to think of traditional argument as verbal dueling with a winner and a loser; in contrast, invitational rhetoric focuses on mutual understanding and mutual influence based on the principles of equality, individual value, and self-determination. It's one way you can develop a dialogical spirit as described in Chapter 3.

1. *Equality:* Rather than imposing your "superior" views on others, you see your listeners as equals. You don't select strategies to overcome their resistance; however, you do identify possible barriers to understanding and try to minimize or neutralize them. In short, you open yourselves to one another's viewpoints.

    For example, say it's an election year. Your classroom contains active supporters of three different candidates. You all have formulated good reasons for your choices. As an invitational rhetor, you share the path you've traveled in making your decision, and you invite your classmates to share theirs.

2. *Nonhierarchical value of all:* By approaching your audience as equals, you respectfully look for the value in their conclusions as well as your own. You don't attempt to demean their position and point out their deficiencies, and you try to maintain a positive relationship with those who differ from you.

invitational rhetoric inviting audiences to enter and understand the rhetor's world and then share their own perspectives; focuses on mutual understanding and mutual influence, not winning or change per se

Back to the election. By not considering yourself intellectually or morally superior by virtue of your viewpoint, you can respectfully recognize the value of your classmates' conclusions, because you work hard to see the point of their reasoning. There's no yelling, no put-downs, and no character assassination of the various candidates.

3. *Self-determination:* Invitational rhetoric may or may not result in change. If your listeners change their opinions or their behaviors, it won't be because you shamed or scared them into accepting your views. And you may modify your own positions by considering their insights. In some instances, you and your listeners may agree to disagree while remaining mutually respectful.

You and your classmates eventually split your votes, but regardless of who's elected, you have insights into the reasoning involved in each position, and you have learned more about working effectively in the political climate that will follow the election.

Including Two Forms

How does invitational rhetoric look in action? This alternative way of approaching issues typically takes two forms: offering perspectives and creating conditions that result in an atmosphere of respect and equality.

1. *Offering perspectives:* You explain what you currently understand or know, and you show a willingness to yield, examine, or revise your conclusions if someone offers a more satisfying perspective. When confronted with hostile or very divergent viewpoints, **re-sourcement** is one way to respond creatively by framing the issue in a different way.

If this sounds complicated, read Gail Grobey's speech in Appendix C. In a narrative format, Gail offers her perspective on not spanking children (to listeners most of whom believed in spanking), and she reframes her daughter's discovery of a prescription pill as an *act of heroism* (saving the dogs from danger) rather than buying into the *ownership frame* (it's mine, and you can't take it away) her daughter presents.

2. *Creating conditions:* You can create conditions in which your audiences feel safe, valued, and free to offer their own perspectives in two ways. First, use **absolute listening**, which is listening without interrupting or inserting yourself into the talk; this allows others to discover their own perspectives. Hear people out without criticism or counterarguments. Second, use **reversibility of perspectives.** While others are sharing their ideas, try to think from their perspectives instead of only your own. The Native American saying "Don't judge people until you've walked a mile in their moccasins" demonstrates perspective taking.

Invitational rhetoric, a form of reasoning often associated with women, is a model of cooperative, dialogical communication in which you and your audiences generate ideas. Because it is rooted in affirmation and respect, it's arguably an ethical way of coming to conclusions. Further, because you're not intent on controlling the ideas of others, you can disagree without figuratively going to war.

re-sourcement creatively framing a divisive issue or viewpoint in a different way that may be less threatening

absolute listening listening without interrupting or inserting oneself into the talk

reversibility of perspectives an attempt to think from the other's perspective as well as one's own

Summary

Whether you are making simple daily decisions or arguing about complex national policy questions, the canon of invention provides you with many resources for making sound decisions. Although it is often impossible to prove a claim beyond any doubt, you can at least interweave a variety of reasoning strategies to support your ideas.

Toulmin's linear model of reasoning shows that claims of fact, definition or classification, value, and policy are based on various kinds of evidence, with a connecting link or warrant and backing that justifies them. Listeners weigh the evidence, data, or grounds to see if it is sufficient and trustworthy enough to lead to the conclusion. To avoid overstating your claim, it is important to limit its scope by using qualifiers. Further, your arguments are more persuasive if you can rebut or counter the objections your listeners have. This also shows that you are familiar with a variety of perspectives on the issue.

Aristotle presented three kinds of proofs thousands of years ago. The first, *logos*, or rational proof, comes from your words. Analogy, both figurative and literal, is reasoning by comparison. Inductive reasoning draws generalizations or conclusions from a number of examples. Then, deductively, generalizations are applied to particular cases. Finally, causal or cause-to-effect reasoning links things that exist in time in such a way that the second results from the first. All these methods require the application of specific tests; otherwise, they can lead to fallacious or faulty conclusions.

Pathos or emotional proofs involve appeals to your listeners' positive and negative emotions as well as their needs. The chapter presented five basic needs: survival, security, belonging and love, esteem, and self-actualization. Emotions combine to form motivations that are both complex and mixed, and emotional appeals need to be tested to see if they make sense.

The third proof, *ethos*, comes from personal credibility. To be believable, you should have good character, good sense, goodwill, and dynamism, but ideas about credibility vary across cultures.

Finally, an alternative way to make sense of complex issues is to practice invitational rhetoric based on equality, individual value, and self-determination rather than on control. You offer your perspectives and create conditions in which others are free to offer theirs. Absolute listening and reversibility of perspectives let you hear and learn from the viewpoints of others. Change may or may not result.

STUDY AND REVIEW

Your online resources for *Public Speaking: Concepts and Skills for a Diverse Society* offer a broad range of study tools that will help you better understand the material in this chapter, complete assignments, and succeed on tests. Your online resources feature

- Speech videos with critical viewing questions, speech outlines, and transcripts
- Interactive versions of this chapter's Stop and Check activities and Application and Critical Thinking Exercises
- Speech Builder Express and InfoTrac College Edition
- Weblinks related to chapter content
- Study and review tools such as self-quizzes, an interactive glossary, and downloadable audio summaries

You can access your online resources at **http://www.cengage.com/login**, using the access code that came with your book or that you bought online at **http://www.iChapters.com**.

KEY TERMS

The terms below are defined in the margins throughout this chapter.

absolute listening 346	argument 327	claim 328
ad hominem 336	assertions 329	common ground 343
ad populum 336	backing 329	deductive reasoning 333
analogy 331	causal reasoning 335	demagogue 339

APPLICATION AND CRITICAL THINKING EXERCISES

1. Watch a movie or television show about a trial, and see if you can diagram the argument or case against the suspect using Toulmin's model. Who is arrested? For what (the claim)? On what evidence (the data or grounds)? What's the warrant (the link: causal reasoning, inductive reasoning, deductive reasoning, parallel case reasoning, testimony by a credible source, emotional arguments)? Is there backing for the warrant? Is the claim or charge limited or qualified? How? What are the rebuttal arguments (the defense)?

2. Stephen Toulmin is a major figure in argumentation. Do an Internet search for "Stephen Toulmin" to find out more about this important thinker whose work is studied by beginning speakers across the nation and the globe. Be prepared to contribute to a class discussion about his ideas.

3. Find a letter to the editor in your local newspaper about a controversial topic. Identify the types of reasoning the author uses and then evaluate his or her arguments. Do they pass the tests for reasoning given in the text? Assess the overall effectiveness of the argument.

4. Find a letter to the editor, a political cartoon, or an ad from a current magazine. How does it appeal to emotions (both positive and negative)? To needs?

5. With a small group of classmates, make a list of possible speech topics that relate to each of the levels of need in Maslow's hierarchy.

6. Watch a movie like *Twelve Angry Men*, or watch a clip of a movie speech found on **www.americanrhetoric.com.** Focus on the persuasiveness of the arguments stemming from logical and emotional appeals and from the credibility of the speaker(s).

7. Visit **http://wiki.idebate.org/index.php/Welcome_to_Debatepedia!** and link to Category Browser/Best Quality Debates. Working with a partner, choose a topic that interests you and, each one taking a side, read through the major arguments. Decide which position has the most compelling arguments and why.

8. Read the speech at the end of this chapter. Stop and answer the questions posed throughout.

SPEECH VIDEO

Read the following speech, "The Benefits of Hunting," for examples of sound and faulty reasoning. For more examples of persuasive reasoning, go to your online resources to watch and critique Gail Grobey's "Spanking," Brittany Farrer's "Limiting Alcohol Ads," and Paul Southwick's "Embryo Adoption."

Student Speech with Questions

This speech contains both sound and faulty reasoning. To guide your analysis, stop throughout your reading and answer the questions inserted between points in the text.

THE BENEFITS OF HUNTING
Anonymous

Animals, I'm sure, have a place in everyone's heart. No one would like to see animals live pitiful lives and die by the hundreds from overpopulation and starvation. Well, this has happened before, and it could very well happen again if hunting is once again abolished by people who are uneducated about its true benefits.

If the welfare of animals means anything to you, it is essential that you listen closely to the biological facts that support hunting as being beneficial to wildlife, for in order to conserve wildlife, we must preserve hunting.

In the next few minutes, I will tell you about the damages resulting when people's right to hunt in certain areas is taken away. I will inform you of the uneducated ideas of animal activists and, finally, explain the differences between hunters and poachers.

a. *What do you think about the use of the phrases "I'm sure," "everyone," and "no one"? What effect does the use of the term "uneducated" have?*
b. *What claim is the speaker making?*

So many people are unaware of the damage that occurs to wildlife when hunting is taken away from a particular area. The best example of this happened in the state of Massachusetts. There, an animal rights group rallied and petitioned against deer hunting. Their efforts led to the banning of hunting in Massachusetts. During the period in which deer hunting was allowed, the deer population was around 100,000. Within the first year after the law was enacted, the population soared to 150,000.

Sounds good? Well, it wasn't! The overabundance of deer created a famine. Deer began to eat forest trees, gardens, and roots. They ate down to the foliage, leaving the plants unable to grow back the next year. Three years after the law went into effect the deer population went from 150,000 to only 9,000. It took the state ten years to return the deer population to normal. Eventually, the hunting ban was reversed, and the deer population has remained at its carrying capacity. I think it is hunting that plays a major role in keeping species from overpopulation.

c. *What kind of reasoning is the speaker using? Does it pass the tests? Do you think her conclusion is obvious? Why or why not?*
d. *She says in her introduction that she will present biological facts about hunting. Does she do so to your satisfaction?*

People often argue that animals were fine before man invented guns. However, before the white men came over here with guns, there weren't sprawling cities like Los Angeles and Portland to take up most of the animals' habitat. In those days, there was far more land for the animals to live on. Today, modernization has pushed the animals into a smaller wildlife area, leaving them less food and less room for breeding. Therefore, it is easier for the animals to overpopulate. Hunting has played a major role in keeping the animal population at a normal number. If hunting is taken away, the animals are sure to overpopulate.

It has been proven that humankind, even in its earliest form, has always hunted animals. Here in North America, before white people and guns came over, Indians hunted animals on a consistent basis. They killed hundreds of buffalo by herding them over cliffs every year. They caught school after school of salmon that migrated up the rivers. These hunts have always played a major role in population management, whether or not you choose to label it as a law of nature.

e. *What argument does the speaker attempt to rebut? Does she do so to your satisfaction?*

However, people argue that Indians needed to hunt animals to live, whereas today's North Americans don't need to kill animals to survive. So what if we can survive on fruit and vegetables? Humans are born omnivorous, meaning it is natural for us to eat both meat and plants. What is inhumane about eating an animal for food? Weren't we designed to do so?

*f. Here is the second argument she attempts to counter or rebut. How well does she suc-
ceed? Explain your answer.*

People also argue that the laws of nature will take care of animals. Hunting has always
been a major part of the laws of nature. Without mountain lions to kill rabbits, the rab-
bit population would be a long-gone species because of overpopulation. Humans as well as
mountain lions are animals. Our predation is as important to other animals, such as deer,
as the mountain lion's predation is to rabbits.

*g. What is the third argument the speaker attempts to refute? What kind of reasoning does
she use?*

*h. Which of the three arguments do you think she did the best job of refuting? Which argu-
ment did she refute the least adequately?*

Animal activists harass hunters all the time. These people have false perceptions of
what hunting really is, and who hunters really are. At a rally against deer hunting, a woman
speaker argued, "Hunters are barbarians who are in it for the kill. Hunters would use machine
guns if they could. Plus, the deer are so cute." I think that argument is pathetic and holds
absolutely no validity.

Another instance of hunter harassment occurred at Yellowstone National Park. An animal
activist was not satisfied with only verbal harassment, so he struck the hunter on the head
twice. Are animal activists really the peaceful and humane people they claim to be? And they
still believe that hunters are bloodthirsty, crazy, and inhumane!

*i. Do these two examples pass the tests for their use? Are they typical? How does the
speaker generalize from them? How might she make her point instead?*

Many of these misperceptions about hunters come from the association of hunters with
poachers. Hunters are not poachers! Poachers are people who kill animals when they want,
regardless of laws and regulations that were set to protect the animals. These are the kind of
people who hunt elephants for their ivory tusks or kill crocodiles for their skins. Poachers kill
deer in areas that are off-limits, during off-limit hunting seasons. These people are criminals
who are extremely harmful to wildlife. Hunters would turn in a poacher in an instant if they
caught one. Poachers give hunting a bad image in the eyes of the public. It's too bad that
the animal activists don't go after the poachers who are extremely harmful to animals, and
stop pointing a finger at hunters who follow the laws and regulations.

*j. Why does the speaker contrast hunters to poachers? In what ways, if any, is this an effec-
tive argument?*

If hunting is banned, just imagine a drive through the mountains on a road covered
with emaciated skeletons of cadaverous deer who died of starvation. No longer can you take
a picture of Bambi, your favorite deer that you saw every year at Yellowstone National Park.
For Bambi and his family were overpopulated, and they slowly wilted away until their final
day. Too bad there weren't a few healthy bucks taken by hunting that year to keep Bambi
and family at a cozy carrying capacity where there was plenty of delicious food for all of
them.

*k. Here, the speaker uses a great deal of pathos. Identify emotional language and images.
Is this effective? Why or why not?*

The argument that animal activists use against hunting is fabricated mainly from
emotions.

If they are personally against killing an animal, I can respect that. But they have no
place trying to ban hunting. It is proven by biological facts that hunting is necessary for
wildlife management. It provides millions of dollars that fund the construction of programs
that help wildlife. It keeps species from overpopulating and starving to death. In order for
wildlife to flourish at an optimum population number, hunting must continue to be a major
part of wildlife management.

A

SPEAKING IN SMALL GROUPS

THROUGHOUT THE WORLD, the ability to work well in small groups is essential in the classroom, in businesses, and in other organizations that regularly accomplish their tasks through cooperative work teams and groups. In fact, in a recent survey conducted by Pennsylvania State University, 71.4 percent of corporate executives polled listed the ability to work in teams as a highly desirable quality in recent graduates.[1]

Working in task-oriented teams often produces excellent results, but it can be frustrating, especially for those participants who are unaware of the dynamics inherent in group work. This appendix first presents some advantages and disadvantages of group work. Next, it gives specific tips for working in two types of groups: investigative groups and problem-solving groups. A description of formats commonly used in public presentations of a group's final product concludes this appendix.

Advantages and Disadvantages of Group Work

You've probably heard the saying "Two heads are better than one." In fact, some people who work on difficult problems believe "the more heads the better." However, if you're trying to accomplish a task with a group plagued by scheduling conflicts, dominating members, or nonparticipants, you may be tempted to work alone. Truth be told, the many advantages of group work must be balanced against the disadvantages.

Advantages of Group Work

Working in groups and teams has several advantages:[2]

▶ *Groups have access to more information and knowledge than do individuals working alone.* It's only reasonable to think that more people equal more experiences and more combined knowledge. For example, a person who has expertise in one area but lacks it in another will need other group members to balance his or her weaknesses. Together, group members can pool resources and generate more information than they could produce individually.

▶ *The various viewpoints that participants bring to the group can help more creative ideas emerge.* By combining personalities and thinking and learning style preferences, the group as a whole can respond more creatively to an issue than if the solution relies on the ideas of only one person. Diversity within a well-functioning group also increases the members' understandings of various cultural perspectives that bear upon the issue.

▶ *Group work provides a deeper level of involvement and learning.* When all the participants do research, discuss their findings, and listen to the information discovered by their teammates, the group can do three to four times as much research in approximately the same time as a single person working alone. Discussions also let group members ask and answer questions that clarify confusing ideas and sharpen critical thinking skills. Consequently, many people learn better in small groups.

▶ *Many people enjoy working in small groups.* Some people are more motivated and have more positive attitudes when they don't deal with a subject or problem alone. Social interactions with others can make teamwork satisfying; not only do group members learn about an issue, they also learn about one another.

▶ *Working in small groups results in the co-creation of meaning.* Because of the nature of information sharing and decision making, small groups are inherently dialogical. Ideally, all members will participate in discussing, refining, and evaluating ideas and solutions.

Disadvantages of Group Work

Despite its advantages, group work has some disadvantages that you should anticipate.

▶ *Working in groups takes more time.* Scheduling meetings and working around the schedules of other busy people takes time, which often frustrates the more task-oriented group members.

▶ *Some members of the group do more work than others.* Some group members may do less work than they would if they were responsible for the entire project. This can result in tension within the group, and often the hard workers resent the slackers.

▶ *Some members of the group may monopolize the discussion and impose their ideas on others.* Dominators can take over a group if the members aren't careful. One reason is linked to personality: Some people are very extroverted and expressive. Another is linked to gender: Women often defer to men in mixed groups.[3]

▶ *There is a tendency toward groupthink.*[4] Groupthink happens when members try to avoid conflict by subtly pressuring themselves and one another to conform to a decision (which may be irrational and unwise). On a national and international level, American military officers in World War II failed to see the signs pointing toward a Japanese attack on Pearl Harbor, and the results were disastrous; in recent years, several world leaders convinced themselves and one another that Saddam Hussein had weapons of mass destruction in Iraq—which required a war to eradicate them. As we now know, the intelligence gathering they relied on was incorrect; no weapons were found. Most decisions your group makes won't have such widespread implications, but you should strive to ensure that you aren't making a bad decision out of politeness or unwillingness to challenge the group's decision.

In summary, although group work offers many advantages, it also has disadvantages. Groups cannot avoid the time factor, but they can make attempts to use their available time together wisely. However, most disadvantages can be minimized if group members are accountable to one another, if all members have a chance to voice their opinion, and if they avoid agreement simply for the sake of peace.

DIVERSITY IN PRACTICE

MALE AND FEMALE TENDENCIES IN GROUP INTERACTIONS

IN HER BOOK *You Just Don't Understand: Women and Men in Conversation,* Deborah Tannen[5] identifies several differences in the conversational styles associated with males and females. John Cowan[6] traces these differences to boys' and girls' playground experiences, which he suggests are "at least a light-year apart." Remember, however, that male- and female-associated characteristics are tendencies, not absolutes, and men and women, especially college students, are probably more alike than different.[7] Nevertheless, Tannen's conclusions are widely discussed, and tendencies such as the following have implications for communication in small group contexts.

▶ Men tend to engage in *Report Talk,* which is informative speaking that relies more on facts, figures, and definitions and less on personalized information. In contrast, women tend to engage in *Rapport Talk* that stresses relationships and personalizes information with examples and stories.

▶ Men's tendency is to pursue interactional goals aimed at gaining power, status, and respect—whether or not they offend others. Women, in contrast, tend to help others and build relationships between people. They are less concerned about winning an argument.

▶ Men tend to speak in a *dominant way,* meaning that they interrupt and display their knowledge and expertise. They also control the topic and set the agenda. On the other hand, women express more agreement, making connections and smoothing relationships. Cowan[8] says that men offer "assertion followed by counterassertion," and women offer "inquiry followed by counterinquiry." Although women suggest more topics than men, men choose which topic to discuss.

▶ Men explain more than women, and their explanations are lengthy. Women can and do explain, but they have fewer opportunities to do so in mixed gender groups.

▶ Men speak more. Conversational time is one-sided in their favor. Women listen more and speak less in mixed gender groups.

To learn more about Professor Tannen's work, visit her website at **www.georgetown .edu/faculty/tannend/** or search the Internet for *Deborah Tannen*. You'll find interviews, excerpts from her books, and other interesting information about gender differences that affect men's and women's talk in small groups.

Investigative Teams

Educators commonly ask students to team up to study a subject and present their findings to the entire class. For example, one study[9] concluded that biology students learn to do "science thinking" in small groups and that their classroom presentations hone the organizational and speaking skills they will use throughout their careers as scientists.

Investigative reporters (students and professionals alike) also team up to probe complex social issues. Because a seven- to ten-minute report (described in Chapter 16) can only overview a controversy, many instructors have students work in teams to study a significant issue in greater depth. Group members then present their conclusions in a more extended period of time. In addition, reporters for a newsmagazine such as U.S. News & World Report commonly work together on a major feature. One or two write the actual story, but the names of additional contributors are listed at the end of the article. Sidebars and smaller, supplementary stories, each written by a different member of the investigative team, surround the featured story.

The advantages of teamwork converge in investigative teams. Obviously, a team can cover a national issue in a national magazine much more thoroughly than a single reporter can. Similarly, students typically learn more and become more involved in a subject when they investigate it with others. The group shares the research burden, which allows a particular student to focus mainly on one area. Not only do team members learn more, others in the class benefit from the variety of perspectives they hear and the in-depth coverage they get when the group shares its findings publicly.

To research and report a topic effectively, the team should have several meetings that progress from an initial get-acquainted session through the research stage to the final presentation.

First Meeting: Getting Acquainted

In your initial meeting, get to know one another and find out each person's interest, knowledge, and expertise regarding your topic. This is a good time to exchange phone numbers or email addresses. Leadership can develop informally, or you can designate someone to guide the meeting and keep people on task. An important role is gatekeeper, the person who makes sure that quiet people participate and that no one dominates the discussion. Another important role is recorder, the member who takes notes (minutes) on what transpires during the meeting.

During this meeting, divide your subject into subtopics, and have each member select specific aspects to research in depth. For instance, you might decide to include a definition, the history, numbers and types of people affected, regions or areas affected, proposed solutions, or arguments for and against each solution.

For the group to be successful, it must hold members accountable. Consequently, before you adjourn, have group members identify a narrowed subtopic and specify the methods (such as interviews or library research) they plan to use to investigate it. Then set a date, place, and time (beginning and ending times) for the next meeting.

Additional Meetings: Discussing the Subject

Begin each new meeting by approving the minutes of the previous meeting. Organize your group's work by writing out an explicit agenda, an ordered list of the items you'll discuss. Proceed by holding team members accountable for summarizing their work and answering questions the others ask. After everyone has contributed, discuss the following: What questions do we still have as a group? Are there gaps in our research? If so, where? What patterns or recurring themes are we finding? Are we beginning to detect a way to organize our final presentation?

Continue to use the gatekeeper and recorder roles. In every meeting, focus on your final goal—to present your material publicly. To achieve this objective, cooperate on organizing ideas and outlining materials into a coherent form. Review organizational patterns (Chapter 9), and think of creative ways to introduce and conclude your presentation (Chapter 10). Identify possible visual aids (assigning a person to create each one), and put someone in charge of requesting the equipment you will need for your presentation.

Before the group separates, have all participants describe what they will do before the next meeting to forward the group's goals. Always conclude by setting a date, place, and time for your next meeting.

Final Meeting: Polishing the Presentation

In previous meetings you researched various aspects of a complex topic. You also used skills from the canon of arrangement or organization to shape your final product. Now, meet once more to finalize all the details. Give each group member a written outline or record of what you've done. Rehearse the actual presentation so that everyone knows her or his role, and iron out any glitches that arise. Check that visuals are made and equipment is ordered, and then congratulate one another on a job well done.

Problem-Solving Teams

What is a problem? Professor Jack Henson[10] defines "problem" as the difference between what is (the present condition) and what should be (the goal). In other words, a problem is the gap between what we have and what we want. We work with others to solve campus, local, national, and global problems. Campus, or local, issues include such things as military recruitment on campus, challenges to free speech, parking problems, and alcohol abuse. National and international issues such as environmental protection, global trade imbalances, elder abuse, and safe water gain our attention. When problems arise, we often form discussion groups, task forces, and committees in which we typically use a problem-solving method described a hundred years ago by the educator John Dewey and modified several times since.

The analytical, linear process presented here of appraising problems and generating solutions is typical of Euro-American culture, and similar methods are used globally. For example, the Africa Region's Knowledge and Learning Center reported that women's groups in Senegal also use a five-step process to solve community problems.[11] In many contexts, a structured, rather than a random, approach results in more effective group work. However, don't think of this process as strictly linear, proceeding only in one direction from point to point; your group may circle back to previous steps, and you may revise as you go along. What follows is a modification of John Dewey's original five steps.

Step One: Define the Problem

It's important at the outset to state the problem clearly. Failure to do so will make your task more difficult later, because it is hard to work out a solution for a problem that is vague. Some problems are simple to define: "Whom shall we recommend to be hired as the new basketball coach?" is an obvious problem to solve after a controversial coach resigns. However, for most problems, you need to narrow the topic and follow these three general suggestions:

▶ State the issue as a policy question, using the word *should*. For example, "Which athlete should we honor as outstanding gymnast?" "What should we do to enhance nighttime safety in the parking lots?"
▶ Leave the question broad enough to allow for a variety of answers—that is, use an open rather than a closed question. The yes or no closed question "Should the student council repair acts of vandalism in the student union building?" is less effective for group discussion than the open question "How should the student council ensure that campus buildings remain free from vandalism?"
▶ State the question as objectively as possible, avoiding emotionally charged language. "How can we get rid of this unfair grading system?" is less effective than "What changes, if any, should be made in the current methods of assigning grades?"

Step Two: Analyze the Problem

After you know the problem, begin collecting pertinent information using the guidelines described in Chapters 7 and 8. Look for the facts—including causes and effects—values, and policies that relate to your topic. Divide the relevant issues among group members and have them consult a variety of sources for information. Asking questions such as these will be helpful:

▶ What are the factual issues involved? What's the history of the problem?
▶ What causes the problem? Which are primary causes? What secondary factors contribute to it?
▶ What effects result from the problem?
▶ What values apply? Are ethical issues involved? In what respects?
▶ Are any relevant policies involved? Any historical precedents?

After completing these two steps, you're ready as a group to explore possible solutions.

Step Three: Set Criteria for Deciding on a Solution

Because solutions must be realistic in terms of time, money, and ease of enactment, set up standards for determining an acceptable solution before you even begin to suggest possible solutions. As part of your consideration, ask yourselves two vital questions:[12] (1) What must we do? That is, what is required? (2) What do we want to do? In other words, what is desired? For example, we must solve the problem with less than $10,000; we want to solve it with less than $5,000. We must have the policy in effect by the beginning of the next school year; we want to have it implemented by the end of the spring term. When you work within budget and time constraints, you'll automatically rule out some solutions as too costly or too time consuming.

Step Four: List Possible Solutions

During this period, your group should generate as many ideas as possible. Because you're seeking possibilities, don't worry if all these suggestions aren't practical. Withhold judgment until later. One common way to generate ideas is to brainstorm, in which group members offer a number of ideas for consideration. Consider using a mind map as described in Chapters 5 and 7 to record these ideas.

Here are some tips for a successful brainstorming session:

- Have a recorder write down all the suggestions, using a whiteboard, overhead transparency, or flip chart.
- Record all the ideas without evaluating them.
- Make sure each person in the group has an opportunity to contribute at least once.
- Piggyback off one another's ideas—that is, encourage group members to use one proposal as a jumping-off point for another.

After a successful brainstorming session in which everyone generates ideas, begin to evaluate each idea against the criteria you decided upon earlier. Often your brainstorming session will lead you to rethink your criteria. So don't hesitate to go back and make necessary revisions.

Step Five: Select the Best Solution

Now that your group has a good idea of the problem, has set criteria for a solution, and has generated a number of ideas, it's time to select the best solution. Begin to evaluate the suggested solutions against the criteria you set. You'll easily eliminate some ideas because they're too expensive, too time consuming, or don't fit your criteria for other obvious reasons. After you have pared down your options, analyze and weigh the merits of those that remain to find the one that members of your group can agree on.

Presenting Your Group's Findings

Whether your group investigated a topic or solved a problem, decide how you will report on your findings, both in writing and orally. First, summarize your work. Then present the information you've discovered or the solution you've chosen, justifying your choice. For problem-solving groups, provide information on why you predict the solution will work, why it will be cost effective, and why it will be easy to implement. Then present your proposal to the audience who will most likely be involved in its implementation. In general, there are three basic ways to present your conclusions.

A Final Report

In this format, one member speaks for the entire group. A group giving an investigative report on a topic such as increasing nighttime safety in campus parking lots all gather data and work together to write up their findings, but only one member of the group actually speaks publicly.

The team members designate a presenter to define the problem for their audience and briefly explain relevant background information. Then the presenter summarizes the decision making process, identifies the criteria decided on for the solution, describes alternative solutions that were considered, and explains and justifies the group's final choice.

To illustrate, let's look at ways a new nighttime parking policy might be announced. To communicate with the college leadership as well as the public, the task committee writes a final report that details the procedures used and gives the underlying rationale for the proposed policy. The committee chairperson then presents it to the board of trustees and to the student council for approval. A press release generated from the final report goes to newspapers in the area. Television stations pick up the story and send reporters to interview the committee spokesperson to gain additional information about the new policy.

A Panel Discussion

In this format, all group members sit on a panel and discuss the issue in dialogical interactions. A leader or moderator asks a series of questions, and members take turns providing insights, with everyone contributing from his or her store of information and opinions. Afterward, the moderator may open the discussion to the audience and encourage listeners to talk with panelists during a question-and-answer period. In this way, the group and the audience cooperate in co-creating meaning.

Each member of a group that studied ways to improve nighttime safety in campus parking lots does research on the topic. They all search for facts, find examples of what other schools have done, get quotations from experts and laypeople, interview or survey college students, professors, and teaching assistants, and discuss among themselves their personal opinions. In a group planning meeting, they share their research findings and identify a series of questions to discuss; then on the day of their presentation, each member contributes to each question during their group's allotted half hour. Afterward, they invite audience questions.

The entire problem-solving group might appear in a "town hall" session on campus. There, in a free-flowing manner, each committee participant discusses the recommended safety policy and the process the group went through to reach it; the committee chair acts as emcee. After the proposal is presented, audience members can ask questions regarding implementation, cost, consequences, and so on.

A Symposium

In this format, each member of the group selects one aspect of the problem and prepares and delivers a speech about it. After the speakers have all finished, the moderator usually opens up the floor for a question-and-answer period.

If a group investigating the topic of nighttime safety in campus parking lots chooses a symposium format, they subdivide the topic, and assign each person one part. The first speaker leads off by describing the problem; the second overviews possible solutions. The third explains the chosen solution, and the fourth relates a case study of a college that implemented a similar policy. The final speaker provides a summary. After they finish, a moderator invites audience questions.

To inform parents of a new nighttime safety policy on campus, the committee might present a symposium during Parents' Weekend. Interested family members then come to hear the task group members discuss their recommendations. One discusses the history of the problem. The next describes the campus-wide discussions that took place over a two-year period. A third details the specifics of the new policy, and the final speaker tells why the committee believes this solution is workable. Parents can then ask questions.

B

SPEAKING ON SPECIAL OCCASIONS

SPECIAL OCCASION SPEECHES are common at celebrations, solemn occasions, and occasions that reaffirm group values. Their general purpose is to commemorate. They also have an integrative function that helps connect people to one another and to their shared goals.[1] Special occasion speeches reinforce and maintain the common belief-attitude-value cluster that influences the group's behaviors.

This appendix provides guidelines for speeches of introduction, farewell, announcement, award presentation and acceptance, nomination, commemoration or goodwill, and eulogy. The Diversity in Practice feature describes some aspects of organizational culture that affect your speech.

Introductions

When people first meet, they ask questions such as "Who is this person?" "What do we have in common?" "What brings her here?" Introductions are short informative speeches that provide people with the facts they need to interact effectively with a newcomer. You may introduce a classmate, a newcomer to your workplace, or a speaker at a special event. Regardless of the type, keep your introduction brief. Chapter 2 provided guidelines for introducing a classmate. Here are some tips for introducing an unfamiliar person to your school or work environment:

▶ Provide the newcomer's name and job title.
▶ Give a few relevant details about the person's educational and occupational background as well as personal characteristics or accomplishments that help the audience know a little more about him or her.
▶ Close by welcoming the newcomer to the group.

Here is a sample introduction of a new faculty member in an elementary school. Notice that it briefly presents her qualifications and provides the current faculty and staff, to whom she's a stranger, with information about her background and some of her interests, which will help them relate to her.

> This year, we are pleased to welcome a new faculty member, Cornelia Baily-Hunter, who will be joining us as our music specialist.
> Cornelia received her B.A. in Music Education from Indiana University, South Bend, and her Masters of Music Education from Penn State. Her vision for the importance of music in a child's life dates back to her elementary school days when a very patient orchestra teacher introduced her to the joys of playing the oboe. She marched in the marching band in high school, joined the college orchestra, and earned tuition money during college by playing in a woodwind quartet that performed at weddings and other social functions. Before moving here to the Southwest to be closer to family, she taught for six years in Pennsylvania.
> Cornelia, we're glad you're here. We know you will be a great addition to the faculty.

To introduce a guest speaker, include some information about the occasion that precipitated the invitation as well as about the actual speaker. Here are some elements to include in such speeches:

▶ Greetings and/or a welcome to the group
▶ A statement about the occasion

◗ Announcement of the speaker's name and topic
◗ A brief account of the speaker's background, education, training, achievements, personality, or any other salient information that relates to the topic or the audience.

Afterward, be prepared to make a few remarks that provide closure. Briefly thank the speaker, and make a simple, short remark relating to the central idea of the speech.

Farewells

Saying good-bye is never easy, because departures cause disruptions that affect those left behind to a greater or lesser degree. This is true whether or not the person was well liked. For example, consider the emotions that arise when a popular professor leaves for a position in another university, a beloved rabbi retires, an unpopular manager is fired, or the seniors on the football team graduate. Because all these departures signal changes in an organization's social patterns, farewell speeches function to ease the inevitable changes that face both the departing individual and the group.

Individuals who leave bid the group or organization farewell, and a group member says good-bye on behalf of those who remain. Both speakers should express emotions—especially appreciation, sadness, affection, and hope for the future. Balance the sadness inherent in the occasion by speaking about happy times; recounting humorous stories is one way to do this.

When you say farewell because you are leaving, include some or all of these elements:

◗ Remind group members of what they've meant to you personally.
◗ List some lessons you learned from being with them.
◗ Tell humorous stories that you'll carry with you as happy memories.
◗ Express both your sadness at leaving and your hopes for the future.
◗ Encourage them to continue upholding the mission values of the organization.
◗ Invite people to write or visit you in your new location.

When you bid farewell to someone who is departing, you speak not only for yourself but also for the group. Remember these elements in your speech:

◗ Recognize the person's accomplishments in the group.
◗ Recognize positive personal characteristics that you will remember.
◗ Use humorous anecdotes.
◗ Express your personal sadness and the group's sense of loss.
◗ Wish the person well in his or her new location.
◗ When appropriate, present a gift as a remembrance.

Announcements

Announcements keep individuals and groups knowledgeable about the goings-on of organizations and groups by providing facts about upcoming events or developments of interest. In clubs and organizations, businesses and faculty meetings, announcements are an agenda staple because they answer the questions "What's happening?" or "What's new?" Essential to these short speeches are details regarding who, where, when, and how much it costs, as the following outline of essential points shows:

◗ First, draw your listeners' attention to the event.
◗ Provide such details as who, what, when, and where the event takes place.
◗ Give both the costs and the benefits of attending.
◗ End with a brief summary of important information.

Here's a sample announcement:

Have fun and do good at the same time by attending the third annual Oregon Food Bank Benefit which will be held Tuesday, August-2, from 5:30–9:00 P.M. at McMenamins Grand Lodge in Forest Grove. Listen to the Big Band sounds of Swing DC and meet some representatives of the Oregon Food Bank, who will be there to take donations of cash or canned goods. The restaurant will donate half of all food and beverage receipts to the food bank. Children are welcome.

So help stop hunger in Oregon a week from Tuesday, from 5:30–9:00 P.M. in Forest Grove. For directions to the lodge, call 503-992-9533, or download a map from www .mapquest.com.

DIVERSITY IN PRACTICE
ORGANIZATIONAL CULTURE

IT'S COMMON to think of organizations as small cultures within the dominant culture; for example, we use the term *corporate culture* to talk about businesses. Your school or workplace has an ethos or personality that derives from its core beliefs, values, attitudes, and behaviors and is often encoded in its mission statement. Organizational culture is comprised of many elements that members of the culture know and newcomers must learn. Here are just a few:[2]

- History—the founders, the founding date, the founding mission
- Political system—the way power is distributed, who leads and who follows, and when
- Distribution of wealth—pay equity, merit pay, bonuses, stock options, and dues or collections
- Art, music, and dress—logos, songs, or uniforms
- Language—jargon or special in-group terminology
- Rituals—banquets, picnics, award ceremonies, installations, commencements
- Folklore—narratives and myths, heroes and villains, described in the stories passed from person to person within the organization.[3]

These last two aspects of culture are particularly relevant to public speaking. In *Theory Z: How American Business Can Meet the Japanese Challenge,* W. B. Ouchi[4] explains that organizational symbols, ceremonies, and myths communicate a group's beliefs and values. The stories that are told and retold and passed from generation to generation explain organizational values, beliefs, and memories. Knowing these symbols and stories is important in understanding the organization; using them in public speaking can be a powerful form of proof to members of the organization.

Awards

Award rituals express the common values of a group; we recognize meritorious work or character traits that embody our ideals. It's common to present recipients with a permanent memento of some sort. When you present an award, emphasize the group's shared beliefs, values, and commitments. In general, award presentations include these elements:

- Name the award and describe its significance. What personal traits or accomplishments does it honor? In whose name is it being presented? Why is it given? How often is it awarded? How are the recipients selected?
- Summarize the selection criteria and reasons the recipient is receiving the award.

▶ Relate the appropriateness of the award to the traits of the recipient.
▶ Express good wishes to the recipient.

Note, however, that some cultural groups rarely single out one individual to praise over others. (New Zealanders, for instance, have the saying "The tall poppy gets mown down.") Consequently, members of these groups may feel uncomfortable when their personal characteristics are publicly acknowledged. If this is the case, honor the entire group rather than a single individual.

Accept an award with a brief speech in which you express gratitude to those who selected you, thank other people who helped you become eligible for such an honor, and reinforce the cultural values that the award demonstrates, as these guidelines and sample acceptance speech show:

▶ Thank those who honored you.
▶ Acknowledge others who helped you.
▶ Personalize what it means to you.
▶ Express appreciation for the honor.

> Thank you, Professor Geffner, for those kind words, and thank you, committee, for selecting me as the Outstanding Speech and Hearing Student this year. As you know, many other students are deserving of honor for their scholarship and their service to the clients in our speech clinic, and I know that each one deserves recognition.
>
> Of course, no student can accomplish anything were it not for the support of a dedicated faculty—and the faculty here at St. John's University is outstanding. I have been impressed not only with their wisdom and skills, but also with the personal interest they all take in the life of each student who majors in speech pathology and audiology. Thanks also to my parents, who supported me both financially and emotionally through these past four years. I appreciate you all.
>
> Next year I will attend graduate school at Northwestern University. I'm sure that when I'm homesick for New York I will remember this honor and be inspired by your confidence in me.
>
> Thank you once again.

Nominations

Nominations are short persuasive speeches that do two things: (1) introduce your candidate to the group, and (2) present brief arguments explaining why he or she should be elected. Be sure to include the following elements:

▶ Name the office, and tell its importance to the organization as a whole.
▶ List the reasons the candidate is right for the office.

Two persuasive organizational patterns discussed in Chapter 17 are especially effective: (1) a direct method or statement of reasons pattern and (2) a criteria satisfaction pattern. When he nominated John Roberts as a new Supreme Court justice, President Bush set the following criteria:[5]

> And so a nominee to that court must be a person of superb credentials and the highest integrity, a person who will faithfully apply the Constitution and keep our founding promise of equal justice under law.

He then explained why his nominee met the criteria:

> John Roberts currently serves on one of the most influential courts in the nation, the United States Court of Appeals for the District of Columbia Circuit. Before he was a respected judge, he was known as one of the most distinguished and talented attorneys in America. John Roberts has devoted his entire professional life to the cause of justice and

is widely admired for his intellect, his sound judgment and personal decency. . . . He's a man of extraordinary accomplishment and ability. He has a good heart. He has the qualities Americans expect in a judge: experience, wisdom, fairness, and civility. He has profound respect for the rule of law and for the liberties guaranteed to every citizen. He will strictly apply the Constitution in laws, not legislate from the bench. He is also a man of character who loves his country and his family. I'm pleased that his wife, Jane, and his two beautiful children, Jack and Josie, could be with us tonight. . . .

Commemorative Events

Commemorative speeches emphasize the audience's ideals, history, and memories; they are common at breakfast, luncheon, and dinner meetings, as well as at conventions and commencement ceremonies. Although their basic purpose is to inspire and to reinforce beliefs and values, these special occasion speeches are often entertaining as well. Each speech is different; however, the following characteristics are typical:

▶ *Build the speech around a theme.* Find out in advance if one has already been selected for the occasion; if so, prepare your remarks around it. If not, select your own inspiring theme. Amari Howard built her classroom speech around the theme "no day but today," words from a song from the Broadway musical *Rent*. Farah Walters,[6] President and Chief Executive Officer, University Hospitals of Cleveland, explains her theme in this excerpt from a keynote address she gave before an organization called WomenSpace.

> Before preparing these remarks, I asked the leadership of WomenSpace if there was anything special that I should address. I was told that there might be some interest in learning a little more about who I am and how I got to be the head of one of America's largest academic medical centers; and I was asked if I would give my assessment of where women are today in the professional world, and where I think women will be in the years ahead. I will touch upon those topics, but in a particular context.
>
> And that context is in the title of my talk—"In Celebration of Options."

▶ *Inspire listeners.* Inspiration is often linked to positive emotions and values such as hope, courage, respect, perseverance, and generosity. Notice the many positive emotions and values in this excerpt from Barbara Bush's[7] commencement address at Wellesley College:

> Wellesley, you see, is not just a place, but an idea, an experiment in excellence in which diversity is not just tolerated, but is embraced. . . . Diversity, like anything worth having, requires effort. Effort to learn about and respect difference, to be compassionate with one another, to cherish our own identity, and to accept unconditionally the same in others. You should all be very proud that this is the Wellesley spirit.

You can watch and evaluate Barbara Bush's speech on **www.americanrhetoric.com.**

▶ *Pay special attention to language.* To make your speech both inspiring and memorable, choose vivid, moving, and interesting words and phrases. Describe scenes in detail so that your hearers can form images in their minds; select words that are rich in connotative meanings. Some of the most famous inspirational lines come from John F. Kennedy's[8] inaugural address:

> Let the word go forth from this time and place, to friend and foe alike, that the torch has been passed to a new generation of Americans . . . proud of our ancient heritage and unwilling to witness or permit the slow undoing of those human rights to which this Nation has always been committed, and to which we are committed today at home and around the world.

Let every nation know, whether it wishes us well or ill, that we shall pay any price, bear any burden, meet any hardship, support any friend, oppose any foe, to assure the survival and the success of liberty.

This we pledge and more. . . .

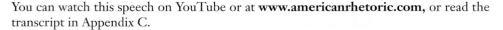

You can watch this speech on YouTube or at **www.americanrhetoric.com,** or read the transcript in Appendix C.

▶ *When appropriate, use humor.* For certain events, such as after-dinner speeches whose major purpose is to entertain, humor is almost essential. This example comes from the opening of psychiatrist Mark Servis's[9] commencement address at the UC Davis School of Medicine:

> . . . I want to talk to you, soon-to-be-full-fledged doctors, about mystery, myth and meaning in medicine. But first I'd love to hear you explain to me the mystery, myth, and meaning of choosing a psychiatrist to speak to you at your graduation. What does it say about this class that a psychiatrist, a shrink, is your choice of speaker? I'm not sure, but I think, in part, it is because you are a daring and bold group, unafraid—and I commend you. But what is going to happen now when someone asks you, or your family members and friends who are here today, "Have you ever seen a psychiatrist?" Think about it, you could be in trouble. Let me encourage you all to not be too literal in your answer to that question.

▶ *Be relatively brief.* These speaking occasions are generally not times to develop an extensive policy speech or to provide detailed information. Rather, they are times to state major themes that reinforce important values.

For further examples, go to **http://dir.yahoo.com/Education/Graduation/Speeches/** and read or watch commencement addresses from a variety of speakers.

Tributes

Tributes are commemorative speeches that highlight and reinforce important cultural beliefs, values, and behaviors. A tribute (called an *encomium* in Latin) praises the qualities of a person (the Basque artist, Jorge Oteiza), thing (dogs), idea (love), organization (NASA), event (D-Day), or group (members of a legendary sports team). Subjects may be living or deceased. A tribute for a living subject should focus on the person's character and achievements; tributes to historical characters should balance the subject's virtues and accomplishments. Keisha Walkes' nomination of Barbara Jordan "Person of the Century" (outlined in Appendix C) has all the elements of a tribute. George Graham Vest, Missouri lawyer and U.S. Senator, gave this tribute to dogs during a lawsuit over a foxhound killed by a sheep farmer[10]:

> Gentlemen of the Jury: The best friend a man has in the world may turn against him and become his enemy. His son or daughter that he has reared with loving care may prove ungrateful. . . . The money that a man has, he may lose. . . . The people who are prone to fall on their knees to do us honor when success is with us, may be the first to throw the stone of malice when failure settles its cloud upon our heads.
>
> The one absolutely unselfish friend that man can have in this selfish world, the one that never deserts him, the one that never proves ungrateful or treacherous is his dog. A man's dog stands by him in prosperity and in poverty, in health and in sickness. He will sleep on the cold ground, where the wintry winds blow and the snow drives fiercely, if only he may be near his master's side. He will kiss the hand that has no food to offer. . . . He guards the sleep of his pauper master as if he were a prince. When all other friends desert, he remains. . . .

If fortune drives the master forth, an outcast in the world, friendless and homeless, the faithful dog asks no higher privilege than that of accompanying him, to guard him against danger, to fight against his enemies. And when the last scene of all comes, and death takes his master in its embrace and his body is laid away in the cold ground, no matter if all other friends pursue their way, there by the graveside will the noble dog be found, his head between his paws, his eyes sad, but open in alert watchfulness, faithful and true even in death.

Needless to say, Vest won the case. Here are some guidelines for a tribute:

▶ In the introduction, tell why the subject is significant or worthy of honor.
▶ Tributes are intended to highlight praiseworthy characteristics, ideas, and behaviors that benefit society. So at the outset, identify a few ideals the subject represents.
▶ Consider using a statement of reasons pattern. For example, a student tribute to the baseball great, Ted Williams, gives three reasons to praise Williams: patriotism, perseverance, and charity.[11]
▶ Develop each point with illustrative incidents from the person's life.
▶ This is not primarily an informative speech, although you will probably have to include information about the subject.

One of the most famous speeches in this category is President Reagan's Tribute to the Challenger Crew which is available on **www.americanrhetoric.com**. See also St. Paul's famous tribute to love in found in the Bible, I Corinthians 13.

Eulogies

Eulogies, speeches that commemorate someone who has died, are perhaps the most difficult kind to give because of the sadness of the occasion. Don't worry about summarizing the person's entire life; instead, highlight things that celebrate the person's personality and the virtues she or he embodied and then focus on sharing your feelings and your experiences to comfort other mourners. For example, here are some lines from Jonah Goldberg's eulogy for his father:[12]

> . . . I think it would be a mistake to think my dad's wisdom and his humor were different facets of his personality. For him, "humor" and "wisdom" were different words for the same thing. After all, a sense of humor is merely the ability to see connections between things we haven't noticed before (while laughter is what we do when we realize that those connections should have been obvious all along). Is wisdom really such a different thing?
>
> Maybe it is, but it never really seemed to be in my dad.
>
> Call it wisdom or humor, my dad saw the world through different lenses. . . . what was obvious for my dad was often insightful, profound, or hilarious to the rest of us. And, conversely, what was obvious to most people could be a complete mystery to him. To call my dad "handy" or overly burdened with street smarts would be a stretch.

Here are some guidelines for preparing a eulogy:

▶ If you're the only person giving a eulogy, consult family members and friends for insights and anecdotes that capture essential personal characteristics or positive traits. This also gives you an opportunity to learn if there is information the family prefers you *not* mention.
▶ Draw from your memories, and share appropriate feelings and experiences.
▶ Keep in mind your goal, which is to appropriately celebrate the deceased person's life by focusing on positive, memorable characteristics and accomplishments.
▶ Humor, used sensitively, can be appropriate and comforting.

▶ Consider using the wave pattern and organize your eulogy around a repeated theme like "Harry was an honest, honorable man . . ." or "John was a devoted friend . . ." or "Molly had enough energy for three people . . ." Support each crest of the wave with an illustrative example.

▶ Often, lines from poetry or the deceased's favorite lyrics work well.

▶ Don't worry about delivery. If you break down or otherwise show your emotions, your audience will be sympathetic. If you think losing control will be a problem, write out and read your eulogy, or speak with the person officiating beforehand and ask him or her to take over if you simply cannot continue. (For an example of appropriate emotion in a eulogy, watch Cher's speech at the memorial service for Sonny Bono, her former husband. It's available at **www.americanrhetoric.com.**)

▶ Keep it short. Unless you're told otherwise, limit your remarks to five to ten minutes.

▶ For additional examples of eulogies, see Famous Eulogies at the Public Speaking Tips website: **http://www.speaking-tips.com/Eulogies/.**

In summary, special occasion speeches function to integrate the members of the group with one another and with the community in which they exist. You'll hear these talks in a variety of organizations—from clubs and volunteer associations to business, educational, and religious institutions. You may have numerous opportunities to introduce newcomers, present awards, give announcements, and make other short speeches on special occasions.

SAMPLE SPEECHES
Student Speeches

Self-Introduction

Text of a speech of self-introduction (Chapter 2).

Mona Bradsher
Mona was assigned to introduce herself by telling something unique. You can watch a video of her delivering her speech on the book's Web site.

My name is Mona Bradsher. I'm a junior, although I'm older than most juniors at our school. In my speech, I want to introduce you to a very persuasive 6-year-old. Through her, you'll learn why I have come back to finish my college degree after a ten-year break from school.

When I was 18, I started college like many of you. But, unlike most of you, I dropped out when I was 20—in the middle of my sophomore year. I left school because I wanted to get married to a man named Jason. I'd met him the summer before, and we had fallen in love. Jason and I did get married and we had a daughter, Sasha.

In my case, the fairy tales were wrong: Jason and I didn't live happily ever after. We divorced just before our fifth wedding anniversary. So there I was—a 25-year-old single mom with a child to raise. My income was pretty low, because I didn't have enough education to get a job that paid well. It was hard to get by on what I could make and the small amount of child support that Jason paid each month. We didn't go out for dinners or movies, but we did eat healthy meals at home. We didn't have money for a nice car, so we used the bus system. When Sasha was sick, I'd have to work extra hours to pay the doctor's bill and the cost of prescriptions. So it was tough, and I worried that as my daughter got older I wouldn't be able to support her on what I made. I felt really trapped.

Last year Sasha started school. One day she came home and told me her teacher had taught them about the importance of education. Sasha's teacher had put up a chart showing the difference between what high school graduates and college graduates make. Her teacher also talked about how education helps every person fulfill his or her individual potential and lead a fuller life. The teacher told all the children that education was the most important gift they could give themselves. So Sasha said to me, "Mommy, now that I'm going to school, why don't you go too?" At first I told Sasha that mommy had to work to pay for our apartment and food, but Sasha would have none of that. She insisted that I should go to school. I don't know how many of you have tried to argue with a very insistent 6-year-old, but take my word for it: You can't win! Because my daughter was so persistent, I checked around and found out there is an educational loan program specifically for older students who want to return to school and complete their education. I qualified, and I'll keep getting the loan as long as I maintain a B average. So far, my average is above that because Sasha and I have a deal: We study together for three hours every night.

And that's why I'm here now. That's why I've come back to finish my degree after a ten-year break. I'm here because my daughter reminded me of the importance of education.

If I can learn an important lesson from a 6-year-old, then I can learn other important lessons from the teachers at our university.

Lifegems: Cremains into Diamonds

Text of a well-researched informative speech. (Chapter 8, Chapter 16)

Chris Russie
Chris gave this informative speech while he was a member of his university's speech team. Competitive speeches require excellent research and source citation within the speech. You can watch a video of Chris delivering his speech on the book's Web site.

Do you know that with use of modern technology you can be made into a perfect and permanent object of incredible beauty? There is one down side, however—first you have to die.

What am I talking about? you may ask yourself. Well, I'll tell you. A new company called LifeGem can take your cremated ashes and make diamonds out of you. Creepy? Perhaps, but before passing judgment, we should examine the company and their diamonds, the process for making these diamonds, and finally the need that such a service fulfills in our society. LifeGem allows people in the search for immortality to find it in some degree, in innovation.

What is LifeGem? LifeGem is a company, but more than that, it is a product and an idea that helps people deal with the loss of the recently departed. According to their Web site, LifeGem.com, this company was founded after three years of intensive research and development. They produce certified, high-quality diamonds from the cremated ashes of people—or their pets.

LifeGem believes that it is important to honor the dead, but that the experience of the survivors is equally important. They hope to be able to provide for families' distinct and individual needs, in producing a memorial to the ones they have lost.

Since the *Chicago Tribune* ran a front-page article about LifeGem on August-20th, the company's Web site has received approximately 20,000 hits daily, according to the September-13th *The Vista* Online.

In their product line, LifeGem carries between .25 carat diamonds for about $2,000—minimum order of two—and 1.0 carat diamonds, which cost about $14,000. Presently the diamonds come in three colors: blue, yellow, and red; in the future, they plan to create clear diamonds as well.

In order to assure customers of the quality of their diamonds and to avoid any bias, LifeGem anonymously sent diamonds to be certified for quality by the European Gemological Laboratory before going public. . . . Greg Herro, head of LifeGem Memorials, claims that an August-21st news release by Reuters reported the diamonds are of the same quality "you would find at Tiffany's." The European Gemological Laboratory, according to the August-22nd *Milwaukee Journal Sentinel*, has since been certifying all of LifeGem's diamonds.

The idea for LifeGem started in 2001, according to the August-20th *Chicago Tribune*, when its creator and current chief operating officer, Rusty VandenBiesen, decided that he didn't want his final resting place to be in a cemetery or in an urn left on a fireplace mantle. He didn't know much about biochemistry or synthetic diamonds, but given that the body is in large part carbon, he figured that it should be possible to make diamonds, if he could find some way to extract a person's carbon.

This might lead one to ask, how are LifeGems made? LifeGem clients take a posthumous trip around the world. This trip has five stages: a European lab, a crematorium in Chicago, another lab in Pennsylvania, back to Europe, and finally, home. After several years of trial and error, an American-owned lab outside of Munich successfully produced diamonds out of a cadaver, claiming that one body could yield up to fifty stones of varying sizes. That number has now been increased to over one hundred stones, according to LifeGem.com. This trip is of course the first and most important step, for without it the rest of our journey would be impossible.

Just after her death, the client is transported to a cremation facility—let's say in Chicago—that has an arrangement with LifeGem. She is then stored for one or two days, according to state law.

After that, she undergoes a special cremation where technicians control oxygen levels in order to minimize the conversion of the carbon into carbon dioxide. Before the incineration has been completed, the technicians halt the process long enough to collect the carbon. The cremation process then continues normally, according to the *Chicago Tribune*. Afterwards, the remains are removed from the chamber. Any foreign material such as shrapnel or bridgework is removed and typically discarded, according to LifeGem.com.

The remains are then processed to a consistent size and shape and placed in an urn of the family's choosing. If there is no urn, the remains are sent home in a cardboard or plastic container.

According to the *Journal Sentinel*, the carbon powder that was extracted during the cremation process is sent to Pennsylvania, where it is heated in a vacuum at 3,000 degrees Celsius or 5,400 degrees Fahrenheit, which turns it into graphite. This graphite, in turn, is sent to the lab in Germany or to the Technological Institute for Superhard and Novel Carbon Materials near Moscow. There it will be placed around a diamond a few thousandths of a millimeter across to aid the crystallization process. Next, it is subjected to intense heat and pressure, roughly eighty thousand times the atmospheric pressure, replicating the forces involved in making a naturally occurring diamond, according to the September-3rd edition of the *Boston Globe*. This whole process takes about 16 weeks, according to Reuters.

The last and final step of this journey, as I am sure you have all suspected, is returning home. LifeGem will now send the client, in her new diamond form, back home to her family.

What possible function can this procedure serve? Our society has a growing demand for nontraditional funerals. According to the National Funeral Directors Association, 38 percent of Americans who died in 2008 were cremated, triple the number from 1973. By the year 2025 the Cremation Association of North America expects that number will jump to nearly 60 percent.

A primary reason for this change in American behavior is the rising cost of traditional funerals. Embalming and high-end coffins have raised the cost of the average funeral to $6,500 (and burial costs are extra). In contrast, cremations can cost less than $1,000, according to the National Funeral Directors Association. LifeGem can produce a single, quarter-carat diamond for $2,000. Even with the requirement of purchasing at least half a carat of diamonds, there is still a significant price difference.

This behavior is not isolated to America. One of LifeGem's goals is to break into the Japanese market, where, according to the *Chicago Tribune*, the national cremation rate is more than 98 percent. This is due, in large part, to the exorbitantly high property values.

Another important feature of American society that such an industry cannot ignore is the way that people shower their pets with love, attention, and, perhaps most importantly for this discussion, money. LifeGem plans to market their services in veterinarians' offices across the U.S. "People would wear a LifeGem to show off the love, light, and energy that came from their animals, too," states Herro. The pet market might in fact turn out to be significant, according to the *Boston Globe*. The company has had about one hundred inquires from people who were interested in the process for a person and more than one hundred inquires about using this process to immortalize a pet.

It seems logical to assume that price is not the only reason for this increase. People want to do something original with themselves, not only in life, but in death as well. This is clearly illustrated in the growing number of new forms of funerals. According to *USA Today*, the remains of Frisbee inventor Ed Headrick are being made into flying discs. Eternal Reefs in Atlanta will mix human ashes and concrete to produce artificial coastal reefs. According to the September-29th *Independent on Sunday* (London), Celestius, Inc. of the U.S. will launch your cremated ashes into space, an option that Gene Rodenberry chose. As you can see, people are being encouraged to be creative with their deaths. Life-Gem provides another way they can do so.

One of Rusty VandenBiesen's hopes was that people could have something very personal to remember their loved ones with. He thought that urns and cemetery plots fail to inspire memories and discussions about loved ones who have passed away. He didn't like the idea of being forgotten.

So as you can see, you can be made into a perfect and permanent object of incredible beauty. LifeGem uses an extensive process to produces high-quality diamonds that do fulfill an actual societal demand. LifeGems provide people with a connection to those who have passed on, and a measure of immortality for those who never want to disappear.

Spanking? There's Gotta Be a Better Way

Text of a narrative speech (Chapter 15).

Gail Grobey
Gail was assigned to give a short narrative speech that made a point. You can watch a video of her delivering her speech on the book's Web site.

My daughter Celeste [displaying a photograph] has always been a rather precocious child. She's picked up all kinds of concepts and language from listening to her future-English-teacher mom talk and has learned how to apply them. When given the opportunity, she'll wax lyrical in her piping 4-year-old voice at some length about the Joker's role as antagonist in Batman and how Robin functions as a foil or why the conflict between the villain and the hero is necessary. She's constantly telling me when I'm stressed about school or work or the mess in the kitchen, "Mom, just breathe. Just find your center and relax in it."

Yes, she's a precocious child, but this time let me place the emphasis on child. Her temper is fierce and daunting, like her mother's! She can get very physical in her anger, striking out destructively at anything she can get her hands on. She can also be manipulative (which is really more like her father)!

At times, my patience is driven to the very end, and so I can understand why some parents turn to spanking. There are times when there seems to be no other alternative, when I can't think of any other way to get through to this completely irrational being. And there are a lot of things about me that would make me the ideal spanking parent: my temper, my impatience, my obsessive need to control. And after all, I was a spanked child. But when she was born, and I saw that tiny body and the light in her eyes, I made a conscious commitment never to strike my child.

As she's grown, that commitment has been challenged. About a year ago, she pranced into my room chanting in the universal language of preschoolers, "Look what I found! You can't have it." I looked down and in her hand was a large, inviting, bright red pill with irresistible yellow writing on it. I recognized it at once as one of my mother's blood pressure pills, and quite naturally, my first impulse was to snatch it.

I also recognized, however, that she was looking for just such a reaction from me. She had lately begun establishing clear patterns of button-pushing. I would say, "Give it to me." To which she would naturally reply, "No!"

And so it would begin. She was prepared to throw and fully enjoy the temper tantrum that would inevitably follow and tax me to the end of my patience. I repressed my impulse to aggressively take command and instead, bent down on one knee and asked her with casual awe, "Wow. Where'd you find it?"

She eyed me suspiciously, backing up. She said, "On the kitchen floor. It's mine. I'm keeping it."

All I could think of was how easy it would be to tip her over the edge into a major fight. (The big ones always begin over something small and silly—me attempting to exercise control over something and her asserting that this is not acceptable. We both get lost in our rage.) It would have been so easy to just grab the pill and move into fight mode. But I held firm to creativity over violence.

"Oh, Celeste," I said, "thank you so much. You are a real hero. You found that dangerous pill and picked it up before the dogs could eat it and make themselves sick. You saved them! What a hero!"

The change on her face was instant. She voluntarily and proudly relinquished the pill and dashed off to tell her grandma what a noble deed she'd just done. I remember saying out loud, "Whew. That was close!" It seems like such a small thing, but I see it as representative of the greater whole.

It's one of my proudest moments as a parent: Celeste and I both walked away with the feeling that we had accomplished something important. She experienced a boost in self-esteem, and I ended up holding firm to my commitment and reinforcing to myself my belief that there is always an alternative way to deal with children, no matter how small the situation or problem. One never needs to resort to violence.

El Equipo Perfecto (The Perfect Team)

Narrative speech delivered in Spanish and interpreted into English (Chapters 12 and 15)

Uriel Plascencia; interpreter, Kelly Bilinski
Uriel's first language is Spanish, so he prepared a narrative speech in Spanish; before the speech, he worked with a fellow student, going over his speech with her. On the day he spoke, she translated his words as he paused between ideas. One key to speaking through an interpreter is to look directly at the audience at all times and to speak at your natural rate. As soon as the interpreter finishes one phrase, go directly into the next. Uriel might use longer phrases in some places and shorter phrases in others, depending on his point. You can view a video of Uriel and Kelly delivering this speech on the book's Web site.

Cuando estaba en mi último año de Preparatoria, yo tuve buenos amigos. Nuestra amistad era muy fuerte que estábamos juntos mucho tiempo. (When I was a senior in high school, I had some very good friends. Our friendship was so strong that we spent a lot of time together.) Nosotros éramos como un equipo en todos los aspectos porque estábamos en las mismas clases, hacíamos juntos nuestra tarea, practicábamos deportes y platicábamos mucho. Nosotros nunca tuvimos problemas serios. (We were like a team in all aspects because we spent time in classes doing our homework, playing sports, and talking. We never seemed to have any serious problems.)

En el principio del segundo semestre, se abrió un campeonato de vóleibol. (In the beginning of the second semester, there were openings for intramural volleyball.) Yo no pensaba estar en estos juegos porque yo estaba muy ocupado con mis estudios. (I didn't think about being in those games because I was very busy with my studies.) Dos de mis amigos hicieron un equipo y me invitaron a formar parte del equipo, yo acepté estar en el equipo. (Two of my friends made a team and they invited me to be a part of the team; I decided to play with them.) Ellos me dijeron la hora y el día de nuestros partidos. (They told me the time and the days that we were supposed to play.) Un día, ellos me llamaron por teléfono para saber si yo iba a venir al partido y yo les dije que sí. (One day, they called me to find out if I was coming to the game, and I said yes.)

Antes del partido, ellos me dijeron que yo iba a jugar el segundo juego. (Before the game, they told me that I was going to play the second set.) Cuando ellos terminaron de jugar el primer juego, yo fui a la cancha para hacer cambios y ellos no quisieron cambiarme. (When they finished playing the first set, I came to the court to switch players, and they didn't want to switch the team.) Ellos no quisieron que yo jugara con ellos. (They didn't want me to play with them.) Yo me sentí un poco mal y traté de entenderlos porque nosotros teníamos planes para el futuro. (I felt a little bad, and I tried to understand because we had plans for the future.) Ellos ganaron el juego y nos fuimos juntos de ahí. Ellos no se disculparon y no me dijeron nada acerca de esto. (They won the game and we left from there together. They didn't apologize or even talk to me about it.)

Ellos me volvieron a llamar por teléfono para saber si yo iba a venir a los juegos finales y yo dije que sí. Yo fui muy emocionado a los juegos finales porque yo quería que fuéramos los campeones. (They called me again to find out if I was coming to the finals and I said yes again. I came to the game very excited because I wanted to win the finals.) Antes del juego, ellos me dijeron qua yo iba a jugar el segundo juego. Ellos me volvieron hacer la misma cosa que última vez. (Before the game, they told me that I was going to play the second set. They made me the same promise as the last time.) Yo fui a la cancha para hacer cambios y ellos no quisieron cambiarme. (I came to the court to switch with another player, but then they didn't want to switch.) Ellos me rechazaron enfrente de muchas personas porque había mucha gente durante los juegos finales. (They rejected me in front of many people because there were a lot of people during the finals.) Ellos insinuaron que no me necesitaban. (They meant they didn't need me.) Yo estaba muy decepcionado y me sentí muy estúpido enfrente de ellos. Yo me fui de la cancha y no pude entender por qué ellos me hicieron esto. (I was very disappointed and I felt so stupid in front of them. I left the court, and I couldn't understand why they made this promise.) Nosotros no habíamos tenido problemas y no supe cuál era el problema. (We hadn't had any problems, and I didn't know what was wrong.) Yo me esperé para ver si ellos ganaban (I waited there to see if they would win) pero no ganaron y me fui inmediatamente de ahí. (but they didn't, and I left immediately.)

Yo estaba pensando todo el día acerca de cuál fue el problema porque yo pensaba que nuestra amistad era más fuerte que un estúpido juego. (I thought the whole day about what was wrong, because I believed our friendship was stronger than a stupid game.) Ellos no podían decir que yo era un mal jugador porque yo era mejor que ellos. (They couldn't say that I was a bad player, because I was actually a better player.) Yo me sentí muy triste porque ellos no me habían hecho algo como esto antes. (I felt very bad because they had made a promise like this before.) Yo traté de entender la situación pero no pude. (I was trying to understand the situation but I couldn't.)

Al siguiente día, (The next day,) uno de mis amigos me estaba buscando para disculparse. El sabía lo que hizo y trató de explicarme y disculparse. (one of these friends was looking for me to apologize. He knew what he had done and he tried to explain to me and apologize.) Yo lo perdoné. (I forgave him.) Cuando me amigo trató de disculparse, yo no lo estaba escuchando. Yo estaba escuchando mi corazón y a Dios. (When my friend was trying to apologize, I didn't listen to him. I was listening to my heart and God.) Yo aprendí de Dios a perdonar y esta es la razón por que yo lo perdoné. (I learned from God to forgive, and this is the reason why I forgave him.) Nosotros somos amigos otra vez. (We are friends again.) El aprendió una lección y estoy seguro que él no lo volverá a hacer a nadie. (He learned a lesson, and I am sure that he won't do this again to anybody.)

How to Write and Pronounce the Vietnamese Alphabet

Demonstration speech (Chapter 16) with a visual aid (Chapter 13)

NamKy Nguyen
NamKy's assignment was to give a short how-to or demonstration speech. He uses a document camera to display the letters as he writes them. A video of NamKy performing his speech is on the book's Web site.

General Purpose: To demonstrate

Specific Purpose: To show my audience how to write and pronounce the Vietnamese alphabet

Central Idea: Vietnamese is easy to write but hard to speak.

Introduction

I. *Xin chào các ban!* Don't worry, I'm fine; I just spoke a bit of Vietnamese.
II. We live near Portland, which has many Vietnamese residents; Seattle has even more, and there are eighty million Vietnamese speakers in Vietnam.
III. Is Vietnamese like Chinese? Korean? No, it uses a modified Latin alphabet.
IV. I have had sixteen years of writing, reading, talking, studying, and dating in Vietnamese, so I think I can consider myself as an expert.
V. In this speech, I'll illustrate the Vietnamese alphabet, pronounce the letters, and teach you some Vietnamese words.

Body

I. First, I will write and pronounce the twenty-nine letters of the Vietnamese alphabet.
    A. [Pronounce each letter] a ă â b c d d *e* ê g h i k l m n o ô ô′ o p q r s t u u′ v x y
    B. Vietnamese is a tonal language; there are six different tones that change meanings.
       1. The six tones are level [*ma*], rising [*má*], falling [*mà*], dipping-rising [*mă*], rising-glottalized [*mã*], and low glottalized [*ma.*].
       2. For example, a level tone on *ma* means "ghost," a rising tone [*má*] means "mom."
       3. The tone changes the meaning; it can be the opposite.
II. Some common Vietnamese words are *Xin chao* [greeting—polite, respectful] and *Cam on* [thank you].

Conclusion

I. Today, I have showed you how to write and pronounce Vietnamese, and I taught you a couple of words.
II. The alphabet wasn't so hard, was it?
III. Have a great time when you meet a Vietnamese person and *Xin chao.*

A Toast to Barbara Jordan

Special occasion speech that emphasizes cultural values (Chapter 17 and Appendix B)

Keisha Walkes
This was a showcase speech given at Missouri State University. Keisha's tribute is a good ex-ample of a speech that aims "to commemorate"; she asked her audience to imagine themselves in a specific ceremonial setting.

General Purpose: To commemorate

Specific Purpose: To pay tribute to the politician, educator, and leader, the late Barbara Jordan

Thesis Statement: Barbara Jordan had a tremendous impact on the views and beliefs of America and on the governance of the United States.

I. President Bush, members of Congress, distinguished guests, ladies and gentlemen: it is my pleasure to welcome you to the first Woman of the Century Awards Gala.
    A. We gather to chat, mingle, exchange pleasantries, and pay tribute to an extraordinary woman who has played many roles in her lifetime.
    B. She has been a politician, educator, inspirational speaker, and leader, whom Senator Barbara Boxer calls a pioneer and riveting orator.
    C. I think of her as the First Lady because of the many firsts she has pioneered.

Transition: Let's get to know something about our honoree.
I. Our awardee was born February-21, 1936, in Houston, Texas; as the daughter of a Baptist minister, she was practically raised in church.
II. She graduated magna cum laude from Texas Southern University in 1956.
   A. She received her law degree from Boston University.
   B. She has honorary doctorate degrees from twenty-five colleges and universities.
III. She has many firsts.
   A. She was part of the first debate team from a Black university to compete in the annual forensics tournament at Baylor College.
   B. She was the first Black elected to the Texas Senate.
   C. She was the first Black woman governor in U.S. history (she served for one day).

Transition: Let's now look at why she is our Woman of the Century.
I. A Woman of the Century should be authentic as a leader.
   A. Jordan struggled to break the color barrier.
   B. She refused to accept her position as a "woman," and she spoke up.
II. A Woman of the Century should have integrity and moral resolve.
   A. Jordan spoke out for upholding the Constitution.
   B. She spoke out against discrimination due to color, gender, or class.
   C. Her powerful words as a member of the Judiciary Committee during Watergate made a difference in history.
III. A Woman of the Century should have initiative.
   A. Jordan emphasized Constitutional rights.
   B. She realized the importance of education about values.
   C. Her words reached many ears and showed that everyone could make a difference.

Transition: Now, the moment we've all been waiting for. [Propose toast]
I. You yourself have agreed that a leader must have courage, must stand up for what he or she believes, and must be able to motivate.
II. Thus, you have chosen this woman as a leader.
III. Ladies and gentlemen, I therefore ask you to join me and raise your glasses in tribute to your leader, your Woman of the Century, the late Barbara Jordan.

Come Watch Lacrosse

This is a simple one point persuasive speech on a topic of importance to the speaker; he uses a statement of reasons pattern (Chapters 6 and 17).

Andrés Lucero
Andrés was assigned to give a one point speech: make a claim a support it by giving three reasons.

Have you ever sat and watched a long, boring baseball game? You all know the deal: ball . . . strike . . . ball . . . strike . . . ten minutes later, a pop up. Well, if you've endured such "entertainment" and agree that there might be more exciting things to do with your time, you should try watching a sport created by Native Americans—one that is fast and exciting, hard hitting, and very strategic. A sport like lacrosse. As you may know, I play lacrosse for the university. Today, I will explain why you should watch a lacrosse game.

Lacrosse is fast and exciting. In fact, it is called the fastest sport in the world, because the clock runs constantly and only stops for a few seconds when the ball goes out of bounds. Unlike baseball or football, players never have time to rest. For that reason, there are many substitutions during the game. Since there is always action on the field, there is never a boring moment. Watching lacrosse is similar to watching a long rally in a tennis match, yet the game itself is as hard hitting as football.

A second reason to watch lacrosse is because it is a very physical game. Since it is a contact sport, not surprisingly, there is lots of rough contact. If I am not careful, I can be seriously injured. I know this from experience. In my first month of college play, I had a painful introduction to Division I lacrosse. On too many occasions, I found myself lying flat on my back, with nothing but sky in view. I discovered that there are many lacrosse players who set up a kill and look to just cream a guy. However, a player does not have to be roughed up. Some players—myself included—try to use strategy to outsmart the opponent.

And this is a third reason you should watch a lacrosse match. Good players and good teams do not just go out and run around the field, they plan what they will do then they execute their plan. When you watch a game, you can see how the entire team works together to make goals. Most of the finesse teams, those who concentrate on strategy, win more often than those who look for ways to injure their opponents.

In conclusion, you now have three good reasons to watch a lacrosse game: it is a fast, hard-hitting sport that requires much strategy to win. So the next time you find yourself in front of the TV watching a ball . . . then a strike . . . then a ball . . . then ten minutes later, a pop up, get up and go watch a lacrosse game—experience it first hand.

Professional Speeches

Tolerance, Love, and Cooperation: When I Think of Ramadan

Goodwill speech (Appendix B) that emphasizes the value of dialogue (Chapter 3) and illustrates the wave pattern (Chapter 9)

Fahri Karakas[1]
Fahri Karakas is on the Faculty of Management at McGill University in Montreal, Canada. This is how he opens his speech, given at the Interfaith Dinner of Dialogue Foundation in Montreal, December 2004. It is a good illustration of the wave pattern.

. . . It is a great pleasure to share this celebration and dinner with you. We are hundreds of people here from various races, different religions, and diverse backgrounds. All of us united, committed, excited, and together under one roof. This is a vivid portrait of the cosmopolitan and multicultural Canadian society. A model of richness as a result of diversity. A living model of democracy and peaceful coexistence. I want to convey my sincere congratulations and thanks to Dialogue Foundation of Montreal for preparing this special occasion for us. I am especially impressed with our friends' sincerity, kindness, generosity, openness, and eagerness to learn. They have been very effective in educating me and others about international religious topics, as well as in promoting an open interfaith dialogue in Montreal.

In the first part, as a practicing Muslim, I would like to share with you a few words on my personal reflections on the month of Ramadan, Ramadan practices, and fasting experiences. Ramadan is commonly called the "Lord of Eleven Months." It is a very special month for Muslims filled with lots of blessings, happiness, love, and sharing.

Personally, I always remember missing Ramadan throughout the year. Ramadan is accepted as our lovely, kind, valued guest. Ramadan is welcomed with great joy, excitement, tranquility, and peace. When I think of Ramadan; I remember all values, people, times, and contexts—all very valuable to me.

When I think of Ramadan, I remember Turkey—my beloved country—the home bed (cradle) of 27 different civilizations. When I think of Ramadan, I remember Istanbul—the city I am in love with, with all its grandeur and mystery.

When I think of Ramadan, I remember special *iftar* (dinner) tents built on every corner in Istanbul—throughout the streets of Uskudar, Sultanahmet, and Eyup. *Iftar* tents are ready, welcoming you everywhere with great warmth. All people eat there as a family, as brothers and sisters, without any borders. Regardless of your status, wealth, race, and religion. All people experiencing perfect equality and sincerity. You are busy? In traffic? Could not reach home? Not have enough money? You just break your fast or have your dinner in the streets.

When I think of Ramadan, I remember my dear mother . . . who cooked a lot of meals, so delicious Turkish cuisine, *tarhana* soups, *boreks*, and *kebaps*, for me. When I think of Ramadan, I remember being awakened by my father in the middle of the night at 4 A.M. for *sahur* (midnight supper). I remember having, sharing our meal as well as our compassion and love together, in an original context in the middle of the night.

When I think of Ramadan, I remember fasting. And I remember—during the day of fasting—especially just before fast breaking, feeling so elevated, so purified, so excited, so awkward, so happy, like a baby. It is a peak experience. . . .

Inaugural

Commemorative speech notable for its effective use of language (Chapter 12, Appendix B)

John F. Kennedy[2]
President Kennedy's 1960 Inaugural speech, composed with the aid of speechwriter Ted Sorensen, is number two on www.americanrhetoric.com's list of 100 best speeches (behind Martin Luther King's "I Have a Dream" speech). It has become the standard to which other presidents aspire. You can watch it online at www.americanrhetoric.com.

Vice President Johnson, Mr. Speaker, Mr. Chief Justice, President Eisenhower, Vice President Nixon, President Truman, Reverend Clergy, fellow citizens:

We observe today not a victory of party, but a celebration of freedom—symbolizing an end, as well as a beginning—signifying renewal, as well as change. For I have sworn before you and Almighty God the same solemn oath our forebears prescribed nearly a century and three-quarters ago.

The world is very different now. For man holds in his mortal hands the power to abolish all forms of human poverty and all forms of human life. And yet the same revolutionary beliefs for which our forebears fought are still at issue around the globe—the belief that the rights of man come not from the generosity of the state, but from the hand of God.

We dare not forget today that we are the heirs of that first revolution. Let the word go forth from this time and place, to friend and foe alike, that the torch has been passed to a new generation of Americans—born in this century, tempered by war, disciplined by a hard and bitter peace, proud of our ancient heritage, and unwilling to witness or permit the slow undoing of those human rights to which this nation has always been committed, and to which we are committed today at home and around the world.

Let every nation know, whether it wishes us well or ill, that we shall pay any price, bear any burden, meet any hardship, support any friend, oppose any foe, to assure the survival and the success of liberty.

This much we pledge—and more.

To those old allies whose cultural and spiritual origins we share, we pledge the loyalty of faithful friends. United there is little we cannot do in a host of cooperative ventures. Divided there is little we can do—for we dare not meet a powerful challenge at odds and split asunder.

To those new states whom we welcome to the ranks of the free, we pledge our word that one form of colonial control shall not have passed away merely to be replaced by a far more iron tyranny. We shall not always expect to find them supporting our view. But we shall always hope to find them strongly supporting their own freedom—and to remember that, in the past, those who foolishly sought power by riding the back of the tiger ended up inside.

To those people in the huts and villages of half the globe struggling to break the bonds of mass misery, we pledge our best efforts to help them help themselves, for whatever period is required—not because the Communists may be doing it, not because we seek their votes, but because it is right. If a free society cannot help the many who are poor, it cannot save the few who are rich.

To our sister republics south of our border, we offer a special pledge: to convert our good words into good deeds, in a new alliance for progress, to assist free men and free governments in casting off the chains of poverty. But this peaceful revolution of hope cannot become the prey of hostile powers. Let all our neighbors know that we shall join with them to oppose aggression or subversion anywhere in the Americas. And let every other power know that this hemisphere intends to remain the master of its own house.

To that world assembly of sovereign states, the United Nations, our last best hope in an age where the instruments of war have far outpaced the instruments of peace, we renew our pledge of support—to prevent it from becoming merely a forum for invective, to strengthen its shield of the new and the weak, and to enlarge the area in which its writ may run.

Finally, to those nations who would make themselves our adversary, we offer not a pledge but a request: that both sides begin anew the quest for peace, before the dark powers of destruction unleashed by science engulf all humanity in planned or accidental self-destruction.

We dare not tempt them with weakness. For only when our arms are sufficient beyond doubt can we be certain beyond doubt that they will never be employed.

But neither can two great and powerful groups of nations take comfort from our present course—both sides overburdened by the cost of modern weapons, both rightly alarmed by the steady spread of the deadly atom, yet both racing to alter that uncertain balance of terror that stays the hand of mankind's final war.

So let us begin anew—remembering on both sides that civility is not a sign of weakness, and sincerity is always subject to proof. Let us never negotiate out of fear, but let us never fear to negotiate.

Let both sides explore what problems unite us instead of belaboring those problems which divide us.

Let both sides, for the first time, formulate serious and precise proposals for the inspection and control of arms, and bring the absolute power to destroy other nations under the absolute control of all nations.

Let both sides seek to invoke the wonders of science instead of its terrors. Together let us explore the stars, conquer the deserts, eradicate disease, tap the ocean depths, and encourage the arts and commerce.

Let both sides unite to heed, in all corners of the earth, the command of Isaiah—to "undo the heavy burdens, and [to] let the oppressed go free."

And, if a beachhead of cooperation may push back the jungle of suspicion, let both sides join in creating a new endeavor—not a new balance of power, but a new world of law—where the strong are just, and the weak secure, and the peace preserved.

All this will not be finished in the first one hundred days. Nor will it be finished in the first one thousand days; nor in the life of this Administration; nor even perhaps in our lifetime on this planet. But let us begin.

In your hands, my fellow citizens, more than mine, will rest the final success or failure of our course. Since this country was founded, each generation of Americans has been summoned to give testimony to its national loyalty. The graves of young Americans who answered the call to service surround the globe.

Now the trumpet summons us again—not as a call to bear arms, though arms we need—not as a call to battle, though embattled we are—but a call to bear the burden of a long twilight struggle, year in and year out, "rejoicing in hope; patient in tribulation," a struggle against the common enemies of man: tyranny, poverty, disease, and war itself.

Can we forge against these enemies a grand and global alliance, North and South, East and West, that can assure a more fruitful life for all mankind? Will you join in that historic effort?

In the long history of the world, only a few generations have been granted the role of defending freedom in its hour of maximum danger. I do not shrink from this responsibility—I welcome it. I do not believe that any of us would exchange places with any other people or any other generation. The energy, the faith, the devotion which we bring to this endeavor will light our country and all who serve it. And the glow from that fire can truly light the world.

And so, my fellow Americans, ask not what your country can do for you; ask what you can do for your country.

My fellow citizens of the world, ask not what America will do for you, but what together we can do for the freedom of man.

Finally, whether you are citizens of America or citizens of the world, ask of us here the same high standards of strength and sacrifice which we ask of you. With a good conscience our only sure reward, with history the final judge of our deeds, let us go forth to lead the land we love, asking His blessing and His help, but knowing that here on earth God's work must truly be our own.

Ain't I a Woman?

This historical speech is famous for Truth's use of the wave and rhetorical questions; it was delivered impromptu, based on Truth's years of speaking out for equality (Chapters 9 and 14).

Sojourner Truth [Isabella Van Wagenen] (1797–1883)
Men in the audience at the Women's Convention (Akron, Ohio, 1851) argued against woman suffrage for three reasons: (1) man's superior intellect; (2) Christ was a man; and (3) the sin of the first woman, Eve. No manuscript exists of Sojourner's speech refuting each point. However, History of Woman Suffrage (1902) gave an eyewitness summary of the points, including Truth's dramatic delivery. This is the most commonly published version:

> Well, children, where there is so much racket there must be something out of kilter. I think that between the Negroes of the South and the women at the North, all talking about rights, the white men will be in a fix pretty soon. But what's all this here talking about?
>
> That man over there says that women need to be helped into carriages, and lifted over ditches, and to have the best place everywhere. Nobody ever helps me into carriages, or over mud-puddles, or gives me any best place!
>
> And ain't I a woman? [*Said raising herself to her full height and her voice to a pitch like rolling thunder.*]
>
> Look at me! Look at my arm! [*She bared her right arm to the shoulder, showing her muscles.*]
> I have ploughed and planted, and gathered into barns, and no man could head me!
> And ain't I a woman?
>
> I could work as much and eat as much as a man—when I could get it—and bear the lash as well!
> And ain't I a woman?

I have borne thirteen children, and seen them most all sold off to slavery, and when I cried out with my mother's grief, none but Jesus heard me!

And ain't I a woman?

Then they talk about this thing in the head; what did they call it? [*someone whispered "Intellect"*]

That's it, honey. What's that got to do with women's rights or Negro's rights? If my cup won't hold but a pint, and yours holds a quart, wouldn't you be mean not to let me have my little half-measure full? [*To loud cheers, she pointed and gave a "keen glance" at the minister who made the argument.*]

Then that little man in black there, he says women can't have as much rights as men, 'cause Christ wasn't a woman! Where did your Christ come from? [*In deep, wonderful tones, outstretched arms and eyes ablaze*]

[*Still louder.*] Where did your Christ come from? From God and a woman! Man had nothing to do with Him.

[*Turning to another man*] . . . If the first woman God ever made was strong enough to turn the world upside down all alone, these women together [*glancing across the platform*] ought to be able to turn it back, and get it right side up again! And now they are asking to do it, the men better let them. [*Sustained cheering*]

Obliged to you for hearing on me, and now old Sojourner has got nothing more to say. [*Roars of applause*]

[*Note: originally reported in dialect and translated into Standard English.*]

REFERENCES

CHAPTER 1

1. Jensen, K. K. & Harris, V. (1999). The public speaking portfolio. *Communication Education, 48,* 221–227.

2. Lunsford, A. (2008, last updated). Scholarly definitions of rhetoric. Retrieved February 4, 2008, from http://www.americanrhetoric.com/rhetoricdefinitions.htm.

3. Hillary for President. (2008, January 7). Morning HUBdate: Rhetoric vs. reality. Press Release. Retrieved February 4, 2008, from www.hillaryclinton.com/news/release/view/?id=5065.

4. These definitions and others can be found on Lunsford, A. A. (2008, last updated). Some definitions of rhetoric. *Rhetoric and Composition.* Retrieved January 3, 2008, from www.stanford.edu/dept/english/courses/sites/lunsford/pages/defs.htm.

5. Allen, M., Berkowitz, S., Hunt, S., & Louden, A. (1999). A meta-analysis of the impact of forensics and communication education on critical thinking. *Communication Education, 48,* 18–30.

6. Call to Serve. (n.d.) Red white & blue jobs: making a difference with your liberal arts degree (p. 1). Partnership for Public Service Booklet.

7. Gray, G. W. (1946). The precepts of Kagmenmi [sic] and Ptah-hotep. *Quarterly Journal of Speech, 31,* 446–454.

8. Witt, P. L. & Behnke, R. R. (2006, April). Anticipatory speech anxiety as a function of public speaking assignment type. *Communication Education, 55,* 167–177.

9. Peterson, M. S. (1997). Personnel interviewers' perceptions of the importance and adequacy of applicant's communication skills. *Communication Education, 46,* 287–291.

10. Darling, A. L. & Dannels, D. P. (2003). Practicing engineers talk about the importance of talk: A report on the role of oral communication in the workplace. *Communication Education, 52,* 1–16.

11. Waugh, T. (2004, June). The tide is turning. Are you ready? *The Practical Accountant, 37,* 16–17. Retrieved February 12, 2005, from InfoTrac College Edition.

12. See the definition of "dialogist publicity" in K. Wahl-Jorgensen. (2001). Letters to the editor as a forum for public deliberation: modes of publicity and democratic debate. *Critical Studies in Media Communication, 18,* 303–320.

13. Conrad, C. (1994). *Strategic organizational communication: Toward the twenty-first century* (3rd ed., p. 31). Fort Worth: Harcourt Brace.

14. Smith, D. (1996, February). Globalization of the general education curriculum. Discussion leader. George Fox University, Newberg, OR.

15. Galvin, K. M., & Cooper, P. J. (2000). Perceptual filters: culture, family, and gender. In K. M. Galvin & P. J. Cooper (Eds.). *Making connections: Readings in relational communication* (2nd ed., pp. 32–33). Los Angeles: Roxbury.

16. Collier, M. J. (2006, October). WSCA presidential address: cultural positioning, reflexivity, and transformative third spaces. *Western Journal of Communication, 70,* 263–269.

17. Hart, R. P., & Burks, D. O. (1972). Rhetorical sensitivity and social interaction. *Speech Monographs, 39,* 90.

18. Pearce, W. B. (1989). *Communication and the human condition.* Carbondale: Southern Illinois University Press.

19. Wallace, K. K. (1955). An ethical basis of communication. *The Speech Teacher, 4,* 1–9.

20. Ong, W. J. (1982). *Orality and literacy: the technologizing of the word.* New York: Methuen.

21. Klopf, D. W. (1997). Cross-cultural apprehension research: procedures and comparisons. In J. A. Daly, J. C. McCroskey, J. Ayers, T. Hopf, & D. M. Ayres. (1997). *Avoiding communication: Shyness, reticence, and communication apprehension* (2nd ed., pp. 269–284). Creskill, NJ: Hampton Press.

22. Lai, A. (2006, June). Eye on religion: cultural signs and caring for Chinese patients. *Southern Medical Journal, 99,* 688–610.

23. Sallinen-Kuparinen, A., McCroskey, J. C., & Richmond, V. P. (1991). Willingness to communicate, communication apprehension, introversion, and self-reported communication competence: Finnish and American Comparisons. *Communication Research Reports, 8,* 54–65.

24. Weider, D. L. & Pratt, S. (1990). On being a recognizable Indian. In D. Carbaugh (Ed.), *Intercultural communication and intercultural contacts* (pp. 45–64). Hillsdale, NJ: Lawrence Erlbaum.

25. Marsella, A. J. (1993). Counseling and psychotherapy with Japanese Americans: cross-cultural considerations. *American Journal of Orthopsiatry, 63,* 200–208.

26. Klopf. Cross cultural apprehension research.

27. Messenger, J. (1960). Anang proverb riddles. *Journal of American Folklore, 73,* 235.

28. Pennebaker, J. W., Rime, B., & Blankenship, V. E. (1996). Stereotypes of emotional expressiveness of northerners and southerners: A cross-cultural test of Montesquieu's Hypothesis. *Journal of Personality and Social Psychology, 70,* 372–380.

29. DePaulo, B. M., Blank, A. L., Swain, G. W. & Hairfield, J. G. (1992). Expressiveness and expressive control. *Personality and Social Psychology Bulletin, 18,* 276–285.

30. Kochman, T. (1990). Cultural pluralism: Black and white styles. In Carbaugh, Op. cit. pp. 219–224.

31. Weider & Pratt. On being a recognizable Indian.

32. Jenefsky, C. (1996). Public speaking as empowerment at Visionary University. *Communication Education, 45,* 343–355. See also M. A. Jaasma. (1997, summer). Classroom apprehension: Does being male or female make a difference? *Communication Reports, 10,* 218–228.

33. Clasen, P. R. W. & Lee, R. (2006). Teaching in a sanitized world: An exploration of the suburban scene in public communication pedagogy. *Communication Education, 55,* 438–463.

34. Stewart, E. C. & Bennett, M. J. (1991). *American cultural patterns: A cross-cultural perspective* (rev. ed.). Yarmouth, ME: Intercultural Press.

35. Kochman, (1990.) Op. cit.; Sullivan, P. A. (1993) Signification and African-American rhetoric: A case study of Jesse Jackson's "Common Ground and Common Sense" speech. *Communication Quarterly, 41,* 1–14; See also A. Wierzbicka. (1991). *Cross-cultural pragmatics: The semantics of human interaction.* Berlin: Mouton de Gruyter.

36. Becker, C. B. (1991). Reasons for the lack of argumentation and debate in the Far East. In L. A. Samovar & R. E. Porter (Eds.), *Intercultural communication: A reader* (6th ed., pp. 234–243). Belmont, CA: Wadsworth.

37. Ugwu-Oju, D. (1993, November 14). Pursuit of happiness. *New York Times Magazine.*

38. Pearce. Communication.

39. Arnett, R. C., & Arneson, P. (1999). *Dialogic civility in a cynical age: Community, hope, and interpersonal relationships.* Albany, NY: SUNY Press.

40. Schwandt, B. & Soraya, S. (1992, August 13–15). Ethnography of communication and "Sprechwissenschaft"—merging of concepts. Paper presented at the Ethnography of Communication Conference, Portland, OR.

41. Bavelas, J. B., Hutchinson, S., Kenwood, C. & Matheson, D. H. (1997). Using face-to-face dialogue as a standard for other communication systems. *Canadian Journal of Communications, 22,* 14 pp. [Online.] Retrieved March 3, 2005, from http://info.wlu.ca/,wwwpress/jrls/cjc/BackIssues/22.1/bavel.html.

42. Bahktin is quoted in A. Wierzbicka. (1991). *Cross-cultural pragmatics: The semantics of human interaction* (p. 149). Berlin: Mouten de Gruyter.

43. Quoted (p.352) in McGuire, M., & Slembek, E. (1987). An emerging critical rhetoric: Hellmut Geissner's Sprechwissenschaft. *Quarterly Journal of Speech, 73,* 349–400.

44. Barnlund, D. (1962). Toward a meaning-centered philosophy of communication. *Journal of Communication, 12*(4), 197–211.

45. Stoner, M. R. (2007, July). PowerPoint in a new key. *Communication Education, 56,* 354–381.

46. The transactional model appears in almost every communication text.

47. Crooks, R. (1998, May 11, last modified). Noise. English Department, Bentley College. Retrieved February 11, 2008, from http://web.bentley.edu/empl/c/rcrooks/toolbox/common_knowledge/general_communication/noise.html.

CHAPTER 2

1. McCroskey, J. C. (1977). Oral communication apprehension: A summary of recent theory and research. *Human Communication Research, 4,* 78–96.

2. Richmond, V. P. & McCroskey, J. C. (1995). *Communication: Apprehension, avoidance, and effectiveness* (4th ed.). Scottsdale, AZ: Gorsuch Scarisbrick.

3. Dwyer, K. K. (1998). Communication apprehension and learning style preference: Correlation and implications for teaching. *Communication Education, 47,* 137–150.

4. Beatty, M. McCroskey, J. C. & Heisel, A. D. (1998). Communication apprehension as temperamental expression: A communibiological paradigm. *Communication Monographs, 65,* 197–219.

5. Robinson, T. E. (1997). Communication apprehension and the basic public speaking course: A national survey of in-class treatment techniques. *Communication Education, 46,* 188–197.

6. Witt, P. L. & Behnke, R. R. (2006). Anticipatory speech anxiety as a function of public speaking assignment type. *Communication Education, 55*(2), 167–177.

7. Bippus, A. M. & Daly, J. A. (1999). What do people think causes stage fright? Naïve attributions about the reasons for public speaking anxiety. *Communication Education, 48,* 63–72.

8. Cicero, M. T. (1981). *Ad herennium: De ratione dicendi. (Rhetorica ad herennium).* (H. Kaplan, Trans.) The Loeb Classical Library. Cambridge, MA: Harvard University Press.

9. Staley, C. C. & Staley, R. S. (2000). Communicating in organizations. In K. Galvin & P. Cooper (Eds.). *Making connections: readings in relational communication,* (2nd ed., pp. 287–294). Los Angeles: Roxbury.

10. Quintilian. (1920–1922). *The instituto oratoria of Quintilian* (4 vols., H. E. Butler, trans.) The Loeb Classical Library. Cambridge, MA: Harvard University Press.

11. Style. (2008). *Compact Oxford English Dictionary.* Accessed June 3, 2008, from www.askoxford.com/concise_oed/style?view5uk.

12. Sawyer, C. R. and Behnke, R. R. (1999). State anxiety patterns for public speaking anxiety and the behavior inhibition system. *Communication Reports, 12,* 33–41.

13. Behnke, R. R & Sawyer, C. R. (2001). Patterns of psychological state anxiety as a function of anxiety sensitivity. *Communication Quarterly, 49,* 84–95.

14. Ibid. See also M. J. Young, R. R. Behnke, & Y. M. Mann. (2004). Anxiety patterns in employment interviews. *Communication Reports, 17,* 49–57.

15. Howell. W. (1990). Coping with internal-monologue. In J. Stewart (Ed.) *Bridges not walls: A book about interpersonal communication* (5th ed, pp. 128–138). New York: McGraw Hill.

16. Mount Sinai Medical Center. (2007). Stress: Diseases and Conditions. Retrieved January 11, 2008, from http://www.mssm.edu/cvi/stress.shtml#q2.

17. Bippus & Daly, Stage fright.

18. Robinson, Communication apprehension.

19. Kane, L. & Helmer, L. (2006, October 6). Conquering podium paralysis: Public speaking skills for doctors. *Medical Economics, 83*(19), 31–32. InfoTrac College Edition.

20. Ayers, J. & Sonandre, D. M. A. (). Performance visualization: does the nature of the speech model matter? *Communication Research Reports, 20*(3), 260–268. Retrieved, April 12, 2008, from Mass Media and Communication Complete database.

21. Mount Sanai Medical Center, Stress.

22. Ayres and Hopf have been studying visualization for many years. See Ayres, J. & Hopf, T. S., (1989). Visualization: Is it more than extra-attention? *Communication Education, 38,* 1–5.; Ayres, J. Hopf, T., & Ayres, D. M. (1994). An examination of whether imaging ability enhances the effectiveness of an intervention designed to reduce speech anxiety. *Communication Education, 43,* 256.

23. Ayers, J. (2005, April). Performance visualization and behavioral disruption: A clarification. *Communication Reports, 18*(1), 55–63.

24. Ayres, J., Hopf, T., & Edwards, P. A. (1999). Vividness and control: Factors in the effectiveness of performance visualization? *Communication Education, 48,* 287–293.

25. MacIntyre, P. J. & MacDonald, J. R. (1998). Public speaking anxiety: Perceived competence and audience congeniality. *Communication Education, 47,* 359–365.

26. Finn, A. N., Sawyer, C. R. & Behnke, R. R. (2003). Audience-perceived anxiety patterns of public speakers. *Communication Quarterly, 51,* 470–482.

27. Stockstill, C. J. & Roach, K. D. (2007). Communication apprehension in high school athletes. Texas Speech Communication Journal, 32(1), 53–64. Retrieved January, 2008, from EBSCO.

CHAPTER 3

1. Plumb. P. (2002, Feb. 25). Seminar: Make disagreements more manageable. *Nation's Cities Weekly,* 25, 7–8. Retrieved March 13, 2005, from InfoTrac College Edition.

2. Jensen, J. V. (1997). *Ethical issues in the communication process.* Mahwah, NJ: Lawrence Erlbaum.

3. Ibid.

4. Pearce, W. B . (1989). *Communication and the human condition.* Carbondale: Southern Illinois Press.

5. Berger, P. (1969). *A rumor of angels: Modern society and the rediscovery of the supernatural.* Garden City, NY: Doubleday.

6. Tannen, D. (1998). *The argument culture: Moving from debate to dialogue.* New York: Random House.

7. Berger, *Rumor.*

8. Gates, H. L. (1992). *Loose cannons: Notes on the culture wars.* New York: Oxford University Press.

9. Pearce, W. B. & Pearce, K. A. (2000). Combining passions and abilities: Toward dialogic virtuosity. *Southern Communication Journal,* 65, 161–175.

10. Pearce, *Communication;.* D. S. Grimes & O. C. Richard. (2003). Could communication form impact organizations; experience with diversity? *The Journal of Business Communication,* 40, 7–28. Retrieved March 15, 2005, from InfoTrac College Edition.

11. Jensen, *Ethical issues.*

12. Yankelovich, D. (1999). *The magic of dialogue: Transforming conflict into cooperation.* New York: Simon & Schuster.

13. Pearce & Pearce, Combining passions.

14. Foss, S. & Griffin, C. (1995). Beyond persuasion: A proposal for an invitational rhetoric. *Communication Monographs,* 62, 2–18.

15. Etzioni, A. (1996). *The new golden rule: Community and morality in a democratic society* (pp. 104–106). New York: Basic Books.

16. Annan, K. (2001, February 5). Idea of "dialogue among civilizations" rooted in fundamental UN values, says Secretary-General in Seaton Hall address [Press release and text of address] [online]. Seton Hall University, School of Diplomacy and International Relations, South Orange, NJ. Retrieved May-3, 2003, from www.un.org/Dialogue/pr/sgsm7705.htm.

17. Yankelovich, *Magic of dialogue.*

18. Mallory, B. L. & Thomas, N. L. (2003, Sept–Oct). When the medium is the message: Promoting ethical action through democratic dialogue. *Change,* 2–9. Retrieved May 22, 2008, from www.collegevalues.org/pdfs/galleyproofsCHANGEfinal.pdf.

19. The mission statement is quoted on the group's home page at www.seedsofpeace.org.

20. Seeds of Peace. About us. Accessed June 3, 2008, from www.seedsofpeace.org/site/PageServer?pagename5aboutus.

21. Shalhoub-Kevorkian, N. (2001, March). Using the dialogue tent to break mental chains: listening and being heard. *Social Service Review,* 75, 135. Retrieved April 27, 2005, from InfoTrac College Edition.

22. Tannen, *Argument culture,* 289.

23. Blakeslee, S. (1992, March). Faulty math heightens fears of breast cancer. *New York Times,* Sec. 4, pp. 1, 2.

24. Gardner, A. (2005, February-1). Women missing out on heart disease diagnoses and treatments. TheBakersfieldChannel.com. [Online.] Retrieved February 9, 2005, from http://kero-tvhealth.ip2m.com/index.cfm?pt5itemDetail&Item_ID5116331&site_cat_id57.

25. Quoted in Bartanen, M. & Frank, D. (1999). Reclaiming a heritage: a proposal for rhetorically grounded academic debate. *Parliamentary Debate: The Journal of the National Parliamentary Debate Association,* 6, 31–54.

26. Barrett, H. (1991). *Rhetoric and civility: human development, narcissism, and the good audience.* Albany, NY: SUNY Press.

27. Jensen, *Ethical issues.*

28. Hexham, I. (1999). Academic plagiarism defined. University of Calgary Department of Religious Studies. Retrieved February 8, 2005, from www.ucalgary.ca/hexham/study/plag.html.

29. Avoiding plagiarism. (Last updated 2001, October-25). UCDavis Student Judiciary Affairs. Retrieved February 9, 2005, from http://sja.ucdavis.edu/avoid.htm#guidelines.

30. Plagiarism and the Internet. (2008). Retrieved May 23, 2008, from www.plagiarism.org/learning_center/plagiarism_the_internet.html.

31. Ibid.

32. Many Internet sites explain plagiarism. See Purdue Online Writing Lab. (2007, September 18, last updated). Avoiding plagiarism. Retrieved June 3, 2008, from http://owl.english.purdue.edu/handouts/research/r_plagiar.html;. See also J. R. Edlund. (2001, October 25, last updated).What is "plagiarism" and why do people do it? University Writing Center. California State University, Los Angeles. [online].

33. Mason, W. (2005, May). Make it newish: E. E. Cummings, plagiarism, and the perils of originality. (E.E. Cummings: A biography) (Book Review). *Harper's Magazine, 310*, 92–102. Retrieved December 10, 2005, from InfoTrac College Edition.

34. Kennedy, R. S. (1980). *Dreams in the mirror: a biography of E. E. Cummings.* Quoted in ibid.

35. Sawyer-Laucanno, C. (2004). *E.E. Cummings, a biography.* Quoted in Mason, p. 100.

36. Purdue Online Writing Lab.

37. Avoiding Plagiarism. (2001). UCDavis.

38. Strandy, L. (2007, December 5). Free trade coffee. First place winner. COMM 100 speech competition. George Fox University, Newberg, Oregon.

39. Valentine, J. (2004). The *dun dun* drum. Student speech included in Appendix C.

40. Frist, B. (2004, August 31). Full text of the remarks of Senate Majority Leader Bill Frist. *The New York Times.* [online] Retrieved September 1, 2004, from www.nytimes.com/2004/08/31/politics/campaign/01TEXT-FRIST>html.

41. This box draws from N. Carbone. (2001, December 3). Thinking and talking about plagiarism. Bedford St. Martins Technotes. Retrieved February 5, 2005, from http://bedfordstmartins.com/technotes/techtiparchive/ttip102401.htm.

42. Hunter, J. (1997). Confessions of an academic honesty woman. Grinnell College Writing Lab. [Online.] Accessed May 30, 2008, from www.grinnell.edu/academic/writinglab/forum/con_hj.pdf.

43. Department of Journalism. (n.d.). Academic Integrity Handbook. University of Arizona. Retrieved June 4, 2008, from http://journalism.arizona.edu/publications/academic_integrity/integrity_handbook.pdf.

44. Cited in the above.

CHAPTER 4

1. The 25 percent efficiency rate is widely quoted. See Roach, C. A. & Wyatt, N. J. (1995). Listening and the rhetorical process. In Stewart, J. *Bridges not walls: a book about interpersonal communication* (9th ed., pp. 171–176). New York: McGraw-Hill.

2. Maes, J. D., Weldy, T. B. & Icenogle, M. L. (1997, January). A managerial perspective: oral communication competency is more important for business students in the workplace. *Journal of Business Communication, 34*, 6–14. Retrieved June 4, 2008, from InfoTrac College Edition.

3. Treuer, P. (2006, July 17, last updated). Listening skills. *Student Handbook.* University of Minnesota Duluth. Retrieved June 4, 2008, from www.d.umn.edu/kmc/student/loon/acad/strat/ss_listening.html.

4. Salopek, J. J. (1999). Is anyone listening? *Training and Development, 53*(9), 58–60. Retrieved February 23, 2005, from InfoTrac College Edition. See also Ramsey, R. D. (2007, November). The most important skills for today's supervisors. *Supervision, 68*(11), 3–5. Accessed March 22, 2008, from InfoTrac College Edition.

5. Lenckus, D. (2005, November 28). Physician apologies, listening skills found to reduce med mal claims. *Business Insurance, 39*(48), 4. Retrieved March 22, 2008, from InfoTrac College Edition.

6. Burley-Allen, M. (2001). Listen up: Listening is a learned skill and supervisors need it to improve their employee relationships. *HR Magazine.* Retrieved June 4, 2008, from InfoTrac College Edition.

7. Owen, J. (2007, June 2). Interior decorator cites listening skills as key to satisfying clients. *The Walton Sun* (Santa Rosa Beach, FL). Retrieved March 22, 2008, from InfoTrac College Edition.

8. GIGA Quotes. (2008, April 9, last revised). Listening. Retrieved June 4, 2008, from www.giga-usa.com/quotes/topics/listening_t001.htm.

9. Janusik, L. (n. d.) Listening and education. International Listening Association. Retrieved June 4, 2008, from www.listen.org/Templates/fact_education.htm#edu.

10. Bentley, S. (1998, February). Listening better: A guide to improving what may be the ultimate staff skill. *Nursing Homes, 47*(2), 56–59. Retrieved March 1, 2005, from InfoTrac College Edition.

11. TAMU Student Counseling Service. (2008). Listening skills. Texas A & M University. Retrieved June 4, 2008, from http://scs.tamu.edu/selfhelp/elibrary/listening_skills.asp

12. Lundsteen, S. W. (1993). Metacognitive listening. In A. D. Wolvin & C. G. Coakley (Eds.). *Perspectives on listening* (pp. 106–123). Norwood, NJ: Ablex.

13. Ibid.

14. Imhof, M. (1998). What makes a good listener? Listening behaviors in instructional settings. *International Journal of Listening, 12*, 81–105. Retrieved March 24, 2008, from EBSCO database.

15. Edwards, R. & McDonald, J. L. (1993). Schema theory and listening. In Wolvin & Coakley, *Perspectives*, 60–77.

16. Tannen, D. (1989). *Talking voices: Repetition, dialogue, and imagery in conversational discourse.* Cambridge: Cambridge University Press.

17. Sitkaram, K. S. & Cogdell, R. T. (1976). *Foundations of intercultural communication.* Columbus, OH: Charles E. Merrill.

18. Ibid.

19. Daniel, J. & Smitherman, G. (1990). How I got over: Communication dynamics in the black community. In Carbaugh, *Intercultural communication.* See also A. L. Smith (Molefi Asanti). (1970). Socio-historical perspectives of black oratory. *Quarterly Journal of Speech, 61*, 264–269.

20. Kiewitz, C., Weaver, J. B. III, Brosius, H-B., & Weimann, G. (1997). Cultural differences in listening style preferences: a comparison of young adults in Germany, Israel, and the United States. *International Journal of Public Opinion Research, 9*, 233–248. Retrieved May 29, 2003, from InfoTrac College Edition.

21. There are many suggestions for good listening. See Imhof, M. (2001). How to listen more efficiently: self-monitoring strategies in listening. *International Journal of Listening, 15*, 2–19. Retrieved March 22, 2008, from EBSCO database. See also See Imhof, M. (1998). What makes, and TAMU Student Counseling Center. (2008). Listening. See also University of Minnesota, Duluth. (2002, February 20). Listening skills. *Student handbook* [online]. Retrieved May 30, 2003, from www.d.umn.edu/student/loon/acad/strat/ss_listening.html.

22. Lundsteen, Metacognitive listening.

23. Read, B. (2006, April 7). A law professor bans laptops from the classroom. *The Chronicle of Higher Education, 52*(31). Retrieved June 5, 2008, from InfoTrac College Edition.

24. OrinKerr.com. (2006, March 23). More on laptops in class [email from June Entman]. Retrieved June 5, 2008, from www.orinkerr.com/2006/03/23/more-on-laptops-in-class/

25. Ridge, A. (1993). A perspective of listening skills. In Wolvin & Coakley, *Perspectives*, 1–14.

26. Boyd, S. D. (2001, October). The human side of teaching: Effective listening. *Techniques, 76*(7), 60. Retrieved March 24, 2008, from InfoTrac.

27. Goodman, G. & Esterly, G. (1990). Questions—the most popular piece of language. In Stewart, *Bridges*, 69–79.

28. Becker, C. B. (1991). Reasons for the lack of argumentation and debate in the Far East. In Samovar & Porter, *Intercultural communication*, 234–243; See also K. Sueda. (1995). Differences in the perception of face: Chinese *mien-tzu* and Japanese *mentsu. World Communication, 24*(1), 23–31.

29. Anonymous reviewer. (2004).

CHAPTER 5

1. Christensen, M. D. (1998, March). An idea is only the bait. *The Writer, 111*, 20–21.

2. Bitzer, L. F. (1999). The rhetorical situation. In J. L. Lucaites, C. M. Condit, & S. Caudill (Eds.), *Contemporary rhetorical theory: A reader* (pp. 217–225). New York: Guilford; see also Vatz, R. E. (1999). The myth of the rhetorical situation. In Lucaites, Condit, & Caudill, *Contemporary rhetorical theory*, 226–231.

3. McKeon, R. (1998). Creativity and the commonplace. In T. B. Ferrell (Ed.), *Landmark essays on contemporary rhetoric* (pp. 33–41). Mahwah, NJ: Hermagoras Press.

4. Weinstein, B. (2008, January 15). The ethics of talking politics at work. *Business-Week*. Retrieved June 9, 2008, from www .businessweek.com/managing/content/ jan2008/ca20080115_994641.htm.

5. Murray, D. M. (1998, May). Write what you don't know. *The Writer, 111*, 7–9.

6. Christensen, Idea.

7. Carrell, L. J. (1997). Diversity in the communication curriculum: Impact on student empathy. *Communication Education, 46*, 234–244.

8. Grant, H. (2007, January). Sabina Xhosa and the new shoes. Address delivered 1 Nov 2006 to Westminster College IBM Lecture, Fulton, Missouri. *Vital Speeches of the Day, 73*(1), 36–40.

9. Scofield, S. (1999, August). An end to writer's block. *The Writer, 111*, 7–9.

10. Augustine. (1958). *On Christian doctrine: Book IV* (D. W. Robertson Jr., Trans.). New York: Liberal Arts Press.

11. Campbell, G. (1963). *The philosophy of rhetoric* (L. Bitzer, Ed.). Carbondale: Southern Illinois University Press. (Original work published 1776)

12. Porrovecchio, M. (personal email, 2005, March 29) reminded me of the influence of Campbell's psychological theories on his rhetoric.

13. Monroe, A. H. (1962). *Principles and types of speech* (5th ed.). Chicago: Scott Foresman.

14. Gwynne, R. (2005, March 12 last updated). Topic organization. University of Tennessee Knoxville. Accessed March 12, 2005. http://web.utk.edu/gwynne/topic_ organization.html.

15. Anonymous reviewer. (2005). College of Marin.

16. Gwynne, Topic organization.

17. Engnell, R. (1999). What is a central idea? Class handout for Introduction to Communication, George Fox University, Newberg, OR.

18. Griffin, C. W. (1998). Improving students' writing strategies; knowing versus doing. *College Teaching, 46*, 48–52. Retrieved April 5, 2008, from InfoTrac College Edition.

CHAPTER 6

1. Media Release. (2007, November 27). OSU's Wright named Oregon's "Professor of the Year" by CASE, Carnegie Foundation. News and Communication Services: Oregon State University [online]. Retrieved January 3, 2008, from http:// oregonstate.edu/dept/ncs/newsarch/2007/ Nov07/dawnwright.html.

2. Holman, P. (1970). *The psychology of speakers and audiences*. Glenview. IL: Scott Foresman.

3. Bitzer, L. F. (1992). The rhetorical situation. *Philosophy & Rhetoric, Supplement 1992, 25*, 1–14. Retrieved June 10, 2008, from Communication and Mass Media Complete database; Garrett, M. & Xiao, X. (1993, Spring). The rhetorical situation revisited. *RSQ: Rhetorical Society Quarterly, 23*(2), 30–40. Retrieved June 10, 2008, from Communication and Mass Media Complete database; Thatcher, B. & Fisanick, C. P. (2000). Guide to understanding the rhetorical situation. Association of Teachers of Technical Writing. Ohio University. Retrieved June 10, 2008, from www.ohiou.edu/attw/teach305j/ guide-rhets.htm.

4. Garret & Xiao, Revisited.

5. Psychologists have written about audience motivations for decades. An early book was H. L. Hollingsworth. (1935). *The psychology of audiences*. New York: American Book Company. See also Holman, The psychology.

6. MSNBC's David Gregory quoted on G. Dickens. (2007, June 28). "Today" fans its company's own Coulter-Edwards flame; Coulter a "flamethrower." NewsBusters. Retrieved February 25, 2008, from http:// newsbusters.org/node/13806

7. New London Group (1996) A pedagogy of multiliteracies: Designing social futures. *Harvard Educational Review 66*(1), 60–92. February 25, 2008, EBSCO

8. Collier, M. J. (1994). Cultural identity and intercultural communication. In Samovar & Porter, *Intercultural communication*, 36–45.

9. Rothenberg, P. S. (Ed.). (1998). *Race, class, and gender in the United States*. New York: St. Martin's Press.

10. Collier, Cultural identity; O'Neil, D. (1999, September 21). Ethnicity and race: An introduction to the nature of social group differentiation and inequality [Online]. Retrieved April 23, 2003, from www.daphne .palomar.edu/ethnicity/default.htm.6

11. Marmor, J. (1996, December). Blurring the lines. *Columns, 16*(8), 22–27.

12. Jameson, D. A. (2007, July). Reconceptualizing cultural identity and its role in intercultural business communication. *The Journal of Business Communication, 44*(3): 199(37). Retrieved through InfoTrac.

13. Halstead, T. (1999, August). A politics for generation X. *Atlantic Monthly, 284*(2), 33ff. Retrieved August 29, 1999, from InfoTrac College Edition.

14. Prensky, M. (1998, October). Bankers trust: Training is all fun and games. *HR Focus, 75*, 10, 11. Retrieved August 30, 1999, from InfoTrac College Edition.

15. Oblinger, D. (2003, July/August). Boomers & Gen Xers & millenials: understanding the new students. EDUCAUSEreview. Retrieved June 9, 2008, from net.educause .edu/ir/library/pdf/erm0342.pdf.

16. Jameson, Reconceptualizing

17. Andersen, J. R., & Nussbaum, J. F. (1987). The public speaking course: A liberal arts perspective. *Communication Education, 35*, 174–182.

18. Rokeach, M. (1972). *Beliefs, attitudes, and values*. San Francisco: Jossey-Bass.

19. Editorial. (2006, July 3). Pander-monium: our view: Congress is angling for votes, not solving problems. *Spokesman-Review* (Spokane, WA). Retrieved June 10, 2008, from InfoTrac College Edition.

20. Ibid.

21. Reider, J. (2008, May 22). Interview. Tavis Smiley. PBS. Retrieved June 10, 2008, from www.pbs.org/kcet/tavissmiley/ archive/200805/20080522_rieder.html.

22. Quoted in ibid.

23. Jaffe, C. I. (1995). Chronemics: communicating mainstream cycles to Russian Old Believer children. *World Communication, 15*, 1–20.

24. Levine, R. (1997). *A geography of time*. New York: Basic Books.

25. McCroskey, J. C. (1993). *An introduction to rhetorical communication* (6th ed.). Englewood Cliffs, NJ: Prentice-Hall.

26. Weider, D. L. & Pratt, S. (1990). On being a recognizable Indian. In D. Carbaugh (Ed.), *Intercultural communication and intercultural contacts* (pp. 45–64). Hillsdale, NJ: Lawrence Erlbaum.

27. Miller, A. N. (2002). An exploration of Kenyan public speaking patterns with implications for the American introductory public speaking course. *Communication Education, 5*(2), 168–182.

CHAPTER 7

1. Educational Testing Service. (2006, November 14). College students fall short in demonstrating the ICT skills necessary for success in college and the workplace: preliminary research finds that many students misjudge the objectivity and authoritativeness of Internet sources. *Internet Wire*. Retrieved May 27, 2008, from InfoTrac-College Edition.

2. Lieggi, L. (1999, July 20). Personal interview. George Fox University, Newberg, OR.

3. Rolfe, A. (2008, May 21). Personal interview. George Fox University, Newberg, OR.

4. University of Maryland. (2006, August, last revised). Primary, secondary, and tertiary sources. Guides to Information Resources. University Libraries. Retrieved May 26, 2008, from www.lib.umd.edu/guides/ primary-sources.html.

5. Rodrigues, D., & Rodrigues, R. J. (2000). *The research paper and the World Wide Web* (2nd ed.). Upper Saddle River, NJ: Prentice-Hall.

6. Unless noted otherwise, the information in this section comes from Finding information on the Internet: A tutorial. (2004, August 18, last updated). UC Berkeley— Teaching Library Internet Workshops. Retrieved August 12, 2005, from www .lib.berkeley.edu/TeachingLib/Guides/ Internet/FindInfo.html.

7. Sherman, C. (2004, February 18). Yahoo! Birth of a new machine. Search Engine Watch. Retrieved August 13, 2005, from http://searchenginewatch.com/searchday/ article.php/3314171.

8. Goldsborough, R. (2006, June). Going beyond the Web's surface. *Teacher Librarian, 33*(5), 52(1). Retrieved May 27, 2008, from InfoTrac College Edition.

9. O'Neill, A. B. & Everhart, C. (1997). Trash or treasure: teaching students how to evaluate Internet resources.

Retrieved June 11, 2008, from www.bcpl .net/~dcurtis/psd/handouts/s3-67/. This resource is older, but a recent article says the questions posed earlier are still valid; see Calkins, S. & Kelley, M. R. (2007, Fall) Evaluating Internet and scholarly sources across the disciplines: two case studies. *College Teaching, 55*(4), 151–156. Retrieved June 11, 2008, from Academic Search Premier database.

10. Hawkes, L. (1999). *A guide to the World Wide Web*. Upper Saddle River, NJ: Prentice-Hall.

11. Wolfe, R. M. & Sharp, L. K. (2005). Vaccination or immunization? The impact of search terms on the Internet. *Journal of Health Communication, 10*, 537–551. Retrieved May 26, 2008, from Communication and Mass Media Complete database.

12. Yu, H. & Young, M. (2004). An impact of web search engines on subject searching in OPAC. *Information Technology and Libraries, 23*, 168–181. Retrieved March 16, 2005, from InfoTrac College Edition.

13. Abram, S. & Luther, J. (2004, May-1). Born with the chip: The next generation will profoundly impact both library service and the culture within the profession. *Library Journal, 129*, 34–38. Retrieved March 16, 2005, from InfoTrac College Edition.

14. Yu & Young, Web search engines.

15. Lieggi, Interview.

16. Miller, Kenyan public speaking patterns, p. 174.

17. Rolfe, Interview.

18. Hawkes, Guide.

19. As of June 11, 2008, Wikipedia was available in 253 languages. http://en.wikipedia .org/wiki/Wikipedia.

20. Reuters. (2005, April 8). Yahoo backs Wikipedia. Retrieved April 9, 2005, from http://today.reuters.co.uk/news/ newsArticle.aspx?type5internetNews &storyID52005-04-08T013855Z_ 01_HOL805922_RTRIDST_0_ OUKIN-TECH-YAHOO.XML.

21. Vara, V. (2005, March 28). From Wikipedia's creator, a new site for anyone, anything. *Wall Street Journal*, B1, B6.

22. Paragraph 107: Fair use. (2004, April 30). Copyright Law of the United States of America. Title 17. Circular 92. Chapter 1. Retrieved June 11, 2008, from www .copyright.gov/title17/92chap1.html.

23. For a case study using the Mozart Effect as the topic, see Calkins & Kelley, Evaluating Internet.

CHAPTER 8

1. For information that supports environmentalists' claims, search InfoTrac College Edition for articles that detail the scientific conclusions.

2. InfoTrac College Edition has many articles about Lomborg. For example, see Walsh, B. (2007, October 15). Eco-rebels. *Time*, *170*(6). 72. Retrieved May 31, 2008; West, W. (2003, February 18). Kay, J. (2008, January). Cold facts.(Cool it: The skeptical environmentalist's guide to global warming by Bjorn Lomborg) (Critical essay).

Commentary, 60(4). (Retrieved May 31, 2008). Eco-doomsayers exact revenge on Lomborg. *Insight on the News, 19*(5), 56–57. Retrieved April 30, 2005.

3. Sayer, J. E. (2007, March). A good speech is "a good man speaking well." Commencement address delivered at the Ohio Institute of Photography and Technology, January 12, 2007. *Vital Speeches, 73,* 3. Retrieved March 1, 2008, from Academic Search Premier.

4. Griffiths, D. (2008, May 17). Uncertain times for quake survivors. BBC News [Online]. Retrieved May 31, 2008, from http://news .bbc.co.uk/2/hi/asia-pacific/7406459.stm.

5. Unless noted otherwise, the information in this box comes from 100 questions and answers about Arab Americans: A journalists' guide. (2001). *Detroit Free Press*. Jobs Page. Retrieved May 31, 2008, from www.freep .com/legacy/jobspage/arabs/

6. Census and religious information from: Arab American Demographics. (2005). Arab American Institute. Retrieved May 28, 2005, from www.aaiusa.org/ demographics.htm.

7. MacIntyre, A. (1981). *After virtue: A study in moral reasoning* (2nd ed.). South Bend, IN: University of Notre Dame Press.

8. Associated Press. (2002, January 31). Prisoner gets $1M heart transplant. CBS News. Retrieved June 11, 2008, from www.cbsnews.com/stories/2002/01/31/ health/main326305.shtml; see also Transplant News. (2002, December 27). Death of inmate who received heart transplant renews debate over organ allocation policies. *BNET: Business Network*. Retrieved June 11, 2008, from http://findarticles. com/p/articles/mi_m0YUG/is_24_12/ ai_n18614748.

9. Miller, A. N. (2002). An exploration of Kenyan public speaking patterns with implications for the American introductory public speaking course. *Communication Education, 51*(2), 178.

10. Associated Press. (2008, March 4). Gang memoir is a total fabrication. CBS News. Retrieved June 13, 2008, from www.cbsnews .com/stories/2008/03/04/entertainment/ main3903246.shtml.

11. The Smoking Gun. (2008, January 8). The man who conned Oprah. Retrieved June 13, 2008, from www.thesmokinggun. com/archive/0104061jamesfrey1.html.

12. Berger, J. (2008, June 1). Prison puppies. *New York Times*. Retrieved June 12, 2008, from www.nytimes.com/2008/06/01/ nyregion/nyregionspecial2/01Rpuppies .html

13. Springen, K. (2004, June 7). Drastically downsized. *Newsweek*, 78. Retrieved June 11, 2008, from InfoTrac College Edition.

14. Schrof , J. M. & Schultz, S. (1999, June-21). Social anxiety. *U.S. News & World Report, 126*(24), 53.

15. Slade, C. (2003). "Seeing reasons": visual argumentation in advertisements. *Argumentation, 17*, 14–160.

16. Jeong, S-H. (2008, March). Visual metaphor in advertising: is the persuasive effect attributable to visual argumentation or metaphorical rhetoric? *Journal of Marketing Communication, 14*(1), 59–73.

17. Jeong, S-H. (2006). Persuasive effect of visual metaphor in advertising: is it attributable to metaphorical rhetoric or visual argumentation? Conference Paper. International Communication Association. Retrieved June 12, 2008, from Communication and Mass Media Complete database.

18. LaWare, M. R. (1998). Encountering visions of Aztlan: Arguments for ethnic pride, community activism and cultural revitalization in Chicano murals. *Argumentation and Advocacy, 34*, 140–153. Retrieved June 13, 2005, from InfoTrac College Edition.

19. Wilson, P. (1983). *Second-hand knowledge: An inquiry into cognitive authority*. Westport, CT: Greenwood.

20. Ibid.

21. Lanier, J. (2008, March-12). Compound puppies: prisoners learn to train dogs. *Independent Tribune*. Retrieved June 12, 2008, from InfoTrac College Edition.

22. Florida/Metro. (1999, May 30). Prison puppies: Ices, Spirit, Moby, and Heather may be locked up, but they aren't criminals—they're learning to be guide dogs. *The Tampa Tribune (Tampa, FL)*. Retrieved June 12, 2008, from InfoTrac College Edition.

23. Tembo, M. S. (1999, April). Your mother is still your mother. *World and I, 14,* 4. Retrieved May 24, 2005, from InfoTrac College Edition.

24. Walters, F. (1992, November 15). In celebration of options: Respect each other's differences. *Vital Speeches of the Day,* 265–269.

25. Pitney, J. J. (1995, November 13). The Tocqueville fraud. *The Weekly Standard,* 1, 44–45.

26. *Business Week*. (2005, March 21). It must be winter in New York: top 20 local markets. Retrieved from www.businessweek.com/ technology/tech_stats/topnet050321.htm.

27. Riley, J. & Ratchford, J. (1998). Americans expected to enjoy 25.6 million hot dogs during baseball season. National Hot Dog and Sausage Council. Retrieved June 6, 2005, from www.hot-dog.org/pr/ pr_opening2000.html.

28. Lewis, R. (2002, August 27) How to Become a Good Googler. CBSnews: The Early Show. Retrieved June 13, 2005, from www.cbsnews.com/stories/2002/08/26/ earlyshow/contributors/reginalewis/ main519808.shtml.

29. Matthews, T. J., Hamilton, M. S., & Hamilton, B. E. (2002, December 11). Mean age of mothers, 1970–2000. National Vital Statistics Reports, *51*(1). Retrieved August 10, 2005, from www.cdc .gov/nchs/data/nvsr/nvsr51/nvsr51_01.pdf.

30. Pay for College. (2008). 2007–2008 college costs: keep rising prices in perspective. CollegeBoard. Retrieved June 13, 2008, from www.collegeboard.com/student/pay/ add-it-up/4494.html.

31. GFK NOP. (2005, June 15). World culture score. Index examines global media habits . . . uncovers who's tuning in, logging on, and hitting the books. Retrieved June 13, 2008, from www.marketresearchworld. net/index.php?option=content&task=view &id=102&Itemid=

32. Quoted directly from Weston, L. P. (2008). The basics: the truth about credit card debt. msn.money. Retrieved June 13, 2008, from http://moneycentral.msn.com/content/Banking/creditcardsmarts/P74808.asp.

33. National Center for Victims of Crime. (2004, February 26). *Crime and victimization in America, statistical overview* [Online]. Retrieved June 13, 2008, from http://www.ncvc.org.

34. U.S. Department of Labor. (2005, June 5). Bureau of Labor Statistics. Retrieved June 13, 2008, from www.bls.gov/cps/wlf-table17-2005.pdf.

35. National Center for Victims of Crime. (2000). Crime and victimization in America: Statistical overview. Retrieved November 13, 2000, from www.ncvc.org.

36. Khan, L. A. (2002, January 15). A century of great awakenings: "We have learned much about ourselves." *Vital Speeches of the Day, 68*(7), 222–225.

37. McLain, F. J. (2001, November-1). The music in your soul. A celebration of life. A speech delivered at fall convocation, Queens College, Charlotte, NC, September 18, 2001. *Vital Speeches of the Day, 68*(2), 59–61.

38. Darling, A. L. & Dannels, D. P. (2003). Practicing engineers talk about the importance of talk: a report on the role of oral communication in the workplace. *Communication Education, 52*(1), 1–16. Retrieved June 1, 2008, from Communication and Mass Media Complete database.

39. Ibid.

40. Dannels, D. P. Communication across the discipline and in the disciplines: speaking in engineering. *Communication Education, 51*(3), 254–268. Retrieved June 1, 2008, from Communication and Mass Media Complete database.

41. Ibid, 263.

CHAPTER 9

1. Miller, G. A. (1956). The magical number seven, plus or minus two: Some limits on our capacity for processing information. *The Psychological Review, 63*, 81–97. Retrieved June 14, 2008, from www.well.com/user/smalin/miller.html.

2. Young People's Trust for the Environment. (2001). Fact sheet: What is a tsunami? Retrieved July 14, 2008, from www.yptenc.org.uk/docs/factsheets/env_facts/tsunami.html.

3. Bloch, M. (1975). *Political language and oratory in traditional society.* London: Academic Press.

4. Miller, A. N. (2002). An exploration of Kenyan public speaking patterns with implications for the American introductory public speaking course. *Communication Education, 51*(2), 168–182.

5. Gandy, D. (2007, July). The secret to becoming very wealthy. Commencement address delivered at St. Leo University (Florida), May 5, 2007. *Vital Speeches of the Day, 73*(7). Retrieved March 1, 2008, from Academic Search Premier database.

6. Jorgensen-Earp, C. (n.d.), "Making other arrangements": Alternative patterns of disposition [Unpublished course handout]. Lynchburg, VA: Lynchburg College.

7. Ibid.

8. Zediker, K. (1993, February). Rediscovering the tradition: Women's history with a relational approach to the basic public speaking course. Panel presentation at the Western States Communication Association, Albuquerque, NM.

9. Truth, S. (1997). Ain't I a Woman? *Modern History Sourcebook.* [online]. Retrieved June 14, 2008, from www.fordham.edu/halsall/mod/sojtruth-woman.html. Original speech delivered 1851, Women's Convention, Akron, OH.

10. Giovanni, N. (2007, April 17). We are Virginia Tech: Remarks at the memorial ceremony for Virginia Tech shooting victims. Retrieved June 14, 2008, from www.americanrhetoric.com/speeches/nikkigiovannivatechmemorial.htm.

11. Anderson, E. R., Jr. (1999, July 1). Solving the health care dilemma: is it good medicine? Speech delivered to the National Leadership Development Conference, Opening Session, Phoenix, Arizona, March 21, 1999. *Vital Speeches of the Day, 65*(18), 571(3). Retrieved June 13, 2008, from InfoTrac College Edition.

12. When I wrote the fifth edition, this information was available online at Impact Publications. (2001). Secret #24: Organize ideas for easy understanding. Winning the Job: Your Career Resource Center. Retrieved June 1, 2005, www.winningthejob.com/page2.php3?ID5150&Item52397; currently, it's in book form, Krannach, C. R. (1998). *101 secrets of highly effective speakers.* Manassas Park, VA: Impact Publications.

CHAPTER 10

1. Quintilian, *instituto oratoria,* Chapter 2.

2. Halperin, E. C. (2007, November). What does it mean? *Vital Speeches of the Day, 73*(11). Retrieved June 14, 2008, from Academic Search Premier database.

3. Davidson, J. (2001, November-15). Relaxing at high speed: You must take time. *Vital Speeches of the Day, 68,* 87–91.

4. Wirth, D. (1999, October-29) *Arachnophobia: Overcoming your fear* [Student Speech]. Goshen, IN: Goshen College.

5. Braithwaite, C. A. (1997). *Sa'ah Naagháí Bak'eh Hòzhóón:* An ethnography of Navajo educational communication practices. *Communication Education, 46,* 219–233.

6. Fanton, J. (2008, March). The case for an international system of justice. Address delivered to the National Press Club, Washington, D.C, December 10, 2007. *Vital Speeches of the Day, 74*(3). Retrieved June 14, 2008, from Academic Search Premier database.

7. Nunn, S. (2007, August). The mountaintop: a world free of nuclear weapons. Speech delivered June 14, 2007, Council on Foreign Relations, Washington, D.C. *Vital Speeches, 73*(8). Retrieved June 14, 2008, from Academic Search Premier database.

8. Ripkin Jr., C. (2007, October). There are no endings. Delivered at the Baseball Hall of Fame induction ceremony, Cooperstown, New York, July 29, 2007. *Vital Speeches of the Day, 73*(10). Retrieved June 14, 2008, from Academic Search Premier database.

9. Abdoo, R. A. (2004, November 15). Lessons in doing the right thing. Speech delivered October 14, 2004. University of Dayton. *Vital Speeches of the Day, 71,* 78–85.

10. Hainer, H. (2008, April). Brand recognition. Delivered to the Chief Executives Club of Boston (Massachusetts), January 31, 2007. *Vital Speeches of the Day, 74*(4). Retrieved June 14, 2008, from Academic Search Premier database.

11. Echo in introductions and conclusions. (n.d.) Instructional web page [Online]. Retrieved December 15, 1999, from www.stlcc.cc.mo.us/fv/webcourses/eng020/testlocation/mensepage/Echo.html.

12. Halperin, What does.

CHAPTER 11

1. Wood, N. (1979). The classical canons in basic speech and English classes. *RQS: Rhetoric Society Quarterly, 9*(4), 188–193. Retrieved June 30, 2008, from Academic Search Premier database.

2. *Preparing the delivery outline.* (1999, December 14). Riverdale School speech class, upper grades. Retrieved January 12, 2001, from www.teleport.com/beanman/english/delivout.html.

3. Thinking and learning skills. (1999). *SNOW.* University of Toronto. Retrieved December 24, 1999, from http://snow.utoronto.ca/learn2/introll.html.

4. Irvine, J. J. & York, D.E. (1995). *Learning styles and culturally diverse students: a literature review.* (ERIC Document Reproduction Service No. ED382 722 UDO3046)

5. Riding, R. & Cheerman, I. (1991). Cognitive styles—an overview and integration. *Educational Psychology, 11,* 193–215.

6. Jorgeson-Earp, C. (n.d.) "Making other arrangements:" Alternative patterns of disposition [Unpublished course handout]. Lynchburg, VA: Lynchburg College.

CHAPTER 12

1. Asen, R. (1999, Winter). Toward a normative conception of difference in public deliberation. *Argumentation and Advocacy, 35*(3), 115–116. Retrieved from InfoTrac College Edition.

2. Davies, I. R. L., Sowden, P. T., Jerrett, D. T., Jerrett, T., & Corbett, G. G. (1998, February). A cross-cultural study of English and Setswana speakers on a colour triads task: a test of the Sapir-Whorf hypothesis. *British Journal of Psychology, 89*(1), 1(15). Retrieved June 19, 2008, from InfoTrac College Edition.

3. Arthur, H., Johnson, G., & Young, A. (2007). Gender differences and color: content and emotion of written descriptions. *Social Behavior and Personality, 35*(6), 827–834. Retrieved June 25, 2008, from SocINDEX database.

4. Gozzi, R. (1990). *New words and a changing American culture.* Columbia, SC: University of South Carolina Press.

5. Burke, K.

6. Pattinson, G. (2005, September 26). Tingo, nakkele, and other wonders. BBC News. Retrieved June 18, 2008, from http://news.bbc.co.uk/2/hi/uk_news/magazine/4248494.stm.

7. Liberman, M. (2004, February 15). 46 Somali words for camel. *Language Log.* Retrieved June 18, 2008, from http://itre.cis.upenn.edu/myl/languagelog/archives/000457.html.

8. Whorf, B. L. (1956). *Language, Thought, and Reality.* Quotations from Benjamin Lee Whorf. Retrieved June 19, 2008, from http://mtsu32.mtsu.edu:11072/Whorf/blwquotes.html.

9. Barfield, O. (1973). *Poetic diction: A study in meaning* (p. 23). Middletown, CT: Wesleyan University Press.

10. Dialects doing well. (1998). InSCIght on Apnet. Retrieved March 12, 2003, from www.apnet.com/inscight/02181009/graphb.htm.

11. Gozzi, New words.

12. Pot. (2002). Merriam-Webster online. Retrieved June 7, 2005, from www.m-w.com/cgi-bin/dictionary/pot.

13. Police officer, Principal, Ibid.

14. Bennett, J., & Yabroff, J. (2008, June-16). Revenge of the Nerdette. *Newsweek Magazine.* Retrieved June 18, 2008, from www.newsweek.com/id/140457.

15. Delwiche, A. (2002, September 29). Propaganda: Euphemisms. Propaganda Critic. Retrieved June 18, 2008, from www.propagandacritic.com/articles/ct.wg.euphemism.html.

16. Johannesen, R. L. (1990). *Ethics in human communication,* 3rd ed. Prospect Heights, IL: Waveland Press.

17. Currey, J., & Mumford, K. (2002, September 18) *Just talk: Guide to inclusive language.* University of Tasmania. Retrieved December-20, 2002, from http://student.admin.utas.edu.au/services/just_talk/Disability/disability.htm.

18. Emory University Department of Religion (2001, December 6). *Statement on inclusive language.* Retrieved June 19, 2008, from www.emory.edu/COLLEGE/RELIGION/about/statement.html.

19. Seiter, J. S., Larsen, J., & Skinner, J. (1998). "Handicapped" or "handi-capable"? The effects of language about persons with disabilities on perceptions of source credibility and persuasiveness. *Communication Reports, 11*(1), 21–31.

20. Frida, D.O. Revenge of the muses: could it be that finally women have had it with demeaning language?" *New York Daily News/Latino.* Retrieved June 22, 32008, from www.nydailynews.com/latino/2007/05/09/2007-05-09_revenge_of_the_muses.html.

21. Currey & Mumford, Just talk.

22. Rieder, J. (2008). *The word of the Lord is upon me: the righteous performance of Martin Luther King, Jr.* Belknap: Harvard University Press.

23. Lessing, D. (2008, February). Not winning the Nobel Prize: Lecture given to the Nobel Peace Prize Committee, Oslo, Norway, December 7, 2007. *Vital Speeches of the Day, 72*(2), Retrieved June 14, 2008, from Academic Search Premier database.

24. Lamm, R. D. (2005). How to make an environmentalist. *Vital Speeches of the Day, 71*(10), 304–306.

25. Carnahan, J. (1999, June 15). *Born to make barrels: Women who put their stamp on history.* Address given at the Trailblazer's Awards Ceremony, University of Missouri, St. Louis. *Vital Speeches of the Day, 65,* 529–531.

26. Brody, W. J. (2007, November). What's promised, what's possible. Speech delivered to the National Press Club. Washington, D.C., September 7, 2007. *Vital Speeches of the Day, 73*(11). Retrieved March 1, 2008, from Academic Search Premier database.

27. Peters, D. (2000, May). Sweet seduction. *Chatelaine, 73*(5), 53. Retrieved December 15, 2002, from InfoTrac College Edition.

28. Reagan, R. (1986, January-31). *Memorial service for the crew of the space shuttle* Challenger. Houston. Retrieved December 15, 2002, from www.eulogywriters.com/challenger.htm.

29. Archambault, D. (1992, May 1). Columbus plus 500 years: Whither the American Indian? *Vital Speeches of the Day, 58,* 491–493.

30. Osborn, M. (1997). The play of metaphors. *Education, 118,* 1, 84–87. Retrieved December 14, from InfoTrac College Edition.

31. Panelist. (2008, June 12). *Life on the Rock* (Encore). EWTN Television.

32. Quoted on www.americanrhetoric.com.

33. Seattle. (1971). The Indian's night promises to be dark. In W. C. Vanderwerth. (Ed.). *Indian oratory: Famous speeches by noted Indian chieftains* (pp. 118–122). Norman, OK: University of Oklahoma Press. (Original work published 1853)

34. Osborn, M. (1967). Archetypal metaphor in rhetoric: The lightdark family. *Quarterly Journal of Speech, 53,* 115–126. See also Osborn, M. (1977). The evolution of the archetypal sea in rhetoric and poetic. *Quarterly Journal of Speech, 63,* 347–363.

35. Seattle. Indian's night.

36. 32.Lustig, M. W., & Koester, J. (1993). *Intercultural competence: Interpersonal communication across cultures.* New York: HarperCollins; see also Simons, G. F., Vazquez, C., & Harris, P. R. (1993). *Transcultural leadership: Empowering the diverse workforce.* Houston: Gulf.

37. Thiederman, S. (1991a). *Bridging cultural barriers for corporate success: How to manage the multicultural workforce.* New York: Lexington; see also Thiederman, S. (1991b). *Profiting in American multicultural market places: How to do business across cultural lines.* New York: Lexington.

38. King, M. L., Jr. (1963). I have a dream. *American Rhetoric* [Online]. Retrieved December 10, 2005, from www.americanrhetoric.com/speeches/Ihaveadream.htm.

CHAPTER 13

1. Neil Wolkodoff is quoted in C. Deherrera. (2002, May). Enhance your career by becoming a speaker. *IDEA Health & Fitness Source, 20*(5), 23–27. Retrieved March 21, 2005, from InfoTrac College Edition.

2. Jeremiah 13.

3. Cicero, De Orator 2:266267. Summarized in Beacham, R. C. (1999). *Spectacle entertainments of early imperial Rome* (p. 38). New Haven: Yale University Press.

4. Reynolds, S. (1996, December). Selling to another language. *Communication World, 14,* 11. Retrieved March 21, 2005, from InfoTrac College Edition.

5. Wall, T. (2004, October). PowerPoint pitfalls that can kill an audience's will to stay awake. *Presentations, 18*(10), 46(1). Retrieved March 21, 2005, from InfoTrac College Edition.

6. Muhovic, E. (2000). *Visual aids for presentations.* [Online.] Center for Managerial Communications, Denver University. Retrieved October 19, 2002, from www.du.edu/emuhovic/visualpresentations.html.

7. Wall, PowerPoint pitfalls.

8. Ibid.

9. Davidson, W., & Kline, S. (1999, March). Ace your presentations. *Journal of Accountancy, 187,* 61. Retrieved October 29, 2002, from InfoTrac College Edition.

10. Anonymous reviewer (1994).

11. Becker, R. A. & Keller- McNulty, S. (1996, May). Presentation myths. *The American Statistician, 50,* 112–116. Retrieved April 23, 2005, from InfoTrac College Edition.

12. See Presentation tips: "Document camera." (2004, February 18). University of Wisconsin–Madison. Retrieved June 26, 2008, from www2.fpm.wisc.edu/support/PresentationTips.htm.

13. *Put more power in your next presentation: Use a document camera.* (2005). Presenters online. Retrieved March 23, 2005, from www.presentersonline.com/technical/tools/documentcamera.shtml.

14. Anonymous reviewer (1994).

15. Doumont, J-L. (2005, Feb.). The cognitive style of PowerPoint: Slides are not all evil. *Technical Communication, 52*(1), 64(7). Retrieved March 20, 2005, from InfoTrac College Edition.

16. Radel, J. (1999, July). *Effective presentations.* The University of Kansas Medical Center on-line tutorial series [Online]. Retrieved March 20, 2005, from http://KUMC.edu/SAH/OTEd/jradel/effective.html.

17. Zielinski, D. (2003, Sept.). Go! Part two: Planes, trains and presenting: Secrets and strategies of speakers on the go. *Presentations, 47*(4), 17–28. Retrieved March 20, 2005, from InfoTrac College Edition.

18. Anonymous reviewer. (1994).

19. Hernandez, T. (2004, Dec.). Digital whiteboards allow design teams to capture plan markups. *Building Design & Construction, 45,* 19–21. Retrieved March 20, 2005, from InfoTrac College Edition.

20. Anonymous reviewer. (1994).

21. Five keys to effective handouts. (1997, October 13). *Buffalo Business First* [online]. Accessed March 22, 2005. http://buffalo.bizjournals.com/buffalo/stories/1997/10/13/smallb3.html.

22. Keller, J. (2003, January 5). Killing me Microsoftly with PowerPoint. *Chicago Tribune*. Retrieved June 26, 2008, from www.robertgaskins.com.

23. Readability. (n.d.) Planning, design, and production [Online]. Retrieved January 3, 2000, from http://ibis.nott.ac.uk/guidelines/ch2/chap2-G-4.html.

24. Jacobs, K. (2005). Which fonts look good in presentations? Retrieved March 24, 2005, from www.microsoft.com/en-us/assistance/HA011243941033.aspx.

25. Ibid.

26. The facts about fonts. (2003, December). *PR Newswire*. Retrieved June 26, 2008, from InfoTrac College Edition.

27. Bennett, J. (2008, April 7). Just go to Helvetica. (Design). *Newsweek*, *151*(14), 54. Retrieved June 26, 2008, from InfoTrac College Edition.

28. Ibid.

29. *Using color to your marketing advantage.* (2005, March-21). Great FX Business Cards Web site. Accessed March 21, 2005. http://www.greatfxbusinesscards.com/colorandemotions.htm.

30. Detz, J. (1998, April-May). Delivery plus content equals successful presentations. *Communication World*, *15*(5), 34–36. Retrieved January 20, 2000, from InfoTrac College Edition.

31. Anonymous reviewer. (1994).

32. Ibid.

CHAPTER 14

1. Hypes, M. G., Turner, E. T., Norris, C. M., & Wollferts, L. C. (1999, January). How to be a successful presenter. *Journal of Physical Education, Recreation & Dance*, *70*(1), 50–53.

2. Unless noted otherwise, most suggestions in this section are taken from Schwartz, A. E. (1988, August). Rehearsing: key to avoiding training chaos. *Training and Development Journal*, *42*(8), 15(3). Retrieved June 27, 2008, from InfoTrac College Edition.

3. Kaye, S. (1999, March). Make an impact with style: presentation tips for leaders. *IIE Solutions*, *31*(3), p. 26(2). Retrieved June 28, 2008, from InfoTrac College Edition.

4. Kampmann, M. & Rosen, J. (1991, January). Speaking with confidence. *Supervisory Management*, *36*(1), 3(1). Retrieved June 27, 2008, from InfoTrac College Edition.

5. Schwartz, Rehearsing.

6. McDonald, C. A. (2008, June). Email interview.

7. Most of the recent work on the canon of memoria is linked to cultural memory, but see Hoogestraat, W. E. (1960). Memory: the lost canon? *Quarterly Journal of Speech*, *46*(2), 141–148. Retrieved June 30, 2008, from Academic Search Premier database.

8. Schwartz, Rehearsing.

9. Kaye, S. (1999, March). Make an impact with style: presentation tips for leaders. IIE Solutions, *31*(3), p. 26(2). Retrieved June 28, 2008, from InfoTrac College Edition.

10. This list draws from Schwartz, Rehearsing.

11. Rieder, J. (2008). *The word of the Lord is upon me: the righteous performance of Martin Luther King, Jr.* Belknap Press/Harvard University Press.

12. Morgan, N. (2004, Winter). Preparing to be real. *Harvard Management Communication Letter*, *1*(1), 3–5. Retrieved June 28, 2008 from InfoTrac College Edition.

13. Schwartz, Rehearsing.

14. Kampmann & Rosen, Speaking with confidence.

15. Hoogestraat, Memory.

16. Anonymous reviewer. (2008).

17. Keefe, J. (1988, August) Drama lessons for speakers. *Meetings & Conventions 33*(9), *30*(1). Retrieved June 27, 2008, from InfoTrac College Edition.

18. Schwartz, Rehearsing.

19. Keefe, Drama lessons.

20. Anonymous reviewer.

21. Montalbo, T. (1980). Churchill: A study in oratory. Seven lessons in speechmaking from one of the greatest orators of all time. The Churchill Centre. Retrieved June 9, 2005, from www.winstonchurchill.org/i4apages/index.cfm?pageid+814

22. Goffman, E. (1959). *The presentation of self in everyday life.* Garden City, NY: Doubleday Anchor.

23. Bippus, A. M. & Daly, J. A. (1999). What do people think causes stage fright? Naïve attributions about the reasons for public speaking anxiety. *Communication Education, 48*, 63–72.

24. Arthur, A. (1997, July). Keeping up public appearances: Master the fine art of public-speaking and give a great presentation every time. *Black Enterprise*, *27*(12), 54. Retrieved December 20, 2002, from InfoTrac College Edition.

25. Goffman, Presentation of self.

26. The classification here comes from Ekman, P. & Friesen, W. V. (1969). The repertoire of nonverbal behavior: Categories, origins, usage, and coding. *Semiotica, I*, 49–98.

27. Morgan, Preparing.

28. Kempmann & Rosen, Speaking with confidence.

29. Richmond, V. P. & McCroskey, J. C. (2000). *Nonverbal behavior in interpersonal relations* (4th ed.). Scottsdale, AZ: Gorsuch Scarisbrick.

30. Montalbo, Churchill.

31. Aristotle, (1954, 1984). *The Rhetoric.* (H. R. Roberts, Trans.). New York: The Modern Library.

32. Summarized in Burgoon, J. K., Buller, D. B., & Woodall, W. G. (1989). *Nonverbal communication: The unspoken dialogue.* New York: Harper & Row; see also Ray, G. B. (1986). Vocally cued personality prototypes: An implicit personality theory approach. *Communication Monographs, 53*, 266–276.

33. Ibid.

34. Morgan, Preparing.

35. Ibid.

36. The next three suggestions come from Toastmasters International. (n.d.). Vocal

variety. Retrieved June 30, 2008, from www.angelfire.com/tn/bektoastmasters/Toastmasters5.html.

37. Davidson, W., & Kline, S. (1999, March). Ace your presentations. *Journal of Accountancy*, *187*(3), 61. Retrieved January 7, 2003, from InfoTrac College Edition.

38. Hypes, Turner, Norris, & Wollferts, Successful presenter.

39. Humphrey, J. (1998, May 15). Executive eloquence: A seven-fold path to inspirational leadership. *Vital Speeches, 64*(15), 468–471. Retrieved June 30, 2008 from InfoTrac College Edition.

40. Hart, R. P., & Burks, D. O. (1972). Rhetorical sensitivity and social interaction. *Speech Monographs, 39*, 90.

41. Branham, R. J., & Pearce, W. B. (1996). The conversational frame in public address. *Communication Quarterly, 44*(4), 423–439.

42. Brookhiser, R. (1999, November 22). Weird Al: A troubled and alarming vice president. *National Review, 60*(22), 32–34. See also Shipman, C. (2000, December/January). Searching for Al. *George Magazine, 102*, 9.

43. Democracy in America (blog). (2008, June 23). Sexism at the *Times? The Economist.* Retrieved July 2, 2008, from www.economist.com/blogs/democracyinamerica/2008/06/sexism_at_the_times.cfm.

44. Anonymous reviewer, 2004.

CHAPTER 15

1. Wicker, B. (1975). *The story-shaped world: Fiction and metaphysics, some variations on a theme.* South Bend, IN: University of Notre Dame Press.

2. Fisher, W. R. (1984). Narration as a human communication paradigm: The case of public moral argument. *Communication Monographs, 51*, 1–22; Fisher, W. R. (1984). The narrative paradigm: An elaboration. *Communication Monographs, 52*, 347–367.

3. Barthes is quoted in Polkinghorne, D. E. (1988). *Narrative knowing and the human sciences* (p. 14). Albany, NY: SUNY Press.

4. Bundgaard, P. F. (2007). The cognitive import of the narrative schema. *Semiotica, 165*(1/4), 247–261. Retrieved July 3, 2008, from Communication and Mass Media Complete database.

5. Bruner, J. (1986). *Actual minds, possible worlds.* Cambridge, MA: Harvard University Press.

6. Cassady, M. (1994). *The art of storytelling: Creative ideas for preparation and performance* (p. 12). Colorado Springs, CO: Meriweather.

7. Anokye, A. D. (1994, Fall). Oral connections to literacy: The narrative. *Journal of Basic Writing, 13*, 46–60.

8. Keeshig-Tobias, L. (1990, January 26). Stop stealing native stories. *Toronto Globe & Mail*, A7.

9. Ibid.

10. Coste, D. (1989). *Narrative as communication.* Minneapolis: University of Minnesota Press.

11. Spangler, D. & Thompson, W. I. (1992). *Reimagination of the world: A critique of*

the new age, science, and popular culture. New York: Bear & Company.

12. Simmons, A. (n.d.). Six stories you need to know how to tell. International Storytelling Center. Retrieved June 15, 2005, from www.storytellingcenter.com/resources/articles/simmons.htm.

13. Aristotle, (1954, 1984). *The Rhetoric.* (H. R. Roberts, Trans.). New York: The Modern Library.

14. Green, M. C. and Brock, T. C. (2000). The role of transportation in the persuasiveness of public narratives. *Journal of Personality and Social Psychology, 79*(5), 701–721.

15. Baum, N. (2003). A land twice promised. Retrieved June 20, 2005, from www.noabaum.com/land.html.

16. Neile, C. S. (2005). Can storytelling save the world. Florida Storytelling Association. Retrieved June 21, 2005, from www.flstory.org/can_storytelling_save.ht.

17. Heuer, A. B. (2001). Storytelling and health care: applied storytelling with stroke survivors. *Diving in the Moon, Trust the Power of Story, 2.* Retrieved July 9, 2008, from www.andreheuer.com/articles/storytelling_health_care_stroke.html.

18. Vergnani, S. A. (2003, March 14). Healing through storytelling. Columbia News Service. Retrieved June 20, 2005, from www.jrn.columbia.edu/studentwork/cns/2003-03-14/16.asp.

19. Quoted, Ibid.

20. Minzescheimer, B. (2007, February 14, last updated). War-torn childhood 'A Long Way Gone,' but not forgotten. *USA Today.* Books. Retrieved July 9, 2008, from www.laurasimms.com

21. Neile, C. S. (2005). International Storytelling Center internship. The Woodrow Wilson National Fellowship Foundation. Retrieved June 20, 2005, from www.woodrow.org/phd/Practicum/neile.html; Neile C. S. (2003). War and peace and story. *Words of Wing, 6.* [online]. Healing Story. Retrieved June 20, 2005, from www.healingstory.org/articles/healing-story-articles.html.

22. Kirkwood, W. G. (1992). Narrative and the rhetoric of possibility. *Communication Monographs, 59,* 30–47.

23. Torrance, J. (1998). *Jackie tales: The magic of creating stories and the art of telling them.* New York: Avon Books.

24. Cassady, *Art of storytelling.*

25. Burke, K. (1983, August 12). Dramatism and logology. *The Times Literary Supplement,* p. 859.

26. Green & Brock, Role of transportation.

27. Cyphert, D. (2007). Presentation technology in the age of electronic eloquence: from visual aid to visual rhetoric. *Communication Education, 56*(2), 168–172.

28. Ibid

29. Tannen, D. Talking voices.

30. Gergen, K. J. (1998). Narrative, moral identity and historical consciousness: A social constructionist account. Available manuscript. Retrieved December 27, 2004, from www.swarthmore.edu/SocSci/kgergen1/web/page/phtml?id5manu3&st+manuscript.

31. McNally, J. R. (1969). Opening assignments: A symposium. *The Speech Teacher, 18,* 18–30.

32. Burke, Dramatism.

33. Fisher, Human communication.

34. Fisher, Narrative paradigm; Fisher, Human communication.

35. Joseph. (1879, April, original publication date). An Indian's view of Indian affairs. *North American Review, 128*(269). 412–433. Retrieved November 8, 2005, from www.washington.edu/uwired/outreach/cspn/sense/part1%20pages/texts/josephview.htm.

CHAPTER 16

1. Elmer-Dewitt, P. (1993, April 12). Electronic superhighways. *Time,* 50–55.

2. Davidson, J. (2005, January 15). Bombarded on all sides: Handling everyday information. (Speech delivered September 29, 2004.) *Vital Speeches of the Day, 71*(7), 212–217.

3. Fancher, M. R. (1993, August 8). Will journalists travel on the information highway? *Seattle Times,* A2.

4. General Assembly of the United Nations. (1948, December 10). Universal Declaration of Human Rights. Retrieved July 4, 2008, from www.un.org/Overview/rights.html.

5. Gluckman, R. (2004, October 18). Beyond the Net's reach: A German firm says it has connected North Korea to the Web, only Pyongyang won't throw the switch. *Newsweek,* 40.

6. Maxwell, L. & McCain, T. A. (1997, July). Gateway or gatekeeper: The implication of copyright and digitalization on education. *Communication Education, 46,* 141–157.

7. Associated Press. (2005, July 7). Reporter jailed for refusal to name leak source. Retrieved July 10, 2008, from www.msnbc.msn.com/id/8417075/

8. U.S. Department of State (2008). Freedom of Information Act (FOIA). Retrieved July 10, 2008, from http://www.state.gov/m/a/ips/

9. Edwards, R. & McDonald, J. L. (1993). Schema theory and listening. In A. D. Wolvin & C. G. Coakley. (Eds.) *Perspectives on Listening* (pp. 60–77). Norwood, NJ: Ablex.

10. Quotation retrieved July 4, 2008, from www.quotedb.com/quotes/1382.

11. Mills, D. W. (2002). Applying what we know: Student learning styles. Retrieved July 4, 2008, from www.csrnet.org/csrnet/articles/student-learning-styles.html.

12. Budiansky, S. (1999, July). The truth about dogs. *Atlantic Monthly, 284*(1), 39–41, 44+.

13. Patterson, M. (n.d.). Demonstrative speech (how to). Brazosport College. Retrieved January 22, 2000, from www.brazosport.cc.tx.us/,/comm/demon.html.

14. Flynn, K, R, (n.d.). Demonstration or "how to" speech topics. Copia-Lincoln Community College. Retrieved June 28, 2005, from www.colin.edu/flynn/Speech/Demo_Speech.htm.

15. Kuzmovich, E. (2005). How to draw a hand. Speech presented to COMM 100 class. George Fox University, Newberg, OR.

16. Nguyen, N. (2005, March). *Ha Noi, Thanh pho yeu dau* (my beloved city). Speech presented to COMM 100 class. George Fox University, Newberg, OR.

17. Salame, J. (2007-2008). The pros and cons of neuroimaging. Competitive speech, George Fox University speech team.

18. Miller, Kenyan public speaking patterns.

19. Rowan, K. (1995). A new pedagogy for explanatory public speaking: Why arrangement should not substitute for invention. *Communication Education, 44*(3), 235–250.

20. von Till, B. (1998, November). Definition speech. San Jose State University. Poster session. National Communication Association meeting, New York City.

21. Boerger, M. A. & Henley, T. B. (1999). The use of analogy in giving instructions. *Psychological Record, 49*(2), 193. Retrieved January 23, 2000, from InfoTrac College Edition.

22. Gardner, H. (1993). *Multiple intelligences: The theory in practice.* New York: Basic Books.

23. Horsfall, S. (2005, Spring) The music of sub-Saharan Africa. Sociology of Music class notes. Texas Wesleyan University. Retrieved June 27, 2005, from http://web.txwesleyan.edu/sociology/horsfall/AfricaMu.html.

24. Goodall, H. L. & Waaigen, C. L. (1986). *The persuasive presentation: A practical guide to professional communication in organizations.* New York: Harper & Row.

25. Rubin, D. L. (1993). Listenability 5 oral-based discourse + considerateness. In Wolvin & Coakley, Perspectives, 261–268.

26. Rowan, New pedagogy.

27. Rubin, Listenability.

28. Thompson, F. T. & Grandgenett, D. J. (1999). Helping disadvantaged learners build effective learning skills. *Education 120*(1), 130–135.

CHAPTER 17

1. Aristotle, (1954, 1984). *The Rhetoric.* (H. R. Roberts, Trans.). New York: The Modern Library.

2. Rubin, D. L. (1993). Listenability 5 oral-based discourse + considerateness. In A. D. Wolvin & C. G. Coakley (Eds.). *Perspectives on listening* (pp. 261–268). Norwood, NJ: Ablex.

3. Ota, A. K. (1993, July 11). Japan's ambassador to U.S. set welcome new tone. *Seattle Times,* A12.

4. Mullins, D. (1993). Guest lecture. St. John's University, Jamaica, NY.

5. Festinger, L. (1957). *A theory of cognitive dissonance.* New York: Row, Peterson.

6. "Attitude." (n.d.). Definition retrieved July 5, 2005, from www.cogsci.princeton.edu/cgi-bin/webwn2.1

7. Park, H. S. (2000). Relationships among attitudes and subjective norms: Testing the Theory of Reasoned Action across cultures. *Communication Studies, 51*(2), 162. Retrieved July 7, 2008, from InfoTrac College Edition.

8. This theory, developed by Fishbein and Ajzen, is summarized in Trafimow, D. & Finlay, K. A. (2001). Evidence for improved sensitivity of within—participants analyses in test of the Theory of Reasoned Action. *The Social Science Journal, 38*(4), 629–638. See also L. A. Muse & C. L. Stamper. (2007). Perceived organizational support: evidence for a mediated association with work performance. *Journal of Managerial Issues, 19*(4), *517*(21). Retrieved July 7, 2008, from InfoTrac College Edition.

9. Poss, J. E. (2001, June.) Developing a new model for cross-cultural research: synthesizing the health beliefs model and the theory of reasoned action. *Advances in Nursing Science, 23*(4), 1–16. Retrieved July 6, 2005, from InfoTrac College Edition.

10. Anonymous reviewer (1994).

11. Monroe, A. H. (1962). *Principles and types of speeches* (5th ed.). Chicago: Scott Foresman.

12. Pugh, T. (2007, Fall). Organ donation. Speech given in COMM 100. George Fox University.

13. Hunt, C. (2002, February). Service and therapy dogs. [Online.] Retrieved July-6, 2005, from www.cofc.edu/,huntc/service.html.

14. Crow, B. (2007). Text reviewer, 5e.

15. Liptak, K. (2006, Fall). Cheerleading IS a sport. Speech given in COMM 100. George Fox University.

CHAPTER 18

1. Quoted in Quindlen, A. (2005, May-30). Life of the closed mind. *Newsweek, 145*(22), 82.

2. Stewart, R. A. & Roach, K. D. (1998). Argumentativeness and the Theory of Reasoned Action, *Communication Quarterly, 46*(2), 177+. Retrieved June 29, 2005, from InfoTrac College Edition.

3. Anonymous reviewer (1994).

4. Aristotle. *Rhetoric*, 1356, 356, 20.

5. Toulmin, S. (1958). *The uses of argument.* Cambridge, UK: Cambridge University Press; Toulmin, S., Rieke, R, & Janik, A. (1984). *An introduction to reasoning* (2nd ed.). New York: Macmillan.

6. Hilliard, A. (1986). Pedagogy in ancient Kemet. In M. Karenga & J. Carruthers (Eds.). *Kemet and the African world view* (p. 257). London: University of Sankore Press.

7. Combs, S. C. (2004). The useless-/usefulness of argumentation: the DAO of disputation. Argumentation and Advocacy, *41*(2), *58*(13). Retrieved June 12, 2006, from InfoTrac College Edition.

8. Ibid.

9. McClain, F. J. (2001, November 1). The music in your soul: A celebration of life. Address delivered at Queens College, Charlotte, NC, September 18, 2001. *Vital Speeches of the Day, 68*(2), 59–61.

10. Voth, B. (1998). A case study in metaphor as argument: A longitudinal analysis of the wall separating church and state. *Argumentation and Advocacy, 34*(3), 127–139. Retrieved March 20, 2002, from InfoTrac College Edition.

11. Jaffe, C. I. (1998, November). Metaphors about the classroom. A paper presented to the National Communication Association, New York City.

12. Wicker, B. (1975). *The story-shaped world: Fiction and metaphysics, some variations on a theme.* South Bend, IN: University of Notre Dame Press.

13. Aristotle (1984). *Poetics* (1459, 5). (I. Bywater, Trans.) New York: The Modern Library. (Original translation published 1954).

14. Hilliard, Pedagogy, 287.

15. Sullivan, P. A. (1993). Signification and African-American rhetoric: a case study of Jesse Jackson's "Common Ground and Common Sense" speech. *Communication Quarterly, 41*(1), 1–15.

16. Morris, H. J. (2002, June 17). League of their own. *U.S. News & World Report, 131,* 21, 50–51.

17. Griffiths, M. (1988). Feminism, feelings, and philosophy. In M. Griffiths & M. Whitford (Eds.). *Feminist perspectives in philosophy* (pp. 131–151). Bloomington: Indiana University Press; Jaggar, A. (1989). Love and knowledge: Emotion in feminist epistemology. In A. Garry & M. Pearsall (Eds.). *Women, knowledge, and reality: Explorations in feminist philosophy* (pp. 129–155). London: Unwin; McMillan, 1982).

18. Jaggar, ibid.

19. Griffiths, Feminism.

20. Frank, D. A. (1997). Diversity in the public space: A response to Stepp. *Argumentation and Advocacy, 33,* 195–197.

21. Dunbar, K. (2000). Gender, science & cognition [Online]. Retrieved July-5, 2005, from www.psych.mcgill.ca/perpg/fac/dunbar/women.html.

22. Asen, R. (1999, Winter). Toward a normative conception of difference in public deliberation. *Argumentation and Advocacy, 35*(3), 115–116. Retrieved from InfoTrac College Edition.

23. Gass, R. (1999). Fallacy list: SpCom 335: Advanced argumentation [Online]. California State University, Fullerton. Retrieved July 5, 2005, from http://commfaculty.fullerton.edu/rgass/fallacy31.htm.

24. Engnell, R. A. (2001). Toward an ethic of evocative language: contemporary uses of Holocaust-related terminology. *Southern Communication Journal, 66,* 312–322.

25. Cribbins, M. (1990). International adoption. [Student speech.] Corvallis: Oregon State University.

26. Suzuki, M. (1992, April 3). Native American symbols in sports. [Student speech.] St. John's University. Jamaica, New York.

27. Roczak, T. (1992, June 9). Green guilt and ecological overload. *New York Times,* A23.

28. Maslow, A. H. (1987). *Motivation and personality* (3rd ed.). San Francisco: Harper & Row. See also

29. Maslow, A. H. (1943). A theory of human motivation. Originally published in *Psychological Review, 50,* 370–396. Posted by C. D. Green. (2000, August). Classics in the history of psychology website. http://psychclassics.yorku.ca/Maslow/motivation.htm.

30. Griffiths, Feminism.

31. Gunn, J. (2007). Hystericizing Huey: emotional appeals, desire, and the psychodynamics of demagoguery. (Huey Pierce Long). *Western Journal of Communication, 71,* 1–27. Retrieved July 2, 2007, from Info-Trac College Edition.

32. Roberts-Miller, P. (2005). Democracy, demagoguery, and critical rhetoric. Rhetoric & Public Affairs, *8*(3), 462. Retrieved July 8, 2008, from Communication and Mass Media Complete database.

33. Ibid

34. Gunn, Hystericizing.

35. Anonymous reviewer. (1994).

36. Aristotle, Rhetoric.

37. Kochman, Cultural pluralism.

38. Anderson, J. W. (1991). A comparison of Arab and American conceptions of "effective persuasion." In L. A. Samovar & R. E. Porter (Eds.). *Intercultural communication: A reader* (5th ed., pp. 96–106). Belmont, CA: Wadsworth.

39. Burke, K. (1983, August-12). Dramatism and logology. *The Times Literary Supplement,* 859.

40. Allen, S. A. (1993, February 15). To be successful you have to deal with reality: An opportunity for minority business. *Vital Speeches, 59,* 271–273.

41. Quintilian, *instituto oratoria.*

42. Ibid., XII: I, 1.

43. Foss, S. K. & Griffin, C. (1995). Beyond persuasion: a proposal for an invitational rhetoric. *Communication Monographs, 62,* 2–18.

TEXT CREDITS

This page constitutes an extension of the copyright page. We have made every effort to trace the ownership of all copyrighted material and to secure permission from copyright holders. In the event of any question arising as to the use of any material, we will be pleased to make the necessary corrections in future printings. Thanks are due to the following authors, publishers, and agents for permission to use the material indicated.

Chapter 1. 2: Source: Hillary for President (2008, January 7), Morning HUBdate: Rhetoric vs. reality. Press Release. Retrieved February 4, 2008 from www.hillaryclinton.com/release/view/?id=5065. **2-3:** These definitions can be found on Lunsford, A.A. (updated last, 2008). Retrieved January 3, 2008 from www.stanford.edu/dept/english/sites/lunsford/pages/defs.htm. **4:** Source: Conrad' C. (1994), "Strategic organizational communication: Toward the twenty-first century", 3rd ed. (Fort Worth: Harcourt Brace), **16:** Used by permission of Alexandria Reed. p. 31. **13:** Used by permission of Liina Teose.

Chapter 2. 19: Used by permission of Reese Wilson. **30-31:** Used by permission of Manfred Tschan. **33–35:** Used by permission of Enriques Ruiz.

Chapter 3. 48: Source: Cited in Department of Journalism, (n.d.), 'Academic Integrity Handbook'. University of Arizona. Retrieved June 4, 2008 from http://journalism.arizona.edu/publications/academic_integrity_handbook.pdf. **50:** Source: Hofman, M. (June 2008), "The best cause of all', 'Inc Magazine', 30(6), 23-24. Retrieved June 4, 2008 from the Business Source Complete database. **50:** Source: Shanhaz, M. (May 2008), "Good vibrations", 'Adweek', 49(16). Retrieved June 4, 2008 from the Business Source Complete database.

Chapter 5. 76: Used by permission of Brad Lau. **78:** Source: Grant, H. (January 2007), "Sabina Xhosa and the new shoes". Address delivered 1 Nov 2006 to Westminster College IBM Lecture, Fulton, Missouri, 'Vital Speeches of the Day', 73(1), pp. 36–40. **81-82:** Used by permission of Linnea Smith. **86:** Used by permission of Linnea Smith.

Chapter 6. 101: Source: www.americanrhetoric.com/speeches/ronaldreaganchallenger.htm **104:** Used by permission of Ron Mitchell. **107:** Used by permission of Amara Sheppard. **109:** Source: Educational Testing Service (Nov 2006), "College students fall short in demonstrating the ICT skills necessary for success in college and the workplace: preliminary research finds that many students misjudge the objectivity and authoritativeness of Internet sources", 'Internet Wire'. Retrieved May 27, 2008 from Info Trac-College Edition.

Chapter 7. 131: Used by permission of Jennifer Salame.

Chapter 8. 137: Source: Griffiths, D., "Uncertain times for quake survivors", 'BBC News' (Online). Retrieved 5/31/08 from http://news.bbc.co.uk/2/hi/asia-pacific/7406459.stm **141:** Source: Berger, J., "Prison Puppies", 'The New York Times', June 1, 2008. **144:** Source: Lanier, J., "Compound puppies: prisoners learn to train dogs", 'Independent Tribune', 3/12/08. **155:** Used by permission of Carrie Weichbrodt.

Chapter 9. 160: Used by permission of Gustave Eiffel. **168:** Source: Anderson, E.R., "Solving the health care dilemma: Is it good medicine?" (7/1/99), 'Vital Speeches of the Day', 65(18), 571(3). **172:** Used by permission of Maria DiMaggio.

Chapter 10. 178: Source: Fanton, J., "The case for a international system of justice" (12/10/07), 'Vital Speeches of the Day', 74(3). **178:** Source: Nunn, S., "The mountaintop: A world free of nuclear weapons" (6/14/07), 'Vital Speeches of the Day', 73(8). **179:** Source: Ripkin Jr., C., "There are no endings" (7/29/07), 'Vital Speeches of the Day', 73(10). **179:** Source: Hainer, H., "Brand recognition" (1/31/07), 'Vital Speeches of the Day', 74(4).

Chapter 11. 197: Used by permission of Emily Smith.

Chapter 12. 212: Source: Frida, D., "Revenge of the muses: Could it be that finally women have had it with demeaning language?", 'New York Daily News/Latino', 6/22/08. **214:** Source: Reider, J., "The word of the Lord is upon me: The righteous performance of Martin Luther King, Jr." (Cambridge: Harvard University Press, 2008). **216:** Source: Lessing, D., "Not winning the Nobel Prize", 'Vital Speeches of the Day', February 2008, 72(2). **217:** Source: Archambault, D., "Columbus plus 500 years: Whither the American Indian", (5/1/1992), 'Vital Speeches of the Day', 58, 491–493. **217:** Source: Brody, W.J., "What's promised, what's possible" 'Vital Speeches of the Day', Nov. 2007, 73(11). **218:** Source: Seattle, 'The Indian's night promises to be dark' in W.C. Vanderwerth, "Indian oratory: Famous speeches by noted Indian chieftains", pp. 118–122. Norman, OK; University of Oklahoma Press, 1971. (Original work published in 1853). **225:** ****Reprinted by arrangement with The Heirs to the Estate of Martin Luther King, Jr., c/o Writer House as agent for the proprietor, New York, NY. Copyright 1963 Dr. Martin Luther King, Jr; copyright renewed 1991 Coretta Scott King.****

Chapter 13. 236: Source: Mark Iles. **250:** Used by permission of Anna Riedl.

Chapter 14. 264: Source: YanHong Krompacky. **264:** Source: Aristotle, "The Rhetoric", H.R. Roberts, (trans.), New York: The Modern Library, 1954, 1984. **266:** Source: Humphrey, J., (5/15/1998) "Executive eloquence: A seven-fold path to inspirational leadership", 'Vital Speeches of the Day', 64, 15, 468–71.

Chapter 15. 271: Source: Barthes, R., "Narrative knowing and the human sciences" (Albany, NY: SUNY Press, 1988), p. 14. **271:** Source: Keeshig-Tobias, L., "Stop stealing native stories", 'Toronto Globe & Mail', 1/26/1990, p. A7. **273:** Source: Baum, N. (2003), "A land twice promised". Retrieved 6/20/05 from www.noabaum.com/land.html. **274:** Source: Vergnani, S.A., "Healing through storytelling", 'Columbia News Service', 6/20/05. **283:** Source: Joseph, "An Indian's View of Indian Affairs" (1879), 'North American Review', 128(269), 412–33.

Chapter 16. 286: Source: General Assembly of the United Nations, 10/12/1948 **291:** From Nguyen, N. (3/05), "Ha Noi Thanh pho yeu dau". Speech presented to COMM 100 class, George Fox University, Newberg, OR. **302:** Used by permission of Joshua Valentine.

Chapter 17. 324: Used by permission of Linnea Strandy.

Chapter 18. 328: Source: Aristotle, "The Rhetoric", H.R. Roberts, (trans.), New York: The Modern Library, 1954, 1984. **331:** Source: Aristotle, "Poetics", I. Bywater, (trans.), New York: The Modern Library, 1954. **331:** From Hilliard, A. (1986), 'Pedagogy in ancient Kemet' in M. Karenga & J. Carruthers

(Eds.), "Kemet and the African World View", p. 287 (London: University of Sankore Press). **338:** From Cribbins, M. (1990), "International adoption", Corvallis, Oregon State University. **339:** Source: Gunn, J., (2007) "Hystericizing Huey: emotional appeals, desires, and the psychodynamics" (Huey Pierce Long), 'Western Journal of Communication', 71, 1–27. **339:** From Roczak, T. (6/9/92), "Green guilt and ecological overload", 'New York Times', p. A23. **339:** From Suzuki, M. (4/3/1992), "Native American symbols in sports", St. Johns University, Jamaica, New York. **340:** From Suzuki, M. (4/3/1992), "Native American symbols in sports", St. Johns University, Jamaica, New York. **340:** From Roczak, T. (6/9/92), "Green guilt and ecological overload", 'New York Times', p. A23. **341:** Source: Gunn, J., (2007) "Hystericizing Huey: emotional appeals, desires, and the psychodynamics" (Huey Pierce Long),

'Western Journal of Communication', 71, 1–27. **342:** Source: Aristotle, "The Rhetoric", H.R. Roberts, (trans.), New York: The Modern Library, 1954, 1984. **343:** Source: Allen, S.A., (2/15/1993) "To be successful you have to deal with reality: An opportunity for minority business", 'Vital Speeches of the Day', 59, 271–73.

Appendix C. 367: Used by permission of Mona Bradsher. **368:** Used by permission of Chris Russie. **370:** Used by permission of Gail Grobey. **371:** Used by permission of Uriel Plascencia; interpreter, translator Kelly Bilinski. **372:** Used by permission of NamKy Nguyen. **373:** Reprinted by permission of Keisha Walkes. **374:** Used by permission of Andres Lucero. **375:** Reprinted by permission of Fahri Karakas. **376:** Source: John F. Kennedy. **378:** Source: Sojourner Truth [Isabella Van Wagenen] (1797–1883).

INDEX